INTERNATIONAL
HUMAN RIGHTS LAW

D0525100

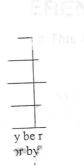

FOR REFERENCE

Do not take This From

y be r
or by

Pearson Education

We work with leading authors to develop the strongest educational materials in law, bringing cutting-edge thinking and best learning practice to a global market.

Under a range of well-known imprints, including Longman, we craft high quality print and electronic publications which help readers to understand and apply their content, whether studying or at work.

To find out about the complete range of our publishing please visit us on the World Wide Web at: www.pearsoneduc.com

INTERNATIONAL
HUMAN RIGHTS LAW

A PRACTICAL APPROACH

―

Javaid Rehman

SENIOR LECTURER IN HUMAN RIGHTS AND PUBLIC LAW,

UNIVERSITY OF LEEDS

An imprint of **Pearson Education**

Harlow, England · London · New York · Reading, Massachusetts · San Francisco
Toronto · Don Mills, Ontario · Sydney · Tokyo · Singapore · Hong Kong · Seoul
Taipei · Cape Town · Madrid · Mexico City · Amsterdam · Munich · Paris · Milan

Pearson Education Limited

Edinburgh Gate
Harlow
Essex CM20 2JE
England

and Associated Companies around the world

Visit us on the World Wide Web at:
www.pearsoneduc.com

First published 2003

ISBN 0 582 43773 3

British Library Cataloguing-in-Publication Data
A catalogue record for this book can be obtained from the British Library.

10 9 8 7 6 5 4 3 2 1
06 05 04 03 02

Typeset by 68
in 10/13pt Sabon
Printed in Great Britain by Henry Ling Ltd,
at the Dorset Press, Dorchester, Dorset

CONTENTS

OVERVIEW OF INTERNATIONAL HUMAN RIGHTS LAW: THEORY AND PRACTICE

PART I INTERNATIONAL LEGAL SYSTEM AND HUMAN RIGHTS

PART IV   GROUP RIGHTS

PART V   CRIMES AGAINST THE DIGNITY OF MANKIND

ACKNOWLEDGEMENTS

The growth and expansion of international human rights law has been truly remarkable. Within a very short time, international human rights law has acquired an important position in legal studies, both at undergraduate and postgraduate levels. The subject has also acquired great relevance for practitioners, and for those representing States, intergovernmental and non-governmental organisations. While human rights law has expanded dramatically, it is surprising (and disappointing) to note that there is a shortage of books and other materials which provide a simple and straightforward analysis of this subject. I first became aware of such a lacuna when I was invited by the University of Peshawar, in association with the Governments of Pakistan and Norway, to teach on a human rights course for the inaugural session of the Human Rights Centre in Peshawar, Pakistan during March–April 2000. Upon my return to the United Kingdom, I was encouraged by many colleagues, friends and students to write a detailed textbook on this subject.

Many people have helped and supported me in writing this book. I am most thankful to Professor John Bell (University of Cambridge) Professor Asif Qureshi (University of Manchester), Siobhan Mullally (University College Cork) and Dr Shaheen Sardar Ali (University of Warwick) for their constant encouragement and for reading the chapters of the book. Professor John Bell's comment have been extremely useful not only in improving the quality of individual chapters, but have also proved instrumental in reshaping the structure and presentation of my ideas. I would also like to thank the reviewers who read the initial draft chapters and provided very encouraging and useful comments for further improvements.

I am also very grateful to a number of colleagues currently working at the University of Leeds for reading parts of the book. I would like to particularly thank Professor Clive Walker, Chloe Wallace, Clare Furniss, Amrita Mukherjee and Penny Robinson for their analysis and extremely positive comments on various chapters. I would like to thank Yaman Akdeniz for his technical computing assistance in completing this study. Maria Eugenia Freitas (currently completing a post-graduate degree at Leeds Metropolitan University) very kindly read through the notes and helped me with their style and referencing. I am very grateful to her for her time and kindness. I would also like to thank my PhD student, Kerem Altiparmak, for updating the case references. Emily Hearn, another of my former students, read through the entire text to eliminate linguistic or grammatical errors; I am grateful to her for this kindness. Having said that, I remain of course responsible for all this work; its inadequacies and imperfections rest solely with me.

In addition to the actual reading of the draft chapters and assistance with the writing of the book, I remain in debt to several colleagues for their overall support and encouragement. A particular debt is owed to Professor Sally Wheeler (former Head of the Department of Law, University of Leeds) for her kindness, support and for her enormous efforts in developing my academic career. I would like to thank Professor Jo Shaw (University of Manchester) for her support and encouragement. Professor Adam Crawford from the Leeds Law Department also very generously supported me in my research. I am very grateful to Caroline Busiman (Law School, University of Westminster) for her kindness and support. My special thanks to Pat Bond, Jill Birch and the copy-editors at Pearson Education for their enormous help and support in completing this study.

Finally, and most importantly I would like to thank my parents for their patience, understanding and love – I would like to dedicate this book to them.

I have tried to state the law as it stood at the beginning of 2002, and where possible up until 31 March 2002.

Javaid Rehman
University of Leeds
March 2002

TABLE OF CASES

International Criminal Tribunal for the Former Yugoslavia

Human Rights Committee

United Nations Committee Against Torture (CAT)

European Court of Human Rights

European Commission of Human Rights

European Court of Justice

Inter-American Court of Human Rights

Inter-American Commission on Human Rights

African Commission on Human and Peoples' Rights

Other International Decisions

DOMESTIC COURTS

Botswana

Canada

India and Pakistan

Israel

Namibia

United Kingdom

United States of America

Zimbabwe

TABLE OF TREATIES

TABLE OF OTHER
DOCUMENTS

———

ABBREVIATIONS

AALR	*Anglo–American Law Review*
ACHR	American Convention on Human Rights
ADHR	American Declaration of the Rights and Duties of Man
AFCHPR	African Charter on Human and Peoples' Rights
AJIL	*American Journal of International Law*
ALJ	*Australian Law Journal*
APJEL	*Asia Pacific Journal of Environmental Law*
AUJILP	*American University Journal of International Law and Policy*
AYBIL	*Australian Yearbook of International Law*
Buff LR	*Buffalo Law Review*
BYIL	*British Year Book of International Law*
Cal. WestILJ	*California Western International Law Journal*
CEDAW	Committee on the Elimination of All Forms of Discrimination against Women
CERD	Committee on the Elimination of All Forms of Racial Discrimination
CHRLR	*Columbia Human Rights Law Review*
CLF	*Criminal Law Forum*
CLJ	*Cambridge Law Journal*
CLP	*Current Legal Problems*
COE	Council of Europe
Col.JTL	*Columbia Journal of Transnational Law*
CSW	Commission on the Status of Women
CYBIL	*Canadian Year Book of International Law*
ECHR	European Convention for the Protection of Human Rights and Fundamental Freedoms
ECOSOC	Economic and Social Council
EHRLR	*European Human Rights Law Review*
EHRR	*European Human Rights Reports*
EJIL	*European Journal of International Law*
ESC	European Social Charter
E.T.S	European Treaty Series
EU	European Union
GA.JICL	*Georgia Journal of International and Comparative Law*

xl

GAOR	General Assembly Official Records
GYBIL	*German Year Book of International Law*
Harvard.ILJ	*Harvard International Law Journal*
HRCP	Human Rights Commission of Pakistan
HRLJ	*Human Rights Law Journal*
HRQ	*Human Rights Quarterly*
ICCPR	International Covenant on Civil and Political Rights
ICESCR	International Covenant on Economic, Social and Cultural Rights
ICJ	International Court of Justice
ICLQ	*International and Comparative Law Quarterly*
IHRR	*International Human Rights Reports*
IJIL	*Indian Journal of International Law*
IJLF	*International Journal of Law and Family*
IJMGR	*International Journal on Minority and Group Rights*
IJRL	*International Journal of Refugee Law*
I.L.M.	International Legal Materials
ILO	International Labour Organisation
ILR	International Law Reports
Iowa LR	*Iowa Law Reports*
Israel L.R.	*Israel Law Reports*
IYHR	*Israel Year Book on Human Rights*
JAL	*Journal of African Law*
JILP	Journal of International Law and Policy
JOLS	*Journal of Law and Society*
LQR	*Law Quarterly Review*
McGill LR	*McGill Law Review*
MLR	*Modern Law Review*
MRG	Minority Rights Group
NILR	*Netherlands International Law Review*
NJHR	*Nordic Journal on Human Rights*
NQHR	*Netherlands Quarterly of Human Rights*
NYIL	*Netherlands Year Book of International Law*
NYUJILP	*New York University Journal of International Law and Politics*
O.A.S.	Organisation of American States
O.A.S.T.S.	Organisation of American States Treaty Series
ODIHR	The Office for Democratic Institutions of Human Rights
OP	Optional Protocol
OSCE	The Organisation for Security and Cooperation in Europe
OAU	Organisation of African Unity
PASIL	*Proceedings of the American Society of International Law*
PCIJ	Permanent Court of International Justice

Race Convention	International Convention on the Elimination of All Forms of Racial Discrimination
Rec. des Cours	*Recueil des Cours de l'Académie de Droit International*
TEu	Treaty of European Union
Tex.ILJ	*Texas International Law Journal*
UDHR	Universal Declaration of Human Rights
U.K.T.S	United Kingdom Treaty Series
UN	United Nations
U.N.T.S	United Nations Treaty Series
UNYBH	United Nations Year Book on Human Rights
Va.JIL	*Virginia Journal of International Law*
Vand.JTL	*Vanderbilt Journal of Transnational Law*
VCLT	Vienna Convention on the Law of Treaties
Yale LJ	*Yale Law Journal*
YBILC	*Year Book of the International Law Commission*
YBUN	Year Book of the United Nations
YEL	*Year Book of European Law*
YJIL	*Yale Journal of International Law*

OVERVIEW OF INTERNATIONAL HUMAN RIGHTS LAW: THEORY AND PRACTICE

HUMAN RIGHTS OF THE INDIVIDUAL IN INTERNATIONAL LAW[1]

The emergence of human rights law in the international sphere is one of the most significant developments to have taken place since the end of the Second World War.[2] International human rights law has challenged and jettisoned the traditional rules relating to State sovereignty. These traditional rules perceived international law as a law primarily related to sovereign States in which non-State actors, in particular individuals, had a tiny role to play. A key aspect of the traditional legal order was the reliance of States upon non-interference in their domestic affairs, which meant that violations of human rights were not a matter of international concern.[3]

---

[1] See A. Cassese, *Human Rights in a Changing World* (Philadelphia: Temple University Press) 1990; K.E. Mahoney and P. Mahoney (eds), *Human Rights in the Twenty-First Century, A global challenge* (Dordrecht: Maritinus Nijhoff Publishers) 1993; A.H. Robertson and J.G. Merrills, *Human Rights in the World: An Introduction to the Study of International Protection of Human Rights*, 4th edn (Manchester: Manchester University Press) 1996; T. Meron (ed.), *Human Rights in International Law: Legal and Policy Issues* (Oxford: Clarendon Press) 1984; L. Henkin (ed.), *The International Bill of Rights: The Covenant on Civil and Political Rights* (New York: Columbia University Press) 1981; M.S. McDougal, H.D. Lasswell, L-C. Chen, *Human Rights and World Public Order: The Basic Policies of an International Law of Human Dignity* (New Haven, Conn.: Yale University Press) 1980; D.J. Harris, *Cases and Materials on International Law*, 5th edn (London: Sweet and Maxwell) 1998, pp. 624–764.

[2] H. Lauterpacht, *International Law and Human Rights* (New York: F. A. Praeger) 1950; S. Oda, 'The Individual in International Law' in M. Sørensen (ed.), *Manual of Public International Law* (London: Macmillan) 1968, pp. 469–530; Robertson and Merrills, above n. 1; these developments are considered in detail in subsequent chapters of this book.

[3] See R.B. Bilder, 'An Overview of International Human Rights Law' in H. Hannum (ed.), *Guide to International Human Rights Practice* (New York: Transnational Publishers) 1999, 3–18 at p. 4.

The rights of the individual, with the limited exceptions of treatment of aliens and arguably that of humanitarian intervention, was a subject that was not addressed by international law.[4] Even in relation to the aforementioned exceptions, international legal order represented the dominance of States without according individuals any specific rights. Thus in the absence of an independent legal personality for the individual, if his rights were violated by a foreign State, it was the State of which the victim was a citizen which was authorised to bring a claim for violation of his rights. In the case of humanitarian intervention, while military force was sometimes used to intervene to protect (primarily religious) minorities such actions were often accompanied (if not dictated) by selfish motives, e.g. territorial gains.[5] Individuals themselves were unable to claim the right of humanitarian intervention nor was there a wholesale recognition of any such right at the global level.[6]

The growth and expansion of human rights law has brought about a radical change in the ideological bases of international law. Such a change is first evident in the universal acknowledgement that gross violations of individual and collective rights cannot be justified on grounds of sovereignty or domestic jurisdiction.[7] These are concerns for the international community as a whole, with the growing recognition that protection of fundamental human rights is an obligation *erga omnes*.[8] Secondly, as we shall consider

---

[4] D. McGoldrick, *Human Rights Committee: Its Role in the Development of the International Covenant on Civil and Political Rights* (Oxford: Clarendon Press) 1991, p. 3.

[5] For a survey of the literature on the subject see F.R. Teson, *Humanitarian Intervention: An Inquiry into Law and Morality* (Irvington-on-Hudson, NY: Transnational Publishers) 1997; N. Ronzitti, *Rescuing Nationals Abroad through Military Coercion and Intervention on Grounds of Humanity* (Dordrecht: Martinus Nijhoff Publishers) 1985; T.M. Franck and N.S. Rodley, 'After Bangladesh: The Law of Humanitarian Intervention by Military Force' 67 *AJIL* (1973) 275; R.B. Lillich (ed.), *Humanitarian Intervention and the United Nations* (Charlottesville: University Press of Virginia) 1973; R.B. Lillich, 'Intervention to Protect Human Rights' 15 *McGill LR* (1965) 205; E. Behanuik, 'The Law of Unilateral Humanitarian Intervention by Armed Force: A Legal Survey' 79 *Military Law Review* (1978) 157; J.-P.L. Fonteyne, 'The Customary International Law Doctrine of Humanitarian Intervention: Its Current Validity under the UN Charter' 4 *Cal.WestILJ* (1974) 203.

[6] Since the ending of the cold war, the Security Council under Chapter VII of the United Nations (UN) has on occasions authorised collective armed intervention in response to gross violations of human rights. See S. Chesterman, *Just War or Just Peace: Humanitarian Intervention and International Law* (Oxford: Clarendon Press) 2001; P. Alston, 'The Security Council and Human Rights: Lessons to be Learned from the Iraq–Kuwait Crisis and its Aftermath' 13 *AYBIL* (1990–91) 107; H. Adelman, 'Humanitarian Intervention: The Case of Kurds' 4 *IJRL* (1992) 4; P. Malanczuk, 'The Kurdish Crises and Allied Intervention in the Aftermath of the Second Gulf War' 2 *EJIL* (1991) 114.

[7] P. Sands and P. Klein, *Bowett's Law of International Institutions*, 5th edn (London: Sweet and Maxwell) 2001, p. 24.

[8] See *Barcelona Traction, Light and Power Company, Limited Case (Belgium v. Spain)*, Judgment 5 February 1970, (1970) ICJ Reports 3, 32; R. Jennings and A. Watts, *Oppenheim's International Law*, 9th edn (Harlow: Longman) 1992, Vol. 1, p. 5.

in this book, the last quarter of the twentieth century saw a mushrooming of international human rights instruments. Specific treaties dealing with the prohibition of racial discrimination and torture, and those defining and promoting children and women's rights have been adopted. Thirdly, the setting up of various mechanisms to publicise, promote and protect human rights has heightened human rights awareness to impact significantly on other areas of international law such as international economic law, business law and environmental law. Fourthly, the procedural advancement of international human rights law has meant that individuals are more directly involved in challenging violations of their rights in international courts, committees and tribunals.

Notwithstanding these advances, in practice human rights law continues to be constrained and limited. Subsequent chapters establish that not only are there substantive weaknesses in existing rights, the application of these rights is impaired by the absences, weaknesses, and limitations of implementation mechanisms and procedures. Our analysis elaborates upon many of these weaknesses and limitations. The lack of enforcement machinery impinges upon all areas of international law, although its impact is felt most vividly in human rights law.

STRUCTURE OF THE BOOK

This book has been divided into five parts and consists of sixteen substantive chapters. These introductory comments are followed by a brief consideration of a number of themes and concepts which consistently recur in this book; a proper understanding of these forms an essential prerequisite to a comprehensive understanding of the subject. Part I of the book, which is entitled international legal system and human rights, provides an overview of the nature of modern international law, the United Nations System and its relationship with modern human rights law. In the light of the *sui generis* character of international law and in recognition of the fact that international human rights is a branch of international law such an analysis appears necessary; an exercise conducted in Chapter 1 of Part I. Chapter 2 (also contained in Part I) deals with the United Nations system and its relationship with the modern human rights regime. This chapter gives consideration to the principal organs of the United Nations with particular reference to their role in protecting human rights. Part II is entitled the International Bill of Rights. It consists of three chapters and considers in depth the Universal Declaration of Human Rights (UDHR),[9] the International Covenant on Civil and Political Rights

---

[9] 10 December, 1948, UN GA Res. 217 A (III), UN Doc. A/810 at 71 (1948).

(ICCPR)[10] and the International Covenant on Economic, Social and Cultural Rights (ICESCR).[11] Part III of the book analyses the regional protection of human rights. The oldest and by far the most advanced regional human rights system is the Council of Europe's European Convention on Human Rights (ECHR).[12] Chapter 6 considers the substantive rights and the implementation mechanisms of ECHR. The work of the Council of Europe in the context of protecting social and economic rights is examined in Chapter 7. Chapter 7 also considers the role of two other regional organisations, the European Union (EU) and Organisation for Security and Cooperation in Europe (OSCE). Both these inter-governmental organisations are increasingly involved in promoting various strands of human rights. Chapter 8 analyses the interesting though complex protection afforded to the Americas by the Inter-American System of Human Rights. The final chapter of Part III, Chapter 9, considers the African Charter on Human and Peoples' Rights (AFCHPR).[13] The AFCHPR is the latest and potentially the most innovative of all regional human rights treaties. A detailed study of this Charter reveals a number of interesting features, which also represent a distinctly African character of human rights protection. Part IV of the book considers the position of individuals belonging to various groups. Although distinctions based on group rights are not simplistic, these chapters focus on racial and religious discrimination, on minorities, indigenous peoples, women and children. The final part, Part V, deals with specific crimes against the dignity of humankind. Chapter 15 analyses the abhorrent (though widely practised) crime of torture against individuals. This chapter presents a detailed survey of efforts on the part of the international community to condemn torture, and cruel, inhuman and degrading treatment or punishment. Chapter 16, the concluding chapter, considers the subject of terrorism and its role in violating fundamental human rights. The evil of terrorism has been confronted by a number of States, in some cases for very long and sustained periods. As we shall consider, although several instruments have been adopted to combat terrorism, recent political events have highlighted the inadequacies of the existing regime to protect human rights from international and national terrorism.

---

[10] Adopted at New York, 16 December, 1966. Entered into force 23 March 1976. GA Res. 2200A (XXI) UN Doc. A/6316 (1966) 999 U.N.T.S. 171; 6 I.L.M. (1967) 368.
[11] Adopted at New York, 16 December, 1966. Entered into force 3 January 1976. GA Res. 2200A (XXI) UN Doc. A/6316 (1966) 993 U.N.T.S. 3; 6 I.L.M. (1967) 360.
[12] Signed in Rome, 4 November 1950. Entered into force 3 September 1953. 213 U.N.T.S. 221; E.T.S. 5.
[13] Adopted on 27 June 1981. Entered into force 21 October, 1986. OAU Doc. CAB/LEG/67/3 Rev. 5, 21 I.L.M (1982) 58.

SOME RECURRENT THEMES

Universalism and regionalism[14]

There has been a long-standing philosophical debate over the nature, categorisation and prioritisation of rights. There is also a debate about the universality of human rights norms. Is the content and scope of rights variable according to regional, religious and political backgrounds or is there a single set of human rights applicable to every individual? The debate upon the issue of universality has been a divisive one with challenges being presented on the basis of regional, cultural and religious distinctions.[15] Proponents of regionalism, for example those purporting Asian or African regionalism, have advocated the establishment of distinct systems.[16] The Islamic States, which form a significant block, have advanced their standards of human rights. The Islamic States claim that primacy should be accorded to the *Sharia*, even if it were to be in conflict with modern norms of human rights law.[17]

The consideration of this debate, its reasoning and outcome is not purely academic but has contributed to varying sets of standards. This book considers these standards and their effectiveness is analysed in the context of international and regional mechanisms for the protection of human rights. At the international level, views differ on such fundamental issues as the rights of

[14] See E. Brems, *Human Rights: Universality and Diversity* (The Hague: Kluwer Law International) 2001; A.D. Renteln, *International Human Rights: Universalism versus Relativism* (Newbury Park: Sage Publications) 1990; A.D. Renteln, 'The Unanswered Challenge of Relativism and Consequences of Human Rights' 7 *HRQ* (1985) 514; H. Gros Espiell, 'The Evolving Concept of Human Rights: Western, Socialist and Third World Approaches' in B.G. Ramcharan (ed.), *Human Rights: Thirty Years after the Universal Declaration: Commemorative Volume on the Occasion of the Thirtieth Anniversary of the Universal Declaration of Human Rights* (The Hague: Martinus Nijhoff Publishers) 1979, pp. 41–65; D. Donoho, 'Relativism Versus Universalism in Human Rights: The Search for Meaningful Standards' 27 *Stanford Law Journal* (1991) 345; A. Eide, 'Making Human Rights Universal: Unfinished Business' 6 *NJHR* (1988) 51; J. Donnelly, 'Cultural Relativism and Universal Human Rights' 6 *HRQ* (1984) 400.
[15] See D.E. Arzt, 'The Application of International Human Rights Law in Islamic States' 12 *HRQ* (1990) 202; D.J. Sullivan, 'Advancing the Freedom of Religion or Belief through the UN Declaration on the Elimination of Religious Intolerance and Discrimination' 82 *AJIL* (1988) 487; A.A. An-Na'im, 'Religious Minorities under Islamic Law and the Limits of Cultural Relativism' 9 *HRQ* (1987) 1.
[16] See I. Nguema, 'Human Rights Perspective in Africa' 11 *HRLJ* (1990) 261; B. Ibhawoh, 'Cultural Relativism and Human Rights: Reconsidering the Africanist Discourse' 19 *NQHR* (2001) 43; S.P. Subedi, 'Are the Principles of Human Rights "Western" Ideas? An Analysis of the Claim of the "Asian" Concept of Human Rights from the Perspectives of Hinduism' 30 *Cal.WestILJ* (1999) 45.
[17] See Report on the Human Rights Situation in the Islamic Republic of Iran by the Special Representatives of the Commission, UN Doc.E/CN. 4/1987/23 (1987). Also see the Reservations made by Islamic States to the Convention on the Elimination of All Forms of Discrimination Against Women (1979) and the Convention on the Rights of the Child (1989). Discussed below Chapters 13 and 14. W.A. Schabas, 'Reservations to the Convention on the Rights of the Child' 18 *HRQ* (1996) 472.

women, children and religious minorities. Another lively though inconclusive debate centres around criminal process and the compatibility of certain punishments with modern human rights values. In some instances (e.g. minority rights) the significant differences have led to failure in formulating comprehensive legally binding instruments. In some others (e.g. the rights of women and children) the strength of international consensus has been diluted due to large-scale reservations placed by States that are parties to the relevant treaties. Subsequent chapters will consider the controversies that exist among States on such issues as the prohibition of capital and corporal punishments.[18]

The existing variations regarding human rights (both in terms of substantive rights and implementation mechanisms) are considered through a study of the European, American and African systems. In addition to the aforementioned regional systems, there are other human rights systems, such as those established under the auspices of the Arab League and the South Asian Association of Regional Cooperation, which adopt a relativist approach.[19] It is equally important to note that in recent years, with the rise of the pan-Islamic movement, Islamic States have propagated a distinct human rights code.[20] There is no single, simple answer to this complex subject. This book recommends that while legitimate variations exist between diverse views of human rights, there is a central core of all human rights values. This central core represents the most fundamental of human rights from which no derogations are permissible.

Interdependence of human rights[21]

The varied perceptions of human rights have also led to claims that there are 'three generations' of human rights. The so-called 'first generation' of human rights is represented by civil and political rights and can be found in treaties such as the ICCPR and ECHR. These rights have traditionally been associated with and have been given priority by western States. The social, economic and cultural rights are equated with the 'second generation' of human rights.

---

[18] See in particular below Chapters 4, 6, 9 and 15.

[19] A. Ahsan, *SAARC: A Perspective* (Dhaka: Dhaka University Press) 1991; A.A. An-Na'im, 'Human Rights in the Arab World: A Regional Perspective' 23 *HRQ* (2001) 701.

[20] See the Islamic Universal Declaration of Human Rights (1981). For further analysis see A.E. Mayer, *Islam and Human Rights: Tradition and Politics* (Boulder, Col.: Westview Press) 1999; J. Rehman, 'Accommodating Religious Identities in an Islamic State: International Law, Freedom of Religion and the Rights of Religious Minorities' 7 *IJMGR* (2000) 139.

[21] See below Chapters 5 and 7. H.J. Steiner and P. Alston (eds), *International Human Rights in Context: Law, Politics, Morals: Text and Materials*, 2nd edn (Oxford: Clarendon Press) 2000, pp. 237–320; C. Scott, 'Reaching Beyond (without Abandoning) the Category of "Economic, Social and Cultural Rights"' 21 *HRQ* (1999) 633; S. Leckie, 'Another Step Towards Indivisibility: Identifying the Key Features of Violations of Economic, Social and Cultural Rights' 20 *HRQ* (1998) 81.

These rights have been canvassed very strongly by the socialist countries and by the developing world. Views on the value and application of the two generations of rights differ markedly. The first generation of rights has often been given priority over second-generation rights. It is generally viewed that civil and political rights could be implemented immediately, whereas economic, social and cultural rights can be introduced only progressively. It is also argued that the application of civil and political rights is less costly (as the State is required to abstain from certain activities, e.g. not to engage in torture), and that civil and political rights are justiciable whereas economic, social and cultural rights are not.

In the last quarter of the twentieth century another generation of human rights, the 'third generation' of rights, emerged. The idea of the third generation of rights has been supported largely by the developing world. This set of rights includes collective group rights and such rights as the right to development, the right to self-determination and the right to environment. In our analysis of the subject, while appreciating the various viewpoints on the nature and scope of human rights, it is important to adopt a holistic approach. This approach follows the principles established by UDHR, which affords recognition to all three generations of rights. This book argues that it is important to accord equal protection importance to all three sets of rights and to acknowledge, 'all human rights are universal, indivisible and interdependent and interrelated'.[22]

The scope of human rights law – individual and minority rights[23]

For much of the period since 1945, the focus of modern international human rights law has been upon the rights of the individual. The issue of minority rights has remained peripheral to human rights, notwithstanding the fact that often individuals are victimised or discriminated against because they belong to a particular ethnic, racial, religious, social or political group. It is therefore not surprising to note that only a limited discussion of the subject of minority rights can be found in classical international human rights textbooks. The events of the last two decades have, alongside significant changes in global political geography, brought a shift in the approach of international community. The tragedies of Rwanda and the former Yugoslavia prompted the United Nations to establish ad hoc tribunals to try and punish those involved

---

[22] United Nations World Conference on Human Rights, *Vienna Declaration and Programme of Action*, (New York: United Nations Department of Public Information) 1993 para 5 (pt 1). Adopted 25 June 1993.

[23] See below Chapters 10–12; see P. Thornberry, *International Law and the Rights of Minorities* (Oxford: Clarendon Press) 1991; J. Rehman, *The Weaknesses in the International Protection of Minority Rights* (The Hague: Kluwer Law International) 2000.

in, *inter alia*, crimes against humanity and genocide.[24] In 1998, the Statute of the International Criminal Court[25] was adopted. Once operative, the International Criminal Court would have the jurisdiction to try individuals for serious violations of human rights, including genocide and crimes against humanity. Having attained the required sixty ratifications on 11 April 2002, the Statute shall enter into force on 1 July 2002.

International and regional organisations have also been active in further standard setting for promoting minorities and indigenous peoples. In 1989 the International Labour Organisation (ILO) adopted the Convention Concerning Indigenous and Tribal Peoples in Independent Countries, ILO No. 169[26] and in December 1992 the United Nations General Assembly approved a resolution on the Rights of Persons belonging to National or Ethnic, Religious and Linguistic Minorities.[27] The Council of Europe, and other regional organisations have also adopted a number of instruments which aim to protect minorities. In the changing global environment, claims from minority groups are having a substantial impact on the theory and practice of human rights law. Minorities differ in their approaches, some claiming constitutional autonomy, while others, more radical in their demands, may resort to violence, destruction and terrorism. In specifically addressing the position of minorities and indigenous peoples, it is submitted that this book is taking an approach appropriate to the legal and political realities of the twenty-first century.

The public/private divide in human rights law[28]

The progression of human rights law has generally been in the direction of according protection to individuals against their States, with the 'anti-State' stance flowing 'from the assumption that individual persons must be protected from the abuse of power of parliaments, governments and public authorities'.[29] As this book will consider in detail, human rights instruments in targeting the State direct their attention towards governments and other public bodies. There is no particular focus on the violations conducted by non-State actors. Does this means that violations of human rights conducted

---

[24] See below Chapters 11 and 12.
[25] Statute of the International Criminal Court, Rome, July 17 1998, A/CONF.183/9.
[26] ILO No. 169, 27 June 1989, 28 I.L.M. (1989) 1382.
[27] 18 December 1992, UN Doc. A/Res/47/135; 32 I.L.M. (1993) 911.
[28] See A. Clapham, *Human Rights in the Private Sphere* (Oxford: Clarendon Press) 1993; M. Forde, 'Non-Governmental Interferences with Human Rights' 56 *BYIL* (1985) 253. These issues are of particular relevance to the protection of such groups as women and children; see below Chapters 13 and 14.
[29] F. Von Prondzynski, *Freedom of Association and Industrial Relations: A Comparative Study* (London: Mansell Publishing Limited) 1987, p. 1.

by private individuals against each other cannot be the subject of scrutiny of international human rights mechanisms?

It is noticeable that many of the violations of individual and group rights are regularly conducted by private individuals themselves against vulnerable groups such as women and children.[30] It would clearly be absurd if these non-State actors were under no obligation to protect human rights in the same way as governments and public officials are. As we shall consider shortly, States are principal subjects of international law and have developed a large network of human rights laws by entering into a range of agreements. While these agreements bind States either in treaty or in customary law, the undertakings are broad; they represent an obligation not only not to violate human rights themselves, but also to undertake to 'ensure'[31] or 'secure'[32] the rights of individuals. The process, by which human rights are to be protected from violations conducted by private individuals, sometimes referred to as the horizontal application of law, has been approved and applied by human rights courts and tribunals. This horizontal application of law aims to provide a comprehensive protection of human rights.[33] States must undertake positive steps to ensure protection from a significant number of violations that take place in the confines of family and private life.

---

[30] See the terminology of the ECHR. ECHR jurisprudence confirms that States can be accountable for acts conducted by private individuals against each other, see *A v. UK*, Judgment of 23 September 1998, 1998-VI RJD 2692; *X and Y v. The Netherlands*, Judgment of 26 March 1985, Series A, No. 91.

[31] See ICCPR Article 2(1); ACHR Article 1.

[32] See ECHR Article 1; according to Article 1 ACHR the 'undertaking is to give effect to [the rights]'.

[33] See the Inter-American Court of Human Rights in the *Velasquez Rodriguez Case*, Judgment of July 29 1988, Inter-Am.Ct.H.R. (Ser. C) No. 4 (1988), para 170.

I

INTERNATIONAL LEGAL SYSTEM AND HUMAN RIGHTS

1

INTERNATIONAL LAW AND HUMAN RIGHTS

INTRODUCTION[1]

In order properly to comprehend the structure of international human rights law, a basic understanding of the nature and operations of international law is required. International human rights law is a branch of international law and shares characteristics and sources of international law. The introductory comments on the nature of international law will be particularly useful for those students who have no previous experience of international law. The chapter considers first the nature and definition of international law. As will be established by our discussion, international law has a character distinct from national laws. International law, unlike national systems, does not base itself on a single unified legislature which makes the laws, an executive organ which enforces them and a judiciary with jurisdiction to decide upon any disputes. This *sui generis* character has led international law to develop itself through a range of sources. Treaty law and custom are well established and classed as recognised sources of international law. There are also others, less conventional and traditionally regarded as subsidiary sources, although as this chapter elaborates the role of General Assembly Resolutions has been significant in developing international law. The chapter concludes with a consideration of those norms of international law from which no derogation is permissible.

---

[1] See A.H. Robertson and J.G. Merrills, *Human Rights in the World: An Introduction to the Study of International Protection of Human Rights*, 4th edn (Manchester: Manchester University Press) 1996; D.J. Harris, *Cases and Materials on International Law*, 5th edn (London: Sweet and Maxwell) 1998, pp. 624–764; A. Cassese, *Human Rights in a Changing World* (Philadelphia: Temple University Press) 1990; M.N. Shaw, *International Law*, 4th edn, (Cambridge: Grotius Publication) 1997, pp. 196–294.

NATURE AND DEFINITION OF INTERNATIONAL LAW

The issues related to the nature and definition of international law are of significant value in establishing the sphere of modern human rights law. As noted in the introductory chapter, international law has traditionally been seen as law that regulates relations between independent and sovereign States, and while the impact of individual human rights has been significant, international law continues to be primarily concerned with the relationship among States. States are the principal subjects of international law, and not only play a key role in the creation of international law but also remain pivotal in its execution and enforcement. International law has been defined by Sir Robert Jennings and Sir Arthur Watts as:

> the body of rules which are legally binding on states in their intercourse with each other. These rules are primarily those which govern the relations of states, but are not the only subjects of international law. International organisations and, to some extent also individuals may be subjects of rights conferred and duties imposed by international law.[2]

Notwithstanding the recognition of a limited role which international organisations and individuals play in the international legal system, the predominant position of States remains firmly established. States retain an exclusive position in the creation of norms of international law. Their exclusive membership of the United Nations ensures their absolute control of the principal organs such as the General Assembly, the Security Council and the Economic and Social Council. It is only the States which could appear before the International Court of Justice in contentious proceedings. As subsequent chapters elaborate, the recognition of international human rights and the enhanced procedural standing has been a product of international treaty agreements, obligations which have been undertaken by States themselves to allow the individual the *locus standi* to make claims to international bodies. In the light of these observations, Professor Cassese's analogy to 'puny Davids confronted by overwhelming Goliaths holding all the instruments of power' when describing the relationship between individuals and States is an accurate one.[3]

CHARACTERISTICS OF INTERNATIONAL LAW

International law is distinct from national legal systems. Unlike domestic legal systems, there is as such no legislature (making laws for the entire international community) nor is there an executive which enforces the decisions

---

[2] R. Jennings and A. Watts, *Oppenheim's International Law*, 9th edn (Harlow: Longman) 1992, Vol. 1, p. 4.

[3] A. Cassese, *International law* (Oxford: Oxford University Press) 2001, p. 4.

made by the legislature.[4] There are also no comparable judicial institutions which would try violations of law and award a judgment against the offender.[5] Our analysis of the position of the United Nations will establish that none of the principal organs are comparable to those that are found on the national level. Thus the United Nations General Assembly, while representing all member States, is not the equivalent to a national legislature. The General Assembly Resolutions, save for limited exceptions, are of a recommendatory nature and as such cannot bind member States. The executive functions of the Security Council are circumscribed both 'legally and politically'.[6] The powers of enforcement actions are triggered not by any mis-demeanour but only through a determination of 'breach of the peace and security'. The consent of State parties remains the critical element in invoking the contentious jurisdiction of the International Court of Justice.

The absence of a legislature, an executive body, and a judiciary with compulsory jurisdiction over all its members, makes international law very different from national legal systems. The absence of a sovereign authority has led critics to doubt whether international law could be termed as 'law'; some would treat it more as an aspect of 'positive morality' than as law. The essence of proper understanding of the nature of law, it is submitted, is to acknowledge its differences from national law and its *sui generis* characteristics. Commenting on these characteristics Professor Shaw notes:

> While the legal structure within all but the most primitive societies is hierarchical and authority is vertical, rather like a pyramid with the sovereign person or unit in a position of supremacy on top, the international system is horizontal consisting of over 180 independent states, all equal in legal theory (in that they all possess the characteristics of sovereignty) and recognising no one in authority over them. The law is above individuals in domestic systems, but international law only exists as between the states. Individuals only have the choice as to whether to obey the law or not. They do not create it. That is done by specific institutions. In international law, on the other hand, it is the states themselves that create the law and obey or disobey it. This, of course, has profound repercussions as regards the sources of law as well as the means for enforcing legal rules.[7]

SOURCES OF INTERNATIONAL LAW

The *sui generis* character of international law is not only evident in its organisation of the system but is also reflected through the manner in which

---

[4] Shaw, above n. 1, at p. 3.

[5] Ibid.

[6] P. Malanczuk, *Akehurst's Modern Introduction to International Law*, 7th edn (London: Routledge) 1997, p. 3.

[7] Shaw, above n. 1, at pp. 5–6.

international laws are created. Within domestic legal systems sources of law can be readily identified. In the case of the United Kingdom, we would consider Acts of Parliament as primary sources of law. As noted earlier, within international law there are no institutions comparable to a domestic legislative body. The absence of any single identifiable legislature is substituted by a range of means, all of which essentially emanate from the consent of States. Concomitant with the absence of a legislative organ, there is also a lack of consensus regarding the list of sources of international law. Article 38(1) of the Statute of the International Court of Justice[8] is often invoked as providing sources of international law. Article 38(1) provides as follow

> The Court, whose function is to decide in accordance with international law such disputes as are submitted to it, shall apply:

(a)   international conventions, whether general or particular, establishing rules expressly recognized by the contesting States;
(b)   international custom, as evidence of a general practice accepted as law;
(c)   the general principles of law recognized by civilised nations;
(d)   subject to the provisions of Article 59, judicial decisions and the teachings of the most highly qualified publicists of the various nations, as subsidiary means for the determination of rules of law.

International conventions

The reference in Article 38(1)(a) is directed to international treaties, which are also varyingly described as covenants, charters, pacts, declarations, protocols and conventions. In our study we will come across various examples of treaties, which include the United Nations Charter,[9] ICCPR[10] and ICESCR,[11] the International Convention on the Elimination of All Forms of Racial Discrimination,[12] and the Convention on the Elimination of All Forms of Discrimination against Women.[13] Treaties represent legally binding obligations undertaken by States parties and represent 'a more modern and more

---

[8] Adopted at San Francisco, 26 June 1945. Entered into force 24 October 1945, 59 Stat. 1055, 3 Bevans 1179.

[9] Adopted at San Francisco 26 June 1945. Entered into force 24 October 1945. 1 U.N.T.S. xvi; U.K.T.S. 67 (1946); 59 Stat. 1031.

[10] Adopted at New York, 16 December 1966. Entered into force 23 March 1976. GA Res. 2200A (XXI) UN Doc. A/6316 (1966) 999 U.N.T.S. 171, 6 I.L.M. (1967) 368.

[11] Adopted at New York, 16 December 1966. Entered into force 3 January 1976. GA Res. 2200A (XXI) UN Doc. A/6316 (1966) 993 U.N.T.S. 3 (1967), 6 I.L.M. (1967) 360.

[12] Adopted 21 December 1965. Entered into force, 4 January 1969. 660 U.N.T.S. 195, 5 I.L.M (1966) 352.

[13] Adopted at New York, 18 December 1979. Entered into force 3 September 1981. UN GA Res. 34/180(XXXIV), GA. Res. 34/180, 34 GAOR, Supp. (No. 46) 194, UN Doc. A/34/46, at 193 (1979), 2 U.K.T.S. (1989); 19 I.L.M (1980) 33.

deliberate method'[14] of creating laws. The most widely recognised definition of a treaty can be found in the Vienna Convention on the Law of Treaties (1969).[15] According to Article 2, a treaty for the purposes of the Vienna Convention is:

> an international agreement concluded between States in written form and governed by international law, whether embodied in a single instrument or in two or more related instruments and whatever its particular designation.[16]

The binding nature of treaties can be likened to contractual agreements in domestic law, although such an analogy is most suited to the so-called treaty-contracts. Treaty-contracts are those treaties which are entered into by two or a few States and deal with a particular matter. By contrast, the law-making treaties create legal obligations, the observance of which does not dissolve treaty obligations. A vital characteristic of law-making treaties is the laying down of rules of general or universal application. It is in this context that the role of treaties as a source of international law is of great significance. Examples of law-making treaties include the United Nations Charter,[17] the Convention on the Prevention and Punishment of the Crime of Genocide,[18] and the Geneva Conventions.[19]

An essential feature of treaty law is that a treaty does not bind non-State parties. However, law-making treaties can in fact bind non-parties, not as a treaty obligation, but as part of customary international law. We shall consider the elements which constitute customary law in the next section. Suffice it to note

---

[14] Shaw, above n. 1, at p. 73.

[15] Concluded at Vienna 23 May 1969. Entered into force 27 January 1980; 58 U.K.T.S (1980), Cmnd 7964; 1154 U.N.T.S. 331.

[16] This definition excludes a number of agreements (e.g. unwritten agreements between States and those between States and international organisations). Such an exclusion however does not mean that these agreements cannot be characterised as binding or as treaties. An agreement would be established so long as the parties intend to create binding legal relationship among themselves. See Shaw, above n. 1, at p. 636.

[17] Signed in San Francisco 26 June 1945. Entered into force 24 October 1945. 1 U.N.T.S. xvi; U.K.T.S 67 (1946); 59 Stat. 1031.

[18] Convention on the Prevention and Punishment of the Crime of Genocide, adopted 9 December 1948. Entered into force 12 January 1951. 78 U.N.T.S. 277. Considered below Chapter 11.

[19] See Geneva Convention (No: I) for the Amelioration of the Condition of the Wounded and Sick in Armed Forces in the Field. Concluded at Geneva, 12 August 1949. Entered into force 21 October 1950. 75 U.N.T.S. 31; Geneva Convention (No: II) for the Amelioration of the Condition of Wounded, Sick and Shipwrecked Members of Armed Forces at Sea Concluded at Geneva, 12 August 1949. Entered into force 21 October 1950. 75 U.N.T.S. 85; Geneva Convention (No: III) Relative to the Treatment of Prisoners of War (without Annexes) Concluded at Geneva 12 August 1949. Entered into force, 21 October 1950. 75 U.N.T.S. 135. Geneva Convention (No: IV) Relative to the Protection of Civilian Persons in Time of War (without annexes) Concluded at Geneva 12 August 1949. Entered into force 21 October 1950, 75 U.N.T.S. 287.

here that a treaty provision could possess the customary force if it fulfils the basic criterion of the establishment of custom – it could reflect customary law if its text declares or its *travaux préparatoires* state, with the requisite *opinio juris*, that its substance is declaratory of existing law. Another significant feature of treaty law is the freedom which it provides to States in their decision to commit themselves to international legal obligations. In the case of multilateral treaties, while a State may be prepared to accept most of the provisions contained in the treaty, it may object to some articles. In these circumstances, it may decide to make a reservation to those provisions it does not wish to be bound by. The effect of a reservation made by a State party is to exclude or modify the obligations of a treaty provision in its application to that State. Article 2(1)(d) of the Vienna Convention on the Law of Treaties defines a reservation as:

> [A] unilateral statement, however phrased or named, made by a State, when signing, ratifying, accepting, approving or acceding to a treaty, whereby it purports to exclude or to modify the legal effect of certain provisions of the treaty in their application to that State.

According to the traditional practice, reservations to multilateral treaties were only accepted as valid if the treaty allowed such a reservation and all the other parties consented to it.[20] However, significant flexibility was added to this practice by the International Court of Justice in its ruling in the *Reservations to the Genocide Convention Case*.[21] In the light of special characteristics of the Genocide Convention, the Court refused to follow the earlier rigid practice. The Court, relying upon the so-called 'Object and purposes' test, stated that it was 'the incompatibility of a reservation with the object and purpose of the Convention that must furnish the criterion'[22] for States that present a reservation as well as for States adhering to it. The indication of the element of subjective judgment has meant disagreements as to the compatibility of a reservation, and consequently the status of a State as a party to a convention. As our subsequent discussion will confirm, the issue of reservations has raised substantial difficulties in not only determining the nature of the obligations undertaken by reserving States, but also the effect such reservations have upon those States which have objected to these reservations. The extensive usage of reservations and the less common deployment of vague expressions to restrict legal obligations are particularly evident with regard to conventions that relate to the rights of women and children.[23]

---

[20] C. Redgwell, 'Universality or Integrity: Some Reflections on Reservations to General Multilateral Treaties' 64 *BYIL* (1993) 245, at p. 236; see also the General Comments by the Human Rights Committee, General Comment No. 24 on Reservations to ICCPR, 15 *HRLJ* (1995) 464; 2 *IHRR* (1995) 10.
[21] *Reservations to the Convention on the Prevention and Punishment of the Crime of Genocide*, Advisory Opinion 28 May 1951 (1951 ICJ Reports, 15).
[22] Ibid. p. 124.
[23] See below Chapters 13 and 14.

Notwithstanding the difficulties that have been generated by reservations, treaties have played a leading role in developing a modern human rights regime. In particular multilateral human rights treaties, as law-making treaties, have established rules of universal application. These fundamental rules emanating from the human rights treaties (e.g. prohibiting torture, genocide and racial inequality) are so firmly grounded as to bind all States (parties and non-parties alike) in customary international law.

International customary law

Article 38(1)(b) refers to this source of international law as 'international custom as evidence of a general practice accepted as law'. International customary law represents a combination of two elements: first, State practice and, second, the acceptance of such practice as law (*opinio juris*). State practice is a term which incorporates not only actions by States but also their abstentions from certain activities. The evidence of State practices can be found, *inter alia*, through the actions of governments, through a survey of statements made by governmental spokesmen to their Parliaments, to foreign governments, and in intergovernmental conferences. The approach adopted by representatives in the United Nations plenary organs such as the General Assembly is a strong indicator of State practices.

In order to establish customary law, State practice in general needs to be uniform and consistent. The International Court of Justice (ICJ) in the *Asylum Case (Colombia* v. *Peru)*[24] noted that a customary law must be 'in accordance with a constant and uniform usage practised by States in question'.[25] The requirements of uniformity and the extensive nature of State practice have been emphasised by the Court in its subsequent case law.[26] There is no requirement of excessive repetition 'or an absolutely rigorous conformity'[27] of a particular practice by States, although it would strengthen the material evidence in confirming the consistency and uniformity. A particular practice, by itself, remains insufficient. In order to distinguish customary law from habits or codes of morality, States need to feel convinced that a certain action is required of them by law. This psychological element in the formation of customary law is termed as *opinio juris*.[28]

---

[24] *Asylum Case (Colombia* v. *Peru)*, Judgment 20 November 1950 (1950) ICJ Reports 266.
[25] Ibid. pp. 276–277.
[26] *Fisheries Case (United Kingdom* v. *Norway)*, Judgment 18 December 1951 (1951) ICJ Reports 116, 131, 138. *North Sea Continental Shelf Cases (Federal Republic of Germany* v. *Denmark; Federal Republic of Germany* v. *Netherlands)*, Judgment 20 February 1969 (1969) ICJ Reports 3.
[27] *Military and Paramilitary Activities in and Against Nicaragua (Nicaragua* v. *United States of America)*, (Merits) Judgment 27 June 1986 (1986) ICJ Reports 14.
[28] A. D'Amato, *The Concept of Custom in International Law* (Ithaca, NY, London: Cornell University Press) 1971, pp. 66–72; O. Elias, 'The Nature of the Subjective Element in Customary International Law' 44 *ICLQ* (1995) 501.

Although not as visible as treaty law, customary law, represents the essential basis upon which the modern human rights regime is formulated. General Assembly Resolutions, if accompanied by the requisite *opinio juris*, can lead to the formation of customary international law. Many of the General Assembly Resolutions have established fundamental principles of human rights. Among the most notable Resolutions are the UDHR,[29] Declaration on the Granting of Independence to Colonial Countries and Peoples (1960)[30] and the Declaration on Principles of International Law Concerning Friendly Relations and Cooperation Among States in Accordance with the Charter of the United Nations (1970).[31] Treaties, as de facto evidence of State practice, aid in the creation of customary law. A treaty provision could possess the customary force if it fulfils the basic criterion of the establishment of custom; it could reflect customary law if its text declares or its *travaux préparatoires* state, with the requisite *opinio juris*, that its substance is declaratory of existing law.[32]

General principles of law

Inserted originally in the Statute of the Permanent Court of Justice[33] for the purpose of providing guidance to the Court in cases of gaps within treaty and customary law, the contemporary position and stature of general principles as a source international law is a matter of some debate. It is also not clear whether these principles are taken from the corpus of international law or are extracted from national legal systems. Akehurst has suggested that there is no reason why principles from both the national and international systems should not be extrapolated to strengthen this source. The approach adopted by international tribunals supports this suggestion. Thus obligations in international law to make reparations have been regarded as part of the corpus of general principles,[34] so have such features taken from national law on

---

[29] Adopted on 10 December 1948, UN GA Res. 217 A(III), UN Doc. A/810 at 71 (1948).

[30] Adopted on 14 December 1960, UN GA. Res. 1514 (XV); UN GAOR 15th Session, Supp. 16, at 66, UN Doc. A/4684 (1961).

[31] Adopted on 24 October 1970, UN GA Res. 2625, 25 UN GAOR, Supp. 28 at 121, UN Doc. A/8028 (1971); 9 I.L.M. (1971) 1292. On the value of General Assembly Resolutions in general international law see B. Sloan, 'General Assembly Resolutions Revisited: (Forty Years Later)' 58 *BYIL* (1987) 39; S.A. Bleicher, 'The Legal Significance of Re-Citation of General Assembly Resolutions' 63 *AJIL* (1969) 444; B. Cheng, 'United Nations Resolutions on Outer Space: "Instant" International Customary Law?' 5 *IJIL* (1965) 23.

[32] M. Akehurst, *A Modern Introduction to International Law*, 6th edn (London: Harper Collins Academic) 1987, pp. 26–27; R.R. Baxter, 'Multilateral Treaties as Evidence of Customary International Law' 41 *BYIL* (1965–66) 275; M. Akehurst, 'Custom as a Source of International Law' 47 *BYIL* (1974–5) 1 at pp. 42–52.

[33] Predecessor to the Statute of the International Court of Justice.

[34] *Chrozow Factory Case* (*Germany* v. *Poland*), PCIJ, Judgment 26 July 1927, Series A, No. 17 (1928) p. 29.

procedure and evidence.[35] General principles have a notable contribution in human rights law. Many principles, particularly those in the criminal justice system (e.g. presumption of innocence and right to free trial), can be identified as general principles of law.

Subsidiary sources of international law

The subsidiary sources of international law include judicial decisions and the teachings of the most highly qualified publicists. Despite this subsidiary position, as we shall consider in this book, judicial decisions have been of great value in developing human rights law. In this regard judicial decisions made by both domestic and international courts are worthy of consideration. The decisions of the International Court of Justice have no binding force except between the parties and in respect of the particular case.[36] Notwithstanding the absence of universal jurisdiction and without the power to establish precedents, the work of the International Court of Justice has been of great significance in developing many areas of international law.[37] The International Court of Justice has played an instrumental role in the development of fundamental principles such as the right to self-determination. The regional human rights courts, notably the European Court of Human Rights, have dispensed judgments which have added to human rights protection. Similar to international and regional courts decisions, domestic courts have, for example, provided important rulings on key concerns such as torture (see e.g. *Filártiga v. Pena-Irala*[38] and the *Pinochet* cases).[39]

The writing and teachings of publicists such as Hugo Grotius had astronomical influence during the formative stages of the modern law of nations. With the rapid growth of treaties and greater recognition of customary law, the influence of jurists in developing international law has declined. Having said

---

[35] *Corfu Channel (United Kingdom* v. *Albania)* (Merits) Judgment 9 April 1949 (1949) ICJ Reports 4, 18.

[36] Article 59 Statute of the International Court of Justice.

[37] See S. Rosenne, *The World Court: What It Is and How it Works* (Dordrecht: Martinus Nijhoff Publishers) 1995; G. Fitzmaurice, *The Law and Procedure of the International Court of Justice* (Cambridge: Grotius Publications) 1986; for a detailed survey see H. Thirlway, 'The Law and Procedure of the International Court of Justice: 1960–1989' 60 *BYIL* (1989) 1, and its following ten volumes at p. 1; E. Schwelb, 'The International Court of Justice and the Human Rights Clauses of the Charter' 66 *AJIL* (1972) 337; N.S. Rodley, 'Human Rights and Humanitarian Intervention: The Case Law of the World Court' 38 *ICLQ* (1989) 321; J. Rehman, 'The Role and Contribution of the World Court in the Progressive Development of International Environmental Law' 5 *APJEL* (2000) 387.

[38] 630 F. 2d 876 (1980); 19 I.L.M 966. US. Circuit Court of Appeals, 2nd Circuit.

[39] *R.* v. *Evans ex p. Pinochet Ugarte* (No. 1) (HL) 25 November 1998 [1998] 3 WLR 1456; *R.* v. *Bow Street Metropolitan Stipendiary Magistrate ex p. Pinochet Ugarte* (No. 2), (HL) 15 January 1999, [1999] 2 WLR 272; *R.* v. *Bow Street Metropolitan Stipendiary Magistrate ex p. Pinochet Ugarte* (No. 3) (HL) 24 March 1999 [1999] 2 WLR 827.

that, as this study establishes, the teachings of jurists remain of value in many areas of international human rights. During the course of this study we shall consistently rely upon authorities such as Oppenheim, Harris and Brownlie.

Additional sources of international law

A notable omission from the list of sources provided by Article 38(1) is a reference to the actions of intergovernmental organisations such as the United Nations (UN), the International Labour Organisation (ILO), the Council of Europe (COE) and the Organisation for Security and Cooperation in Europe (OSCE). We have already considered the significance of United Nations General Assembly Resolutions as sources of international law; the influence of the Assembly's Resolutions in developing and re-shaping principles of international law is a theme referred to throughout this book. Other organs of the United Nations (e.g. the Security Council and the Economic and Social Council) represent important vehicles for advancing norms of international law and international human rights law. The OSCE has adopted a number of instruments which, although not legally binding *per se* (and recognised as 'soft-law'), are important expressions of State practice. Instruments such the Helsinki Final Act have, in the case of the former Soviet Union, been of greater significance than binding human rights treaties.[40] Another example of 'soft-law' is the Standard Minimum Rules for the Treatment of Prisoners which, as we shall see, established important standards in the treatment of prisoners and young offenders.[41]

JUS COGENS AND HUMAN RIGHTS LAW

As noted in our earlier discussion, through treaties or customary law States establish or develop international law. At the same time, the discretion to formulate new laws is not unlimited and there remain certain rules of international law from which no derogation or reservation is permissible. In strict legal terms these rules have attained the status of norms of *jus cogens*. The elaboration of the doctrine of *jus cogens* is provided by the 1969 Vienna Convention on the Law of Treaties.[42] According to Article 53 of the Convention:

---

[40] See below Chapter 7.

[41] Standard Minimum Rules for the Treatment of Prisoners, adopted by the First United Nations Congress on the Prevention of Crime and the Treatment of Offenders, held in Geneva 1955, and approved by UN ECOSOC Resolution 663 C (XXIV) 31 July 1957. (Amended – New Rule 95 added – by ECOSOC Resolution 2076 (LXII) 13 May 1977.

[42] For a consideration of the meaning of *jus cogens* see Articles 53 and 64 of the Vienna Convention on the Law of Treaties; see E. Schwelb, 'Some Aspects of International *Jus Cogens* as Formulated by the International Law Commission' 61 *AJIL* (1967) 946; M.M. Whiteman, '*Jus Cogens* in International Law, with a Projected list' 7 *GA.JICL* (1977) 609.

A treaty is void if, at the time of its conclusion, it conflicts with a peremptory norm of general international law. For the purposes of the present convention, a peremptory norm of general international law is a norm accepted and recognised by the international community of States as a whole as a norm from which no derogation is permitted and which can be modified only by a subsequent norm of general international law having the same character.

Two important features of Article 53 need to be noted. First, the provisions of Article 53 are now subsumed into customary law thereby binding all States, parties and non-parties to the Vienna Convention. Secondly, the restrictions contained within Article 53 apply equally to other sources such as customary law or general principles of international law. Although there is no specification as to what constitutes such a norm, fundamental rights such as the right of all peoples to self-determination, and the prohibition of slavery, genocide, torture and racial discrimination represent settled *jus cogens* examples. This point is well established by various commentaries on the subject. According to the Commentary of the International Law Commission's analysis of 'best and settled rules' of *jus cogens*, these include prohibitions of:

(b) a treaty contemplating the performance of any other act criminal under international law and

(c) a treaty contemplating or conniving at the commission of acts, such as trade in slaves, piracy or genocide.[43]

In Professor Brownlie's categorisation, the 'least controversial examples are the prohibition of the use of force, the law of genocide, the principle of racial non-discrimination, crimes against humanity and the rules prohibiting trade in slaves and piracy'.[44] To this, we can add the prohibition on torture, the right to life, and liberty and security of the person.

---

[43] See *YBILC* (1966) vol. II. pp. 247–248; I. Brownlie, *Principles of Public International law*, 4th edn (Oxford: Clarendon Press) 1990, p. 513.

[44] Ibid.

2

THE UNITED NATIONS SYSTEM AND THE MODERN HUMAN RIGHTS REGIME (1945–)[1]

INTRODUCTION

> If we fail to use the Charter and the organization we have created with it, we shall betray all of those who died in order that we might live in freedom and in safety.... This Charter is no more perfect than our own Constitution, but like that Constitution it must be made to live.[2]

The progression of international human rights law is generally related to the developments that took place at the end of the Second World War. After the war, the United Nations was established to 'save succeeding generations from the scourge of war ... and to reaffirm faith in fundamental human rights'.[3] The United Nations Charter,[4] which represents the constitution of the organisation, is also an international treaty the provisions of which bind all

---

[1] See P. Alston (ed.), *The United Nations and Human Rights: A Critical Appraisal* (Oxford: Clarendon Press) 1992; S.C. Khare, *Human Rights and United Nations* (New Delhi: Metropolitan Book Co.) 1977; J.P. Humphrey, *Human Rights and the United Nations* (Toronto: Published for the Canadian Institute of International Affairs by Baxter Pub. Co.) 1963; T. Meron, *Human rights law-making in the United Nations: A Critique of Instruments and Process* (Oxford: Clarendon Press) 1986; H.J. Steiner and P. Alston, *International Human Rights in Context: Law, Politics, Morals: Text and Materials*, 2nd edn (Oxford: Clarendon Press) 2000, pp. 592–704; D.J. Harris, *Cases and Materials on International Law*, 5th edn (London: Sweet and Maxwell) 1998, pp. 624–631; M.N. Shaw, *International Law*, 4th edn (Cambridge: Grotius Publication) 1997, pp. 824–931.
[2] President Harry S. Truman, Address to the Delegates in San Francisco at the adoption of the United Nations Charter (1948), cited in R.C. Hottelet, 'Ups and Down in UN History' 5 *Washington University Journal of Law and Policy* (2001) 17 at p. 17.
[3] Preamble of the United Nations Charter (1945).
[4] Adopted in San Francisco 26 June 1945. Entered into force 24 October 1945. 1 U.N.T.S xvi; U.K.T.S 67 (1946); 59 Stat. 1031.

States that are parties to it.[5] The Charter assigns a range of functions to the United Nations, and although there are references to human rights, there has been considerable debate over the priorities which dictate the role and performance of this organisation. The UN Charter contains a number of references to human rights. According to the preamble of the Charter:

> We the peoples of the United Nations, determined ... to reaffirm faith in fundamental human rights, in the dignity and worth of the human person, in the equal rights of men and women and of nations large and small ... have resolved to combine our efforts to accomplish these aims.[6]

Article 1(3) states that one of the purposes of the United Nations is the promotion and encouragement of respect for human rights and fundamental freedoms for all 'without distinction as to race, sex, language or religion'. According to Article 8, the United Nations shall place no restrictions on the eligibility of men and women to participate in any capacity in its principal and subsidiary organs. According to Article 55, the United Nations shall 'promote universal respect for, and the observance of, human rights and fundamental freedoms for all without distinction as to race, sex, language or religion'. In accordance with Article 56 'all members of the United Nations pledge themselves to take joint and separate action in co-operation with the Organisation for the achievement of the purposes set forth in Article 55'. Articles 56 and 55 should be read together to formulate what one learned commentator has termed as '[probably] the only clear legal obligations' in the Charter on members to promote respect for human rights'.[7]

The Charter also devolves authority on the Economic and Social Council (ECOSOC) to initiate studies and reports in relation to 'international economic, social, cultural, educational, health, and related matters and may make recommendations with respect to any such matters to the General Assembly, to the Members of the United Nations, and to the specialised agencies concerned'.[8] According to Article 62(2) ECOSOC may 'make recommendations for the purpose of promoting respect for, and observance of, human rights and fundamental freedoms for all'. The trusteeship system incorporated in the United Nations Charter also carries with it the notion of equality and human rights for all.[9] One of the objectives of the trusteeship system has been

---

[5] The substantive provisions of the Charter also bind non-State parties in general international law. See P. Sands and P. Klein, *Bowett's Law of International Institutions*, 5th edn (London: Sweet and Maxwell) 2001, p. 24.

[6] Preamble of the United Nations Charter (1945).

[7] J.P. Humphrey, 'The UN Charter and the Universal Declaration of Human Rights' in E. Luard (ed.), *The International Protection of Human Rights* (London: Thames & Hudson) 1967, 39–56 at p. 42. For further analysis of the human rights obligations see E. Schwelb, 'The International Court of Justice and the Human Rights Clauses of the Charter' 66 *AJIL* (1972) 337.

[8] Article 62(1).

[9] For further consideration of trusteeship see below.

'to encourage respect for human rights and for fundamental freedoms for all without distinction as to race, sex, language, or religion, and to encourage recognition of the interdependence of the peoples of the world'.[10]

In addition to these explicit references to human rights, there is more implicit recognition of the role which the UN organs can play in promoting human rights. Thus in accordance with Article 10, the General Assembly may discuss (and has discussed on a number of occasions) matters within the scope of the Charter including human rights issues. Article 66(2), which grants authority to ECOSOC with the approval of the General Assembly to 'perform services', has been used as the basis of various UN human rights initiatives including awards and fellowship programmes and human rights seminars.[11]

LIMITATIONS OF THE CHARTER

Notwithstanding these references to human rights, it must not be assumed that human rights, equality and self-determination were the primary concerns of the politicians who engaged themselves in the drafting of the United Nations Charter.[12] The Dumbarton Oaks proposals of 1944 (representing the blueprint for the establishment of a world organisation) made only one general reference to human rights.[13] The major powers, prominently the United States and the United Kingdom, had been reluctant to sanctify the cause of complete equality and non-discrimination.[14] They were also not fully committed to an international regime of human rights. A Chinese proposal to uphold the principle of equality proved unacceptable to the United States, British and Soviet delegates at Dumbarton Oaks and hence was eliminated.[15] It was eventually the pressure from various NGOs and lobbying from a number of States that highlighted the necessity for greater recognition of human rights provisions in the Charter. At the time of its drafting several proposals were put forward including one from Panama for the incorporation of a bill

---

[10] Article 76(c).

[11] Humphrey, above n. 7, at p. 46.

[12] See L. Henkin, 'International Law: Politics, Values and Functions' 216 (IV) Rec. des Cours (1989) 13, at p. 215.

[13] See Ch. 9 Sect. A(I) Dumbarton Oaks Proposals UNCIO iv, 13; Text in L.M. Goodrich, E. Hambro, and A. Patricia Simons, *Charter of the United Nations: Commentary and Documents* (New York: Columbia University Press) 1969, pp. 664–672; A.H. Robertson and J.G. Merrills, *Human Rights in the World: An Introduction to the Study of International Protection of Human Rights*, 4th edn (Manchester: Manchester University Press) 1996, p. 26.

[14] A.D. Renteln, *International Human Rights: Universalism versus Relativism* (Newbury Park: Sage Publications) 1990, p. 21.

[15] P.G. Lauren, 'First Principles of Racial Equality: History and the Politics and Diplomacy of Human Rights Provisions in the United Nations Charter' 5 HRQ (1983) 1 at p. 2.

of rights within the Charter.[16] None of these proposals materialised. One proposal, however, which was accepted and has proved significant, is for the inclusion in Article 68 of the Charter of an authorisation for ECOSOC to establish a Commission on Human Rights.[17] The Commission which was formed in 1946 held its first meeting in January 1947. After its establishment, ECOSOC entrusted the Commission with the task of submitting proposals, recommendations and reports with a view to formulating an International Bill of Rights.[18]

The Charter does not establish any particular regime of human rights protection and the emphasis is upon the non-intervention in the affairs of member States of the United Nations.[19] The main focus of the Charter is the promotion of international peace and security. With regard to the right to equality and non-discrimination, it must be emphasised that at the time when the Charter came into operation in October 1945 there were serious impediments to the establishment of a regime based on equality and non-discrimination: colonialism persisted in large measure; racial, religious and sex-based apartheid was widely practiced; and the right to self-determination of all peoples, although inscribed in the text of the Charter, was considered by many to be a pious hope rather than a firmly established legal right.[20]

Notwithstanding these shortcomings, over the years the United Nations (as an organisation of almost universal membership) has confirmed its

---

[16] See J. Huston, 'Human Rights Enforcement Issues at the United Nations Conference on International Organization' 53 *Iowa LR* (1967) 272; P. Alston, 'The Commission on Human Rights' in P. Alston (ed.), above n. 1, at p. 127; Document of the United Nations Conference on International Organisation (1945) vi 545–9; A.H. Robertson and J.G. Merrills, *Human Rights in the World: An Introduction to the Study of International Protection of Human Rights*, 4th edn (Manchester: Manchester University Press) 1996, p. 26; G. Alfredsson and A. Eide, 'Introduction' in G. Alfredsson and A. Eide (eds), *The Universal Declaration of Human Rights: A Common Standard of Achievement* (The Hague: Martinus Nijhoff Publishers) 1999, xxv–xxxv at p. xxvii.

[17] J. Humphrey, 'The Universal Declaration of Human Rights: Its History, Impact and Juridical Character' in B.G. Ramcharan (ed.), *Human Rights: Thirty Years after the Universal Declaration: Commemorative Volume on the Occasion of the Thirtieth Anniversary of the Universal Declaration of Human Rights* (The Hague: Martinus Nijhoff Publishers) 1979, 21–37 at p. 21.

[18] See ECOSOC Res. 5(I) and 9(II). ECOSOC OR 1st Year, 2nd Session, pp. 400–402.

[19] See Article 2(7) of the United Nations Charter, which provides that 'Nothing contained in the present Charter shall authorize the United Nations to intervene in matters which are essentially within the domestic jurisdiction of any state or shall require the Members to submit such matters to settlement under the present Charter; but this principle shall not prejudice the application of enforcement measures under Chapter VII'. Article 2(7) has been given great prominence by States. According to one commentator 'the discussion of the San Francisco Conference on the Charter indicates that there was a general agreement that the general prohibition of intervention in domestic affairs is an overriding principle or limitation, and controls each and every organ of the U.N.' A. Boulesbaa, *The U.N. Convention on Torture and Prospects for Enforcement* (The Hague: Martinus Nijhoff Publishers) 1999, pp. 92–93.

[20] Y. Blum, 'Reflections on the Changing Concept of Self-Determination' 10 *Israel Law Review* (1975) 509 at p. 511; R. Emerson, 'Self-Determination' 65 *AJIL* (1971) 459 at p. 471. See below Chapter 12.

influence in international legal and political developments. Since the establishment of the organisation in 1945 the role of the United Nations has been
critical in the global promotion and protection of human rights. The role has
been performed through a wide range of mechanisms and methods – some
proving more effective than the others. The UN consists of the following
principal organs: the General Assembly, the Security Council, the Economic
and Social and Council (ECOSOC), the International Court of Justice, The
Trusteeship Council, and the Secretariat. In order to gain an adequate understanding of the United Nations' involvement with international human rights
law, it is important we consider each of its principal organs in turn.

THE GENERAL ASSEMBLY[21]

The General Assembly is the plenary organ of the United Nations currently
representing 189 States.[22] The UN Charter establishes the General Assembly
as a platform where all States can debate any relevant matter with the
Assembly having a broad competence to consider human rights issues. All
members of the UN are represented in the General Assembly. Each member
may have up to five representatives but only one vote. Decisions on important
questions require a two-thirds majority vote, others a simple majority. A
non-exhaustive definition of 'important questions' is given in Article 18(2).
These include election, suspension or expulsion of members, election of non-
permanent members of the Security Council and recommendations in relation
to the maintenance of international peace. The single vote for each State
means no account is taken of size, economic strength or world influence so the
vote of, for example, the USA has the same value as that of, say, Bangladesh.
This may be seen as unrealistic but on the other hand it does mean that
decisions of the General Assembly are genuinely representative of world
opinion.[23]

---

[21] See Sands and Klein, above n. 5, at pp. 27–39; S. Bailey, *The General Assembly of the United
Nations: A Study of Procedure and Practice* (Praeger: New York) 1964; M.J. Peterson, *The
General Assembly in World Politics* (Boston: Allen and Unwin) 1986; B. Sloan, *United Nations
General Assembly resolutions in our changing World* (Ardsley-on-Hudson, NY: Transnational
Publishers) 1991; J. Andrassy, 'Uniting for Peace' 50 *AJIL* (1956) 563; T. Rowe, 'Human Rights
Issues in the UN General Assembly 1946–1966' 14 *Journal of Conflict Resolution* (1970) 425;
D.H.N. Johnson, 'The Effect of Resolutions of the General Assembly of the United Nations'
32 *BYIL* (1955–56) 97; A. Cassese, 'The General Assembly: Historical Perspective 1945–1989'
in P. Alston (ed.), above n. 1, pp. 25–54; J. Quinn, 'The General Assembly in the 1990s' ibid.
pp. 55–106.
[22] For a list of the UN member States and the dates of their membership, see
http://www.un.org/Overview/unmember.html (1 May 2002).
[23] For a list of the UN member States and the dates of their membership, see
http://www.un.org/Overview/unmember.html (1 May 2002).

The rules relating to the membership of the General Assembly are contained in Article 4 of the Charter. Article 4 provides:

1. Membership in the United Nations is open to all other peace-loving states which accept the obligations contained in the present Charter and, in the judgement of the Organization, are able and willing to carry out these obligations.
2. The admission of any such state to membership in the United Nations will be effected by a decision of the General Assembly upon the recommendation of the Security Council.

In practice, however, the issue of admission and expulsion has been surrounded by political rivalries, particularly during the cold war years.[24] According to Article 5 of the UN Charter a member of the United Nations may be suspended on recommendation of the Security Council. Article 6 allows for the expulsion of a member from the UN where that member has persistently violated principles of the UN. According to the provisions of the Charter, the powers of the General Assembly are (with one exception) of deliberative or recommendatory nature. The exception concerns the internal budgetary obligations of member States.[25] The authority to discuss and make recommendations derives largely from Articles 10–13 of the UN Charter although, as we shall see, the scope of its authority has been enhanced considerably through subsequent developments of international law.

Articles 10 and 11 authorise the General Assembly to discuss 'any questions or on any matters'[26]within the scope of the UN Charter (except where the Security Council is dealing with the same subject)[27] and make appropriate recommendations to the State(s) concerned and the Security Council.[28] In accordance with the mandate provided under Article 13 of the UN Charter, the General Assembly has commissioned a number of studies for the purpose of promoting international cooperation in various fields and 'assisting in the realisation of human rights'.

In strict interpretation of the provisions of the Charter, the General Assembly is not a legislative body. It is not to be treated as a substitute for the Security Council nor has it been accorded a primary role in the promotion and protection of international human rights. A number of factors, however, led the General Assembly to become a forum of enormous significance.[29] During

---

[24] See Article 4 UN Charter; G. Abi-Saab, 'Membership and Voting in the United Nations' in H. Fox (ed.), *Membership and Voting in the United Nations* (London: BIICL) 1997, pp. 19–39.
[25] See Article 17 UN Charter.
[26] Article 10 UN Charter.
[27] Article 12 UN Charter.
[28] Article 11(2) UN Charter.
[29] A. Cassese, 'The General Assembly: Historical Perspective 1945–1989' in P. Alston (ed.), above n. 1, pp. 25–54, at p. 29.

the cold war, the inability of the Security Council to attain consensus on areas affecting peace and security provided the General Assembly with the opportunity to exert political authority. A step towards establishing such authority was taken by the Assembly when it adopted the Uniting for Peace Resolution on 3 November 1950.[30] The Resolution provides that:

> if the Security Council, because of lack of unanimity of the permanent members fails to exercise its primary responsibility for the maintenance of international peace and security, breach of the peace, or act of aggression, the General Assembly shall consider the matter immediately with a view to making appropriate recommendations to Members for collective measures, including in the case of breach of peace or act of aggression the use of armed force when necessary, to maintain or restore international peace and security.

Through the adoption of this Resolution, the Assembly assumed a role in the determination of threats to peace and security, including making recommendations on the usage of armed force. While invoked sparingly, the Resolution nevertheless enhanced the position of the Assembly *vis-à-vis* the Security Council. A second factor influential in enhancing the power of the General Assembly arose as a consequence of the increased membership of the new States from Asia and Africa. These new States (which came to form the majority of UN membership) have influenced not only the role and proceedings of the General Assembly but also international law generally. While General Assembly Resolutions are recommendatory and cannot as such establish binding legal obligations, they do present evidence of State practice. State practices provide an important ingredient in the development of binding customary law.[31] The developing world has also used the Resolutions to advance their agenda with regard to international law. In this context it is important to note the highly authoritative General Assembly Resolutions such as the Declaration on the Granting of Independence to Colonial Countries and Peoples (1960)[32] and the Declaration on Principles of International Law Concerning Friendly Relations and Cooperation Among States in Accordance with the Charter of the United Nations (1970).[33] Reference can also be made to other General Assembly Resolutions which have been used to advance the political aspirations of the developing world. These would include *inter alia* the Charter of

---

[30] Adopted 3 November 1950, UN GA Res. 377(V), GAOR, 5th Sess. Supp. 20, at 10.

[31] For the elements required to establish customary international law, see above Chapter 1.

[32] Adopted on 14 December 1960, UN GA. Res. 1514 (XV); UN GAOR 15th Sess., Supp. 16, at 66, UN Doc. A/4684 (1961).

[33] Adopted on 24 October 1970, UN GA Res. 2625, 25 UN GAOR, Supp. 28 at 121, UN Doc. A/8028 (1971); 9 I.L.M. (1971) 1292. On the value of General Assembly Resolutions in general international law see B. Sloan, 'General Assembly Resolutions Revisited: (Forty Years Later)' 58 *BYIL* (1987) 39; S.A. Bleicher, 'The Legal Significance of Re-Citation of General Assembly Resolutions' 63 *AJIL* (1969) 444; B. Cheng, 'United Nations Resolutions on Outer Space: "Instant" International Customary Law?' 5 *IJIL* (1965) 23.

Economic Rights and Duties of States[34] the Declaration on the Establishment of a New International Economic Order[35] and the Declaration on the Right to Development[36] containing claims of economic self-determination and sovereignty of national resources.[37]

A distinct, though important role, is played by the General Assembly in preparing, drafting and adopting international treaties. While annexed to General Assembly Resolutions, these treaties are opened for accession by member States and, as legal obligations, bind States which are party to the treaties. The normal Assembly voting procedures are used to adopt these treaties.[38] Examples of such annexations include the International Covenants[39] and the International Convention on the Elimination of All Forms of Racial Discrimination.[40] When considering the implementation mechanism of the various UN sponsored treaties, we see that the General Assembly plays a vital role in receiving and reviewing the compliance of States with their international obligations.[41]

THE SECURITY COUNCIL[42]

The Security Council, like the General Assembly, is one of the principal organs of the United Nations. The Security Council acts as the executive body of the United Nations with its primary responsibility being to maintain international peace and security.[43] The Security Council has fifteen members,

---

[34] GA Res. 3281(XXIX) 14 I.L.M. (1975) 251.

[35] GA Res. 3201 (S-VI) 13 I.L.M. (1974) 715.

[36] GA Res. 128, UN GAOR, 41 Sess., Supp. 53 at 186, UN Doc. A/Res/41/128.

[37] See A. Cassese, *International Law* (Oxford: Clarendon Press) 2001, p. 400.

[38] Shaw, above n. 1, at p. 638.

[39] ICCPR. Adopted at New York, 16 December 1966. Entered into force 23 March 1976. GA Res. 2200A (XXI) UN Doc. A/6316 (1966) 999 U.N.T.S. 171; 6 I.L.M. (1967) 368. ICESCR. Adopted at New York, 16 December 1966. Entered into force 3 January 1976. GA Res. 2200A (XXI) UN Doc. A/6316 (1966) 993 U.N.T.S. 3, 6 I.L.M. (1967) 360.

[40] Adopted 21 December 1965. Entered into force, 4 January 1969. 660 U.N.T.S. 195, 5 I.L.M. (1966) 352.

[41] See S. Davidson, *Human Rights* (Buckingham: Open University Press) 1993, p. 67.

[42] See Sands and Klein, above n. 5, at pp. 39–55; S.D. Bailey, 'The Security Council' in P. Alston (ed.), above n. 1, pp. 304–336; S.D. Bailey, *Voting in the Security Council* (Bloomington, Ind.: Indiana University Press) 1969; S.D. Bailey, *The Procedure of the UN Security Council* (Oxford : Clarendon Press) 1988; R. Higgins, 'The Place of International Law in the Settlement of Disputes by the Security Council' 64 *AJIL* (1970) 1; R.A. Brand, 'Security Council Resolutions: When do they Give Rise to Enforceable Legal Rights? The United Nations Charter, the Byrd Amendment and a Self Executing Treaty Analysis' 9 *Cornell International Law Journal* (1976) 298; M.C. Woods, 'Security Council Working Methods and Procedures: Recent Developments' 45 *ICLQ* (1996) 100; B. Fassbender, *UN Security Council Reform and the Right of Veto: A Constitutional Perspective* (The Hague: Kluwer Law International) 1998; D. Sarooshi, *The United Nations and the Development of Collective Security: The delegation by the UN Security Council of its Chapter VII Powers* (Oxford: Clarendon Press) 1999.

[43] See Article 24(1) UN Charter.

five of which are permanent. The permanent members of the Council are China, France, the Russian Federation, the United Kingdom and the United States. The other ten members are elected by the Assembly for two years. They are elected by a two-thirds majority vote of the General Assembly. The UN Charter Article 23(1) refers to equitable geographical distribution and there is an informal agreement that there should be five from Afro-Asian States, one from Eastern Europe, two from Latin America and one from Western Europe and other States (e.g. Canada, Australia). The justification for the five permanent members is that concerted action in the face of opposition from one or more of the major powers would be an unrealistic expectation. The five in question can all be described as major powers. Amendment of the Charter would require the consent of the five concerned[44] and a consensus on who should be included instead would be very hard to obtain. The tacit acceptance that Russia could succeed to the seat that the Charter allocated to the former Soviet Union illustrates a reluctance to open up discussion of the general issue of which of the States are appropriate permanent members.

The Security Council (unlike the General Assembly) does not hold regular meetings. Instead, it can be called together at any time on short notice. Any country (member or non-member) or the Secretary-General may bring to the Security Council's attention a dispute or threat to peace and security. The voting system in the Security Council is different to that of the General Assembly. To pass a resolution in the Security Council, an affirmative vote of nine members is required. However, a negative vote by any of the permanent members on a resolution that relates to a non-procedural matter would veto the resolution.[45] The power to veto resolutions was incorporated into the Charter to prevent the Council taking any substantial decision detrimental to the interests of any of the permanent members. The power of veto was used extensively at the height of the cold war, leading to an inability on the part of the Security Council to take any effective steps to maintain peace and security or to prevent extensive violations of human rights.

According to Article 24 of the UN Charter, member States agree to confer primary responsibility upon the Security Council for the maintenance of

---

[44] See Article 108 of the UN Charter.
[45] See Article 27 the UN Charter. Abstention should be distinguished from absence. In 1950 the Soviet Union boycotted meetings because the government of China had not been permitted to take its country's place on the Security Council. At this point the Korean War broke out and the Security Council authorised military action by UN members, action which the Soviet Union would certainly have vetoed if it had been present. It subsequently argued that the action was illegal, as being present and abstaining was very different from not being present at all. On the other hand, Article 28 of the Charter imposes a duty on members to be represented at all times and if the Soviet argument was correct a State could prevent the Council from acting at all by absenting itself. The situation has never been repeated.

international peace and security. By virtue of Article 25, member States undertake to accept and carry out the decisions of the Council. The powers conferred upon the Security Council are elaborated in subsequent chapters of the Charter. Chapter VI (Articles 33–38) assigns recommendatory powers to the Security Council in relation to the peaceful settlement of disputes whereas Chapter VII (Articles 39–51) confers upon the Council the authority to deal with threats to peace, breaches of the peace and acts of aggression. Acting under Chapter VII, the Security Council has an absolute discretion in the determination of whether there exists a threat to peace and security under Chapter VII.[46] The Council also has significant enforcement powers, namely economic sanctions or military action.

The role played by the Security Council under Chapters VI and VIII has important implications for human rights. After the collapse of the Soviet Union and the thaw in East–West relations there had been expectations that the Security Council would work as a more effective body to promote and protect human rights. With the authorisation of the Security Council, allied forces were successful in expelling Iraqi forces from Kuwait. Subsequently the Security Council passed Resolution 688 (1991) against Iraqi repression of the Kurdish people which was relied upon by the allied powers to establish a 'safe-haven' and maintain a 'no-fly zone' in Northern Iraq.[47] The Security Council has also made extensive use of its resolutions and enforcement powers in the territories of former Yugoslavia,[48] Somalia,[49] Haiti[50] and more recently in East Timor. In the absence of an international criminal court, the Security Council also undertook the unprecedented step of establishing ad hoc tribunals for the trials of those accused of gross violations of human rights in Rwanda and the former Yugoslavia.

---

[46] See the *Prosecutor* v. *Tadic*, Case IT-94-1-AR72, Decision on the Defence Motion for Interlocutory Appeal on Jurisdiction, 2 October 1995, paras. 29–30; V. Gowlland-Debbass, 'The Relationship Between the International Court of Justice and Security Council in the Light of the Lockerbie Case' 88 *AJIL* (1994) 643 at p. 662.

[47] In this regard note the absence of a specific authorisation by the Security Council to establish the safe-havens. See T.M. Franck, 'When, If Ever, May States Deploy Military Force without Prior Security Council Authorization' 5 *Washington Journal of Law and Policy* (2001) 51 at pp. 62–63; also see Shaw, above n. 1, at pp. 874–875.

[48] See SC Res. 757 (30 May 1992); SC Res. 770 (13 August 1992); SC Res. 787 (16 November 1992); SC Res. 815 (30 March 1993); SC 819 (16 April 1993); SC Res. 824 (1993).

[49] See SC Res. 733 (23 June 1992) adopted at the 3039th mtg. by unanimous vote; SC Res. 751 (24 April 1992) and adopted at the 3069th mtg.; SC Res. 775 (28 August 1992) adopted 3110th mtg. by unanimous vote and SC Res. 794 (3 December 1992) adopted at 3145 mtg.

[50] See SC Res. 841 (16 June 1993); SC Res. 940 (31 July 1994).

THE ECONOMIC AND SOCIAL COUNCIL (ECOSOC)[51]

ECOSOC is concerned with a number of economic and general welfare issues. These include trade, developmental and social matters including population, children, housing and racial discrimination. While the mandate of the ECOSOC covers wide-ranging issues, its actual powers are limited to recommendations which are not binding on States. ECOSOC consists of 54 members, who are elected for a three-year term of office. Until 1991 ECOSOC had two annual sessions, each lasting for four weeks. However, the General Assembly in May 1991 decided that from 1992 ECOSOC would hold an organisational session of up to four days in New York in early February of each year and one substantive session of four to five weeks, to take place, between May and July, and alternate between New York and Geneva. Unlike the position within the Security Council, no provisions are made for the permanent membership of ECOSOC, although in practice the permanent members (within the Security Council) are repeatedly elected.[52] It is also the case that the issue of being elected to the ECOSOC is not as politically volatile as compared to its own subsidiary organs such as the Human Rights Commission. In the ECOSOC sessions it is the usual practice for a State to be represented by its permanent representative stationed either in New York or Geneva. In the light of the rapidly declining prestige of the Council, the most articulate political and governmental representatives prefer to be part of the Commission as opposed to the Council.

According to Article 62 of the UN Charter, ECOSOC may initiate or make studies on a range of subjects and may make recommendations to the General Assembly, members of the UN and to relevant specialised agencies. The UN Charter makes provisions for the ECOSOC to consult NGOs in its work. ECOSOC may also prepare draft conventions and call international conferences. The functional commissions of ECOSOC include the Commission on Human Rights and the Commission on the Status of Women.[53] ECOSOC also

---

[51] See D. O'Donovan, 'The Economic and Social Council' in P. Alston (ed.), above n. 1, pp. 107–125; G.J. Mangone, *UN Administration of Economic and Social programs* (New York: Columbia University Press) 1966; L.D. Stinebower, *The Economic and Social Council: An Instrument of International Cooperation* (New York, NY: Commission to Study the Organization of Peace) 1946; A. Loveday, 'Suggestions for the Reform of the United Nations Economic and Social Machinery' 7 *International Organization* (1953) 325; W.R. Malinowski, 'Centralization and Decentralization in the United Nations Economic and Social Activities' 16 *International Organization* (1962) 521.

[52] D. O'Donovan, 'The Economic and Social Council' in P. Alston (ed.), above n. 1, pp. 107–125, at p. 108.

[53] In all there are nine functional commissions. Apart from the Commission on Human Rights and the Commission on the Status of Women, there are the following: Statistical Commission, Commission on Population and Development, Commission for Social Development, Commission on Narcotic Drugs, Commission on Crime Prevention and Criminal Justice, Commission on Science and Technology for Development and Commission on Sustainable Development.

has a number of regional commissions[54] and several standing committees and expert bodies.[55] It also runs a number of programmes such as the UN Environment Programme and has established bodies such as the UN High Commissioner for Refugees. The UN work on human rights has focused around ECOSOC and its subsidiary organs, in particular the Commission on Human Rights to which we shall now turn our attention.

The Commission on Human Rights and the Sub-Commission on the Promotion and Protection of Human Rights[56]

The UN Charter requires that ECOSOC 'shall set up Commissions in the economic and social field and for the promotion of human rights'.[57] In its first meeting in 1946 the Council established two functional commissions: the Commission on Human Rights and the Commission on the Status of Women. Over the years the representation of the Commission has grown and it currently consists of 53 individuals who sit in their capacity as governmental representatives.[58] The Commission meets for an annual session of six weeks in Geneva during March and April. The proceedings of the Commission are reported to the General Assembly via ECOSOC.

Since the Commission members are nominated by their governments, their political positions often mirror those of their governments. Professor Harris correctly makes the point that 'the Commission is a highly political animal, with its initiatives and priorities reflecting bloc interests'.[59] By the same token, the presence of governmental representatives and the positions they adopt in the proceeding of the Commission raises the profile and significance of the institution. The initial terms of reference of the Human Rights Commission

---

[54] The five Regional Commissions: Economic Commission for Africa (Addis Ababa, Ethiopia), Economic and Social Commission for Asia and the Pacific (Bangkok, Thailand), Economic Commission for Europe (Geneva, Switzerland), Economic Commission for Latin America and the Caribbean (Santiago, Chile) and Economic and Social Commission for Western Asia (Beirut, Lebanon).

[55] The five standing committees and expert bodies are: Committee for Programme and Coordination, Commission on Human Settlements, Committee on Non-Governmental Organisations, Committee on Negotiations with Intergovernmental Agencies and Committee on Energy and Natural Resources. In addition the Council has a number of expert bodies on subjects including development planning, natural resources, and economic, social and cultural rights.

[56] See P. Alston, 'The Commission on Human Rights' in P. Alston (ed.), above n. 1, at pp. 126–210; A. Eide, 'The Sub-Commission on Prevention of Discrimination and Protection of Minorities' ibid. pp. 211–264.

[57] Article 46 UN Charter.

[58] The allocation of these seats is on a geographical basis. The current membership is based on the following: 15 African States, 13 Asian States, 11 Latin American States, 5 Eastern European States and 10 Western European and Other States.

[59] Harris, above n. 1, at p. 628.

were that the Commission should submit proposals, recommendations and reports to ECOSOC concerning:

(a) An international bill of rights
(b) International Declarations or Conventions on Civil Liberties, the Status of women, freedom of information and similar matters
(c) The Protection of Minorities
(d) The Prevention of discrimination on grounds of race, sex, language or religion
(e) Any other matter concerning human rights not covered by items (a), (b), (c), (d).[60]

Further extensions to the mandate of the Human Rights Commission have taken place.[61] Among the Commission's significant achievements has been its standard-setting through preparation of human rights instruments. The list of accomplishments in this regard is extensive. The Jewel in the Crown is the Commission's work in the drafting of the Universal Declaration of Human Rights[62] and the two International Covenants.[63] There are other human rights treaties including the International Convention on the Elimination of All forms of Racial Discrimination (1966),[64] the Convention on the Rights of the Child (1989)[65] and the Convention on the Elimination of All Forms of Discrimination against Women.[66] The Commission has engaged itself in the preparation *inter alia* of the Declaration on the Elimination of All Forms of Intolerance and of Discrimination Based on Religion or Belief,[67] and the Declaration on the Rights of Persons Belonging to National or Ethnic, Religious and Linguistic Minorities.[68] In addition, as we shall consider further, it has authorised the setting-up of various working groups and special rapporteurs.

The Commission has a subsidiary organ, the Sub-Commission on the Promotion and Protection of Human Rights. Until 1999, the Sub-

[60] ECOSOC Res. 5(1) of 16 February 1946 and Resolution 5(11) of 21 June 1946.
[61] ECOSOC Res. E/1979/36.
[62] 10 December 1948, UN GA Res. 217 A(III), UN Doc. A/810 at 71 (1948).
[63] ICCPR. Adopted at New York, 16 December 1966. Entered into force 23 March 1976. GA Res. 2200A (XXI) UN Doc. A/6316 (1966) 999 U.N.T.S. 171; 6 I.L.M. (1967) 368. ICESCR. Adopted at New York, 16 December 1966. Entered into force 3 January 1976. GA Res. 2200A (XXI) UN Doc. A/6316 (1966) 993 U.N.T.S. 3, 6 I.L.M. (1967) 360.
[64] Adopted 21 December 1965. Entered into force, 4 January 1969. 660 U.N.T.S. 195, 5 I.L.M. (1966) 352.
[65] Adopted in New York, 20 November 1989. Entered into force 2 September 1990. UN GA Res. 44/25 Annex (XLIV), 44 UN GAOR Supp. (No. 49) 167, UN Doc. A/44/49 (1989) at 166; 1577 U.N.T.S. 3. 28 I.L.M (1989) 1448.
[66] Adopted at New York, 18 December 1979. Entered into force 3 September 1981. UN GA Res. 34/180(XXXIV), GA. Res. 34/180, 34 GAOR, Supp. (No. 46) 194, UN Doc. A/34/46, at 193 (1979), 2 U.K.T.S. (1989); 19 I.L.M (1980) 33.
[67] Adopted by the General Assembly on 25 November 1981. GA Res. 55, UN GAOR, 36 Sess., Supp. 51 at 171, UN Doc. A/36/684. See below Chapter 10.
[68] Adopted by the General Assembly 18 December 1992, GA Res. 135, UN GAOR 47 Sess. Supp. 49 at 210, UN Doc. A/Res/47/135. 32 I.L.M. (1993) 911. See below Chapter 11.

Commission was known as the Sub-Commission on the Prevention of Discrimination and the Protection of Minorities. The Sub-Commission consists of 26 members who serve in their individual capacity independently of their governments. The Sub-Commission was established by ECOSOC in 1947. The terms of reference under which the Sub-Commission works are:

(a) to undertake studies particularly in the light of the Universal Declaration ... and to make recommendations to the Commission on Human Rights concerning the prevention of discrimination of any kind relating to human rights and fundamental freedoms and protection of racial, national, religious and linguistic minorities; and

(b) to perform any other functions which may be entrusted to it by [ECOSOC] or the Commission on Human Rights.

The Sub-Commission members are elected by the Human Rights Commission on regional distribution from among individuals nominated by governments. Unlike the Human Rights Commission, the members of the Sub-Commission work in an independent capacity. The Sub-Commission has one annual session of three weeks (during late July to early August) preceded by working groups lasting for one or two weeks, which are attended by non-governmental organisations and by governmental observers.

The activities of the Commission and the Sub-Commission represent the focal point in terms of the practices and procedures of human rights activities within the United Nations. As this book establishes, the Commission has made a significant contribution to standard-setting, and more recently to the monitoring and implementation of human rights obligations. In addition the Commission has engaged itself in such activities as studies and seminars, fellowship programmes and the provision of advisory services. The Commission has been criticised on several occasions for its political bias and for its lack of sensitivity on major human rights issues. However, Alston's comments are pertinent when he notes that the Human Rights Commission 'has firmly established itself as a single most important United Nations organ in the human rights field, despite its subordinate status as one of several specialised "functional" commissions answerable to the Economic and Social Council and through it, to the General Assembly'.[69]

The petitioning system

For the first twenty years, the Human Rights Commission confined itself to standard-setting mechanisms. In 1947 the Commission adopted the statement (which was subsequently heavily criticised) that it had 'no power to take any

---

[69] P. Alston, 'The Commission on Human Rights' in P. Alston (ed.), above n. 1, 126–210 at p. 126.

action in regard to any complaints concerning human rights'.[70] Until 1967 the Commission refused to consider complaints of human rights violations in member States of the United Nations. Substantial issues confronted the domestic policies of major States, including the United States, the United Kingdom and France. These included the existence of colonialism and difficult race relations. In addition, until 1967 it had been anticipated that the Commission would focus on standard setting and that effective implementation of International Covenants would redress the human rights situation. The limitations of review led one critic to note that by mid 1960s the system had become 'the world's most elaborate waste-paper basket'.[71] However, in the 1960s there was also a discernible change in the political environment. A number of States had emerged which were anxious to promote international action against colonialism and racial discrimination. The increased membership of the UN also allowed them to have greater representation in the Commission. In 1966, ECOSOC decided almost to double the size of the original membership of the Commission to 32 members, 20 of whom came from the developing world.[72] Perceiving racial oppression and apartheid as a great threat to world peace, these State representatives were strong advocates of an international petitioning system receiving and acting upon complaints of racial discrimination and apartheid. The successful and rapid adoption of the Convention on the Elimination of All Forms of Racial Discrimination was a major encouragement.

In 1967, ECOSOC passed Resolution 1235 (XLII) which has proved to be of enormous significance. In this Resolution ECOSOC authorised the Human Rights Commission and its Sub-Commission on the Prevention of Discrimination and the Protection of Minorities to 'examine information relevant to gross violations of human rights and fundamental freedoms, as exemplified by the policy of apartheid as practised in the Republic of South Africa ... and racial discrimination as practised notably in Southern Rhodesia, contained in the communications listed by the Secretary-General to [ECOSOC] Resolution 728F' and 'to make a thorough study of situations which reveals a consistent pattern of violations of human rights, and report, with recommendations thereon, to the Economic and Social Council'.[73]

The procedures adopted under Resolution 1235 (unlike Resolution 1503) are not confidential and are of a public nature. They can be commenced by the

---

[70] E/259 (1947) paras 21–22; See T.J.M. Zuijdwijk, *Petitioning the United Nations: A Study in Human Rights* (Aldershot: Gower) 1982, pp. 1–14; J.Th. Moller, 'The Right to Petition: General Assembly Resolution 217B' in G. Alfredsson and A. Eide (eds), *The Universal Declaration of Human Rights: A Common Standard of Achievement* (The Hague: Martinus Nijhoff Publishers) 1999, 653–659 at p. 653.

[71] J. Humphrey, 'The Right of Petition in the United Nations' 2/3 *Human Rights Journal* (1971) at p. 463.

[72] P. Alston, 'The Commission on Human Rights' in P. Alston (ed.), above n. 1, 126–210 at p. 143.

[73] ESCOR 42nd Sess., Supp. 1 (1967).

Sub-Commission or by a State themselves and operate in variety of ways. These may be country-specific mandates, may consider States with similar patterns of violations or target gross violations of human rights. The resolutions originate in the Sub-Commission and are passed on to the Commission. The Sub-Commission's resolutions can highlight the issue of human rights violation in a particular country. The Sub-Commission may also request the UN Secretary-General to prepare a report on a particular country; this report may contain extensive information.[74] The Commission makes the ultimate decisions as to the action on these resolutions and also retains the authority (subject to the approval of ECOSOC) for the appointment of a rapporteur or any other mechanism for studying a given country situation or acting on a thematic basis.

In reliance upon Resolution 1235, the Commission has established a number of public procedures.[75] These include investigations into alleged violations of human rights in various States. The Commission has also created various working groups, special Rapporteurs and expert bodies to monitor human rights situations. One of the earliest activities in this regard (and indeed the first of the thematic mechanisms) was the establishment of the Working Group on Enforced and Involuntary Disappearances in 1980.[76] Since its establishment, the Working Group has considered 50,000 cases from over seventy countries. The Working Group is mandated to examine questions concerning enforced or involuntary disappearances. Its primary role is to provide assistance to families of the disappeared and detained persons to ascertain the fate of their family members.[77] The Working Group works on individual cases, country reports, and the general phenomenon of disappearances, including the question of impunity. Members of the group have also conducted visits to various countries including Mexico, Bolivia, Peru, the Philippines and Somalia.[78] The Working Group has called for investigations, and the prosecution and punishment of those responsible for disappearances. The contributions and role of the Working Group encouraged the General Assembly to adopt the Declaration on the Protection of All Persons from Enforced Disappearances.[79] The Declaration expanded the Working Group's mandate to monitor compliance with duties under the Declaration, including the obligation to establish civil liability as well as criminal responsibility for disappearances.

---

[74] N.S. Rodley, 'United Nations Non-Treaty Procedures for Dealing with Human Rights Violations' in H. Hannum (ed.), *Guide to International Human Rights Practice*, 3rd edn (New York: Transnational Publishers) 1999, 61– 83 at p. 63.

[75] Harris, above n. 1, at p. 629.

[76] See N.S. Rodley, *The Treatment of Prisoners in International Law*, 2nd edn (Oxford: Clarendon Press) 1999, pp. 270–276.

[77] See United Nations, *Enforced or Involuntary Disappearances: Fact Sheet No. 6* (Rev. 2) (Geneva: United Nations), pp. 5–6.

[78] See Rodley, above n. 76, at p. 274.

[79] Adopted by the General Assembly 16 December 1992, GA Res. 133, UN GAOR, 47 Sess., Supp. 49 at 207; UN Doc. A/Res/47/133. 32 I.L.M. (1993) 903.

Another valuable thematic mechanism established under the Resolution 1235 procedure is the Working Group on Arbitrary Detention. The Working Group was set up by the Commission in 1991 and operates under the following mandate:

(a) To investigate cases of detention imposed arbitrarily or otherwise inconsistently with relevant international standards set forth in the Universal Declaration of Human Rights or in the relevant international legal instruments accepted by the States concerned provided that no final decision has been taken in such cases by domestic courts in conformity with domestic law;

(b) To seek and receive information from Governments and intergovernmental and non-governmental organisations, and receive information from the individuals concerned, their families or their representatives

(c) To present a comprehensive report to the Commission at its annual session

The Working Group may investigate cases of arbitrary deprivation of liberty, and accepts communications from detained individuals or their families as well as from governments and intergovernmental and non-governmental organisations (NGOs). It is the only non-treaty based mechanism whose mandate expressly provides for consideration of individual complaints. If the Working Group decides after its investigation that arbitrary detention has been established then it makes recommendations to the government concerned. It transmits these recommendations to the complainant three weeks after sending them to the relevant government. The opinions and recommendations of the Working Group are published in an annex to the report presented by the group to the Commission on Human Rights at each of its annual sessions.

In addition to the thematic mandates accorded to the Working Group on Enforced and Involuntary Disappearances and the Working Group on Arbitrary Deprivation of Liberty, a number of other mandates are in force although the tasks are entrusted to individual experts described varyingly as Special Rapporteurs, Independent Experts, Representatives of the Secretary-General or Representatives of the Commission. Fourteen of these experts are in charge of country mandates which include Afghanistan (since 1984), Iran (1984), Iraq (1991), the former Yugoslavia (1992), Myanmar (1992), Cambodia (1993) Equatorial Guinea (1993) the Palestinian Occupied Territories (1993) Somalia (1993) Sudan (1993) the Democratic Republic of Congo (1994) Burundi (1995) Haiti (1995) and Rwanda (1997).

Among the Rapporteurs are the Special Rapporteur on Extra-Judicial, Summary and Arbitrary Execution (1982), Torture (1985), Religious Intolerance (1986), Mercenaries (1987), Sale of Children, Child Prostitution and Pornography (1990), Internally-Displaced Persons (1992), Contemporary Forms of Racism and Xenophobia (1993), Freedom of Opinion and Expression (1993) Children in Armed Conflict (1993), Extreme Poverty

(1998), the Right to Development (1998), the Right to Education (1998), the Rights of Migrants (1999) the Right to Adequate Housing (2000), the Right to Food (2000) Human Rights Defenders (2000) and Structural Adjustment Policies and Foreign Debt (2000).

The country-specific mandates are reviewed annually whereas thematic mandates are reviewed every three years. The functions of the Special Rapporteurs include study and research into the area, conduct country visits and on-site investigations, receive, consider and deal with complaints from victims and intervene on their behalf.[80] The nature of their mandate often requires them to make urgent appeals to the appropriate government in case of imminent human rights violations. The Special Rapporteurs and Independent Experts have performed valuable tasks in promoting good practice in the field of human rights. At the same time they are ultimately reliant upon the cooperation of the States and governments themselves. Their mandates are limited to reporting to the Commission and they do not have any means to enforce their views. Commenting on some of the contributions and limitations of the work of Rapporteurs, a United Nations document notes:

> Through their reports to the Commission, the experts highlight situations of concern. Their reports often provide an invaluable analysis of the human rights situation in a specific country or on a specific theme. Some reports bring to the attention of the international community issues that are not adequately on the international agenda. Many reports name victims and describe the allegations of violations of their human rights. Throughout the year, many experts intervene on behalf of victims. While the work of experts is often a major driving force contributing to change, it is difficult to attribute concrete results in the field of human rights to one factor. Much depends on how Governments, the civil society in a particular country and the international community react to the violations and to the findings, conclusions and recommendations of experts.
>
> The continuous examination of a particular situation, however, signals to victims that their plight is not forgotten by the international community and provides them with the opportunity to voice their grievances. The perpetrators of human rights violations know that they are being watched. The authorities concerned know that the assessment of their human rights record will have an impact on political, developmental and humanitarian considerations. This sometimes brings improved accountability and therefore change for the better.[81]

---

[80] United Nations, *Seventeen frequently asked questions about United Nations Special Rapporteurs: Fact Sheet No: 27* (United Nations: Geneva) 2001, pp. 8–9.
[81] Ibid. pp. 12–13.

Resolution 1503 procedure[82]

At the time of the adoption of ECOSOC Resolution 1235 the intention was primarily to focus on pariah States such as South Africa, Namibia and the Portuguese African Colonies. At that time NGOs were not authorised to make representations and submissions regarding violations taking place in any member State of the United Nations.[83] However, in 1967, the Sub-Commission recommended to the Commission that they should establish a special committee of experts to consider in addition to the South African situation, situations in Haiti (under François Duvalier) and in Greece (under the Colonels). This submission encouraged the Commission to develop a confidential procedure to consider information from a variety of sources. Resolution 1503 (XLVIII) was adopted as an ECOSOC Resolution on 27 May, 1970.[84] The procedure allows the Commission and its Sub-Commission to consider in private those communications received by the Secretary-General and referring to the Commission those 'situations which appear to reveal a consistent pattern of gross and reliably attested violations of human rights'.[85]

Resolution 1503 is a 'petition-information' system because the objective is to use complaints as a means by which to assist the Commission in identifying situations involving a 'consistent pattern of gross and reliably attested violations'. The violation of an individual's human rights is a piece of evidence and his case, in combination with other related cases, would be of sufficient importance to spur the United Nations to some form of action.

The following procedure must be followed:

• Communications are to be sent to the offices of the United Nations High Commission on Human Rights in Geneva.
• UN Secretariat will acknowledge receipt of communication.
• UN Secretariat sends communication to the government concerned and summarises the contents in a monthly confidential list. Governmental replies are also placed in a monthly list.

---

[82] T. Van Boven, 'United Nations and Human Rights: A Critical Appraisal' in A. Cassese (ed.), *UN Law: Fundamental Rights* (Alpen aan den Rijn: Sijthof and Noordhoff) 1979, pp. 119–135; M. Schreiber, 'La Protection des droits de l'homme' 145(II) Rec. des Cours (1975) 299 at p. 351; J.P. Humphrey, 'The United Nations Sub-Commission on the Prevention of Discrimination and the Protection of Minorities' 62 *AJIL* (1968) 869; M.J. Bossuyt, 'The Development of Special Procedures of the United Nations Commission on Human Rights' 6 *HRLJ* (1985) 179.
[83] N.S. Rodley, 'United Nations Non-Treaty Procedures for Dealing with Human Rights Violations' in H. Hannum (ed.), above n. 74, at p. 65.
[84] Resolution 1503 (XLVIII) 27 May 1970, ECOSOC.
[85] Ibid. para 1.

- Working Group of the Sub-Commission begins the procedure by sorting through various complaints received in the preceding year.[86] The Working Group on Communications consists of five Sub-Commission members and each one takes responsibility for a group of rights. The Working Group holds closed meetings once a year for ten days before the session of the Sub-Commission to consider the communications submitted, including the replies of the relevant government. A majority among the Working Group (that is at least three members) need to be of the view that the communication reveals a consistent pattern of gross violations of human rights before the situation can be forwarded to Sub-Commission.[87] Only a very small percentage of communications (around 1 per cent) are regarded by the Working Group as revealing a consistent pattern of gross violations of human rights and to be of sufficient merit to be referred to the Sub-Commission.

- Sub-Commission decides in closed sessions which of the situations referred to it should be forwarded to the Commission. On average, the Sub-Commission has passed a list of eight to ten countries to the Commission every year, with situations in over seventy-five countries having been to the Commission since the establishment of the procedure.[88] The relevant government is at this stage invited to make comments and observations, although the complainant is not invited or even informed.

- The Sub-Commission establishes a communications Working Group which is required to draft recommendations made by the Commission as to any proposed action.

Communications must be written within a reasonable period of time of the exhaustion of domestic remedies.[89] Generous rules in terms of petitioners of communications are applied; any one – an individual or a group – may apply provided he or she is a victim or has a direct or reliable knowledge of the alleged violations. Most often the petitions are submitted by NGOs. They must also not be anonymous, lacking in evidence, abusive, manifestly of a political nature or exclusively based on reports from the media.[90]

---

[86] Ibid. para 1.

[87] Ibid. para 5.

[88] N.S. Rodley, 'United Nations Non-Treaty Procedures for Dealing with Human Rights Violations' in H. Hannum (ed.), above n. 74 at p. 67.

[89] See ibid. para 6(b)(ii).

[90] The Human Rights Committee has distinguished Resolution 1503 as a procedure dealing with *situations* and therefore not precluding its consideration of *cases* based on the same matter. See Report of the Human Rights Committee, GAOR, XXXIII, Supp. No. 40 (A/33/40) para 582.

The overriding feature of the communication must be that it reveals a consistent pattern of gross violations of human rights.[91] Thus it needs to show a significant number of cases of violations of human rights, for example, imposition of the death penalty without a fair trial, torture, prolonged detention, etc. It may also be possible to make a number of communications revealing a pattern of violation of rights. The petitioner needs to provide detailed facts, such as names, places and authorities concerned, backed by sufficient evidence such as the testimony of victims, etc. He must show that violations have taken place and that all domestic remedies that are effective and not unreasonably prolonged have been exhausted. It also needs to be shown that the situation is not being dealt with by an international procedure. To establish the pattern of violations, reliance should be placed on violations of the rights as provided for in the international bill of rights or other major human rights treaties.

The communication should also consist of a covering letter referring to Resolution 1503; a summary of allegations and all relevant facts; and all documents, annexes, testimonials, etc. The Commission takes several days to consider the complaints which have been forwarded to it by the Sub-Commission. At the end of its consideration, the chairperson of the Commission announces the names of the countries that have been considered. In the light of its consideration the Commission may submit to ECOSOC its 'report and recommendations'. The confidential nature of the procedure means that all actions under Resolution 1503 'shall remain confidential until such time as the Commission may decide to make recommendations to ECOSOC'.[92] The Commission may keep the situation under review, it may appoint an envoy to seek further information on the spot and report back, or appoint an ad hoc committee aimed at finding a friendly solution.[93] The Commission may also transfer this action to Resolution 1235, thus allowing 'a thorough study by the Commission and a report and recommendations thereon to the Council'.[94]

---

[91] The previous history of the Sub-Commission's determination of what constitutes 'a consistent pattern' has been disappointing. The case of the former East Pakistan could be presented as an example. The civil war in the former East Pakistan lasted for nine months (from March–December 1971). During August 1971, when the matter was considered by the Sub-Commission under Resolution 1503, the Sub-Commission agreed with the Pakistani representative that in August 1971 'insufficient time had elapsed to draw the conclusion that "a consistent pattern of violation of human rights" had occurred. See the Commission on Human Rights, Sub-Commission on the Prevention of Discrimination and Protection of Minorities.' UN Doc. E/CN. 4/Sub.2/SR 633 (1971) p. 143. See Boulesbaa, above n. 19, at p. 105; also see J. Rehman, *The Weaknesses in the International Protection of Minority Rights* (The Hague: Kluwer Law International) 2000, pp. 92–93; J. Salzberg, 'UN Prevention of Human Rights Violations: The Bangladesh Case' 27 *International Organization* (1973) 115.

[92] Resolution 1503 (XLVIII) 27 May 1970; ECOSOC para 8.

[93] Ibid. para 6(b).

[94] ESC Res. 1503 (1970) para 6 (a).

In the final analysis it is worth reiterating that in the absence of 'going public', Resolution 1503 remains a secret and confidential procedure.[95]

The Commission on the Status of Women[96]

The Commission on the Status of Women (CSW) is one of the nine functional commissions of the ECOSOC. The CSW currently consists of 45 members who are elected by ECOSOC for a four-year term. Like the Commission on Human Rights members are appointed by their governments and the representation is on a geographically equitable basis. The meetings of the Commission are held annually in Vienna for eight working days. The CSW was a product of ECOSOC Resolution 11(II) of June 1946 to prepare reports and recommendations for the Council to advance and promote women's rights. In practice the most prominent achievement of the CSW has been in the field of standard setting. While it has played a pivotal role in the drafting of a number of instruments including the Convention on the Political Rights of Women[97] and the Convention on the Nationality of Married Women[98], its single most significant achievement is the work on the drafting of the Convention on the Elimination of All Forms of Discrimination Against Women.[99] The CSW has a continuing involvement with the Convention as it receives reports from the Committee on the Elimination of All Forms of Discrimination Against Women (CEDAW) under the 1979 Convention.[100] The CSW has been involved in information gathering, cooperation with other international agencies, and preparing recommendations and reports on the rights of women in political, economic, civil, social and educational fields. Like the Commission on Human Rights, it is also possible for this Commission to appoint a sessional working group to review confidential communications 'which appear to reveal a consistent pattern of reliably attested injustice and discriminatory practice against women', and to prepare a report which will indicate the categories in which communications are most frequently submitted to the Commission.[101]

---

[95] Ibid. para 8.

[96] See L. Reanda, 'The Commission on the Status of Women' in P. Alston (ed.), above n. 1, pp. 265–303.

[97] Opened for signature and ratification by General Assembly resolution 640 (VII) of 20 December 1952. Entry into force 7 July 1954.

[98] Opened for signature and ratification by General Assembly resolution 1040 (XI) of 29 January 1957. Entry into force 11 August 1958.

[99] See below Chapter 13.

[100] Article 21(2).

[101] L. Reanda, 'The Commission on the Status of Women' in P. Alston (ed.), above n. 1, at p. 274.

INTERNATIONAL COURT OF JUSTICE[102]

The International Court of Justice (ICJ) is 'the principal judicial organ of the United Nations'.[103] The ICJ was established in 1946 as the successor to the Permanent Court of International Justice (PCIJ). The Statute of the ICJ forms an integral part of the UN Charter and all UN members are automatically members of the ICJ.[104] The Court consists of 15 judges elected by concurrent votes of the Security Council and the General Assembly. The jurisdiction of the ICJ is either contentious or advisory. Only States can be parties to the contentious jurisdiction, a jurisdiction that is based upon the consent of the parties in dispute.[105] In contentious cases, the judgment of the Court is final and binds only States which are parties to the case.[106] The ICJ is also authorised to deliver advisory opinions. A request for such an opinion could be brought forth by a number of organs including the General Assembly or the Security Council, although the advisory jurisdiction is not open to States. In effecting the advisory jurisdiction, the objective of the Court is to 'offer legal advice to the organ and institutions requesting the opinion'.[107]

As the principal judicial organ of the UN, the ICJ's task is to decide upon matters involving judicial disputes. It is neither the Court's role to create new law, nor to decide upon matters without a legal basis. Having said that, in reality it is often difficult to isolate legal from political matters, a situation that becomes apparent in cases involving allegations of human rights violations. Furthermore, the limitation of adjudication rather than the development of law is also unrealistic. The decisions and advisory opinions of the Court are of great value and have in a number of instances been greatly significant in the advancement of international law. Indeed so significant has been the Court that its principal provision for adjudication of a dispute is regarded as providing the catalogue of primary sources of international law.[108]

---

[102] See Chapter XIV UN Charter. See S. Rosenne, *The World Court: What It Is and How it Works* (Dordrecht: Martinus Nijhoff Publishers) 1995; G. Fitzmaurice, *The Law and Procedure of the International Court of Justice* (Cambridge: Grotius Publications) 1986; for a detailed survey see H. Thirlway, 'The Law and Procedure of the International Court of .Justice: 1960–1989' 60 *BYIL* (1989) 1, and its following ten volumes at p. 1; E. Schwelb, 'The International Court of Justice and the Human Rights Clauses of the Charter' 66 *AJIL* (1972) 337; N.S. Rodley, 'Human Rights and Humanitarian Intervention: The Case Law of the World Court' 38 *ICLQ* (1989) 321; J. Rehman, 'The Role and Contribution of the World Court in the Progressive Development of International Environmental Law' 5 *APJEL* (2000) 387.

[103] Article 92, UN Charter.

[104] According to Article 93(1) 'All members of the United Nations are ipso facto parties to the Statute of the ICJ' and Article 94(1) provides that 'Each member of the United Nations undertakes to comply with the decisions of the ICJ in any case to which it is a party'.

[105] See Article 36 Statute of the ICJ.

[106] Ibid. Article 59.

[107] *Legality of the Use by a State of Nuclear Weapons in Armed Conflict*, Advisory Opinion 8 July 1996, (1996) ICJ Reports 66, paras 15 and 35.

[108] See above Chapter 1.

Since its establishment, the Court has not been used as extensively as one might have expected. Nevertheless, in so far as human rights issues are concerned there is an enormous body jurisprudence which has been accumulated over the years. Among the innumerable judgments and advisory opinions where the Court has expanded on the jurisprudence of international human rights norms, reference could be made to the *Reservations to the Genocide Convention Case*,[109] the *Barcelona Traction case*,[110] the *Namibia case*,[111] the *Tehran Hostages case*[112] and the *East Timor case*.[113]

THE TRUSTEESHIP COUNCIL[114]

The work of the Trusteeship Council is predominantly of historical interest though it has significant contemporary implications for modern developments of international human rights law. The objectives of the trusteeship system included *inter alia*:

> to encourage respect for human rights and for fundamental freedoms for all without distinction as to race, sex, language, or religion, and to encourage recognition of the interdependence of the peoples of the world

After the formation of the UN, former mandatory territories under the Covenant of the League of Nations were placed under the protection of the UN trusteeship system, with a council in charge of supervising the system. The only mandatory territory not placed under the trusteeship system or granted independence was South West Africa. The issue became a subject of contention, in the process creating substantial human rights jurisprudence in the areas of racial non-discrimination and the right to self-determination. The International Court of Justice provided four advisory opinions and one judgment. The matter was also the subject of a series of General Assembly Resolutions. The main aim of the Council was to supervise the social advancement of the people of

---

[109] *Reservations to the Convention on the Prevention and Punishment of the Crime of Genocide,* Advisory Opinion 28 May 1951 (1951) ICJ Reports, 15.

[110] See *Barcelona Traction, Light and Power Company, Limited (Belgium* v. *Spain)*, Preliminary Objection, Judgment 24 July 1964 (1964) ICJ Reports 6.

[111] *Legal Consequences for States of the Continued Presence of South Africa in Namibia (South West Africa) notwithstanding Security Council Resolution 276* (1970), Advisory Opinion 21 June 1971, (1971) ICJ Reports 16.

[112] See *United States Diplomatic and Consular Staff in Tehran (United States of America* v. *Iran)*, Judgment 24 May 1980 (1980) ICJ Reports 3.

[113] *East Timor Case (Portugal* v. *Australia)*, Judgment 30 June 1995 (1995) ICJ Reports 90.

[114] See Sands and Klein, above n. 5, at pp. 63–68; J.L. Kunz, 'Chapter XI of the United Nations Charter in Action' 48 *AJIL* (1954) 103; M. Reisman, 'Reflections on State Responsibility for Violations of Explicit Protectorate, Mandate and Trusteeship Obligations' 10 *Michigan Journal of International Law* (1989) 231; R.E. Gordon, 'Some Legal Problems with Trusteeship' 28 *Cornell Journal of International Law* (1995) 231.

trust territories, with the aim ultimately of preparing them for self-government and independence. Originally there were eleven trust territories, mostly in Africa and the Pacific Ocean, but the last of these – Palau – gained independence in 1994. Consequently, on 1 November 1994 the Council suspended its operations. Although currently in suspension, the system may have a future role to play for those territories where the State and government have collapsed leading to a situation of complete anarchy. It might be worth considering whether a State such as Afghanistan for example (ravaged by years of civil war and suffering from famine and natural calamities) should be placed under trust to an international organisation or a willing State.

THE SECRETARIAT[115]

Headed by the Secretary-General, the Secretariat provides staff for the day-to-day functioning of the UN. The Secretary-General is appointed by the General Assembly on the unanimous recommendation of the Security Council.[116] The charter does not specify a term of office but by convention he or she serves for five years and may then be reappointed for a further five years. Article 98 provides that the Secretary-General shall carry out such functions as may be assigned to him by either the General Assembly or the Security Council and Article 99 gives him an independent role: he may bring to the attention of the Security Council any matter which, in his opinion, may threaten international peace and security. He or she may propose issues to be discussed by the General Assembly or any other organ of the United Nations. The Secretary-General often acts as a 'referee' in disputes between member States and on a number of occasions his 'good offices' have been used to mediate in international disputes. Since the creation of the UN, a total of seven Secretary-Generals have been appointed, the current incumbent being Kofi Annan from Ghana. The Secretary-General can play a notable part in the future developments of international law. One recent example is that of the publication of Agenda for Peace by the former Secretary-General, Dr Boutros Boutros-Ghali, which has encouraged States to re-evaluate their practices to secure peace and human rights.[117]

The role of the Secretary-General in human rights, although variable and dependent on individual personalities, is potentially very significant. Successive Secretary-Generals have maintained that it is within their mandate to use their offices to raise and resolve human rights concerns. Many examples of the

---

[115] See B.G. Ramcharan, *Humanitarian Good Offices in International Law: The Good Offices of the United Nations Secretary-General in the Field of Human Rights* (The Hague: Martinus Nijhoff Publishers) 1983; T.C. Van Boven, 'The Role of the United Nations Secretariat' in P. Alston (ed.), above n. 1, pp. 549–579.

[116] See Article 97 of the UN Charter.

[117] Shaw, above n. 1, at p. 834.

involvement of the Secretary-General could be found in his intervention to prevent serious violations of human rights, the most recent being the initiatives of Kofi Annan to condemn the terrorist attacks of 11 September 2001 and to make efforts to end all forms of terrorism. He has made substantial attempts to encourage the international community to provide humanitarian assistance to the Afghan people and on 27 September 2001 launched a $584 million appeal to help the Afghans in their current crisis.[118] Other notable examples include the Secretary-General's involvement during the invasion of Kuwait (1990–1991), attempts during 1998 to enforce the compliance of Iraq with the Security Council's Resolutions, the 1999 agreement with Libya leading to the Lockerbie bombing trials and the efforts to resolve the East Timor conflict (2000). At the same time, it cannot be stated with certainty in which human rights situations the Secretary-General would exercise his good offices. There is also no definitive and specific procedure invoking the good offices of the Secretary-General.[119] Applications should be made to him or her via the High Commission on Human Rights in Geneva or in New York.[120] In practice, in terms of petitioning it would perhaps be more useful to approach the United Nations High Commissioner on Human Rights. The High Commissioner has a specific mandate in this regard; significant information is available about the activities of the High Commissioner on the UN web-site.[121]

---

[118] See UN Web-Site http://www.un.org/News/dh/latest/sg_afghan.htm (1 November 2001).

[119] N.S. Rodley, 'United Nations Non-Treaty Procedures for Dealing with Human Rights Violations' in H. Hannum (ed.), above n. 74, at p. 80.

[120] Ibid.

[121] For details of the web-site see appendix I.

II

THE INTERNATIONAL BILL OF RIGHTS

3

THE UNIVERSAL DECLARATION OF HUMAN RIGHTS[1]

INTRODUCTION

We have noted that the United Nations Charter contains a number of references to 'human rights', though no elaboration is provided to the meaning of the concept within the Charter itself. It has also been noted that efforts by certain States, notably Panama, to have a 'Bill of Rights' included within the United Nations Charter proved unsuccessful.[2] After the coming into operation of the United Nations Charter, there was a move to spell out the meaning of the concept of 'human rights' in greater detail. In 1945, the preparatory

---

[1] See G. Alfredsson and A. Eide (eds), *The Universal Declaration of Human Rights: A Common Standard of Achievement* (The Hague: Kluwer Law International) 1999; J. Morsink, *The Universal Declaration of Human Rights: Origins, Drafting and Intent* (Philadelphia: University of Pennsylvania Press) 1999; B. van der Heijden and B. Tahzib-Lie (eds), *Reflections on the Universal Declaration of Human Rights: A Fiftieth Anniversary Anthology* (The Hague: Martinus Nijhoff Publishers) 1998; M.G. Johnson, *The Universal Declaration of Human Rights: A history of its Creation and Implementation, 1948–1998* (Paris: UNESCO Pub.) 1998; P. Baehr, C. Flinterman and M. Senders (eds), *Innovation and Inspiration: Fifty Years of the Universal Declaration of Human Rights* (Amsterdam: Royal Academy of Arts and Sciences) 1999; J. Humphrey, 'The Universal Declaration of Human Rights: Its History, Impact and Juridical Character' in B.G. Ramcharan (ed.), *Human Rights: Thirty Years after the Universal Declaration: Commemorative Volume on the Occasion of the Thirtieth Anniversary of the Universal Declaration of Human Rights* (The Hague: Martinus Nijhoff Publishers) 1979, pp. 21–37; E. Schwelb, 'The Influence of the Universal Declaration of Human Rights on International and National Law' *PASIL* (1959) 217.
[2] See above Chapter 2; also see J.P. Humphrey, 'The UN Charter and the Universal Declaration of Human Rights' in E. Laurd (ed.), *The International Protection of Human Rights* (London: Thames & Hudson) 1967, 39–56 at p. 47.

commission recommended that ECOSOC should establish a Commission on Human Rights which would then prepare a Bill of Rights. The recommendation was approved by the General Assembly and a Human Rights Commission was established in 1946. The first regular sessions of the Human Rights Commission began on 27 January 1947. The Human Rights Commission immediately got down to its first task, that is the drafting of the International Bill of Rights. A consideration of the proceedings of the Human Rights Commission (and a specifically established Drafting Committee) represents divisions as to the form the International Bill of Rights should take. The primary divisions were among those who wanted a declaration and those in favour of a binding convention or treaty.[3] In the second session of the Human Rights Commission late in 1947, it was decided that the International Bill of Rights should have three parts: a declaration; a Convention; and 'measures of implementation' (i.e. a system of international supervision).[4] It was subsequently decided to split the Covenant into two separate Covenants.

The Declaration was adopted on 10 December 1948 with forty-eight votes in favour, none against and eight abstentions.[5] The UDHR was adopted by Resolution 217(III) which consisted of five parts. Part A consisted of the UDHR whereas part B was entitled the Right to Petition.[6] In part C of the Resolution, the General Assembly called upon the United Nations Sub-Commission 'to make a thorough study of the problem of minorities, in order that the United Nations may be able to take effective measures for the protection of racial, national, religious or linguistic minorities'.[7] Part D related to the publicity to be given to the UDHR and Part E was entitled 'Preparation of a Draft Covenant on Human Rights and Draft Measures of Implementation'. The Declaration has thirty articles covering the most important fundamental human rights. The General Assembly adopted the Declaration as a 'common standard of achievement for all peoples and all nations'. The catalogue of rights contained within the Declaration, provides for both civil and political rights as well as economic, social and cultural rights. These rights are contained in the following Articles:

[3] H.J. Steiner and P. Alston, *International Human Rights in Context: Law, Politics and Morals: Text and Materials*, 2nd edn (Oxford: Clarendon Press) 2000, p. 138.
[4] Humphrey, above n. 1, at pp. 22–23.
[5] 10 December, 1948, UN GA Res. 217 A(III), UN Doc. A/810 at 71 (1948). Byelorussia, Czechoslovakia, Poland, Ukraine, USSR, Yugoslavia, Saudi Arabia, and South Africa.
[6] See T.J.M. Zuijdwijk, *Petitioning the United Nations: A Study in Human Rights* (Aldershot: Gower) 1982, pp. 90–93.
[7] G.A. Resolution 217 C(III) (1948) para 5. See A. Eide, 'The Sub-Commission on Prevention of Discrimination and Protection of Minorities' in P. Alston (ed.), *United Nations and Human Rights: A Critical Appraisal* (Oxford: Clarendon Press) 211–264, at p. 220; A. Eide, 'The Non-inclusion of Minority Rights: Resolution 217C (III)' in G. Alfredsson and A. Eide (eds), *The Universal Declaration of Human Rights: A Common Standard of Achievement* (The Hague: Kluwer Law International) 1998, 701–723 at p. 723.

Article 1   Recognition of being born free and equal in dignity and rights
Article 2   Right to equality
Article 3   Right to life, liberty and security of person
Article 4   Freedom from slavery or servitude
Article 5   Freedom from torture or cruel, inhuman or degrading treatment or punishment
Article 6   Right to recognition everywhere as a person before the law.
Article 7   Right to equality before the law
Article 8   Right to an effective remedy by competent national tribunals
Article 9   Right not to be subjected to arbitrary arrest, detention or exile
Article 10   Right to fair trial
Article 11   Presumption of innocence and prohibition of retroactive criminal law
Article 12   Prohibition of arbitrary interference with privacy, family, home or correspondence
Article 13   Right to freedom of movement
Article 14   Right to seek asylum
Article 15   Right to a nationality
Article 16   Right to marry and found a family
Article 17   Right to own property
Article 18   Right to freedom of thought, conscience and religion
Article 19   Right to freedom of opinion and expression
Article 20   Right to freedom of peaceful assembly
Article 21   Right to participate in the governance of the State, and the right to democracy
Article 22   Right to social security
Article 23   Right to work
Article 24   Right to rest and leisure
Article 25   Right to a decent standard of living
Article 26   Right to education
Article 27   Right to cultural life
Article 28   Right to social and international order suitable for the realisation of human rights

RANGE OF RIGHTS CONTAINED AND THE RATIONALE FOR INTERNATIONAL CONSENSUS

The Declaration contains a remarkable range of rights. It includes classical civil and political rights,[8] social, economic and cultural rights[9] and group or people's rights.[10] The civil and political rights bear a resemblance to those

---

[8] Also known as first generation rights. See above Introduction.

[9] Also referred to as second generation rights. See above Introduction.

[10] Also known as third generation rights or solidarity rights. See above Introduction. Also See P. Alston, 'The Commission on Human Rights' in P. Alston (ed.), above n. 7, at p. 188.

rights contained in the eighteenth and nineteenth-century classical human rights documents; like the French Declaration of the Rights of Man, the Universal Declaration thrives on the rights to liberty, equality and fraternity.[11] The Declaration provides a comprehensive set of civil and political rights. These rights, also known as first generation rights, include the right to equality, to life, to an effective remedy by national tribunals, to fair trial, to freedom of assembly, opinion and expression, and thought, conscience and religion. The Declaration condemns torture and slavery and prohibits arbitrary interference with privacy, family, home or correspondence. The Declaration also contains certain civil and political rights which have remained controversial. One example is the right to property. The right to property, although included in Article 17 of the UDHR, could not be provided for either in the ICCPR (1966) or in the ICESCR (1966).[12] Another example is that of the right to seek asylum.[13]

In addition to the aforementioned civil and political rights, the Declaration contains a number of social, economic and cultural rights. These rights, also referred to as second generation rights, include the right to social security, to work, to rest and leisure and the right to education. The right to cultural life is accorded by Article 27. Article 28 takes a broad approach and provides for the third generation rights of a suitable international order and the right to peace. According to this Article, everyone is entitled to a social and international order in which the rights and freedoms set forth in this Declaration can be fully realised.

This cataloguing of rights in a single document appears even more remarkable when considered in light of the great consensus showed in adopting the document. Various reasons for such a consensus can be put forward, some more obvious than others. First and most importantly, it was relatively easy to find acceptance among UN States because of the belief that the Declaration, as a General Assembly Resolution, was a non-binding instrument.[14] International consensus would have been much harder had State representatives been faced with the prospect of accepting legally binding obligations. Second, at the time of adoption of the Declaration, there were far fewer member States, making it relatively more easy to find common ground. As we shall be considering, soon after the adoption of the Declaration rapid changes in

---

[11] See S.P. Marks, 'From the "Single Confused Page" to the Decalogue for Six Billion Persons: The Roots of the Universal Declaration of Human Rights in the French Revolution' 20 *HRQ* (1998) 459.

[12] C. Krause and G. Alfredsson, 'Article 17' in G. Alfredsson and A. Eide (eds), above n. 1, pp. 359–378.

[13] R.B. Lillich, 'Civil Rights' in T. Meron (ed.), *Human Rights in International Law: Legal and Policy Issues* (Oxford: Clarendon Press) 1984, 115–170 at p. 152; M. Kjǽrum, 'Article 14' in G. Alfredsson and A. Eide (eds), above n. 1, 279–295 at p. 285.

[14] Schwelb, above n. 1, at p. 218.

global political geography took place. The former colonies emerged as new States and did not share the same priorities and claims of the founder member States. Finally, a range of strategies was adopted by the drafters to achieve consensus and have the Declaration adopted by the international community. Pointing to these strategies, Samnøy mentions the exclusion of controversial issues and the use of generalised and vague terminology.[15]

NATURE OF OBLIGATIONS AND RELEVANCE FOR HUMAN RIGHTS PRACTITIONER

As already indicated, the Declaration was adopted by General Assembly Resolution 217 (III) and was not intended to be legally binding. The intention of those who drafted the Declaration was to provide guidelines which States would aim to achieve. Thus according to Mrs Eleanor Roosevelt, the Chairman of the Human Rights Commission, 'it [the Declaration] is not, and does not purport to be a statement of law or of legal obligation'; it is instead 'a common standard of achievement for all peoples of all nations'. Given the prima facie non-binding character of the Declaration, the immediate question arises as to the practical relevance of consideration of this instrument. The most direct answer to this question is that, despite the intention being to draft guidelines, over a period of time the substantive provisions of the Declaration have become binding on all States. The binding authority derives from sources described below.

UDHR as an authoritative interpretation of the Charter

The United Nations Charter, while making references to human rights does not itself provide a catalogue of human rights. After the enforcement of the Charter, it was intended that a detailed bill of rights would provide an explanation as to the definition of human rights. As the first part of such a Bill, the Declaration is arguably an authoritative interpretation of the meaning of human rights as prescribed within the United Nations Charter. This argument is substantiated both from the *travaux préparatoires* of the Declaration and from its text. The preamble to the Declaration makes reference to Articles 55 and 56 of the United Nations Charter. As one leading authority has pointed out such references can lead to the argument that 'each right contained in the Universal Declaration is effectively incorporated into the Charter'.[16]

---

[15] Å. Samnøy, 'The Origins of the Universal Declaration of Human Rights' in G. Alfredsson and A. Eide (eds), above n. 1, 3–22 at p. 14.
[16] See N.S. Rodley, *The Treatment of Prisoners in International Law*, 2nd edn (Oxford: Clarendon Press) 1999, p. 63.

During the drafting stages of the Declaration, representatives of a number of States treated the Declaration as a document interpreting human rights provisions of the Charter. The Chinese representative was of the view that, while the United Nations Charter placed member States under an obligation to observe human rights, the Universal Declaration 'stated these rights explicitly'.[17] According to Professor Réne Cassin of France, a member of the Commission and the Drafting Committee, the Universal Declaration 'could be considered as an authoritative interpretation of the Charter'.[18] Similarly the Chilean representative remarked that 'violations by any State of the rights enumerated in the Declaration would mean violation of the principles of the United Nations'.[19] Among the Islamic States, the Egyptian representative took the view that the Declaration was an 'authoritative interpretation of the [UN] Charter',[20] supported by the Syrian and Pakistan delegates. Ironically, it was the concern that the non-binding General Assembly Resolution might in fact come to have binding effect (through its recognition as an authoritative interpretation of the UN Charter's human rights provisions) that produced substantial disquiet on the part of South Africa, leading ultimately to its abstention from the vote.[21]

UDHR as part of customary international law

A significant proportion of this book deals with human rights treaties, such as the ICCPR,[22] the ICESCR,[23] the ECHR,[24] and the AFCHPR.[25] As we saw in Chapter 1, treaties are legally binding obligations undertaken by State parties.[26] However, treaty law represents one aspect, albeit a significant one, of the international law-making process. We have also noted that other sources of international law include international customary law and general principles of law. International customary law, which binds all States, consists of two key ingredients: State practice and the conviction that such practice amounts to law (*opinio juris*).[27]

---

[17] Cited in Humphrey, above n. 2, at p. 50.
[18] Ibid. p. 51.
[19] A/C.3/SR 91 at 97.
[20] UN Doc. A/C.3/SR 92 at 12. See D.E. Arzt, 'The Application of International Human Rights Law in Islamic States' 12 *HRQ* (1990) 202 at pp. 215–216.
[21] See Humphrey, above n. 2, at pp. 32–33.
[22] Adopted at New York, 16 December 1966. Entered into force 23 March 1976. GA Res. 2200A (XXI) UN Doc. A/6316 (1966) 999 U.N.T.S. 171; 6 I.L.M. (1967) 368.
[23] Adopted at New York, 16 December 1966. Entered into force 3 January 1976. GA Res. 2200A (XXI) UN Doc. A/6316 (1966) 993 U.N.T.S. 3; 6 I.L.M. (1967) 360.
[24] Signed at Rome, 4 November 1950. Entered into force 3 September 1953. 213 U.N.T.S. 221; E.T.S. 5.
[25] Adopted on 27 June 1981. Entered into force 21 October 1986. OAU Doc. CAB/LEG/67/3 Rev. 5, 21 I.L.M (1982) 58.
[26] See above Chapter 1.
[27] Ibid.

In the light of existing State practices it can be strongly argued that a vast majority of the provisions of the Declaration now represent customary international law.[28] There is overwhelming evidence of State practice, with the requisite *opinio juris*, to confirm the customary binding nature of many of the provisions of the Declaration.[29] Such evidence can be derived from its constant reaffirmation by the General Assembly.[30] According to one source, in the first twenty-one years after its adoption, the Declaration was cited no fewer than seventy-five times by the General Assembly, an exercise that has remained prevalent in the subsequent human rights activities of the Assembly.[31] There is also a consistent referral to the Universal Declaration in international instruments, in bilateral agreements[32] and multilateral human rights treaties.[33] In the context of multilateral human rights treaties it is important to note that the International Covenants and three regional human rights treaties make specific reference to the Declaration. In his consideration, Professor Brownlie points to the Final Act of the Conference on Security and Cooperation in Europe,[34] and the Proclamation of Tehran[35] whereby States express their intention to follow the principles of the Universal Declaration on Human Rights.[36] To this one could add the Vienna Declaration and Programme of Action, which was adopted by a consensus of representatives

---

[28] According to one authority 'the Universal Declaration is the ius constituendum of the United Nations Charter to the term "human rights" and most of the international lawyers support the opinion that its principles are customary international law'. H-J. Heintze, 'The UN Convention and the Network of International Human Rights Protection by the United Nations' in M. Freeman and P. Veerman (eds), *Ideologies of Children's Rights* (Dordrecht: Martinus Nijhoff Publishers) 1992, 71–78, at p. 72.

[29] See e.g. the Preambles to European Convention on Human Rights (1950) and the African Charter on Human and People's Rights (1981).

[30] See the Colonial Declaration, which provides 'All States shall observe faithfully and strictly the provisions of the Charter of the United Nations, Universal Declaration of Human Rights and the present Declaration'. GA Resolution 1514 (XV) 1960.

[31] S. Bleicher, 'The Legal Significance of Re-citation of General Assembly Resolutions' 63 *AJIL* (1969) 444 at p. 449; T.J.M. Zuijdwijk, above n. 6, at p. 101.

[32] See e.g. the Franco–Tunisian Convention (1955) *UNYBH* (1955) 340, at p. 342.

[33] See A.H. Robertson and J.G. Merrills, *Human Rights in the World: An Introduction to the Study of International Protection of Human Rights*, 4th. edn., (Manchester: Manchester University Press) 1996, p. 29; J. Humphrey, 'The International Bill of Rights: Scope and Implementation' 17 *William and Mary Law Review* (1975) 527; Humphrey, above n. 1, at pp. 28–29.

[34] See the Final Act of the Conference on Security and Cooperation in Europe, Adopted by the Conference on Security and Co-operation in Europe at Helsinki, August 1, 1975. Reprinted in 14 I.L.M (1975) 1292. Discussed below Chapter 7.

[35] See the Proclamation of Tehran, *The Final Act of the United Nations Conference on Human Rights*, Tehran, 22 April–13 May, 1968, UN Doc. A/CONF. 32/41 (New York: United Nations) E. 68, XIV. 2.

[36] I. Brownlie (ed.), *Basic Documents on Human Rights*, 2nd edn (Oxford: Clarendon Press) 1981, p. 21.

from 171 States.[37] In addition to containing numerous references to the Universal Declaration, it emphasises

> That the Universal Declaration of Human Rights, which constitutes a common standard of achievement for all peoples and all nations, is the source of inspiration and has been the basis for the United Nations in making advances in standard setting as contained in the existing international human rights instruments, in particular the International Covenant on Civil and Political Rights and the International Covenant of Economic, Social and Cultural Rights.[38]

Further recognition by States of the binding nature of the Declaration found in the replication of its provisions in their national constitutions or in referrals to it in their constitutional documents.[39] National and international tribunals have also relied upon the Declaration, treating it as a binding document.[40]

While endorsing the customary value of many of the rights contained in the Declaration, at the same time some caution is recommended. As we shall see during the course of this study, not all rights contained in the Universal Declaration have generated a sufficient degree of consensus to be recognised as binding in customary law. There is debate about the legal value and content of a number of rights, in particular of economic, social and cultural rights.[41] Thus questions have been raised about the legal and juridical value of such rights as the right to rest and leisure, the right to a decent standard of living, and the right to participate in the cultural life of the community. In the light of divisions it is sensible to take account of the views of one leading authority when he writes 'it must not be assumed without more that any and every human right referred to [in UDHR] is part of customary international law'.[42]

---

[37] *Vienna Declaration and Programme of Action* (New York: United Nations Department of Public Information) 1993. Adopted by the United Nations World Conference on Human Rights, 25 June 1993.

[38] Ibid. Preamble to the Declaration.

[39] See e.g. the Constitution of Bosnia and Herzegovina (1995).

[40] See e.g. *United States Diplomatic and Consular Staff in Tehran* (*United States of America* v. *Iran*), Judgment 24 May 1980, (1980) ICJ Reports 3, where the International Court notes 'Wrongfully to deprive human beings of their freedom and to subject them to physical constraint in conditions of hardship is in itself manifestly incompatible with ... the fundamental principles enunciated in the Universal Declaration of Human Rights' ibid. para 91. Commenting on the Tehran case, Professor Rodley, makes the valid point that '[a] more natural interpretation is that the Court was simply stating that the Declaration as a whole propounds fundamental principles recognised by general international law' N.S. Rodley, 'Human Rights and Humanitarian Intervention: The Case Law of the World Court' 38 *ICLQ* (1989) 321 at p. 326. See also *Filártiga* v. *Peña-Irala* 630 F. 2d 876 (1980); 19 I.L.M (1980) 966. US Circuit Court of Appeals, 2nd Circuit.

[41] See below Chapter 5.

[42] P. Thornberry, *International Law and the Rights of Minorities* (Oxford: Clarendon Press) 1991, p. 322.

UDHR binding states with its *jus cogens* character

The chapters in the book confirm that a number of the rights contained in the UDHR have become so firmly established in international law that they are now treated as having a *jus cogens* character. We have already noted that no specification has been provided on the norms forming *jus cogens*. At the same time several of the fundamental rights enunciated in the Declaration, such as the right to equality (Article 2), right to life, liberty and security (Article 3), freedom from slavery or servitude (Article 4), freedom from torture or cruel, inhuman or degrading treatment or punishment (Article 5), the right to a fair trial (Article 10), the presumption of innocence and the prohibition of retroactive criminal law (Article 11), represents aspects of the norm of *jus cogens*.

The existence of such substantial affirmation of the rights has led many commentators to take the position that the normative provisions of the Declaration form part of *jus cogens*, and thereby bind all States.[43] As this book analyses in detail, the fundamental rights of the Declaration now form part and parcel of every human rights instrument. It is well established that it is not possible to derogate from these rights. At the same time, a number of rights are arguably not even part of customary law and categorising those as part of the *jus cogens* would be inaccurate. There is significant debate on the customary position not only on economic, social and cultural rights such as the right to social security (Article 22), right to rest and leisure (Article 24), right to a decent standard of living (Article 25), and right to participate in cultural life (Article 27) but also on civil and political rights which include the right to seek asylum (Article 14) and upon the various facets of the right to freedom of thought, conscience and religion (Article 18).[44]

---

[43] See M.S. McDougal, H.D. Lasswell and L-C. Chen, *Human Rights and World Public Order: The Basic Policies of an International Law of Human Dignity* (New Haven and London: Yale University Press) 1980, p. 64.

[44] See below Chapters 10 and 11.

4

INTERNATIONAL COVENANT ON CIVIL AND POLITICAL RIGHTS[1]

INTRODUCTION

After the adoption of the Universal Declaration of Human Rights (UDHR),[2] the next stage was to establish legally binding principles on international human rights. In its Resolution 217B and E(III) of 10 December 1948, the General Assembly, through the ECOSOC, requested the Human Right Commission to continue to give priority to the drafting of the International Covenant and measures of implementation.[3] Originally it had been intended to draft a single Covenant covering all the fundamental rights. However, with the onset of the cold war and the rise of new nation States (with their own priorities) it became impossible to incorporate all the rights within one

---

[1] S. Joseph, J. Schultz and M. Castan, *The International Covenant on Civil and Political Rights: Cases and Material and Commentary* (Oxford: Clarendon Press) 2000; D. McGoldrick, *The Human Rights Committee: Its Role in the Development of the International Covenant on Civil and Political Rights* (Oxford: Clarendon Press) 1991; D.J. Harris and S. Joseph (eds), *The International Covenant on Civil and Political Rights and United Kingdom Law* (Oxford: Clarendon Press) 1995; M. Nowak, *U.N. Covenant on Civil and Political Rights: CCPR Commentary* (Kehl: Arlington: N.P. Engel) 1993; M.J. Bossuyt, *Guide to the 'Travaux Préparatoires' of the International Covenant on Civil and Political Rights* (Dordrecht: Martinus Nijhoff Publishers) 1987; P.R. Ghandhi, *The Human Rights Committee and the Right of Individual Communication: Law and Practice* (Aldershot: Ashgate Publishing Ltd.) 1998; D.J. Harris, *Cases and Materials on International Law*, 5th edn (London: Sweet and Maxwell) 1998, pp. 624–764; H.J. Steiner and P. Alston, *International Human Rights in Context : Law, Politics, Morals: Text and Materials*, 2nd edn (Oxford: Clarendon Press) 2000, pp. 592–704.
[2] 10 December 1948, UN GA Res. 217 A(III), UN Doc. A/810 at 71 (1948).
[3] Ghandhi, above n. 1, at p. 3.

document.[4] The western States put emphasis on civil and political rights whereas the focus of the socialist and newly independent States was on economic, social and cultural rights and the right to self-determination. There were divisions and difficulties around having civil and political rights alongside economic, social and cultural rights, within the text of a single treaty. Those in favour of a single covenant argued that:

> human rights could not be clearly divided into different categories, nor could they be so classified as to represent a hierarchy of values. All rights should be promoted and protected at the same time. Without economic, social and cultural rights, civil and political rights might be purely nominal in character; without civil and political rights, economic, social and cultural rights could not be ensured.[5]

However, the opposing camp prioritised civil and political rights as more significant. They also pointed to the progressive nature of the social and economic rights, some even doubting that they were rights in the true sense. A critical issue related to the implementation mechanism. While it was thought possible to set up a scheme to implement civil and political rights, the same was not thought to be feasible for social and economic rights.[6]

It was ultimately decided to have two different treaties, one covering pri-marily civil and political rights (i.e. ICCPR)[7] and the other economic, social and cultural rights (i.e. ICESCR).[8] As we shall analyse in detail, although some rights contained within these treaties overlap, there are nevertheless substantial differences in the content, nature of obligations and the implementation mech-anisms. The ICCPR and the ICESCR were approved by the Third Committee of the General Assembly in December 1966. Each Covenant required 35 ratifications and both came into force in 1976. The Optional Protocol was approved in 1966 and required 10 ratifications. As of 31 March 2002, there were 148 States parties to the ICCPR. In addition, 101 States have made dec-larations pursuant to the First Optional Protocol to the ICCPR. The Second Optional Protocol, aimed at the Abolition of the Death Penalty, was adopted

---

[4] See Steiner and Alston (eds), above n. 1, at p. 139.

[5] Annotations on the Text of the Draft International Covenants on Human Rights, UN Doc. A/2929 (1955), 7 para. 8.

[6] McGoldrick, above n. 1, at pp. 11–13; for a consideration of implementation mechanism in the Covenants see J.Th. Moller, 'The Right to Petition: General Assembly Resolution 217B' in G. Alfredsson and A. Eide, 'Introduction' in G. Alfredsson and A. Eide (eds), *The Universal Declaration of Human Rights: A Common Standard of Achievement* (The Hague: Martinus Nijhoff Publishers) 1999, pp. 653–659.

[7] Adopted at New York, 16 December, 1966. Entered into force 23 March 1976. GA Res. 2200A (XXI) UN Doc. A/6316 (1966) 999 U.N.T.S. 171; 6 I.L.M. (1967) 368.

[8] Adopted at New York, 16 December, 1966. Entered into force 3 January 1976. GA Res. 2200A (XXI) UN Doc. A/6316 (1966) 993 U.N.T.S. 3; 6 I.L.M. (1967) 360.

and opened for signature, accession or ratification on 15 December 1989.[9] It came into operation on 11 July 1991. There are currently 46 States parties to this Protocol. The ICCPR consists of a preamble and 53 articles, which are divided into eight parts. The ICCPR consists of the following rights:

Article 1	The right to self-determination
Article 6	The right to life
Article 7	Freedom from torture or cruel, inhuman or degrading treatment or punishment
Article 8	Freedom from slavery and the slave trade
Article 9	The right to liberty and security
Article 10	The right of detained persons to be treated with humanity
Article 11	Freedom from imprisonment for debt
Article 12	Freedom of movement and choice of residence
Article 13	Freedom of aliens from arbitrary expulsion
Article 14	Right to a fair trial
Article 15	Prohibition against retroactivity of criminal law
Article 16	Right to recognition everywhere as a person before the law
Article 17	Right to privacy for every individual
Article 18	Right of freedom of thought, conscience and religion
Article 19	Right of opinion and expression
Article 20	Prohibition of propaganda for war and of incitement to national, racial or religious hatred
Article 21	Right of peaceful assembly
Article 22	Freedom of association
Article 23	Right to marry and found a family
Article 24	Rights of the child
Article 25	Political rights
Article 26	Equality before the law
Article 27	Rights of persons belonging to minorities

The ICCPR has many rights which are covered by UDHR or other international and regional human rights treaties. However, unlike the UDHR, the ICCPR does not accord protection to the right to property (covered by UDHR and ECHR First Protocol).[10] For the most part the ICCPR grants rights to all individuals who are within the territories of state parties and are subject to their jurisdiction, regardless of their constitutional or political status. Thus the protection covers nationals, aliens, refugees and illegal immigrants. The reference in the ICCPR to 'everyone' or 'all persons' in relation to a majority

---

[9] Annex to GA Res. 44/128. Reprinted in 29 I.L.M (1990) 1464. See generally W. Schabas, *The Abolition of Death Penalty in International Law*, 2nd edn (Cambridge: Cambridge University Press) 1997.

[10] See Chapters 3 and 6 respectively. ECHR, First Protocol (adopted 20 March 1952) entered into force 18 May 1954, ETS 9.

of rights confirms this view.[11] In order to ensure the rights within the Covenant, States parties undertake to provide for an effective remedy, by competent and judicial authorities, and to ensure the enforcement of these remedies by competent authorities.[12]

THE INTERNATIONAL COVENANTS AND THE RIGHT TO SELF-DETERMINATION[13]

Both the ICCPR and the ICESCR begin with identical provisions on the right to self-determination. Article 1 of the Covenants provides that

(1) All peoples have the right of self-determination. By virtue of that right they freely determine their political status and freely pursue their economic, social and cultural development.

(2) All peoples may, for their own ends, freely dispose of their natural wealth and resources without prejudice to any obligations arising out of international economic co-operation, based upon the principle of mutual benefit, and international law. In no case may a people be deprived of its own means of subsistence.

(3) The States Parties to the present Covenant, including those having responsibility for the administration of Non-Self-Governing and Trust Territories, shall promote the realization of the right of self-determination, and shall respect that right, in conformity with the provisions of the Charter of the United Nations.

Self-determination is a difficult right to define in international law and there is significant controversy as to the exact parameters of this right. The implementation of the right to self-determination has also raised controversy and debate. In the drafting process, several States questioned the value of this right in the post-colonial world. Many States were particularly concerned that minority groups within independent States may use this right as a basis of their claim to secession. In its General Comment, the Human Rights

---

[11] McGoldrick, above n. 1, at pp. 20–21.

[12] Article 2(3).

[13] See R. McCorquodale, 'The Right of Self-Determination' in Harris and Joseph (eds), above n. 1, pp. 91–119; A. Cassese, *Self-Determination of Peoples: A Legal Reappraisal* (Cambridge: Cambridge University Press) 1995; H. Hannum, *Autonomy, Sovereignty and Self-Determination: The Accommodation of Conflicting Rights* (Philadelphia: University of Pennsylvania Press) 1990; C. Tomuschat (ed.), *Modern Law of Self-Determination* (Dordrecht: Martinus Nijhoff Publishers) 1993; H. Hannum, 'Rethinking Self-Determination' 34 *Va.JIL* (1993) 1; M. Koskenniemi, 'National Self-Determination Today: Problems of Legal Theory and Practice' 43 *ICLQ* (1994) 241; V.P. Nanda, 'Self-Determination in International Law: The Tragic Tale of Two Cities – Islamabad (West Pakistan) and Dacca (East Pakistan)' 66 *AJIL* (1972) 321; E. Suzuki, 'Self-Determination and World Public Order: Community Response to Territorial Separation' 16 *Va.JIL* (1976) 779; P. Thornberry, 'Self-Determination, Minorities, Human Rights: A Review of International Instruments' 38 *ICLQ* (1989) 867; R. White, 'Self-Determination: Time for a Reassessment' 28 *NILR* (1981) 147. For further analysis see below Chapter 12.

Committee (the committee in charge of implementing the Covenant) has been assertive and has advocated a continuing obligation to advance the right to self-determination.[14] At the same time the Committee has shown a lack of satisfaction in the coverage of this right in State reports. The Committee notes:

> Although the reporting obligations of all States parties include article 1, only some reports give detailed explanations regarding each of its paragraphs. The Committee has noted that many of them completely ignore article 1, provide inadequate information in regard to it or confine themselves to a reference to election laws. The Committee considers it highly desirable that States parties' reports should contain information on each paragraph of article 1.[15]

It has urged States parties to present their constitutional and political processes which allow for the exercise of this right to self-determination.[16] On the other hand, it seems certain that violations of Article 1 cannot be the subject of a complaint under the First Optional Protocol.[17] In a number of cases the Human Rights Committee has taken the position that as a right belonging to peoples, it is not open to individuals to claim to be victims of the violation of the right to self-determination.[18] Equally, reservations have been entered upon the Article. India, at the time of its ratification, entered a reservation to Article 1 according to which:

> The Government of the Republic of India declares that the words the 'right of self-determination' appearing in this Article apply only to the peoples under the foreign domination and that these words do not apply to sovereign independent States or to a section of a people or nation – which is the essence of national integrity.[19]

GENERAL NATURE OF OBLIGATIONS[20]

Articles 2–5 of both the Covenants constitute Part II, containing in each instance an undertaking to respect or to take steps to secure progressively the

---

[14] The Right to Self-determination of Peoples (Art. 1) 13/04/84. CCPR General Comment 12. (General Comments) para 3.

[15] Ibid.

[16] Ibid. para 4.

[17] S. Lewis-Anthony, 'Treaty-Based Procedures for Making Human Rights Complaints within the UN System' in H. Hannum (ed.), *Guide to International Human Rights Practice*, 3rd edn (New York: Transnational Publishers) 1999, 41–59, at p. 44.

[18] See *Lubicon Lake Band* v. *Canada*, Communication No. 167/1984 (26 March 1990), U.N. Doc. Supp. No. 40 (A/45/40) at 1 (1990). Also see General Comment 23(50) Article 27, U.N. Doc. CCPR/C/21/Rev. 1/Add.5 (1994) at para 3.1.

[19] UN Centre for Human Rights, Human Rights: Status of International Instruments (1987) 9 UN Sales No. E.87.XIV.2.

[20] See Joseph, Schultz and Castan, above n. 1, at pp. 3–29; McGoldrick, above n. 1, at pp. 3–43; D. Harris, 'The International Covenant on Civil and Political Rights and the UK' in D.J. Harris and S. Joseph (eds), above n. 1, pp. 1–67.

substantive rights which follow in Part III together with certain other provisions. According to Article 2(1) of the ICCPR 'each State Party undertakes to respect and to ensure to allow individuals within its territory and subject to its jurisdiction the rights recognised in the present Covenant'.

While there is an obligation undertaken by States to 'respect and to ensure rights recognised in the Covenant' there is no obligation to incorporate the treaty into domestic law.[21] The Human Rights Committee has tried to investigate the exact status which the Covenant has in relation to the constitutional regimes of States parties. In elaborating the provisions of this article, the Committee has noted that, in order to ensure the rights, States are under an obligation to undertake positive and specific action. In its General Comment, the Committee considered it:

> necessary to draw the attention of States parties to the fact that the obligation under the Covenant is not confined to the respect of human rights, but that States parties have also undertaken to ensure the enjoyment of these rights to all individuals under their jurisdiction. This aspect calls for specific activities by the States parties to enable individuals to enjoy their rights. This is obvious in a number of articles (e.g. article 3 [on the equal rights between men and women to the enjoyment of the rights] in the ICCPR) but in principle this undertaking relates to all rights set forth in the Covenant.[22]

Article 2(2) provides that the States parties undertake to guarantee that the rights enunciated in the present Covenant will be exercised without discrimination of any kind as to race, colour, sex, language, religion, political or other opinion, national or social origin, property, birth or other status.[23] Equality upon the basis of gender is also an issue addressed in Article 3 according to which States parties undertake to ensure the equal rights of men and women to the enjoyment of all civil and political rights set forth in the present Covenant. Article 4 is a provision permitting State parties to make derogations from the ICCPR 'in time of public emergency which threatens the life of the nations'. The capacity to make derogations is, however, limited to 'strict exigencies of the situation'.[24] No derogations are permissible from Articles 6, 7, 8 (paras 1 and 2), 11, 15, 16 and 18. The scope of derogation has also been narrowly construed by the Committee

---

[21] See ICCPR General Comment No: 3 Implementation at the National Level (Article 2) 31/07/81 13th Sess., 1981, para 1. Several States parties, including the United Kingdom have not incorporated the ICCPR in their domestic laws. For the United Kingdom's position see R. Higgins, 'The Role of Domestic Courts in the Enforcement of International Human Rights: The United Kingdom' in B. Conforti and F. Francioni (eds), *Enforcing International Human Rights in Domestic Courts* (The Hague: Maritnus Nijhoff Publishers) 1997, pp. 37–58.

[22] General Comment 3 (13), Doc. A/36/40, p. 108.

[23] For further elaboration of the Committee on the Article see Equality of Rights between Men and Women (Article 3) 29/03/2000 General Comment No: 28 CCPR/C/21/Rev. 1/Add 10.

[24] Article 4(1).

and it retains the ultimate discretion in construing whether a particular derogation satisfies the requirement.[25]

ANALYSIS OF SUBSTANTIVE RIGHTS

The right to life, prohibition of torture and the issues concerning capital punishment[26]

The right to life, contained in Article 6, represents the most fundamental of all human rights.[27] It has been protected by all international and regional human rights instruments.[28] According to Article 6(1) 'Every human being has the inherent right to life. This right shall be protected by law. No one shall be arbitrarily deprived of life.' The Committee has pronounced it as the supreme right and the provisions of the treaty establish firmly that no derogations are permissible from this right.[29] Article 6 does not provide an absolute prohibition of taking life but only 'arbitrary' deprivation of life, which raises questions about the nature and scope of the right to life. According to Professor Shestack:

> Surely the right to life guaranteed by Article 6(1) of [ICCPR] would seem to be so basic as to be considered absolute. Yet Article 6(1) only offers protection against

---

[25] General Comment No: 5 Derogation of Rights (Article 4) (13th Sess., 1981) 31/07/81. The Committee has taken the view that 'measures taken under article 4 are of an exceptional and temporary nature and may only last as long as the life of the nation concerned is threatened and that, in times of emergency, the protection of human rights becomes all the more important, particularly those rights from which no derogations can be made. The Committee also considers that it is equally important for States parties, in times of public emergency, to inform the other States parties of the nature and extent of the derogations they have made and of the reasons therefore and, further, to fulfil their reporting obligations under article 40 of the Covenant by indicating the nature and extent of each right derogated from together with the relevant documentation'. Ibid. para 3. See also See R. Higgins, 'Derogations under Human Rights Treaties' 48 *BYIL* (1976–77) 281 at p. 281; A. Kiss, 'Permissible Limitations on Rights' in L. Henkin (ed.), *The International Bill of Rights: The Covenant on Civil and Political Rights* (New York: Columbia University Press) 1981, pp. 290–310.

[26] See W.P. Gromley, 'The Right to Life and the Rule of Non-Derogability: Peremptory Norms and Jus Cogens' in B.G. Ramcharan (ed.), *The Right to Life in International Law* (Dordrecht: Martinus Nijhoff Publishers) 1985, pp. 120–159; N.S. Rodley, *The Treatment of Prisoners in International Law*, 2nd edn (Oxford: Clarendon Press) 1999; S. Joseph, 'The Right to Life' in D.J. Harris and S. Joseph (eds), above n. 1, pp 153–183; Joseph, Schultz and Castan, above n. 1, at pp. 108–243.

[27] Y. Dinstein, 'The Right to Life, Physical Integrity and Liberty' in L. Henkin (ed.), above n. 25, pp. 114–137; P. Sieghart, *The Lawful Rights of Mankind: An Introduction to the International Legal Code of Human Rights* (Oxford: Clarendon Press) 1985, p. 107.

[28] See Article 3 UDHR; Article 2 ECHR; Article I UDHR, Article 4 ACHR; Article 4 AFCHPR.

[29] See Article 4(2) ICCPR; General Comment No: 6; also see General Comment No: 14, *Nuclear Weapons and the Right to Life* (Article 6) (23rd Sess.) 1984, para 1.

'arbitrary' deprivation of life. What is the effect of this qualification on the nature of the rights involved?[30]

Some elaboration has been provided by the Committee on the meaning of 'arbitrary'. In *Guerrero v. Columbia*[31] (also referred to as the *Camargo* case), the Colombian police had raided a house in which they believed a kidnapped person was being detained. The kidnapped person was not found in the house. However, the police waited for the suspected kidnappers and seven individuals, who were not proved to be connected with the kidnap, were shot without warning on their arrival at the house. The forensic evidence repudiated initial police claims that the deceased persons had died while resisting arrest. On the contrary, forensic evidence was produced confirming that the individuals concerned had been shot from point-blank range and without any warning. They had also been shot down at varying intervals. Guerrero, the victim herself, had been shot several times after she had died of a heart attack.[32] The police action was justified by the State because of a Legislative Decree No. 0070. This decree provided the Colombian police with a defence to any criminal charge 'in the course of operations planned with the object of preventing and curbing kidnapping'[33] for so long as the national territory remained 'in a state of siege'.[34] The Committee found that the police in this incident could not justify their action on the basis of the national legislation. According to the Committee, the police action had resulted in arbitrary deprivation of life violating Article 6 of the ICCPR. In the *Guerrero* case the Committee, while expanding on the concept of 'arbitrary', noted that the mere fact that the taking of life is lawful under national law does not by itself prevent it from being 'arbitrary'. In its views the Committee implies that there are limited exceptions to the right to life (that is self-defence, arrest and the prevention of escape) applicable in nationl and international law.[35]

---

[30] J. Shestack, 'The Jurisprudence of Human Rights' in T. Meron (ed.), *Human Rights in International Law: Legal and Policy Issues* (Oxford: Clarendon Press) 1984, 69–113 at p. 71.

[31] *Husband of Maria Fanny Suarez de Guerrero v. Colombia*, Communication No. R.11/45 (5 February 1979), UN Doc. Supp. No. 40 (A/37/40) at 137 (1982).

[32] The Committee's decision on the issue of causing Guerrero's death remains unclear. See McGoldrick, above n. 1, at p. 341.

[33] The Decree Doc. A/37/40, 137, paras. 1.4, 7.1, 7.2.

[34] Ibid. para 1.5.

[35] The same exceptions to right to life are provided in other instruments see e.g. ECHR Article 2(2); see Rodley, above n. 26, at pp. 181–184; also see Harris, above n. 1, at p. 654. For exposition of the meaning of 'Arbitrary' as used in Article 4(1) see the Inter-American Commission on Human Rights report in Case 10.559 (Peru) 136 at pp. 147–148. The case is discussed by S. Davidson, 'The Civil and Political Rights Protected in the Inter-American Human Rights System' in D.J. Harris and S. Livingstone (eds), *The Inter-American System of Human Rights* (Oxford: Clarendon Press) 1998, 213–288, at p. 218.

In *Baboeram-Adhin and Others* v. *Suriname*,[36] the State attempted to justify the execution of 15 individuals on the basis that the men were killed while
trying to escape after an unsuccessful coup attempt. The Committee in the
absence of adequate evidence provided by the State found a violation of
Article 6. The Committee took the view that:

> it was evident from the facts that fifteen prominent persons had lost their lives as
> a result of deliberate action by the military police that the deprivation of life was
> intentional. The state party has failed to submit any evidence proving that these
> persons were shot while trying to escape.[37]

The Committee has also found violations of Article 6 where capital punishment has been imposed in absentia,[38] or has been imposed in a discriminatory or arbitrary manner in conjunction with a breach of the right to fair
trial,[39] or there has been a failure by the State to inform the victim of an
appeal hearing until after it had been conducted,[40] or the manner of execution
is inhuman or degrading.[41] Article 6 does not abolish capital punishment but
provides that:

> [i]n Countries which have not abolished the death penalty, sentence of death may
> be imposed only for the most serious crimes in accordance with the law in force
> at the time of the commission of the crime. ... This penalty can only be carried out
> pursuant to a final judgment rendered by a competent court.

Issues surrounding capital punishment have been and continue to be complex;
we will address them shortly. In so far as other aspects of the right to life are
concerned, no specific guidelines are provided as to the points in time at which
life terminates or commences. Abortion *per se* is not contrary to the provisions
of the ICCPR and attempts to incorporate a prohibition on abortion proved
unsuccessful.[42] Similarly, from the jurisprudence of the Committee, it would

---

[36] *K. Baboeram-Adhin, and J. Kamperveen et al.* v. *Suriname*, Communication Nos. 146/1983
and 148–54/1983, UN Doc. CCPR/C/21/D/146/l983 (1984), U.N. Doc. CCPR/C/OP/2 AT 5
(1990), para. 6.3.
[37] Para 14.1.
[38] *Daniel Monguya Mbenge* v. *Zaire*, Communication No. 16/1977 (8 September 1977), U.N.
Doc. Supp. No. 40 (A/38/40) at 134 (1983).
[39] *Lloydell Richards* v. *Jamaica*, Communication No. 535/1993, UN Doc. CCPR/C/59/D/535/1993
(31 March 1997), paras 7.2, 7.5; *Earl Pratt and Ivan Morgan* v. *Jamaica*, Communication No.
210/1986 and 225/1987 (6 April 1989), UN Doc. Supp. No. 40 (A/44/40) at 222 (1989); *Little* v.
Jamaica, Communication No. 283/l988 (19 November 1991), UN Doc. CCPR/C/43/D/283/l988
(1991), paras 8.4 and 3.2; *Pinto* v. *Trinidad and Tobago*, Communication No. 232/1987 (20 July
1990), Report of the HRC, Vol. II (A/45/40), 1990, at 69, paras 12.5–12.6.
[40] *Thomas* v. *Jamaica*, Communication No. 321/1988 (3 November 1993), UN Doc.
CCPR/C/49/D/321/1988 (1993).
[41] McGoldrick, above n. 1, at p. 346; within the ECHR see *Soering* v. *United Kingdom*,
Judgment of 7 July 1989, Series A, No. 161.
[42] L.A. Rehof, 'Article 3' in Alfredsson and Eide (eds), above n. 6, 89–101, at p. 96.

appear that voluntary euthanasia is not unlawful. Article 7 is a very significant Article, the provisions of which are non-derogable,[43] and has been addressed by the Committee in State reports, in its General Comment and in the Optional Protocol.[44] A useful example of the Committee's jurisprudence under the Optional Protocol is provided through the *Conteris v. Uruguay case*.[45] Mr Conteris was a Methodist pastor, a journalist and a university professor who had been arrested and detained by the Uruguayan police because of his previous connections with the Tupamaros movement. He was held incommunicado for three months and subjected to various forms of physical torture, including hanging by the wrists and burning. After having been forced to sign a confession he was sentenced by a military court to 15 years' imprisonment. After a change in government he was subsequently released. The Committee found violations of several articles of ICCPR. These were Article 7, Article 9(1), 9(2), 9(3), 9(4), 10(1), 14(1) and 14(3).

While reporting on this Article, the Committee requires States Parties not only to describe the steps undertaken for the general protection of Article 7 but in addition to:

> provide detailed information on safeguards for the special protection of particularly vulnerable persons. It should be noted that keeping under systematic review interrogation rules, instructions, methods and practices as well as arrangements for the custody and treatment of persons subjected to any form of arrest, detention or imprisonment is an effective means of preventing cases of torture and ill-treatment. To guarantee the effective protection of detained persons, provisions should be made for detainees to be held in places officially recognized as places of detention and for their names and places of detention, as well as for the names of persons responsible for their detention, to be kept in registers readily available and accessible to those concerned, including relatives and friends. To the same effect, the time and place of all interrogations should be recorded, together with the names of all those present and this information should also be available for purposes of judicial or administrative proceedings. Provisions should also be made against incommunicado detention. In that connection, States parties should ensure that any places of detention be free from any equipment liable to be used for inflicting torture or ill-treatment. The protection of the detainee also requires that prompt and regular access be given to doctors and lawyers and, under appropriate supervision when the investigation so requires, to family members.[46]

---

[43] Rodley, above n. 26, at p. 83.

[44] General Comment Concerning Prohibition of Torture and Cruel Treatment or Punishment (Article 7): 10/04/92. CCPR General Comment No: 20.

[45] *Hiber Conteris v. Uruguay*, Communication No. 139/1983 (17 July 1985), UN Doc. Supp. No. 40 (A/40/40) at 196 (1985).

[46] General Comment Concerning Prohibition of Torture and Cruel Treatment or Punishment (Article 7): 10/04/92, para 11.

In its consideration of periodic reports, the Committee has requested States parties to provide detailed information on the measures taken to implement this Article. States have been asked to ensure compliance with international standards such as the UN Standard Minimum Rules for the Treatment of Prisoners, the UN Code of Conduct for Law Enforcement Officials or the UN Standard Minimum Rules for the Administration of Juvenile Justice ('The Beijing Rules'). The Committee has questioned various forms of punishments and practices such as interrogation techniques,[47] the use of illegally obtained information,[48] stoning and flogging,[49] collective punishment for those found guilty,[50] and loss of nationality.[51]

At the same time it has to be conceded that the Committee has tended to avoid (or be consistent in dealing with) the problematic issue of distinguishing between the various facets of Article 7, that is 'torture', 'cruel', 'inhuman' or 'degrading treatment or punishment'. Instead it has relied generally on the broad prohibitions contained in the Article.[52] There also remain the difficult issues in relation to the nature of punishment and what constitutes inhuman and degrading treatment. Issues of cultural relativism have inhibited the development of a consensus on subjects such as corporal punishment.[53] Further controversial issues are raised in debates surrounding capital punishment and extradition to States where the convicted person may be given a death penalty. The position in international law is not established and State practices are inconsistent. As noted earlier, in 1989 the United Nations adopted the Second Optional Protocol to the ICCPR, Aiming at the Abolition of the Death Penalty,[54] a treaty that has not yet been widely ratified. Nearly half of the world's States retain capital punishment as a sentence for a range of offences, some of which may not (in objective terms) be regarded as the 'most serious crimes'.[55] In view of the numbers and influence of the retentionist States one leading authority on the subject has noted that 'it is hardly surprising that general international law does not expressly require the abolition of the death penalty'.[56]

---

[47] SR 65 para 3 (Tomuschat on Czechoslovakia), SR 69 para 18 (Graefrath), SR 148 paras 3–6 (Lallah on UK).

[48] SR 69 para 32 (Tarnopolsky on UK), SR 98 para 64 (Tomuschat on Yugoslavia), SR 143 para 28 (Tomuschat on Austria).

[49] See Human Rights Committee, 64th Sess., *Concluding Observations of the Human Rights Committee: Libyan Arab Jamahiriya.* 06/11/98. CCPR/C/79/Add.101. (Concluding Observations/Comments), para 11.

[50] Ibid. para 12.

[51] SR 129 para 5 (Bouziri on Chile).

[52] Cf. the position in ECHR, below Chapter 6; Rodley, above n. 26, at p. 96.

[53] See General Comment 7(16) para 2. Cf. ECHR.

[54] Annex to GA Res. 44/128. Reprinted in 29 I.L.M (1990) 1464. For details of ratification see Appendix II.

[55] Criminal laws of some States includes capital punishments for activities such as blasphemy, adultery, sodomy, etc.

[56] Rodley, above n. 26, at p. 96.

With regard to the issue of whether a significant delay in the execution of a convicted person (the so-called death row phenomenon) *per se* constitutes inhuman, cruel and degrading treatment which violates Article 7, there exist substantial disagreements – even among international tribunals. The European Court of Human Rights has held that extradition of an individual in circumstances where he is likely to spend long periods awaiting execution would amount to cruel, inhuman or degrading treatment.[57] A similar position was adopted by the United Kingdom's Privy Council in *Pratt and Morgan* v. *Jamaica*.[58] However the Human Rights Committee has taken a different approach on the subject in *Pratt and Morgan* v. *Jamaica*[59] and *NG* v. *Canada*.[60] The case of *NG* is a striking one in that the Committee relied on the manner of execution (gas asphyxiation) rather than the fact of execution as a ground for finding a violation of Article 7. In 1985, Mr NG, the author, a resident of the US, was convicted in Canada of shooting a security guard. In 1990, the Canadian courts ordered his extradition to the US (California) to stand trial for kidnapping and twelve other murders. The Canadian government, after a substantial review of the case took the decision not to exercise their power to obtain assurances that the death penalty would not be imposed as a condition of extradition. In 1991, the author appealed to the Committee claiming that his extradition was in violation of Article 6 and 7 of the ICCPR. The Human Rights Committee took the view that Canada's decision to extradite Mr NG in the present circumstances did not violate Article 6. The Committee endorsed the Canadian Minister of Justice's position that there was 'the absence of exceptional circumstances, the availability (in California) of due process and of appeal against conviction and the importance of not providing a safe haven for those accused of murder'.[61]However, in finding a violation of Article 7, the Committee did take the position that:

> the author has provided detailed information that execution by gas asphyxiation may cause prolonged suffering and agony and does not result in death as swiftly as possible, as asphyxiation by cyanide gas may take over 10 minutes. The State party had the opportunity to refute these allegations on the facts; it has failed to do so. Rather, the State party has confined itself to arguing that in the absence of a norm of international law which expressly prohibits asphyxiation by cyanide gas, 'it would be interfering to an unwarranted degree with the internal laws and practices of the United States to refuse to extradite a fugitive to face the possible

---

[57] See *Soering* v. *United Kingdom*, Judgment of 7 July 1989, Series A, No. 161; See below Chapter 6.
[58] *Pratt* v. *Attorney General of Jamaica* (PC (Jam)) Privy Council (Jamaica), 2 November 1993 [1994] AC 1 at 35.
[59] *Earl Pratt and Ivan Morgan* v. *Jamaica*, Communication No. 210/1986 and 225/1987 (6 April 1989), UN Doc. Supp. No. 40 (A/44/40) at 222 (1989).
[60] *Chitat Ng* v. *Canada*, Communication No. 469/1991 (7 January 1994), UN Doc. CCPR/C/49/D/469/1991 (1994).
[61] Ibid., para 15.6.

imposition of the death penalty by cyanide gas asphyxiation'. The Committee concludes that execution by gas asphyxiation, should the death penalty be imposed on the author, would not meet the test of 'least possible physical and mental suffering', and constitutes cruel and inhuman treatment, in violation of article 7 of the Covenant.[62]

Rights to liberty and security of person, prohibitions of arbitrary detentions and unfair trials[63]

Denials of liberty and security of person and arbitrary detentions have been sources of substantial concern. A recent United Nations document correctly expresses this concern in that '[a]ll countries are confronted by the practice of arbitrary detention. It knows no boundaries, and thousands of persons are subjected to arbitrary detention each year.'[64] We noted above that the continued practices of arbitrary and unlawful detention led the Commission on Human Rights to establish a Working Group on Arbitrary Detention.[65] Article 9 protects the valuable right of liberty and security of the person. The Article confirms that, in pursuance of this right,

no one shall be subjected to arbitrary arrest or detention. No one shall be deprived of his liberty except on such grounds and in accordance with such procedures as are established by law.[66]

The Article goes on to provide procedural guarantees for the detained person.[67] The reasons for arrest must be given at the time of arrest and the arrested person must be promptly informed of the charges against him.[68] Persons arrested or detained for criminal offences are to be brought promptly before a judge and must be tried within a reasonable period or released.[69] Persons deprived of their liberty are entitled to challenge the legality of their detention and in case of unlawful detention are entitled to the right of compensation.[70]

---

[62] Ibid. paras 16.3 and 16.4.
[63] See Joseph, Schultz and Castan, above n. 1, at pp. 206–339; R.B. Lillich, 'Civil Rights' in T. Meron (ed.), above n. 30, pp. 115–170; Y. Dinstein, 'The Right to Life, Physical Integrity and Liberty' in L. Henkin (ed.), above n. 25, pp. 114–137; L.A. Rehof, 'Article 3' in Alfredsson and Eide (eds), above n. 6, 89 –101 at p. 89; Harris, above n. 1, pp. 637–680; Steiner and Alston, above n. 1, pp. 136–237; McGoldrick, above n. 1, at pp. 362–458.
[64] United Nations, *The Working Group on Arbitrary Detentions: Fact Sheet No: 26* (Geneva: United Nations).
[65] See above Chapter 2.
[66] Article 9(1).
[67] Article 9(2)–(5).
[68] Article 9(2).
[69] Article 9(3).
[70] Article 9(4) and 9(5).

A useful example of a State violation of rights contained in Article 9 and the Human Rights Committee's analysis is provided by the case of *Mukong v. Cameroon*.[71] M was a journalist and long-standing critic of the government. He had been campaigning for multiparty democracy in Cameroon for a long time. In 1988 he was arrested and detained after a BBC broadcast in which he had criticised the Cameroonian government. The reason given for his arrest was that he had made subversive comments contrary to a State Ordinance. He was subsequently charged with offences under the Ordinance. He was released only to be rearrested in 1990 for his campaign for the creation of a multiparty democracy. M appealed to the Committee claiming violations of various provisions of the Covenant. In its response the Committee found violations of Articles 7, 9 and 14, and it took the view that M's detention in the period during 1988–1990 and subsequently in 1990 were in violation of Article 9.

In another case *Carballal v. Uruguay*,[72] Carballal was arrested on 4 January 1976 and held incommunicado for more than five months. During his detention, for long periods he was tied and blindfolded and kept in secret places. Attempts to have recourse to habeas corpus proved unsuccessful. He was brought before a military judge on 5 May 1976 and again on 28 June but was detained for over a year. The Committee found *inter alia* violations of Article 9(1), 9(2), 9(3), and 9(4).

Article 10 provides for the right of detained persons to be treated with humanity. The Committee has given this Article a broad ambit, noting its application to anyone who has been deprived of his liberty including such people as those who are detained in prisons and hospitals, in particular psychiatric or mental hospitals.[73] It has insisted that:

[t]reating all persons deprived of their liberty with humanity and with respect for their dignity is a fundamental and universally applicable rule. Consequently, the application of this rule, as a minimum, cannot be dependent on the material resources available in the State party. This rule must be applied without distinction of any kind, such as race, colour, sex, language, religion, political or other opinion, national or social origin, property, birth or other status.[74]

Article 14 represents the core of the criminal justice system within international law. Compliance with the provisions of Article 14 are an essential prerequisite to ensuring fairness in criminal proceedings. The Committee has elaborated on the right to fair trial through its General Comment, review of

---

[71] *Womah Mukong v. Cameroon*, Communication No. 458/1991 (10 August 1994), UN Doc. CCPR/C/51/D/458/1991 (1994).

[72] *Leopoldo Buffo Carballal v. Uruguay*, Communication No. 33/1978 (8 April 1981), UN Doc. CCPR/C/OP/1 at 63 (1984).

[73] General Comment No: 21 (44th Sess.) 1992, para 2.

[74] General Comment No: 21 (44th Sess.) 1992, para 4.

State reports and decisions from individual communications.[75] The Article ordains that all persons be equal before courts and tribunals.[76] The concept of equality of arms is applicable not only in the courts and judicial tribunals but there also needs to be 'equality of the citizen *vis-à-vis* the executive'.[77] Unlike the European Court of Human Rights, the Committee has not elaborated significantly on the meaning of 'criminal charge' or 'rights and obligation in a suit at law';[78] the committee has, however, formulated substantial jurisprudence on fair and public hearings by a competent, independent and impartial tribunal. The Committee has viewed with concern developments such as the setting-up of special or military courts,[79] *Sharia* courts,[80] State security courts,[81] temporary appointments of judges,[82] and threats to the independence of the judiciary and the liberty of advocates freely to exercise their profession.[83]

The Committee has also put emphasis on the independence of the judiciary and the separation of State organs, in particular the executive from the judiciary. Attached to the right to fair trial is the presumption of innocence. In criminal trials, in order to secure conviction the prosecution must establish its case beyond reasonable doubt.[84] In order to ensure a fair trial, Article 14 provides for a number of minimum guarantees. These consist of: being informed promptly and in detail in a language which the accused understands;[85] having adequate time and facilities for the preparation of a defence;[86] being tried without undue delay;[87] being tried in person and being

---

[75] General Comment No: 13 Equality before the courts and the right to a fair and public hearing by an Independent Court Established by Law (Article 14) 13/04/84.

[76] Article 14(1).

[77] SR 187 para 26 (Tomuschat on Poland).

[78] For further consideration see *Y. L. v. Canada*, Communication No. 112/1981 (8 April 1986), UN Doc. Supp. No. 40 (A/41/40) at 145 (1986) *a*; also see *Larry James Pinkney v. Canada*, Communication No. 27/1978 (2 April 1980), UN Doc. CCPR/C/OP/1 at 12 (1984). On the European Court of Human Rights, see below Chapter 6.

[79] See Concluding Observations by the Human Rights Committee: Peru. 15/11/2000. CCPR/CO/70/PER. (Concluding Observations/Comments) 70th Sess., para 12.

[80] See SR 200 para 8 (Graefrath on Iraq).

[81] SR 282 para 22 (Opsahl on Mali).

[82] See the Concluding Observations/Comments of the Human Rights Committee: Syrian Arab Republic CCPR/CO/71/SYR, para 15.

[83] See Human Rights Committee, 64th Sess., *Concluding Observations of the Human Rights Committee: Libyan Arab Jamahiriya.* 06/11/98. CCPR/C/79/Add.101. (Concluding Observations/Comments), para 14; Concluding Observations of the Human Rights Committee: Democratic People's Republic of Korea. 27/07/2001. CCPR/CO/72/PRK. (Concluding Observations/Comments) 72nd Sess., para 8.

[84] See General Comment 13 (21) para 7.

[85] Article 14(3)(a).

[86] Article 14(3)(b).

[87] Article 14(3)(c).

able adequately to defend his case;[88] and not being forced into making a guilty plea.[89] The Committee acting under the First Optional Protocol has on a number of occasions elaborated on the meaning and content of this right. In *Pratt and Morgan v. Jamaica*, the Committee found a breach of Article 14 when it took 20 hours (thereby meaning waiting for the accused until 45 minutes before his scheduled execution) before communication of a reprieve was received.[90] In another case involving appeal against imposition of the death penalty in Jamaica, the Committee found a violation of Article 14(3)(d). In this case the victim claimed that his lawyer had, without consulting him, withdrawn his appeal against conviction. The victim contended that had he foreseen the likely action of his lawyer, he would have sought another counsel. In finding violations of the Article, the Committee took the view that,

> while article 14, paragraph 3(d) does not entitle the accused to choose counsel provided to him free of charge, measures must be taken to ensure that counsel, once assigned, provides effective representation in the interests of justice. This includes consulting with, and informing, the accused if he intends to withdraw an appeal or to argue before the appeals court that the appeal has no merit.[91]

Rights to privacy, freedom of expression, conscience, opinion, assembly and association[92]

Among the essential ingredients of modern human rights law are rights to privacy, and freedom of expression, opinion, assembly and association. These rights are protected by all international and regional human rights instruments. Within the ICCPR, these rights can be found in Articles 17–20. Article 17 protects the important right to privacy, family, home and correspondence. The article has been elaborated further by the Committee's General Comment

---

[88] Article 14(3)(d)(e).

[89] Article 14(3)(g).

[90] *Earl Pratt and Ivan Morgan v. Jamaica*, Communication No. 210/1986 and 225/1987 (6 April 1989), UN Doc. Supp. No. 40 (A/44/40) at 222 (1989), para 137; Rodley, above n. 26, at p. 235.

[91] *Kelly v. Jamaica*, Communication No. 253/1987 (8 April 1991) Annual Report 1991 (A/46/40), Annex XI.D.

[92] McGoldrick, above n. 1, at pp. 459–497; J.P. Humphrey, 'Political and Related Rights' in T. Meron (ed.), above n. 30, pp. 171–203; J. Michael, 'Privacy' in D.J. Harris and S. Joseph (eds), above n. 1, pp. 333–353; P. Cumper, 'Freedom of thought, Conscience and Religion' ibid. pp. 355–389; D. Feldman, 'Freedom of Expression' ibid. pp. 391–437; K. Ewing, 'Freedom of Association and Trade Union Rights' ibid. pp. 465–489; Joseph, Schultz and Castan, above n. 1, at pp. 348–441.

and also by its case law under the Optional Protocol.[93] In the *Aumeeruddy-Cziffra case*,[94] a number of Mauritian women claimed violations of their rights under *inter alia* Articles 17(1), 2(1), 3 and 26 of ICCPR. They claimed that the laws were being applied discriminatorily by the Mauritian immigration authorities, who were discriminating between Mauritian men on the one hand and Mauritian women who had married foreign men on the other hand. The claim in relation to Article 17(1) arose because of the interference with their rights to family life. The Committee reviewed the existing laws and found violations of the right to family life. It also found that the existing distinction in Mauritius breached the non-discriminatory provisions contained in the ICCPR. In *Toonen* v. *Australia*,[95] a claim that the Tasmanian Criminal Code making private homosexual conduct a criminal offence was upheld to be in breach of Article 17.

Article 19 represents the right of opinion and expression. It is an important right; parallel rights can be found in Article 19 UDHR, Article 10 ECHR and Article 9 ACHR. Article 19(1) provides that 'everyone shall have the right to hold opinions without interference'. Thus the right to hold an opinion is an absolute right and no interference from any source is permissible. By contrast, the provisions relating to freedom of expression are subject to restrictions. According to Article 19(2):

---

[93] In its General Comment on this Article the Committee notes 'Article 17 provides for the right of every person to be protected against arbitrary or unlawful interference with his privacy, family, home or correspondence as well as against unlawful attacks on his honour and reputation. In the view of the Committee this right is required to be guaranteed against all such interferences and attacks whether they emanate from State authorities or from natural or legal persons. The obligations imposed by this article require the State to adopt legislative and other measures to give effect to the prohibition against such interferences and attacks as well as to the protection of this right'. It goes on to provide that 'relevant legislation must specify in detail the precise circumstances in which such interferences may be permitted. A decision to make use of such authorized interference must be made only by the authority designated under the law, and on a case-by-case basis. Compliance with article 17 requires that the integrity and confidentiality of correspondence should be guaranteed *de jure* and *de facto*. Correspondence should be delivered to the addressee without interception and without being opened or otherwise read. Surveillance, whether electronic or otherwise, interceptions of telephonic, telegraphic and other forms of communication, wire-tapping and recording of conversations should be prohibited. Searches of a person's home should be restricted to a search for necessary evidence and should not be allowed to amount to harassment. So far as personal and body search is concerned, effective measures should ensure that such searches are carried out in a manner consistent with the dignity of the person who is being searched. Persons being subjected to body search by State officials, or medical personnel acting at the request of the State, should only be examined by persons of the same sex'. Human Rights Committee, General Comment No: 16 The Right to Respect of Privacy, Family, Home and Correspondence, and Protection of Honour and Reputation (Article 17): 08/04/88. (32nd Sess., 1988), paras 1 and 8.
[94] *Shirin Aumeeruddy-Cziffra and 19 other Mauritian women v. Mauritius*, Communication No. 35/1978 (9 April 1981), UN Doc. CCPR/C/OP/1 at 67 (1984).
[95] *Toonen* v. *Australia*, Communication No. 488/1992 (4 April 1994), UN Doc CCPR/C/50/D/488/1992 (1994).

Everyone shall have the right to freedom of expression; this right shall include freedom to seek, receive and impart information and ideas of all kinds, regardless of frontiers, either orally, in writing or in print, in the form of art, or through any other media of his choice.

However, restrictions are provided by Article 19(3) which states:

The exercise of the rights provided for in paragraph 2 of this article carries with it special duties and responsibilities. It may therefore be subject to certain restrictions, but these shall only be such as are provided by law and are necessary

a) For respect of the rights or reputations of others
b) For the protection of national security or of public order (ordre public), or of public health or morals.

In their survey of reports the Committee has examined and raised concerns over many issues, for example banning or censorship,[96] governmental controls of various forms,[97] limitations on certain groups such as civil servants and armed forces,[98] and imposition of criminal liability for producing published works.[99] The Committee has also been unhappy over the applicable limitations embodied in criminal laws for offences including blasphemy or blasphemous libel,[100] sedition,[101] subversive propaganda,[102] etc. In *Hertzberg and Others* v. *Finland*,[103] the authors of the communication alleged violation of their rights of freedom of expression and opinion by the State-controlled broadcasting company (FBC). Their claim was that Article 19 rights were breached in relation to the sanctions imposed on expression and information through censorship of radio and TV programmes on homosexuality. In its defence, Finland relied *inter alia* upon protection of public morals and claimed that these actions were fully supported by public opinion. Furthermore, the State also argued that the decision on sanctions represented the internal ruling of the autonomous broadcasting company. The Committee took account of the Finnish argument pertaining to the defence of public morals. It came to the conclusion that 'since a certain "margin of discretion" must be accorded to the responsible national authorities'[104] in issues concerning public morals, the application of Article 19(3) meant that no violation had taken place of the

---

[96] SR 26 para 10 (Vincent-Evans on Syria).
[97] SR 89 para 41 (Esperson on Iran).
[98] SR 321 para 27 para 27 (Movchan on the Netherlands).
[99] SR 54 para 36 (Tarnopolsky on Denmark).
[100] SR 161 para 23 (Bouziri on Belize, then UK Dependency).
[101] See e.g. SR 402 para 6 (Tarnopolsky on Australia).
[102] See e.g. SR 222 para 32 (Tomuschat on Columbia).
[103] *Leo R- Hertzberg, Uit Mansson, Astrid Nikula and Marko and Tuovi Putkonen, represented by SETA (Organization for Sexual Equality) v. Finland*, Communication No. R.14/61 (7 August 1979), UN Doc. Supp. No. 40 (A/37/40) at 161 (1982).
[104] Ibid. paras 10.3.

freedom of opinion and expression. The Committee's view is in line with other international bodies such as the European Court of Human Rights.[105]

Another related concern for human rights law has been the advocacy of religious and racial hatred and propaganda for war. The prohibition of such forms of expression is provided for by Article 20. Elaborating on the provisions of this Article, the Committee in its General Comment has noted that:

> Not all reports submitted by States parties have provided sufficient information as to the implementation of Article 20 of the Covenant. ... State parties are obliged to adopt the necessary legislative measures prohibiting the actions referred to therein. However the reports have shown that in some States such actions are neither prohibited by law nor are appropriate efforts intended or made to prohibit them. Furthermore, many reports failed to give sufficient information concerning the relevant national legislation.[106]

A number of States have entered reservations to this article pointing to the vagueness of the provisions and the lack of definition of the terms: 'propaganda' and 'war'. These States include France, Australia, Finland, Denmark, the Netherlands, Luxembourg, Iceland, New Zealand, Norway and Sweden.[107] Article 20(2) prohibits by law any advocacy of national, racial or religious hatred that constitutes incitement to discrimination, hostility or violence. While in itself a worthy aspiration, there nevertheless remains potential for conflict with Article 19, freedom of opinion and expression, and in this regard a careful balance needs to be established.[108]

The interaction between principles of equality and non-discrimination with minority rights[109]

The strong focus of modern human rights law on the principles of equality and non-discrimination necessitates constant referrals and analysis. In their application to ICCPR, equality and non-discrimination represent the most dominant subjects; a following Chapter, in presenting a detailed analysis, considers the value of Articles 2, 3, 25 and 26 of the Covenant.[110] For the present purposes,

---

[105] See *Handyside* v. *United Kingdom*, Judgment of 7 December 1976, Series A, No. 24; below Chapter 6.

[106] Human Rights Committee, *General Comment No 11: Prohibition of Propaganda for War and Inciting National, Racial or Religious Hatred* (Article 20) 29/07/83 (19th Sess., 1983).

[107] McGoldrick, above n. 1, at p. 494.

[108] McGoldrick, above n. 1, at pp. 486–490.

[109] Joseph, Schultz and Castan, above n. 1, at pp. 518–595; Lord Lester and S. Joseph in Harris and Joseph (eds), above n. 1, pp. 597–627; B.G. Ramcharan, 'Equality and Non-Discrimination' in L. Henkin (ed.), above n. 25, at pp. 246–269; P. Thornberry, *International Law and the Rights of Minorities* (Oxford: Clarendon Press) 1991, pp. 141–319; for detailed consideration of the issues in international law, see below Chapters 10–12.

[110] See below Chapter 10.

two points need to be made. First, the principles of equality and non-discrimination as utilised in the Covenant incorporate de facto equality, thereby sanctioning affirmative action policies.[111] Secondly, equality and non-discrimination represent independent rights and (unlike ECHR Article 14) do not need to be linked to violations of substantive rights.[112] Thus, in the cases of *Broeks* v. *The Netherlands*[113] and *Zwaan De Vries* v. *The Netherlands*[114] the Committee found the social security legislation discriminated against women and thereby contravened Article 26. This view was taken notwithstanding the absence of a substantive right to social security in the Covenant.

While the emphasis on the individual's right to equal treatment and non-discrimination is overwhelming, modern international law has remained reluctant to accord collective rights to minority groups.[115] The dominant themes of non-discrimination were for a long time regarded as a substitute for minority rights, an approach confirmed by the non-incorporation of minority rights articles in the United Nations Charter, UDHR and the ECHR. This point is reiterated by the United Nations Special Rapporteur Francesco Capotorti who, while preparing his study pursuant to Article 27 of ICCPR, comments that the prevention of discrimination and the implementation of special measures to protect minorities 'are merely two aspects of the same problem; that of fully ensuring equal rights to all persons'.[116] Article 27 itself is structurally incoherent and does not accord minorities collective rights. Having said that, the ICCPR is unique among international law treaties for its inclusion of an article which provides rights on the basis of an individual's minority characteristic. Article 27 provides that:

> In those States in which ethnic, religious or linguistic minorities exist, persons belonging to such minorities shall not be denied the right, in community with the other members of their group, to enjoy their own culture, to profess and practise their own religion, or to use their own language.

---

[111] See e.g. the Human Rights Committee, General Comment 25, *The Right to Participate in Public Affairs, Voting Rights and the Right of Equal Access to Public Service* (Article 25) (12/07/96) para 23.

[112] Note however the developments since the adoption of Protocol 12 to the ECHR. See below Chapter 6.

[113] *S. W.M. Broeks* v. *The Netherlands*, Communication No. 172/1984 (9 April 1987), UN Doc. Supp. No. 40 (A/42/40) at 139 (1987).

[114] *F.H. Zwaan-de Vries* v. *The Netherlands*, Communication No. 182/1984 (9 April 1987), UN Doc. Supp. No. 40 (A/42/40) at 160 (1987).

[115] See below Chapter 11.

[116] F. Capotorti, *Special Rapporteur, Study on the Rights of Persons Belonging to Ethnic, Religious and Linguistic Minorities*, UN Sales NoE.78.XIV.I (1978) Reprinted in 1991 by the United Nations Centre for Human Rights, UN Sales NoE.91.XIV.2, 26.

A number of communications have involved a discussion of the provisions of Article 27,[117] though the case that has attracted most attention is that of *Lovelace* v. *Canada*.[118] Mrs Lovelace had lost her status as a Maliseet Indian after her marriage to a non-Indian according to the Indian Act of Canada.[119] She claimed that an Indian man who married a non-Indian woman would not have lost his status and that the law was discriminatory. The essence of the original communication filed by her had been that this loss of status and deprivation of the right to return to her original reserve lands had been in breach of Articles 2(1), 3, 23(1), 23(4), 26 and 27 of the Covenant.

In relation to admissibility, she had argued that she was not obliged to exhaust the domestic remedies that are provided in Article 5(2)(a) of the Optional Protocol since the Canadian Supreme Court had already declared that regardless of any inconsistencies with the Canadian Bill of Rights and legislation prohibiting discrimination, the relevant provisions[120] remained operative.[121] The communication was declared admissible in August 1979 and the Committee provided its interim decision in July 1980. In giving its decision, the Committee took the view that the denial of opportunity to Sandra Lovelace to return to her reserves was essentially a breach of Article 27. After having found a violation of Article 27, the Committee considered it unnecessary to examine general provisions of discrimination contained in Articles 2, 3 and 26.[122] However, in an individual opinion, Mr Bouziri was of the view that there had also been violations of Articles 2(1), 3, 23(1) and (4), and 26 since the provisions of the Indian Act were discriminatory, especially on the basis of gender.[123]

Kitok v. *Sweden*[124] is another example of issues arising out of minority or indigenous rights. In this case, the petitioner alleged that he had inherited rights in reindeer breeding, land and water in Sorkaitum Sam village but, through the operation of a Swedish law, he was denied the power to exercise those rights resulting from the loss of his membership of Sam

---

[117] See e.g. *Ivan Kitok* v. *Sweden*, Communication No. 197/1985 (27 July 1988), UN Doc. Supp. No. 40 (A/43/40) at 221 (1988); *Lubicon Lake Band* v. *Canada*, Communication No. 167/1984 (26 March 1990), UN Doc. Supp. No. 40 (A/45/40) at 1 (1990).

[118] *Sandra Lovelace* v. *Canada*, Communication No. 24/1977 (30 July 1981), UN Doc. CCPR/C/OP/1 at 83 (1984). For commentaries see A.F. Bayefsky, 'The Human Rights Committee and the Case of Sandra Lovelace' 20 *CYBIL* (1982) 244; D. McGoldrick, 'Canadian Indians, Cultural Rights and the Human Rights Committee' 40 *ICLQ* (1991) 658.

[119] S.12(1)(b); Can. Rev. Stat., C.1–6.

[120] Ibid.

[121] *A-G of Canada* v. *Jeanette Lavelle, Richard Isaac et al* v. *Yvonne Bedard (1974), SCR 1349.*

[122] paras 13.2–13.19.

[123] Ibid. p. 175.

[124] *Ivan Kitok* v. *Sweden*, Communication No. 197/1985 (27 July 1988), UN Doc. Supp. No. 40 (A/43/40) at 221 (1988); Prior decisions CCPR/C/WG/27/D/197 1985; CCPR/C/29D/197 1985 (admissibility 25 March 1987).

village. The communication alleged violations of Articles 1 and 27 of the ICCPR. The Committee declared his claim inadmissible under Article 1 viewing that the

> author, as an individual, could not claim to be the victim of a violation of the right to self-determination. Whereas the Optional Protocol provides recourse to individuals claiming that their rights have been violated, Article 1 deals with rights conferred upon people as such.[125]

As far as the provisions of Article 27 were concerned, the Committee decided to consider the communication on its merits. However, it observed that the overall provisions of Swedish law were consistent with the spirit of Article 27.

THE HUMAN RIGHTS COMMITTEE[126]

The Human Rights Committee is a body of experts in charge of the implementation of the ICCPR. It works on a part-time basis. The functions of the Committee are detailed in ICCPR, the First Optional Protocol, and rules of procedure. Part IV of the ICCPR provides for the setting up of the Committee and elaborates on its role and activities. The Committee consists of 18 members elected from among nationals of States Parties to the ICCPR.[127] These members are anticipated to be of a high moral character with established competence in the field of human rights.[128] The members of the Committee are elected to serve in their personal capacity for four-year terms.[129] They are eligible for re-nomination. The elections to the Committee take place by secret ballot of States parties to the Covenant, at meetings that are convened by the United Nations Secretary-General. In the elections:

---

[125] Para 6.3.

[126] See above McGoldrick, above n. 1; Ghandhi, above n. 1; T. Opsahl, 'The Human Rights Committee' in Alston (ed.), *The United Nations and Human Rights* (Oxford: Clarendon Press) 1992, pp. 369–443; L. Heffernan, 'A Comparative View of Individual Petitions Procedures under the European Convention on Human Rights and the International Covenant on Civil and Political Rights' 19 *HRQ* (1997) 78; B.G. Ramcharan, 'Implementing the International Covenants on Human Rights' in B.G. Ramcharan (ed.), *Human Rights: Thirty Years after the Universal Declaration Commemorative Volume on the Occasion of the Thirtieth Anniversary of the Universal Declaration of Human Rights* (The Hague: Martinus Nijhoff Publishers) 1979, pp. 159–195; A. De Zayas, J.Th. Möller and T. Opsahl, 'Application of the International Covenant on Civil and Political Rights under the Optional Protocol by the Human Rights Committee' 28 *GYBIL* (1985) 9; P.R. Ghandhi, 'The Human Rights Committee and the Right of Individual Communication' 57 *BYIL* (1986) 201; J. Rehman, 'The Role of the International Community in Dealing with Individual Petitions under the Optional Protocol' 9 *JOLS* (1992) 13.

[127] Article 28(1) Rule 18 of Rules of Procedure provided that the 'members of the Committee shall be the 18 persons appointed in accordance with articles 28–34 of the Covenant'.

[128] Article 28(2).

[129] Article 28(3).

consideration shall be given to equitable geographic distribution of membership and to the representation of the different forms of civilization and of the principal legal systems.[130]

Each State party is entitled to nominate a maximum of two persons, who should also be its nationals.[131] The Committee may not include more than one national from the same State.[132]The persons elected are those nominees who obtain the largest majority of votes and an absolute majority of votes of the representatives of States parties present and voting.[133] The Committee meets three times a year in spring,[134] summer and autumn[135] for three weeks' sessions. As noted earlier, the Committee members serve in their personal capacity and not as representatives of their States. This independent stance is reinforced by the requirement that each member must make a solemn declaration on appointment that they will perform their functions impartially and conscientiously. While it is important for members of the Committee to be independent, the Covenant itself does not provide a condition for them to have complete independence from their governments. The Committee members have included individuals having various governmental positions, including ministers and members of Parliament. As part-time workers, the Committee members receive emoluments.[136]

There are three main mechanisms of implementation carried out by the Committee. First, there is the compulsory reporting procedure whereby all States parties are obliged to present reports showing compliance with the ICCPR. Secondly, there exists an inter-State complaints procedure. Finally, an individual complaints procedure is in place. We shall be dealing with each of these mechanisms in greater detail in the remainder of this chapter.

THE REPORTING PROCEDURE

There are three types of reports: initial, supplementary and periodic reports. Initial reports are required after one year of the entry into force for the State party concerned, and periodic reports follow after every five years.[137] As we shall consider, the Committee has provided guidelines for initial and periodic reports.[138] Notwithstanding these guidelines the reports are often incomplete.

---

[130] Article 31(2).
[131] Article 29(2).
[132] Article 31(1).
[133] Article 30(4).
[134] In New York.
[135] In Geneva.
[136] Article 35.
[137] See below.
[138] See Guidelines Regarding the Form and Content of Reports from States Parties under Article 40 of the Covenant. Doc.CCPR/C/5; Doc A/32/44.

Additional guidelines have been provided for periodic reports. Only Article 40(3) deals with the provision of information by specialised agencies. No provisions are made explicitly for NGOs to provide information,[139] nor has the committee decided to allow specialised agencies and NGOs to comment on the States' reports.[140] However, it has been possible to acquire information from various non-governmental sources. NGOs are allowed to submit information to individual members of the Committee in their individual capacity.

The reporting procedure, it should be emphasised, is the principal mechanism of implementation and is the only compulsory procedure to which all States parties must comply. The obligation falling upon each State is to report upon the 'measures [it] has adopted' to give effect to the provisions of the ICCPR and also, under Article 40(2), to report on 'the factors and difficulties, if any, affecting the implementation of the Covenant'. Initial reports are made within one year of entry of the Covenant for that State. The reports are to be considered by the Committee. The role of the Committee is to 'study' the reports and to transmit its reports, and such general comments as it may consider appropriate, to the States parties.[141] The Committee may also submit to ECOSOC those general comments in addition to the State reports received from States parties.

The Committee has decided that subsequent reports are to be required every five years.[142] Since 1992 the Committee has allowed itself the authority to request a report at any time it considers appropriate and to allow the chairperson to request a special report in exceptional cases or in cases of emergency. Under this procedure, urgent reports have been required from a number of States.[143] Prior to the consideration of the State report, the report is scrutinised by a working group of the Committee. The working group prepares a list of questions arising from the analysis of the report and these questions are then put to the State representative. The questions typically involve omissions from the report, follow-up from the previous report and any other issues arising from the report. The list of questions may be made public once the session has started. The consideration of a report takes place over two to three public meetings. A representative of the reporting State is invited to introduce the report and answer questions as contained in the list prepared by the working group. The Committee also receives information from other informal sources. It may seek additional information from the State party concerned through

---

[139] See UN Doc. E/2575.

[140] Harris, above n. 1, at p. 648.

[141] Cited in McGoldrick, above n. 1, at p. 9.

[142] UN Doc. CCPR/C/19/Rev.1

[143] In 1992 special reports were asked for by the Committee from Bosnia-Herzegovina, Croatia and the Federal Republic of Yugoslavia; in 1993 from Angola and Burundi; and in 1994 from Haiti and Rwanda.

supplementary reports.[144] At the completion of the session, the Committee proceeds to draft and adopt its comments. The comments represent the Committee's view on a State party's report. It consists of the positive and negative features in the reports, concerns and constraints. It also includes suggestions and recommendations. Periodic reports follow a similar pattern, with the Committee continually emphasising the elaboration of the follow-up procedures in the light of the Committee's comments on the previous report.[145] According to Article 40(5) the Committee is to 'submit to the General Assembly of the United Nations through ECOSOC annual reports of its activities'. Within the United Nations, the third committee considers the Annual Reports of the Committee. A procedure was devised in 1985 to deal with supplementary reports.[146]

Reporting guidelines

While the reporting procedure appears an attractive mechanism for monitoring progress, in practice there are substantial difficulties and hurdles. The States' reports are frequently delayed and are often incomplete, failing to provide the required information. In the light of these hurdles, the Committee has also made a significant concession to those States which submit supplementary reports. Thus if a State party submits additional or supplementary information within a year of its initial or periodic report, the Committee makes provision for deferring the periodicity of report.[147]

In order to assist States regarding the required content of the reports, in 1977 the Committee set out general guidelines.[148] According to these guidelines, reports should describe measures adopted giving effect to the rights in the Convention. Reports should also refer to the difficulties and other factors affecting the implementation of the rights. The guidelines also require States to outline their legislative, administrative or other mechanisms in place with regard to the rights contained in the ICCPR and to include information on restrictions of these rights. According to these guidelines States parties are reminded of their obligations to ensure the rights contained within the Convention. Such obligations may entail affirmative action policies and may relate to situations within the private sphere. In 1981 and 1995 these guidelines were supplemented by additional sets of guidelines. The 1995

---

[144] While seeking additional information from the State party, the Committee has used a method of asking questions on a topic-by-topic basis.

[145] Ghandhi, above n. 1, at p. 24.

[146] Doc A/41/40, para. 45.

[147] Doc A/3740, Ax IV; adopted by Human Rights Committee at its 380th meeting 28 July, 1982.

[148] See General Guidelines Regarding the Form and Content of Reports from States Parties under Article 40 of the Covenant GAOR 32nd Sess. No. 44 (A/32/44). Report of the Human Rights Committee.

guidelines emphasise that the reports should include factors 'affecting the difficulties experienced in the implementation of the Covenant, including any factors affecting the equal enjoyment by women of that right'.[149] Guidelines have also been provided for periodic reports under Article 40(1)(b). The effect of these efforts has, however, been limited and various examples could be found of incomplete or inadequate compliance with the reporting procedures. Since there are no sanctions attached to non-compliance, the powers of the Committee remain limited.

GENERAL COMMENTS[150]

The Human Rights Committee is also entitled to provide General Comments, comments which relate to various rights within the Covenant and are non-country specific.[151] The practice of producing General Comments began in 1981. The overall purpose behind these General Comments is to:

> make the Committee's experience available for the benefit of all States Parties, so as to promote more effective implementation of the Covenant; to draw the attention of States parties to insufficiencies disclosed by a large number of reports; to suggest improvements in the reporting procedure; to clarify the requirements of the Covenant; and to stimulate the activities of States Parties and International Organisations in the promotion and protection of human rights. General Comments are intended also to be of interest to other States, especially those preparing to become parties to the Covenant. They are intended, in addition, to strengthen cooperation amongst States in the universal protection and promotion of human rights.[152]

In its initial set of General Comments, the Committee considered aspects of the reporting obligations of States, procedures and the obligations on States parties under Article 2 to undertake specific activities to enable individuals to enjoy their rights. General Comments have been made on Articles 1–4, 6, 7, 9, 10, 12, 14, 17–20, 23–25, 27 and 41. The General Comments delivered have been addressed to all States parties, and in its consideration of States reports the Committee has increasingly referred to these General Comments. The General Comments not only act as an invaluable guide to the interpretation of particular articles, but also have added considerably to the existing jurisprudence regarding civil and political rights. We have already considered the value of the General Comments in our analysis of the substantive rights of

---

[149] UN Doc. CCPR/C/20Rev. para 6.
[150] See T. Opsahl, 'The General Comments of the Human Rights Committee' in J. Jekewitz et al., *Des Menschen Recht Zwischen Freiheit Und Verantwortung, Festschrift für Karl Josef Partsch zum 75. Geburstag* (Berlin: Duncker and Humblot) 1989, pp. 273–286.
[151] ICCPR Article 40(4).
[152] Ghandhi, above n. 1, at p. 25.

the Covenant, but the significance of these Comments upon controversial subjects such as the rights of the child,[153] minorities[154] and freedom of religion[155] cannot be overstated.

INTER-STATE APPLICATIONS[156]

The second mode of implementation is the inter-State complaints procedure as authorised under Articles 41 and 42 of the ICCPR. Although part of the same treaty, the procedure is optional with States interested in using this mechanism being required to make an additional declaration.[157] Both parties, the complainant and the State against whom the complaint is made, must have made a declaration under Article 41. According to this procedure a State (A) which considers another State (B) is violating the Covenant can bring that fact to the attention of the State Party concerned. State (B) must respond to the allegations within three months.[158] If, however, the matter has not been resolved within six months of the receipt of the initial communication, either State may bring the matter to the attention of the Committee.[159] The Committee must decide whether all local remedies have been exhausted before considering the case in closed sessions.[160] The Committee's task is to make an attempt to resolve the dispute through its good offices.[161] The Committee is obliged to produce a written report within twelve months of the date of receipt of notice of complaint. If a solution is reached, then the Committee's report will be brief and confined to facts and the solution reached.[162] If a friendly solution has not been reached then the Committee is required to confine its report to a brief statement of facts. The written submissions and a record of the oral submissions made by the States parties involved are to be attached to the report.[163]

According to Article 42 (if the matter is not resolved amicably) the Committee may, with the consent of the States parties concerned, appoint a five-member ad hoc conciliation commission.[164] The Commission is required

---

[153] Human Rights Committee, *General Comment No: 17, Rights of the Child (Art. 24)*: 35th Sess., 1989, 07/04/89.

[154] Human Rights Committee, *General Comment No: 23, The Rights of Minorities (Art. 27)*: 50th Sess., 1994, 08/04/94.

[155] Human Rights Committee, *General Comment No: 22, The Right to Freedom of Thought, Conscience and Religion (Art. 18)*: 48th Sess. 1993, 30/07/93.

[156] See S. Leckie, 'The Inter-State Complaint Procedure in International Law: Hopeful Prospects or Wishful thinking?' 10 *HRQ* (1988) 249.

[157] Article 41(1).

[158] Article 41(1)(a).

[159] Article 41(1)(b).

[160] Article 41(1)(c)(d).

[161] Article 41(1)(e).

[162] Article 41(1)(h)(i).

[163] Article 41(1)(h)(ii).

[164] Article 42(1)(a)(b).

to report its findings to the Chairman of the Committee within twelve months of having taken up the matter.[165] If no solution has been reached then the Commission report must state the facts and indicate 'its views on the possibilities of an amicable solution'.[166] A conciliation commission has the power to make recommendations, however, these recommendations are not binding upon States. In each case the matter will be referred to the General Assembly – through ECOSOC being informed, in due course, by the Committee in its annual report. Like other international procedures of a similar nature the inter-State complaints procedure has not proved to be of any major significance. Inter-State proceedings, in the words of one commentator, 'are undeniably complex, cumbersome and elongated'.[167] States often feel reluctant to challenge other States for political and diplomatic reasons. As yet the inter-State complaints procedure has not been used.[168]

THE INDIVIDUAL COMPLAINTS PROCEDURE[169]

A third mechanism, and by far the most significant in so far as individuals are concerned, is the individual complaints procedure under the first optional protocol to the ICCPR. At the time of drafting of the ICCPR it had been proposed to incorporate a mechanism of individual complaints within the Covenant itself, an effort which proved abortive in the light of widely differing views and disagreements. The Protocol, which emerged as a separate treaty, came into operation on 23 March 1976 and by 31 March 2002 there were 101 States parties to it – covering a population of well over one billion people from all continents of the world. Under this Protocol, the Committee has provided consideration to more than 1,000 cases emerging from 69 States parties.

According to Article 1 of the Protocol, a State party to the Covenant that also becomes a party to the Protocol:

> recognises the competence of the Committee to receive and consider communications from individuals subject to its jurisdiction who claim to be victims of violation by that State Party of any of the rights set forth in the Covenant. No Communication shall be received by the Committee if it concerns a State Party to the Covenant which is not a party to the present Protocol.[170]

The Communication should be sent to the Secretariat of the Office of the High Commissioner for Human Rights. Communications must be in written form. There is no restriction of language and, unlike the European system,

---

[165] Article 42(7).
[166] Article 42(7)(c).
[167] Ghandhi, above n. 1, at p. 26.
[168] Ibid. at p. 27.
[169] For a detailed consideration see Ghandhi, above n. 1.
[170] Article 1, Protocol 1.

there is no time limit on submission after the exhaustion of domestic remedies. However, prior to submission, and in accordance with Article 2, the individual who claims to be the victim of violations of his or her rights must have exhausted all available domestic remedies.

The communication must provide essential prerequisite information. This consists of the name, address and nationality of the victim and the author. The State against which the complaint is being made must be identified clearly. When a State is not a party to the Optional Protocol, the Secretary-General returns the communications with the notification that the State concerned is not a party to the Protocol. There should also be identification of the breach and the articles which are alleged to have been breached. There must also be a statement to the effect that, having satisfied the admissibility requirements (i.e. the exhaustion of domestic remedies), the same matter is not being considered by another international procedure etc.[171] The communication must be signed and dated. Article 3 of the Protocol provides that the Committee shall consider inadmissible any communication which is anonymous or which the Committee considers to be an abuse of the right of submission or incompatible with the provisions of the Covenant. Article 5(2) provides for the exclusion of those communications where the same matter is the subject of another international investigation or settlement.

Consideration of the communication under the OP is confidential at the merit and admissibility stage. On receipt of the communication, it is screened by a member of the Secretariat of the offices of the High Commissioner for Human Rights. The communication is registered by the Secretariat and is forwarded to the Human Rights Committee's Special Rapporteur for New Communications.[172] The Special Rapporteur, a member of the Committee, provides the initial scrutiny and ensures that the necessary information is provided or contained in the communication. He seeks observations or further information from the relevant State party and the individual, and then passes them to the five-member Working Group on Communications. The latter meets for one week before the session and can declare a communication admissible so long as the Working Group is unanimous.[173] Otherwise the issue of admissibility is considered by the whole committee.[174]The general practice is that the recommendations of the Working Group are normally followed by the Committee.[175]

---

[171] Article 5(2)(a)(b).

[172] For the terms of reference for the Special Rapportuer on New Communications, see GAOR, 46th Sess., Supplement No. 40 (A/45/40) Report of the Human Rights Committee, p. 218.

[173] Rule 87(2).

[174] S. Lewis-Anthony, 'Treaty-Based Procedures for Making Human Rights Complaints within the UN System' in H. Hannum (ed.), above n. 17, at p. 47.

[175] Ghandhi, above n. 1, at p. 75.

The Committee is under an obligation to bring any communication submitted to it to the attention of the concerned State party.[176] Within six months the State party must provide the Committee with written explanations or statements clarifying the matter.[177] Cases found to be admissible are considered on their merits after further consultation with the State party and the author of the Communication. The Committee holds closed meetings when examining individual communications and the pleadings are treated as confidential. The Committee formulates its views in the light of all the written information made available to it by the individual and by the State party concerned. There are thus no apparent mechanisms for oral on-site investigations.[178]

The Human Rights Committee presents its views through consensus, though individual members can write concurring or dissenting opinions.[179] The Committee forwards its formulated views to the State party and to the individual. According to Article 6, the Committee includes in its annual report under Article 45 of the Covenant a summary of its activities under the Optional Protocol. The Committee's views are not legally binding, carrying only moral and political obligations.[180] The terminology, such as using 'communications' rather than 'complaints' and 'views' as opposed to 'decisions', confirms the limited nature of the mandate of the Human Rights Committee.

The Committee's views have not been readily endorsed by States parties and the lack of compliance with the views of the Committee has been a source of some concern. Between 1982 and 1990, the committee sent out letters to the States parties concerned, requesting that they take action in response to its views. This process has proved to be unsatisfactory. From 1990 onwards the Committee has undertaken greater efforts to ensure compliance. A Committee member is now designated as a Special Rapporteur to follow the implementation process through. The Committee's practice in cases of violation is to require the State concerned to inform the Committee of any actions undertaken in response to the Committee's findings. In order to ensure monitoring of State compliance, the special Rapporteur has a wide mandate: to make 'such contacts and take such action as appropriate for the due performance of the follow-up mandate'.[181] In pursuit of this mandate the Special Rapporteur has contacted a number of permanent representatives or missions of States

---

[176] Article 4(1).

[177] Article 4(2).

[178] S. Lewis-Anthony, 'Treaty-Based Procedures for Making Human Rights Complaints within the UN System' in Hannum (ed.), above n. 17, at p. 48.

[179] For the difficulties surrounding decision making by consensus, see Ghandhi, above n. 1, at pp. 32–35.

[180] De Zayas, Möller and Opsahl, above n. 126, at p. 11.

[181] Rules of Procedure Rule 95(2).

parties to discuss the actions taken by the State.[182] A further initiative to ensure compliance involves on-site visits.[183] In August 1995, the Special Rapporteur conducted his first – and as yet only – on-site investigation mission to monitor the compliance of Jamaica with the Committee's view on administration of Justice in cases involving the death penalty and death row phenomena. It must be noted that lack of funding for such visits can be a discouraging factor for planning future initiatives. The Committee's annual report submitted to the General Assembly includes not only reference to those States which have not complied with the Committee's views but also information on the follow-up activities. States are also required to provide information on action undertaken in response to the Committee's view in their periodic reports submitted under Article 40 of the Covenant.

Admissibility requirements under the Optional Protocol

Who may submit a petition?

According to Article 1 of the OP, the Committee may receive communications from:

> individuals subject to [the State Party's] jurisdiction who claim to be victims of a violation by the State party of any of the rights set forth in the Covenant.

There is no requirement of nationality provided that the victim has been within the jurisdiction of the State. The Committee, therefore, is authorised to receive communication from nationals, aliens, refugees or anyone else so long as the individual concerned is subject to jurisdiction.[184] Organisations or associations, as such, are not entitled to submit communications.[185] The person submitting the communication is identified as the 'author'.[186] Only one or several 'individuals' (acting either on their own behalf or through his/their representatives) may submit a communication under Article 1 of the Protocol. The committee has taken the term 'representative' to mean a 'duly appointed representative', for example the alleged victim's lawyer.[187] The Committee, however, has adopted a flexible approach in circumstances where it has not

---

[182] S. Lewis-Anthony, 'Treaty-Based Procedures for Making Human Rights Complaints within the UN System' in H. Hannum (ed.), above n. 17, at p. 49.

[183] Ibid.

[184] See *Miguel Angel Estrella* v. *Uruguay*, Communication No. 74/1980 (17 July 1980), UN Doc. Supp. No. 40 (A/38/40) at 150 (1983).

[185] *Disabled and handicapped persons in Italy* v. *Italy*, Communication No. 163/1984 (10 April 1984), UN Doc. CCPR/C/OP/1 at 47(1984); *J. R. T. and the W. G. Party* v. *Canada*, Communication No. 104/1981(6 April 1983), UN Doc. CCPR/C/OP/1 at 25 (1984) (an unincorporated political party).

[186] McGoldrick, above n. 1, at p. 170.

[187] UN Doc. A/33/40 para 580.

been possible for the victim to submit the communication because of arbitrary detention, being held incommunicado, strict mail censorship, an incapacitating illness consequent upon detention, or death occurring as a result of State actions or omissions.[188] In these circumstances the Committee has allowed others to petition on behalf of the victim provided there is a strong enough link between the individual and the complainant, and that the victim has (or would have) consented himself or herself to such an action. This position is reconfirmed by Rule 90 of the Committee Rules of Procedure according to which a 'communication should normally be submitted by the individual himself or by his representative' although it may be submitted on behalf of the alleged victim 'when it appears that he is unable to submit [it] himself'.[189]

In *Massera* v. *Uruguay* the author's communication on behalf of her husband, her stepfather, and her mother was held admissible.[190] Similarly, communications on behalf of daughter,[191] an uncle and aunt,[192] a son-in-law[193] and a niece[194] have been admissible by reason of close family connections. The onus is upon the authors to establish sufficient linkage with the victim and convince the Committee that he or she has (or would have) authorised submission to the Committee. The Committee has not limited the acceptance of communications from close family members. At present NGOs are not authorised to present communications on behalf of the alleged victim, and organisations in general may not act as authors of communications since Articles 1 and 2 of the Protocol explicitly refer to 'individuals'.

Are actio popularis *communications permissible?*

Under the provisions of the Protocol a person can claim to be the 'victim' only if his or her rights are actually being affected. It is undeniably a matter of degree how concretely this requirement should be taken. However, it is clear that no individual could in the abstract – by way of *actio popularis* – challenge

---

[188] See *Herrera Rubio* v. *Colombia*, Communication No. 161/1983 (2 November 1987), UN Doc. Supp. No. 40 (A/43/40) at 190 (1988; *Miango* v. *Zaire*, Communication No. 194/1985 (27 October 1987), UN Doc. Supp. No. 40 (A/43/40) at 218 (1988). See Ghandhi, above n. 1, at p. 85.

[189] Rule 90(b) Rules of Procedure.

[190] *Moriana Hernandez Valentini de Bazzano, Luis Maria Bazzano Ambrosini, Martha Valentini de Massera and Jose Luis Massera* v. *Uruguay*, Communication No. R.1/5 (15 February 1977), UN Doc. Supp. No. 40 (A/34/40) at 124 (1979).

[191] *Maria del Carmen Almeida de Quinteros, on behalf of her daughter, Elena Quinteros Almeida, and on her own behalf* v. *Uruguay*, Communication No. 107/1981 (17 September 1981), UN Doc. Supp. No. 40 (A/38/40) at 216 (1983).

[192] *Beatriz Weismann Lanza and Alcides Lanza Perdomo* v. *Uruguay*, Communication No. R. 2/8 (20 February 1977), UN Doc. Supp. No. 40 (A/35/40) at 111 (1980).

[193] *Daniel Monguya Mbenge* v. *Zaire*, Communication No. 16/1977 (8 September 1977), UN Doc. Supp. No. 40 (A/38/40) at 134 (1983).

[194] *Beatriz Weismann Lanza and Alcides Lanza Perdomo* v. *Uruguay*, Communication No. R. 2/8 (20 February 1977), UN Doc. Supp. No. 40 (A/35/40) at 111 (1980).

a law or practice claiming it to be contrary to the Covenant.[195] If the law has not already been concretely applied to the detriment of the individual, it must in any event be applicable in such a way that the alleged victim's risk of being affected is more than a theoretical possibility.[196] In *Shirin Aumeeruddy-Cziffra and 19 Other Mauritian Women* v. *Mauritius*,[197] the authors of the communication complained that two pieces of legislation on immigration and deportation resulted in gender discrimination, violating the right to found a family and home and removed the protection of courts of law, breaching Articles 2–4, 17, 23, 25 and 26 of the Covenant. To further their complaints, the authors argued that, under the new laws,

> alien husbands of Mauritian women lost their residence status in Mauritius and must now apply for a resident permit which may be refused or removed at any time. These new laws, however, do not affect the status of alien women married to Mauritian husbands who retain their legal right to residence in the country. The authors further contend that under the new laws alien husbands of Mautirian woman may be deported under a ministerial order which is not subject to Judicial Review.[198]

At the time of the communication, seventeen authors were unmarried and only three co-authors were married to foreign husbands. The Committee applying the test of 'alleged victim's risk being more than a theoretical possibility' held that only those women directly affected by Mauritian legislation could claim to be victims. This excluded the seventeen unmarried Mauritian women. The Committee however held the three married women to be 'victims'. Despite the apparently narrow view taken in the Mauritian women's case, the existence of a risk will suffice and the petitioner need not show that the law has in fact been applied to their detriment.

The existence of risk was used as a criterion in *Toonen* v. *Australia*[199] where a practising homosexual was regarded as a 'victim' when he challenged a law criminalising homosexual acts, a law that not been enforced for ten years. Justifying its views, the Committee noted that 'the threat of enforcement and the pervasive impact of the public opinion had affected [the author] and continued to affect him personally'.[200] The existence of risk is also a critical factor in cases where the victim faces being extradited to a non-State party

---

[195] See *A. R. S.* v. *Canada*, Communication No. 91/1981 (28 October 1981), UN Doc. CCPR/C/OP/1 at 29, 30 (1984). Contrast with the requirement laid down in ACHR (Article 44). below Chapter 8.

[196] *Shirin Aumeeruddy-Cziffra and 19 other Mauritian women* v. *Mauritius*, Communication No. 35/1978 (9 April 1981), UN Doc. CCPR/C/OP/1 at 67 (1984), para 9.2.

[197] Ibid.

[198] Ibid.

[199] *Toonen* v. *Australia*, Communication No. 488/1992 (4 April 1994), UN Doc. CCPR/C/50/D/488/1992 (1994).

[200] Ibid. para 8.2

with a strong possibility of facing torture. In *Kindler* v. *Canada*, the Committee noted:

> A State party would itself be in violation of the Covenant if it handed over a person to another State in circumstances in which it was foreseeable that torture would take place. The foreseeability of the consequence would mean that there was a present violation by the State party, even though the consequence would not occur until later on.[201]

Communications ratione materia

The Committee's competence to examine communications is limited to violations of rights contained within the ICCPR. Other alleged violations (not contained in the Convention) are not admissible.[202] Thus allegations of being over-taxed (based on racial discrimination),[203] right to property,[204] the right to asylum,[205] or the right to conscientious objection are outside the remit of the Committee's consideration.[206] However, an overlap with rights contained in other international instruments does not render the alleged violation inadmissible.[207]

Against whom?

It is only possible to bring an action against a State party and not an international or regional organisation.[208] It is also important to verify that the concerned State is a party to both the ICCPR and the Optional Protocol. Once a State is identified as having accepted obligations under the ICCPR and the Protocol, there are two additional issues which have generated complexities. First, sometimes it can be difficult to identify whether a particular organ is part of the State or a private body, and in this regard our earlier discussion (on

---

[201] *Kindler* v. *Canada*, Communication No. 470/1991 (11 November 1993), UN Doc. CCPR/C/48/D/470/1991 (1993), p. 141 (para 6.2).

[202] *K. L.* v. *Denmark*, Communication No. 59/1979 (26 March 1980), UN Doc. CCPR/C/OP/1 at 24 (1984); *C. E.* v. *Canada*, Communication No. 13/1977 (25 August 1977), UN Doc. CCPR/C/OP/1 at 16 (1984).

[203] *I. M.* v. *Norway*, Communication No. 129/1982 (6 April 1983), UN Doc. CCPR/C/OP/1 at 41 (1984).

[204] *K. L.* v. *Denmark*, Communication No. 59/1979 (26 March 1980), UN Doc. CCPR/C/OP/1 at 24 (1984).

[205] *V. M. R. B.* v. *Canada*, Communication No. 236/1987 (18 July 1988), UN Doc. Supp. No. 40 (A/43/40) at 258 (1988).

[206] *L. T. K.* v. *Finland*, Communication No. 185/1984 (9 July 1985), UN Doc. Supp. No. 40 (A/40/40) at 240 (1985).

[207] See *S. W. M. Broeks* v. *The Netherlands*, Communication No. 172/1984 (9 April 1987), UN Doc. Supp. No. 40 (A/42/40) at 139 (1987), 160; McGoldrick, above n. 1, pp. 163–165.

[208] *H.d.P* v. *The Netherlands*, Communication No. 217/1986 (24 March 1988), UN Doc. CCPR/C/OP/1 at 70 (1984). Similar to ECHR decision *CFDT* v. *European Communities/their Members* A. 8030/77, 13 D & R 231 (1978) (European Commission).

public/private divide) needs to be recalled. State responsibility extends to officially or semi-officially controlled agencies (for example, an industrial board[209] or a broadcasting corporation).[210] Secondly, since the undertaking on the part of the State is 'to respect and to ensure all individuals ... the rights', it is also possible to hold the State accountable in situations where although the breach was conducted by a private party, the State had nevertheless the duty to prevent that breach.[211]

Communications ratione temporis

In accordance with the general rules of international law, alleged breaches of the Covenant which occurred before the Covenant and the Protocol had entered into force[212] with regard to the State party concerned are beyond the scope of consideration.[213] If, however, the alleged violations continued after the relevant date,[214] or the alleged offences began and continued even though the initial arrest took place before the entry into force for the relevant State of the Covenant and the Protocol,[215] or the alleged offences have produced long-term effects, the communication could be declared admissible.

Communications between petitioner and the State complained against

(Interpretation of Article 1 of the Protocol in relation to Article 2(1) of the Covenant – meaning of 'within its territory and subject to its jurisdiction').

According to Article 2(1) of the Covenant, 'each State Party undertakes to respect and ensure to all individuals within its territory and subject to its jurisdiction the rights recognised in the present Covenant without distinction of any kind'. In contrast Article 1 of the Protocol refers to the requirement of

---

[209] *B. d. B. et al.* v. *The Netherlands*, Communication No. 273/1989 (30 March 1989), UN Doc. Supp. No. 40 (A/44/40) at 286 (1989).

[210] *Leo R- Hertzberg, Uit Mansson, Astrid Nikula and Marko and Tuovi Putkonen, represented by SETA (Organization for Sexual Equality)* v. *Finland*, Communication No. R.14/61 (7 August 1979), UN Doc. Supp. No. 40 (A/37/40) at 161 (1982).

[211] See the Committee's approach in *Herrera Rubio* v. *Colombia*, Communication No. 161/1983 (2 November 1987), UN Doc. Supp. No. 40 (A/43/40) at 190 (1988) and *Alfredo Rafael and Samuel Humberto Sanjuán Arévalo* v. *Colombia*, Communication No. 181/1984 (3 November 1989), UN Doc. Supp. No. 40 (A/45/40) at 31 (1990).

[212] *Miguel A. Millán Sequeira* v. *Uruguay*, Communication No. 6/1977 (29 July 1980), UN Doc. CCPR/C/OP/1 at 52 (1984); *Lucia Sala de Touron* v. *Uruguay*, Communication No. 32/1978 (31 March 1981), UN Doc. CCPR/C/OP/1 at 61 (1984).

[213] *A. R. S.* v. *Canada*, Communication No. 91/1981 (28 October 1981), UN Doc. CCPR/C/OP/1 at 29 (1984).

[214] *William Torres Ramirez* v. *Uruguay*, Communication No. 4/1977 (26 August 1977), UN Doc. CCPR/C/OP/1 at 3 (1984).

[215] *Luciano Weinberger Weisz* v. *Uruguay*, Communication No. 28/1978 (29 October 1980), UN Doc. CCPR/C/OP/1 at 57 (1984); *Leopoldo Buffo Carballal* v. *Uruguay*, Communication No. 33/1978 (8 April 1981), UN Doc. CCPR/C/OP/1 at 63 (1984).

'jurisdiction' but not to that of territory. The Committee has adopted a broad approach to the meaning of jurisdiction. Thus in a number of circumstances, complaints have been held admissible for individuals not physically within the territory of the State concerned. In *Samuel Lichtensztejn* v. *Uruguay*[216] the Committee held a petition admissible by a Uruguayan citizen who was resident in Canada in relation to the non-renewal of her passport. According to the Committee the words, 'subject to its jurisdiction, in Article 1 of the Protocol, refer to the relationship between the individual and the State concerned, and not to the place where the violation occurred'.[217]

Thus, depending on the nature of the alleged complaint, it is possible for the victim to be outside the territory of the State party. Therefore refusal to renew a passport in another State would result in the denial of the right to freedom of movement. Abduction in the territory of another State,[218] or atrocities committed after occupation of foreign land also provide examples.[219] Furthermore the victim does not have to be in the territory or jurisdiction of the concerned State at the time of the alleged violation or at the time of the filing of the communication. The decision in the *Lilian Celiberti de Casariego case*[220] confirms that the Committee sees no problem in declaring a communication from a refugee admissible.[221] It would also appear that a communication would be held admissible on the basis that at the relevant time the individual concerned was under the effective control of the respondent State, regardless of the theoretical territorial boundaries.

Admissibility and procedural requirements connected with the content of the petition

Effect on admissibility of the existence of international procedures (Article 5(2)(a))

According to this Article a communication cannot be considered if it contains the same matter as that which is being examined by another international

[216] *Samuel Lichtensztejn* v. *Uruguay*, Communication No. 77/1980 (30 September 1980), UN Doc. Supp. No. 40 (A/38/40) at 166 (1983).

[217] *Delia Saldias de Lopez* v. *Uruguay*, Communication No. 52/1979 (29 July 1981), UN Doc. CCPR/C/OP/1 at 88 (1984).

[218] Ibid. *Attorney-General of the Government of Israel* v. *Eichmann* 36 ILR (1961) 5; J.E.S. Fawcett, 'The Eichmann Case' 58 *BYIL* (1962) 181; L.C. Green, 'The Eichmann Case' 23 *MLR* (1960) 507.

[219] See Committee Against Torture, *Initial Reports of States parties Due in 1997*: Kuwait. 15/10/97. CAT/C/37/Add.1. (State Party Report) paras 53, 54.

[220] *Lilian Celiberti de Casariego* v. *Uruguay*, Communication No. R.13/56 (17 July 1979), UN Doc. Supp. No. 40 (A/36/40) at 185 (1981).

[221] In fact most communications seem to be presented by individuals in similar situations.

procedure, for example by the European Court of Human Rights[222] or by the Inter-American Commission on Human Rights.[223] This limitation does not apply to the State reporting system such as those prescribed by Article 16 of the ICESCR[224] or considerations under the ECOSOC Resolution 1503 procedure,[225] the ILO Freedom of Association Committee,[226] those pending before the United Nations Working Group on Enforced or Involuntary Disappearance established by the Commission on Human Rights in its Resolution 20(XXXVI) 29 February 1980,[227] or the Country-Studies by the Inter-American Commission on Human Rights.[228] Only procedures implemented by inter-State or intergovernmental organisations fall under this provision. Those established by NGOs, such as inter-parliamentary councils, do not affect admissibility, nor do procedures such as the e.g. petition system of the General Assembly Special Committee against Apartheid, and those of several ad hoc fact-finding bodies on human rights in particular countries.[229] The examination of State reports under the ICESCR does not come within the terms of Article 5(2)(a).[230] Equally there is nothing to prevent an applicant exhausting another international procedure and then submitting a communication to the Committee. Similarly the Committee is not precluded from consideration of a communication which has been withdrawn from another international procedure[231] or submitted by an unrelated third party.

Even in the case of communications being considered by another international procedure, the Committee has adopted generous rulings. In one case, the Committee determined that a two-line reference to the author in a list of over 100 persons detained did not breach the provisions of Article 5(2)(a).[232] In *Miguel A.*

[222] See *D.F. et al. v. Sweden*, Communication No. 183/1984 (26 March 1985), UN Doc. Supp. No. 40 (A/40/40) at 228 (1985).

[223] See *Miguel A. Millán Sequeira v. Uruguay*, Communication No. 6/1977 (29 July 1980), UN Doc. CCPR/C/OP/1 at 52 (1984).

[224] *S. W. M. Broeks v. The Netherlands*, Communication No. 172/1984 (9 April 1987), UN Doc. Supp. No. 40 (A/42/40) at 139 (1987).

[225] *A et al. v. S*, Communication No. 1/1976 (26 January 1978), UN Doc. CCPR/C/OP/1 at 17 (1984).

[226] *John Khemraadi Baboeram et al v. Suriname*, Communication No. 146/1983 and 148 to 154/1983 (4 April 1985), UN Doc. Supp. No. 40 (A/40/40) at 187 (1985).

[227] *Basilio Laureano Atachahua v. Peru*, Communication No. 540/1993 (16 April 1996), CCPR/C/56/D/540/1993.

[228] Harris, above n. 1, at p. 650.

[229] See Doc. A/33/40 para 582.

[230] McGoldrick, above n. 1, at p. 183.

[231] *Raul Sendic Antonaccio v. Uruguay*, Communication No. R.14/63 (28 November 1979), UN Doc. Supp. No. 40 (A/37/40) at 114 (1982). According to the Human Rights Committee 'same matter refers to having "identical parties to the complaints advanced and facts adduced in support of them"' *V. O. v. Norway*, Communication No. 168/1984 (17 July 1985), UN Doc. CCPR/C/OP/1 at 48 (1984), para 6(a).

[232] *Miguel A. Millán Sequeira v. Uruguay*, Communication No. 6/1977 (29 July 1980), UN Doc. CCPR/C/OP/1 at 52 (1984).

Millán Sequeira v. *Uruguay* the Committee also decided that a communication submitted to the Inter-American Commission on Human Rights prior to the entry into force of the ICCPR and OP could not relate to the event alleged to have taken place after that date. Similarly the rule was not breached by a subsequent opening of the case by an unrelated third party.[233] A case which has already been examined under another procedure on international investigation could not concern the same matter if it was submitted to that particular procedure prior to the entry into force of the Protocol and the Covenant for that particular State.[234]

Effect on admissibility by non-exhaustion of domestic remedies (Article 5(2)(b))

One of the most significant admissibility requirements is that the victim must have exhausted all domestic remedies before attempting to have recourse to the Committee.[235] Thus in the event of available (and not unreasonably prolonged) domestic remedies, the Committee is barred from considering the communication. While not stated explicitly, the Committee has considered this provision in the light of existing principles of general international law. Unlike ECHR, there are no time limits and the approach of the Committee has been flexible and generous. The applicant has the initial burden of proof to show that he has exhausted domestic remedies. After having established the prima facie case, the burden of proof shifts to the State to refute the alleged violations. If the domestic remedies are ineffective,[236] unreasonable in nature or excessively onerous,[237] unduly prolonged[238] or are no longer open or are, in fact, unavailable[239] to the victim then he is not under obligation to exhaust these remedies. Similarly there is no obligation on the victim to resort to extraordinary remedies.[240]

In the absence of evidence suggesting the existence of ineffective and unreasonably prolonged remedies, the Committee has declined to accept general

---

[233] *Lilian Celiberti de Casariego* v. *Uruguay*, Communication No. 56/1979 (29 July 1981), UN Doc. CCPR/C/OP/1 at 92 (1984).

[234] *Alberto Grille Motta* v. *Uruguay*, Communication No. 11/1977 (29 July 1980), UN Doc. CCPR/C/OP/1 at 54 (1984).

[235] *N. S.* v. *Canada*, Communication No. 26/1978 (28 July 1978), UN Doc. CCPR/C/OP/1 at 19 (1984).

[236] *Guillermo Ignacio Dermit Barbato and Hugo Haroldo Dermit Barbato* v. *Uruguay*, Communication No. 84/1981, 27 February 1981, UN Doc. Supp. No. 40 (A/38/40) at 124 (1983).

[237] See *T.K* v. *France*, Communication No. 220/1987 (08 December1989). CCPR/C/37/D/220/1987; *H.K.* v. *France*, Communication No. 222/1987 (08 December 1989). CCPR/C/37/D/222/1987.

[238] *Alba Pietraroia* v. *Uruguay*, Communication No. 44/1979 (27 March 1981), UN Doc. CCPR/C/OP/1 at 65 (1984).

[239] *Eduardo Bleier* v. *Uruguay*, Communication No. R.7/30 (23 May 1978), UN Doc. Supp. No. 40 (A/37/40) at 130 (1982).

[240] *Earl Pratt and Ivan Morgan* v. *Jamaica*, Communication No. 210/1986 and 225/1987 (6 April 1989), UN Doc. Supp. No. 40 (A/44/40) at 222 (1989).

statements from the State party concerned regarding the non-exhaustion of domestic remedies. The Committee has noted on a number of occasions that the State is required to show that remedies are available and effective.[241]

The Committee has also placed the burden of proof on the State party to rebut the allegations made by the individual because it is the State which is in a stronger position and has access to pertinent information. In *Eduardo Bleier v. Uruguay*, the Committee said in relation to the burden of proof that this cannot rest on the author of the communication, especially considering that the author and the State do not always have equal access to the evidence, and that frequently the State party alone has access to the information. It is implicit in Article 4(2) of the OP that the State party has the duty to investigate in good faith that all the allegations are corroborated by evidence submitted by the author. In cases where the author has submitted allegations supported by substantial witness testimony, and where clarification of the case depends on information exclusively in the hands of the State party, the committee may consider allegations as substantial in the absence of satisfactory evidence and explanation by State party.[242] Similarly in *William Torres Ramirez v. Uruguay*, a general denial by Uruguay of non-exhaustion of domestic remedies was declared to be entirely insufficient.[243] The author's allegations, where they have been either uncontested or the details are of a general character, have often been accepted unconditionally. This approach of the Committee in relation to burden of proof issues is commendable, commenting on which Davidson notes that the Human Rights Committee has signalled

> quite clearly in its jurisprudence that it is the State which must show which remedies are specifically available to a complainant when it denies that local remedies have not been exhausted.[244]

Other admissibility requirements

In general the victim needs to establish a prima facie case. In other words, the communication must not be 'entirely without foundation or merit in legal principle'.[245] Thus, where a petitioner is complaining, for example of breach

---

[241] 'It is incumbent on the State party to prove the effectiveness of remedies the non-exhaustion of which it claims' and the availability of the alleged remedy must be 'reasonably evident'; *C. F. et al. v. Canada*, Communication No. 113/1981, 25 July 1983 (19th Sess.), 12 April 1985 (24th Sess.), UN Doc. CCPR/C/OP/1 at 13 (1984).

[242] *Eduardo Bleier v. Uruguay*, Communication No. R.7/30 (23 May 1978), UN Doc. Supp. No. 40 (A/37/40) at 130 (1982), para 13.

[243] *William Torres Ramirez v. Uruguay*, Communication No. 4/1977 (26 August 1977), UN Doc. CCPR/C/OP/1 at 3 (1984).

[244] S. Davidson, *The Inter-American Court of Human Rights* (Aldershot: Dartmouth) 1992, at pp. 71–72.

[245] Ghandhi, above n. 1, at p. 181.

of the right to fair trial and racial discrimination, he needs to substantiate his claims with some evidence.[246] According to Article 3 of the Optional Protocol, the Committee is barred from considering any communication that is anonymous. The author of the communication is required to identify himself or herself, though the Committee may agree (depending on the circumstances) not to reveal his or her identity to the State. The communication must also not abuse the right of submission, or be incompatible with the provisions of the Covenant.[247] Communications have rarely been held inadmissible because of abuse of the right to petition.[248]

CONCLUSIONS

Since the procedure came into effect in March 1979, the Committee has found 282 violations of various rights contained in the ICCPR. An analysis of the jurisprudence of the Committee provides an impressive exhibition of the manner in which a body with limited resources and powers could nevertheless exert influence to protect the rights of individuals. The Committee has, over the last two decades, emerged as the most important organ striving for the universal enforcement of human rights within the framework of the United Nations. Imaginative and ambitious ideas have been taken up. Reference could be made to the provisions for informing the respondent State of desirable interim measures 'to avoid irreparable damage to the victim'[249] and the publication of its final decisions without abridgement in spite of Article 6 of the Protocol providing merely for a 'summary of its activities'.[250] In contrast to the ECHR, the grounds for rejecting individual communications are restrictively applied. There is no time limit, again in contrast to the ECHR's six-month rule. While the Committee has utilised concepts found in other human

---

[246] *C. L. D.* v. *France*, Communication No. 228/1987 (18 July 1988), UN Doc. Supp. No. 40 (A/43/40) at 252 (1988).

[247] Article 3 Optional Protocol.

[248] See *K. L.* v. *Denmark*, Communication No. 59/1979 (26 March 1980), UN Doc. CCPR/C/OP/1 at 24 (1984). The Committee found the author's submission an abuse of the right to petition. K.L.'s communication related to the author's taxable income with the author claiming violation of Articles 14 and 26 of ICCPR. He had previously submitted a similar communication, which had been held inadmissible because of lack of factual evidence and substantiation of the actual violation of the rights. In the present instance there was a similar lack of substantiation. It was held inadmissible and an abuse of the right to petition.

[249] Rule 86 of the Rules of Procedure provides authority to the Committee before forwarding its [final] views on the communication to the relevant State party to inform that State 'of its views as to whether interim measures may be desirable to avoid irreparable damage to the victim of the alleged violation'. See *O. E.* v. *S*, Communication No. 22/1977 (25 January 1978), UN Doc. CCPR/C/OP/1 at 5 (1984); *Alberto Altesor* v. *Uruguay*, Communication No. 10/1977 (26 July 1978), UN Doc. CCPR/C/OP/1 at 6 (1984).

[250] Article 6 Optional Protocol.

rights systems, such as the ECHR's doctrine of 'margin of appreciation',[251] it has been very restrictive in granting discretionary powers which are likely to be misused.[252] With regard to submitting communications, the costs of petitioning are relatively small and there are no specific requirements relating to the language in which communications ought to be made. Despite these positive features, there are significant difficulties faced by the Committee.

It is not a court of law and its views are not binding upon the relevant parties.[253] There is no possibility of sanctions (comparable to ECHR) attached to the Committee's decisions nor are any provisions made for the appointment of an ad hoc investigation committee (as in ECOSOC Resolution 1503)[254] nor for the appointment of an ad hoc conciliation commission as in its own inter-State procedure.[255] There are no judicial sanctions attached to the Committee's views although the basic spirit of the Protocol and the purpose for which the Committee was established must not be overlooked. The Committee was never perceived to be a Supreme Court for international protection of human rights. The Protocol and any international human rights system can only work effectively in cooperation with State parties' involvement and cooperation. Although limited to those States that are parties to the Protocol, the procedure presents the only attempt within the UN system to deal with cases from individuals in a quasi-judicial procedure and to render an opinion upon the merits of the case.

Before concluding, a number of concerns and limitations faced by the Committee under the Optional Protocol have to be mentioned. First, the absence of sanctions attached to the Committee's views does in fact mean that the full potential of the international system of human rights protection is not realised. While the Committee has persuaded many states to change their laws and administrative practices, the overall position has appropriately been described as 'disappointing'.[256] It is certainly unsatisfactory when compared to the European human rights system. Second, attached to this lack of sanctions is the concern regarding non-cooperation with, or even non-recognition of, the Committee's decisions. We have already considered the Committee's

---

[251] *Leo R- Hertzberg, Uit Mansson, Astrid Nikula and Marko and Tuovi Putkonen, represented by SETA (Organization for Sexual Equality)* v. *Finland*, Communication No. R.14/61 (7 August 1979), UN Doc. Supp. No. 40 (A/37/40) at 161 (1982). See below Chapter 6.

[252] According to Professor Harris 'No margin of appreciation doctrine is applied under the International Covenant on Civil and Political Rights either, largely for fear of State abuse' See D. Harris, 'Regional Protection of Human Rights: The Inter-American Achievement' in D.J. Harris and S. Livingstone (eds), above n. 35, 1–29 at p. 10, n. 52.

[253] J. Crawford, 'The UN Human Rights Treaty System: A System in Crisis' in P. Alston and J. Crawford (eds), *The Future of UN Human Rights Treaty Monitoring* (Cambridge: Cambridge University Press) 2000, 1–12, at p. 2.

[254] See above Chapter 2.

[255] See above inter-State procedure.

[256] McGoldrick, above n. 1, at p. 202.

efforts to ensure compliance and cooperation. These efforts are only partially successful. Last but not least, the Committee, like other UN bodies, is facing a substantial crisis of personnel and funding. In its work it is facing a huge backlog of at least three years.[257] There is an urgent need to support the Committee with additional funds, and it would be useful to hold a number of extraordinary sessions to reduce or remove the current backlog.

---

[257] H.J. Steiner, 'Individual Claims in a World of Massive Violations: What Role for the Human Rights Committee' in P. Alston and J. Crawford (eds), above n. 253, 15–53 at p. 33.

5

THE INTERNATIONAL COVENANT ON ECONOMIC, SOCIAL AND CULTURAL RIGHTS[1]

INTRODUCTION

All human rights are universal, indivisible and interdependent and interrelated. The international community must treat human rights globally in a fair and equal manner, on the same footing, and with the same emphasis.[2]

The Vienna Declaration and Programme of Action (1993) clearly recognises the interrelationship and interdependence of civil and political rights and the social, economic and cultural rights. This recognition is present in varying degrees in all the major human rights instruments. As we have already noted

---

[1] H.J. Steiner and P. Alston, *International Human Rights in Context: Law, Politics, Morals: Text and Materials*, 2nd edn (Oxford: Clarendon Press) 2000, pp. 237–320; M. Craven, *The International Covenant on Economic, Social and Cultural Rights: A Perspective on its Development* (Oxford: Clarendon Press) 1995; D.J. Harris, *Cases and Materials on International Law*, 5th edn (London: Sweet and Maxwell) 1998, pp. 689–699; G. Peces-Barba, 'Reflections on Economic, Social and Cultural Rights' 2 *HRLJ* (1981) 281; D. Beetham, 'What Future for Economic and Social Rights?' 53 *Political Studies* (1995) 41 at p. 51; A. Eide, 'The Realisation of Social and Economic Rights and the Minimum Threshold Approach' 10 *HRLJ* (1989) 35; D.M. Trubeck, 'Economic, Social and Cultural Rights in the third World' in T. Meron (ed.), *Human Rights in International Law: Legal and Policy Issues* (Oxford: Clarendon Press) 1984, pp. 205–271.

[2] Vienna Declaration and Programme of Action (New York: United Nations Department of Public Information) 1993 para 5 (pt 1). Adopted by the United Nations World Conference on Human Rights, 25 June, 1993. Also see C. Scott, 'Reaching Beyond (without Abandoning) the Category of "Economic, Social and Cultural Rights"' 21 *HRQ* (1999) 633.

the UDHR[3] affirms the existence of the three generations of rights.[4] The ICCPR also retains as its primary Article the right to self-determination, which is a collective right, the right of peoples.[5] It also contains articles on equal protection of the law (Article 26), right to freedom of association (Article 22(1)), right to life (Article 6(1)) and rights of minorities including their cultural rights (Article 27). Similarly other international and regional human rights instruments reiterate the overlap between social, economic and cultural rights, and civil and political rights. Regional human rights treaties primarily represented by the ECHR,[6] the American Convention on Human Rights (ACHR),[7] and the AFCHPR[8] indulge in various ways to protect social, economic and cultural rights, while retaining a focus on civil and political rights.

ARGUMENTS OVER THE SUPERIORITY OF RIGHTS

Notwithstanding this interaction, there have been divisions over the status of economic, social and cultural rights. A variety of arguments continue to be put forward asserting the superiority of civil and political rights. Civil and political rights are advocated as being more important since they arguably form a critical basis for protecting human rights.[9] This assumption of the superiority of civil and political rights has, as Leckie notes, led to gross violations and neglect of economic and social rights. He notes:

> when people die of hunger or thirst, or when thousands of urban poor and rural dwellers are evicted from their homes, the world still tends to blame nameless economic or 'developmental' forces, or the simple inevitability of human deprivation, before placing liability at the doorstep of the state. Worse yet, societies increasingly blame victims of such violations for creating their own dismal fates, and in some countries, they are even characterized as criminals on this basis alone.[10]

Attached to the assumption of the superiority of civil and political rights is the claim that these rights establish immediate binding obligations, whereas

---

[3] 10 December, 1948, UN GA Res. 217 A(III), UN Doc. A/810 at 71 (1948).

[4] See above Chapter 3.

[5] Adopted at New York, 16 December, 1966. Entered into force 23 March 1976. GA Res. 2200A (XXI) UN Doc. A/6316 (1966) 999 U.N.T.S. 171; 6 I.L.M. (1967) 368.

[6] Signed at Rome, 4 November 1950. Entered into force 3 September 1953. 213 U.N.T.S. 221; E.T.S. 5.

[7] Signed at San Jose, 22 November 1969. Entered into force 18 July 1978. 1144 U.N.T.S 123; O.A.S.T.S. No.36, O.A.S. Off. Rec. OEA/Ser.L/V/11.23, doc. rev, (1979); 9 I.L.M. (1970) 673.

[8] Adopted on 27 June 1981. Entered into force 21 October 1986. OAU Doc. CAB/LEG/67/3 Rev. 5, 21 I.L.M. (1982) 58.

[9] S. Leckie, 'Another Step Towards Indivisibility: Identifying the Key Features of Violations of Economic, Social and Cultural Rights' 20 *HRQ* (1998) 81 at p. 82.

[10] Ibid.

the language of social and economic rights largely represents undertakings of a progressive nature.[11] 'Progressive achievement' is thus described as the linchpin of ICESCR.[12]

A view very commonly held by commentators and State representatives is that in order to ensure civil and political rights, governments are required to abstain from certain activities (for example not to conduct torture or to deprive people of their liberty). In comparison, economic, social and cultural rights are believed to require a State's intervention and are therefore seen as positive rights. While in some instances this distinction can be made out, in other cases of protecting civil and political rights, active State action is definitely required.[13] Associated with this point is the claim that civil and political rights are easier to enforce and implement since the cost implications are not so significant. Furthermore, it is argued that economic, social and cultural rights obligations are much more difficult to implement since they remain dependent on the economic strength of the State in question. While it is true that some economic and social obligations (for example, to provide everyone with a decent standard of living, to ensure that no one is hungry or unemployed) represent substantial commitments, fulfilling many of the civil and political rights can be equally onerous. Thus, for example, satisfying all the various aspects of the right to fair trial can be very demanding financially.

Those advocating superiority of civil and political rights point to the differences in approach within the substantive provisions as well as in the measures of implementation. We have already noted the approach adopted in ICCPR while dealing with civil and political rights. Contrast these provisions with those of ICESCR. Whereas the ICCPR relies on an authoritative terminology such as 'everyone has the right', 'no one shall be', and has provided definitive rights, the ICESCR relies on imprecise terminology; the usage of such terms as 'recognition' arguably makes it more difficult to regard the rights as legally enforceable. The ICESCR has also been criticised for advancing relatively

---

[11] See Harris, above n. 1, at p. 695; D.M. Trubeck, 'Economic, Social and Cultural Rights in the Third World' in T. Meron (ed.), above n. 1, at pp. 210–212.
[12] P. Alston and G. Quinn, 'The Nature and Scope of State Parties' Obligations under the International Covenant on Economic, Social and Cultural Rights' 9 *HRQ* (1987) 156 at p. 172; According to Robertson and Merrills, 'It is thus quite clear that this is what is known as a promotional convention, that is to say, it does not set out rights which the parties are required to implement immediately, but rather lists standards which they undertake to promote and which they pledge to secure progressively, to the greatest extent possible, having regard to their resources' A.H. Robertson and J.G. Merrills, *Human Rights in the World: An Introduction to the Study of International Protection of Human Rights*, 4th edn (Manchester: Manchester University Press) 1996, at p. 276; also see D. McGoldrick, *The Human Rights Committee: Its Role in the Development of the International Covenant on Civil and Political Rights* (Oxford: Clarendon Press) 1991, pp. 11–13. G. Van Bueren, 'Combating Child Poverty – Human Rights Approaches' 21 *HRQ* (1999) 680 at p. 684.
[13] Beetham, above n. 1, at p. 51.

novel claims as 'rights'. Commentators have doubted the existence of such economic 'rights' as the 'right to food'.[14]

The apparently weak and vague nature of the provisions contained within the ICESCR has led some critics to question whether the treaty provides for legally binding and enforceable rights. Although not completely accurate, there is a measure of truth in the views of these critics. As we shall analyse in the course of this chapter, the implementation mechanisms applicable to the ICE-SCR are much weaker than those of the ICCPR and the system, unlike that of the ICCPR, does not have an inter-State or individual's complaints procedure.

GENERAL NATURE OF OBLIGATIONS: PROGRESSIVE REALISATION OF RIGHTS

In Article 2 of the Covenant, the nature of the obligations undertaken by States parties is spelled out. According to Article 2 (1):

> Each State Party to the present Covenant undertakes to take steps, individually and through international assistance and co-operation, especially economic and technical, to the maximum of its available resources, with a view to achieving progressively the full realisation of the rights recognised in the present Covenant by all appropriate means, including particularly the adoption of legislative measures.

Some commentators doubt whether the Covenant imposes obligations carrying immediate legal affect. The matter has been controversial, although the correct view appears to be that the Article imposes legal obligations that are required to be given immediate legal affect by the State party concerned. Thus according to the Limburg Principles:[15]

> [t]he obligation 'to achieve progressively the full realisation of the rights' requires States parties to move as expeditiously as possible towards the realisation of the rights. Under no circumstances shall this be interpreted as implying for States the right to defer indefinitely efforts to ensure full realisation. On the contrary all States parties have the obligation to begin immediately to take steps to fulfil their obligations under the Covenant.[16]

---

[14] R.L. Brad, 'The Right to Food' 70 *Iowa Law Review* (1985) 1279. C.f. G.J.H. Van Hoof, 'The Legal Nature of Economic, Social and Cultural Rights: A Rebuttal of Some Traditional Views' in P. Alston and K. Tomasevski (eds), *The Right to Food* (Boston: Martinus Nijhoff Publishers) 1990, pp. 97–110.

[15] These principles represent guidelines on the implementation of the Covenant. *The Limburg Principles on the Implementation of the International Covenant on Economic, Social and Cultural Rights*, UN ECCOR. Res. Commission on Human Rights, 43rd Sess., Agenda Item 8, UN Doc. E/CN. 4/1987/17Annex (1987), reprinted as 'The Limburg Principles on the Implementation of the International Covenant on Economic, Social and Cultural Rights' 9 *HRQ* (1987) 122.

[16] Limburg Principles, principle 21. See also *the Statement to the Committee on Economic, Social and Cultural Rights* by B.G. Ramcharan, Deputy High Commissioners, ICESCR, 25th Sess., 23 April 2001.

These obligations, however, are limited to 'taking steps' with a view to 'achieving progressively the full realisation of the rights' that are recognised in the treaty. It is interesting to note the contrasting provisions of ICCPR which impose an obligation on States to 'respect and to ensure'. The provisions of Article 2(1) have been further explored by the Committee's General Comment on the Nature of State Parties Obligation (Article 2, para 1) where the Committee notes 'while the Covenant provides for progressive realisation and acknowledges the constraints due to the limits of available resources, it also imposes various obligations which are of immediate effect'.[17] The Committee has emphasised that even in situations where there are inadequate resources, the obligation remains on the State party to try to ensure the enjoyment of rights.[18]

While legislative means are required, they do not represent the only means of ensuring implementation and it is a matter for the State concerned to determine whatever means (legislative or otherwise) would be required to provide the rights contained within the Covenant. In its third General Comment, the Committee observed that the phrase

'by all appropriate means' must be given its full and natural meaning which each State party must decide for itself which means are the most appropriate under the circumstances with respect to each of the rights, the 'appropriateness' of the means chosen will not always be self-evident. It is therefore desirable that States parties reports should indicate not only the measures that have been taken but considered to be most 'appropriate' under the circumstances. However the ultimate determination as to whether all appropriate measures have been taken remains for the Committee to make.[19]

Article 2(2) represents the crucial non-discriminatory provision within the Covenant. According to this provision the rights contained within the treaty are to be provided without 'any discrimination on the basis of race, colour, sex, language, religion, political or other opinion, national or social origin, property, birth or other status'. As we shall be analysing in the course of this study, the norm of non-discrimination informs the entirety of human rights law. The effective application of a regime of equality and non-discrimination is particularly important in the context of ensuring economic, social and cultural rights. The significance of this principle is underlined by Craven when he notes:

It is very much apparent that a notion of equality runs through the heart of the Covenant. The Covenant assumes the creation or maintenance of state welfare

---

[17] ICESCR General Comment 3, *The Nature of States Parties Obligations* (Article 2, para 1) General Comment No. 3 (14/12/90). UN Doc. E/1991/23, Annex III UN ESCOR, Supp. (No. 3), 84, para 1.
[18] UN Doc. E/1991/23, para 11.
[19] ICESCR General Comment 3, above n. 17, para 4.

institutions and social safety nets (for example the provision of housing, food, clothing and social security) and as such is openly redistributionist.[20]

States are required not only to provide *de jure* equality, but are allowed to introduce distinctions among various sections of the community in order to ensure de facto equality. According to one commentator the policy of affirmative action has been sanctioned by the terminology of Article 2(1) itself.[21] Article 3 restates the fundamental requirement for equality of provision of the rights contained in the Covenant. Commenting on this article, Principle 45 of the Limburg Principle observes that '[I]n the application of article 3 due regard should be paid to the Declaration and Convention on the Elimination of All Forms of Discrimination against Women and other relevant instruments and the activities of (CEDAW) under the said Convention'.[22] Article 4 provides for a general limitation clause which is applicable to the substantive rights contained in Part III of the treaty. Article 5 contains what can be termed as a 'saving clause' which in effect states that treaty provisions cannot be used as a justification for the violation of the rights either contained therein or already established elsewhere.[23]

SELF-DETERMINATION AND ECONOMIC AND SOCIAL RIGHTS

Article 1 of the Covenant deals with the important right of self-determination. As noted earlier, the provisions within the Article are identical to those of Article 1 in the ICCPR.[24] The analysis here will focus on those aspects of self-determination which are directly relevant to economic and social rights. The right to self-determination, which includes economic self-determination, has been clearly established as a right in international law and forms a part of the norms of *jus cogens*.[25] In conceptualising the economic and social dimensions of this right, it is important to mention that the impetus for the development of a legally binding right of self-determination has come from the developing and the socialist worlds. The *travaux préparatoires* of the human rights covenants confirm that a number of developing States were at the forefront of incorporating the right to economic self-determination. For these States, a cardinal aspect of self-determination was the right to permanent sovereignty over natural wealth and resources along with a right to the nationalisation of property.[26]

---

[20] Craven, above n. 1, at p. 161.
[21] Ibid. pp. 157–158.
[22] Limburg Principles, principle 45.
[23] Alston and Quinn, above n. 12, at p. 192.
[24] See above Chapter 4.
[25] On *jus cogens* see above Chapter 1. For further discussion on the relationship of self-determination with *jus cogens* see below Chapter 12.
[26] See M.N. Shaw, *International Law*, 4th edn (Cambridge: Grotius Publication) 1997, p. 34.

In so far as economic self-determination is concerned, this position is established within Article 1 of the Covenant. According to Article 1(1):

> All Peoples have the right of self-determination. By virtue of that right they freely … pursue their economic … development. All Peoples may, for their own ends, freely dispose of their natural wealth and resources without prejudice to any obligations arising out of international economic co-operation, based upon the principle of mutual benefit, and international law. In no case may a people be deprived of its own means of subsistence.

Article 1(3) goes on to assert the point that

> Developing countries, with due regard to human rights and their national economy, may determine to what extent they would guarantee the economic rights recognised in the present Covenant to non-nationals.

The ideal of permanent sovereignty and the right to exploit nationally based resources has led to substantial controversies over the issue of expropriation and nationalisation of foreign property. Developed States have insisted that any expropriation of foreign property needs to comply with 'minimum international standards'[27] and be based on compensation that is 'prompt, adequate and effective'.[28] In contrast the developing countries advanced the so-called 'New International Economic Order', which authorised an unfettered discretion over natural resources including a right to nationalisation.[29] This vision of permanent sovereignty over natural resources was evidenced in the Charter of Economic Rights and Duties of States[30] and the Declaration on the Establishment of a New Economic Order.[31] The Declaration on the Establishment of a New Economic Order contains provisions asserting permanent sovereignty over natural resources. Para 4(2)(e) asserts the right to:

> full permanent sovereignty of every State over its natural resources and economic activities. In order to safeguard these resources, each State is entitled to exercise effective control over them and their exploitation with means suitable to its own situation, including the right to nationalisation or transfer of ownership to its nationals, this right being an expression of the full permanent sovereignty of the State. No State may be subjected to economic, political or any other type of coercion to prevent the free and full exercise of this inalienable right.

---

[27] See D.J. Harris, *Cases and Materials on International Law*, 5th edn (London: Sweet and Maxwell) 1998, p. 548.
[28] Derived from a formula devised by a former United States Secretary of State, Cordell Hull, and known generally as the Hull formula (1938), according to which 'no government is entitled to expropriate private property, for whatever purpose, without provision for prompt, adequate and effective payment therefore'. Text in 32 *AJIL* (1938), Supp., 192.
[29] See R. Jennings and A. Watts, *Oppenheim's International Law*, 9th edn (Harlow: Longman) 1992, Vol. 1, p. 17.
[30] GA Res. 3281(XXIX) 14 I.L.M. (1975) 251.
[31] GA Res. 3201 (S–VI) 13 I.L.M. (1974) 715.

Article 25 of ICESCR, alongside the above mentioned provisions of Article 1, was deployed by the developing world to advance claims of economic sovereignty and self-determination. According to Article 25, nothing in the ICESCR shall be interpreted to impair 'the inherent right of all people to enjoy and utilise fully and freely their natural wealth and resources'.[32] While substantial differences exist regarding a suitable agenda for economic reform, in so far as the issues of expropriation are concerned the last two decades have seen the traditional distinctions appear to blur. The developing States have become more conscious of the value of foreign investment and have come round to the idea of providing guarantees of adequate compensation so as to attract foreign investors. This eagerness to attract foreign investment has also been influenced by the collapse of socialist planned economies, accompanied by a growing recognition that expropriation and nationalisation of foreign property is damaging for a continuing flow of foreign capital investments. Having said that, the exact position on expropriation within *lex lata* is not fully established[33] and the modern jurisprudence on arbitration awards for nationalisation and expropriation of foreign property does not eradicate the uncertainties.[34]

ANALYSIS OF THE STRUCTURE AND SUBSTANTIVE RIGHTS

The ICESCR was adopted at the same time as the ICCPR and entered into force on 3 January 1976.[35] Attempts to establish a complaints procedure based on an optional protocol (similar to ICCPR's first Optional Protocol) have, thus far, been unsuccessful. The ICESCR is divided into five parts. Part I (Article 1) deals with the right to self-determination. Part II (Articles 2–5) provides *inter alia* for the general nature of States parties obligations; Part III (Articles 6–15) provides for specific substantive rights; Part IV provides for implementation; Part V provides general provisions of a legal nature. As we shall see, the Covenant is supplied with an implementation mechanism. The body in charge of implementation is called the Committee on the International Covenant on Economic, Social and

---

[32] See Article 25.

[33] See A.H. Qureshi, *International Economic Law* (London: Sweet and Maxwell) 1999, 376; cf. P. Malanczuk, *Akehurst's Modern Introduction to International Law*, 7th edn (London: Routledge) 1997, p. 237. Also see J. Rehman, 'Islamic Perspectives on International Economic Law' in A.H. Qureshi (ed.), *Perspectives on International Economic Law* (The Hague: Kluwer Law International) 2002, pp. 235–258.

[34] See in particular the jurisprudence of the Iran–United States Tribunal, M. Fitzmaurice and M. Pellonpää, 'Taking property in the Practice of Iran-United States Claim Tribunal' 19 *NYIL* (1988) 53; A. Mouri, *The International Law of Expropriation as Reflected in the Work of the Iran–United States Claims Tribunal* (Dordrecht: Martinus Nijhoff Publishers) 1994.

[35] Adopted at New York, 16 December 1966. Entered into force 3 January 1976. GA Res. 2200A (XXI) UN Doc. A/6316 (1966) 993 U.N.T.S. 3; 6 I.L.M. (1967) 360.

Cultural Rights (the Committee). In addition to the work of the Committee, the jurisprudence on the subject has been enhanced by a number of sources including the Limburg Principles on the Implementation of the International Covenant on Economic, Social and Cultural Rights[36] and the Maastricht Guidelines on Violations of Economic, Social and Cultural Rights.[37] As their respective titles indicate, these documents articulate principles and guidelines on the Convention rights and violations of these rights.

The Covenant sets out the following substantive rights:

Article 1   The right to self-determination
Article 6   The right to work
Article 7   The right to just and favourable conditions of work
Article 8   The right to form trade unions and the right to strike
Article 9   The right to social security, including social insurance
Article 10   The right to protection and assistance to the family, including special assistance for mothers and children
Article 11   The right to an adequate standard of living including adequate food, clothing and housing, and continuous improvement of living conditions
Article 12   The right to the enjoyment of the highest attainable standard of physical and mental health
Article 13   The right to education, primary education being compulsory and available to all, and secondary and higher education being generally available. Adult education to be encouraged and improvements to be made to the system of schooling
Article 14   Compulsory (free of charge) primary education to be introduced within two years of acceptance of the treaty
Article 15   The right to take part in cultural life and to enjoy the benefits of scientific progress

The right to work and rights of workers

Article 6 provides for the right to work which includes 'the right of everyone to the opportunity to gain his living by work which he freely chooses or accepts' and also states that the State 'will take appropriate steps to safeguard this right'.[38] The right to work is a very significant right as, in the words of Seighart, work represents 'an essential condition of human survival'.[39] It is also protected

---

[36] The text of the Limburg Principles published in UN Doc.E/CN.4/1987/17, Annex. Reprinted in 9 *HRQ* (1987) 122.
[37] See 20 *HRQ* (1998) 691; V. Dankwa, C. Flinterman and S. Leckie, 'Commentary to the Maastricht Guidelines on Violations of Economic, Social and Cultural Rights' 20 *HRQ* (1998) 705.
[38] Article 6(1).
[39] P. Sieghart, *The Lawful Rights of Mankind: An Introduction to the International Legal Code of Human Rights* (Oxford: Clarendon Press) 1985, p. 123.

by other international human rights instruments including the UDHR,[40] the American Declaration of the Rights and Duties of Man (ADHR)[41] and the European Social Charter (ESC).[42] Craven rightly observes that:

> not only is [work] crucial to the enjoyment of 'survival rights' such as food, clothing or housing it affects the level of sophistication of many other human rights such as the right to education, culture and health.[43]

The phenomenon of arbitrary discrimination and denial of the right to work has been deployed to victimise individuals and groups in many parts of the world. Ethnic minorities and women in a number of States are deprived of equal opportunities or free choices in employment.[44] The Committee has criticised violations of the Convention provisions whereby women require permission from their husbands before being able to work outside their homes,[45] or there are racial or ethnic motivations behind discrimination in granting employment.[46]

According to Article 6(2) steps are to be taken by State parties to the present Covenant to achieve the full realisation of this right. The steps shall include technical and vocational guidance and training programmes, policies and techniques to achieve steady economic, social and cultural development, and full and productive employment under conditions safeguarding fundamental political and economic freedoms to the individual. Article 7 expands on the subject of working conditions and remuneration and provides for a recognition of the right to:

> enjoyment of just and favourable conditions of work which ensure, in particular:
>
> (a) Remuneration which provides all workers, as a minimum, with:
>
> > (i)   Fair wages and equal remuneration for work of equal value without distinction of any kind, in particular women being guaranteed conditions of work not inferior to those enjoyed by men, with equal pay for equal work;
> >
> > (ii) A decent living for themselves and their families in accordance with the provisions of the present Covenant;

---

[40] 10 December 1948, UN GA Res. 217 A(III), UN Doc. A/810 at 71 (1948).

[41] Resolution XXX, Final Act of the Ninth International Conference of American States, Bogota, Colombia, 30 March–2 May 1948, 48. O.A.S Res. XXX. O.A.S. Off. Rec. OEA/Ser. L/V/1.4 Rev. (1965). See below Chapter 8.

[42] Adopted at Turin 18 October 1961. Entered into force, 26 February 1965. 529 U.N.T.S 89; ETS 35. See below Chapter 7.

[43] Craven, above n. 1, at p. 194.

[44] See e.g. Discrimination against religious and ethnic groups in States. Minority Rights Group (ed.), *World Directory of Minorities* (London: Minority Rights Group) 1997.

[45] See the Concluding Observations on report of Iran E/C.12/1993/7 at 3, para 6.

[46] See the Summary Records on the Part of the thirtieth meeting on Report by Dominican Republic (06/03/1996) E/C.12/1996/SR.30 para 17.

Article 7 emphasises fairness in remuneration for work which is of equal value. In order to satisfy the requirement of fair wages, the Committee has advocated a system of minimum wages conforming largely to the ILO Minimum Wage-Fixing Convention of 1970.[47] It lays stress upon an equitable system based on fairness in remuneration between men and women.[48] Article 7(a) is also concerned with the adequacy of rights to allow a decent living for individuals and their families.[49] The various elements of the right to just and favourable conditions of work include equal remuneration between men and women,[50] a decent living for workers and their families,[51] safe and healthy conditions of work,[52] equal opportunities in employment including merit-based opportunities for promotion,[53] rest, leisure and reasonable limitation of hours of work along with paid periodic holidays.[54] The review of these rights by the Committee has raised a number of concerns. In its analysis of State reports, the Committee has expressed unhappiness and dissatisfaction over the employment of people it has termed as 'irregular workers'. These are workers who perform the same tasks as other employees, but their employment is not officially recognised; they are on a lower wage and they do not have any health or unemployment benefits.[55]

A related concern has been the treatment of migrant workers in labour markets as well as in societies in general. In a recent report prepared by the Secretary-General, several States acknowledged the maltreatment of migrants and particularly migrant women:

> Mexico noted that women migrant workers were vulnerable to physical and/or psychological violence, racism, xenophobia and other forms of discrimination. Mexico also reported that women migrant workers were subjected to violations of their rights by border-patrol officials, including battering, rape and kidnapping. Costa Rica indicated that the fact that many women migrant workers were undocumented made them vulnerable to abuse, including sexual harassment and sexual violence. Kuwait acknowledged that there might be rare cases of violence against women ...[56]

Article 8 affords the right to form and join trade unions to everyone. The Article also states that no restrictions should be placed on the exercise of this

---

[47] ILO Minimum Wage-Fixing Convention 1970 (No. 131) 825 U.N.T.S. 77 e. 234.
[48] Article 7(a)(i).
[49] Article 7(a)(ii).
[50] Ibid.
[51] Ibid.
[52] Article 7(b)
[53] Article 7(c).
[54] Ibid.
[55] See Concluding Observations of the Committee on Economic, Social and Cultural Rights: Japan. 31/08/2001. E/C.12/1/Add.67. (Concluding Observations/Comments), para 61.
[56] See Report prepared by the Secretary-General, *Violence against Women Migrant Workers*, A/56/329.

right other than those that are necessary for national security, public order or for protecting the rights of others.[57] The right to strike, although controversial, was incorporated by the Third Committee as the majority considered that it was indispensable for the protection of the interests and rights of workers, up to a point whereby the absence of this right would render meaningless any guarantee of trade union rights.[58] This right to strike is subject to limitations laid down in Article 8(1)(a), that is rights may be limited in the interests of national security, public order or the rights and freedoms of others. The right to strike provisions stand out in human rights treaties as only the European Social Charter has similar explicit provisions.[59] The Committee has suggested that the right to strike should be incorporated as part of the contract of employment.[60]

Article 8 can be regarded as an extension of the right to Freedom of Association and it also overlaps with Civil and Political Rights; the terminology of the Article is reminiscent of the obligations within civil and political rights. The wording of the Article emphasises that the rights need to be given immediate effect. According to Article 8(2) this article shall not prevent the imposition of lawful restrictions on the exercise of these rights by members of the armed forces or of the police or of the administration of the State. Article 8(2) restricts members of armed forces, following the lead by the ECHR which also has similar restrictions.[61]

Social security and family rights

According to Article 9, the States parties recognise the right of everyone to security, which includes social insurance. Article 10 deals with the important subject of promoting and protecting the family. In encouraging States parties to provide all possible assistance to families, the Article treats family as 'the natural and fundamental group unit of society', a terminology applied in other international and regional human rights treaties.[62] The Article notes the value of family in the education and upbringing of children. A corollary to the family unit is the institution of marriage, which, according to the Article, must be entered into with the free consent of the intending spouses.[63]

Article 10(2) states that special protection should be accorded to mothers during a reasonable period before and after childbirth. During such period,

---

[57] Article 8(2).
[58] See Mosorov (USSR) E/CN.4/SR.298 at p. 8 (1952); Bracco (Uruguay) E/CN.4/SR.229 at 3 (1952); Brena (Uruguay) A/C.3/SR. 719.
[59] See below Chapter 7.
[60] See Konate on the Report from Jamaica E/C.12/1990/SR.15 at p. 6, para 25.
[61] ECHR Article 11(2).
[62] See Article 23(1) ICCPR; Article 18 AFCHPR; Article 17 ACHR.
[63] Article 10(1).

working mothers should be given paid leave or leave with adequate social security benefits. According to 10(3) special measures of protection and assistance need to be taken on behalf of all children and young persons without any discrimination for reasons of parentage or other conditions. Children and young persons are to be protected from economic and social exploitation. Their employment in work harmful to their morals or health, dangerous to life, or likely to hamper their normal development should be punishable by law. States are also required to set age limits below which the paid employment of child labour should be prohibited and punishable by law.

In the light of the frequent abuse which women and children suffer, the protection of their rights has become a special concern for human rights law. In contemporary societies the exploitation of children is conducted through such abominable practices as prostitution, sexual slavery, labour and servitude. Child labour and exploitation is an institutionalised practice in many parts of the world. According to conservative estimates, between 50–100 million, 10-to 14-year-old children are currently in full-time employment. The actual figures are likely to be much higher.[64] The prostitution and sale of children (especially young girls) and their sexual abuse is also a deplorable but not uncommon occurrence. The provisions of Article 10(3) have been further reinforced by a number of recent initiatives. Notable among these are the enforcement of the Convention on the Rights of the Child,[65] and the more recent Protocol on the Sale of Children, Child Pornography and Child Prostitution.[66]

Adequate standard of living and mental and physical health

Article 11 provides for the right to an adequate standard of living. According to Article 11(1) States parties recognise the

> right of everyone to an adequate standard of living for himself and his family, including adequate food, clothing and housing, and to the continuous improvement of living conditions.

The important provisions of this Article have been the subject of a General Comment as well as a thorough investigation by the Committee.[67] In its obser-

---

[64] G. Van Bueren, *The International Law on the Rights of the Child* (Dordrecht: Martinus Nijhoff Publishers) 1995, p. 263; also see D.E. Ehrenberg, 'The Labor Link: Applying the International Trading System to Enforce Violations of Forced and Child Labour' 20 *YJIL* (1995) 361.

[65] Adopted at New York, 20 November 1989. Entered into force 2 September, 1990. UN GA Res. 44/25 Annex (XLIV), 44 UN GAOR Supp. (No. 49) 167, UN Doc. A/44/49 (1989) at 166; 1577 U.N.T.S. 3. 28 I.L.M. (1989) 1448.

[66] Adopted by the General Assembly 25 May, 2000. GA. Res. 263, UN GAOR, 54 Sess., Supp. 49; UN Doc. A/Res/54/263. See M. J. Dennis, 'Newly Adopted Protocols to the Convention on the Rights of the Child' 94 *AJIL* (2000) 789.

[67] CESCR General Comment 7, *The Right to Adequate Housing: Forced Evictions* (Article 11(1)) General Comment No. 7 (20/05/97).

vations the Committee points to the importance of adequate housing as a fundamental human right and has treated forced eviction as a violation of the Article. In reviewing the report from the Dominican Republic the Committee asserted:

> The information that had reached members of the committee concerning massive expulsion of nearly 15,000 families in the course of the last five years, the deplorable conditions in which the families had to live, and the condition in which the expulsions had taken place were sufficiently serious for it to be considered that the guarantees in Article 11 of the Covenant had not been respected.[68]

In its sixth session, the Committee found that evictions of large numbers of people had led Panama 'not only [to infringe] upon the right to adequate housing but also on the inhabitants' right to privacy and security of the home'.[69] The Committee's members have criticised States for reduction in low-cost housing or for shortage of low-income housing.[70] Article 11(2) details certain provisions to advance the right of individuals to freedom from hunger. The article has been the subject of a General Comment where the Committee notes:[71]

> The right to adequate food, like any other human right, imposes three types or levels of obligations on States parties: the obligations to *respect*, to *protect* and to *fulfil*. In turn, the obligation to *fulfil* incorporates both an obligation to facilitate and an obligation to provide. The obligation to *respect* existing access to adequate food requires States parties not to take any measures that result in preventing such access. The obligation to *protect* requires measures by the State to ensure that enterprises or individuals do not deprive individuals of their access to adequate food. The obligation to *fulfil* (facilitate) means the State must pro-actively engage in activities intended to strengthen people's access to and utilisation of resources and means to ensure their livelihood, including food security. Finally, whenever an individual or group is unable, for reasons beyond their control, to enjoy the right to adequate food by the means at their disposal, States have the obligation to *fulfil* (provide) that right directly. This obligation also applies for persons who are victims of natural or other disasters.[72]

The obligation which the Committee has termed 'the obligation to fulfil' represents a substantial commitment. This particular obligation to fulfil the

---

[68] UN Doc E/C.12/1990/8, para 249.
[69] UN Doc E/C.12/1991/4, para 135.
[70] See e.g. Romero E/C.12/1988/SR.12 at 10–11, para 52 and Concluding Observations on report of Italy E/1993/22 at 50, para 192.
[71] CESCR General Comment 12, *The Right to Adequate Food* (Article 11) General Comment No. 12 E/C.12/199/5 (12/05/99).
[72] (Emphasis provided.) *The Right to Adequate Food* (Art. 11) 12/05/99. E/C.12/1999/5, ICESCR General Comment 12. (General Comments), para 15. See also Brad, above n. 14.

right to food has not been the subject of extensive investigation on the part of the international community. Were such an investigation conducted, many States would find themselves breaching fundamental norms of human rights law. In a recent study conducted by Dr Boulesbaa, after having reviewed a whole host of international instruments and case law, the author regards a failure or deliberate omission in providing for the right to food as akin to the violation of the provisions of the United Nations Convention against Torture and Other Cruel, Inhuman or Degrading Treatment or Punishment.[73]

Article 12 provides for the right to the highest attainable standard of physical and mental health. The steps required for the realisation of these rights include formulating adequate provisions for the reduction of the stillbirth rate and of infant mortality, for the healthy development of children,[74] the improvement of industrial and environmental hygiene for everyone,[75] preventative measures and treatment of epidemic, endemic and other diseases,[76] and making available the required medical care to everyone.[77]

The right to health has been the object of General Comment by the Committee on the International Covenant on Economic, Social and Cultural Rights.[78] The Committee's views are extremely pertinent when it notes:

> Health is a fundamental human right indispensable for the exercise of other human rights. Every human being is entitled to the enjoyment of the highest attainable standard of health conducive to living a life in dignity. The realisation of the right to health may be pursued through numerous, complementary approaches, such as the formulation of health policies, or the implementation of health programmes developed by the World Health Organisation (WHO), or the adoption of specific legal instruments. Moreover, the right to health includes certain components which are legally enforceable.[79]

Elaborating on Article 12(1) which provides a definition of the right to health the committee observes:

> The right to health is not to be understood as a right to be healthy. The right to health contains both freedoms and entitlements. The freedoms include the right to control one's health and body, including sexual and reproductive freedom, and the right to be free from interference, such as the right to be free from torture, non-consensual medical treatment and experimentation. By contrast, the entitlements

---

[73] A. Boulesbaa, *The UN Convention on Torture and Prospects for Enforcement* (The Hague: Martinus Nijhoff Publishers) 1999, pp. 9–15. Provisions of the Convention discussed below Chapter 15.
[74] Article 12(a).
[75] Article 12(b).
[76] Article 12(c).
[77] Article 12(d).
[78] ICESCR General Comment 14, *The Right to Highest Attainable Standard of Health* (Article 12) General Comment No. 14 (11/08/00) (E/C.12/200/4).
[79] Ibid. para 1.

include the right to a system of health protection which provides equality of opportunity for people to enjoy the highest attainable level of health.[80]

In its General Comment the Committee emphasises the availability and accessibility of health care for all individuals, a provision which should also be sensitive to medical ethics and distinct cultures.[81] The Committee then considers specialist topics relating to the health care of groups such as women, children, the disabled, the elderly and indigenous peoples.[82]

Education rights

Article 13 provides for the right of everyone to education. This is an Article which, in the words of the Committee, 'is the most wide-ranging and comprehensive article on the right to education in international human rights law'.[83] Article 13, in reinforcing the value of education in the advancement of human rights, forms part of a substantial jurisprudence which international and regional organisations have accumulated on this subject. In addition to the UDHR, there are specific provisions in the International Convention on the Elimination of All Forms of Racial Discrimination,[84] the Convention on the Elimination of All forms of Discrimination against Women,[85] the Convention against Torture and Other Cruel, Inhuman or Degrading Treatment or Punishment,[86] the Convention on the Rights of the Child[87] and the International Convention on the Protection of the Rights of All Migrant Workers and Members of their Families.[88] In 1945 the United Nations Educational, Scientific and Cultural Organisation (UNESCO), a specialised agency of the United Nations, was established with the purpose of contributing 'to peace and security by collaborating among the nations through

---

[80] Ibid. para 8.

[81] Ibid. para 12.

[82] Ibid. para 21–27; also see P. Graham, 'The Child's Right to Health' in M. Freeman and P. Veerman, (eds), *Ideologies of Children's Rights* (Dordrecht: Martinus Nijhoff Publishers) 1992, pp. 203–211.

[83] ICESCR General Comment 13, *The Right to Education* (Article 13) General Comment No. 13 (8/12/99) (E/C.12/1999/10) para. 2.

[84] Adopted 21 December 1965. Entered into force, 4 January 1969. 660 U.N.T.S. 195, 5 I.L.M. (1966) 352.

[85] Adopted at New York, 18 December 1979. Entered into force 3 September 1981. UN GA Res. 34/180(XXXIV), GA. Res. 34/180, 34 GAOR, Supp. (No. 46) 194, UN Doc. A/34/46, at 193 (1979), 2 U.K.T.S. (1989); 19 I.L.M. (1980) 33.

[86] Adopted and opened for signature, ratification and accession on 10 December 1984 by GA Res. 39/46, 39 UN GAOR, Supp. No. 51, UN Doc. A/39/51, at 197 (1984). Entry into force 26 June 1987. 1465 U.N.T.S. 85; 23 I.L.M. (1984) 1027.

[87] See Articles 19(1), 23(2) and 28.

[88] Adopted 18 December 1990. GA Res. 45/158 reprinted 30 I.L.M. (1991) 517. See Articles 30 and 43.

education, science and culture'.[89] The Convention against Discrimination in Education was adopted by the General Conference of UNESCO in December, 1960.[90] The value of education in human development and the contribution which it makes in the advancement of human rights is a feature given credence by the Council of Europe,[91] the European Union,[92] the Organisation of American States[93] and the Organisation of African Unity.[94] More recently, on 23 December 1994 the United Nations General Assembly adopted a resolution proclaiming 'the United Nations Decade for Human Rights Education (1 January 1995–31 Decemer 2004)'. In this resolution, the Assembly welcomed a plan of action for the decade with a request to the

---

[89] See the UNESCO Constitution 1945 Article 1(1).

[90] Adopted 14 December 1960. Entered into force 22 May 1962. 429 U.N.T.S. 93.

[91] See e.g. Resolution (78)41 on the Teaching of Human Rights (adopted by the Committee of Ministers, November 1978); The Declaration Regarding Intolerance – A Threat to Democracy (adopted by the Committee of Ministers, April 1982); Declaration on the Freedom of Expression and Information (adopted by the Committee of Ministers, 29 April 1982); Recommendation R(81) 17 to Member States on Adult Education Policy (adopted by the Committee of Ministers, November 1981); Recommendation R(79)16 to Member States on the Promotion of Human Rights Research in the Member States of the Council of Europe (adopted by the Committee of Ministers, September 1979); Recommendation R(83)13 to Member States on the Role of Secondary School in Preparing Young People for Life (adopted by the Committee of Ministers, September 1983).

[92] See e.g. the Resolution of the European Parliament on Freedom of Education in the European Community (March 1984); Resolution of the Council and the Representatives of the Governments of the Member States meeting within the Council on the fight against racism and xenophobia (May 1990); Decision of the European Parliament and of the Council adopting the third phase of the 'Youth for Europe' programme (818/95/EC, March 1995); Resolution of the Council and of the Representatives of Member States' Governments meeting within the Council on the response of educational systems to the problems of racism and xenophobia (95/C/312/01, October 1995).

[93] See the 'Pact of San José', Charter of the O.A.S. (as amended). Signed 1948. Entered into force 13 December 1951. For integrated text 33 ILM (1994) 981. See the American Declaration of the Rights and Duties of Man O.A.S. Res. XXX, adopted by the Ninth International Conference of American States (1948), reprinted in Basic Documents Pertaining to Human Rights in the Inter-American System, OEA/Ser.L.V/II.82 doc.6 rev.1, 17 (1992) (Article 12); American Convention on Human Rights (ACHR) Signed November 1969. Entered into force 18 July 1978. O.A.S.T.S. Off. Rec. OEA/Ser.L/V/11.23, doc.21, rev. (1979). I.L.M. (1970) 673 (Article 26); the Additional Protocol to American Convention in the Area of Economic, Social and Cultural Rights 'Protocol of San Salvador' O.A.S. Treaty Series No. 69 (1988), entered into force November 16 1999, reprinted in Basic Documents Pertaining to Human Rights in the Inter-American System, OEA/Ser.L.V/II.82 doc.6 rev.1 at 67 (1992) (Article 13) and the Inter-American Convention on the Prevention, Punishment and Eradication of Violence against Women, signed on 9 June 1994. Entered into force 3 March 1995. Reprinted in 33 I.L.M (1994) 1534 (Article 8). For further consideration of these treaties see below Chapter 8.

[94] See the African Charter on Human and Peoples' Rights (AFCHPR) (Article 25 O.A.U. Doc. CAB/LEG/67/3 Rev. 5. Reprinted 21 I.L.M. (1982) 58; 7 *HRLJ* (1986) 403. The African Charter on the Rights and Welfare of the Child adopted July 1990, entered into force 29 October 1999, O.A.U Doc. CAB/LEG/TSG/Rev.1. Article 11(2) and the Resolution on Human and Peoples' Education (CM/Res. 1420 (LVI), adopted by the Council of Ministers of the Organisation of African Unity, 56th Ordinary Session, Dakar, Senegal, 22–28 June 1992).

High Commission on Human Rights to ensure facilitation of the implementation of this plan.[95]

As the most comprehensive statement on the subject, Article 13 represents a synthesis of the right to education. In accordance with the provisions for the thorough realisation of this right, States parties are committed to ensuring free, compulsory primary education – and education in a range of forms including technical and vocational secondary education, higher education which is accessible to everyone on the basis of capacity and merit, and adequate provisions for adult education. The aim is a system of schooling operating at all levels. Article 13(3) provides autonomy to parents (or the legal guardians) to select private schooling for their children. The provisions of Article 13 are further reinforced by Article 14. According to Article 14 all States parties undertake to adopt a detailed plan of action for the implementation of compulsory free education for everyone within two years (from the time of the ratification and acceptance of the treaty) if it does not already have such a system in place.

Both Articles 13 and 14 have been the subject of General Comments.[96] In its General Comment No. 13, the Committee strongly supports the value of this right. It notes:

> Education is both a human right in itself and an indispensable means of realising other human rights. As an empowerment right, education is the primary vehicle by which economically and socially marginalised adults and children can lift themselves out of poverty and obtain the means to participate fully in their communities. Education has a vital role in empowering women, safeguarding children from exploitative and hazardous labour and sexual exploitation, promoting human rights and democracy, protecting the environment, and controlling population growth. Increasingly, education is recognised as one of the best financial investments States can make. But the importance of education is not just practical: a well-educated, enlightened and active mind, able to wander freely and widely, is one of the joys and rewards of human existence.[97]

The Committee then goes on to expand on the various facets of this right. In relation to the provisions of this right, the Committee observes that, although variable, education should be made available to all without discrimination. Educational institutions should be physically and economically accessible to everyone. The remainder of General Comment No. 13 is dedicated to

---

[95] For a detailed consideration see United Nations, *The Right to Human Rights Education: The United Nations Decade for Human Rights Education (1995–2004)* (New York and Geneva: United Nations) 1999.

[96] ICESCR General Comment 11, *Plans of Action for Primary Education* (Article 14) General Comment No. 11 (10/05/99) (E/C.12/1999/4); CESCR General Comment 13, *The Right to Education* (Article 13) General Comment No. 13 (8/12/99) (E/C.12/1999/10).

[97] ICESCR General Comment 13, *The Right to Education* (Article 13) General Comment No. 13 (8/12/99) (E/C.12/1999/10) para 1.

expanding further on various levels of education (for example secondary, technical, higher education). General Comment No. 11, on Plans of Action for Primary Education, represents a very useful guide to Article 14's provisions.[98] The Committee in this comment analyses the meaning of various terms and elaborates on the obligations undertaken by the States parties under this Article. According to the Committee, the term 'compulsory' is meant

> to highlight the fact that neither parents, nor guardians, nor the State are entitled to treat as optional the decision as to whether the child should have access to primary education. Similarly, the prohibition of gender discrimination in access to education, required also by articles 2 and 3 of the Covenant, is further underlined by this requirement. It should be emphasised, however, that the education offered must be adequate in quality, relevant to the child and must promote the realisation of the child's other rights.[99]

It also goes on to note that 'free of charge' is meant to ensure that education is free, without any costs falling on the child, the parents or the guardians.[100] The Committee elaborates upon the State's obligations by noting that the States are required to formulate a plan of action covering all the requisite action necessary for the comprehensive realisation of this right within two years of their becoming a party to the treaty.[101] Furthermore a State cannot avoid obligations on the grounds of lack of necessary resources. In situations where a State party lacks the necessary resources, there is also an obligation on the international community to provide support.[102]

Cultural rights

The rubric of the treaty accords great prominence to culture; the treaty is entitled the International Covenant on Social, Economic and Cultural Rights. However, in reality it is not until Article 15 that cultural life is addressed directly. According to Article 15, States parties recognise the right of everyone to take part in cultural life. There is also a recognition on the part of States to allow the individual the benefit of scientific progress and its applications[103] and to allow him to benefit from 'the protection of the moral and material interests from any scientific, literary or artistic production of which he is author'.[104] Steps undertaken by States to realise this right include 'those

[98] ICESCR General Comment 11, *Plans of Action for Primary Education* (Article 14) General Comment No. 11 (10/05/99) (E/C.12/1999/4).
[99] Ibid. para 6.
[100] Ibid. para 7.
[101] Ibid. para 8.
[102] Ibid. para 9.
[103] Article 15(1)(b).
[104] Article 15(1)(c).

necessary for the conservation, the development and the diffusion of science and culture'.[105]

Culture represents a quintessential part of human existence; the absence of a cultural association makes it difficult to forge common identities and establish social values. While a number of references could be found to cultural rights within human rights treaties, international law has remained deficient in according recognition to cultural rights as collective group rights; the comments noted earlier in relation to minority rights are pertinent here.[106] For many States the fear is that in the name of culture, minority groups would campaign for autonomy, leading to secession and the break-up of existing State structures. In the context of the individualistic human rights law, it is thus no surprise that cultural rights within the Covenant fail to receive preeminence.

IMPLEMENTATION MACHINERY[107]

Apart from the difficulties in the substantive nature of the rights, the mechanisms to implement economic, social and cultural rights have not proved satisfactory. Under Articles 16–25 States parties are under an obligation to provide periodic reports. This reporting procedure is the only mechanism for the implementation of the Covenant.[108] In accordance with Article 16, the State parties are under an obligation to submit reports to ECOSOC via the Secretary-General of the United Nations[109] on the measures they have adopted to give effect to the rights in the Covenant.[110] The reports need to be informative of the progress made in achieving the observance of the rights within the treaty.[111] The United Nations Secretary-General is also required to

---

[105] Article 15(2).

[106] See above Chapter 4.

[107] See *The Limburg Principles on the Implementation of the International Covenant on Economic, Social and Cultural Rights*; P. Alston, 'The Committee on Economic, Social and Cultural Rights' in P. Alston (ed.), *The United Nations and Human Rights: A Critical Appraisal* (Oxford: Clarendon Press) 1992, pp. 473–507; M. O'Flaherty, *Human Rights and the UN: Practice before the Treaty Bodies* (London: Sweet and Maxwell) 1996, pp. 53–82; S. Leckie, 'The Committee on Economic, Social and Cultural Rights: Catalyst for Change in a System Needing Reform' in P. Alston and J. Crawford (eds), *The Future of UN Human Rights Treaty Monitoring* (Cambridge: Cambridge University Press) 2000, pp. 129–144.

[108] Proposals for having a complaints procedure have thus far been unsuccessful. See P. Alston, *Establishing a right to petition under the Covenant on Economic, Social and Cultural Rights*, Collected Courses of the Academy of European Law: The Protection of Human Rights in Europe (Florence: European University Institute), vol. IV, book 2 (1993) p. 115.

[109] Article 16(2)(a).

[110] Article 16(1).

[111] Ibid.

transmit copies of these reports to the relevant specialised agencies.[112] According to Article 17, States may indicate factors and difficulties affecting the degree of fulfilment of the obligations. Initial reports must be submitted within two years of the Covenant coming into operation for the State, thereafter every five years.[113]

The Covenant as such does not provide for the creation of a treaty body, and the responsibility for the implementation has been assigned to ECOSOC.[114] In order to perform its task of implementing the Covenant, ECOSOC set up a fifteen-member sessional working group initially consisting of governmental representatives and subsequently of experts appointed by governments. The working group was not able to perform effectively, its track record being termed as 'disappointing'.[115] Among the many criticisms made of the working group, the foremost ones were that its examination of reports was inadequate, superficial and politicised. It was claimed that the working group's conclusions lacked substance and failed to inform the States of the extent to which they were complying with their obligations in terms of the Covenant. Furthermore, the attendance of members was irregular and members were not fully involved in the proceedings of the working-group sessions.[116] Specialised agencies were also critical of the working group, claiming that they were not adequately involved in the work of the group; the reports failed to provide a summary or to provide any recommendations on substantive issues.[117]

---

[112] Article 16(2)(b). The implementation mechanism instituted by ECOSOC and Article 18 of the ICESCR allow specialised agencies to arrange with ECOSOC to submit reports which 'may include particulars of decisions and recommendations on such implementation adopted by [the specialised agencies] competent organs'. In pursuance of this mandate, the ILO has submitted a series of papers and reports see e.g. 26th report of the ILO (11/11/99), Implementation of ICESCR E/C.12/1999/SA/1; Report of the ILO (1805/98 E/1998/17) (Report of the UN Agencies/Organs); Background paper submitted by the ILO (21/04/98; E/C.12/1998/8); 18th Session, Day of General Discussion: Globalisation and its Impact on the Enjoyment of Economic and Social Rights (11 May 1998).

[113] ECOSOC Res. 1988/4, UN Doc. E/C/12/1989/4. When the Covenant came into effect, States parties were required to present initial reports every three years dealing with only a third of the rights recognised in Part III of the Covenant (i.e. Articles 6–9, 10–12 and 13–15). A cycle of reporting for the States parties thus took 9 years, denying any updated analysis of a States' obligation of all the rights contained in the Covenant. However the change to submission of the complete initial State report after 2 years of the enforcement of the Covenant and thereafter every 5 years was brought into operation in order to enhance the effectiveness of the reporting procedures.

[114] See O'Flaherty, above n. 107, at p. 62.

[115] P. Alston, 'Out of the Abyss: The Challenges Confronting the New UN Committee on Economic, Social and Cultural Rights' 9 *HRQ* (1987) 332 at p. 333.

[116] See the International Commission of Jurists, *Commentary: Implementation of the International Covenant on Economic, Social and Cultural Rights – ECOSOC Working Group*, ICJ Review No. 27, December 1981, 28; Westerveen, 'Towards a System for Supervising States' Compliance with the Right to Food' in P. Alston and K. Tomasevski (eds), *The Right to Food* (Boston: Martinus Nijhoff Publishers) 1990, p. 119.

[117] See P. Alston, 'The Committee on Economic, Social and Cultural Rights' in Alston (ed.), above n. 107, 473, at pp. 480–481.

As a response to these criticisms, in 1985, ECOSOC established the Committee on Economic, Social and Cultural Rights.[118] The Committee held its first session in March 1987,[119] and has to date held twenty-seven sessions.[120] The Committee consists of eighteen members elected by ECOSOC from a list submitted by State parties for a term of four years. Elections of half of the Committee take place every two years, with members being entitled to be re-elected. Only States parties are entitled to nominate persons for election to the Committee.[121] The members of the Committee serve in their personal capacity and (unlike the members of the sessional working group) not as State representatives.[122] The representation of the Committee is based on the criterion of equitable geographical distribution.

Aims and objectives of the state reporting system

In order to counter the deficiencies in the State reporting the Committee has elaborated on the aim of reporting, a task undertaken by the Committee in its first General Comment.[123] In its General Comment, the Committee considered

> that it would be incorrect to assume that reporting is essentially a procedural matter designed solely to satisfy each State party's formal obligation to report to the appropriate international monitoring body. On the contrary, in accordance with the letter and spirit of the Covenant the process of preparation and submission of reports by States can, and indeed should, serve to achieve a variety of objectives.[124]

The Committee articulated the following objectives:

- (particularly in relation to the initial reports) to ensure that a comprehensive review is undertaken with respect to national legislation, administrative rules and procedures, and practices in an effort to ensure the fullest possible conformity with the Covenant.
- to ensure that the State party monitors the actual situation with respect to each of the rights on a regular basis and is thus aware of the extent to which the various rights are, or are not, being enjoyed by all individuals within its territory or under its jurisdiction.
- to enable the Government to demonstrate that such principled policy making has in fact been undertaken.

---

[118] ECOSOC Resolution 1985/17 (1985).
[119] P. Alston and B. Simma, 'First Session of the UN Committee on Economic, Social and Cultural Rights' 81 *AJIL* (1987) 747.
[120] See the twenty-seventh session of the Committee, held during 12–30 May 2002.
[121] ESC Res. 1985/17, para c.
[122] ESC Res. 1985/17, para b.
[123] CESCR General Comment 1, *Reporting by States Parties* General Comment No. 1 (24/02/89).
[124] Ibid, para 1.

- to facilitate public scrutiny of government policies with respect to economic, social and cultural rights and to encourage the involvement of the various economic, social and cultural sectors of society in the formulation, implementation and review of the relevant policies.
- to provide a basis on which the State party itself, as well as the Committee, can effectively evaluate the extent to which progress has been made towards the realisation of the obligations contained in the Covenant. For this purpose, it may be useful for States to identify specific benchmarks or goals against which their performance in a given area can be assessed.
- to enable the State party itself to develop a better understanding of the problems and shortcomings encountered in efforts to realise progressively the full range of economic, social and cultural rights.
- to enable the Committee, and the States parties as a whole, to facilitate the exchange of information among States and to develop a better understanding of the common problems faced by States and to reach a fuller appreciation of the type of measures which might be taken to promote effective realisation of each of the rights contained in the Covenant.[125]

Procedure

The Committee meets twice annually for three-week sessions, its primary task being to examine State reports.[126] The meetings are held in Geneva during April–May and November–December of each year. In one session the Committee normally considers up to six reports. Once a report is submitted, the Committee makes a decision about the session in which consideration shall take place. After the submission of the report, it is likely to take 12–18 months for the report to be considered. The reports which the Committee has agreed should be reviewed are passed on to a five-member working group of the Committee. The working group holds closed meetings at the end of each session, making an initial consideration of the reports due for full consideration at the next session.

In its consideration, the working group draws up a list of issues with the information before it, utilising information acquired from various intergovernmental and non-governmental sources. The rationale behind this list is to

identify in advance the questions which might most usefully be discussed with the representative of the reporting States. The aim is to improve the efficiency of the system and to facilitate the task of States' representatives by providing advance notice of many of the principal issues which will arise in the examination of the reports.[127]

---

[125] Ibid. paras 2–9.
[126] The Committee has had a number of additional extraordinary sessions.
[127] UN Doc. E/1995/22, Chap. III, para 23.

State parties are required to respond in writing to these questions prior to the consideration of the report. The reports are reviewed in a public session with the consideration of a single State report normally spreading over two days. Reports are normally introduced by the State representative. The discussion by the Committee is based around the list of questions previously prepared by its working group and issues arising therefrom. During the session, the State representative is given the opportunity to respond to the questions on the list. After their consideration, the Committee members summarise their views and make suggestions and recommendations. The consideration normally lasts for around three meetings, each three hours long. Following consideration of a State's report, the Committee produces its Concluding Observations, a practice it has followed since its second session.[128] Concluding Observations are issued as a public document in which various aspects of the report are analysed and these usually consist of positive features in the report, the identification of difficulties and the concerns of the Committee. Suggestions and Recommendations are also made within the Concluding Observations. The Committee may include requests for the provision of additional information which had been made to the State representatives during the consideration of the report. Concluding Observations are issued at the end of each session and are included in the annual report of the Committee to ECOSOC. Since 1993 NGOs have been allowed by the Committee to make oral presentations at the start of each session. This provides the NGOs with an opportunity to comment on the reports which are due to be considered by the Committee. The NGOs have often produced alternative reports which represent a different and more accurate picture. It is not surprising that the Committee has benefited enormously from these alternative reports and other sources of information emanating from the NGOs. According to Leckie, the merits of alternative reports include:

> [drawing] attention to inaccuracies and distortions in a governmental report; they can provide new information and offer ideas for more appropriate policies and legis-lation. The preparation of alternative reports can also act as a catalyst in the emer-gence of new coalition and movements between previously unconnected groups.[129]

In many respects the Committee's nature and role appears similar to those of the Human Rights Committee. However, unlike the Human Rights Committee, this Committee is not responsible to States parties but to ECOSOC, a main organ of the United Nations.[130] The primary difficulty in the implementation of the Covenant stems from the parties' reluctance to

---

[128] Craven, above n. 1, at p. 87.

[129] S. Leckie, 'The Committee on Economic, Social and Cultural Rights: Catalyst for Change in a System Needing Reform' in P. Alston and J. Crawford (eds), above n. 107, at p. 134.

[130] For consideration of ECOSOC see Chapter 2 above.

comply with their reporting obligations. Reports submitted by the States are often significantly overdue and have the characteristic of being excessively brief, incomplete or outdated. The other difficulties of implementation include the vast scope and indeed the vagueness that characterises the rights themselves.[131] An associated issue is the ambivalence of many States towards economic, social and cultural rights of this nature. The relative lack of jurisprudence and case law from international and domestic tribunals has not been helpful,[132] and there has been the added problem of obtaining adequate and relevant information from States parties. There has been reluctance in developing the jurisprudence related to economic, social and cultural rights in comparison to civil and political rights; the breadth of the Convention rights makes the Committee's analysis more difficult. Many of the economic and social rights concepts have not been considered in any depth at the domestic or international level. The development of such a jurisprudence has been one of the primary preoccupations of the Committee, a practice which, as we shall consider, is conducted in a variety of ways.

INNOVATIVE PROCEDURES

To make its work more effective the Committee has adopted a number of innovative procedures. The original provision in Article 17 required States parties to submit an initial report within one year of the Covenant's entering into force. However the Committee, adopting a realist approach, devised rules to extend the date of submission to two years and thereafter every five years. Furthermore, in order to deal with inordinate delays with the submission of reports, in its sixth session the Committee appealed to the Council to allow it to list those States which had failed to submit their initial reports despite the passage of ten years. This, in effect, was an attempt to embarrass or blacklist certain States. In addition, the Committee also adopted procedures of streamlining for consideration notwithstanding substantial delay on the part of some states in submitting initial or periodic reports.[133] Although it is anticipated that the State representative would be present at the time of consideration of the reports, the inability of States to send representatives has been rejected by the Committee as an invalid ground to delay consideration of the State reports.

NGOs play an important role in the promotion and protection of human rights. Considering their potential value in promoting economic, social and cultural rights, it is disappointing to note that no specific provision had been made

---

[131] P. Alston and B. Simma, 'Second Session of the UN Committee on Economic, Social and Cultural Rights' 82 *AJIL* (1988) 603 at p. 606.

[132] See Alston, above n. 115, at 351.

[133] UN Doc. E/1992/23, 99 para 245.

for the NGOs to make a contribution to the Covenant's reporting and supervisory procedures.[134] The Committee, however, has made attempts to overcome this limitation. In recognition of the usefulness of the NGOs' work – especially the production of alternative reports – the Committee has invited 'all concerned bodies and individuals to submit relevant and appropriate documentation to it'.[135] The Committee has also established procedures to invite the governments to provide additional information and to engage in dialogue on particular issues. 1994 saw the Committee seeking additional information from Panama, the Dominican Republic and the Philippines on the subject of forced eviction.[136] Similarly, additional information has been sought from a number of other States, including the UK.

As from its third session, on the invitation of ECOSOC, the Committee has begun to prepare General Comments on various articles and provisions of the Covenant. We have already noted the reasoning and rationale behind formulating General Comments for the ICCPR.[137] The Committee's decision to adopt General Comments has been based on the same rationale. The primary objective of the General Comments, according to the Committee, is to assist State parties to fulfil their obligations;[138] in particular:

> to make the experience gained so far through the examination of these reports available for the benefit of all States parties in order to assist and promote their further implementation of the Covenant; to draw the attention of the States parties to insufficiencies disclosed by a large number of reports; to suggest improvements in the reporting procedures and to stimulate activities of the States parties, the international organisations and specialised agencies concerned in achieving progressively and effectively the full realisation of the rights recognised in the Covenant.[139]

A number of significant Comments have been adopted by the Committee. These include, General Comment No. 1 (1989) on Reporting by States Parties,[140] General Comment No. 2 (1990) on International Technical Assistance Measures (Article 22),[141] General Comment No. 3 (1990) on the Nature of States Parties' Obligations (Article 2, paragraph 1 of the Covenant),[142] General Comment No. 7 (1997) on the Right to Adequate Housing: Forced Evictions (Article 11, paragraph 1, of the Covenant),[143]

---

[134] See Alston, above n. 115, at p. 367.
[135] E/1992/23 at 100 para 386 (Report of the Committee, sixth session).
[136] Robertson and Merrills, above n. 12, at p. 281.
[137] See above Chapter 4.
[138] E/1998/14 Committee's Second Session, 63 para 367.
[139] E/1993/22 Report of the Committee's Seventh Session UN Doc. E/1993/22. 19, para 49.
[140] Third Session 1989, UN Doc. E/1989/22.
[141] Fourth Session, 1991, UN Doc. E/1990/23 (adopted February 1990).
[142] Fifth Session, 1990, UN Doc. E/1991/23 (adopted December 1990).
[143] Sixteenth Session, 1997 UN Doc. E/1998/22, annex I, adopted November, 1997.

General Comment No. 5 (1994) on Persons with Disabilities;[144] and General Comment No. 6 (1995) on the Economic, Social and Cultural Rights of Older Persons.[145]

In addition, the Committee has set aside one day in every session for a general discussion on a specific issue or issues, which allows specialised agencies and NGOs to contribute more effectively to the work of the Committee.[146] This reserved day is usually the Monday of the Committee's final week.[147] According to the Committee the function of this day is twofold: 'the day assists the Committee in developing in greater depth its understanding of the issues; and it enables the Committee to encourage inputs into its work from all interested parties'.[148] The 'specific issue' agenda item for the proceedings of this day was established as early as the third session when the Committee considered the issue of the right to food. In the fourth session the day of general discussion was devoted to the right of housing. In 1994 the Committee discussed the role of social security measures, with particular reference to transition to a market economy and human rights education. In 1998 the one day of general discussion was dedicated to globalisation and its impact on the enjoyment of economic and social rights.[149] The exercise has been productive. Commenting on some of these positive aspects Alston notes:

> The discussions have provided an invaluable means by which the Committee has been able to open up its dialogue and has given it the opportunity to invite a much wider range of inputs from individuals or groups that feel they have something to offer to the Committee. The general discussion also enables the Committee to discuss broader, sometimes more theoretical issues which are directly relevant to its role of examining State reports and especially to the task of elaborating General Comments.[150]

One of the most positive achievements of the Committee's work has been its close association and coordination with UN agencies and the Special Rapporteurs. The Committee was addressed in 1993 by the Special Rapporteur on the Issue of Impunity, from the Sub-Commission on Prevention of Discrimination and Protection of Minorities, and in 1994 by a delegate from the World Health Organisation (WHO) in the context of human rights and HIV/AIDS. In 2001 the Committee was addressed by the Deputy High Commissioner, Dr Bertrand Ramcharan. The Committee has also initiated the

---

[144] Eleventh Session 1994 UN Doc. E/C.12/1994/13 (1994) adopted November, 1994.

[145] Thirteenth Session 1995 UN Doc. E/C.12/1995/16/ Rev. 1 (1995) adopted 24 November, 1995.

[146] Alston and Simma, above n. 131 at p. 608.

[147] See O'Flaherty, above n. 107, at p. 79.

[148] UN Doc. E/1995/22, para 44.

[149] See Background paper submitted by ILO 21/04/98; E/C.12/1998/8.

[150] P. Alston, 'The Committee on Economic, Social and Cultural Rights' in P. Alston (ed.), above n. 107, pp. 493–494.

concept of fact-finding missions for its members to visit States and assess for themselves situations involving violations of economic and social rights. In further investigations of the issue of forced eviction in 1995, the Committee sent a fact-finding mission (which thus far remains the only mission) to Panama which reported back to the Committee during the same year.[151]

CONCLUSIONS

The analysis of economic, social and cultural rights contained in the ICESCR reveals many limitations and shortcomings. A particularly disturbing aspect has been the debate about the nature of many of the rights contained in the Covenant; whether they create immediate binding obligations or a mere programme of action. Through a consideration of the provisions of the ICESCR, the Committee's Observations and General Comments, this chapter has established that economic, social and cultural rights retain the same legal value and binding effect as civil and political rights. At the same time, on a pragmatic level, it has to be conceded that the implementation of economic and social rights thus far has not been straightforward. The implementation mechanisms themselves have had to be revised and we are still awaiting the adoption of an individuals' complaints procedure.

The Committee, since its establishment in 1985, has done a commendable job in monitoring the Covenant. Of particular value have been its views emerging from its analysis of State reports and General Comments. In its consideration of State reports, the Committee has taken a broad approach which encompasses human rights obligations incurred through the acceptance of ICESCR. Thus:

> in addition to asking questions on the status of ethnic minorities, natural children, women and men or discrimination on the basis of religion, alternative political philosophies and class bias [the Committee] has directed itself to the situation of those in particular regional areas, aliens (including the stateless, migrant workers and refugees) unmarried couples, and parents, people with AIDS, or physical and mental disabilities, homosexuals, the poor and the elderly.[152]

In particular the Committee has stressed the need for comprehensive reviews of national legislation and administrative rules regarding the rights contained in the Covenant and of adequate scrutiny of governmental policies. The Committee has also highlighted the need for greater coordination in policy making which would provide a basis for effective evaluation of the progress made in achieving the rights. Through its work the Committee has facilitated a better understanding of the problems and issues involved in the implementation of the

---

[151] See United Nations, *The Committee on Economic, Social and Cultural Rights*, Fact Sheet No. 16, Rev.1, (Geneva: United Nations) 1991.
[152] Craven, above n. 1, at pp. 169–170. (footnotes omitted).

Covenant as well as promoting the exchange of information among States. Changes have also been introduced which have improved the work of the Committee. As noted earlier, the system of presenting initial reports at three-year intervals, each dealing with one-third of the rights, was changed by the Committee to a single comprehensive report to be submitted every five years.

With regard to the role and position of NGOs in the present context, NGOs have been the principal advocates of the vindication of individual human rights. Although, over the years, their contribution (again largely through positive actions undertaken by the Committee) has become more effective in the implementation of the ICESCR, there continues to be some reluctance on the part of many NGOs to engage themselves in promoting economic, social and cultural rights. A predisposition in favour of civil and political rights is perhaps to be attributed to the origins and issues addressed by many of the NGOs. NGOs based in the developing world, in particular, have often treated violations of economic and social rights as ancillary to the breaches of civil and political rights.[153] This bias in the work of the NGOs needs to be removed.

The focus of the present chapter has been on ICESCR. Subsequent chapters of this book establish that economic, social and cultural rights have blended into civil and political rights, a feature particularly evident from a survey of the jurisprudence of the regional treaties of Europe, the Americas and Africa. The regional human rights systems have also accorded a degree of prominence to economic and social rights through the adoption of such treaties as the European Social Charter,[154] the additional Protocol to European Social Charter (1996)[155] and the Additional Protocol to the American Convention on Human Rights in the Area of Economic, Social and Cultural Rights (1988).[156]

---

[153] According to Alston 'for a variety of historical, ideological, pragmatic and other reasons, there remains a considerable reluctance on the part of many, if not most, human rights NGOs to become involved in this field. This is particularly the case with respect to those NGOs based in the West that do not have significant constituencies in the Third World. In the case of limited mandate organisations such as Amnesty International or Index on Censorship, the justification is the desire to maintain a narrow and precise focus. Other NGOs that purport to be concerned with either "the rights contained in the Universal Declaration" or "internationally recognised human rights" face a much more difficult task to justify their neglect of economic, social, and cultural rights. The situation in Central America today, for example, cannot be adequately or productively analysed without taking full account of both sides of the human rights equation. In this sense, the much vaunted interdependence of the two sets of rights is not simply a hollow UN slogan designed to conceal an ideological split, but is an accurate reflection of the realities of the situation'. Alston, above n. 115, at p. 372 (footnotes omitted).

[154] Adopted at Turin 18 October 1961. Entered into force, 26 February 1965. 529 U.N.T.S 89; ETS 35. See below Chapter 7.

[155] Adopted 3 May 1996. Entered into force, 3 July 1999. ETS No. 163. See below Chapter 7.

[156] Additional Protocol to the American Convention on Human Rights in the Area of Economic, Social and Cultural Rights, 'Protocol of San Salvador' O.A.S. Treaty Series No. 69 (1988), entered into force 16 November 1999; 28 I.L.M. (1989) 156. See below Chapter 8.

III

REGIONAL PROTECTION OF HUMAN RIGHTS

6

EUROPEAN
HUMAN RIGHTS – I[1]

INTRODUCTION

European human rights law is not the product of a single monolithic mechanism. Instead there are several institutions which have established mechanisms for protecting human rights.[2] The role of at least three organisations is worthy of consideration: the Council of Europe, the European Union (EU) and the Organisation for Security and Cooperation in Europe (OCSE). The Council of Europe, the oldest of these institutions, has also had the most significant role in promoting human rights at the European level. The European Union, which remains politically the most viable and influential body, has had only an indirect part to play in protecting human rights. However, increasingly

---

[1] See R. Clayton et al., *The Law of Human Rights* (Oxford: Clarendon Press) 2000; D.J. Harris, M. O'Boyle and C. Warbrick, *Law of the European Convention on Human Rights* (London: Butterworths) 1995; A. Mowbray and D.J. Harris, *Cases and Materials on the European Convention on Human Rights* (London: Butterworths) 2001; M.W. Janis, R.S. Kay and A.W. Bradley, *European Human Rights Law: Text and Materials*, 2nd edn (Oxford: Clarendon Press) 2000; R. Blackburn and J. Polakiewicz. (eds), *The European Convention on Human Rights: The Influence of ECHR on the Legal and Political Systems of Member States 1950–2000* (Oxford: Oxford University Press) 2001; Lord Lester and D. Pannick, *Human Rights: Law and Practice* (London: Butterworths) 1999; A. Loux and W. Finnie, *Human Rights and Scots Law: Comparative Perspectives on the Incorporation of the ECHR* (Oxford: Hart) 1999; L.J. Clements, N. Mole and A. Simmons, *European Human Rights: Taking a case under the Convention*, 2nd edn (London: Sweet and Maxwell) 1999; T. Barkhuysen, M.L. Van Emmerik and P.H.P.H.M.C. Van Kempen, *The Execution of Strasbourg and Geneva Human Rights Decisions in the National Legal Order* (The Hague: Martinus Nijhoff Publishers) 1999; P. van Dijk (ed.), *Theory and Practice of the European Convention on Human Rights*, 3rd edn (The Hague: Kluwer Law International) 1998.

[2] These institutions sometimes act in parallel, while at other times they overlap with one another.

human rights issues are being absorbed into the programmes of the rapidly expanding EU. Although having largely operated as an organisation aimed at promoting security and peace within Europe, the OSCE has taken a number of valuable human rights initiatives which are worthy of consideration.

Limitations of space make it impossible to study the work of each of the aforementioned organisations in great detail. Two chapters of this book are nevertheless dedicated to the study of European human rights law. The present chapter focuses on the position of the Council of Europe's European Convention on Human Rights (ECHR), an instrument which focuses largely on the provisions of civil and political rights. The next chapter, Chapter 7, considers the Council of Europe's European Social Charter (ESC). It then goes on to analyse the position and role of the EU and the OSCE in the protection of human rights.

THE COUNCIL OF EUROPE AND PROTECTION OF CIVIL AND POLITICAL RIGHTS

The Council of Europe is an intergovernmental organisation established in 1949 with the objective, *inter alia*, of strengthening democracy, human rights and the rule of law.[3] In its initial years, the membership of the Council of Europe was confined to the western democratic European countries. It excluded Spain and Portugal until the mid-1970s. However, with the collapse of communism, several members of central and eastern Europe have joined the Council. The current membership of the Council of Europe is forty-three, including all EU member States. The Council of Europe has produced various important regional human rights treaties, the most prominent one being the ECHR.[4] The ECHR was adopted in 1950 and came into operation in 1953; it currently provides protection to well over 800 million people. The institutions of the ECHR, the Court and the Committee of Ministers are based in Strasbourg, France.

During the Second World War (1939–1945) Europe had been the scene of the most serious human rights violations. At the end of the War, it had become a major objective of the allied powers to punish those who had been involved in crimes against humanity during the War and to uphold human rights in the region. A regional human rights treaty protecting the fundamental civil and political rights was meant to act as a bulwark against the recurrence of the worst forms of human rights violations. Those signing the treaty also aimed to encourage the extension of democracy in communist Europe and to suppress the spread of dictatorships and totalitarian ideologies in other parts of Europe.

---

[3] According to Article 3 of the Statute each member State 'must accept the principles of rule of law and the enjoyment by all persons within its jurisdiction of human rights and fundamental freedoms'. See Statute of the Council of Europe, adopted 5 May 1949. Entered into force August 1949. E.T.S. 1.
[4] Signed at Rome, 4 November 1950. Entered into force 3 September 1953. 213 U.N.T.S. 221; E.T.S. 5. The Convention has over years been amended through 12 additional protocols.

As we have already noted, the UDHR was adopted in December 1948 by the United Nations General Assembly.[5] A natural progression from the Declaration on Human Rights was the formulation of a binding treaty with measures of implementation. Although it was not until 1966 that the International Covenants were adopted, consensus was easier to attain among the western liberal States to draft a regional human rights treaty. The ECHR, despite being a regional convention, reflects the influence of and similarities with the principles contained in the Universal Declaration. The preamble of the ECHR, for example, refers to the Universal Declaration. Fundamental rights in the ECHR such as the prohibition of torture, the right to liberty and security and the right to a fair trial draw inspiration from similar provisions of the Declaration. However, there are also significant differences in the substantive provisions of the articles. Whereas the Universal Declaration considers civil, political, social, economic and cultural rights, the ECHR predominantly promotes and protects the civil and political rights.[6] This difference reflects the diversity of Constitutions adopted in Europe at the time – see for example the French Constitution of 1946, the Italian Constitution of 1948 and the German Basic Law of 1949.

The ECHR is divided into three sections. Section I provides a description and definition of the rights and fundamental freedoms provided in the treaty. Section II provides for the establishment of a court of human rights and explains the procedures, while Section III considers miscellaneous provisions such as reservations, denunciation, signature and ratification.[7] The substantive guarantees provided in the Convention are expanded by a number of additional Protocols.

The ECHR and its Protocols do not cover several important rights. The Convention, unlike the ICCPR, does not provide for the right to self-determination, which is recognised as one of the principal rights in international human rights instruments.[8] The coverage of the ECHR on minority or group rights is particularly thin.[9] There is also the failure to provide for economic, social and cultural rights. Despite these omissions in the protection of rights, over the past fifty years the rights contained in the

---

[5] See above Chapter 3.

[6] The Counterpart of the ECHR is the European Social Charter which is considered in Chapter 7.

[7] K. Starmer, *European Human Rights Law: The Human Rights Act 1998 and the European Convention on Human Rights* (London: Legal Action Group) 1999, lxxi.

[8] See below Chapter 12.

[9] The ECHR (or its Protocols) does not contain particular provisions protecting the rights of minorities. Some remedial action was taken by the Council of Europe to adopt a Framework Convention for the Protection of National Minorities; opened for signature 1 February 1995, entered into force 1 February 1998. E.T.S. 157; 34 I.L.M. (1995) 351. See G. Gilbert, 'The Council of Europe and Minority Rights' 18 *HRQ* (1996) 160. For consideration of these treaties see below Chapter 11.

Convention have been utilised to protect individual rights. The Convention had been treated as a living instrument and has been interpreted in keeping with the changing values and traditions of European society.[10] The ECHR, although a regional instrument, has also had an enormous impact upon the development of norms in general international law.[11]

Rights contained in the Convention

Article 2	Right to life
Article 3	Prohibition of torture
Article 4	Prohibition of slavery and forced labour
Article 5	Right to liberty and security
Article 6	Right to a fair trial
Article 7	No punishment without law
Article 8	Right to respect private and family life
Article 9	Freedom of thought, conscience and religion
Article 10	Freedom of expression
Article 11	Freedom of assembly and association
Article 12	Right to marry
Article 13	Right to an effective remedy
Article 14	Prohibition of discrimination
Article 15	Derogation in time of emergency
Article 16	Restrictions on political activities of aliens
Article 17	Prohibition of abuse of the rights
Article 18	Limitation on use of restrictions on rights

Protocol No. 1[12]

Article 1	Protection of property
Article 2	Right to education
Article 3	Free elections

Protocol No. 4[13]

Article 1	Prohibition of imprisonment for debt
Article 2	Freedom of movement
Article 3	Prohibition of expulsion of nationals
Article 4	Prohibition of collective expulsion

---

[10] See on issues of corporal punishment, *Tyrer* v. *United Kingdom*, Judgment of 25 April 1978, Series A, No. 26; homosexuality, *Dudgeon* v. *United Kingdom*, Judgment of 22 October 1981, Series A. No. 45.

[11] Thus e.g. Privy Council in *Pratt* v. *Attorney General of Jamaica* (PC (Jam)) Privy Council (Jamaica), 2 November 1993 [1994] AC 1 at 35 approved the European Court of Human Rights view expressed on the 'death-row' phenomenon.

[12] ETS No. 9, 213 U.N.T.S. 262. Entered into force May 18 1954.

[13] ETS 46. Entered into force May 2 1968.

Protocol No. 6

Article 1   Abolition of death penalty[14]

Protocol No. 7

Article 1   Expulsion of aliens[15]
Article 2   The right to review by a higher tribunal
Article 3   Compensation for miscarriage of justice
Article 4   *Ne bis in idem*
Article 5   Equality of rights and responsibilities between spouses during and after their marriage

Protocol No. 12

General prohibition of discrimination[16]

ANALYSIS OF SUBSTANTIVE RIGHTS

The right to life and the prohibition of torture, cruel, inhuman, degrading treatment or punishment[17]

As we have already considered, the right to life is peremptory, and the most fundamental of all human rights.[18] Within the Convention, the right to life is protected by Article 2, a right which is non-derogable even in times of war and public emergency.[19] The taking of life is prohibited save in the limited circumstances provided within the article, a subject which we shall consider shortly. In relation to the substance of the right to life, the State is under two kinds of obligations. First, there is a negative obligation not to take life and not to deprive an individual of his life save in limited circumstances which must be strictly in accordance with law. The second obligation is of a positive nature which entails taking effective steps to protect the life of the individual concerned. Positive obligations include protecting individuals from agents of the State such as the police and security forces as well as non-State actors

---

[14] ETS 114. Entered into force March 1 1985.
[15] ETS 117. Entered into force Nov. 1 1988.
[16] Adopted 26 June 2000. Opened for Signature 4 November 2000.
[17] See D.J. Harris, 'The Right to Life Under the European Convention on Human Rights' 1 *Maastricht Journal of European Comparative Law* (1994) 122; F. Ni Aolain, 'The Evolving Jurisprudence of the European Convention Concerning the Right to Life' 19(1) *NQHR* (2001) 21; see also N.S. Rodley, *The Treatment of Prisoners in International Law*, 2nd edn (Oxford: Clarendon Press) 1999.
[18] See above Chapter 4.
[19] Harris, O'Boyle and Warbrick, above n. 1, at p. 37. Derogations are permissible in circumstances provided by Article 15(2). Article 15(2) provides that derogations from the Article are permissible 'in respect of deaths resulting from lawful acts of war'.

including terrorist organisations and other private individuals. The duty to take reasonable measures to protect life includes a duty to put in place 'effective criminal law provisions to deter the commission of offences against the person backed up by law-enforcement machinery for the prevention, suppression and sanctioning of breaches of such provisions'.[20] It also means requiring the proper investigation of all suspicious deaths.[21]

While these two components are firmly established the remit of the obligation is not very clear. Thus while the positive obligation includes taking reasonable steps to enforce the law to protect the citizens, the State cannot be expected to protect individuals from every attack.[22] Similarly, the breadth of obligations which might affect the right to life is uncertain. For instance, a question mark remains over the issue of State liability with regard to poor housing, lack of food, lack of medical attention, environmental pollution, road worthiness and workplace safety. This issue was considered but left unanswered in a case in which the parents of a seriously disabled child claimed that their daughter had not been allowed free medical treatment.[23]

In the context of Article 2, the meaning of the term 'life' has been the subject of considerable debate, especially regarding the point at which life begins and ends. There is, for instance, substantial controversy regarding the rights of an unborn child.[24] In *Paton v. UK*,[25] the European Commission held that the abortion of a ten-week old foetus under British law to protect the physical and mental health of the mother was not in breach of Article 2. In *H v. Norway*,[26] the Commission took the view that the abortion of a fourteen-week old foetus

---

[20] *Osman v. United Kingdom*, Judgment of 28 October 1998, 1998-VIII RJD 3124, para 115. See also *Velasquez Rodriguez Case*, Judgment of July 29, 1988, Inter-Am.Ct.H.R. (Ser. C) No. 4 (1988), paras 170–172.

[21] *McCann and Others v. United Kingdom*, Judgment of 27 September 1995, Series A, No. 324; *Kaya v. Turkey*, Judgment of 19 February 1998, 1998-I RJD 297.

[22] *W v. United Kingdom*, App. No. 9348/81, 32 DR 190 (1983).

[23] On the facts of the case, the child had been provided adequate treatment *X v. Ireland*, App. No. 6839/74, 7 DR 78 (1976); in another case, which concerned the operation of a public vaccination scheme leading to the death of some young children, the Commission held the possibility of liability when a State undertakes involvement in a public vaccination scheme. On facts, the application was held inadmissible as 'appropriate steps' had been taken for safe administration of the scheme; *X v. United Kingdom*, App. No. 7154/75, 14 DR 31 (1978).

[24] *Open Door Counselling v. Ireland*, Judgment of 29 October 1992, Series A, No. 246, 142 NLJ (1696); also see *Brugggemann and Scheuten v. FRG*, App. No. 6959/75, 10 DR 100 (1977). L.A. Rehof, 'Article 3' in G. Alfredsson and A. Eide (eds), *The Universal Declaration of Human Rights: A Common Standard of Achievement* (The Hague: Martinus Nijhoff Publishers) 1999, 89–101 at p. 97; for a consideration at the international level see P. Alston, 'The Unborn Child and Abortion under the Draft Convention on the Rights of the Child' 12 *HRQ* (1990) 156. D. Shelton, 'Abortion and the Right to Life in the Inter-American System: The Case of "Baby Boy"' 2 *HRLJ* (1981) 309; also see below Chapter 14.

[25] *Paton v. United Kingdom*, App. No. 8416/79 19 DR 244 (1980).

[26] *H v. Norway*, App No. 17004/90 (1992) unreported.

was not contrary to Article 2 on the grounds that 'pregnancy, birth or care for the child may place the woman in a difficult situation of life'. The Commission considered the wide differences on the issue of abortion and allowed for a certain margin of appreciation. The decision is broader than *Paton* because abortion was later in time and the reasons given were social and did not relate to health or medical condition. From the cases mentioned above, the Commission appears to have taken the view that Article 2 is applicable only to persons who are already born.[27] In *H v. Norway*, however, the Commission did note that in certain circumstances Article 2 does offer protection to the unborn child, without indicating what those circumstances were. As it stands, currently the grounds for abortion are very wide and, in *Open Door Counselling* v. *Ireland*, the Human Rights Court itself left open the possibility of Article 2's placing restrictions on abortion.[28] Controversy arises in relation to the point when a person dies and the rights of individuals who are dying. Article 2 has also raised complexities in relation to euthanasia.[29]

The general exceptions to the Article are provided in Article 2(2). These are exhaustive and must be narrowly construed. Article 2(2)(a) provides for death occurring as a result of self-defence. *McCann and Others* v. *UK*[30] was the first case dealt with by the Court concerning Article 2.[31] In this case three members of the provisional IRA were shot dead by British soldiers in Gibraltar. It was suspected that these IRA activists had remote control devices for a bomb to be detonated in a public place. The resulting damage, it was feared, would cause serious loss of life. The Commission, by 11 to 6 votes, held that shooting was justified under Article 2(2). The Court, however, disagreed. According to the Court the exception covers, but is not limited to, intentional taking of life. The question was the extent to which the State's response was proportionate to perceived threats posed by IRA members. In all the circumstances of the case (including the planning and conduct of the operations by the British Security forces and the decision to let the IRA members enter Gibraltar from Spain) it held that the UK had sanctioned

---

[27] H. Fenwick, *Civil Liberties*, 2nd edn (London: Cavendish Publishing Ltd) 1998, p. 37.

[28] *Open Door Counselling* v. *Ireland*, Judgment of 29 October 1992, Series A, No. 246.

[29] In *Widner* v. *Switzerland*, the Commission held Article 2 does not require passive euthanasia (by which a person is allowed to die by not being given treatment) to be a crime, App. No. 120527/92 (1993) unreported. A similar situation would appear to prevail in other human rights systems. On the position of euthanasia in the Inter-American Human Rights System, see S. Davidson, 'The Civil and Political Rights Protected in the Inter-American Human Rights System' in D.J. Harris and S. Livingstone (eds), *The Inter-American System of Human Rights* (Oxford: Clarendon Press) 1998, 213–288 at p. 218.

[30] *McCann and Others* v. *United Kingdom*, Judgment of 27 September 1995, Series A, No. 324.

[31] Aolain, above n. 17, at pp. 28–31; see S. Joseph, 'Denouncement of the Death on the Rock: The Right to Life of Terrorists' 14 *NQHR* (1996) 5.

killing by its agents in circumstances giving rise to a breach of Article 2. The Court noted:

> In sum, having regard to the decision not to prevent the suspects from travelling into Gibraltar, to the failure of the authorities to make sufficient allowances for the possibility that their intelligence assessments might, in some respects at least, be erroneous, and to the automatic recourse to lethal force when the soldiers opened fire, the Court is not persuaded that the killing of the three terrorists constituted the use of force which was no more than absolutely necessary in defence of person from unlawful violence within the meaning of Article 2(2)(a) of the Convention.[32]

The case emphasises a strict proportionality test under Article 2(2). Therefore the use of deadly force to effect an arrest would never be justified except in circumstances where there was no uncertainty that the suspects would kill if allowed to escape. The other exceptions provided in Article 2(2) are quelling a riot[33] and to effect an arrest or prevent an escape.[34] It also needs to be emphasised that Article 2 does not prohibit capital punishment. In 1983 Protocol 6, which prohibits the death penalty, was adopted. The Protocol came into force in 1985 and is ratified by a majority of member States.

According to Article 3 'No one shall be subjected to torture or to inhuman or degrading treatment or punishment'.[35] The rights contained in Article 3 are of a non-derogable nature even in times of war and public emergencies.[36] The prohibition of torture and inhuman or degrading treatment or punishment is expressed in a very strong language and no exceptions as such are attached to it. In *Chahal* v. *UK*,[37] the European Court of Human Rights addressed this subject in clear and unambiguous language noting:

> The Convention prohibits in absolute terms torture or inhuman or degrading treatment or punishment, irrespective of the victim's conduct ... Article 3 makes no provision for exceptions and no derogation from it is permissible under Article 15 even in the event of a public emergency to the life of the nation.[38]

The concept of torture was originally envisaged in narrow terms, but has gradually been extended as society's tolerance of official brutality has changed. In addition, the abolition of the death penalty in most countries within Europe has reduced tolerance to State violence. The various cat-

---

[32] Para 213.
[33] *Stewart* v. *United Kingdom*, App. No. 10044/82, 39 DR 162 (1984).
[34] *Farrell* v. *United Kingdom*, App. No. 9013/30, 30 DR 96 (1982).
[35] The Article draws its inspiration from Article 5 of the Universal Declaration on Human Rights (1948) and the American Declaration of Human Rights (1948). It also has close associations with Article 7 of the ICCPR and Articles 5 of the ACHR (1969) and AFCHPR (1981).
[36] Harris, O'Boyle and Warbrick, above n. 1, at p. 55.
[37] *Chahal* v. *United Kingdom*, Judgment of 15 November 1996, 1996-V RJD 1831.
[38] Ibid. para 79.

egories of prohibition have different applications and the Article has been used in a variety of circumstances. In the case of *Ireland* v. *United Kingdom*,[39] the Court provided some useful guidelines regarding the provisions of Article 3. The Court, in formulating a narrow approach, took the view that 'torture' means deliberate inhuman treatment causing very serious and cruel suffering, whereas 'inhuman treatment or punishment', meant treatment or punishment that causes intense physical and mental suffering. In the Court's analysis, degrading treatment or punishment was treatment or punishment that arouses in a victim a feeling of fear or anguish and inferiority capable of humiliating and debasing the victim, possibly breaking his or her physical or moral resistance. The meaning and scope of the Article can be illustrated through the facts of the *Ireland* v. *UK* case. The case is particularly useful in distinguishing torture from inhuman and degrading treatment or punishment.[40]

In this case the Irish Government had brought proceedings against the UK alleging that persons taken into custody pursuant to the Civil Authorities (Special Powers) Act, Northern Ireland, 1922 were subjected to a treatment which in Convention terms amounted to torture, inhuman and degrading treatment contrary to Article 3. The Irish government also alleged that internment without trial amounted to a violation of the right to liberty and security of the person as provided in Article 5, and the right to fair trial accorded in Article 6 of the Convention. In addition there was a claim of a violation of Article 14 (that is, that the powers of detention and internment were exercised in a discriminatory manner). A particular source of concern were the methods of interrogation used by the British Security forces in Northern Ireland. They were engaged in the so-called 'interrogation in depth', that is the use of five techniques which included: 'wall-standing' long periods of standing in a stressed position; 'hooding', placing black hoods on the prisoners' heads; subjecting to noise; deprivation of sleep; and deprivation of food and drink.

The European Commission in its report delivered to the Committee of Ministers in February 1976 took the view that measures of detention without trial were not in violation of Article 5. According to the Commission, the measures undertaken by the British Government complied with the derogation entered under Article 15, which were not applied in a discriminatory manner. The Commission did not find violations of Article 14 but it did find that the use of the five techniques of interrogation constituted 'torture and

---

[39] *Ireland* v. *United Kingdom*, Judgment of 28 January 1978, Series A, No. 25.
[40] A.H. Robertson and J.G. Merrills, *Human Rights in the World: An Introduction to the Study of International Protection of Human Rights*, 4th edn (Manchester: Manchester University Press) 1996, at pp. 139–140.

inhuman treatment' contrary to Article 3.[41] The Commission's view, however, was not endorsed by the European Court of Human Rights. When the case, after being referred by the Irish Government was considered by the Court, the Court drew a distinction between the various facets of Article 3, that is, between 'torture' on the one hand and 'inhuman' and 'degrading' treatment on the other. Torture as defined by the Court meant 'deliberate' inhuman treatment causing very serious and cruel suffering. Applying this test, it held that the use of the 'five techniques' and physical assault did not amount to torture, although it constituted 'inhuman and degrading treatment'.[42] In concurrence with the Commission, the Court found that the measures of detention and internment without trial were covered by the Article 15 derogation made by the United Kingdom, and that their application was not in contravention of non-discriminatory provisions of Article 14.

While a treatment needs to reach a minimum threshold before being designated as inhuman, the crucial factor which distinguishes it from torture is the absence of a deliberate intent to cause suffering. Inhuman treatment could be the result of conditions or treatment in a place of detention[43], withholding of food, water and medical treatment, rapes and assault[44] preventative detention, failure to provide medical treatment,[45] extradition or deportation,[46] mental torture and solitary confinement. In assessing whether punishment is inhuman, subjective consideration needs to be given to various factors including the physical and mental suffering, the applicant's sex, age, health and sensibilities etc. Degrading treatment arises from an ordinary everyday meaning and would include gross humiliation through racial discrimination.[47] In order to constitute degrading punishment, the humiliation and debasement involved must attain a particular level depending on, *inter alia*, the circumstances of the

---

[41] According to the Commission 'the systematic application of techniques for the purpose of inducing a person to give information shows a clear resemblance to those methods of systematic torture which have been known over the ages ... [T]he Commission sees in them a modern system of torture falling in the same category as those systems which have been applied in previous times as a means of obtaining information and confession'. *Ireland* v. *United Kingdom*, Series B, No. 23–I Com Rep (1971), para 794.

[42] The restrictive views adopted by the Court in relation to the meaning of torture have been criticised heavily. See R.J. Spjut, 'Torture under the European Convention on Human Rights' 73 *AJIL* (1979) 267; AI News Release (AI Index02/04/78) 19 January.

[43] *Denmark, Norway, Sweden* v. *Greece*, 12 YB 1 (1969). Overcrowding and inadequate heating, toilets, sleeping arrangements, food, recreation.

[44] *Ireland* v. *United Kingdom*, Judgment of 28 January 1978, Series A, No. 25. *Cyprus* v. *Turkey*, App. No. 8007/77, 13 DR 85 (1978).

[45] *Guzzardi* v. *Italy*, Judgment of 6 November 1980, Series A. No. 39; *Hurtado* v. *Switzerland*, Judgment of 28 January 1994, Series A, No. 280-A.

[46] *Soering* v. *United Kingdom*, Judgment of 7 July 1989, Series A, No. 161; *Chahal* v. *United Kingdom*, Judgment of 15 November 1996, 1996-V RJD 1831

[47] *Abdulaziz, Cabales and Balkandali* v. *United Kingdom*, Judgment of 28 May 1985, Series A, No. 94.

case, such as the nature and context of the punishment itself and the manner and methods of its execution.[48]

Article 3 has been applied in a range of circumstances. Indeed, in many instances its provisions have been invoked to accord rights otherwise not contained in the Convention. While the Convention does not provide for a right not to be extradited, not to be deported, to a nationality, to political asylum or a right of aboard (for a non-national), the various facets of this Article have been used to assist applicants claiming some of these rights. Instances of violation of Article 3 may be deportation of a person who would be deprived of proper medical treatment,[49] or would be likely to suffer from cruel or degrading punishment or be separated from his family as a result of extradition.[50]

A striking example of the wide ambit of Article 3 to cover rights not expressly provided for in the Convention is illustrated through the *Soering case*. In *Soering* v. *UK*[51] the applicant, who was a West German national, murdered his girlfriends' parents, with the complicity of his girlfriend. These offences were committed in the US State of Virginia, where he and his girlfriend were students. After having committed these offences they fled to the United Kingdom. The United States Government, under the terms of the Extradition Treaty of 1972 between the United States and the United Kingdom, applied for the applicant and his girlfriend to be extradited to the United States. The girlfriend was extradited and, having pleaded guilty as an accessory to the murder, was sentenced to 90 years' imprisonment. In the case of the applicant, the United Kingdom, while agreeing to extradite him, had sought assurances that if convicted he would not be given the death penalty. The applicant however appealed to the Strasbourg institutions. The death penalty *per se* is not prohibited by the Convention and the UK by extraditing Mr Soering to the USA was not breaching any provisions of the Convention or general international law. The applicant's primary claim was based on the prospect of his suffering from inhuman or degrading treatment under Article 3 while waiting for his execution in the state of Virginia.

The European Court of Human Rights, in upholding Soering's claim, took the view that if he was extradited to Virginia there would be a real risk of his being placed on death row, which would constitute a violation of Article 3. The Court acknowledged that the imposition of death penalty *per se* is not in

---

[48] *Tyrer* v. *United Kingdom*, Judgment of 25 April 1978, Series A, No. 26; cf. *Campbell and Cosans* v. *United Kingdom*, Judgment of 25 February 1982, Series A, No. 48.

[49] *D* v. *United Kingdom*, Judgment of 2 May 1997, 1997-III RJD 777.

[50] See *Chahal* v. *United Kingdom*, Judgment of 15 November 1996, 1996-V RJD 1831.

[51] (1989) 11 EHRR 439. See C. Van Den Wyngaert, 'Applying the European Convention on Human Rights to Extradition: Opening Pandora's Box' 39 *ICLQ* (1990) 757; R.B. Lillich, 'The Soering Case' 85 *AJIL* (1991) 128.

breach of Article 3. However, Article 3 prohibition could be breached in conditions where the death penalty was imposed only after a 6–8 years' waiting period (the so called 'death row' phenomenon). That he was 18 when the offences were committed and there was psychiatric evidence of his mental instability were mitigating factors in favour of the applicant. Thus, in the words of the Court:

> having regard to the very long period of time spent on death row in such extreme conditions, with ever present and mounting anguish of awaiting execution of the death penalty, and to the personal circumstance of the applicant, especially his age and mental state at the time of the offence, the applicant's extradition to the United States would expose him to a real risk of treatment going beyond the threshold set by Article 3.[52]

As in the case of *Soering*, there must exist a real risk as opposed to a mere possibility of facing inhuman or degrading treatment. The Court in *Soering* attempted to narrow down the ambit of its decision with the proviso that such a ruling would be only made in view of 'the serious and irreparable nature of the alleged suffering risked'.[53] The narrow dicta has been followed in *Cruz Varas and others* v. *Sweden*[54] and *Vilvarajah and others* v. *UK*.[55]

The right to liberty and security

Article 5 of the Convention deals with the right to Liberty and to Security of the Person. This provision is designed to control the exercise of powers of arrest and detention, and is something which liberal constitutions have sought to achieve for several centuries.[56] It protects liberty as well as security of the person. Articles 5(2)–(5) set out the procedures for such protection. According to Article 5(1) no deprivation of liberty is acceptable save in accordance with a procedure prescribed by law.[57] In *Winterwerp* v.

---

[52] Ibid. p. 111. Soering, as a remarkable decision was followed in *Pratt* v. *Attorney General of Jamaica* (PC (Jam)) Privy Council (Jamaica), 2 November 1993, [1994] AC 1, where the Privy Council in approving the European Court's approach held 'in any case in which execution is to take place more than five years after sentence there will be strong grounds for believing that the delay is such as to constitute "inhuman or degrading punishment or treatment"'. As we have noted, the Human Rights Committee under the first Optional Protocol has held that death row, *per se* does not amount to cruel, inhuman or degrading treatment or punishment. (See *NG* v. *Canada* discussed in Chapter 4) *Chitat Ng* v. *Canada*, Communication No. 469/1991 (7 January 1994), UN Doc. CCPR/C/49/D/469/1991 (1994) para 8.4; also see *Barret and Sutcliffe* v. *Jamaica*, HRC Report GAOR, 47th Session, Supp. 40, p. 246 at p. 250.
[53] Judgment 7 July, Series A. No. 161 para 90.
[54] *Cruz Varas and others* v. *Sweden*, Judgment of 20 March 1991, Series A, No. 201.
[55] *Vilvarajah and others* v. *United Kingdom*, Judgment of 30 October 1991, Series A, No. 215.
[56] See e.g. the Magna Carta 1215 c. 29.
[57] Cf. the *lettres de cachet* under the Ancien Regime in France.

The Netherlands,[58] the Court held that this meant that procedures must be, first, in accordance with national and conventional law including 'general principles contained in the Convention' and, second, they must not be 'arbitrary'. Article 5 applies even where the detention period is very short.

According to Article 5(1)(a) detention after conviction must be in accordance with applicable municipal law and with the Convention. This provision means that there must be a court judgment that justifies it and that the procedure that is followed to effect the detention is lawful.[59] Article 5 does not require 'lawful conviction' but 'lawful detention'. The Conviction in para 5(1)(a) means, 'finding of guilt' and is taken to be a conviction by a trial court.

Article 5(1)(b) means arrest or detention for non-compliance with lawful orders of a court or such arrest or detention in order to secure fulfilment of any obligation prescribed by law.[60] According to Article 5(1)(c) lawful arrest or detention of a person is effected for the purpose of bringing him before the competent legal authority on reasonable suspicion of having committed an offence or where it is considered reasonably necessary to prevent him committing an offence or fleeing after having done so. In cases of detention after arrest but before conviction, it is imperative that the arrested person be brought promptly to trial and that the trial takes place in reasonable time. For an arrest to be lawful there must be reasonable suspicion on the part of the person conducting the arrest that the person being arrested has committed or is likely to commit an offence. At the same time an 'honest belief' alone without an objective basis justifying arrest and detention is insufficient.[61] Article 5(1)(d) deals with the detention of minors. The term 'minor' has an autonomous Convention meaning, although it is generally taken to mean a person below the age of 18. Detention must also be for a lawful purpose. Article 5(1)(e) aims to protect society from vagrants, alcoholics, drug addicts and persons carrying infectious diseases. They may be restrained as a matter of social control (or even for their own protection), rather than because they have committed a criminal offence. Article 5(1)(f) allows the arrest or detention of a person to prevent his unauthorised entry into a country or the arrest and detention of a person against whom action is being taken with a view to extradition and deportation. However, these individuals are given the right to have their detention or arrest reviewed in accordance with national laws.

The safeguards for the arrested persons are contained in Article 5(2). Reasons for arrest (in a language which the arrested person understands) need

---

[58] *Winterwerp v. the Netherlands*, Judgment of 24 October 1979, Series A, No. 33.

[59] Harris, O'Boyle and Warbrick, above n. 1, at p. 107.

[60] *Engel v. The Netherlands*, Judgment of 8 June 1976, Series A, No. 22, para. 69.

[61] *Fox, Campbell and Hartley v. United Kingdom*, Judgment of 30 August 1990, Series A, No. 182, para 32.

to be given promptly but not immediately.[62] Article 5(3) provides for the right to be brought promptly before judicial authorities. An arrested person is entitled to trial within a reasonable time or release pending trial.[63]

The right to a fair trial

The right to a fair trial deals with the most significant right of any criminal justice system. In the light of the significance of Article 6, which provides the right to fair trial, it is not surprising that more applications have been received relating to Article 6 than to any other provision of the Convention. The primary issue relates to the extent to which Strasbourg institutions should monitor national judicial systems to ensure the right to fair trial. There is also the question of the margin of appreciation in view of the substantial variations of criminal justice proceedings. Significant differences exist between common law and civil law systems reflecting adversarial and inquisitorial systems of justice. Within common law systems (that is, England and Ireland) criminal investigation is conducted entirely by the police.[64] In some civil law countries, the first investigation is conducted by the police, although after the identification of the suspect the case is handed over to an investigating judge who then decides whether a prosecution should be brought.[65]

From an analysis of the jurisprudence of the Convention, a number of significant principles have emerged relating to the right to fair trial. First, the scope of Article 6(1) extends not only to guarantees of fair trial but also to access to the Courts themselves.[66] Second, this access to the Court must be 'effective'.[67] Third, the right to a fair hearing, in criminal proceedings, includes a right to be present during hearings and there is equality of opportunity to present one's case in accordance with established principles of natural justice. A significant feature of natural justice is that justice must not only be done, it must also be seen to be done. In *Piersack* v. *Belgium*[68] it was held that a breach of Article 6(1) had taken place with the appointment of a presiding trial judge who had earlier been the head of the section of the public prosecutor's depart-

---

[62] Ibid. para 32 (1990); *Murray* v. *United Kingdom*, Judgment of 28 October 1994, Series A, No. 300-A. Given social mobility, especially under the provisions of the European Union, this provision is of importance and requires the State to make available translators where possible.

[63] *Brogan and others* v. *United Kingdom*, Judgment of 29 November 1988, Series A, No. 145-B.

[64] See J. Sprack, *Emmins on Criminal Procedure*, 8th edn (London: Blackstones Press) 2000.

[65] For the French Pre-trial System see J. Bell, 'The French Pre-trial System' in C. Walker and K. Starmer (eds), *Miscarriages of Justice: A Review of Justice in Error* (London: Blackstones Press) 1999, pp. 354–376. Cf. in Germany, there is no investigating Judge.

[66] *Golder* v. *United Kingdom*, Judgment of 21 February 1975, Series A, No. 18.

[67] *Airey* v. *Ireland*, Judgment of 9 October 1979, Series A, No. 32; P. Thornberry, 'Poverty, Litigation and Fundamental Rights–A European Perspective' 29 *ICLQ* (1980) 250.

[68] *Piersack* v. *Belgium*, Judgment of 1 October 1982, Series A, No. 53.

ment, and had investigated the applicant's case and instituted proceedings against him. Although there was no evidence that as a judge he had acted with bias, his position was still unacceptable and regarded as a violation of Article 6.

Fourth, in accordance with Article 6(2), there is a right to be presumed innocent until proven guilty. This presumption was breached in *Allenet de Ribemont v. France*,[69] when a senior politician (Minister of Interior) made comments at a press conference to the effect that the applicant was one of the instigators of the murder. The Court held that Article 6(2) applied and the provisions of the Article had been breached. Although not yet charged, the applicant had been arrested and the statement was akin to a declaration of guilt which, first, encouraged the public to believe that the applicant was guilty and, secondly, prejudiced the assessment of the facts by the court. The provisions here concern the actions of the State and do not, as such, affect the way in which allegations of criminal wrongdoing are reported in the media.

Fifth, regard must be had to Article 6(3) which provides further guarantees of rights in criminal cases. Sixth, the person charged with criminal offences must have 'adequate time and facilities for the preparation of his defence'. This provision pre-empts hasty trials. The term 'adequate facilities' means 'that the defendant had opportunity to organise his defence in an appropriate way and without restriction as to the possibility to put all relevant defence arguments before the trial court'. The provision also entails the person's right to be informed promptly, in a language which he understands and in detail, of the nature and cause of the action against him. He should also have adequate time and facilities to prepare his defence, to defend himself in person or through legal assistance of his own choosing; or if he has not sufficient means to pay for legal assistance, to be given it free when the interests of justice so require.

Seventh, the right to a fair hearing needs to analysed as a whole. In *Barbera Messegue and Jabardo v. Spain*,[70] a culmination of factors such as the accused being driven over 300 miles the night before trial, and unexpected changes in the constitution and brevity of the trial led the Court to find breach of Article 6(1).[71] Eighth, fair trial also includes the right to trial within a reasonable time; excessive delay in holding trial or being kept in detention would be a violation of that Article. The hearing should be in public and neither of the

---

[69] *Allenet de Ribemont v. France*, Judgment of 10 February 1995, Series A, No. 308.

[70] *Barbera Messegue and Jabardo v. Spain*, Judgment of 6 December 1988, Series A, No. 146.

[71] Cf. in *Standford v. United Kingdom*, Judgment of 25 January 1994, Series A, No. 182-A, para 24. It was disputed that the accused was not able effectively to participate in the proceedings because he had not been able to hear witnesses. However, when proceedings were looked into their entirety, including the fact that the accused had an experienced counsel and with whom he had been able to communicate and who had defended him well, it was held that the accused had had a fair trial.

parties should be placed at a disadvantage.[72] There should also be fairness in the provisions of evidence (for example, the exclusion of illegally obtained evidence, the exclusion of hearsay evidence, to allow the defence's access to evidence, the freedom from self-incrimination).[73] The Article also provides for a right to be able to cross-examine, to have a reasoned judgment, and in criminal cases a right to be legally represented and have access to legal aid.

Privacy, family life, home and correspondence

Article 8 protects an interesting set of rights. According to Article 8(1), everyone has the right to respect for his private and family life, his home and his correspondence. The jurisprudence of the Convention confirms that 'private life', 'family life', 'home' and 'correspondence' are distinct though often overlapping interests. 'Private life' covers a wide range of issues, for example identity, moral and physical integrity, personal relationships and sexual relations.[74] In *Dudgeon v. UK*, a homosexual relationship between adult men was regarded as a 'most intimate aspect' of 'private life'.[75] In the category of personal and physical identity we can include cases concerning transsexuals, or those concerning changes of names, appearances and birth certificates. 'Private life', however, has been accorded a wide meaning. The collection and usage of information, census details, photographs, medical data, fingerprinting and telephone tapping are all potential intrusions into private life.

According to the provisions of this Article, 'home' has a broad meaning and has sometimes been taken to cover residence and business premises. Once the existence of a 'home' is established then the applicant is entitled to certain rights, for example the right to access and occupation, not to be expelled or evicted. Interests in the 'home' include the right to a peaceful enjoyment of residence, freedom or relief from noise, pollution etc.[76] In *Lopes Ostra v. Spain*[77] the applicant was successful in claiming that failure by the State to act to prevent or to protect him from serious pollution (fumes from waste disposal plant dealing with waste from a tannery) constituted a failure to respect his home and private life. A failure to provide information about the risks inherent in

---

[72] *Borgers v. Belgium*, Judgment of 30 October 1991, Series A, No. 214-B.

[73] *Funke and others v. France*, Judgment of 25 February 1993, Series A, No. 256-A; *Saunders v. United Kingdom*, Judgment of 17 December 1996, 1996-VI RJD 2044.

[74] See I. Karstan, 'Atypical Families and the Human Rights Act: The Rights of Unmarried Fathers, Same Sex Couples and Transsexuals' 3 *EHRLR* (1999) 195.

[75] *Dudgeon v. United Kingdom*, Judgment of 22 October 1981, Series A, No. 45.

[76] See *Rees v. United Kingdom*, Judgment of 17 October 1986, Series A, No. 106, paras 42–46; cf. *B v. France*, Judgment of 25 March 1992, Series A, No. 232-C, paras 49–62.

[77] *Lopes Ostra v. Spain*, Judgment of 9 December 1994, Series A, No. 303-C. See R. Desgagné, 'Integrating Environmental Values into the European Convention on Human Rights' 89 *AJIL* (1995) 263.

residing at a hazardous and unsafe place would result in breaching the provisions of Article 8. In *Guerra* v. *Italy*,[78] a group of individuals from an Italian village successfully brought a claim for violation of Article 8. They complained of local government's maladministration in failing to provide essential information about the risks contained in a nearby chemicals factory. The chemicals factory was high risk and had a history of accidents. Although on a previous occasion an explosion in the factory had led to the hospitalisation of 150 people with arsenic poisoning, none of the applicants in the present case had suffered a direct injury. The Court held that there was a violation of the Article, adjudicating that once the authorities became aware of the essential information and the risks and dangers involved in running the factory, they had delayed informing the applicants, thereby depriving them of the opportunity to assess the risks they and their families ran by continuing to live in the vicinity of the factory.[79]

'Correspondence' could be of a sensitive nature which needs to be protected (lawyer–client, lawyer–prisoner correspondence).[80] In *Malone* v. *UK*,[81] Mr Malone, an antique dealer had been tried and acquitted of charges of dishonesty. In 1978 he brought proceedings against the police alleging that since 1971 he had been under police surveillance, which included having his telephone tapped and his telephone calls metered. Mr Malone also claimed that his correspondence had been intercepted and tampered with and sought a declaration from the English High Court. He argued, *inter alia*, that the interception, monitoring or recording of conversations during his telephone calls without his consent was unlawful, and violated Article 8 of the Convention. His claim in the English High Court was dismissed. He then went to the European Court of Human Rights, which upheld his claim that there had been a violation of Article 8. According to the Court:

> In view of the attendant obscurity and uncertainty as to the state of the law in this essential respect, the Court cannot but reach a similar conclusion to that of the Commission. In the opinion of the Court, the law of England and Wales does not indicate with reasonable clarity the scope and manner of exercise of the relevant discretion conferred on the public authorities. To that extent, the minimum degree

---

[78] *Guerra and others* v. *Italy*, Judgment of 19 February 1998, (1998) 26 EHRR 357.

[79] See *McGinley and Egan* v. *United Kingdom*, Judgment of 9 June 1998, 1998-III RJD 1334; *L.C.B* v. *United Kingdom*, Judgment of 9 June 1998, 1998-III RJD 1390. (1998) 26 EHRR 212. For a survey of literature see D. Hart, 'Environmental Rights' in R. English and P. Havers (eds), *An Introduction to Human Rights and the Common Law* (Oxford: Hart Publishers) 2000, pp. 159–183; R. Churchill, 'Environmental Rights in Existing Human Rights Treaties' in A. Boyle and M Anderson (eds), *Human Rights Approaches to Environmental Protection* (Oxford: Clarendon Press) 1996, pp. 89–108.

[80] See *Silver and others* v. *United Kingdom*, Judgment of 25 March 1983, Series A, No. 61, paras 91, 93–95; *Campbell* v. *United Kingdom*, Judgment of 25 March 1992, Series A, No. 223.

[81] *Malone* v. *United Kingdom*, Judgment of 2 August 1984, Series A, No. 82; see N. Taylor and C.P. Walker, 'Bugs in the System', 1(2) *Journal of Civil Liberties* (1996) 105.

of legal protection to which citizens are entitled under the rule of law in a democratic society is lacking.

The Article places wide and far-reaching obligations on States parties in
safeguarding respect for family life. The obligations are of a positive nature,
an important illustration of which is provided by the case of *X and Y v. The
Netherlands*.[82] In this case, there had been a sexual assault on a 16-year-old
mentally handicapped girl by an adult male of sound mind. It had not been
possible to bring a criminal charge against the accused because of a procedural
gap in Dutch law. In the absence of criminal prosecution, the Dutch government had pointed to the possibility of civil remedies available to the girl. The
European Court acknowledged the margin of appreciation which the State
had and the difficulties which resulted as a consequence of actions by a private individual as opposed to public bodies. However, according to the Court,
civil remedies were inadequate and the absence of effective criminal sanctions in these circumstances constituted a breach by the Dutch government of
the obligation to respect the girl's right to private life. Thus, according to the
Court, positive obligations under Article 8 included ensuring the existence
of civil remedies as well as criminal law provisions against sexual attacks.

Family life has also been given an extensive meaning. In *Marckx v.
Belgium*[83] it was held that Belgium had a positive obligation to make legislative provisions which safeguarded an illegitimate child's integration into the
family, a failure of which led to the violation of Articles 8 and 14. Violations
under Article 14 took place because of discrimination between legitimate and
illegitimate children. Violation of Article 8 occurred as the discriminatory
treatment was inconsistent with Belgium's duty to respect the mother's right
to family life.

The Convention does not provide and protect the right to enter and stay in
a member State. However, if the deportation of a family member makes it
impossible to maintain the family, then the concerned State is under an
obligation not to exclude that particular member. In *Berrehab v. The
Netherlands*,[84] the applicant was a Moroccan national whose right to stay in
the Netherlands was dependent on remaining married to a Dutch national. It
was held that a violation of Article 8 had taken place when, after his divorce,
his residence permit was not renewed. The violation had taken place because
his removal from the Netherlands would make it impossible for him to maintain family ties with his daughter. In *Moustaquim v. Belgium*,[85] a deportation

---

[82] *X and Y v. The Netherlands*, Judgment of 26 March 1985, Series A, No. 91. See G. Van
Bueren, 'Protecting Children's Rights in Europe–A Test Case Strategy' 1 *EHRLR* (1996) 171.
[83] *Marckx v. Belgium*, Judgment of 13 June 1979, Series A, No. 31.
[84] *Berrehab v. The Netherlands*, Judgment of 21 June 1988, Series A, No. 138.
[85] *Moustaquim v. Belgium*, Judgment of 18 February 1991, Series A, No. 193.

order served on a young Moroccan national (second-generation immigrant in Belgium) violated Article 8(1). The applicant had been brought to Belgium as an infant and spent his childhood in his new country alongside seven of his brothers and sisters. He had strong families ties in Belgium and those ties could be enjoyed only while he remained in Belgium. This wide interpretation has led to changes in the immigration laws of several signatory States.

Freedoms of religion, expression, assembly and association

Article 9 provides for freedom of thought, conscience and religion. As we analyse in a subsequent chapter, this is a difficult right to provide and protect within general international law.[86] In so far as the Convention is concerned, the phrases 'thought, conscience and religion' as used in the Article were initially difficult to define. In *X and Church of Scientology* v. *Sweden*[87] the European Commission was faced with the question as to whether advertisement by the Church was to be attributed a commercial or religious purpose. After deciding that this advertisement was for commercial purposes, and therefore not a manifestation of religion protected by article, the Commission did not find it necessary to discuss whether scientology is a religion. As a substantive right the Commission and Court have insisted that freedom of religion occupies the position of a fundamental right. At the same time it has been difficult to balance this right when in conflict with other human rights such as the right to freedom of expression[88] or the right to private and family life.

Article 10 contains the very important right to the freedom of expression. Article 10(1) provides that:

> Everyone has the right to freedom of expression. This right shall include freedom to hold opinions and to receive and impart information and ideas without inter-ference by public authority and regardless of frontiers.

However, the right is not unlimited and the State has a wide margin of appreciation to restrict expression, as illustrated in *Handyside* v. *UK*.[89] In *Handyside*, the applicant had published a book called *The Little Red Schoolbook*, intended for school children aged 12 years and above. The book was meant to be for reference on issues such as education, learning, teachers and pupils, and contained a section on sex with subheadings such as pornography, contraceptives, and some other sexually intimate exercises. The applicant was convicted of having committed offences contrary to the Obscene

---

[86] See below Chapter 10.

[87] *X and Church of Scientology* v. *Sweden*. App. No. 7805/77, 16 DR 68 (1979), at 72.

[88] *Otto-Preminger Institute* v. *Austria*, Judgment of 20 September 1994, Series A, No. 295-A, paras 47, 49.

[89] *Handyside* v. *United Kingdom*, Judgment of 7 December 1976, Series A, No. 24.

Publications Act 1964. When the case came up before the European Court of Human Rights, the Court took into account the variety of views that prevailed among the countries of the Council of Europe and, in particular, the importance of allowing domestic institutions the powers to decide in accordance with their moral and ethical values. Having regard to this margin of appreciation, the Court decided that there had been no violation of Article 10.[90]

Despite the existence of a margin of appreciation, it is not in every case that the Strasbourg institutions have allowed the domestic authorities to determine the rights and freedoms of individuals. In the *Sunday Times* v. *UK* cases,[91] the applicants claimed that a court order prohibiting the publication of an article concerning 'thalidomide children' (that is, children who were born deformed by reason of their mothers having taken thalidomide as a tranquilliser during pregnancy) constituted a violation of their right as guaranteed by Article 10 of the Convention. The order had been made on the ground that the relevant article might prejudice the proceedings which were pending before the English Courts. The European Court of Human Rights held that the United Kingdom had violated the provisions of the Convention and ordered payment of a significant amount to the applicants for their costs.

Article 11 provides for freedom of assembly and association as related freedoms. Peaceful assembly includes public meetings, demonstrations, marches, picketing and processions. Assembly needs to be peaceful, although any incidental breaches of peace would not render the assembly unlawful. The requirement of notification and permission is not normally regarded as interference, but bans, because of the seriousness of the interference, require justification under Article 11(2). The interference under Article 11(2) must be 'in accordance with the law'. Freedom of association means that individuals are not to be compelled to become members of particular associations and there should be no discrimination against individuals who join specific organisations. Under the Convention, individuals have the freedom to form trade unions, and the State remains under an obligation to allow the establishment of trade unions. The State cannot make membership of a particular trade union compulsory. Breaches of the Convention law would be conducted through restrictive policies, or using public powers of interference.

---

[90] The same approach characterised the Court's position in *Muller and others* v. *Switzerland*, Judgment of 24 May 1988, Series A, No. 133 (which concerned an artistic work) and *Otto-Preminger Institute* v. *Austria*, Judgment of 20 September 1994, Series A., No. 295-A (which related to the display of a film).

[91] *Sunday Times* v. *United Kingdom*, Judgment of 26 April 1979, Series A, No. 30; *Sunday Times* v. *United Kingdom* (No. 2), Judgment of 26 November 1991, Series A, No. 217. (1979) 2 *EHRR* 245.

Non-discrimination issues under the Convention

Article 14 provides for the universally recognised norm of non-discrimination.[92] Unlike Article 26 of the ICCPR, however, Article 14 has been restricted to protecting persons against discrimination only in respect of rights contained within the Convention. In the sense of not being an independent article, it is called a 'parasitic article'. These limitations of Article 14 have now been redressed by the adoption of Protocol 12, which extends beyond the rights provided in the Convention to 'any right set forth by law'.[93] Protocol 12 removes the precondition that the rights affected must be contained within the Convention or one of the Protocols ratified by the State party. Article 14 protects against discrimination, instead of promoting equality, although it would appear that different treatment of people in similar circumstances may be justified under Article 14.[94]

INSTITUTIONAL MECHANISMS AND IMPLEMENTATION MACHINERY

At the time of the enforcement of the ECHR, the institutional bodies comprised the European Commission of Human Rights, the European Court of Human Rights and the Committee of Ministers. On 1 November 1998, when Protocol 11 came into operation, the Commission was abolished and the functions of the Commission were merged into those of a permanent and full-time Court. The decision-making powers of the Committee of Ministers were also abolished by the eleventh Protocol and the role of the Committee is now limited to supervising the executions of judgments.[95] The new Court of Human Rights performs the functions, both of the previously existent Commission and its own function, thereby deciding upon both issues of admissibility and merits of the cases. The Court sits in Committees of 3 Judges, Chambers of 7 Judges and a Grand Chamber of 17 Judges. In a particular case, the judge of the respondent State will sit *ex officio* as part of the Chamber or the Grand Chamber. If the judge is unable to sit, the Court will choose someone from that State to sit in the capacity of judge.[96] The ECHR also makes provisions for the

---

[92] See Harris, O'Boyle and Warbrick, above n. 1, at pp. 462–487; J.A. Goldston, 'Race Discrimination in Europe: Problems and Prospects' 4 *EHRLR* (1999) 462.

[93] Article 1, Protocol 12 provides as follows: 'The enjoyment of any right set forth by law shall be secured without discrimination on any ground such as sex, race, colour, language, religion, political or other opinion, national or social origin, association with a national minority, property, birth or other status'.

[94] *Rasmussen v. Denmark*, Judgment of 28 November 1984, Series A, No. 87.

[95] ECHR Article 46(2). For a useful comparison with the Inter-American human rights system see D. Harris, 'Regional Protection of Human Rights: The Inter-American Achievement' D. Harris and S. Livingstone (eds), above n. 29, at pp. 1–29.

[96] Article 27(2).

possibilities of third-party intervention by a State or another interested party with the request, or with leave, of the president of the Chamber.[97]

COMPLAINTS PROCEDURE UNDER PROTOCOL 11

Preliminary procedures

The appropriate language for initiating proceedings is French or English. The President of the Court, however, has a discretion to allow parties to use any language in the preliminary stage of a case. Individual petitioners can lodge complaints of their own accord since lawyers are not required for proceedings before the Court. The Rules of the Court also make provision for legal aid for individual applicants. The funding is based on the financial assistance provided by the Council of Europe. Requests for legal aid should be made to the Court and decisions are based on the test of whether a particular individual would be eligible to obtain legal aid in his or her State. The financial assistance provided is not extensive but does allow for essential expenses including travel and living expenses in pursuit of a claim before the Court.[98]

Complaints procedure

The complaints procedure under the amended Convention is as follows.[99] The application should be addressed to the Registrar of the European Court of Human Rights, with whom all subsequent correspondence should be conducted. Once an application is registered with the secretariat, a Judge Rapporteur is assigned by a Chamber. The Judge Rapporteur makes a request for factual or other additional information and prepares a report on admissibility. The Judge Rapporteur may refer the case to the committee of three judges, proposing dismissal. Alternatively, if he considers that the application raises a significant issue, he may then refer it directly to the Chamber. After a consideration of the application, the committee of three judges may by a unanimous vote declare the application inadmissible or strike it off the list. A unanimous decision of inadmissibility means the end of the case as no appeals

---

[97] ECHR Article 36 and Rule 61. *Amicus curiae* had previously been submitted in a number of occasions, e.g. *Chahal v. United Kingdom*, Judgment of 15 November 1996, 1996-V RJD 1831; *Chahal v. UK* (1997) 23 *EHRR* 413.

[98] K. Boyle, 'Europe: The Council of Europe, the OSCE, and the European Union' in H. Hannum (ed.), *Guide to International Human Rights Practice*, 3rd edn (New York: Transnational Publishers) 1999, 135–161 at p. 146.

[99] These changes were introduced through Protocol 11 (in effect 1 November 1998). Protocol 11 to the European Convention for the Protection of Human Rights and Fundamental Freedoms, adopted 11 May 1994. Entered into force 1 November 1998. E.T.S. 35; 33 I.L.M. (1994) 960; 15 *HRLJ* (1984) 86.

can be made against the committee's decision.[100] The unsuccessful applicant would then be sent a short note informing him of the decision of the committee. However, if no such decision is taken then the application is to be referred to a Chamber which has the task of deciding upon the admissibility as well as the merits of the case.[101] The government is informed and invited to present its observations on admissibility, which may lead to a friendly settlement. The government normally has six weeks to make comments or observations and to answer any pertinent questions. The latter may involve issues surrounding, for example, the exhaustion of domestic remedies etc. The applicant is forwarded copies of the government's responses. A report is formulated which forms the basis of subsequent action. The applicant and the government may also make oral submissions before the chamber at the admissibility stage. The chamber, whose deliberations are in private, then formulates (and communicates) its views on admissibility. It needs to be noted that all inter-State cases are to be decided by a Chamber.[102]

Post-admissibility procedures

Once an application is declared admissible there are two possible courses of action which can be pursued simultaneously – attempts to reach a friendly settlement and decision on the merits of the case. As under the previous procedure, once an application has been declared admissible, attempts are to be made to reach a friendly settlement.[103] On the instructions of the Chamber, the Registrar of the Court contacts the parties to see if there are possibilities of a friendly settlement. With this objective in mind, separate or joint meetings could be organised. In the meantime, the Chamber continues to examine the merits of the case. It may invite the parties to furnish additional information and evidence. The Chamber may ask for additional evidence or written observations. It can also hold additional hearings of the case in order to decide upon its merits. Prior to giving a judgment, the Chamber may in certain circumstances relinquish its jurisdiction to the Grand Chamber. Such a relinquishment of jurisdiction takes place where a case raises serious questions regarding the interpretation of the Convention or where resolution of a question before the Chamber might have a result inconsistent with a previous judgment.[104] However, relinquishment is not possible if one party to the case objects.

The judgment by the Chamber becomes final in three circumstances: First, where the Parties declare non-intention in referring the case to the Grand

---

[100] ECHR Article 28.
[101] ECHR Article 29(1).
[102] ECHR Article 29(2).
[103] ECHR Articles 38 and 39.
[104] ECHR Article 30.

Chamber,[105] secondly, where three months have elapsed since the Chamber has given its judgment,[106] and finally where a referral request has been turned down by a panel of Judges.[107] Within three months of the decision any party may, in 'exceptional cases', request a referral to the Grand Chamber. The application is to be heard by a panel of five Judges and accepted if 'the case raises a serious question affecting the interpretation or application of the Convention or a serious issue of general importance'.[108] The judgments of the Grand Chamber are final.[109]

INTER-STATE APPLICATIONS

The ECHR does not have a State reporting procedure (similar in nature to international human rights treaty based bodies)[110] but has inter-State and individual complaints procedures for redress of grievances. The inter-State procedure allows a contracting State party to refer alleged breaches by another State party of the rights contained in the Convention (or the Protocols) to the Court.[111] In inter-State cases the only applicable admissibility requirements are *ratione materiae, ratione personae, ratione loci, ratione temporis*, exhaustion of domestic remedies and the six months rule.[112] There is no limitation of the rule that 'substantially the same matter has already been examined'[113]and 'contains no new relevant information'.[114] Nor is there the application of the rule of 'manifestly ill-founded'[115] or 'abusive' or 'politically motivated' or 'abuse of the right of petition'.[116]

There is no requirement of nationality or whether particular interests are at stake.[117] Unlike the ICCPR, there is not the requirement of making an additional declaration for the system to be operative; the right to complain

---

[105] ECHR Article 44(2)(a).
[106] ECHR Article 44(2)(b).
[107] ECHR Article 44(2)(c).
[108] ECHR Article 43(2).
[109] ECHR Article 44(1).
[110] See however ECHR Article 52 on reporting. Also see A.A.C. Trindade, 'Reporting in the Inter-American System of Human Rights Protection' in P. Alston and J. Crawford (eds), *The Future of UN Human Rights Treaty Monitoring* (Cambridge: Cambridge University Press) 2000, 333–346 at p. 334.
[111] ECHR Article 33.
[112] Harris, O'Boyle and Warbrick, above n. 1, at p. 604.
[113] Article 35(1) and (2).
[114] *Cyprus v. Turkey*, App. No. 8007/77, 13 DR 85 (1978), at 154–155 (1978); *Ireland v. United Kingdom*, Series B, No. 23–I Com Rep (1971), p. 670.
[115] *France, Norway, Denmark, Sweden, the Netherlands v. Turkey*, App. Nos. 9940–9944/82, 35 DR 143 at 160–162 (1983).
[116] *Cyprus v. Turkey*, App. No. 8007/77, 13 DR 85 at 154–155 (1978).
[117] *Austria v. Italy*, App. No 788/60, 4 YB 140 (1961).

flows directly from ratification of the Convention.[118] A State may refer any alleged breach of the Convention. On the other hand, as we consider shortly, the individual can only claim breaches of the 'rights' contained in the Convention.[119] It also appears to be the case that in inter-State cases the principle of reciprocity does not apply. Therefore a State would not be barred from complaining under an article because it has entered into a reservation to the provision or has not ratified the (allegedly broken) provision of a Protocol.[120]

It is equally irrelevant whether one state (or its government) has not been recognised by the other. Other differences from individual applications are that a State could challenge legislative measures in *abstracto*.[121] On the other hand, individuals must satisfy the victim requirement. In inter-State cases, applications are communicated automatically to the respondent government after the admissibility stage and there are separate proceedings on questions of admissibility and merits. Like other comparable treaty-based inter-State procedures, this procedure has not been used extensively, although there has been some jurisprudence. A number of reasons can be advanced for the lack of popularity of the inter-State procedures. It is often seen as politically motivated and tends to strain relations (or is a product of strained relations) among States. Furthermore, it is not perceived as the most efficient method of resolving a dispute.[122]

INDIVIDUAL COMPLAINTS

In contrast to the inter-State procedure, the individual complaints procedure has provided a significant amount of jurisprudence. As of 1 November 1998 when the Protocol 11 came into operation the individual complaints procedure has become automatic and a compulsory procedure for all States parties. According to Article 34:

> The Court may receive applications from any person, non-governmental organisation or group of individuals claiming to be the victim of a violation by one of the High Contracting Parties of the rights set forth in the Convention or the protocols thereto. The High Contracting Parties undertake not to hinder in any way the effective exercise of this right.

---

[118] Ibid.

[119] P.R. Ghandhi, *The Human Rights Committee and the Right of Individual Communication: Law and Practice* (Aldershot: Ashgate Publishing Ltd) 1998, p. 27.

[120] *France, Norway, Denmark, Sweden, the Netherlands v. Turkey*, No 9940–9944/82, 35 DR 143 at 168–169 (1983) where France was not barred from bringing a case against Turkey which concerned issues that were covered by the French reservation.

[121] Harris, O'Boyle and Warbrick, above n. 1, at p. 607.

[122] See e.g. *Ireland v. United Kingdom*, Judgment of 28 January 1978, Series A. No. 25. Case discussed below.

Complaints under Article 34 may be brought only by a person, a non-governmental organisation or group of individuals. This would include companies, minority shareholders, trusts, professional associations, trade unions, etc. Non-governmental organisations or groups of individuals are broad categories but they do not cover, for example, municipalities or local government organisation. In relation to individual complaints, over 90 per cent of the complaints are declared inadmissible and thus it is imperative to understand and comply with the admissibility requirements.

Ratione personae

Complaints may be brought by only a person, a non-governmental organisation or groups of individuals claiming to be victims of the violation of a Convention right.

Complaints against whom?

Complaints may be brought only against a State or State bodies. This would cover the activities of such public bodies as the courts, the security forces, or local or provincial governments.[123] A complaint could not be brought against the actions of private persons or private bodies, for example a newspaper. It is sometimes difficult to identify whether a particular body is a private organisation or a State body. Complex issues of State responsibility can arise in relation to the liability of such organisations as railway or broadcasting corporations. In these situations, factors such as autonomy, financial independence and control over recruitment may determine the extent to which the organisation is acting as a non-State actor.

Actions by private individuals or private bodies may give rise to State responsibility in circumstances where the State is required to secure particular rights, for example, the right to freedom of expression, to association, the right to form and join trade unions, the right to education and the prohibition of inhuman or degrading treatment. In *Costello-Roberts* v. *UK*,[124] the issue before the European Court of Human Rights was whether the State was responsible for corporal punishment in private schools, allegedly in breach of Article 3 and 8. In answering positively, the Court noted three points. First, the State has an obligation to secure for children their right to education under Article 2 of the 1st Protocol and that a school's disciplinary system fell within the ambit of the right to education. Secondly, in the UK, the right to education was ensured and guaranteed equally to pupils studying both at private

---

[123] Harris, O'Boyle and Warbrick, above n. 1, at p. 630.
[124] *Costello-Roberts* v. *United Kingdom*, Judgment of 25 March 1993, Series A, No. 247-C.

and public schools, and thirdly, the State cannot be absolved of the obligations imposed on it by delegating them to private organisations or individuals.[125]

An even more radical case of imposition of State liability for actions of private individuals is exemplified through *A v. UK*.[126] In this case a stepfather who had engaged in activities of beating his 9 year-old step-son was charged with occasioning actual bodily harm in the English Courts. The stepfather had successfully relied on the defence of reasonable chastisement and was acquitted. The European Court of Human Rights, however, rejected this defence and held that a breach of Article 3 had been committed. The Court held the United Kingdom Government responsible because children and other vulnerable people were entitled to protection even from private individuals and the State was under an obligation to provide this protection.

It is also important to recognise that individuals cannot bring actions against those States that have not ratified the Convention or the relevant Protocol. Furthermore, the defendant must be a State party, and not an international agency, an international or regional organisation such as the United Nations or the European Union.[127] In inter-State cases both States parties must have ratified the Convention.

Requirement of victim

The petitioner under Article 34 must claim to be directly affected or there must be a significant risk of being directly affected.[128] It is insufficient to establish a mere possibility, suspicion, or conjuncture of future risk.[129] In *Open Door Counselling and Dublin Well Women v. Ireland*,[130] which concerned a Supreme Court injunction against the provision of information by applicant companies concerning abortion facilities outside Ireland, the Commission and the Court were of the view that women of child-bearing age could be regarded as victims as they belonged to a class of women which may be directly affected. In *Times Newspaper Ltd v. UK*,[131] the view was taken

---

[125] Ibid. para 30.

[126] Judgment of 23 September 1998, 1998-VI RJD 2692; *The Times*, 1 October 1998. In the context of the Human Rights Act see J. Cooper, 'Horizonatility: The Application of Human Rights Standards in Private Disputes' in R. English and P. Havers (eds), above n. 79, at pp. 53–69; M. Hunt, 'The "Horizontal Effect" of the Human Rights Act' *Public Law* (1998) 423.

[127] *CFDT v. European Communities*, App. No. 8030/77, 13 DR 231 (1978).

[128] See *Klass and others v. Germany*, Judgment of 6 September 1978, Series A, No. 28, where it was held by the Court that all users and potential users of telecommunication and postal services were 'directly affected' by legislation providing for secret surveillance. They thereby satisfied the victim requirement, despite the fact that they had not been subjected to such surveillance. Also consider *Norris v. Ireland*, Judgment of 26 October 1988, Series A, No. 142.

[129] *Tauria v. France*, App. No. 28204/95, DR 83-A 113 (1995).

[130] *Open Door Counselling v. Ireland*, Judgment of 29 October 1992, Series A, No. 246.

[131] *Times Newspaper v. United Kingdom*, App. No. 14631/89, 65 DR 307(1990).

that a newspaper publisher could be regarded as a victim of Article 10 violation (even without proceedings having been taken against him) where the law was not clear enough to be able to predict the risk of prosecution. In subsequent case law, the requirement of victim has been more narrowly construed.

There also remains the possibility of being classed as an indirect victim, for example the widow of a person killed by terrorists and close family members or friends. This is applicable particularly in relation to serious violations of rights, for example those under Articles 2 or 3. The meaning of indirect victim has been taken to mean those who are prejudiced by violations or have personal interests, for examples parents, guardians, etc.

Competence *ratione materiae*

Under the competence *ratione materiae*, the individual cannot complain of breach of rights not contained in the Convention. Regardless of the extreme desirability in a particular instance or regardless of the serious nature of human rights violations, individuals cannot rely on those rights which are not contained in the Convention or the Protocols. Thus, for example, individuals are not able to complain of the violation of such rights as those to pensions, social security, nationality or political asylum. However, as noted above, the Convention rights have sometimes been given a very broad meaning and applied in a range of circumstances. Thus, for example, while there is no right of political asylum and freedom from expulsion or extradition, applicants have been able to rely on Article 3.

A distinction between individual and inter-State petitions is also worthy of note. In inter-State complaints a State can complain about any violation of the provisions of the Convention, whereas individuals can complain only about the rights contained within the Convention.

Competence *ratione loci*

Competence *ratione loci* limits the competence of the Court to analysing those alleged breaches that take place within the 'jurisdiction' of a particular state. Having said that, 'jurisdiction' is not necessarily synonymous with territory, for example it would include State responsibility for acts conducted by agents outside their territory. This issue was considered in *Cyprus* v. *Turkey*.[132] In this case, the Turkish Government argued for the application to be declared inadmissible *ratione loci*. The Turkish Government's argument was that it could not be held responsible for acts outside its national territory. The European Commission in rejecting the Turkish Governments argument took

---

[132] *Cyprus* v. *Turkey*, App. No. 8007/77, 13 DR 85 (1978).

the view that the term 'jurisdiction' was not synonymous with territory. The real question related to authority and control of the State wherever exercised. Since the Turkish forces had landed in Cyprus and operated under the direction of the Turkish State, their actions extended the de facto jurisdiction of the Turkish State. The concept of jurisdiction was further highlighted in *Loizidou* v. *Turkey*, where the Court noted:

> Although article 1 set limits on the reach of the Convention, the concept of 'jurisdiction' under this provision is not restricted to the national territory of the High Contracting Parties. According to its established case law, for example, the Court has held that extradition or expulsion of a person by a contracting State may give rise to an issue under article 3, and hence engage the responsibility of the State under the Convention (see, the *Soering* v. *U.K.* judgment of 7 July 1989, Series A, no. 161, pp. 35–36, para 91; the *Cruz Varas* v. *Sweden* judgment of 20 March 1991, Series A, no. 201, p. 28, paras. 69 and 70; and the *Vilvarajah and Other* v. *U.K.* judgment of 30 December 1991, Series A, no. 215, p. 34, para 103). In addition, the responsibility of Contracting Parties can be involved because of acts of their authorities, whether performed within or outside national boundaries, which produce effects outside their territory (see the *Drozd and Janousek* v. *France and Spain* judgment of 26 June 1992, Series A, No. 240, p. 29, para 9.1).[133]

Exhaustion of domestic remedies

Once the initial requirements are satisfied the Court has to ascertain whether the particular application satisfies the criterion of admissibility in the light of Article 35 of the Convention. Article 35 provides as follows:

> (1) The Court may only deal with the matter after all domestic remedies have been exhausted, according to the generally recognised rules of international law, and within a period of six months from the date on which the final decision was taken.

As we already noted, the Article 35(1) rule on the exhaustion of domestic remedies is based on the rule of general international law that the State must have the opportunity to redress the alleged wrong. The task of ensuring that there are available 'adequate' and 'effective' remedies is an important requirement falling upon all contracting States parties. This requirement is intended to reduce the mass of complaints. It is more appropriate that, in the first instance, the domestic courts be given the opportunity to provide remedies to the alleged wrongs.

Thus the complainant is required to take actions to redress his grievances at the national level. The applicant must pursue all possible and available remedies that are likely to be adequate and effective. The meaning of remedies 'likely to be adequate and effective' would depend on the breach in question

---

[133] *Loizidou* v. *Turkey* (Preliminary Objections), Judgment of 23 March 1995, Series A, No. 310, para 62.

and on the State jurisdiction. In principle, the applicant must appeal to the highest court of appeal against an unfavourable decision. In States where there is a written constitution, the applicant should take his case through to the constitutional court – to the highest court of appeal. Mere doubt as to the prospect of failure is inadequate, although at the same time he need not go against settled and established legal opinion. The applicant need not pursue his case in the domestic forum if it is clear from established case law that pursuing a particular remedy would be ineffective.[134]

Six months rule

The six months rule means that the application must be submitted to the Court within six months of the exhaustion of domestic remedies. Accordingly, the Court is restricted to dealing with cases only within a period of six months from the date when the final decision was taken at the domestic level. The rule is intended to prevent old cases reappearing before the admissibility institutions. The six months will start running from the date of the final decision marking the exhaustion of all domestic remedies. The court may refuse to accept the petition under this heading if after the initial letter to pursue the action there is a substantial period of inaction before the applicant submits further information.

Other restrictions

(2)   The Court shall not deal with any application submitted under Article 34 that
(a)   is anonymous; or
(b)   is substantially the same as a matter that has already been examined by the Court or has already been submitted to another procedure of international investigation or settlement and contains no relevant new information
(3)   The Court shall declare inadmissible any individual application submitted under Article 34 which it considers incompatible with the provisions of the Convention or the protocols thereto, manifestly ill-founded, or an abuse of the right of application.
(4)   The Court shall reject any application which it considers inadmissible under this Article. It may do so at any stage of the proceedings.

The applicant is required to disclose his or her identity but could request that that identity not be disclosed to the public.[135] Also the application must not represent substantially the same matter as an earlier application; the Court will reject the application if the factual basis of the new application is the same

---

[134] *Johnston and others v. Ireland*, Judgment of 18 December 1986, Series A, No. 112, and *Open Door Counselling v. Ireland*, Judgment of 29 October 1992, Series A, No. 246.
[135] Rule 47(3).

as the previous one[136] or it is under consideration by another body. It does not matter if there are new legal arguments involved. The purpose of this rule is to prevent duplication of examination by international bodies. The term 'international investigation' has been taken to mean such bodies as the Human Rights Committee, other enforcement bodies (for example, ILO) and the European Court of Justice. It is equally irrelevant whether a particular body can render binding decisions. The application will be rejected if it is manifestly ill-founded or abuses the right of application.[137] The application will be held to be manifestly ill-founded if it discloses no breach of the rights contained in the Convention or if the complainant fails to substantiate his application or has ceased to be the victim. The application would also be rejected if it is an abuse of the right of petition such as being insulting, using provocative language, derogatory, or being mere political propaganda. However, even though there is substance in the complaint, the mere fact that it is initiated to gain political ground renders it manifestly ill-founded. This provision is intended to prevent situations where attempts are being made to mislead the Court, or there is a deliberate refusal to cooperate with the Court.

REMEDIES BEFORE THE COURT

The European Court of Human Rights judgments are of a declaratory nature and cannot of themselves repeal inconsistent national law or judgment.[138] Equally the State is not obliged to give direct effect to the decisions of the Court in their national laws. The defendant State therefore remains free to implement them in accordance with the rules of its national legal system.[139] The one case where a State has patently refused to accept or comply with the European Court's Judgment is *Brogan* v. *UK*.[140] In this case the United Kingdom informed the Committee of Ministers that it could not repeal its legislation on prevention of terrorism. The United Kingdom then made a derogation provision under Article 15, which was subsequently upheld by the Committee of Ministers.[141] In relation to the provision of remedies Article 41 provides as follows:

> If the Court finds that there has been a violation of the Convention or the protocols thereto, and if the internal law of the High Contracting Party concerned

---

[136] See *X* v. *United Kingdom*, App. No. 8206/78 25 DR 147 (1981).
[137] Article 34(3).
[138] *Marckx* v. *Belgium*, Judgment of 13 June 1979, Series A, No. 31, para 58 cited in Harris, O'Boyle and Warbrick, above n. 1, at p. 26.
[139] Sometimes it is unclear whether steps (e.g. the legislation) goes far enough. See R.R. Churchill and J.R. Young, 'Compliance with Judgments of the European Court of Human Rights and Decisions of the Committee of Ministers: The Experience of the UK' 62 *BYIL* (1991) 283.
[140] *Brogan and others* v. *United Kingdom*, Judgment of 29 November 1988, Series A, No. 145-B.
[141] *Brannigan and McBride* v. *United Kingdom*, Judgment of 26 May 1993, Series A, No. 258-B, para 5. See Harris, O'Boyle and Warbrick, above n. 1, at p. 31.

allows only partial reparation to be made, the Court shall, if necessary, afford just satisfaction to the injured party.

On the finding of a breach, the Court's powers are limited to the awarding of compensation and the granting of legal costs. As regards the award of compensation, the Court has made awards under two heads: pecuniary and non-pecuniary damage (for example loss of past and future earnings, loss to property, loss of opportunity) and costs and expenses. In proceedings before the Court it is not possible to obtain specific relief. In *Selcuk and Asker* v. *Turkey*[142] applicants asked to be re-established in the village, a request that was turned down by the Court.[143]

SIGNIFICANT PRINCIPLES EMERGENT FROM THE ECHR

Reservations: Article 57

In accordance with general international law, the ECHR allows States parties to make reservations to treaty provisions. Article 57 of ECHR provides:

(1) Any State may, when signing this Convention or when depositing its instrument of ratification, make a reservation in respect of any particular provision of the Convention to the extent that any law then in force in its territory is not in conformity with the provision. Reservations of a general character shall not be permitted under this article.
(2) Any reservation made under this article shall contain a brief statement of the law concerned.

Derogation in time of emergency: Article 15

In exceptional circumstances States parties are permitted to take certain measures which interfere with or restrict the enjoyment of the rights provided in the Convention and the Protocols. In legal terms such restrictions and interference are termed as derogations. The permissibility of such restrictions is authorised by Article 15(1) of the Convention which provides:

In time of war or other public emergency threatening the life of the nation any High Contracting Party may take measures derogating from its obligations ...

[142] *Selcuk and Asker* v. *Turkey*, Judgment of 24 April 1998, 1998-II RJD 891.
[143] D. Shelton, *Remedies in International Human Rights Law* (Oxford: Oxford University Press) 1999, p. 203.

However these derogation provisions are subject to a number of conditions. These include, first, that these provisions have to be narrowly construed and are legitimate only to the extent that they are required by the exigencies of the situation. Second, that they are not inconsistent with other obligations of international law. Article 15(2) provides that it is not permissible to derogate from the provisions relating to the right to life (except in respect of deaths resulting from lawful acts of war), from the right not to be tortured etc., the right not to be enslaved, and the right not to be subjected to retrospective criminal penalties. Third, the Secretary-General of the Council of Europe is to be informed of the measures which are taken with a detailed explanation of the reasons that led to such derogations.

Margin of appreciation

The Convention has been reliant on a concept which is termed as the margin of appreciation. In essence it grants the domestic courts and institutions a measure of discretion to deal with a particular issue in accordance with their own moral, political, ideological and legal viewpoint. The notion of the margin of appreciation could best be illustrated by the dicta of the Court in the *Handyside* v. *UK case*.[144] The Court noted:

> the machinery of protection established by the Convention is subsidiary to the national systems safeguarding human rights. The Convention leaves to each Contracting State, in the first place, the task of securing the rights and freedoms it enshrines. The institutions created by it make their own contribution to this task but they become involved only through contentious proceedings and once all domestic remedies have been exhausted ... It is not possible to find in the domestic law of the various Contracting States a uniform European conception of morals. The view taken by their respective laws of the requirements of morals varies from time to time and from place to place, especially in our era which is characterised by rapid and far-reaching evolution of opinions on the subject ... By reason of their direct and continuous contact with the vital forces of their countries, State authorities are in principle in a better position than the international judge to give an opinion on the exact content of these requirements as well as on the necessity of a 'restriction' or 'penalty' intended to meet them.[145]

CONCLUSIONS

The ECHR remains the most valuable treaty adopted by the Council of Europe. After fifty years of existence the ECHR has firmly established itself as

---

[144] *Handyside* v. *United Kingdom*, Judgment of 7 December 1976, Series A, No. 24.
[145] Ibid. para 48.

the leading human rights treaty. During the course of this chapter we have surveyed a range of rights that are protected by the ECHR. A number of modifications and advancements have been made by subsequent Protocols to the substantive protection of rights. A significant addition to the protection of human rights would be through the application of the most recent protocol, Protocol 12. The case law of the Convention is also impressive in the sense that the judgments of the European Court of Human Rights have influenced many States to change their laws or reformulate their administrative policies. Such a situation compares favourably with other systems protecting human rights, where the system of implementation is hampered by absence of bodies with the authority to deliver binding judgments. However, the success of the Convention and the ever expanding number of States parties to the treaty exacerbated the difficulties in dealing with the cases. The induction of Protocol 11 aimed to simplify the institutional mechanisms. It was also designed to allow individuals within member States access to the European Court of Human Rights, and to curtail the functions of the Committee of Ministers. The reformed system, thus far, appears to be producing its intended results.

While the Convention has been hugely successful in the past fifty years, a number of challenges are presented. First, there has been a significant change in the social, ideological and political values within Europe; the question arises as to the extent the text of the Convention could be used to interpret these rapidly changing values. The second and more significant issue relates to the position and nature of obligations that are undertaken by the States which were formerly part of the communist or socialist bloc. A number of these States have faced difficulties in complying with the standards of protecting civil and political rights accepted within the western States. In the light of their endemic political and economic problems there is almost an acceptance of their inability to match objective standards on protecting civil and political rights; such an approach, however, is a dangerous one since it may lead to different standards even with the context of a regional treaty.

7

EUROPE AND HUMAN RIGHTS – II[1]

INTRODUCTION

At the end of the Second World War, Europe needed an institutional frame-work to protect individual rights. At the same time the shattered infrastruc-ture was in urgent need of redevelopment. Thus, in addition to the protection of civil and political rights, there was also a desire for economic stability and prosperity.[2] Post-war Europe, however, was soon to be engulfed into an ideological and political conflict, and security considerations necessitated the establishment of a strong military alliance. In the light of these security con-siderations, the Conference on Security and Cooperation in Europe (CSCE) was developed. The CSCE, as we shall consider in due course, has expanded into an active organisation, the Organisation for Security and Cooperation in Europe (OSCE). At the time of its inception in 1949, the Council of Europe's membership was largely drawn from western liberal States. The aims of the organisation were directed towards acting as a bulwark against the spread of communism and totalitarianism and to protect largely well-established civil and political rights. It did not take long, however, to recognise that civil and

---

[1] See L. Betten and N. Grief, *EU Law and Human Rights* (London: Longman) 1998; L. Betten and D. Mac Devitt, *The Protection of Fundamental Social Rights in the European Union* (The Hague: Kluwer Law International) 1996; D. Gomien, D. Harris and L. Zwaak, *Law and Practice of the European Convention on Human Rights and the European Social Charter* (Strasbourg: Council of Europe Pub) 1996; A.H. Robertson and J.G. Merrills, *Human Rights in the World: An Introduction to the Study of International Protection of Human Rights*, 4th edn (Manchester: Manchester University Press) 1996, pp. 160–196. H.J. Steiner and P. Alston, *International Human Rights in Context: Law, Politics, Morals: Text and Materials*, 2nd edn (Oxford: Clarendon Press) 2000, pp. 789–797.
[2] See A. Cassese, *International Law* (Oxford: Oxford University Press) 2001, p. 398.

169

political rights could not be protected without the promotion of economic and social rights. With the objective of promoting economic and social rights, the Council of Europe undertook to establish a regional treaty. The process of drafting took seven years and resulted in the adoption of the European Social Charter (ESC) (1961).[3] The Charter, as we shall consider in this chapter, has been criticised for its limited vision in according adequate substantive rights. More significantly, there were substantial shortcomings in the implementation procedures, which necessitated a thorough revision. The amended and revised Charter was adopted in 1996.[4]

Parallel to these moves in the Council of Europe, the project of economic integration took shape with the signature of the ECSC Treaty of Paris and, more importantly, the 1957 Treaty of Rome establishing the European Economic Community.[5] It must be emphasised that the Treaty of Rome envisaged an economic, rather than a political union and any rights conferred on individuals were incidental to that project. Over the years, however, the European Economic Community (or European Union as it is now known) has moved towards creating and protecting more explicit rights of citizenship and to a lesser extent what it terms as 'fundamental' rights. It has a direct role to play in relation to discrimination on grounds of nationality and gender-based discrimination.

In the light of the broad nature of organisations such as the EU and OSCE, the present chapter will concentrate on elucidating their role in relation to the protection of human rights. This chapter has been divided into five sections. After these introductory comments, the next section considers the Council of Europe's European Social Charter. The third section analyses the role and protection of human rights within the framework of the European Union, while the penultimate section considers the OSCE and its contribution to the promotion of human rights. The chapter ends with some concluding observations.

EUROPEAN SOCIAL CHARTER 1961[6]

A major criticism of the European Convention on Human Rights has been its almost exclusive focus on the protection of civil and political rights. As has

---

[3] Adopted at Turin 18 October 1961. Entered into force, 26 February 1965. 529 U.N.T.S 89; ETS 35.

[4] Adopted 3 May 1996. Entered into force, 3 July 1999. ETS 163. See below this chapter.

[5] See the Consolidated version of the treaty establishing the European Economic Community, signed at Rome, 25 March 1957, as amended by subsequent treaties through to the Treaty of Amsterdam (1997), effective 1 May 1999. 1997 O.J. (C 340) 3. Reprinted in 37 I.L.M 79 May (1998).

[6] D.J. Harris, *The European Social Charter* (Charlottesville: University Press of Virginia) 1984; D.J. Harris, 'A Fresh Impetus for the European Social Charter' 41 *ICLQ* (1992) 659; D.J. Harris, 'The System of Supervision of the European Social Charter–Problems and Options for the Future' in L. Betten (ed.), *The Future of European Social Policy*, 2nd edn (Deventer: Kluwer Law and Taxation Publishers) 1991, pp. 1–34.

been noted, over the years this criticism has been addressed, albeit to a limited extent, through two key processes. First, a number of rights have been added through additional Protocols to the ECHR which have a strong economic and social dimension.[7] Secondly, the broad interpretation accorded to many of the civil and political rights has highlighted the strong inter-linkage between these rights and economic, social and cultural rights.[8] Notwithstanding this indirect involvement, there has been a growing demand to have an effective regional treaty providing a more direct focus on social and economic rights.

The European Social Charter was adopted in Turin in 1961 by eleven Council of Europe member States. The substantive rights and implementation mechanisms of the Charter have been modified through a series of amendments. The ESC consists of a preamble, five parts and an appendix. The first additional Protocol, adopted in 1988, added several rights to the treaty. Further additions and amendments have been conducted to the implementation machinery through the Amending Protocols of 1991 and 1995. Part I of the Charter establishes a number of principles, which contracting parties accept as policy aims. It does not establish specific legal obligations and includes such aims as the opportunity for everyone to earn his living in an occupation freely entered into, the right to just conditions of work, the right to safe and healthy working conditions, fair remuneration, children and young persons having the right to special protection, and employed women, in case of maternity, having the right to special protection.

Part II of the Charter lists a number of substantive rights. These substantive provisions are a consolidation and extension of the policy aim. The Charter is unique in the sense that it provides States with the discretion of not accepting all the provisions of the treaty. According to Part III (Article A) of the revised Charter, a State party undertakes *inter alia*:

(b) to consider itself bound by at least six of the following nine articles of Part II of this Charter: Articles 1, 5, 6, 7, 12, 13, 16, 19 and 20;

(c) to consider itself bound by an additional number of articles or numbered paragraphs of Part II of the Charter which it may select, provided that the total number of articles or numbered paragraphs by which it is bound is not less than sixteen articles or sixty-three numbered paragraphs.

Rights contained within the ESC

Article 1 The right to work
Article 2 The right to just conditions of work
Article 3 The right to safe and healthy working conditions

---

[7] See e.g. the Right to Property and the Right to education (Protocol 1, Articles 1 and 2) Protocol 12, etc.
[8] See above Chapter 6.

Article 4   The right to a fair remuneration
Article 5   The right to organise
Article 6   The right to bargain collectively
Article 7   The right of children and young persons to protection
Article 8   The right of employed women to protection of maternity
Article 9   The right to vocational guidance
Article 10 The right to vocational training
Article 11 The right to protection of health
Article 12 The right to social security
Article 13 The right to social and medical assistance
Article 14 The right to benefit from social welfare services
Article 15 The right of physically or mentally disabled persons to vocational training, rehabilitation and social resettlement
Article 16 The right of the family to social, legal and economic protection
Article 17 The right of children and young persons to social and economic protection
Article 18 The right to engage in a gainful occupation in the territory of other Contracting Parties
Article 19 The right of migrant workers and their families to protection and assistance
Article 20 The right to equal opportunities and equal treatment in matters of employment and occupation without discrimination on the grounds of sex
Article 21 The right to information and consultation
Article 22 The right to take part in the determination and improvement of the working conditions and working environment
Article 23 The right of elderly persons to social protection
Article 24 The right to protection in cases of termination of employment.
Article 25 The right of workers to protection of claims in the event of the insolvency of their employer
Article 26 The right of all workers to dignity at work
Article 27 The right of all persons with family responsibilities and who are engaged or wish to engage in employment to do so without being subject to discrimination and as far as possible without conflict between their employment and family responsibilities
Article 28 The right of workers' representatives to protection in the undertaking and facilities to be accorded to them
Article 29 The right to be informed and consulted in collective redundancy procedures
Article 30 The right to protection against poverty and social exclusion
Article 31 The right to housing

The ESC contains a number of rights which are valuable to workers and employees. The right to just conditions of work,[9] for example, provides an

---

[9] Article 2.

undertaking from the States parties *inter alia* to allow individual employees reasonable daily and weekly working hours.[10] It also allows for public holidays with pay, and a minimum of four weeks' annual holiday with pay.[11] Through the right to safe and healthy working conditions States parties undertake to:

> formulate, implement and periodically review a coherent national policy on occupational safety, occupational health and the working environment. The primary aim of this policy shall be to improve occupational safety and health and to prevent accidents and injury to health arising out of, linked with or occurring in the course of work, particularly by minimising the causes of hazards inherent in the working environment.[12]

An interesting and positive feature of the Charter is its protection of children and young persons at work.[13] In accordance with Article 7, States parties undertake to set a minimum age of 15 for allowing employment, subject to exceptions of light work, which does not affect their health, moral or education.[14] States also agree that persons in compulsory education are not to be employed in such a manner as would deprive them of the full benefit of their education.[15] In providing the right of employed women to maternity protection, States undertake to:

> provide either by paid leave, by adequate social security benefits or by benefits from public funds for employed women to take leave before and after childbirth up to a total of at least fourteen weeks.[16]

Other useful Articles secure the right to social security,[17] the right to social and medical assistance[18] and the right to social welfare services.[19] In the light of a substantial elderly population of Europe, it is important to have provisions protecting their rights.[20] While the Charter provides some protection to migrant workers and their families,[21] one of its disappointing features is its approach which limits the provision of rights to nationals of contracting parties only.[22]

---

[10] Article 2(1).
[11] Article 2(2).
[12] Article 3(1).
[13] Article 7.
[14] Article 7(1).
[15] Article 7(2).
[16] Article 8(1).
[17] Article 12.
[18] Article 13.
[19] Article 14.
[20] Article 15.
[21] Article 19.
[22] See Appendix to the Revised European Social Charter; Scope of the Revised European Social Charter in terms of persons protected.

Implementation mechanism[23]

The ESC as a regional treaty dealing with economic and social rights parallels the ICESCR,[24] which, as we have considered, operates at the international level.[25] The ESC mirrors similar weaknesses of implementation. The implementation mechanism of the ESC has recently been revised and now provides for a complaints procedure in addition to the reporting system. Primary monitoring of the treaty is conducted by a system of regular reports submitted by the State parties. State parties are required to submit reports on the implementation of the Charter every two years.[26] It needs to be noted that while the ESC requirement is for biannual reports of Articles which States parties have accepted, the Committee of Ministers and the Council of Europe have decided on the reporting of all 'non-core' articles every four years.

There also remains the possibility of occasional reports on unaccepted provisions.[27] These reports allow the Committee of Independent Experts (CIE) to clarify the meaning of particular provisions and to comment on the problems that a State envisions in accepting those provisions.[28] Requests for such reports have been rare, and there have thus far been only four occasions when States have been called upon to submit such reports.

Two bodies are primarily involved in the monitoring of State reports: The Committee of Independent Experts (CIE)[29] and the Governmental Committee. CIE is elected by the Committee of Ministers for a term of six years.[30] It consists of:

> at least nine members elected by the Parliamentary Assembly by a majority of votes cast from a list of experts of the highest integrity and of recognised competence in national and international social questions, nominated by the Contracting Parties.[31]

Members of the Committee sit in their individual capacity and are required not to perform any functions incompatible with the requirements of independence, impartiality and availability inherent in their office.[32] The other body, the

---

[23] D.J. Harris, 'Lessons from the Reporting System of the European Social Charter' in P. Alston and J. Crawford (eds), *The Future of UN Human Rights Treaty Monitoring* (Cambridge: Cambridge University Press) 2000, pp. 347–360; D.J. Harris, 'The System of Supervision of the European Social Charter–Problems and Options for the Future' in L. Betten (ed.), above n. 6, pp. 1–34.
[24] Adopted at New York, 16 December 1966. Entered into force 3 January 1976. GA Res. 2200A (XXI) UN Doc. A/6316 (1966) 993 U.N.T.S. 3, 6 I.L.M. (1967) 360.
[25] See above Chapter 5.
[26] Article 21.
[27] Article 22.
[28] D.J. Harris, 'Lessons from the Reporting System of the European Social Charter' in P. Alston and J. Crawford (eds), above n. 23, at p. 350.
[29] In 1999, CIE changed its name to the European Committee of Social Rights. The Committee, however, is still generally known as CIE, a title which is used for the purposes of the present chapter.
[30] Article 25(2).
[31] Article 25(1).
[32] Article 25(4).

Governmental Committee, consists of one representative of each of the Contracting parties.[33] Members of the Governmental Committee are usually civil servants, in charge of the national ministry responsible for implementing the ESC.[34] The Committee is authorised to allow no more than two international organisations of employers and no more than two international trade union organisations to send observers in a consultative capacity to its meetings.[35] It may also, at its discretion, consult those representatives of non-governmental organisations with consultative status with the Council of Europe and having a particular competence in matters relating to the Charter.[36]

The process is initiated through submission of the report to the Secretary General for its examination by CIE. At the time of sending the report to the Secretary General, the relevant State party is required to forward copies of this report to 'such of its national organisations as are members of the inter-national organisations of employers and trade unions invited ... to be represented at the meetings of the Governmental Committee'.[37] Any comments, formulated by these organisations and sent to the Secretary General are made available to the State party concerned for its response.[38] The CIE may ask for additional information or clarification from the States parties.[39]

The CIE provides a legal assessment of a State's compliance with the provisions which it has accepted.[40] The conclusions made by the Committee are made available as a public document, and are communicated to the Parliamentary Assembly of the Council of Europe and to any other relevant organisations. Once this stage is over, State reports, and the assessment made by the CIE on these reports, are transmitted to the Governmental Committee. The Governmental Committee examines those assessments where there are indications of non-compliance with the provisions of the Charter and, on the basis of social, economic and other policy considerations, prepares recommendations for the Committee of Ministers to adopt. The recommendations prepared by Governmental Experts are also passed on to the Parliamentary Assembly of the Council of Europe, which transmits its views to the Council of Ministers. In the light of comments made by Governmental Experts and the Parliamentary Assembly, the Committee of Ministers issues recommendations to States which fail to comply with the Charter.

---

[33] Article 27(2).
[34] D.J. Harris, 'Lessons from the Reporting System of the European Social Charter' in P. Alston and J. Crawford (eds), above n. 23, at p. 355.
[35] Ibid.
[36] Ibid.
[37] Article 23(1).
[38] Article 23(1).
[39] Article 24(3).
[40] Article 24(2).

The Committee of Ministers adopts, by a majority of two-thirds of those voting, with entitlement to voting limited to the Contracting Parties, on the basis of the report of the Governmental Committee, a resolution covering the entire supervision cycle and containing individual recommendations to the Contracting Parties concerned.[41] The Secretary General of the Council of Europe transmits to the Parliamentary Assembly, with a view to the holding of periodical plenary debates, the reports of the Committee of Independent Experts and of the Governmental Committee, as well as the resolutions of the Committee of Ministers.[42]

From the above description, the implementation mechanism might appear to be a straightforward one. However, in practice substantial difficulties arise because of a weak and cumbersome system of monitoring the treaty. Many reasons can be advanced for the weaknesses in implementing the ESC. Giving the mandate to the Committee of Ministers was inappropriate because of the political nature of the body. Politicians have been reluctant to criticise States for fear of generating political tensions. Under the provisions of the original Charter, the Committee has to adopt recommendations by a two-thirds majority of its members. In the light of the limited membership of this Charter, for many years the Charter's Contracting Parties represented only around one-third of the Council of Europe's membership. This resulted in non-State parties criticising practices in a State which had committed itself to fulfilling the Charter's obligations. There were other problems, generated by the antagonism between the CIE and the Governmental Experts. A confrontation took place in the very first cycle of reporting, when the CIE found 57 breaches from the seven States involved. In reaction to this, the Governmental Committee produced its own less demanding interpretation of the Charter.[43]

National trade unions and employers' organisations are given the right to comment on national reports. However, their role was limited in that they may only sit as observers at the meetings of the Committee of Governmental representatives. There are also no explicit provisions to the effect that their comments shall be taken into account by the supervisory bodies. This minor role for the employers' and workers' representatives is another reason for the Charter's lack of popularity.

In response to these problems and in the context of the decision taken in November 1990 to revise the Charter, a number of improvements were made in the supervisory system, as well as an extension in the range and content of the rights. The 1991 Amending Protocol changed the voting requirements in the Committee of Ministers from a two-thirds majority of member States to a two-

[41] Article 28(1).
[42] Article 29.
[43] D.J. Harris, 'Lessons from the Reporting System of the European Social Charter' in P. Alston and J. Crawford (eds), above n. 23, at p. 353.

thirds majority of Contracting Parties, strengthening the role of the Committee of Independent Experts and improving the consultation procedures with employers' and trade unions' representatives as well as with NGOs.[44] In addition, the 1991 Protocol enables the Committee of Experts to make direct contact with contracting parties in order to request clarification and additional information concerning their reports. Under the original provisions, the Experts could only conclude that certain situations were unclear and therefore that they were not sure whether the Charter had been infringed. They would have to wait two years to get the relevant information, which might still be inconclusive.

The second major improvement is a better definition of the Governmental Committee. The aim of this is to avoid what used to happen previously, namely that the Governmental representatives more or less repeated the work of the experts and usually came to different conclusions. This offered the Committee of Ministers an opportunity to abstain from any further actions, as there was no clear indication of a breach of the Charter. The amendment provides that in the light of the reports of experts of the contracting parties, the Governmental Committee shall select the situations which should, in its view, be the subject of recommendations by the Committee of Ministers. In addition to a better description of the role of the Governmental Committee, there has been a shift in the hitherto confrontational position adopted by the CIE towards the Governmental Committee. The CIE has also, in the words of Professor Harris, 'adopted a somewhat more measured approach. It is much slower to find a new party in breach of its obligations in its early reports. It has also moderated its approach to the application of some particularly delicate provisions or issues'.[45]

A recent reform is the addition of a collective complaints procedure to the present control mechanism which came into effect after ratification by five Contracting Parties to the Charter. The procedure does not allow individuals to make complaints. However, complaints can be lodged by management, labour and non-governmental organisations (NGOs) against Contracting Parties allegedly failing to comply with their obligations under the Charter. Complaints can be made regarding general situations and not about particular or individual cases. The Revised European Social Charter adopted by the Committee of Ministers and opened for signature on 3 May 1996 came into force in July 1998. The complaints procedure adds a new dimension and importance to the Social Charter; its impact is likely to be a beneficial one in generating greater interest in the Charter.

Many of the rights contained in the ESC have been addressed at various levels, and in some cases much more strongly at the European level through the

---

[44] See Article 28(1)
[45] D.J. Harris, 'The System of Supervision of the European Social Charter–Problems and Options for the Future' in L. Betten (ed.), above n. 6, 1–34, at p. 10.

European Union. This statement can be tested by contrasting Articles 2, 3, 7, 8, 20, 21, 25 and 29 of the ESC to comparable European Council Directives.[46] In a few instances, even the ECHR jurisprudence has been of greater assistance to disgruntled workers or employees. Despite the shortcomings in the Charter, there are a number of positive features. Although reports are usually delayed (not an unusual feature of international reporting procedure), the States parties to ESC have made a point of making a definitive submission.[47] This action represents a major contrast with the situation at the international level, in particular in economic and social rights reporting. It is also to the credit of the CIE that they review each of the State reports completely objectively and independently.

THE EUROPEAN UNION[48]

While the Council of Europe was focused on maintaining peace within Europe by means of cooperation in the field of human rights, the European Economic

---

[46] Compare the following: Article 2 ESC with Council Directive 93/104/EC of 23 November 1993 concerning certain aspects of the organisation of working time; Article 3 ESC with Article 137 TEC creating a legal basis for health and safety legislation, and there are too many subsequent Directives to number Article 7 ESC with Council Directive 94/33/EC of 22 June 1994 on the protection of young people at work; Article 8 ESC with Council Directive 92/85/EEC of 19 October 1992 on the introduction of measures to encourage improvements in the safety and health at work of pregnant workers and workers who have recently given birth or are breastfeeding; Article 20 ESC with Article 141 TEC; Council Directive 75/117/EEC of 10 February 1975 on the approximation of the laws of the Member States relating to the application of the principle of equal pay for men and women; Council Directive 76/207/EEC of 9 February 1976 on the implementation of the principle of equal treatment for men and women as regards access to employment, vocational training and promotion, and working conditions; Council Directive 97/80/EC of 15 December 1997 on the burden of proof in cases of discrimination based on sex (also a couple of Directives on discrimination in social security); Article 21 ESC with Council Directive 91/533/EEC of 14 October 1991 on an employer's obligation to inform employees of the conditions applicable to the contract or employment relationship; Council Directive 94/45/EC of 22 September 1994 on the establishment of a European Works Council or a procedure in Community-scale undertakings and Community-scale groups of undertakings for the purposes of informing and consulting employees; Article 25 ESC with Council Directive 80/987/EEC of 20 October 1980 on the approximation of the laws of the Member States relating to the protection of employees in the event of the insolvency of their employer and Article 29 ESC with Council Directive 98/59/EC of 20 July 1998 on the approximation of the laws of the Member States relating to collective redundancies.

[47] D.J. Harris, 'Lessons from the Reporting System of the European Social Charter' in P. Alston and J. Crawford (eds), above n. 23, at p. 353.

[48] P. Alston (ed.), *EU and Human Rights* (Oxford: Oxford University Press) 1999; J. Shaw, *Law of the European Union* (Basingstoke: Palgrave) 2000, pp. 331–369; T.C. Hartley, 'The Constitutional Foundations of the European Union' 117 *LQR* (2001) 225; F. Jacobs, 'The Protection of Human Rights in the Members States of the EC: The Impact of Case-Law' in J. O'Reilley (ed.), *Human Rights and Constitutional Law* (Dublin: Round Hall Press) 1992, pp. 243–250; A. Clapham, 'A Human Rights Policy for the European Community' 10 *YEL* (1990) 309; M.H. Mendelson, 'The European Court of Justice and Human Rights' 1 *YEL* (1981) 125; M.H. Mendelson, 'The Impact of European Community Law on the Implementation of European Convention on Human Rights' 3 *YEL* (1983) 99; J. McBride and L. Neville Brown, 'The United Kingdom, the European Community and the European Convention on Human Rights' 1 *YEL* (1981) 167.

Community (which later became part of the EU) was founded in order to unite Europe economically. The Treaty of Rome only indirectly concerned itself with human rights.[49] Among the few related provisions was Article 48 of the Treaty, which provided for the right of freedom of movement for community workers and Article 119 that established equal pay for equal work for men and women. The different approaches taken by the COE and the EC meant that, historically, the protection afforded under Community law was different from the rights afforded under the ECHR. Within the Community sphere, rights and protection were accorded to the individual not 'by virtue of his or her humanity, but [by reason of] one's status as a community national.'[50] Furthermore it was argued that:

> the essentially economic character of the Communities ... [made] the possibility of their encroaching upon fundamental human values, such as life, personal liberty, freedom of opinion, conscience etc, very unlikely.[51]

Given this apathy towards human rights, the contemporary interest in the subject in so far as the Union is concerned calls for an explanation. A cumulation of internal and external factors has elevated human rights into a major issue. In the last quarter of the twentieth century, the community perceptions broadened and the protection of fundamental rights is now a significant concern. Since its establishment, the membership and influence of the European Community (now the European Union) has expanded and the Union is now actively engaged in taking initiatives for human rights protection. As an acknowledgement of their human rights commitments, all EU member States have become parties to the ECHR, ESC and the OSCE. The promotion and protection of human rights, not only within the EU but elsewhere too, features prominently in meetings of the EU foreign ministers.

In the last decade, the Union itself has been directly affected by serious concerns, such as an influx of refugees and threats to the territorial integrity of some of its Member States. Equally, the acts of genocide, ethnic cleansing and substantial violations of fundamental rights in central and eastern Europe, particularly in the former Yugoslavia and in the Balkans, have been particularly disturbing for the EU. Such distressing activities on the doorstep of the Union have raised substantial concerns regarding the effectiveness of the organisation in protecting human rights. The escalation of violence in the

---

[49] See the Consolidated version of the treaty establishing the European Economic Community, signed at Rome, 25 March 1957, as amended by subsequent treaties through the Treaty of Amsterdam (1997), effective 1 May 1999. 1997 O.J. (C 340) 3. Reprinted in 37 I.L.M 79 May (1998).

[50] P. Twomey, 'The European Union: Three Pillars without a Human Rights Foundation' in D. O'Keeffe and P. Twomey (eds), *Legal issues of the Maastricht Treaty* (London: Wiley) 1994, 121–131 at p. 122.

[51] A.G. Toth, 'The Individual and European Law' 24 *ICLQ* (1975) 659 at p. 667.

Balkans has, from time to time, also threatened to engulf Member States.[52] Constitutional reform within Member States, particularly the United Kingdom, also provided an impetus to revisiting the subject at EU level.[53]

The Union's expanding influence and interference with individual rights led to demands for greater accountability. The human rights debate has become entwined with the problems of the perceived democratic deficit within an increasingly powerful and bureaucratic Union. The concerns regarding the ineffectiveness of the apparatus to protect fundamental human rights have been addressed by Union institutions, albeit partially, through a variety of methods. The issues of redress are analysed in greater detail in the following pages.

Institutional structures and protection of human rights

The legal and institutional structure of the EU is relatively complex and beyond the scope of this book. However, a basic grasp of the relevant institutions and legal instruments is necessary in order to understand what follows. This outline is intended for those who have never studied EU law; the need for a concise treatment means that this account is necessarily simplified and many subtleties are ignored.

EU law, at first sight, appears to be just another branch of international law, in that it is based on a series of treaties, starting with the Treaty of Rome in 1957 and ending with the recently signed (but not, at the time of writing, ratified) Treaty of Nice 2000. These treaties provide the foundation for all EU law making. The nature and composition of the institutions, the legislative procedures, and, importantly, the substantive areas in which the EU is competent to act, are all laid down in the Treaties. This means that the EU can do nothing if not authorised to do so by the founding Treaties, or by secondary legislation which is ultimately derived from the founding Treaties.

In general terms, the Treaties have been consolidated into two Treaties: the Treaty establishing the European Community (abbreviated to TEC) and the Treaty establishing the European Union (abbreviated to TEU). The difference between the EC and the EU was laid down in the Treaty of European Union, signed at Maastricht in 1992.[54] This Treaty created the European Union, an entity made up of three pillars. The first and most important pillar is the

---

[52] D. McGoldrick, 'The Tale of Yugoslavia: Lessons for Accommodating National Identity in National and International Law' in S. Tierney (ed.), *Accommodating National Identity: New Approaches in International and Domestic Law* (The Hague: Kluwer Law International) 2000, pp. 13–63.

[53] See e.g. the position in the UK with the Human Rights Act (1998), and also in other States such as Spain, Belgium and the Netherlands.

[54] See the Consolidated version of the Treaty on European Union (1992), as amended by the Treaty of Amsterdam (1997), effective 1 May 1999. 1997 O.J. (C 340) 1. Reprinted in 37 I.L.M (1998) 56.

European Community, the successor to the European Economic Community created in Rome in 1957 and focused upon the creation of an internal market. The second pillar concerns cooperation in foreign and security policy, and the third concerns cooperation in police and criminal matters. The distinction between the first pillar and the other two pillars is important, because the law-making procedures and the way in which the law operates differ considerably. Human rights issues arise in the context of all three pillars.

While the EU may appear to be another branch of international law, in fact – at least when it comes to the first pillar – the reality is more complex. Two doctrines, developed by the Court of Justice, combine to give EC law its particular force within national legal systems. The doctrine of the supremacy of EC law, first declared in *Costa* v. *ENEL*,[55] states that EC law should take priority over any domestic law, even domestic constitutional law. The doctrine of direct effect of EC law, first expressed in *Van Gend en Loos*,[56] states that EC law, if it fulfils certain conditions relating to clarity and unconditionality, can take effect within domestic legal systems even if national governments and legislatures have not properly transposed it into national legislation. Together, these doctrines give EC law a supreme role in national legal systems, even if national governments or legislatures oppose aspects of that law.

A number of institutions are involved in the EU legislative and policy-making procedures. The three main legislative institutions are the Commission, the Council of Ministers and the European Parliament. The Commission is made up of 20 independent Commissioners, nominated by Member States and approved by the European Parliament, but who are supposed to act independently of their State of origin, in the interests of the Union. The Commission has significant policy-making and law enforcement functions, and its role in the legislative process is that of making legislative proposals. The main legislative body is the Council of Ministers. It is made up of ministerial representatives from all Member State governments, and has the biggest role in legislating. It often has to do this in cooperation with the European Parliament, whose role in the legislative procedure has increased considerably during the past ten years. Members of the European Parliament are directly elected by European citizens and represent their interests.

The most important non-legislative institution, whose role has been crucial in the development of human rights competence in the EU, is the Court of Justice. The Court is made up of judges drawn from the Member States. Their jurisdiction is limited, in that individuals generally do not have the right to bring cases directly before the Court of Justice. The exception to this is staff cases, where the staff of the Community institutions can bring cases against

---

[55] Case 6/64 [1964] ECR 585.
[56] *Van Gend en Loos* v. *Nederlandse Tariefcommissie*, Case 26/62 [1963] ECR 3.

their employers. Other than this, the Court hears cases in a number of different situations. It hears cases brought by the Commission against Member States, accusing them of failing to implement Community law.[57] National courts may refer questions of Community law to the Court in order to help them decide cases.[58] The Court also has the power, if asked to do so by one of the institutions or another interested party, to judicially review acts of the Community institutions.[59] Human rights issues are most usually raised in the context of these last two types of action. As well as the Court of Justice, there exists a Court of First Instance. This Court hears staff cases and judicial review cases in the first instance. The parties can then appeal to the Court of Justice. The scope of the Court of First Instance's competence is set to be broadened if the Treaty of Nice is ratified.

European Court of Justice and human rights

The inadequate recognition given to fundamental rights in the founding treaty of the European Economic Community and a lack of interest in human rights was mirrored in the earlier jurisprudence of the European Court of Justice. During the early years of the Community the Court was evasive and refused to rule on human rights issues, on the grounds that human rights were not included in the Treaty of Rome.[60] Over the years, however, the Court of Justice has undergone a significant change in its attitude towards human rights protection, largely prompted by its dialogues with national constitutional courts. This shift is evident in its case law. In 1960, in a case concerning the German constitutional protection of the right to private property and the right to pursue a business activity, the Court took the view that Community law: 'does not contain any general principles, express or otherwise, guaranteeing the maintenance of vested rights.'[61] Fifteen years later, in the groundbreaking *Nold* judgment, the Court, dealing with a very similar situation involving one of the parties in the 1960 litigation, stated that 'fundamental rights form an integral part of the general principles of law, the observance of which it ensures'[62] and that '... it cannot therefore uphold measures which are incompatible with fundamental rights recognised and protected by the constitutions of (Member) States.'[63]

---

[57] Article 226 TEC.
[58] Article 234 TEC.
[59] Article 230 TEC.
[60] Betten and Grief, above n. 1, at p. 54.
[61] Joined Cases 36–38 and 40/59 *Geitling and Nold* [1960] ECR 423 at p. 439.
[62] Case 4/73 *Nold* v. *Commission of European Communities* [1974] ECR 491, para 13.
[63] Ibid. para 14.

In the *Nold* case the European Court of Justice took the position that:

> international treaties for the protection of human rights on which the Member States have collaborated, or of which they are signatories, can supply guidelines which should be followed within the framework of community law.[64]

In another German case, *Hauer v. Land Rheinland-Pfalz*,[65] the applicant challenged a decision of the German authorities refusing her permission to plant vines on her land. The question referred by the German authorities to the ECJ led the Court to consider whether a council regulation which prohibited the new planting of vines for a period of three years infringed the right to property guaranteed by Article 1 of the 1st Protocol of the ECHR. The Court held that although the Protocol declares that every person is entitled to the peaceful enjoyment of their possession, it allows restrictions upon the use of property provided they are deemed necessary for the protection of general interests. After considering the constitutional rules of the Member States, the Court held the applicant's rights to property had not been infringed since the planting restrictions in question were justified by objectives of general interest pursued by the Community – the immediate elimination of production surpluses and the long-term restructuring of the European wine industry.

The fact that these cases concerned the German constitution should not be seen as coincidental. At the time of the *Nold* judgment, the Court of Justice and the German constitutional court were engaged in a debate (which continues to this day) concerning the reluctance of the German constitutional court to accept the supremacy of a body whose acts cannot be reviewed for violation of the wide-ranging fundamental rights contained within the German Basic Law. In the *Internationale Handesgesellschaft* case, the Court of Justice accepted explicitly that the German constitution court could review Community acts for violations of fundamental rights, but made it clear that it, rather than national constitutional courts, maintained that competence.[66]

A further step was taken in *Rutili v. Minister for the Interior*.[67] In *Rutili*, French authorities prohibited an Italian national involved in political activities from residing in certain *départments* (regions). The ECJ held that limitations cannot be imposed on the right of a national of any Member State to enter the territory of another Member State, to stay there and to move freely within it

---

[64] Ibid. para 14.

[65] *Hauer v. Land Rheinland-Pfalz*, Case 44/79 [1979] ECR 3727.

[66] *Internationale Handelsgesellschaft mbH v. Einfuhr- und Vorratsstelle fur Getreide und Futtermittel*, Case 11/70 [1970] ECR 1125. In this case the Court of Justice acknowledged (at p. 1134) that the 'protection of (human rights), whilst inspired by the constitutional traditions common to Member States, must be ensured within the framework of the structure and objectives of the Community.'

[67] *Rutili (Roland), Gennevilliers (France) v. Ministry of the Interior of the France*, Case 36/75 [1975] ECR 1219

unless his presence or conduct constitutes a genuine and sufficiently serious threat to public policy, concluding that:

> these limitations are a specific manifestation of the more general principle, enshrined in Articles 8, 9, 10 and 11 of ECHR ... which provide that no restrictions in the interests of national security or public safety shall be placed on the rights secured by the above quoted articles other than such as are necessary for the protection of those interests 'in a democratic society'.

The Court of Justice made it clear that provisions of Community law must be construed and applied by Member States with reference to principles of fundamental rights. Besides highlighting the Convention as a source of general principles to which it will have recourse, the ECJ's ruling suggested that provisions of Community law must be construed and applied by Member States with reference to those principles.

In a series of subsequent cases the ECJ went further in applying substantive principles of international human rights law. In *R* v. *Kirk (Kent)*[68] the Court applied the principles of non-retroactivity of penal provisions (as in Article 7 ECHR) in the context of disputes concerning the validity of the British regulations prohibiting Danish vessels from fishing within the UK's twelve-miles fishery zone. In *Johnston* v. *CCRUC* which concerned the legality of the policy of not issuing firearms to female members of the RUC, one question involved the applicant's right to effective judicial remedy. The ECJ ruled that Article 6 of the Equal Treatment Directive had to be interpreted in the light of the principle of judicial control, which reflects a general principle of law underlying the constitutional traditions common to Member States and is laid down in Articles 6 & 13 of ECHR. The Court was of the view that:

> By virtue of Article 6 [of the Directive], interpreted in the light of the general principles stated above, all persons have the right to obtain an effective remedy in a competent court against measures which they consider to be contrary to the principle of equal treatment for men and women.[69]

It followed that Article 53(2) of the Sex Discrimination (NI) order 1976, according to which a certificate issued by the Secretary of State was conclusive evidence that derogation from the equality principle was justified, was contrary to the principle of effective judicial control. It has increasingly been acknowledged by the Court of Justice that, when acting within the framework of Community law, authorities within the domestic sphere are obliged to follow human rights principles. This view was taken a step further by Advocate General Jacobs in *Konstantinidis* v. *Stadt Altensteig-Standesamt*[70] when he

---

[68] *R.* v. *Kirk (Kent)*, Case 63/83 [1984] ECR 2689.
[69] *Johnston* v. *Chief Constable of the Royal Ulster Constabulary*, Case 222/84 [1986] ECR 1651, para. 19.
[70] *Konstantinidis* v. *Stadt Altensteig-Standesamt*, Case 168/91 [1993] ECR–I 1191.

noted that a person relying upon Articles 48, 52 or 59 TEC in relation to employment in another Member State is

> entitled to assume that, where ever he goes to earn his living in the European Community, he will be treated in accordance with a common code of fundamental values, in particular those laid down in the European Convention on Human Rights.[71]

Despite this positive movement, one significant gap in human rights protection remains. The EU cannot be held accountable for human rights violations before the European Court of Human Rights, because the Union is not a party to the Convention.[72] It was hugely disappointing for human rights advocates when the Court of Justice ruled out the possibility of accession of the EU to the Convention, on the grounds that the Treaties did not give the Union competence to do so.[73]

Human rights and the EU treaties

The role of the Court of Justice in developing a human rights competence can be understood as a defensive tactic to bolster its argument that Community law is supreme throughout the Member States. Nevertheless, for many years it remained the only Community level forum in which human rights issues were discussed. It was not until the Maastricht Treaty of European Union (TEU) in 1992 that human rights were formally placed on the institutional agenda.[74] In many ways, Maastricht was to prove a significant watershed in the development of human rights protection within what was thenceforth to be known as the EU. Most symbolically, the obligation to protect human rights was inserted into the preamble of the founding Treaty. This had no legal effect whatsoever, but it represented a first step towards the inclusion of some sort of human rights dimension into an apparently solely economic entity. This obligation was to be played out in two contexts: the EU's Foreign and Development Policy and the development of citizenship of the Union.

The TEU introduced, under what is known as the Second Pillar, a Common Foreign and Security Policy (CFSP). This policy allows for Member States,

---

[71] Ibid. p. 1211.

[72] *CFDT v. European Communities*, App. No. 8030/77, 13 DR 231 (1978). See D.J. Harris, M. O'Boyle, C. Warbrick, *Law of the European Convention on Human Rights* (London: Butterworths) 1995, at p. 27.

[73] Opinion 2/94 ECJ OJ 1994 NOC 174/8; CELS, Occasional Paper, *The Human Rights Opinion of the ECJ and its Constitutional Implications*, 1996; K. Economides and J.H.H. Weiler, 'Accession of the European Communities to the European Convention on Human Rights: Commission Memorandum' 42 *MLR* (1979) 683; D. McGoldrick, *International Relations Law of the European Union* (London: Longman) 1997, pp. 174–180.

[74] For a general discussion see P. Twomey, 'The European Union: Three Pillars without a Human Rights Foundation' in D. O'Keeffe and P. Twomey (eds), above n. 50, pp. 121–131

acting intergovernmentally, to take common action in the face of world events. One of the objectives of this Policy is, under Article 11 TEU, stated to be the development and consolidation of democracy, the rule of law and respect for human rights and fundamental freedoms. Thus the TEU gives Member States the power to act internationally in order to secure the respect of human rights.

This power, however, is limited by the weaknesses and difficulties which have plagued the CFSP itself. While the CFSP is perhaps more effective than is sometimes acknowledged, its human rights dimension has been accused of lacking in consistency.[75] More hopeful was the inclusion within development cooperation policy of human rights conditionality, whereby Community aid or trade agreements are made conditional on the achievement of certain levels of human rights protection. This policy was institutionalised at Maastricht but had been incorporated into the Lomé Convention in 1990 and generalised by means of the Council Resolution of 28 November 1991 on human rights clauses in cooperation agreements. This resolution requires a carrot and stick approach to be taken. Financial resources are to be made available to beneficiary states to enable them to promote democracy and human rights. However, if human rights violations are identified, the EU has the power to withdraw aid until the problems are rectified.

One important criticism that has been made of the emphasis on human rights in external relations, however, is the fact that standards of protection are required of third countries nationals which the EU itself does not grant to its own citizens. This potential hypocrisy is starkly illustrated within the Maastricht Treaty itself. In this treaty, the EU took an irreversible step towards the protection of individual rights by creating the concept of Citizenship of the Union. While this concept is an important symbol of the aspirations of the Union beyond the economic dimension, the citizenship provisions have been seen as somewhat hollow.[76] One important gap in the provisions is that no reference is made to the fundamental rights of those citizens, despite proposals from the European Parliament and the Spanish government that citizenship should incorporate a fundamental rights dimension. It would appear that giving EU citizens fundamental rights which could, potentially, be different from those granted by the Member States was a loss of sovereignty too far.

Further, the development of the Third Pillar, known as Justice and Home Affairs, gave powers to the Union which it could be argued cried out for some sort of human rights dimension. These provisions related in the main

---

[75] A. Clapham, 'Human Rights in the Common Foreign Policy' in P. Alston (ed.), above n. 48, pp. 627–683,
[76] H.U. Jesserun d'Oliveira, 'Union Citizenship: Pie in the Sky?' in R. Dehousse (ed.), *Europe After Maastricht: An Ever Closer Union?* (Munchen: Law Books in Europe) 1994, pp. 58–84.

to agreements surrounding issues of immigration, asylum and free movement within the territory of the Union, including police cooperation and the Schengen Information System – a data-sharing system operated by the police and immigration services of the various Member States. The Member States are not limited in these actions by human rights considerations. Under Article 35 TEU, the jurisdiction of the Court of Justice was excluded from all questions as to the validity of operations carried out by Member States with regard to the maintenance of law and order and the safeguarding of internal security, including all operations carried out by the police or other law enforcement services. This means that the review power developed by the Court of Justice and outlined in the previous section did not apply here.[77]

While the Maastricht Treaty was of fundamental importance, there remained significant problems with its provisions. The modifications made by the Amsterdam Treaty, signed in 1997, in the main addressed the more symbolic issues of protection.[78] As well as the mention of human rights within the preamble of the Treaty, human rights and fundamental freedoms, as guaranteed by the ECHR and the constitutional traditions of the Member States, were recognised under Article 6(2) TEU as being one of the foundations of the Union. The Court of Justice, under Article 46(d) TEU, can in the context of its existing powers of judicial review (which, in the main, are focused on First Pillar activity) review acts of the institutions against the principles contained in Article 6(2). Moreover, the obligation on Member States to comply with human rights standards gained a very few teeth: Article 7 provided that Member States who persistently violated human rights standards could have their rights of membership suspended. Further, Article 49 TEU made respect of human rights standards a condition of entry for new States applying to join the EU.

Aside from the explicitly human-rights-based dimension, other important steps were taken at Amsterdam. The Social Chapter of the Treaty, first inserted at Maastricht but weakened by the opt-out of the UK, was strengthened at Amsterdam. A new Article 13 TEC was added, giving the Community the power to legislate against discrimination on a wide range of grounds. With a burst of unprecedented speed, perhaps spurred to action by the worrying gains of the Far Right in Austria, two Directives and an Action Plan were passed under Article 13, prohibiting racial

---

[77] T. Eicke, 'European Charter of Fundamental Rights–Unique Opportunity or Unwelcome Distraction' 3 *EHRLR* (2000) 280.

[78] For a general discussion of the contribution of the Amsterdam Treaty to human rights in the EU, see D. McGoldrick, 'The European Union after Amsterdam: An Organisation with General Human Rights Competence' in D. O'Keeffe and P. Twomey (ed.), *Legal Issues of the Amsterdam Treaty* (Oxford: Hart Pub.) 1999, pp. 249–270.

discrimination in all circumstances, and discrimination in the workplace on the grounds of sex, race, age, disability, religion and, to a limited extent, sexual orientation.[79]

Nevertheless, the limitations of EU human rights protection continue to be visible. Two major issues are indicated below. First, Article 6(2) TEU states that the rights to be protected are those contained within the ECHR and the constitutional traditions of the Member States. This vague formula allows the Court of Justice to maintain a significant level of power as to the rights which it will protect. The fact that the rights protected extend beyond those contained within the ECHR is a recognition of the limited nature of the Convention and the changing perceptions of fundamental rights. To that extent, the flexible approach which this represents is to be commended. However, the problem of distilling rights from constitutional traditions is significant. In some cases, the Court has adopted an almost mathematical approach. In others, however, clashes become apparent: what, for example, of the Irish constitutional protection of the right to life of the unborn child in conjunction with the, usually implicit and limited, freedom to choose to have an abortion which exists in many other Member States.[80]

In other cases the question is whether a fundamental right is in fact violated. Mention should be made here of the ongoing Banana Saga, where the German constitutional court required that the application of Regulation 404/93 on trade preferences should be modified in order to take account of the right of protection of private property, despite a finding by the Court of Justice that the Regulation did not violate fundamental rights.[81] This decision, taken in conjunction with the German Constitutional Court's earlier decision about the Maastricht Treaty,[82] demonstrates that the German court remains determined to have the last word on whether rights protected in the Basic Law are violated. Therefore, some sort of clarity is required as to the specific fundamental rights protected, as well as the jurisdiction of the various courts, in order that the power of the Court of Justice does not remain untrammelled.

Second, the extent of the protection that can be provided is limited. The Court of Justice's power of review extends to Community acts and (under its

---

[79] Council Directive 2000/43/EC of 29 June 2000 implementing the principle of equal treatment between persons irrespective of racial or ethnic origin (OJ L 180 19/7/2000, p. 22); Council Directive 2000/78/EC of 27 November 2000 establishing a general framework for equal treatment in employment and occupation (OJ L 303 2/12/2000, p. 16); Council Decision 2000/750/EC of 27 November 2000 establishing a Community action programme to combat discrimination (2001 to 2006) (OJ L 303 2/12/2000, p. 23).

[80] Difficulties have already been encountered on this issue – see *Society for the Protection of Unborn Children (Ireland)(SPUC)* v. *Grogan*, Case-159/90 [1991] ECR I-4685 and *Open Door Counselling* v. *Ireland*, Judgment of 29 October 1992, Series A, No. 246.

[81] *Federal Republic of Germany* v. *Council of the European Union*, Case 280/93 [1994] ECR I-4973.

[82] *Brunner* v. *European Union Treaty* (2 Bv R 2134/92 & 2159/92) [1994] 1 CMLR 57.

own case law) to acts of the Member States when they are acting within an area of Community competence. The Court has no power to act against Member States violating the rights of Union citizens or residents in areas where the Community has no competence. Further, the power is very limited when it comes to Second and Third Pillar issues. Under the Treaty of Amsterdam, immigration, asylum and free movement matters were moved to the First Pillar, under Title IV TEC. However, Article 68 TEC limits the scope of action of the Court of Justice, in that requests for preliminary rulings may be made only by the national court of last resort (rather than by any court) and the Court of Justice is given no jurisdiction in areas relating to the maintenance of law and order and the safeguarding of internal security.[83] The fundamental rights protected by the Court are thus perhaps better understood as obligations on the Community and on States in certain circumstances, rather than as clear rights possessed by individuals.

In other areas, while the rhetoric of human rights can be found in abundance, the enforcement of their positive inclusion within the full range of Community policy remains impossible. The acquisition of a full set of fundamental rights for Community citizens and residents, enforceable by the Court of Justice and national courts against both Community institutions and Member States, would appear to be the next obvious step.

The Charter of Fundamental Rights

To take the next step towards a full set of fundamental rights was, however, fraught with difficulty. The concern about State sovereignty which prevented the inclusion of a human rights dimension in the Maastricht citizenship provisions persists, and has in many ways intensified. A number of Member States, while prepared to countenance the preparation of a declaration of rights, would not accept a binding Charter. Further, the divergences between national constitutional traditions which gave the Court so much discretion, in turn made the task of agreeing on an acceptable text all the more difficult. However, in June 1999, at the European Council in Cologne, EU heads of state committed themselves to the establishment of a Charter.[84] A body (confusingly known as the Convention) was set up, under the presidency of the former German President Roman Herzog, and included representatives from Member State governments, the Commission, the European Parliament and national Parliaments, and that body produced a draft Chapter in October 2000. That draft was adopted by all fifteen Member States at Nice in December 2000.

---

[83] Ibid.
[84] Conclusions of the European Council in Cologne, 3 and 4 June 1999, Annex IV.

A striking aspect of the Charter is its scope. By focusing on fundamental rights rather than on the traditional, liberal democratic view of human rights, social and economic rights were included. The Convention had made it clear that they intended not to create new rights but to make explicit those rights which already exist, whether within the ECHR, other European or international agreements, or within the constitutions of Member States.

The 54 Articles of the Charter are divided into 6 chapters: dignity, freedoms, equality, solidarity, citizens' rights and justice. Chapter One, on dignity, covers the uncontroversial areas of the right to life, prohibition of torture, and prohibition of slavery and forced labour. These rights are covered by the International Covenant on Civil and Political Rights and by all regional human rights treaties. Article 3, however, introduces a number of rights, hitherto unestablished within the traditional framework of human rights. Article 3(2) provides:

> In the fields of medicine and biology, the following must be respected in particular:
>
> –the free and informed consent of the person concerned, according to the procedures laid down by law,
> –the prohibition of eugenic practices, in particular those aiming at the selection of persons,
> –the prohibition on making the human body and its parts as such a source of financial gain,
> –the prohibition of the reproductive cloning of human beings.

While clearly influenced by the Council of Europe's Convention on Human Rights and Bio-Medicine,[85] the extent to which these provisions would influence developments in the European Union with regard to the field of medicine and biotechnology remains uncertain. The Charter prohibits only reproductive cloning. However, there is neither an authorisation nor prohibition of any other forms of cloning.

Chapter Two, on freedoms, is generally unproblematic. The rights to liberty and security, to privacy, the right to marry, and freedom of conscience, expression and assembly are familiar from international treaties including the ECHR. The social and economic rights included here involve the right to education, the right to work, the freedom to conduct a business and the right to property. We have already highlighted the distinctions which have traditionally been placed between civil and political rights and social and economic rights. Thus, for example, the right to education, often considered as an economic and social right, is provided in the UDHR (Article 26) and the International Covenant on Economic, Social and Cultural Rights (Article 13). It is not provided for in the

---

[85] ETS 164 and Additional Protocol ETS 168; See L.A. Rehof, 'Article 3' in G. Alfredsson and A. Eide (eds), *The Universal Declaration of Human Rights: A Common Standard of Achievement* (The Hague: Kluwer Law International) 1999, 89–101 at p. 98

International Covenant on Civil and Political Rights. Similarly, the right to education could not be established in the ECHR, although it was subsequently grafted on to it by the first Protocol to the treaty.[86] It is, therefore, positive to note the inclusion of civil, political, economic, social and cultural rights under the umbrella of one human rights document.

The idea of freedom also incorporates the right to asylum and protection against removal, expulsion and extradition in certain circumstances. The right to seek asylum has generated difficulties in international and domestic laws.[87] Although incorporated into Article 14 of the Universal Declaration of Human Rights, its subsequent affirmation within human rights treaties has been problematic. International law has similarly shown great weakness in forbidding expulsions and providing protection to individuals from extradition to States where they are likely to face serious risks. Although the ECHR (Protocol 4, Article 4) prohibits the collective expulsion of aliens, traditionally there has been a reluctance to condemn expulsions. Two recent and useful standard-setting norms aim to establish a more comprehensive regime protecting non-nationals against arbitrary expulsions. First, the African Charter on Human and Peoples' Rights (AFCHPR).[88] provides, in Article 12(5), that:

> The mass expulsion of non-nationals shall be prohibited. Mass expulsion shall be that which is aimed at national, racial, ethnic or religious groups.

The other provision, which has an application at the international level, is incorporated in the Statute of the International Criminal Court,[89] which, in its definition of crimes against humanity includes deportation or the forcible transfer of population.[90] The Extradition and deportation of an individual has already raised complex issues of cultural relativism, and the European Court of Human Rights has had to deal with them in cases such as *Soering* v. *UK*[91] and *Chahal* v. *UK*.[92] Given that, under Title IV TEC, the Community is required to agree joint asylum and immigration policies, the inclusion of the right to asylum and protection against expulsion within the Charter could prove significant. It might equally dilute some of the insensitivity shown by the provisions of the recent European Union directive on the mutual recognition of decisions

---

[86] See Protocol 1 of ECHR, Article 2. See above Chapter 5.
[87] For an analysis by the International Court of Justice see the *Asylum Case (Columbia v. Peru)* ICJ Reports 1950, p. 266.
[88] Adopted on 27 June 1981. Entered into force 21 October 1986. OAU Doc. CAB/LEG/67/3 Rev. 5, 21 I.L.M (1982) 58. See below Chapter 9.
[89] Statute of the International Criminal Court, Rome, July 17 1998, A/CONF.183/9; 37 ILM (1998) 999.
[90] See Article 7(2)(d) Statute of the International Criminal Court also see J.-M. Henckaerts, *Mass Expulsion in Modern International Law and Practice* (The Hague: Martinus Nijhoff Publishers) 1995.
[91] *Soering* v. *United Kingdom*, Judgment of 7 July 1989, Series A, No. 161.
[92] *Chahal* v. *United Kingdom*, Judgment of 15 November 1996, 1996-V RJD 1831.

on the expulsions of third country nationals; without substantial procedural human rights scrutiny, this Directive is likely to prejudice the position of third country nationals residing within the Union.[93] Finally, within the section on freedoms, the freedom of the arts and sciences, including academic freedom, and the much-needed but much-disputed right to the protection of personal data is incorporated under this heading.

Chapter Three is shorter and concerns equality. Article 21 prohibits discrimination on a wide range of grounds in an explicitly non-exclusive list. Further articles make more specific statements about cultural, religious and linguistic diversity, and the cases of men and women, children, the elderly and persons with disabilities. These articles generally cover the ground of already existing binding legislation, particularly the new Framework Directive discussed earlier, although the extension of the rights beyond the workplace is significant. It is noticeable, however, that while discrimination on grounds of sexual orientation is prohibited under the general Article 21, no more specific provisions on sexual orientation or transgendered people are included. Equally, no provisions making a direct reference to minorities or minority rights can be found. Given the recent upsurge in the issue of minority rights, it is disappointing not to have a detailed article on the rights of ethnic and religious minorities resident within the European Union.[94]

Chapter Four marks the point where more controversial material was included. Rights relating to solidarity, which are in the main social rights, were not accepted as fundamental rights by all Member States. The ambitions that some parties had for this chapter have not been realised, and the rights contained within it are somewhat limited. Essentially, they cover workers' rights, such as collective bargaining, health and safety and the right not to be unfairly dismissed, which are already contained within Community law. A number of the provisions contain references to the legal regimes of Member States, and the principle of subsidiarity appears to have been firmly in the forefront of the drafters' minds. The rights to social security, health care and consumer protection are couched in particularly broad terms. The extent to which the jurisprudence of relevant provisions of the European Social Charter and the ECHR will influence the developments of the rights contained within this Chapter remains uncertain.

Chapter Five, on citizens' rights, might again have been hoped to be significant, given the criticisms that have been made of the existing concept of Citizenship of the Union. However, it remains limited. The majority of the rights in Chapter Five are already contained within binding Community law:

---

[93] See Council Directive 2001/40/EC of 28 May 2001 on the Mutual Recognition of Decisions on the Expulsions of Third Country Nationals (OJL149/34 28/05/2001).
[94] See below Chapter 11.

the citizenship rights of Articles 17–22 TEC (which, it is made clear, apply only to citizens of the Union) and the provisions concerning the right of access to documents.

Finally, in Chapter Six, the rights to justice bring us back to familiar territory. Here we can find the right to a fair trial, the right to a defence, the right to a proportionate penalty and the right not to be tried twice for the same offence. The rights contained in this Chapter are already a firmly established part of the International Criminal justice system. The ECHR covers such rights as the right to fair trial in considerable detail and the European Commission and Court on Human Rights have built substantial jurisprudence on the subject over the last five decades.

Chapter Seven represents a very important part of the Charter. It not only provides the level of protection but also explains the scope of the Charter rights. According to Article 51(1):

> The provisions of this Charter are addressed to the institutions and bodies of the Union with due regard for the principle of subsidiarity and to the Member States only when they are implementing Union law. They shall therefore respect the rights, observe the principles and promote the application thereof in accordance with their respective powers.

In relation to the level and sphere of protection it is reassuring that the Charter adopts a wider and all-embracing approach. Thus, according to Article 53:

> Nothing in this Charter shall be interpreted as restricting or adversely affecting human rights and fundamental freedoms as recognised, in their respective fields of application, by Union law and international law and by international agreements to which the Union, the Community or all the Member States are party, including the European Convention for the Protection of Human Rights and Fundamental Freedoms, and by the Member States' constitutions.

The question of the enforceability or otherwise of the Charter was a particular subject of discussion. Given the fact that the Court of Justice maintains a power to enforce human rights against Member States and institutions, it might be thought that a non-binding Charter would be impracticable.[95] However, a number of Member States (notably, but not exclusively, the UK) objected to the Charter having any binding status at all, despite the limited scope of Article 51. More fundamental, however, was the concern as to the symbolic power which a binding Charter would have as a part of a putative EU constitution and as a claim to EU sovereignty. At the Nice Conference, where concerns of national interest and political horse-trading reigned

---

[95] S. Fredman, C. McCrudden and M. Freedland, 'An EU Charter of Fundamental Rights' *Public Law* (2000) 178 at p. 185.

supreme, anything having the potential to decrease the power of Member States was not likely to meet with much success.

The Charter, therefore, remains purely declaratory and, in theory at least, of purely political import. It was, however, drafted with the idea in mind that it could, at some point in the future, become binding.[96] Further, despite the intentions of the Member States, the existing competence of the Union and of the Court of Justice raises the possibility that the provisions will have some legal impact. That possibility looked very real when, in his opinion in Case 173/99 *BECTU* v. *Secretary of State for Trade and Industry*,[97] Advocate-General Tizzano made explicit reference to Article 31(2) of the Charter, which states that workers have the right to paid annual leave. He further argued that, while the Charter is not itself binding, the statement of existing rights which it constitutes cannot be ignored in cases concerned with the nature and scope of a fundamental right elaborated in other, binding Community legislation. In cases such as the *BECTU case*, where the precise scope and application of the right is in dispute, the Charter is intended to serve as a substantive point of reference. This wide-ranging approach was, however, rejected by the Court of Justice. In its decision of 26 June 2001, the Court referred only to the 1989 Community Charter of the Fundamental Social Rights of Workers, and stated that the right to paid annual leave was 'a particularly important principle of Community social law' rather than, as Tizzano A-G had argued, a fundamental social right.[98] In a second case concerning the interpretation of the Working Time Directive, the same Advocate-General suggested that it was possible that that Directive itself could be challenged for infringing a fundamental social right.[99] It may, however, be significant that he argued that such a challenge would fail, and, in the light of the Court's decision in the *BECTU case*, it is unlikely that such an argument would succeed at present.

This role of the Charter is likely to be extended. In its human rights jurisdiction, while the Court of Justice may continue to claim the right to search national constitutional traditions for specific rights, the Charter may supersede the ECHR as the principal point of reference for deciding what rights are to be protected. In this context, the weakness of a non-binding Charter can be seen. The Court of Justice maintains its right to review on human rights

---

[96] See, in particular, the speech of Roman Herzog, annexed to the report of the first meeting of the Convention held on 17/12/1999 (CHARTRE 4105/00), where he stated that 'we should constantly keep the objective in mind that the Charter which we are drafting must one day, in the not too distant future, become legally binding'.

[97] *Broadcasting, Entertainment, Cinematographic and Theatre Union (BECTU)* v. *Secretary of State for Trade and Industry*, Case C-173/99, Preliminary Ruling, 8 February 2001.

[98] *R. (on the application of Broadcasting, Entertainment, Cinematographic and Theatre Union)* v. *Secretary of State for Trade and Industry*, Case C-173/99 [2001] 3 C.M.L.R. 7.

[99] *R. Bowden and Others* v. *Tuffnells Parcels Express Ltd*, Case C-133/00, opinion delivered on 8 May 2001.

grounds, and will make use of the Charter in doing that, but it also maintains the right to depart from the Charter if it so chooses. In a similar vein, while the Charter can be referred to in the context of the broader human rights dimension referred to above,[100] it does not bind the Union, which can either ignore rights contained within the Charter or enforce rights not contained therein.

Critical comments

The non-binding and unenforceable nature of the Charter is one aspect which has given rise to criticism. Weiler calls a non-binding Charter 'a symbol of European impotence and refusal to take rights seriously.'[101] The existence of a non-binding Charter does not add significantly to existing protection (apart, perhaps, from those substantive rights which are recognised within the Charter but not within the ECHR and which may be used by the Court of Justice in the exercise of its power of review). It may also be taken by critics as yet another vacuous declaration of enumerated rights. While the Convention claimed that the Charter was drafted in the hope that it would become binding, much of it is drafted in grand, abstract and general terms (this is particularly noticeable in the solidarity provisions). Weiler argues that a commitment to human rights protection within the EU requires not yet another Declaration of Fundamental Rights, but the elaboration of a human rights policy, complete with a Commissioner, a staff and a budget, which is committed to searching out and facilitating the punishment of human rights violations.

These criticisms have to be taken on board. The non-binding nature of the Charter suggests that it is intended to be nothing more than a statement of principle, albeit the first statement of principle on human rights made by EU Member States in that capacity. Having said that, there are nevertheless positive features in the Charter. The breadth of the rights in the document and the inclusion of social and economic as well as civil and political rights is to be applauded. It is extremely encouraging to note the inclusion of a number of novel rights, which presumably have been incorporated as a response to new challenges from globalisation and more technology. The Charter also covers some of the more difficult areas. The inclusion of, for example, a right to asylum is also potentially helpful. However, a number of nettles have not been grasped, and some significant omissions have already been alluded to.

---

[100] Indeed, even before the Charter was officially adopted by the Convention, its provisions were referred to in the report of the 'Three Wise Men' on the EU's sanctions against Austria (September 2001).

[101] J. Weiler, 'Does the European Union Truly Need a Charter of Rights' 6 *European Law Journal* (2000) 96.

It is to be hoped that the Court of Justice will take the opportunity to make full use of the Charter within its existing jurisdiction. Nevertheless, the failure of the Member States to extend the scope of human rights protection within, and by, the EU is regrettable. Whether the hope of the Convention, that the Charter will at some point in the not too distant future become binding, will be realised remains to be seen. The Charter may yet prove to be the first step along the long road towards really effective human rights protection within Europe, or it may remain an interesting but ultimately toothless document.

THE OSCE[102]

The Organisation for Security and Cooperation in Europe (OSCE) is similar in nature to the European Union in the sense that both intergovernmental organisations, while not designed for promoting human rights *per se*, have nevertheless become involved with the subject at the European level. There are, however, significant differences between the OSCE and both the EU and Council of Europe. The OSCE is not a legal body and, unlike the EU and the Council of Europe, its foundations have not been laid on legally binding treaties.[103] The principles that emerge from the OSCE process are commitments as opposed to legal rights and obligations. This means that unlike treaties these commitments cannot, as such, be incorporated into domestic law and national courts are unable to rely upon these principles. Despite the absence of a legally binding regime, the OSCE has been highly successful; it is arguably the non-binding character of the regime which encouraged States such the former Soviet Union to accept the fundamental principles of the organisation.[104]

The OSCE, which prior to 1 January 1995 was known as the Conference on the Security and Cooperation in Europe (CSCE), represents the largest regional security organisation in the world. It has 55 participating States from Europe, Central Asia and North America and is engaged *inter alia* in early

---

[102] R. Brett, 'Human Rights and the OSCE' 18 *HRQ* (1996) 668; Robertson and Merrills, above n. 1, at pp. 179–190; P. Sands and P. Klein, *Bowett's Law of International Institutions*, 5th edn (London: Sweet and Maxwell) 2001, pp. 199–201; Van Dijk, 'The Final Act of Helsinki–Basis for a Pan-European System' 11 *NYIL* (1980) 97; A. Bloed (ed.), *From Helsinki to Vienna: Basic Documents of the Helsinki Process* (Dordrecht: Martinus Nijhoff Publishers in cooperation with the Europa Instituut, Utrecht) 1990; http:/www.osce.org.

[103] Brett, above n. 102, at p. 671.

[104] Brett correctly makes the point that '[I]t should not be forgotten that the Helsinki Final Act rather than the International Covenant on Civil and Political Rights (to which the Soviet Union was also a party and which came into force at about the same time) was the basis for the human rights groups that sprang up in the USSR itself as well as in Central Europe. Participating States were able to reach agreement on the Helsinki Final Act precisely because it would not be a legally binding document. The pursuit of legal rigour may sometimes be less useful to the cause of human rights in practice than political compromise'. Brett, above n. 102, at pp. 676–677.

warnings, the prevention of conflicts and rehabilitation after a conflict has taken place. The development of the organisation can be broken down into two phases. The first period corresponds roughly to 1973–1990 which reflected tensions – through to increasing détente between the West and Eastern Europe. The second phase, since 1990, has witnessed the breakdown of the Soviet Union and the Warsaw Pact and considerable institutional development of the organisation.

The initial developments of the organisation are rooted in the Conference on Security and Cooperation in Helsinki. The Conference, which began in 1973 with 33 participant States, including the United States and Canada, concluded in 1975 with the adoption of the Helsinki Final Act[105] and comprises four parts often referred to as 'baskets'. 'Basket I' relates to questions concerning security in Europe; 'Basket II' is concerned with economic issues; 'Basket III' addresses humanitarian and other issues; and 'Basket IV' deals with the follow-up process after the Conference. The Final Act as such is not a document dedicated to human rights, although 'Basket I' does contain important references to human rights. Principle VII 'Basket I' is entitled 'Respect for human rights and fundamental freedoms, including freedom of thought, conscience, religion or belief'. This principle represents a commitment by the participating States to respect human rights, which include freedom of religion without distinctions as to race, sex, language etc. Principle VII also contains an understanding that the participatory States

> will promote and encourage the effective exercise of civil, political, economic, social, cultural and other rights and freedoms all of which derive from the inherent dignity of the human person and are essential for his free and full development.[106]

According to Principle VIII, participating States are committed to respecting equal rights of peoples and their right to self-determination. 'Basket III', entitled 'Cooperation in humanitarian and other fields', is of considerable relevance.[107] It considers such issues as reunification of families[108] and marriages between citizens of different States,[109] travel for personal and professional reasons,[110] transfrontier information[111] and flows and cooperation in

---

[105] Conference and Security and Cooperation in Europe: Final Act (Helsinki Accord) 1 August, 1975, 14 ILM (1975) 1292. The agreement is often referred to as the Helsinki Accords. See Russell (1976) AJIL 242; A. Bloed and P. Van Dijk (eds), *Essays on Human Rights in the Helsinki Process* (Dordrecht: Martinus Nijhoff Publishers) 1985; T. Buergenthal, 'The CSCE Rights System' 25 *George Washington Journal of International Law and Economics* (1991–1992) 333.
[106] Principle VII.
[107] Basket III. For the text see I. Brownlie (ed.), *Basic Documents on Human Rights*, 3rd edn (Oxford: Clarendon Press) 1992, pp. 428–447.
[108] Para 1(b).
[109] Para 1(c).
[110] Para 1(e).
[111] Para 2(a)–(c).

culture and education.[112] The Helsinki Conference was followed by a number of follow-up intergovernmental Conferences. These were held in Belgrade (1977–78),[113] Madrid (1980–1983),[114] Vienna (1986–1989)[115] and Helsinki (1992).[116]

The second, more vibrant phase began with the conclusion of the Vienna meeting of the CSCE conference. The Vienna Meeting, which had started in November 1986 concluded in January 1989. The Concluding Document of the Vienna Meeting represents a considerable advance on human rights issues. Such developments can be seen in the light of easing tensions between the western and eastern European States and a willingness to address the subject of human rights within the Communist regimes.

The Concluding Document deals with a range of issues including security, culture, trade, education and the environment. In relation to human rights, the participating States agree to provide effective exercise of human rights guarantees and to establish provisions for effective remedies. The Concluding Document also aims to protect the freedom of religion, freedom of movement and the rights of national minorities. The Vienna Meeting added a significant dimension to the human rights protection. It provided for a four-stage monitoring process, for which it considers questions relating to the 'human dimension'. The four-stage monitoring procedure is initiated by an exchange of information on matters relating to human rights through diplomatic channels. The second stage is conducted by holding bilateral meetings with other participating States and requesting them to exchange questions on human rights. In the third stage, any State may bring relevant cases to the attention of other participating States. In the final stage participating States may broach the relevant issues at the Conference of Human Dimension as well as at the CSCE follow-up meetings.

Further improvements (both in the substantive recognition of rights and the procedures to implement these rights) were to take place in subsequent Documents, in particular the Copenhagen Document.[117] Within the Document, participating States show a range of commitments which include

---

[112] Paras 3 and 4.

[113] See Conference on Security and Cooperation in Europe: Concluding Document on the Belgrade Meeting in Follow-up to the Conference 8 March 1977. Reprinted 17 I.L.M (1978) 414.

[114] See Conference on Security and Cooperation in Europe: Concluding Document of the Madrid Session Meeting 9 September 1983. Reprinted 22 I.L.M. (1983) 1395.

[115] See Conference on Security and Cooperation in Europe: Concluding Document of the Vienna Meeting 15 January 1989. Reprinted 28 I.L.M. (1989) 531.

[116] See Conference on Security and Cooperation in Europe: Declaration and Decisions from Helsinki Summit, 10 July 1992. Reprinted 31 I.L.M. (1992) 1385.

[117] See Document of the Copenhagen Meeting of the Conference on the Human Dimension of the Conference for Security and Cooperation in Europe. Adopted by the CSCE at Copenhagen 29 June 1990. Reprinted 29 I.L.M. (1990) 1305.

respect for the rule of law, justice and democracy.[118] There is an affirmation of fundamental rights and freedoms, freedom of expression,[119] right to association,[120] right of everyone to leave any country[121] and the right to peacefully enjoy his property.[122] A number of civil and political rights (for example, the prohibition of torture and capital punishment) are also reaffirmed. The Copenhagen Document shows a particular interest in the position of national minorities. Although the document is reluctant to define minorities it nevertheless emphasises linguistic, cultural and religious rights. In relation to implementation, the Copenhagen Document tightens up the mechanism by providing specific deadlines within which participating States are to act. In addition the participating States:

> Examined practical proposals for new measures aimed at improving the implementation of the commitments relating to the human dimension of the CSCE. In this regard, they considered proposals related to the sending of observers to examine situations and specific cases, the appointment of rapporteurs to investigate and suggest appropriate solutions …[123]

A number of these proposals (such as the provisions for on-site investigations by independent experts) have been given effect.[124] The use of independent experts was the first step towards involvement of what was previously a purely intergovernmental procedure. The procedure was invoked by the United Kingdom on behalf of the '"12" European Community States' and the United States in support of investigating attacks on unarmed civilians in Croatia and Bosnia and has also been used by several eastern European States.[125] Other procedures have also been introduced such as the biennial review meeting with the authority to draw attention to violations of human rights.

The Copenhagen Document was followed by the Paris Charter for a New Europe (the Paris Charter) in 1990.[126] The adoption of the Charter was also accompanied by a number of institutional and structural changes. The Paris Charter has led to the creation of the posts of Secretary General and the High Commissioner for National Minorities. It also set up a schedule of meetings, which have led to further developments in the field of human rights. In

---

[118] See I(1)(2)(5.1).

[119] See II(9.1).

[120] See II(9.3).

[121] See II(9.5).

[122] See II (9.6).

[123] Copenhagen Document para 43.

[124] See Conference on Security and Cooperation in Europe: Document of the Moscow Meeting on the Human Dimension, Emphasizing Respect for Human Rights, Pluralistic Democracy, the Rule of Law, and Procedures for Fact-Finding, 3 October 1991 (reprinted 30 ILM (1991)1670).

[125] See Brett, above n. 102, at p. 682.

[126] See Conference on Security and Cooperation in Europe adopted at Paris, 21 November 1990. Reprinted 30 ILM (1991)190.

subsequent years further institutional and procedural developments have taken place. The Office for Democratic Institutions of Human Rights (ODIHR), established initially to monitor elections, was given the mandate to provide information on the implementation of human rights within the participating States. ODIHR also maintains a list of experts who can be used for mediation, fact-finding and conciliation purposes. An individual/group complaints mechanism has also been initiated through the contact point in the ODIHR for issues concerning, for example the Roma or the Sinti.

The fourth follow-up meeting was held in 1992 in Helsinki, in a politically transformed environment. The break-up of the Soviet Union and the civil war in Yugoslavia had raised increasing concerns not only over security issues but also on the human rights front. These issues were addressed in the concluding Document. In this Document minority and groups rights are given a distinct recognition and the scope of domestic jurisdiction further curtailed in so far as the protection of human rights is concerned. The Helsinki Document also established the post of High Commissioner on National Minorities with the primary objective of bringing pressure on States to improve their individual and collective group rights record.[127] As we have already noted, at the beginning of 1995 the Conference, in the light of its achievement, reformed itself to be recognised as an Organisation. Subsequent summits in Lisbon (December 1996) and Istanbul (November 1999) have led to the adoption of Declarations and Charters on the Security in Europe.

Human rights involvement through visits

As noted above, human rights protection was not envisaged as a primary function of the work of the CSCE. The past decade has seen a remarkable transformation in the role of the organisation. In this regard a number of procedures have already been referred to, although some mechanisms need a further brief survey. These include the short and long-term visits. In relation to the short-term visits, the OSCE sends a mission to a country to conduct a survey and to report back to the OSCE. Long-term visits are intended to monitor the human rights situation in a country over a period of time. These visits are conducted by around eight individuals nominated by the OSCE and the visit lasts for up to six months. A number of missions have been conducted including those in Georgia, Estonia, Moldova, Latvia, Tajikistan, Ukraine and Chechnya.

---

[127] See CSCE Helsinki Decisions 35 I.L.M. (1992) 1385; A. de Zayas, 'The International Judicial Protection of Peoples and Minorities' in C. Brölmann, R. Lefeber and M. Zieck, (eds), *Peoples and Minorities in International Law* (Dordrecht: Martinus Nijhoff Publishers) 1993, 253–287 at p. 282; A. Bloed, 'The OSCE and the Issue of National Minorities' in A. Phillips and A. Rosas (eds), *Universal Minority Rights* (Turku/Åbo, London: Åbo Akademi University Institute for Human Rights, Minority Rights Group (International)) 1995, pp. 77–86.

High Commissioner for National Minorities

One of the most complex problems confronting the CSCE was the subject of minority rights, particularly within Central and Eastern Europe. The difficulties in addressing the issue of group rights are dealt with in subsequent chapters. Suffice it to note that within the United Nations and European human rights system collective group rights are accorded only very limited recognition. The disintegration of the Soviet Union, and the escalation of civil wars in many parts of central and eastern Europe, reinvigorated the subject. In order to deal with the situation in 1992, the CSCE established the High Commissioner for National Minorities (HCNM). The primary responsibility of the HCNM is conflict prevention. The HCNM is a person of 'eminent international personality ... from whom an impartial performance of the function may be expected'.[128] The HCNM is appointed for a three-year term which is renewable once.[129] Since his appointment, the HCNM has done a commendable task not only in attempting to resolve disputes but has also been instrumental in easing ethnic, racial and religious tensions in many parts of central and eastern Europe. With the involvement of American and British forces in Afghanistan, and highly volatile situation developing in States bordering Afghanistan, it would appear that the HCNM's role may well remain critical in the near future.

CONCLUSIONS

This chapter has analysed the position of three different institutions, all operating in the field of human rights. The comparisons between the work of the ESC and the EU produce interesting results. Since its establishment, the ESC has been operational with an insufficiently effective system of implementation. Two proposals have been put forward to make the system more effective. First, to establish a European Court of Social Rights (along similar lines to the European Court of Human Rights) and, second, to add the rights of the ESC in the form of an additional protocol to the ECHR. Both these proposals have failed to command serious consideration by the Council of Europe. Over the years some positive developments have taken place to improve the implementation mechanism of the ESC through the introduction of a collective complaints procedure. However, judging from the record of the past forty years, it remains clear that much needs to be done. A more serious threat to the ESC is that it remains undervalued and largely unknown even among European lawyers. By way of contrast to the ESC, the EU represents a well established and effective organisation. The growth and expansion of the sphere of the

---

[128] See Helsinki Summit, July 1992 above n. 127 (Helsinki) Decision 8.
[129] Ibid. Decision 9.

Union in areas affecting economic, social and cultural rights is making it difficult to sustain a largely benign human rights treaty such as the ESC.

The development of the OSCE from a purely security organisation to an entity which is actively engaged in the promotion and protection of human rights has to be welcomed. The OSCE has set up a number of institutions, which have, in a short time proved their worth. A key institution is the HCNM who has raised major security concerns and has engaged in dispute resolution and highlighted major problems faced by minority groups of the region. Given recent political events at the turn of the century, the HCNM will continue to have an important role. The lawlessness in some of the territories of eastern Europe provides a safe-haven for terrorist organisations to operate from; in the twenty-first century, the HCNM as well as the OSCE will have to confront the issue of terrorism directly.[130]

---

[130] For further consideration of the subject of terrorism in international human rights law, see below Chapter 16.

8

THE INTER-AMERICAN SYSTEM FOR THE PROTECTION OF HUMAN RIGHTS[1]

INTRODUCTION

The origins of American Unity and a movement towards humanitarian and liberal notions date back to the nineteenth century.[2] One of the earliest attempts to forge inter-State cooperation was through the establishment of the International Union of American Republics in 1890. American unity had already been manifested by the proclamation of the so-called Monroe Doctrine, preventing any intervention from Europe in the affairs of the Americas.[3] These expressions of American unity were once more exhibited

---

[1] See D.J. Harris and S. Livingstone (eds), *The Inter-American System of Human Rights* (Oxford: Clarendon Press) 1998; C. Medina Quiroga, *The Battle of Human Rights: Gross, Systematic Violations and the Inter-American System* (Dordrecht: Martinus Nijhoff Publishers) 1988; T. Buergenthal, 'The Inter-American System for the Protection of Human Rights' in T. Meron (ed.), *Human Rights in International Law: Legal and Policy Issues* (Oxford: Clarendon Press) 1984, pp. 439–493; A.H. Robertson and J.G. Merrills, *Human Rights in the World: An Introduction to the Study of International Protection of Human Rights*, 4th edn (Manchester: Manchester University Press) 1996, pp. 197–237; S. Davidson, *Human Rights* (Buckingham: Open University Press) 1993, pp. 126–151; T. Buergenthal, 'The Advisory Practice of the Inter-American Human Rights Court' 79 *AJIL* (1985) 1; T. Buergenthal and D. Shelton, *Protecting Human Rights in the Americas: Cases and Materials*, 4th edn (Kehl, Arlington, Va., USA: N.P. Engel) 1995; L.E. Frost, 'The Evolution of the Inter-American Court of Human Rights: Reflections of Present and Former Judges' 14 *HRQ* (1992) 171; D. Shelton, 'The Jurisprudence of the Inter-American Court of Human Rights' 10 *AUJILP* (1994) 333.
[2] Robertson and Merrills, above n. 1, at p. 197.
[3] Ibid. p. 197.

with the establishment of the Pan-American Union at the end of the nine-teenth century. However, it was at the end of the Second World War that sig-nificant steps were undertaken in so far as the promotion and protection of human rights was concerned. At the ninth International Conference of American States in Bogotá, Colombia (1948) it was decided to replace the Pan-American Union with the Organisation of American States (O.A.S.).[4] The O.A.S. is a body comparable to the Council of Europe in terms of its institutional work for the promotion and protection of human rights in the Americas.[5]

The constitutional texts of the O.A.S. are reflected through an array of documents. This includes the Charter itself as amended by its four protocols (Buenos Aires (1967),[6] Cartagena de Indias (1985)[7] Washington (1992)[8] and Managua (1993).[9] Further substantiation in the human rights field is provided by the American Declaration of the Rights and Duties of Man 1948,[10] the American Convention on Human Rights 1969,[11] the Inter-American Convention to Prevent and Punish Torture (1985),[12] the Additional Protocol to the American Convention on Human Rights in the Area of Economic, Social and Cultural Rights (Pact of San Salvador) (1988),[13] the Protocol to Abolish the Death Penalty (1990),[14] the Inter-American Convention on

---

[4] Also known as the 'Pact of San José' Charter of the O.A.S. (as amended). Signed 1948. Entered into force 13 December 1951. For integrated text 33 I.L.M. (1994) 981.

[5] For the Council of Europe see Chapter 6.

[6] 721 U.N.T.S. O.A.S.T.S. 1-A (entered into force 27 February 1970). This Protocol incorpo-rated the Inter-American Commission on Human Rights as an organ of the O.A.S. (Article 51).

[7] O.A.S. Treaty Series No. 66, 25 I.L.M. 527 (entered into force 16 November, 1998).

[8] I-E Rev. OEA Documentos Officiales OEA/Ser.A/2 Add.3 (SEPF) 33 I.L.M. 1005 (entered into force 25 September 1997).

[9] I-F Rev. OEA Documentos Officiales OEA/Ser.A/2 Add.4 (SEPF) 33 I.L.M. 1009 (entered into force 29 January 1996).

[10] Resolution XXX, Final Act of the Ninth International Conference of American States, Bogotá, Colombia, 30 March–2 May 1948, 48. OEA/Ser/L.V/11.7, at 17 (1988).

[11] Signed November 1969. Entered into force 18 July 1978. O.A.S.T.S. Off. Rec. OEA/Ser.L/V/11.23, doc.21, rev. (1979). 9 I.L.M. (1970) 673.

[12] Signed 9 December 1985. Entered into force 28 February 1987. O.A.S.T.S. 67, GA Doc/Ser.P, AG/doc. 2023/85 rev.1 (1986) pp. 46–54, 25 I.L.M. (1986) 519. See F. Kaplan, 'Combating Inter-American Convention to Prevent and Punish Torture' 25 *Brooklyn Journal of International Law* (1989) 399; S. Davidson, 'No More Broken Bodies or Minds: The Definition and Control of Torture in the Late Twentieth Century' 6 *Canterbury Law Review* (1995) 25.

[13] Additional Protocol to the American Convention on Human Rights in the Area of Economic, Social and Cultural Rights, 'Protocol of San Salvador' O.A.S.T.S. 69 (1988), entered into force November 16 1999, reprinted in Basic Documents Pertaining to Human Rights in the Inter-American System, OEA/Ser.L.V/II.82 doc.6 rev.1 at 67 (1992); 28 I.L.M. (1989) 156.

[14] Protocol to the American Convention on Human Rights to Abolish the Death Penalty, O.A.S.T.S. 73 (1990), adopted 8 June 1990, reprinted in Basic Documents Pertaining to Human Rights in the Inter-American System, OEA/Ser.L.V/II.82 doc.6 rev.1 at 80 (1992); 29 I.L.M. (1990) 1447.

Forced Disappearance of Persons (1994)[15] and the Inter-American Convention on the Prevention, Punishment and Eradication of Violence against Women (1994).[16]

The Inter-American system is rather distinctive from other regional systems in that its origins lie in two distinct though interrelated instruments. First, there is the O.A.S. Charter system of human rights, which relies upon the O.A.S. Charter and the American Declaration of the Rights and Duties of Man. Secondly, human rights protection is provided by the American Convention on Human Rights to those States members of the O.A.S. which have voluntarily become parties to Convention.[17] The two institutional systems operate through an interrelated organ, the Inter-American Commission on Human Rights. In both instances, the Inter-American Commission is vested with authority to receive communications from individuals and groups alleging violations of human rights contained within the American Declaration or the American Convention on Human Rights.

THE O.A.S. CHARTER SYSTEM AND THE AMERICAN DECLARATION OF THE RIGHTS AND DUTIES OF MAN

The O.A.S. is a regional Organisation and comes within the ambit of a regional Organisation as provided in Article 52 of the United Nations Charter. The O.A.S. Charter System has similarities with that of the UN System.[18] Like the UN Charter, the O.A.S. Charter contains a number of references to human or fundamental rights. According to Article 3(l) 'the American States proclaim the fundamental rights of the individual without distinction as to race, nationality, creed or sex'. Article 17 of the Charter goes on to provide:

> Each State has the right to develop its cultural, political, and economic life freely and naturally. In this free development, the State shall respect the rights of the individual and the principles of universal morality.

The Charter does not elaborate upon the meaning of the term 'rights of the individual' as used in Article 3(l) and 17. The task of expanding on the meaning of human rights was undertaken by a declaration, the American Declaration of the Rights and Duties of Man, which was adopted at the same

---

[15] Signed 9 June 1994. Entered into force 28 March 1996. 33 I.L.M. (1994) 1529.

[16] Signed 9 June 1994. Entered into force 3 March 1995. 33 I.L.M. (1994) 1534.

[17] It needs to be noted that there is no obligation on O.A.S. Member States to becoming parties to ACHR. Out of the 35 O.A.S. members, 10 have not become parties to the Convention.

[18] Davidson, above n. 1, at p. 127; also see V. Gomez, 'The Interaction between the Political Actors of the O.A.S., the Commission and the Court' in D.J. Harris and S. Livingstone (eds), above n. 1, pp. 173–211.

time as the adoption of the Charter.[19] This Declaration contains a variety of rights and also provides a set of duties of the individual to society. The following rights and duties are contained within the Declaration:

Article I	Right to life, liberty and personal security
Article II	Right to equality before law
Article III	Right to religious freedom and worship
Article IV	Right to freedom of investigation, opinion, expression and dissemination
Article V	Right to protection of honour, personal reputation, and private and family life
Article VI	Right to a family and to protection thereof
Article VII	Right to protection for mothers and children
Article VIII	Right to residence and movement
Article IX	Right to the inviolability of the home
Article X	Right to the inviolability and transmission of correspondence
Article XI	Right to the preservation of health and to well-being
Article XII	Right to education
Article XIII	Right to the benefits of culture
Article XIV	Right to work and to fair remuneration
Article XV	Right to leisure time and to the use thereof
Article XVI	Right to social security
Article XVII	Right to recognition of juridical personality and civil rights
Article XVIII	Right to a fair trial
Article XIX	Right to nationality
Article XX	Right to vote and to participate in government
Article XXI	Right of assembly
Article XXII	Right of association
Article XXIII	Right to property
Article XXIV	Right of petition
Article XXV	Right of protection from arbitrary arrest
Article XXVI	Right to due process of law
Article XXVII	Right of asylum
Article XXVIII	Scope of the rights of man
Article XXIX	Duties towards society
Article XXX	Duties toward children and parents
Article XXXI	Duty to receive instruction
Article XXXII	Duty to vote
Article XXXIII	Duty to obey the law
Article XXXIV	Duty to serve the community and the nation
Article XXXV	Duties with respect to social security and welfare
Article XXXVI	Duty to pay taxes

---

[19] American Declaration of the Rights and Duties of Man, O.A.S. Res. XXX, adopted by the Ninth International Conference of American States (1948), reprinted in Basic Documents Pertaining to Human Rights in the Inter-American System, OEA/Ser.L.V/II.82 doc.6 rev.1, 17 (1992).

Article XXXVII   Duty to work
Article XXIX   Duty to refrain from political activities in a foreign country.

The role and position of the Declaration is comparable to UDHR.[20] Both the documents were drafted after the atrocities of the Second World War and attempt to uphold liberal democratic traditions of fundamental human rights. Among the significant differences is the list of duties for the individual contained in the American Declaration. The American Declaration (like the UDHR) was not intended to be legally binding. Like the UDHR, the legal status of the American Declaration has been a matter of some debate.

Both the Inter-American Commission on Human Rights and Inter-American Court of Human Rights have treated the Declaration as being an authoritative interpretation of the Charter and thus having a binding effect. The Court in its Advisory Opinion No. 10 observed that:[21]

> by means of an authoritative interpretation, the member States of the Organization have signalled their agreement that the Declaration contains and defines the fundamental rights referred to in the Charter. Thus the Charter of the Organization cannot be interpreted and applied as far as human rights are concerned without reading its norms, consistent with the practice of the organs of the OAS, to the corresponding provisions of the Declaration [and that] for the member States of the Organization, the Declaration is the text that defines the human rights referred in the Charter.[22]

The Court in this opinion was inclined to take this view primarily because of the recognised position of the American Declaration in the revised Statute of the Inter-American Commission, which places the Declaration on a par with ACHR.[23] At the same time, such an elevated status for the Declaration has generated criticism from States which accepted the Declaration as a political statement only rather than a legally binding instrument. The continuous objections from these States also make it difficult to establish the view that the Declaration represents regional customary law.[24]

THE INTER-AMERICAN COMMISSION ON HUMAN RIGHTS

Background: one Commission for the two systems

The jurisdiction of the Inter-American Commission on Human Rights extends to all O.A.S. member States. The Commission which was established

---

[20] See Chapter 2.
[21] *Interpretation of the American Declaration of the Rights and Duties of Man Within the Framework of Article 64 of the American Convention on Human Rights*, Advisory Opinion OC-10/89, July 14, 1989, Inter-Am. Ct. H.R. (Ser. A) No. 10 (1989).
[22] Ibid. para 45.
[23] Article 2 provided 'for the purposes of the Statute human rights are understood to be set forth in the American Declaration of the Rights and Duties of Man'.
[24] For elaboration on customary law, see above Chapter 1.

in 1959 is a product not of a binding treaty agreement but of a resolution of ministers of foreign affairs.[25] The Commission started its work in May 1960 in pursuance of its Statute, which was adopted during the same year.[26] The Statute, as noted above, considered the American Declaration as providing a detailed expression to human rights. Although mandated since 1965 (with the addition of a new Article 9) to receive and deal with individual communications, the Commission concentrated on its advisory and recommendatory role. There remained a reluctance to move towards the consideration of individual applications and the justification presented was that the Commission's sources and influence could be more effectively utilised in identifying human rights violations, holding meetings in any member State of the O.A.S., and conducting on-site investigations leading to country studies.[27]

For several years after its creation the status and position of the Inter-American Commission remained unclear. The Statute of the Commission defines it as an 'autonomous entity' of the O.A.S. It therefore meant that the Statute failed to provide the Commission with any exact legal status. The position was rectified by the Buenos Aires Protocol of 1967 which in amending the O.A.S. Charter recognised the Commission as one of the 'principal organs'[28] of the organisation, through which it aimed to attain its purposes. The revised Charter came into operation in 1970.

With the Inter-American Commission becoming an institutional organ of the O.A.S. Charter, the debate on the content of human rights and, in particular, the value of the ADHR intensified.[29] It was also not clear whether there would be two Commissions in operation catering independently for the O.A.S. Charter system and the American Convention respectively. The Inter-American Commission's new Statute (which came into force in 1979, following the coming into operation of the ACHR) confirmed the existence

---

[25] See Resolution VIII of the Fifth Meeting of Consultation of Ministers of Foreign Affairs, Final Act, Santiago, Chile (12–18) August 1959. O.A.S. Off Rec. OEA/Ser F/II.5 (Doc 89, English, Rev. 2) October, 1959 at 10–11.

[26] Statute of the Inter-American Commission on Human Rights, O.A.S. Res. 447 (IX-0/79), O.A.S. Off. Rec. OEA/Ser.P/IX.0.2/80, Vol. 1 at 88, Annual Report of the Inter-American Commission on Human Rights, OEA/Ser.L/V/11.50 doc.13 rev. 1 at 10 (1980), reprinted in Basic Documents Pertaining to Human Rights in the Inter-American System, OEA/Ser.L.V/II.82 doc.6 rev.1 at 93 (1992).

[27] C. Cerna, 'The Inter-American Commission on Human Rights: Its Organisation and Examination of Petitions and Communications' in D.J. Harris and S. Livingstone (eds), above n. 1, 65–113 at p. 67.

[28] Article 52(2) O.A.S. Charter.

[29] Article 111 of the revised Charter provided that 'an inter-American Convention on human rights shall determined the structure, competence and procedure of the (Inter-American) Commission as well as those of other organs responsible for these matters'.

of a single Commission to serve both the OAS Charter and the American Convention.[30] Article 1(2) of the Commission's Statute provides:

> For the purposes of the present Statute, human rights are understood to be:
>
> a) the rights set forth in the American Convention on Human Rights in relation to the states parties thereto;
>
> b) the rights set forth in the American Declaration of the Rights and Duties of Man in relation to the other member states.

This meant, first, that all member States of O.A.S. not parties to ACHR continued to be bound by standards of the Charter. Secondly, the mechanisms established by the Commission as a Charter institution were preserved. This also endowed a rather treaty-like status to the American Declaration. The Commission also has a specific mandate to oversee all human rights obligations undertaken by O.A.S. States.[31]

Structure and organisation of the Commission

According to Article 34 of the ACHR, the Commission comprises seven members who are nationals of the O.A.S. The members of the Commission must be people with a 'high moral character with recognised competence in the field of human rights'.[32] They serve in their personal capacity for a period of four years and may be re-elected but on only one occasion. Members act in an independent capacity and not as State representatives.[33] Although not a requirement, most members have a legal background. The Commission represents all members of the O.A.S., and is not confined to the State parties of the ACHR.[34]

Members of the Commission are elected by the General Assembly of the O.A.S. The procedure for the election of members of the Commission requires that at least six months prior to the completion of the terms of office of the member, the Secretary General is required to request to each member of the O.A.S. in writing to propose its list of candidates within 90 days.[35] Each government may propose up to three candidates who may be nationals of

---

[30] Statute of the Inter-American Commission on Human Rights, O.A.S. Res. 447 (IX-0/79), O.A.S. Off. Rec. OEA/Ser.P/IX.0.2/80, Vol. 1 at 88, Annual Report of the Inter-American Commission on Human Rights, OEA/Ser.L/V/11.50 doc.13 rev. 1 at 10 (1980), reprinted in Basic Documents Pertaining to Human Rights in the Inter-American System, OEA/Ser.L.V/II.82 doc.6 rev.1 at 93 (1992). See R. Norris, 'The New Statute of the Inter-American Commission on Human Rights' 1 *HRLJ* (1980) 379.

[31] D. Shelton, *Remedies in International Human Rights Law* (Oxford: Oxford University Press) 1999, p. 122.

[32] Article 34 ACHR; Article 2(1) Statute of the Commission.

[33] Article 35 ACHR; Article 2(2) Statute of the Commission.

[34] Article 35 ACHR.

[35] Article 4 of Statute of the Commission.

their own State or any other member State. If three names are put forward then at least one is required to be a non-national.[36] Members are then elected by secret ballot, with candidates obtaining the highest number of votes being declared elected.[37] The Commission is supported by a secretariat, which carries out its day-to-day work. It prepares the working programme for each session and implements the Commission's decisions. It also prepares the draft reports and resolutions.

The Commission sessions are held generally in Washington, but may also be held in any other State member of the O.A.S. The ordinary sessions are held twice every year, each session lasting for three weeks; in the course of these individual communications are given consideration.[38] In addition there are also one or two extraordinary sessions each year. During the proceedings of the Commission oral hearings are conducted in which representations can be made by individuals and NGOs.[39] The role and functions of the Commission are described in Articles 41 of ACHR which provides that

> The main function of the Commission shall be to promote respect for and defense of human rights. In the exercise of its mandate, it shall have the following functions and powers:
>
> a)   to develop an awareness of human rights among the peoples of America;
> b)   to make recommendations to the governments of the member states, when it considers such action advisable, for the adoption of progressive measures in favour of human rights within the framework of their domestic law and constitutional provisions as well as appropriate measures to further the observance of those rights;
> c)   to prepare such studies or reports as it considers advisable in the performance of its duties;
> d)   to request the governments of the member states to supply it with information on the measures adopted by them in matters of human rights;
> e)   to respond, through the General Secretariat of the Organisation of American States, to inquiries made by the member states on matters related to human rights and, within the limits of its possibilities, to provide those states with the advisory services they request;
> f)   to take action on petitions and other communications pursuant to its authority under the provisions of Articles 44 through 51 of this Convention; and
> g)   to submit an annual report to the General Assembly of the Organisation of American States.

---

[36] Article 3(2) of Statute of the Commission.

[37] Article 5 of Statute of the Commission.

[38] C. Cerna, 'The Inter-American Commission on Human Rights: Its Organisation and Examination of Petitions and Communications' in D.J. Harris and S. Livingstone (eds), above n. 1, 65–113 at p. 74.

[39] Shelton, above n. 31, p. 122.

These are the functions which the Commission used to perform prior to the ACHR becoming effective. As is evident, these are of a promotional character which includes making recommendations to member governments and requesting information on the human rights issues. The Commission also has the authority to prepare reports on the human rights situation in any State of the O.A.S., and can use information from individuals and NGOs to prepare such reports. It submits annual reports to the O.A.S. General Assembly, which includes resolutions on individual cases, reports on various States and recommendations for progress in human rights situations.[40] Articles 44–47 relate to those functions which apply specifically to the States parties to the ACHR. They focus on the individual and inter-State complaints procedures.

Complaints procedure

The procedure for acting upon individual complaints from the O.A.S. Charter system and ACHR systems can be found in different sources. In the case of the O.A.S. Charter system the complaints procedure is provided by regulation 51–54 of the Commission's Regulations[41] whereas the complaint procedures under the ACHR are contained in Articles 44–55 of the Convention. Notwithstanding these sources the actual practice of the two bodies is similar, though differences can be found in the post-admissibility stages. The differences result from the institutional structuring of the two institutions. While in the case of ACHR, the Commission has the option of transmitting cases to the Court, providing the relevant State has accepted the jurisdiction of the Court,[42] no such possibilities exist in the case of O.A.S. Charter system. The absence of a Court also means that the final decisions in the O.A.S. Charter systems are made by the Commission. The Commission, unlike the Court, cannot dispense legally binding judgment. Secondly unlike the ACHR system, no obligations exist for the Commission to secure a friendly settlement.[43]

THE AMERICAN CONVENTION ON HUMAN RIGHTS (ACHR)

The ACHR, also known as the Pact of San José, along with its protocols represents the second part of the inter-American human rights system. ACHR was adopted in 1969 and entered into force in 1978. In 1988 an additional protocol was concluded extending the range of rights it covered. In 1990,

---

[40] Ibid. p. 122.
[41] Regulations of the Inter-American Commission on Human Rights, reprinted in *Basic Documents Pertaining to Human Rights in the Inter-American System*, OEA/Ser.L.V/II.82 Doc.6 rev.at 103 (1992).
[42] Article 14 ACHR.
[43] Davidson, above n. 1, at p. 135.

another protocol was adopted which aimed at the abolition of the death penalty. There have been several sources of inspiration for ACHR, including the International Covenants and the ECHR. In terms of the implementation mechanisms, similarities can be traced between the European Convention and its American counterpart. At the time of its inception, the ACHR followed the pattern of ECHR, being managed by a Commission and Court. However, whereas the European Commission was abolished after the 11th Protocol came into operation, the ACHR continues to rely upon its Commission and Court. The functions of the Inter-American Commission include admissibility and a possible friendly settlement. The recommendations of the Inter-American Commission are conducted on merit but are not legally binding. The functions of the Court are largely of a judicial decision-making nature. There are two processes of complaint allowed by the Convention. First, there is the contentious procedure, which allows both individuals (and other non-State actors) to institute proceedings against a State party to the Convention and an inter-State complaints procedure. Second, there is the possibility of invoking the advisory jurisdiction of the Court.

In the light of the influence of the comparable international and regional human rights instruments, it is not surprising that many of the rights contained in the American Convention overlap or relate very closely to those of other regional and international human rights treaties. The ACHR contains traditional civil and political rights as well as economic, social and cultural rights. Many similarities can be found within the rights contained in the Convention, the International Covenants and the ECHR, although there are a number of significant differences. The ACHR contains a number of rights, not found in either the International Covenants or the ECHR. Having said that, the anticipation with which they were implemented is more or less the same as in other international covenants.[44] The economic rights contained in the ACHR are supplemented by the Protocol. It is interesting to note that the differences in implementation follow the pattern of International Covenants and the European Human Rights System. According to Article 1(1) of ACHR, States parties are to 'respect the rights and freedoms' and to 'ensure to all persons subject to their jurisdiction the free and full exercise of those rights and freedoms'. By contrast, Article 1 of the Protocol provides that the States parties take appropriate measures 'for the purpose of achieving progressively ... the full observance of the rights recognised in the protocol'.

The following rights are contained in the Convention:

Article 3	Right to recognition before the law
Article 4	Right to life
Article 5	Right to humane treatment

---

[44] Ibid. pp. 136–137.

Article 6   Freedom from slavery and servitude
Article 7   Right to liberty and security
Article 8   Right to a fair trial
Article 9   Freedom from retroactively of the criminal law
Article 10   Right to compensation
Article 11   Right to privacy
Article 12   Freedom of conscience and religion
Article 13   Freedom of thought and expression
Article 14   Right to reply
Article 15   Freedom of assembly
Article 16   Freedom of association
Article 17   Freedom to marry and found a family
Article 18   Right to a name
Article 19   Rights of the child
Article 20   Right to nationality
Article 21   Right to property
Article 22   Freedom of movement and residence
Article 23   Right to participate in government
Article 24   Right to equal protection
Article 25   Right to juridical protection
Article 26   Economic, social and cultural rights

ANALYSIS OF SUBSTANTIVE RIGHTS

Right to life, liberty, the prohibition of enforced disappearances and torture

Article 4 protects the fundamental right to life; Article 4(1) provides that 'Every person has the right to have his life respected'. The remainder of the Article, however, raises a number of issues without providing any definitive statement. It notes that the right to life 'shall be protected by law, and in general from the moment of conception'. The question as to whether abortion is a violation of the Convention has been considered by the Inter-American Commission in a case arising from the US, which is not a party to the Convention. After considering the *travaux préparatoires* of the American Declaration, the Commission concluded that abortion of a foetus did not lead to a violation of the Declaration. The Commission also held obiter that the term 'in general' allowed a discretion to States to determine the validity of their respective abortion laws.[45]

Article 4(1), like Article 6(1) of ICCPR goes on to prohibit 'arbitrary' taking of life. The Inter-American Court has adopted a strict approach, defining 'arbitrary' to mean that any taking of life must not be the result of a

[45] See the *Baby Boy Case*, Case No. 2141 (United States), Res. 23/81, OEA/Ser. L/V/II.54, Doc. 9, rev. 1, Oct. 16, 1981. For commentary on the case see D. Shelton, 'Abortion and the Right to Life in the Inter-American System: The Case of "Baby Boy"' 2 *HRLJ* (1981) 309.

disproportionate use of force by public authorities.[46] In line with the ECHR, the Inter-American Court has pronounced on the existence of a positive and negative obligation on State parties.[47] Like the ICCPR, Article 4(2) represents what has been described as an 'abolitionist trend'.[48] It allows the death penalty for only the most serious offences, with the prohibition on reintroduction of this penalty in States which have already abolished capital punishment and the prohibition of its extension to crimes to which it currently does not apply. Enforced disappearances have been an unfortunate recurrent theme in the history of the States of Latin America. The Inter-American institutions have included the phenomenon of enforced disappearances as representing acts of torture or cruel, inhuman or degrading punishment or treatment.[49] Similarly, prolonged periods of detention incommunicado,[50] rape,[51] putting hoods on the victims so as to suffocate;[52] mock burials and mock executions;[53] enforcement of malnutrition and starvation[54] have all been categorised as torture.

As already noted, the O.A.S. system in recognising the significance of prohibiting, condemning and punishing all forms of torture adopted a regional convention in 1985.[55] Article 1 of the Convention defines torture as follows:

> For the purposes of this Convention, torture shall be understood to be any act intentionally performed whereby physical or mental pain or suffering is inflicted on a person for purposes of criminal investigation, as a means of intimidation, as personal punishment, as a preventive measure, as a penalty, or for any other purpose. Torture shall also be understood to be the use of methods upon a person intended to obliterate the personality of the victim or to diminish his physical or mental capacities, even if they do not cause physical pain or mental anguish.
>
> The concept of torture shall not include physical or mental pain or suffering that is inherent in or solely the consequence of lawful measures, provided that

---

[46] *Neira Alegria Case*, Judgment of January 19 1995, Inter-Am.Ct.H.R. (Ser. C) No. 20 (1995).

[47] *Velasquez Rodriguez Case*, Judgment of July 29 1988, Inter-Am.Ct.H.R. (Ser. C) No. 4 (1988).

[48] S. Davidson, 'The Civil and Political Rights Protected in the Inter-American Human Rights System' in D.J. Harris and S. Livingstone (eds), above n. 1, 213–288 at p. 222.

[49] See *Lissardi and Rossi v. Guatemala*, Case 10.508, Report No. 25/94, Inter-Am.C.H.R., OEA/Ser.L/V/II.88 rev.1 Doc. 9 at 51 (1995).

[50] *Velasquez Rodriguez Case*, Judgment of July 29 1988, Inter-Am.Ct.H.R. (Ser. C) No. 4 (1988).

[51] *Caracoles Community v. Bolivia*, Case 7481, Res. No. 30/82, March 8 1982, OAS/Ser.L/V/II.57, Doc. 6 Rev. 1, at 20 September 1982, at 36 and *Raquel Martí de Mejía v. Perú*, Case 10.970, Report No. 5/96, Inter-Am.C.H.R., OEA/Ser.L/V/II.91 Doc. 7 at 157 (1996),

[52] *Lovato v. El Salvador*, Case 10.574, Report No. 5/94, Inter-Am.C.H.R., OEA/Ser.L/V/II.85 Doc. 9 rev. at 174 (1994).

[53] *Barrera v. Bolivia*, Case No. 7824, Res. No. 33/82, Inter-Am.C.H.R., O.A.S./Ser.L/V/II.57, Doc. 6 rev. (1982) 44.

[54] *Roslik et al. v. Uruguay*, Case 9274, Res. No. 11/84, October 3 1984, O.A.S./Ser.L/V/II.66, doc.10 rev. 1, at 121.

[55] See Kaplan, above n. 12, at p. 399; Davidson, above n. 12, at p. 25.

they do not include the performance of the acts or use of the methods referred to in this article.

The Inter-American Commission (unlike the ECHR) has not distinguished between torture, inhuman and degrading treatment.[56] In a recent case relating to rape, in elaborating upon the meaning of torture, the Inter-American Commission has noted that there should be *mens rea* and *actus reas*, and that the act must be committed either by a public official or by an individual at the instigation of an officer.[57]

Enforced disappearances bear a strong relationship with torture but essential prerequisites to these disappearances are also loss of personal liberty and inhumane treatment. The ACHR protects both the right to personal liberty and security[58] and provides for a right to humane treatment.[59] Article 7, in according the right to personal liberty, prohibits arbitrary arrests, imprisonment and loss of liberty save for reasons established by law. Whereas the right to liberty is breached in the absence of lawful arrests[60] and for failure to comply with national laws,[61] the right to security is violated by threatening individuals with arbitrary arrests and detention.[62]

Equality and non-discrimination

Article 1(1) in placing obligations on States parties provides for the State to respect the rights of all persons and to ensure to all persons

> subject to their jurisdiction the free and full exercise of those rights and freedoms, without any discrimination for reasons of race, color, sex, language, religion, political or other opinion, national or social origin, economic status, birth, or any other social condition.

The obligations in the article are further reinforced through the provisions of Article 24, which affirms that 'all persons are equal before the law. Consequently, they are entitled, without discrimination, to equal protection of the law'. Equality, as is emphasised throughout this book, is the norm with the *jus cogens* character. This Article prohibits discriminatory practices in the

---

[56] S. Davidson, 'The Civil and Political Rights Protected in the Inter-American Human Rights System' in D.J. Harris and S. Livingstone (eds), above n. 1, 213–288, at p. 230.
[57] *Raquel Martí de Mejía* v. *Perú*, Case 10.970, Report No. 5/96, Inter-Am.C.H.R., OEA/Ser.L/V/II.91 Doc. 7 at 157 (1996), at 182–8.
[58] Article 7.
[59] Article 5. According to Article 5(1) 'Every person has the right to have his physical, mental and moral integrity respected'.
[60] Article 5(1).
[61] *Gangaram Panday Case*, Judgment of January 21 1994, Inter-Am.Ct.H.R. (Ser. C) No. 16 (1994).
[62] *Garcia* v. *Peru*, Case 11.006, Report No. 1/95, Inter-Am.C.H.R., OEA/Ser.L/V/II.88 rev.1 Doc. 9 at 71 (1995).

provision of rights contained in the Convention and no derogations are permissible from the norm of non-discrimination. The value behind this principle of equality and non-discrimination was reiterated by the American Court in Advisory Opinion No. 4 Proposed Amendment to Naturalisation Provisions of the Political Constitution of Costa Rica[63] when it stated 'equality springs directly from the oneness of the human family and is linked to the essential dignity of the individual'.[64] The Court went on to approve the affirmative action policies in order to generate de facto equality and cited with approval the European Court of Human Rights in the *Belgian Linguistic Case*.[65]

Equality before the law has a substantial association with principles of natural justice and most significantly to the right to fair trial, a right protected by Article 8 of the Convention. Article 8(1) in providing the right to fair trial states:

> Every person has the right to a hearing, with due guarantees and within a reasonable time, by a competent, independent, and impartial tribunal, previously established by law, in the substantiation of any accusation of a criminal nature made against him or for the determination of his rights and obligations of a civil, labor, fiscal, or any other nature.

The right to fair trial also includes in criminal cases a right to be presumed innocent until proven guilty.[66] It also incorporates the right of the accused to be assisted, without charge, by an interpreter,[67] prior notification of the charge,[68] adequate time and means for the preparation of defence,[69] right of assistance through counsel,[70] the right to examine witnesses and to obtain the appearance of witnesses of experts,[71] the right not to be compelled to be a witness against himself[72] (or not to make confession through coercion),[73] a right to appeal.[74] The right to fair trial provides guarantees against the rule of double jeopardy,[75] and ensures that a trial should be held in public unless a closed trial is necessary to protect the interests of justice.[76] The right to fair trial is strengthened by Article 10 which provides that 'Every person has the

---

[63] Proposed Amendments to the Naturalization Provisions of the Constitution of Costa Rica, Advisory Opinion OC-4/84, January 19, 1984, Inter-Am. Ct. H.R. (Ser. A) No. 4 (1984).
[64] Ibid. para 54.
[65] *Belgian Linguistic Case* (No. 2), Judgment of 23 July 1968, Series A, No. 6, cited ibid. para 57.
[66] Article 8(2).
[67] Article 8(2)(a).
[68] Article 8(2)(b).
[69] Article 8(2)(c).
[70] Article 8(2)(e).
[71] Article 8(2)(f).
[72] Article 8(2(g)).
[73] Article 8(3).
[74] Article 8(2)(h).
[75] Article 8(4).
[76] Article 8(5).

right to be compensated in accordance with the law in the event he has been sentenced by a final judgment through a miscarriage of justice'.

Privacy, religion, thought, expression, assembly and association

This section considers a number of rights which are distinct from one another but with overlapping features. Freedom of religion is inextricably related to freedom of thought and expression. A similar relationship could be found in cases of freedom of assembly and association. The right to privacy and honour is protected by Article 11 of the Convention. Violation of honour, according to the American Commission, represents not only moral and spiritual indignation but could also include physical abuse.[77] Article 11 bears similarities to Article 8 of the ECHR, and the Inter-American Commission has been influenced in its approach by the decisions of the European Court of Human Rights. Although unlike the ECHR the ACHR does not provide an explicit clause justifying restrictions based on public interest, national security or public safety, such restrictions are implied in the provisions of the Article and would be authorised by the Commission. Articles 12 and 13 in granting freedom of religion and thought are more explicit in recognising the authority of the State to place limitations. At the same time the Commission and Court have made it clear that any discretion given to the State has to be construed narrowly.[78] Pursing this narrowly construed discretion the Court found that the practice of compulsory licensing of journalists in Costa Rica could not be justified on grounds of public order.[79]

Specialist rights

The ACHR contains a number of rights which have been of special concern for States from the Americas. Among these can be included the right to reply

---

[77] See *Rivas* v. *El Salvador*, Case 10.772, Report No. 6/94, Inter-Am.C.H.R., OEA/Ser.L/V/II.85 Doc. 9 rev. at 181 (1994). Discussed by S. Davidson, 'The Civil and Political Rights Protected in the Inter-American Human Rights System' in D.J. Harris and S. Livingstone (eds), above n. 1, 213–288 at p. 256.

[78] See *Steve Clark* v. *Grenada*, Case 10.325, Report No. 2/96, Inter-Am.C.H.R., OEA/Ser.L/V/II.91 Doc. 7 at 113 (1996).

[79] Compulsory Membership in an Association Prescribed by Law for the Practice of Journalism (Arts 13 and 29 of the American Convention on Human Rights), Advisory Opinion OC-5/85, November 13 1985, Inter-Am. Ct. H.R. (Ser. A) No. 5 (1985). Also see *Nicolas Estiverne* v. *Haiti*, Case 9.855, Res. No 20/88, March 24 1988, OEA/Ser.L/V/II.74, Doc. 10 rev. 1, at 146; *Spadafora Franco* v. *Panama*, Case 9.726, Res. No 25/87, September 23 1987, OEA/Ser.L/V/II.74, Doc. 10 rev. 1, at 174.

and the right to a name. Article 18 represents an interesting provision and in conferring the right to a name, notes:

> Every person has the right to a given name and to the surnames of his parents or that of one of them. The law shall regulate the manner in which this right shall be ensured for all, by the use of assumed names if necessary.

Although the right to a name is provided for in other international instruments, the inclusion of this right has been campaigned for particularly strongly by Latin American States. As we shall consider in due course, the Article relating to the right to an identity was introduced by Argentina for incorporation into the Convention on the Rights of the Child. Argentina campaigned for the incorporation of the right to identity as a reaction to its so-called 'dirty war'.[80] These sentiments were no doubt the driving force for the incorporation of this right in the ACHR. The American Commission has confirmed the relevance of this Article for Argentina by holding irregular adoptions of the children of *desaparecidos*, disappearances and kidnapping as violating Article 18.[81]

The right to property as an important right is contained in Article 21. This right is contained in the UDHR, the first Protocol of the ECHR and the African Charter, although due to a number of controversies could not be included in the international covenants. The provision is extremely useful for a region which has been vulnerable to denial of property rights, expropriation and nationalisation. The American Commission has accorded this right a special significance and has regarded it as of great value for the enjoyment of other human rights.[82] While the overall rationale behind an Article dealing with the right to property appears acceptable, what is less certain is the inclusion of Article 21(3) which provides that 'Usury and any other form of exploitation of man by man shall be prohibited by law'. A possible reason for the inclusion of the provision may be to prevent usury on tangible property. Nevertheless, the article perhaps appears more in tune with the values put forward by Islamic States on the prohibition of *riba* than with the American States.[83]

The right to freedom of movement and residence also signifies a useful right, and is represented in other international human rights instruments. Of particular

---

[80] D. Fottrell, 'Children's Rights' in A. Hegarty and S. Leonard (eds), *Human Rights: An Agenda for the Twenty First Century* (London: Cavendish Press) 1999, 167–179 at p. 172; D. Freestone, 'The United Nations Convention on the Rights of the Child' in D. Freestone (ed.), *Children and the Law: Essays in Honour of Professor H.K. Bevan* (Hull: Hull University Press) 1990, 288–323 at p. 290. See Chapter 14 below.

[81] See IACHR 'A Study about the Situation of Minor Children who were Separated from their Parents and are claimed by Members of their Legitimate Families' [1988] *Inter-American Year Book on Human Rights* 476 at 480.

[82] See *Marín* et al. v. *Nicaragua*, Case 10.770, Report No. 12/94, Inter-Am.C.H.R., OEA/Ser.L/V/II.85 Doc. 9 rev. at 293 (1994).

[83] See J. Rehman, 'Islamic Perspectives on International Economic Law' in A.H. Qureshi (ed.), *Perspectives on International Economic Law* (The Hague: Kluwer Law International) 2002, pp. 235–258.

value, in this regard in the context of the Americas is the provision of the right to seek and gain asylum.[84] The *Asylum Case (Columbia* v. *Peru)*[85] before the International Court of Justice confirms that the issues concerning asylum have formed a sensitive aspect in the complex political matrix of the region.[86]

Economic, social and cultural rights

The ACHR is one of the first civil and political rights treaties to explicitly incorporate economic, social and cultural rights.[87] Article 26 provides that:

> The States Parties undertake to adopt measures, both internally and through international cooperation, especially those of an economic and technical nature, with a view to achieving progressively, by legislation or other appropriate means, the full realization of the rights implicit in the economic, social, educational, scientific, and cultural standards set forth in the Charter of the Organization of American States as amended by the Protocol of Buenos Aires.

The provisions in this Article have been supplemented by the Protocol on Economic, Social and Cultural rights.[88] Although the overall picture in dealing with cultural rights has not been promising, particularly in relation to indigenous peoples, the Commission has taken the view that within international law there exists a prohibition on unrestricted assimilation of cultural and indigenous rights and that

> special legal protection is recognized for the use of language, the observance of their religion, and in general, all those aspects related to the preservation of their cultural identity. To this should be added the aspects linked to productive organization, which includes, among other things, the issue of the ancestral and communal lands.[89]

PROCEDURES UNDER THE AMERICAN CONVENTION ON HUMAN RIGHTS

State reporting

There is no reporting procedure under ACHR similar to the ones conducted by the treaty-based bodies. There are, however, limited provisions in relation

---

[84] Article 22(7) provides 'Every person has the right to seek and be granted asylum in a foreign territory, in accordance with the legislation of the State and international conventions, in the event he is being pursued for political offenses or related common crimes'.

[85] *Asylum Case (Colombia* v. *Peru)*, Judgment 20 November 1950 (1950) ICJ Reports 266.

[86] See M.N. Shaw, *International Law*, 4th edn (Cambridge: Grotius Publication) 1997, p. 60.

[87] See M. Craven, 'The Protection of Economic, Social and Cultural Rights under the Inter-American System of Human Rights' in D.J. Harris and S. Livingstone (eds), above n. 1, at pp. 289–321.

[88] Ibid.

[89] See O.A.S. Docs. OEA/Ser. L/V/II.62, doc. 10 rev. 3 (1983) and OEA/Ser.LV/II.62, doc.26 (1984).

to reporting contained in Articles 42 and 43 of the treaty. These Articles provide as follows:

Article 42

The States Parties shall transmit to the Commission a copy of each of the reports and studies that they submit annually to the Executive Committees of the Inter-American Economic and Social Council and the Inter-American Council for Education, Science, and Culture, in their respective fields, so that the Commission may watch over the promotion of the rights implicit in the economic, social, educational, scientific, and cultural standards set forth in the Charter of the Organization of American States as amended by the Protocol of Buenos Aires.

Article 43

The States Parties undertake to provide the Commission with such information as it may request of them as to the manner in which their domestic law ensures the effective application of any provisions of this Convention.

Individual complaints procedure

Petitions are to be submitted in writing, stating the facts of the case, the details of the victim, the name of the State alleged to have violated the rights, and the alleged breaches. It is also important for the petition to confirm that domestic remedies have been exhausted and the communication satisfies other admissibility requirements. It is equally significant to assess the financial implications of the petitioning to the Commission. For invoking the Inter-American procedure, legal aid is not generally available.[90]

Article 44 provides for the procedure for individual complaints. According to Article 44:

Any person or groups of persons, or any non-governmental entity legally recognized in one or more member States of the Organization, may lodge petitions with the Commission containing denunciations or complaints of violations of the Convention by a State party.

It must be noted that the States becoming parties to ACHR automatically recognise the competence of the Commission to receive complaints from persons alleging violation of their rights. The petitioning system is also automatic for the States of the O.A.S. Charter. The differences between the ACHR and the Optional Protocol of the ICCPR and the ECHR are worthy of consideration. While according to Article 34 of the ECHR only 'victims' may be authors of communications, Article 44 provides that 'any person or group of persons, or any non-governmental entity legally recognized in one or more member

---

[90] See C. Cerna, 'The Inter-American Commission on Human Rights: Its Organisation and Examination of Petitions and Communications' in D.J. Harris and S. Livingstone (eds), above n. 1, 65–113 at p. 79.

states of the Organization, may lodge petitions with the Commission containing denunciations or complaints of victims of this convention by a State party'. Similarly since any person, NGO or legally recognised entity may lodge a petition regardless of their being a victim of a violation, the ACHR is generous in that *actio popularis* applications are permissible.[91] 'Person' means a person who is alive and does not include entities such as banks and corporations.[92]

Inter-State application

Like the ICCPR, the ECHR and the AFCHPR, the ACHR provides for an inter-State complaints mechanism. However, unlike ECHR (and in line with ICCPR), the State is required to make a declaration recognising the competence of the Commission to receive and examine communications from another State. Article 45(1) provides for this procedure, according to which:

> Any State party may, when it deposits its instrument of ratification of or adherence to this Convention, or at any later time, declare that it recognizes the competence of the Commission to receive and examine communications in which a State Party alleges that another State party has committed a violation of a human right set forth in this Convention.

Communications under this procedure are only acceptable on the basis of reciprocity.[93] By way of contrast to the European human rights system, the inter-State application procedure has never been used.[94]

Admissibility requirements

The procedure for admissibility of individual and inter-State complaints is provided for in Articles 46–47. Article 46 provides as follows:

> Admission by the Commission of a petition or communication lodged in accordance with Articles 44 or 45 shall be subject to the following requirements:
>
> (a) that the remedies under domestic law have been pursued and exhausted in accordance with generally recognized principles of international law;
> (b) that the petition or communication is lodged within a period of six months from the date on which the party alleging violation of his rights was notified of the final judgment;

---

[91] Shelton, above n. 1, at p. 342.
[92] See C. Cerna, 'The Inter-American Commission on Human Rights: Its Organisation and Examination of Petitions and Communications' in D.J. Harris and S. Livingstone (eds), above n. 1, 65–113 at p. 78.
[93] See Article 45(2).
[94] D. Harris, 'Regional Protection of Human Rights: The Inter-American Achievement' in D.J. Harris and S. Livingstone (eds), above n. 1, 1–29 at p. 3.

(c) that the subject of the petition or communication is not pending in another international proceeding for settlement; and

(d) that, in the case of Article 44, the petition contains the name, nationality, profession, domicile, and signature of the person or persons or of the legal representative of the entity lodging the petition.

2. The provisions of paragraphs 1(a) and 1(b) of this article shall not be applicable when:

(a) the domestic legislation of the state concerned does not afford due process of law for the protection of the right or rights that have allegedly been violated;

(b) the party alleging violation of his rights has been denied access to the remedies under domestic law or has been prevented from exhausting them; or

(c) there has been unwarranted delay in rendering a final judgment under the aforementioned remedies.

The admissibility requirements of Article 46 are supplemented by those of Article 47 which provides that:

The Commission shall consider inadmissible any petition or communication submitted under Articles 44 or 45 if:

(a) any of the requirements indicated in Article 46 has not been met;

(b) the petition or communication does not state facts that tend to establish a violation of the rights guaranteed by this Convention;

(c) the statements of the petitioner or of the state indicate that the petition or communication is manifestly groundless or obviously out of order; or

(d) the petition or communication is substantially the same as one previously studied by the Commission or by another international organization.

As analysis throughout this book has shown, in order to invoke any international human rights procedure certain prerequisites must be met. The ACHR, in common with other human rights systems, contains certain conditions. According to the provisions of the ACHR, the petitioner must have pursued and exhausted all domestic remedies, although as Shelton points out this requirement is 'less stringent than other human rights systems'.[95] In accordance with the general principles of international law, the petitioner is only required to pursue and exhaust those remedies which would adequately and effectively redress his grievances. He is not obliged to apply to domestic courts where there are no adequate remedies or if there is an 'unwarranted delay'.[96] The Commission has developed in its jurisprudence the meaning of the term 'unwarranted delay'.[97] The petitioner is also not obliged to follow his case in the domestic courts where

---

[95] Shelton, above n. 1, at p. 344.

[96] Article 46(2)(c).

[97] See *Fabricio Proano et al.* v. *Ecuador*, Case 9.641, Res. No 14/89, April 12 1989, OEA/Ser.L/V/II.76, Doc.10, at 104; see *Rojas DeNegri and Quintana* v. *Chile*, Case 9.755, Res. No. 01a/88, September 12 1988, OEA/Ser.L/V/II.74, Doc. 10 rev. 1, at 132.

he or she is being denied access to remedies[98] or is being prevented from exhausting domestic remedies,[99] or there has been a denial of justice because of lack of independent judicial determination of the case.[100]

As regards the burden of establishing whether adequate or effective domestic remedies exist and need to be pursued as a prerequisite, the Commission has tended to follow an approach favouring the petitioner.[101] This approach is closer in line to the one adopted by the Human Rights Committee, as opposed to the one adopted by the former European Commission on Human Rights. Such a liberal approach is probably due to the difficulties which an individual is likely to encounter in satisfying the principle, particularly regarding the provision of adequate evidence in his favour. The Inter-American Court has endorsed the Commission's approach. In the *Velasquez Rodriguez case*,[102] the Court noted 'a State claiming non-exhaustion of local remedies has an obligation to prove that domestic remedies remain to be exhausted and that they are effective'.[103]

The petitioner is also obliged to submit his claim to the Commission within a period of six months of the final decision within the domestic court.[104] The procedure has many similarities with those of the ECHR. Like the ECHR requirement, in the present instance the six months will start running from the date of final decision involving the exhaustion of all domestic remedies; the period starts from the actual notification of the judgment. The Commission may refuse to accept the petition under this heading if, after the initial letter to pursue the action, there is a substantial period of inaction before the applicant submits further information. On the other hand, the Commission has shown flexibility in the application of the six months rule where expiry of time limit is attributable to the State,[105] or in cases of continuing violations such as detention[106] or disappearances of the victims.[107]

---

[98] Article 46(2)(b).

[99] Ibid.

[100] C. Cerna, 'The Inter-American Commission on Human Rights: Its Organisation and Examination of Petitions and Communications' in D.J. Harris and S. Livingstone (eds), above n. 1, 65–113 at p. 87.

[101] The Commission's Regulations provide 'When the petitioner contends that he is unable to prove exhaustion as indicated in this Article, it shall be up to the government against which this petition has been lodged to demonstrate to the Commission that the remedies under domestic law have not previously been exhausted, unless it is clearly evident from the background information contained in the petition'. The Commission's Regulation Article 37(3).

[102] *Velasquez Rodriguez Case*, Judgment of July 29 1988, Inter-Am.Ct.H.R. (Ser. C) No. 4 (1988).

[103] Ibid. Preliminary Objections para 88.

[104] Article 46(1)(b).

[105] See Commission's Regulations Article 38(2).

[106] See *Bustos* v. *Argentina*, Case 2.488, Res. No. 15/81, March 6 1981, OAS/Ser.L./V/II.54, Doc. 9 rev. 1, at 19 and *Cano* v. *Argentina*, Case 3482, Res. No. 16/81, March 6 1981, OAS/Ser.L/V/II.54, Doc. 9 rev. 1, at 23.

[107] See *Mignone* v. *Argentina*, Case 2.209, Res. No. 21/78, November 18 1978; OEA/Ser.L/V/II.50, Doc. 13, rev. 1, at 49; *San Vincente* v. *Argentina*, Case 2.266, Res. No. 22/78, November 18 1978; OEA/Ser.L/V/II.50, Doc. 13, rev. 1, at 52. Resolution No. 21/78, 22/78.

Article 46(1)(c) requires that the 'subject of the petition or communication is not pending in another international proceeding'. This requirement is placed to avoid the petitioner instituting parallel proceedings under another international procedure. However, this limitation does not apply where the case is being considered by the United Nations Working Group on Enforced and Involuntary Disappearances,[108] or under the ILO Procedures[109] or simultaneous applications have been made by an unrelated third party.[110]

Procedure

If the communication is held admissible under Article 46 then the Commission goes on to consider whether it satisfies conditions in Article 47. The communication would fail if any of the requirements of Article 46 are not met. It would also fail if no violation of any of the rights in the Convention is found. Similarly there would be a failure if the petition is manifestly groundless or out of order. Finally it would be inadmissible if the communication is substantially the same as one already studied by the Commission or studied by any other international Organisation.

Once the communication is held to be prima facie admissible, there are two stages. In accordance with Article 48 the primary function of the Commission is to receive all necessary information and evidence up to and during the proceedings of the case.[111] On receipt of relevant information or after the passage of an established period, the Commission decides whether grounds exist for the consideration of the petition; and in cases where they do not, the Commission is authorised to close the case.[112] The second function for the Commission (which takes place if the case has not been closed[113] or if the petition has not been held admissible)[114] is to place itself at the disposal of parties with a view to reaching a friendly settlement.[115]

---

[108] See *Munoz Yaranga et al.* v. *Peru*, Cases 9501–9512, Res. No 1–19/88, 24 March 1988, OEA/Ser.L/V/II.74, Doc. 10 rev. 1, pp. 235–274.

[109] See the Commission's report, fifty-fourth Session 1981.

[110] *Lilian Celiberti de Casariego* v. *Uruguay*, Communication No. 56/1979 (29 July 1981), UN Doc. CCPR/C/OP/1 at 92 (1984).

[111] Article 48(1)(a) and Article 48(1)(e) (ACHR). (For the provision of information, time limits are prescribed. See Article 34 of the Commission's Regulations.)

[112] Article 48(1)(b) (ACHR).

[113] Article 48(1)(b) (ACHR).

[114] Article 48(1)(c) (ACHR).

[115] Article 48(1)(f). While the Court has recognised that the Commission has some discretion in reaching for a friendly settlement (see *Velasquez Rodriguez*, Preliminary Objections para 42) it has been critical of the Commission for its reluctance in using the provision, since according to the provision, such action represents a mandatory requirement (see *Caballero Delgado and Santana Case*, Preliminary Objections, Judgment of January 21 1994, Inter-Am.Ct.H.R. (Ser. C) No. 17 (1994).

If a friendly settlement is reached, in accordance with Article 49, the Commission then needs to draw up a report consisting of a brief statement of facts and the solution reached, which is transmitted to the Secretary General of the O.A.S. However, if it is not possible to reach a settlement, the Commission must draw up a report under Article 50 stating the facts and its conclusions and transmit it to the relevant State party concerned within 180 days.[116]

Under Article 50(1) (and in cases where settlement is not reached) the Commission may make a recommendation or proposal which must not be published.[117] With the transmission of the report there commences a three-month period during which the parties could settle the case, or the case could be referred to the Court either by the Commission or the State party itself.[118] If any of these actions do not take place, then the Commission has the option of presenting its opinion and recommendations as to the remedial course of action. In making such recommendation, the Commission is required to prescribe a time frame within which these remedial actions need to be taken.[119] After the expiry of the three-month period, the Commission must decide whether the State has undertaken proper action and whether to publish its report.[120] There is no guidance in the rules of procedure as to when the Commission must refer a case to the Court. From the jurisprudence of the Court, it can be said that cases raising complex or controversial legal issues ought to be referred to the Court.[121]

THE INTER-AMERICAN COURT OF HUMAN RIGHTS[122]

The Inter-American Court of Human Rights was established in pursuance of the ACHR. The Court has its permanent seat in San José, Costa Rica. The provisions relating to the Court are provided in Chapter VIII of the ACHR. According to Article 52, the Court is to consist of seven judges. Only States parties to the O.A.S. Charter make the nominations, although the nominated person need not hold the nationality of the State proposing his or her appointment.[123]

---

[116] See Article 50.

[117] See Article 50(2).

[118] Article 51(1).

[119] Article 51(1) and Article 51(2).

[120] See Article 51.

[121] *Compulsory Membership in an Association Prescribed by Law for the Practice of Journalism* (Arts 13 and 29 of the American Convention on Human Rights), Advisory Opinion OC-5/85, November 13 1985, Inter-Am. Ct. H.R. (Ser. A) No. 5 (1985).

[122] S. Davidson, *The Inter-American Court of Human Rights* (Aldershot: Dartmouth) 1992; C.A. Dunshee de Abranches, 'La Corte Interamericana de Derechos Humanos' in *La Convencióan Americana sobre Derechos Humanos* (Washington) 1990, pp. 91–147; C.M. Cerna, 'The Structure and Functioning of the Inter-American Court of Human Rights (1979–1992) 63 *BYIL* (1992) 135.

[123] Article 52(2) ACHR; Article 4(2) Statute.

Membership of the Court is limited to a maximum of one judge having the nationality of a given State.[124] The judges act in their individual capacity for a period of six years and are re-electable only once.[125] They are 'jurists of the highest moral authority and of recognised competence in the field of human rights, who possess qualifications required for the exercise of the highest judicial functions'. As noted above the judges are nominated and elected for a term of six years by States parties to the American Convention.

There remains the possibility of appointing ad hoc judges; the circumstances of such appointments are provided in Article 55:

1   If a judge is a national of any of the States Parties to a case submitted to the Court, he shall retain his right to hear that case.
2   If one of the judges called upon to hear a case should be a national of one of the States Parties to the case, any other State Party in the case may appoint a person of its choice to serve on the Court as an ad hoc judge.
3   If among the judges called upon to hear a case none is a national of any of the States Parties to the case, each of the latter may appoint an ad hoc judge.
4   An ad hoc judge shall possess the qualifications indicated in Article 52.
5   If several States Parties to the Convention should have the same interest in a case, they shall be considered as a single party for purposes of the above provisions. In case of doubt, the Court shall decide.

The Court does not sit throughout the year but has two regular sessions.[126] However there remains the possibility of asking for a special session and the Court has the power to order provisional measures and make an interim judgment. The quorum of the Court is five members and, unlike the ECHR, there is no possibility of formulating the Chambers.[127]

FORMS OF JURISDICTION

Contentious jurisdiction

The Court has two forms of jurisdictions: a contentious and an advisory jurisdiction. Contentious jurisdiction itself is of two types: inter-State or individual complaints although, as noted, the inter-State procedure has not yet been invoked. States may accept the contentious jurisdiction of the Court either unconditionally, conditionally or in specific cases.[128] In other words this

---

[124] Article 52(2) ACHR.
[125] Article 54(1) ACHR; Article 5(1) of the Statute.
[126] Article 22(1) Statute; Article 11 Rules.
[127] Davidson, above n. 122, at p. 46.
[128] Article 62(2).

jurisdiction is optional.[129] It must also be noted that only States and the Commission may submit a case to the Court.[130] The individual (unlike the new procedure under the ECHR) has no *locus standi* before the Court although the lawyer for the petitioners has been listed in all stages. For the Court to exercise its contentious jurisdiction, the proceedings before the Commission must have been completed, and the case must be referred by the Commission or the State within three months after the initial report on the matter is transmitted to the parties. The Commission notifies the individuals if the case is submitted to the Court and the individual is given an opportunity to make observations. It needs to be noted that unlike the ECHR, the contentious jurisdiction of the Inter-American Court is very recent and the first case where breaches were found was decided in 1988. This leaves the position that a number of Articles within the Convention have yet to be tested before the Court.[131]

According to Article 62, the Contentious jurisdiction may only be initiated if the State party or States parties concerned have accepted the Court's jurisdiction in such matters.[132] As noted above, the Court's jurisdiction cannot be invoked unless the procedures before the Commission have been fully completed.[133] Proceedings before the Court can be instituted through the filing of a petition to the Secretary General of the Court stating, *inter alia*, the grounds and violations of human rights.[134] Once an application has been received the Secretary of the Court notifies the Commission and all concerned State parties.[135] There is, at this point, a possibility of filing preliminary objections. On the receipt of these objections the Court may, at its discretion, either deal with these preliminary objections or join these with the merits of the case.[136] After submission of written memorials, the Court allows the parties to make oral submission during the hearing of the case.

Once the case has been referred to the court, it has the competence of reviewing the Commission's factual as well as admissibility findings *de novo*.[137] Unlike the European Court of Human Rights, the Inter-American Court has addressed the issue of measuring damages for personal injury and wrongful death.[138] However, neither European nor the Inter-American Court

---

[129] Not all parties to ACHR have accepted the jurisdiction of the Court.
[130] Article 61.
[131] A.A.C. Trindade, 'The Operation of the Inter-American Court of Human Rights' in D.J. Harris and S. Livingstone (eds), above n. 1, 133–150 at p. 141.
[132] Article 62(3).
[133] *Viviana Gallardo et al. case*, Advisory Opinion No. G 101/81, Inter-Am.Ct.H.R. (Ser. A) (1984).
[134] Articles 25(1) and 25(2) Rules of the Statute of the Court; Article 61 ACHR.
[135] Article 26 Rules of the Statute of the Court.
[136] Davidson, above n. 122, at p. 52.
[137] See Shelton, above n. 1, at p. 342.
[138] See *Velasquez Rodriguez Case*, Judgment of July 29 1988, Inter-Am.Ct.H.R. (Ser. C) No. 4 (1988); *El Amparo Case*, Judgment of January 18 1995, Inter-Am.Ct.H.R. (Ser. C) No. 19 (1995).

has awarded punitive damages yet. The *Velasquez Rodriguez*[139] and *Godínez Cruz* cases[140] were the first contentious cases before the Court, thereby allowing it the opportunity to expand on the Convention's provisions for reparations. Both the cases were brought against Honduras for the disappearances of the aforementioned individuals. In expanding on the meaning of reparations the Court observed

> Reparation of harm brought about by the violation of an international obligation consists in full restitution (restitutio in integrum) which includes the restoration of the prior situation, the reparation of the consequences of the violation, and indemnification and patrimonial and non-patrimonial damages, including emotional harm.[141]

Having stated the general position, the Court articulated a number of important principles on reparations. It adopted the approach that international law (as opposed to national law) should provide the criterion for awarding reparations. It recognised the value in awarding damages for emotional harm in instances of human rights violations, which in its view should be based on principles of equity, although it rejected the claim for punitive damages. The Court emphasised a duty upon the States to punish those responsible for the disappearances and to prevent future recurrence of any such violations. In rejecting the contentions made by the Honduras government that damages should be paid out at a level equivalent to accidental death, the Court awarded damages including loss of earnings which the victim would have earned until the point of death. The salary was based upon what the victim was earning at the time of his disappearance inclusive of the progressive increase of salary. In relation to the payment of damages, the Court ordered a payment within 90 days as lump sum. Alternatively, the State could make the payment in six months, though it would be subject to interest. In subsequent proceedings the Court ordered Honduras to compensate the victim for the loss in value of *Lempira* from the point of judgment.[142]

In a later case the issue of awarding damages was further elaborated. In *Aloeboetoe et al. case*,[143] the State of Surinam accepted liability for the detention, abuse and murder of seven unarmed Bush men, suspected by the State

---

[139] *Velasquez Rodriguez Case*, Judgment of July 29 1988, Inter-Am.Ct.H.R. (Ser. C) No. 4 (1988).

[140] *Godínez Cruz Case*, Judgment of January 20 1989, Inter-Am.Ct.H.R. (Ser. C) No. 5 (1989).

[141] *Velasquez Rodriguez Case*, para 26.

[142] See D. Shelton, 'Reparations in the Inter-American System' in D.J. Harris and S. Livingstone (eds), above n. 1, 151–172 at p. 156.

[143] *Aloeboetoe et al. Case*, Reparations (Art. 63(1) American Convention on Human Rights) Judgment of September 10 1993, Inter-Am.Ct.H.R. (Ser. C) No. 15 (1994). Text in International Human Rights Reports, 1(2), 1994, 208. Also see S. Davidson, 'Remedies for violations of the American Convention on Human Rights' 46 *ICLQ* (1995) 405.

police of subversive activities. The Court in awarding damages also took the innovative step of identifying the victims' successors through the application of the tribal customary laws of the Saramcas tribe and also dealt with the issue of moral damage for psychological harm.[144] In the *Neira Alegria case*[145] the Court found a violation of Article 4 conducted by Peru. The case concerned the disappearance of three prisoners after a cell block in which they were detained was destroyed. The Court awarded compensation that was to be fixed by agreement with the Commission. The Court, however, reserved the right to review and approve the agreement and to determine the amount in case of failure of any agreements.

Article 63 deals with the judgments of the Court. Article 63(1) provides:

> If the Court finds that there has been a violation of a right or freedom protected by this Convention, the Court shall rule that the injured party be ensured the enjoyment of his right or freedom that was violated. It shall also rule, if appropriate, that the consequence of the measure or situation that constituted the breach of such right or freedom be remedied and that fair compensation be paid to the injured party.

Like the ECHR, the American Court's decision are also of a declaratory nature, in that while the Court declares a violation of particular rights of the Convention, it does not institute the required changes at the domestic level. The decisions of the court are binding on State parties.[146] The Contracting parties agree to abide by its judgment[147] and compensatory damages can be executed in the country concerned in accordance with domestic procedures governing the execution of the judgments against the State.[148] The Court's judgment is final, and it is not possible to appeal against it.[149]

Unlike the Committee of Ministers (which operates within the ECHR system) there is no single body in charge of executing the judgment and supervising its enforcement. If a State refuses to abide by the judgment of the Court, the Court is limited to documenting it in its annual report. The Court also has the power to award Provisional measures.[150] It has the power to do so in emergency cases where there is a real threat of violation taking

---

[144] See Shelton, above n. 1, at pp. 364–370.
[145] *Neira Alegria Case*, Judgment of January 19 1995, Inter-Am.Ct.H.R. (Ser. C) No. 20 (1995). American Society of International Law, *Human Rights Interest Group Newsletter*, 5(1), 1995, 29.
[146] Article 63(1).
[147] Article 68(1).
[148] Article 68(2).
[149] Article 66(1) and Article 67 ACHR.
[150] Article 63(2).

place in the imminent future – Article 63(2).[151] These provisions were invoked in the *Velasquez Rodriguez* case.

Advisory jurisdiction[152]

The second element of Court's jurisdiction is its Advisory jurisdiction. The rules regarding Advisory jurisdiction are provided in Article 64 of the Convention which provides:

1. The member states of the organisation may consult the Court regarding the interpretation of this Convention or of other treaties concerning the protection of human rights in the American states. Within their spheres of competence, the organs listed in Chapter X of the Charter of the Organisation of American States, as amended by the Protocol of Buenos Aires, may in like manner consult the Court.
2. The Court, at the request of a member state of the organisation, may provide that state with opinion regarding the compatibility of any of its domestic laws with the aforesaid international instruments.

From the above provision it is clear that the Court may provide an advisory opinion on the interpretation of the ACHR and other human rights treaties, concerning the protection of human rights in American States.[153] Any State member of the O.A.S. may request an advisory opinion; such requests are not restricted to States parties to the Convention. While States not parties to the ACHR may be less interested in this particular Convention, nevertheless they do continue to have an interest in the interpretation of other human rights treaty obligations which they have incurred.[154] These opinions not only relate to the interpretation of instruments referred in Article 64, but any member State could also seek an opinion as to whether its domestic legislation is comparable or not. The only main requirement is 'legitimate institutional interest' in the questions posed to the Court by this request.[155] The advisory opinions of the Court are not restricted to parties of O.A.S. member States but also authorise any organ of O.A.S. listed in Chapter X of the Charter.[156]

---

[151] The Commission has asserted a similar power; see C. Cerna, 'The Inter-American Commission on Human Rights: Its Organisation and Examination of Petitions and Communications' in D.J. Harris and S. Livingstone (eds), above n. 1, 65–113 at p. 107; *Roach and Pinkerton v. United States*, Case 9.647, Res. No. 3/87, OEA/Ser.L/V/II.71, Doc. 9 rev. 1, at 147.

[152] See T. Buergenthal, 'The Advisory Practice' above n. 1, at p. 1.

[153] Article 64(1).

[154] Davidson, above n. 122, at p. 101.

[155] *The Effect of Reservations on the Entry Into Force of the American Convention on Human Rights (Arts 74 and 75)*, Advisory Opinion OC-2/82, September 24 1982, Inter-Am. Ct. H.R. (Ser. A) No. 2 (1982).

[156] Ibid.

The Court, however, has emphasised that the organ petitioning for an advisory opinion must have a requisite *locus standi* to seek such a ruling.[157] The Inter-American Commission has been unequivocally recognised by the Court as having the competence to request advisory opinions,[158] and in practice has been the only organ to invoke the Court's advisory jurisdiction.[159] The procedure for invoking the advisory jurisdiction is initiated by making an application to the Court along with written observations. The Court then sets a date for a public hearing. The ultimate decision to provide an advisory opinion is at the discretion of the Court. By virtue of the Courts' *amicus curiae* provisions, NGOs, academics and private individuals have been involved in the process of the Court's jurisdiction.[160]

Technically these opinions are advisory; however, through examination of the competence of the Court and its powers to interpret a particular provision, it can be said that an opinion has considerable authority. For a State to disregard the advisory opinion of the Court is akin to breaching its obligations under the Convention. The Court's advisory jurisdiction has been used much more frequently than its contentious jurisdiction. A wide range of issues have been addressed by the Court in its advisory opinions. The Court has advised upon the relationship and interaction of various systems of human rights protection with the opinion that the Convention creates immediate binding obligations for the ratifying State.[161] It pronounced on the limitation of death penalty,[162] it has interpreted the provisions of the Convention[163] and has pronounced that the suspension of the remedies of *amparo* and habeas corpus (even in times of emergencies) as incompatible with the provisions of the Convention.[164]

---

[157] Ibid.

[158] As the Court noted in *Entry into force of the American Convention for a State Ratifying or Adhering with a Reservation case* '[U]nlike some other OAS organs, the Commission enjoys, as a practical matter, an absolute right to request advisory opinions within the framework of Article 64(1) of the Convention' para. 16.

[159] A.A.C. Trindade, 'The Operation of the Inter-American Court of Human Rights' in D.J. Harris and S. Livingstone (eds), above n. 1, 133–150 at p. 142.

[160] See Shelton, above n. 1, at p. 342.

[161] *'Other Treaties' Subject to the Consultative Jurisdiction of the Court (Art. 64 of the American Convention on Human Rights)*, Advisory Opinion OC-1/82, September 24 1982, Inter-Am. Ct. H.R. (Ser. A) No. 1 (1982) and *The Effect of Reservations on the Entry Into Force of the American Convention on Human Rights (Arts 74 and 75)*, Advisory Opinion OC-2/82, September 24 1982, Inter-Am. Ct. H.R. (Ser. A) No. 2 (1982).

[162] *Restrictions to the Death Penalty (Arts 4(2) and 4(4) of the American Convention on Human Rights)*, Advisory Opinion OC-3/83, September 8 1983, Inter-Am. Ct. H.R. (Ser. A) No. 3 (1983).

[163] *The Word 'Laws' in Article 30 of the American Convention on Human Rights*, Advisory Opinion OC-6/86, May 9 1986, Inter-Am. Ct. H.R. (Ser. A) No. 6 (1986).

[164] *Habeas Corpus in Emergency Situations (Arts 27(2) and 7(6) of the American Convention on Human Rights)*, Advisory Opinion OC-8/87, January 30 1987, Inter-Am. Ct. H.R. (Ser. A) No. 8 (1987) and *Judicial Guarantees in States of Emergency (Arts 27(2), 25 and 8 of the American Convention on Human Rights)*, Advisory Opinion OC-9/87, October 6 1987, Inter-Am. Ct. H.R. (Ser. A) No. 9 (1987).

In the first case considered by the Court, the *'Other Treaties' case*,[165] the issue concerned the actual scope of the advisory jurisdiction of the Court, particularly the meaning of the reference in Article 64(1) to 'other treaties concerning the protection of human rights in the American System'. Peru had asked for an advisory opinion, asking whether 'other treaties' meant treaties adopted within the framework of the Inter-American System or was more general and included, for example, the UN Covenants and other non-American human rights treaties to which States outside the Americas may be parties. The Court took the view that any human rights treaty may be the subject of an advisory opinion although according to the Court there may be circumstances where it could refuse such a request if the case involved a non-American State's obligations. In the *Restrictions to the Death Penalty case*[166] two primary issues were dealt with by the Court. Guatemala had made a reservation to Article 4(4) concerning the imposition of the death penalty, and the case emerged from a disagreement between the Commission and Guatemala. The first primary issue was whether, in the absence of Guatemala having accepted the jurisdiction of the Court, was it still open to the Court to address the question. The Court took the view that since the case fell within the scope and competence of the Commission, the Court had jurisdiction to deal with the case. Secondly, on the substantive matter the Court followed a much more traditional judicial approach. It held that Guatemala's reservations should be construed in a manner that was compatible with the objects and purposes of the Convention and at the same time leaving Guatemala's obligations under Article 4(4) intact.

In the *Interpretation of the American Declaration case*,[167] Columbia had asked for an advisory opinion of the Court regarding the status of the American Declaration on the Rights and Duties of Man posing the question whether, under Article 64(1) of the ACHR, it qualified as a treaty. The Court, reversing the Commission's earlier approach, took the view that it could not be regarded as a treaty. On the other hand, the Court did advance the position that the Declaration is an authoritative interpretation of the human rights provisions of the O.A.S. Charter and in that sense is a source of international obligations. The importance given to the Declaration is valuable when the human rights record of the non-State parties of the ACHR is to be considered.

---

[165] *'Other Treaties' Subject to the Consultative Jurisdiction of the Court (Art. 64 of the American Convention on Human Rights)*, Advisory Opinion OC-1/82, September 24 1982, Inter-Am. Ct. H.R. (Ser. A) No. 1 (1982).

[166] *Restrictions to the Death Penalty (Arts 4(2) and 4(4) of the American Convention on Human Rights)*, Advisory Opinion OC-3/83, September 8 1983, Inter-Am. Ct. H.R. (Ser. A) No. 3 (1983).

[167] *Interpretation of the American Declaration of the Rights and Duties of Man Within the Framework of Article 64 of the American Convention on Human Rights*, Advisory Opinion OC-10/89, July 14 1989, Inter-Am. Ct. H.R. (Ser. A) No. 10 (1989).

FACT FINDING MISSIONS OF THE INTER-AMERICAN COMMISSION

Article 18(g) of the Statute of the Inter-American Commission provides the Commission with a fact-finding investigative jurisdiction. It compares favourably to other fact-finding processes, in particular the UN fact-finding missions.[168] Since its establishment the Commission has conducted well over sixty *in loco* investigations of alleged violations of human rights in States belonging to the O.A.S. Commenting on the value of this investigation Trindade notes:

> the IACHR has undertaken extensive fact-finding exercises, probably to a larger extent than any other international supervisory organ at least in so far as *in loco* observations are concerned. These are of particular significance as *in loco* investigations in Chile of 1974, the report on forced disappearances in Argentina of 1979, the report on the population of Miskito origin in Nicaragua of 1984, and the reports on Haiti of 1993–1994, among others ... The reports resulting from these missions have been instrumental in asserting the facts of a situation. Moreover, the publicity given to the reports has served to achieve certain of the objectives of a reporting system such as the monitoring of human rights, public scrutiny of legislative measures and administrative practices, exchange of information and the fostering of a better understanding of the problems encountered.[169]

CONCLUSIONS

The promotion and protection of individual human rights within the Americas has been problematic. The region has witnessed substantial violations of human rights: torture, disappearances and mass killings. Repressive military regimes of the region violated human rights, and victimised and persecuted unashamedly their political opponents. Confronted by hostile or uncooperative regimes it is to the credit of the inter-American system not only to have remained operational but also, in a number of instances, to have produced positive contributions to the protection of human rights.

This chapter has traced the developments through which the two largely incoherent inter-American systems are gradually progressing towards greater consistency and regularisation. Having said that, reliance upon the two distinct systems is unsatisfactory. The unsatisfactory nature of human rights

---

[168] See M.C. Bassiouni, 'Appraising UN Justice Related Fact-Finding Mission' 5 *Washington University Journal of Law and Policy* (2001) 37; T.M. Franck and H.S. Fairley, 'Procedural Due Process in Human Rights Fact-Finding by International Agencies' 74 *AJIL* (1980) 308; D. Weissbrodt and J. McCarthy, 'Fact-Finding by International Human Rights Organizations' 22 *Va.JIL* (1981) 1.

[169] A.A.C. Trindade, 'Reporting in the Inter-American System of Human Rights Protection' in P. Alston and J. Crawford (eds), *The Future of UN Human Rights Treaty Monitoring* (Cambridge: Cambridge University Press) 2000, 333–346 at p. 342.

protection is particularly evident in those States parties of the O.A.S. which have not ratified the ACHR. The refusal to accept the obligations under the American Convention results in the failure of the Inter-American court to deal with the cases and to provide legally binding judgments. As Trindade correctly notes:

> The basis of the Court's compulsory jurisdiction provides yet another illustration of the unfortunate lack of automatic application of international jurisdiction. The Inter-American System of human rights protection will considerably advance the day that all OAS member States can become parties to the American Convention (and its two Protocols) without reservations and all States Parties to the Convention accept unconditionally the Court's jurisdiction.[170]

Another important limitation is the lack of provisions in the Inter-American system to ensure compliance with the judgments of the Court. According to Article 65, the Court is required to submit to the General Assembly of the O.A.S. a report on its working during the previous year, in particular the cases which have not complied with the Court's judgment.[171] Non-compliance or inadequate compliance continues to remain a substantial problem in human rights law. In this respect, the largely political sanctions to ensure compliance represent an unsatisfactory feature of the Convention.[172]

---

[170] A.A.C. Trindade, 'The Operation of the Inter-American Court of Human Rights' in D.J. Harris and S. Livingstone (eds), above n. 1, 133–150 at p. 136.

[171] Article 65 ACHR.

[172] See V. Gomez, 'The Interaction between the Political Actors of the OAS, the Commission and the Court' in D.J. Harris and S. Livingstone (ed.), above n. 1, 173–211 at pp. 191–192.

9

AFRICAN CHARTER ON HUMAN AND PEOPLE'S RIGHTS[1]

INTRODUCTION

Historically termed the 'Dark Continent', from pre-colonial to modern times Africa has witnessed substantial violations of human rights. In pre-colonial Africa, unfortunate practices such as human sacrifices, torture and infanticide were performed.[2] During the period of colonisation, Africa was economically and politically exploited and served as a ready source of produce for the slave trade and European expansionism.[3] For Africa, the transition from colonialism to independent Statehood has been a painful one. Post-colonial Africa has witnessed substantial violations of individual and collective rights. The repressive one-party political systems and the dictatorial regimes of men

---

[1] U.O. Umozurike, *The African Charter on Human and Peoples' Rights* (The Hague: Kluwer Law International) 1997; E.K. Quashigah and O.C. Okafor (eds), *Legitimate Governance in Africa: International and Domestic Legal Perspectives* (The Hague: Kluwer Law International) 1999; A.H. Robertson and J.G. Merrills, *Human Rights in the World: An Introduction to the Study of International Protection of Human Rights*, 4th edn (Manchester: Manchester University Press) 1996, pp. 242–266; S. Davidson, *Human Rights* (Buckingham: Open University) 1993, pp. 152–162; C. Flinterman and E. Ankumah, 'The African Charter on Human and Peoples' Rights' in H. Hannum (ed.), *Guide to International Human Rights Practice*, 3rd edn (New York: Transnational Publishers) 1999, pp. 163–174; H.J. Steiner and P. Alston, *International Human Rights in Context : Law, Politics, Morals: Text and Materials*, 2nd edn (Oxford: Clarendon Press) 2000, pp. 920–937; M. Mutua, 'The African Human Rights Court: A Two Legged Stool?' 21 *HRQ* (1999) 342.

[2] Umozurike, above n. 1, at pp. 15–18.

[3] See A. Cassese, *International Law in a Divided World* (Oxford: Clarendon Press) 1990, p. 52; R. Howard, 'Evaluating Human Rights in Africa: Some Problems of Implicit Comparisons' 6 *HRQ* (1984) 160 at p. 170.

like Idi Amin of Uganda (1971–1979), Francisco Marcias Nguema of Equatorial Guinea (1969–1979) and Jean Bokassa of the former Central African Empire (1966–1979) have been instrumental in the denial of all fundamental rights. Worst still, several African States notably Rwanda, Burundi and the Sudan have been overcome by waves of ethnic cleansing and genocide.

Amidst the gross violations of individual and collective rights, human rights have not been a noted strong point of African governments or African intergovernmental organisations.[4] Effective protection of human rights has only rarely influenced the policies of the Organisation of African Unity (OAU), the principal regional African organisation.[5] The OAU Charter, the primary constitutional document of the Organisation does not make any explicit references to human rights, although States parties do undertake to 'promote international co-operation, having due regard to the Charter of the United Nations and the Universal Declaration of Human Rights'.[6] The absence of any specialised Commissions relating to human rights is also conspicuous but not accidental.[7] The apathy towards the effective promotion of human rights since its establishment confirms a genuine distaste on the part of the OAU for this subject.

One major exception has been the adoption by the OAU of the African Charter on Human and Peoples' Rights (AFCHPR).[8] The African Charter is

---

[4] For a historical position see U.O. Umozurike, 'The African Charter on Human and Peoples' Rights' 77 *AJIL* (1983) 902; U.O. Umozurike, 'The Domestic Jurisdiction Clause in the O.A.U. Charter' 311 *African Affairs* (1979) at 199; R.M. D'Sa, 'Human and Peoples' Rights: Distinctive Features of the African Charter' 29 *JAL* (1985) 72 at p. 73.

[5] The OAU is the regional organisation which represents the African States and was responsible for the adoption of the African Charter on Human and Peoples' Rights. The Charter of the Organisation of African Unity (OAU) was adopted by the Summit Conference of the Heads of States and Governments in 1963. The OAU is based on the principles of Sovereign equality, non-interference, absolute dedication to the total emancipation of the African territories which are still dependant and a policy of non-alignment with regard to all blocs. Article 2 of the OAU Charter includes among its aims *inter alia* 'to promote the unity and solidarity of the African States … eradicate all forms of colonialism from the continent of Africa and to defend their sovereignty, their territorial integrity and independence. The legal basis for adopting the African Charter can be found in 21(b) of the OAU Charter which asks member States 'to coordinate and intensify their collaboration and efforts to achieve a better life for the peoples of Africa'. According to 21(e) which requires States to 'promote international co-operation having due regard to the Charter of the United Nations and the Universal Declaration of Human Rights'. The Organs of the OAU are the Assembly of Heads of States and Governments which is the Supreme organ and meets at least once a year; Council of Foreign Ministers meets at least twice a year and its main function is to prepare or execute decisions of the Assembly; the General Secretariat; and the Commission of Mediation, Conciliation and Arbitration. For the text of the OAU Charter see, I. Brownlie (ed.), *Basic Documents in International Law*, 2nd edn (Oxford: Oxford University Press) 1981, pp. 68–76.

[6] Ibid. Article 2(1)(e) OAU Charter.

[7] Ibid. Article 20 OAU Charter.

[8] Adopted on 27 June 1981. Entered into force 21 October 1986. OAU Doc. CAB/LEG/67/3 Rev. 5, 21 I.L.M (1982) 58; 7 *HRLJ* (1986) 403.

also known as the Banjul Charter after Banjul, Gambia's Capital city, where the Charter was drafted. The Charter was adopted in June 1981 at the eighteenth conference of Heads of State and Governments of the OAU. It came into operation in October 1986. All States parties to the OAU are eligible to become parties to the Charter.[9] This chapter deals with African human rights law, with its primary focus upon the protection accorded through the African Charter on Human and Peoples' Rights (the Charter).

DISTINCTIVE FEATURES OF THE CHARTER[10]

Incorporation of three generations of rights

Earlier chapters have considered the divisions and bifurcations between the three generations of rights. The Charter is the only human rights treaty to accord explicit protection to civil and political rights, social economic rights and collective groups rights. This Charter contains an elaborate list of traditional civil and political rights. These rights bear strong similarities to the ones contained in other international and regional treaties and include such fundamental rights as the right to equality before the law, the right to liberty, the right to a fair trial, freedom of conscience including religious freedom, freedom of association and freedom of assembly. In addition to the civil and political rights, there is a set of economic, social and cultural rights. These include the right to education, the right to participate in the cultural life of one's community, and the right of the aged and disabled to special measures of protection.

Furthermore, and more exceptionally, the Charter also contains a number of collective rights, the so-called 'third-generation' rights. The idea of people's rights, in particular, the right to economic and political self-determination forms a vital element within the constitutional workings of independent African States; it is also strongly represented within the African Charter, which as its title confirms is the only treaty upholding the rights of people alongside individual human rights. The Charter contains the important and well-established rights of peoples such as the right to existence and the right to self-determination. In addition there are other innovative (though equally valuable) rights such as the 'right to a general satisfactory environment'.[11]

---

[9] C.A. Odinkalu and C. Christensen, 'The African Commission on Human and People's Rights: The Development of its Non-State Communication Procedures' 20 *HRQ* (1998) 235 at pp. 236–237.

[10] D'Sa, above n. 4, at p. 73.

[11] A. Boyle and M Anderson (eds), *Human Rights Approaches to Environmental Protection* (Oxford: Clarendon Press) 1996; P.W. Birnie and A.E. Boyle, *International Law and the Environment* (Oxford: Oxford University Press) 1992, pp. 188–214; J. Rehman, 'The Role and Contribution of the World Court in the Progressive Development of International Environmental Law' 5 *APJEL* (2000) 387.

Environmental rights are increasingly being associated as part of the framework of international human rights law. There is now a substantial jurisprudence on the right to a safe environment and the contribution of the African Charter to the subject must be acknowledged. As a pioneering treaty provision in international human rights law, Article 24 of the Charter has done much to highlight a generally satisfactory environment as being a human right.[12]

Duties of the individual

The idea of duties, once again a distinctive feature of African societies, is unprecedented in so far as human rights treaties are concerned.[13] Furthermore, the African Charter sets these out explicitly within Chapter II, Articles 27–29. It has been contended that the Charter includes a section on duties for the same reason as it includes a group of articles on economic and social rights. The primary reason had been that the States concerned wished to put forward a distinctive conception of human rights in which civil and political rights were seen to be counterbalanced by duties of social solidarity. Three general principles emerge from these provisions regarding the duties. First, that every individual has duties towards his family and society, towards State, 'other legally recognised communities', and the international community. Secondly, the rights and freedoms of each individual must be exercised with due regard to the rights of others, collective security, morality and common interests. Thirdly, that everyone has the duty to respect and consider others without discrimination and to promote mutual respect and tolerance. The individual also owes a duty to his family, national community, nation, and the African region as a whole.

'Claw-back' clauses

The provisions of the Charter, while distinctive in the manner described, have been the objects of criticism. Criticisms have been levelled against the vague nature of its provisions and its so-called 'claw-back' provisions, which authorise the State to deprive the individual of his or her rights.[14] The 'claw-back' clauses are used in relation to Articles 5–12 and have similarities

---

[12] For regional environmental treaties within Africa see the Bamako Convention on the Ban of the Import into Africa and the Control of Transboundary Movement and Management of Hazardous Wastes within Africa (1991) www.lexmercatoria.org (20 March 2002).

[13] We have noted the existence of provisions on the duties of the individuals in the American Declaration of the Rights and Duties of Man (1948); see above Chapter 8.

[14] C.E. Welch. Jr., 'The African Commission on Human and Peoples' Rights: A Five Year Report and Assessment' 14 *HRQ* (1992) 43 at p. 46.

to derogations, save that in the case of the latter, circumstances are explicitly stated in which rights may be limited. In so far as 'claw-back' clauses are concerned, a wide range of discretion is conferred upon the State to exclude enjoyment of rights.[15] In each instance, the State is permitted to justify limitations on the rights by reference to its own domestic laws. As we shall consider, these 'claw-back' clauses feature in many of the rights within the Charter.

ANALYSING THE SUBSTANTIVE RIGHTS IN THE CHARTER

The Charter can be divided into three parts. Part one contains the rights and duties of the individual, part two considers the role and functions of the African Commission on Human and Peoples' Rights, (the Commission), and part three covers general procedural provisions. The principal executive organ for the implementation of the Charter has thus far been the Commission. However, it has recently been decided to establish an African Court on Human and Peoples' Rights.[16] The Court will complement the work of the Commission. According to Article 1, States parties recognise the rights, duties and freedoms in the Charter and undertake to adopt legislative or any other measures of compliance. The subsequent Articles provide a list of rights contained in the Charter. These are as follows:

Article 2	The right to non-discrimination
Article 3	The right to equality before the law
Article 4	The right to respect for life and the integrity of the person
Article 5	Freedom from exploitation and degradation, including slavery, torture and cruel, inhuman or degrading punishment
Article 6	The right to liberty and security of the person
Article 7(1)	The right to a fair trial
Article 7(2)	Freedom from retrospective punishment
Article 8	Freedom of conscience, the profession and free practice of religion
Article 9(1)	The right to receive information

---

[15] See R. Higgins, 'Derogations under Human Rights Treaties' 48 *BYIL* (1976–77) 281; A. Kiss, 'Permissible Limitations on Rights' in L. Henkin (ed.), *The International Bill of Rights: The Covenant on Civil and Political Rights* (New York: Columbia University Press) 1981, pp. 290–310.

[16] See *Protocol to the African Charter on Human and Peoples' Rights on the Establishment of an African Court on Human and Peoples' Rights* adopted 10 June 1998, OAU. Doc. CAB/LEG/66/5. Not yet in force. Also see the *Draft Protocol to the African Charter on Human and Peoples' Rights on the Establishment of an African Court on Human and Peoples Rights by the Assembly of Heads of State and Governments of the Organization of the African Unity, Conference of Ministers/Attorney-General on the Establishment of an African Court of Human and Peoples' Rights* OAU/LEG/MIN/AFCHPR/PROT (1) Rev. 2 (1997). Also see G.J. Naldi and K. Magliveras, 'Reinforcing the African System of Human Rights: The Protocol on the Establishment of a Regional Court of Human and Peoples' Rights' 16 *NQHR* (1998) 431.

Article 9(2)	The right to express and disseminate opinions
Article 10	Freedom of association
Article 11	Freedom of assembly
Article 12(1)	Freedom of movement
Article 12(2)	Right to leave any country and the right to return
Article 12(3)	Right to seek and obtain asylum
Article 12(5)	Prohibition of mass expulsion
Article 13(1)	The right to participate in government
Article 13(2)	The right to equal access to the public services
Article 13(3)	The right of equal access to public property and to public services
Article 14	The right to property
Article 15	The right to work
Article 16	The right to health
Article 17(1)	The right to education
Article 17(2)	The right to participate in the cultural life of one's community
Article 17(3)	The duty of the State to promote and protect the moral and traditional values
Article 18(1)	Recognition of family as the natural unity and basis of society
Article 18(2)	Family to be assisted as a custodian of morals and traditional values
Article 18(3)	Protection of the rights of women and children
Article 18(4)	Rights of the aged and disabled
Article 19	Peoples' right to equality
Article 20(1)	Peoples' right to existence
Article 20(1)–(3)	Peoples' right to self-determination
Article 21(1)	Peoples' right to dispose wealth and natural resources
Article 22	Peoples' right to economic, social and cultural development
Article 23	Peoples' right to national and international peace and security
Article 24	Peoples' right to a general satisfactory environment

Non-discrimination and equality

Article 2 of the Charter reiterates the right to non-discrimination. This right, as we have noted throughout this book, represents the core of modern human rights law. It is very correctly established as the leading right within the context of a region which has suffered from substantial acts of discrimination and from inequalities. Article 2 provides:

> Every individual shall be entitled to the enjoyment of the rights and freedoms recognised and guaranteed in the present Charter without distinction of any kind such as race, ethnic group, colour, sex, language, religion, political or any other opinion, national and social origin, fortune, birth or other status.

The terminology of the Article and the prohibited categories of discrimination are very similar to those employed in other human rights treaties. Like other human rights instruments, distinctions based on race, ethnicity, colour, sex, religion, language, political opinions, national and social origins, or birth are not permitted. The analysis of the provisions of this Article allows us to make a number of specific comments. First, the terms used in the Article are not exhaustive; other possible grounds of discrimination, for example age, disability and sexual orientation are also covered though not stated. Secondly, the usage of the term 'fortune' represents an innovate basis of non-discrimination. From the *travaux préparatoires*, the rationale for employing this term is not fully established. According to the *Oxford Advanced Learners Dictionary*, 'fortune' means 'chance, especially regarded as a power affecting peoples' lives'.[17] It has been suggested by one commentator that its addition 'implied African recognition that enforcement of rights may depend upon a person's general circumstances or status in society'.[18] Thirdly, among this broad right to non-discrimination, certain sections of the community nevertheless deserve special attention. In the light of the frequent discrimination faced by women and children, protection of their rights on the basis of equality is an important concern.[19]

The right to non-discrimination is further reinforced by the provisions of Article 3 which emphasise equality of all individuals before the law,[20] and equal protection for everyone before the law.[21] As noted above, equality and non-discrimination represent fundamental principles of all international, regional and domestic frameworks. Equality includes *de jure* and de facto equality confirming Umozurike's point that 'the Charter refers to substantive or relative and not material, formal or absolute equality'.[22] The notion of equality, therefore, allows for reverse discrimination or affirmative action policies.

Non-discrimination and equality as broad overarching principles also encapsulate the concept of fairness in trial and freedom from retrospective punishment. The right to fair trial is covered by Article 7. Article 7(1) provides every individual with the right 'to have his cause heard'. This Article includes the right of appeal to competent national organs and affirms the right to be presumed innocent until proved guilty by a competent court or tribunal. It also affirms the right to a defence, including the right to be defended by counsel of his choice; and the right to be tried within a reasonable time by an impartial court or tribunal. Article 8 contains the cardinal principle of

---

[17] *Oxford Advanced Learner's Dictionary of Current English* (Oxford: Oxford University Press) 1989, p. 486.

[18] Davidson, above n. 1, at p. 154.

[19] See G. Van Bueren, *The International Law on the Rights of the Child* (Dordrecht: Martinus Nijhoff Publishers) 1995, at p. 402.

[20] Article 3(1).

[21] Article 3(2).

[22] Umozurike, above n. 1, at p. 30.

natural justice that no one may be condemned for an act or omission which
did not constitute a legally punishable offence at the time it was committed.
It provides that no penalty may be inflicted for an offence for which no provision was made at the time it was committed. Punishment is personal and can
be imposed only on the offender.

Right to life and prohibitions of torture and slavery

The right to life, as the supreme human right, has been protected by Article 4
of the Charter which provides as follows:

> Human beings are inviolable. Every human being shall be entitled to respect for
> his life and the integrity of his person. No one may be arbitrarily deprived of this
> right.

The Article in recognising the inviolability of human life confirms the entitlement of everyone to the right to life and integrity of person. At the same time,
the Article is structured in an awkward manner and does not address some
fundamental issues. There is no explanation of the meaning of the term 'life'
and it is not clear as to the extent to which the rights of the unborn child are
protected. Furthermore, following the ICCPR, the Charter does not prohibit
all forms of deprivation of life. Only 'arbitrary' deprivation of life is prohibited, although the meaning of 'arbitrary' is not defined. Some guidance
may be obtained from the jurisprudence of the Human Rights Committee,
which has spelled out the meaning in its consideration of individual cases and
State reports.[23] Unlike, the ICCPR, no limitations are placed on the usage of
capital punishment. The imposition of the death penalty remains a controversial subject in international law, and a majority of African States retain this
sentence within their territories.

Article 5 provides for the right to the respect of the dignity in human beings.
It also prohibits slavery, the slave trade, and cruel, inhuman or degrading
treatment or punishment. The prohibitions on torture, inhuman degrading
treatment or punishment as norms of *jus cogens* and principles of customary
international law, have been affirmed in all the international human rights
instruments. The meaning of the term 'torture' and 'inhuman' or 'degrading
treatment or punishment' has been expanded further by the Committee
against Torture (CAT), and by regional human rights bodies (such as the
European Commission and the European Court of Human Rights).[24] Cruel,
inhuman and degrading treatment and punishment has been addressed in
considerable detail by the European Court of Human Rights in the context of
corporal punishment. While the jurisprudence of the African Commission on

[23] See above Chapter 4.
[24] See below Chapter 15.

this subject is not substantial, domestic African courts have relied upon the ECHR's prohibition on corporal punishment. The Zimbabwean Supreme Court decision in *State* v. *Ncube and Others*, represents the formulation of important principles. In this case, three persons had been found guilty of offences against children (rape of an unspecified number over a period of two and a half years). All three men were sentenced to significant terms of imprisonment with labour and were also each sentenced to a whipping of six strokes. Their appeal to the Supreme Court which concerned the sentence was upheld. According to the Court, whipping as a punishment violated s. 15(1) of the Zimbabwean Constitution, a provision which prohibits torture and inhuman or degrading treatment or punishment.[25] In arriving at this decision the Court considered Article 3 of ECHR, comparative criminal and other case law including *Tyrer* v. *UK*[26] and concluded that whipping was an affront to human dignity.[27]

It also needs to be appreciated that cruel, inhuman and degrading treatment is a subject impinging heavily upon cultural or religious relativism. For those States practising *Sharia*, punishments such as flogging, physical amputations and executions raise issues of compatibility with modern norms of human rights law. Some of the African States have been criticised for allowing such practices as female circumcision or for criminalising adult homosexuality.[28] The African Charter clearly prohibits slavery and slave trade. However various practices of servitude, in particular child labour, continue to take place. In addition to the prohibition of slavery and subjugation, the Charter provides for the right to liberty and security of person. Article 6 notes:

> Every individual shall have the right to liberty and to the security of his person. No one may be deprived of his freedom except for reasons and conditions previously laid down by law. In particular, no one may be arbitrarily arrested or detained.

Right to liberty and security of person is an important human right, and forms an essential ingredient of the human rights corpus. The Article, while providing protection, is unsatisfactory because of its vague and uncertain terminology. The use of the term 'except for reasons and conditions previously

---

[25] [1987] (2) ZLR 246 (SC) 267 B–C; 1988 (2) SA 702 (ZSC) 717 B–D; summaries of the case in International Commission of Jurists, *The Review*, No. 41 December 1988, 61; 14 *Commonwealth Law Bulletin* (1988) 593.

[26] *Tyrer* v. *United Kingdom*, Judgment of 25 April 1978, Series A, No. 26.

[27] 1988 LRC (Const) 442; also see *State* v. *A Juvenile* [1989] (2) ZLR 61 (Court of Appeal of Botswana holding Corporal punishment of Juveniles unconstitutional under Section 7 of the Constitution which prohibits inhuman or degrading punishment. Namibian Supreme Court held corporal punishment unconstitutional in *Ex parte Att. General in re Corporal Punishment by Organs of State* 1991(3) AS 76 NMSC.

[28] See *William Courson* v. *Zimbabwe*, Communication No 136/94, para 21.

laid down by law' represents an example of the 'claw-back' clause type referred to earlier. The 'reasons and conditions' are not provided anywhere in the Charter thus making it impossible to assess their conformity with other international human rights instruments. There is also the unhelpful employment of the concept of 'arbitrary' in the arrest and detention of individuals.

Freedom of religion, expression, association and movement

Article 8 of the Charter provides for the right to freedom of conscience and religion. According to the Article:

> Freedom of conscience, the profession and free practice of religion shall be guaranteed. No one may, subject to law and order, be submitted to measures restricting the exercise of these freedoms.

The right to freedom of religion constitutes an invaluable right in the context of a region which continues to suffer from serious persecutions based on religious differences.[29] Notwithstanding the value of this right, the provisions of the Article themselves have left a great deal to be desired. The meaning of 'free practice' is unclear as it does not establish whether it incorporates the freedom to change religion or if it allows proselytism. Furthermore the use of the 'claw-back' clause of 'subject to law and order' can lead to unreasonable and unacceptable restrictions upon this freedom. Article 9 provides for an interesting and rather unusual right, the right to receive information. The Article also provides for a right of expression and the freedom to disseminate one's opinion. At the same time, the provisions of the Article can be highly restrictive as the ultimate discretion to determine the boundaries of right to receive information and give expression is retained. Article 10 accords the right to association. Article 10(2) states that, subject to the obligation of solidarity provided for in Article 29, no one may be compelled to join an association. According to Article 11 all individuals have the right to assembly. This right again is subject to a 'claw-back' clause of being subject to 'necessary restrictions provided for by law in particular those enacted in the interest of national security, the safety, health, ethics and rights and freedoms of others'.

Article 12 provides for freedom of movement and residence within the borders of a State. It also confirms that the individual has the right to leave any country including his own, and to return to his country.[30] Within this article

---

[29] J. Maxted and A. Zegey, 'North Africa, West and the Horn of Africa' in Minority Rights Group (eds), *World Directory of Minorities* (London: Minority Rights Group) 1997, pp. 388–463; T. Hodges, *Jehovah's Witnesses in Africa* (London: Minority Rights Group) 1985; T. Parfitt, *The Jews of Africa and Asia: Contemporary: Anti-Semitism and Other Pressures* (London: Minority Rights Group) 1987; P. Verney et al., *Sudan: Conflict and Minorities* (London: Minority Rights Group) 1995.
[30] Article 12(2).

there is also the right to seek and obtain asylum and for non-nationals not to be expelled, unless due to a decision made in accordance with the law. Mass expulsion (aimed at expelling national, racial, ethnic or religious groups) is prohibited. This prohibition represents a highly valuable ordinance and is aimed at preventing recurrences similar to the expulsion of Asians from Uganda under Amin.[31]

Nationality has been a problematic area of international human rights law and denial of citizenship as a tool for discrimination has been applied by a number of States, including those from Africa. International Conventions, including the International Convention on the Elimination of All Forms of Racial Discrimination and the African Charter, do not specifically prohibit discrimination on the basis of nationality. However, mass expulsion as the most acute form of discrimination has been conducted against many ethnic, religious and racial groups in Africa. The induction of such a provision is a positive development of regional human rights law.

Property rights in the Charter

Article 14 of the Charter states that the right to property shall be guaranteed, and may only be restricted in the interest of public need or in the general interest of the community. In addition, expropriation of property would have to be in accordance with the provisions of the law. The grounds for expropriation are not elaborated upon nor are any examples provided. The right to property has been a controversial one.[32] The UDHR contains the right to property, as does Protocol 1 of the ECHR and the ACHR. The Right to property, however, proved too divisive and it was not possible to incorporate it within the International Covenants. Socialist and developing countries argued against providing absolute guarantees for property rights. They campaigned for a right to be able to expropriate and nationalise foreign assets and to restrict the rights of foreign nationals more generally. A confirmation of this view is provided by Article 2(3) of the ICESCR which provides:

> Developing countries, with due regard to human rights and their national economy, may determine to what extent they would guarantee the economic rights recognized in the present Covenant to non-nationals.

Issues regarding the disposal of property and natural wealth are further addressed within the Charter in the context of peoples' rights. Article 21

---

[31] While traditional human rights instruments had not focused on expulsions it would now appear that mass expulsions on the basis of race, religion or ethnicity constituted a crime against humanity.

[32] See C. Krause and G. Alfredsson, 'Article 17' in G. Alfredsson and A. Eide (eds), *The Universal Declaration of Human Rights: A Common Standard of Achievement* (The Hague: Kluwer Law International) 1999, pp. 359–378.

provides all peoples with a right freely to dispose of their wealth and natural resources. At the same time, as we shall consider in the next section, the term 'peoples' is used as being almost synonymous to that of the 'State', thereby allowing African governments an almost unquestionable discretion in relation to the usage, expropriation and exploitation of natural resources and property. Article 21 provides as follows:

(1) All peoples shall freely dispose of their wealth and natural resources. This right shall be exercised in the exclusive interest of the people. In no case shall a people be deprived of it.
(2) In case of spoliation the dispossessed people shall have the right to the lawful recovery of its property as well as to an adequate compensation.
(3) The free disposal of wealth and natural resources shall be exercised without prejudice to the obligation of promoting international economic cooperation based on mutual respect, equitable exchange and the principles of international law.
(4) States parties to the present Charter shall individually and collectively exercise the right to free disposal of their wealth and natural resources with a view to strengthening African unity and solidarity.
(5) States parties to the present Charter shall undertake to eliminate all forms of foreign economic exploitation particularly that practiced by international monopolies so as to enable their peoples to fully benefit from the advantages derived from their national resources.

Economic, social and cultural rights

In addition to civil and political rights, the African Charter also contains a number of economic, social and cultural rights. As we have already noted, the efforts to incorporate economic, social and cultural rights alongside civil and political rights within a single United Nations Covenant proved futile. It is therefore to the Charter's credit for having provided a combination of these rights, which also confirms the distinctive African concept of human rights.

Article 15 of the Charter provides for the right to work. This right is contained in the UDHR, and the ICESCR. Among regional instruments it can be found in the ESC and the TEU. Unlike any of the international and regional human rights instruments, Article 15 fails to deal with this right in any great detail. Furthermore, the right to work is not guaranteed *per se*, but guarantees that once employed a worker would have a right to work in equitable and satisfactory conditions and shall receive equal pay for equal work. Equal pay for equal work is also aimed at ensuring equality for women.

The Charter provides for the right to enjoy the best attainable state of physical and mental health. The provisions place State parties under an obligation to provide health and medical services for their population. The right to health is an important right although compliance with this obligation remains problematic. Article 16, in providing for this right, states:

(1) Every individual shall have the right to enjoy the best attainable state of physical and mental health.

(2) States parties to the present Charter shall take the necessary measures to protect the health of their people and to ensure that they receive medical attention when they are sick.

Article 17 covers a wide range of interrelated rights. According to the Article, individuals are accorded the right to education, though there is no specification of the content of this right. The Article provides individuals with the right to participate freely in the cultural life of the community and imposes an obligation on the State to promote and protect the morals and traditional values recognised by the community. The provision of free exercise in community life is presumably intended for minority groups within States; while there is no reference to minorities in the entire Charter, this provision is useful.

Article 18 is wide ranging and covers at least four rights. It recognises family as the natural unit and basis of society, and establishes a duty upon the State to take care of the physical health and morals of the family. In its acknowledgement of family as the natural and fundamental unit, the provisions draw upon Articles 23 ICCPR and Article 17 ACHR.[33] Article 18(2) reinforces these obligations with the duty on the State to assist the family unit in establishing it as the custodian of morals and traditional values. Article 18(3) is a comprehensive clause concerning prohibition of discrimination against women. According to this provision:

The State shall ensure the elimination of every discrimination against women and also ensure the protection of the rights of the women and the child as stipulated in international declarations and conventions.

These provisions appear to place far-reaching obligations in relation to protecting the rights of women and children. In the light of the construction of the Article, it has been contended that parties to the Charter are automatically bound by treaty law on women and children regardless of whether or not they have been ratified by the State.[34] Although an ambitious interpretation, this is a step in the right direction and would also encourage the African Commission and the new African Court to draw inspiration from the jurisprudence of human rights bodies, in particular the CEDAW and CRC.

---

[33] According to Article 17(1) of the ACHR 'The family is the natural and fundamental group unit of society and is entitled to protection by Society and the State'. For further consideration of ACHR see above Chapter 8.

[34] Davidson, above n. 1, at p. 154.

While the African Commission has not yet dealt with case law emerging from non-discrimination of women, the landmark decision remains of *Unity Dow* v. *The Attorney-General of Botswana.*[35] In this case the Court of Appeal of Botswana held that a Statute which discriminated against women was unconstitutional law. The Citizenship Act 1984 denied Botswana citizenship to Botswanaes women married to a foreign husband, but granted it to Botswanaes men who were married to foreign women. The Court held that the provision was discriminatory and thus contrary to the Constitution of Botswana.

Article 18(3) also provides for the protection of the right of the child and places an obligation to follow the principles enshrined in international treaty law. In order further to substantiate the legal regime in the rights of the child, African States themselves have entered a specialised treaty concerning children, the African Charter on the Rights and Welfare of the Child 1990.[36] In 1990, the OAU also adopted strategies for the African Decade for Child survival, Protection and Development 1990–2000. Article 18(4) provides that the aged and the disabled have the right to special measures of protection.

THE MEANING OF PEOPLES' RIGHTS IN THE AFRICAN HUMAN RIGHTS LAW[37]

The impact of the concept of Peoples' right to self-determination is nowhere more evident than in the African continent; Africa has emancipated itself from the shackles of colonialism, racial oppression and apartheid through a reliance upon this concept. The term 'peoples' and 'the right to self-determination' therefore forms a vital element within the constitutional working of independent African States as well as in the regional approach represented collectively. A number of State constitutions support the principle of peoples rights, and the regional approach is reflected through a wide range of treaties including the Charter of the OAU and the African Charter.

The preamble of the OAU Charter reaffirms the 'inalienable right of all people to control their own destiny'.[38] The purposes of the Charter includes a commitment to intensify the collaboration of African States to achieve

---

[35] *Unity Dow* v. *The Attorney-General of Botswana*, Decisions of the High Court and Court of Appeal (Botswana), [1991] Law Reports of the Commonwealth (Const.) 574 (High Court); affirmed [1992] Law Reports of the Commonwealth 623 (Court of Appeal).

[36] Adopted in July 1990, entered into force 29 October 1999, O.A.U. Doc. CAB/LEG/TSG/Rev.1.

[37] For a detailed consideration see J. Rehman, 'The Concept of "Peoples" in International Law with Special Reference to Africa' in B.T. Bakut and S. Dutt (eds), *Development in Africa for the 21st Century* (London: Palgrave) 2000, pp. 201–214; R. Kiwanuka, 'The Meaning of "People" in the African Charter on Human and Peoples' Rights' 82 *AJIL* (1988) 80.

[38] Preamble OAU Charter.

'a better life for the Peoples of Africa'.[39] Even though the OAU Charter supports the principles enshrined in the UN Charter and UDHR, the OAU does not have any particular vision on individual human rights or collective group rights.[40] The references to peoples are framed largely in the context of the right to sovereign State equality, and moves to eradicate colonialism.[41] There is no consideration of the right to self-determination apart from an emphasis on non-interference in the domestic affairs of States, and the guarantee for the 'respect for the sovereignty and territorial integrity of each State and its inalienable right to independent existence'.[42]

The latter provision is the reconfirmation of the *uti possidetis juris* principle. The origins of the principle of *uti possidetis* could be traced back to the early nineteenth century, whereby the newly independent successor States of the former Spanish Empire in South and Central America were considered to have inherited the administrative divisions of the colonial empire as their new territorial boundaries.[43] The doctrine has come to be accepted as having universal significance and global application; in essence the application of the principle meant that the demarcations of boundaries under the colonial regimes corresponded to the boundaries of the new States that emerged.[44]

The *uti possidetis juris* principle received complete support from the African Heads of State at the time of adoption of the OAU Charter. Indeed, at the inaugural session of the Treaty, the Prime Minister of Ethiopia, echoing the sentiments of other heads of government, commented 'it is in the interest of all

---

[39] Article 2(1)(b) OAU Charter.
[40] O. Ojo and A. Sesay, 'The OAU and Human Rights: Prospects for the 1980's and Beyond' 8 *HRQ* (1986) 89 at p. 96.
[41] Article 2(1)(c) and (d) OAU Charter.
[42] Article 3(3) OAU Charter.
[43] M.N. Shaw, *International Law*, 3rd edn (Cambridge: Grotius Publication) 1997, p. 302.
[44] See Article 3(3) of the *OAU Charter*; Principle III of the *Helsinki Final Act 1975*, 1975 ILM 1292; Article 62 2(2)(a) VCLT 1969, 58 U.K.T.S, 1980, Cmnd 7964; Article 2 of the Vienna Convention on the Succession of States in Respect of Treaties (1978) 17 I.L.M 1488, 72 *AJIL* 971. For judicial acknowledgement of the principles see *Frontier Dispute Case (Burkina Faso v. Mali)* 1986 ICJ Reports 554; G. Naldi, 'The Case Concerning the Frontier Dispute (Burkina Faso/Republic of Mali): *Uti Possidetis* in an African Perspective' 36 *ICLQ* (1987) 893; *Temple of Preah Vihear Case (Merits) (Cambodia)*, 1962 ICJ Rep 6, 16, 29; *Rann of Kutch Arbitration* 1968, 50 ILR 2, 408; *Guinea-Guinea Bissau Maritime Delimitation Case* 77 ILR 1985, 635, 637; *Arbitration Tribunal in Guinea-Bissau v. Senegal*, 1990 83 ILR 1, 35; *Land, Islands and Maritime Frontier Case: El Salvador v. Honduras (Nicaragua Intervening)* 1992 ICJ Rep 351, 380; also see *Sovereignty over Certain Frontier Land (Belgium v. the Netherlands)* ICJ Rep 1959, 209, in particular Judge Moeno Quitana's dissenting opinion, 252; *Avis Nos. 2 and 3 of the Arbitration Commission of the Yugoslavia Conference*, 31 I.L.M. 1497, 1499; *Taba Award (Egypt)* 80 ILR 1989, 224 in particular arbitrator Lapidoth's dissenting opinion; also see J. Klabbers and R. Lefeber, 'Africa: Lost between Self-Determination and *Uti-Possidetis*', in C. Brölmann, R. Lefeber, M. Zieck (eds.), *Peoples and Minorities in International Law* (Dordrecht: Martinus Nijhoff Publishers) 1993, pp. 33–76. See also J. Rehman, 'Re-Assessing the Right to Self-Determination: Lessons from the Indian Experience' 29 *AALR* (2000) 454.

Africans now to respect the frontiers drawn on the maps, whether they are good or bad, by the former colonisers'.[45] Thus while the OAU Charter fails to elaborate on the subject of people's rights to self-determination, it nevertheless affirms the African position on the inviolability and sanctity of boundaries inherited by the new States.

In contrast to the OAU, the African Charter has a much stronger focus on the subject of the rights of peoples. As the rubric of the treaty reflects, there is a special position accorded to peoples' rights. Indeed, the African Charter has the distinction of being the only international instrument to provide a detailed exposition of the rights of peoples. The peoples' rights, according to the Charter are spelt out in Articles 19–24 of the Treaty. These are the right of all peoples to equality,[46] to existence[47] and self-determination,[48] to dispose freely of wealth and natural resources,[49] to economic, social and cultural development,[50] to national and international peace and security,[51] and to a 'general satisfactory environment'.[52]

Notwithstanding a detailed exposition of the rights of peoples, the drafters of the African Charter deliberately avoid the complex issue of the definition of the term 'peoples'. The only affirmative view that emerges from a close scrutiny of the provisions of the Charter is that there is no single uniform meaning that could be attributed to the term 'peoples'. The Charter presents a variable approach, depending on the issue in question. Thus, as we have already noted on the subject of the disposal of wealth and natural resources in Article 21, the overlap between State and peoples is so strong that the terms could be used almost interchangeably. Similarly, according to Article 23(1), 'All Peoples shall have the right to national and international peace and security' – a right normally assigned to States.[53]

On the other hand, the African Charter has provisions dealing with peoples' rights to equality and existence. As we have considered throughout this book, the right to equality and non-discrimination forms the basis of modern human rights law. The right to equality is an individual right, although it may also be applied to support particular group members qua individuals. In comparison to equality, the right to existence has a more direct application to groups within States. The right to existence is designed to protect 'national, ethnical

---

[45] Cited in J. Klabbers and R. Lefeber, 'Africa: Lost between Self-Determination and *Uti-Possidetis*', in C. Brölmann, R. Lefeber, M. Zieck (eds), above n. 44, at p. 57.

[46] Article 19.

[47] Article 20(1).

[48] Article 20(1)–(3)

[49] Article 21.

[50] Article 22.

[51] Article 23.

[52] Article 24.

[53] Cf. The provisions contained in the Universal Declaration of Human Rights (1948).

or religious groups' from genocide and physical extermination.[54] Therefore in the context of the right to equality and existence, the only permissible view that could be formed is that 'peoples' represent collectivities such as ethnic, national or religious minorities within independent States.

Article 20 of the African Charter, which provides for the right to existence, also accords peoples 'the unquestionable and inalienable right to self-determination'. The contrasting nature of the two rights and the manner of their proposed application, however, needs some analysis. The references to self-determination are closely associated with colonialism and oppression. It is only colonised and oppressed peoples who have the 'right to free themselves from the bonds of domination'.[55] Although the term 'oppression' is not defined, the limitation of being under colonial or minority racist regimes is firmly engrained. It is certainly not permissible for minorities or indigenous peoples to seek foreign assistance to further any claims towards self-determination. This impermissibly of relating minorities or indigenous peoples with self-determination has been confirmed by the jurisprudence of the African Commission, which operates in pursuance of the Charter.

The African Commission, as we shall analyse in greater detail below, considers Communications concerning group and peoples' rights. However, Article 56(2) of the Charter implies that in order for the Communication to be admissible, allegations of violations of group rights must be compatible with the provisions of the Charter of the OAU relating to respect of sovereignty and territorial integrity of the member States of that organisation. In *Katangese Peoples' Congress* v. *Zaire*[56] Mr Gerard Moke, the author, was the President of the Katangese Peoples' Congress. He claimed that Zaire violated the Katangese peoples' right to self-determination. In its admissibility decision taken at its sixteenth ordinary session in October 1993, the Commission declared that the communication had 'no merit' under the African Charter because it was not compatible with Article 56(2) of the Charter. In its decision, the Commission first reasoned that the definition of 'peoples' and the content of the right are controversial, and then took the view that the issue in the present Communication was not self-determination for all Zairians as a people, but specifically for the Katangese. The Commission held that in these circumstances, it was obliged 'to uphold the sovereignty and territorial integrity of Zaire, a member of the OAU and a party to the African Charter on Human and Peoples' Rights.' Another case related to the situation in Senegal, where rebels were trying to secede from the State.[57] In this case, the

---

[54] See below Chapters 11 and 12.
[55] Article 20(2).
[56] Communication 75/92.
[57] Tenth Annual Activity Report of the African Commission on Human and Peoples' Rights 1996–1997, ACHPR/RPT/10th at 4.

Commission refused to uphold this claim *inter alia* on the basis that such a claim by the Casamance group may prompt other groups in the region to bring similar legal challenges. The Commission has made attempts to encourage the government to reach a settlement with the dissident group.

THE AFRICAN COMMISSION[58]

The African Commission is the main executive organ and is also in charge of implementing the provisions of the Charter.[59] The Commission consists of eleven members and are chosen from among 'African personalities of highest reputation known for their high morality, integrity, impartiality and competence in matters of human and peoples' rights; particular consideration being given to persons having legal experience'.[60] The Commission members are elected by Heads of States and Governments of the OAU, for a renewable term of six years, from a list of persons nominated by State parties.[61] The Commission then appoints a chairman and a vice-chairman for a two-year term. The OAU is the parent body and the Commission is required to report to it.[62] The Commission holds a session twice each year: in spring and in autumn. The members of the Commission sit in their personal capacity. While each State party can nominate up to two individuals, no two members of the Commission may be nationals of the same State.[63] On 29 July 1987 an Assembly of Heads of State and Governments of OAU for the first time elected eleven members of the Commission.

While the OAU is responsible for financing the Commission,[64] the Commission has been assigned a role establishing its independence from its parent body. This independence of the Commission members is represented in various ways. The members make a solemn declaration of impartiality and faithfulness,[65] and the headquarters of the Commission are in a country other than the one having OAU organs. Members of the Commission also enjoy diplomatic privileges and immunities.[66] A number of Rules of Procedure have been set up to deal with the organisation of the Commission's work, conduct of business, publication of documents and participation in the Commission's

---

[58] See R. Murray, *The African Commission on Human and People's Rights and International Law* (Oxford: Hart Pub.) 2000; Odinkalu and Christensen, above n. 9, at p. 235; Welch. Jr., above n. 14, at p. 42.
[59] Article 30.
[60] Article 31.
[61] Articles 33, 36.
[62] Article 34.
[63] Article 34.
[64] Articles 41 and 42.
[65] Article 31(1).
[66] Article 43.

sessions by State representatives. As a general rule sittings in the Commission are to be private although final summary minutes of sessions, public or private, shall be 'intended for general distribution unless, under exceptional circumstances, the Commission decides otherwise'.[67] The Commission's reports to the OAU Assembly are confidential unless the Assembly itself decides otherwise, while the annual report of the Commission is to be published following consideration by the Assembly.[68] The voting on draft resolutions, if a vote is requested, is by a simple majority. According to Article 41, the Secretary-General of the OAU is to appoint the Commission's Secretary.

It should be noted that the Commission's recommendations concerning protection activities require the endorsement of either the Assembly of Heads of State or OAU. However, no such approval is required in relation to promotional activities. The Commission is mandated to perform a number of functions. These are provided for in Article 45 and consist of:

(a) Promotional Role (Article 45(1)).
(b) Role of protecting human and peoples' rights (Article 45(2)).
(c) Interpreting the provisions of the Charter at the request of a State party, an institution of the OAU or an African Organisation recognised by the OAU (Article 45(3)).
(d) Performing any other tasks that may be entrusted to it by the Assembly of Heads of State and Government (Article 45(4)).

According to Article 45(1) the promotional functions of the Commission consist of promoting Human and Peoples' Rights and in particular:

(a) to collect documents, undertake studies and researches on African problems in the field of human and peoples' rights, organise seminars, symposia and conferences, disseminate information, encourage national and local institutions concerned with human and peoples' rights, and should the case arise, give its views or make recommendations to Governments.
(b) to formulate and lay down, principles and rules aimed at solving legal problems relating to human and peoples' rights and fundamental freedoms upon which African Governments may base their legislations.
(c) co-operate with other African and international institutions concerned with the promotion and protection of human and peoples' rights.

In the performance of its duties, the Commission 'may resort to any appropriate method of investigation' and may hear from the OAU Secretary-General 'or any other person capable of enlightening it'. In its promotional programme the Commission has formulated a Programme of Action which

---

[67] Ibid. 51.
[68] Rules 78, 80.

consists of research and information for quasi-legislative cooperation.[69] A number of seminars have been organised involving such agencies and NGOs as UNESCO and the International Commission of Jurists.[70]

PROTECTING HUMAN AND PEOPLES' RIGHTS

The African Charter provides for a State reporting procedure, an inter-State complaints procedure, and what it terms as 'Other Communications' procedure. The State reporting procedure is contained in Article 62, the Inter-State procedure is dealt with in Articles 47–54, while the 'Other Communications' procedure is provided for in Articles 55–59.

State reporting procedure

The Commission obtains reports from State parties with a view to ascertaining whether or not each State party has taken administrative, legislative or other measures to implement the Charter. According to Article 62, each State party is obliged to submit every two years from the date of the Charter's enforcement 'a report on the legislature or other measures taken with a view to give effect to the rights and freedoms recognised and guaranteed' by the Charter. The reports are handled by Assembly of Heads of State and Governments of OAU. The reporting procedure has been treated as 'the back-bone of the mission of the Commission'.[71]

The Charter does not specify any details as to the body to which the reports are to be submitted or provide guidelines on the structure of these reports and what subsequent action is required regarding these reports. The African Commission has provided certain guidelines on reporting procedures.[72] The reports need to provide detailed legislative measures and actual implementation for human rights protection. After submission, the reports are examined in public by the Commission. The Commission and the State representatives engage in a dialogue with the purpose of assisting and encouraging States in implementation of the Charter. After consultation on a report, the Commission communicates its observations and comments to the relevant State party. Despite these guidelines and efforts for improvements, States have been reluctant to produce reports. The rules of procedure in the African

---

[69] See the Activity Report of the African Commission on Human and Peoples' Rights 9 *HRLJ* (1988) 326.

[70] Murray, above n. 58, at p. 15.

[71] I. Badawi El-Sheikh, 'The African Commission on Human and Peoples Rights: Prospects and Problems' 7 *NQHR* (1989) 272 at p. 281.

[72] See F.D. Gaer, 'First Fruits: Reporting By States under the African Charter on Human and Peoples Rights' 10 *NQHR* (1992) 29.

Charter do not attach sanctions for non-compliance with reporting procedures.[73] The few reports that have been produced are not satisfactory.

Inter-State procedure

In addition to State reporting, the second principal function of the Commission is to ensure the protection of human rights through its complaints procedure. The Charter envisages two modes of inter-State complaints. First, under Article 47 of the Charter if one State party has reason to believe that another State party has violated its obligations under the Charter, it may refer the matter to the State concerned by written communication. According to Article 47, this communication shall also be addressed to the Secretary-General of OAU and Chairman of the Commission. Within three months of the receipt of the communication, the State to which communication has been addressed shall give the inquiring State written explanation or statement clarifying the issue. This should include all possible information and action on redress. If within three months from the date on which the original communication was received by a State the issue is not settled satisfactorily through negotiations or other peaceful means, then either State may bring the matter before the Commission.[74] The Commission then requests further information from the State against whom complaint has been made. Parties can appear before the Commission and/or present written or oral statements. There also remains the possibility of an on-site investigation. The Charter makes clear that the primary objective is to secure a friendly settlement. Not only is this the basic aim of the Commission but, under Article 47, a complainant is encouraged to approach the other party directly with a view to settling the matter without involving the Commission. In advance of the European and American Conventions, Article 47 reflects the African States' preference for informed methods of dispute settlement. However, such an approach is prone to criticism as being 'too State-centric'[75] with the Commission appearing to settle 'inter-State disputes rather than serving as a watchdog of human rights transgressions'.[76] The only State complaint received thus far has been from Libya against the United States concerning the removal of Libyan soldiers from Chad. The communication was held inadmissible as the USA is not a party to the treaty.

The alternative mechanism of inter-State complaints is contained in Article 49. According to this procedure, a State party may refer the matter directly to the Commission if it considers that another State party has violated any of the provisions of the Charter. The reference to the Commission would be by a

---

[73] Umozurike, above n. 1, at pp. 71–72.
[74] Article 48.
[75] Ojo and Sesay, above n. 40, at p. 89.
[76] Ibid. p. 96.

communication to the Chairman of the Commission to the Secretary-General of the OAU and the relevant State party. In line with other international procedures the Commission can only deal with the matter if all local remedies have been exhausted.[77] However, there remains the usual exemption to those cases where remedies are 'unduly prolonged'.[78]

The Commission has wide powers. It can ask States to provide information and they are entitled to appear before it and submit oral and written representations. Article 52 provides that when the Commission has obtained from States concerned 'and from other sources' all the information it deems necessary, its task is to make attempts to reach 'an amicable solution based on the respect of Human and Peoples' Rights'.[79] Failing this, the Commission is required to prepare a report (containing facts and its findings) and send it to the States concerned and to Heads of State and Government. According to Article 53, while transmitting its report the Commission may make appropriate recommendations to the Assembly of Heads of State and Government. The Commission is also required to submit a general report on its activities to each ordinary session of Assembly of Heads of States and Government.[80]

Other communications

In addition to the inter-State mechanisms for protecting human rights, the African Charter also has another complaints procedure which is entitled 'Other Communications'. Much like its European Counterpart, this procedure has been more readily used. By the end of 2001, the Commission had received well over 200 communications. Article 55 of the Charter provides that the Commission's secretary is to prepare a list of non-State communications and to pass them to members of the Commission.[81] The decision on whether to consider the communication is conducted by the Commission members by a simple majority vote.[82]

The powers of the Commission under Article 55 are mandatory, that is the African Commission's Competence to deal with individual or other non-State Communications is accepted automatically, as soon as a State ratifies the Charter. The following are the conditions of admissibility:

- The Communication must indicate the author(s) even if they request anonymity.[83]

---

[77] Article 50.
[78] Ibid.
[79] Article 52.
[80] Article 54.
[81] Article 55(1).
[82] Article 55(2).
[83] Article 56(1).

The Commission requires the authors to provide their names and addresses even if they desire to remain anonymous in respect of the State party concerned. It must be noted in the present context that there are no limitations regarding who may file a petition. Unlike the position in ECHR, there is no victim requirement. There is no requirement that the authors are the victims or family members of the victim.[84] The author does not need to be a national of the State party to the Charter[85] and does not even need to be based within the State against whom the complaint is made.[86] Several Communications have, unsurprisingly, been put forward by NGOs – a concession which carries the risk of opening floodgates. A number of communications have been held inadmissible as they were either instituted against non-African States, non-State parties or against non-State entities.[87]

- The Communications must be compatible with the Charter of OAU 'or' the African Charter.[88]

The difficulties in providing a literal reading to the term 'or' have been pointed out.[89] It would appear that a sensible construction of the provisions requires the communication to be compatible to both the Charter of the OAU and the African Charter. It also means that attempts on the part of minority groups or indigenous peoples to claim a right to self-determination would not be admissible since these arguably conflict with OAU provisions on the territorial integrity and sovereignty of the State. In this context our discussion earlier in the chapter needs to be recalled. The Commission has used these provisions to hold Communications inadmissible if they fail to show a prima facie violation of any of the Articles[90] or make a general allegation[91] or have failed to be specific.[92]

- The Communications must not be insulting, nor written in a disparaging manner which is directed against the State or its institutions or against the OAU.[93]

The Commission has used this requirement to hold Communications inadmissible where an allegation has been of the order, for example, of the

---

[84] *Free Legal Assistance Group, Lawyers Committee for Human Rights, Union InterAfricaine des Droits de l'Homme, Les Temoins de Jehovah v. Zaire*, Communication Nos. 25/89, 47/90, 56/91, 100/93, 9th Annual Activity Report of the African Commission on Human and Peoples' Rights, 1995/96, ACHPR/RPT/9th reprinted 4 IHRR (1997) 89, 92.

[85] *Lawyers Committee for Human Rights v. Tanzania*, Communication No. 66/92.

[86] *Maria Baes v. Zaire*, Communication No. 31/89 (admissibility)

[87] See *Mohammed El-Nekheily v. OAU*, Communication No.12/88.

[88] Article 56(2).

[89] Odinkalu and Christensen, above n. 9, at p. 252.

[90] *Frederick Korvah v. Liberia*, Communication No. 1/88, (admissibility) (1988).

[91] *Hadjali Mohand v. Algeria*, Communication No. 13/88 (admissibility) (1988).

[92] Ibid.

[93] Article 56(3).

'President (of Cameroon) must respond to charges of crimes against humanity' or 'regime of torturers'. While the requirement of a Communication to be non-insulting is not uncommon, the Commission has nevertheless been criticised for showing bias and approaching the issues very subjectively.[94]

• Communications are not based exclusively on news disseminated through the mass media.

This is a rather unusual requirement, that the complaint must not be based exclusively on events as portrayed by the mass media. This requirement, while aimed at preventing spurious petitions, possibly represents a distinctly African approach.

• Communications are sent after exhausting all local remedies, unless the remedies are unduly prolonged.

We have already noted that exhaustion of all available remedies as an admissibility requirement is part and parcel of all international procedures. A number of exceptions apply to this general rule. There would be no requirement to exhaust local remedies where all opportunities of redress have been closed[95] or where the procedures are excessively prolonged or cumbersome.[96] In a number of instances, however, the approach adopted by the African Commission has been much narrower. This position is reflected by the case of the *Kenya Human Rights Commission* v. *Kenya*.[97] In this case the University staff in Kenya decided to form an umbrella trade union named the Universities Academic Staff Union (UASU) and submitted the application for registration in May 1992. Not having heard from the University authorities for six months they decided to go on strike. Their application for registration was rejected by the University Registrar in 1993. The University Staff instituted legal proceedings to challenge the decision made by the Registrar. Although, the proceedings were still before the Kenyan courts, President Moi alleged that the Kenyan government would never allow the registration of UASU, a statement that was repeated a number of times. Despite this almost confirmed position of the government, in October 1995 the Commission decided that although 'the President gave indication that any challenge would not be effective' the complainant had to await the outcome of national procedures and thus declared the Communication inadmissible. Such an attitude is unfortunate

---

[94] Odinkalu and Christensen, above n. 9, at p. 255.

[95] *Civil Liberties Organization* v. *Nigeria*, Communication No. 67/91 (1993) (Section 4 of the State Security (Detention of Persons) Decree barring an legal challenge.

[96] *Louis Emgba Mekongo* v. *Cameroon*, Communication No. 59/91 (1994) (case pending for twelve years). *Lawyers' Committee for Human Rights* v. *Tanzania*, Communication No. 66/92 (1994) (rejection of bail applications and delay in appeal procedures).

[97] Communication 135/94 *Kenya Human Rights Commission* v. *Kenya* (admissibility) 4 IHRR (1997) 86.

and fails to comply with the recognised exceptions whereby the authors of the Communication are exempted from utilising those remedies which would prove to be 'inadequate' or 'ineffective'.

The Commission's more recent jurisprudence tends to be more in line with that of other international bodies. The Commission has pronounced on occasions the meaning of 'effective' remedies. Thus in one case where appeal against death sentence lay before the Governor, it was held that such an appeal created 'a discretionary, extraordinary remedy which was of a non-judicial nature'. The Commission therefore held that it was not necessary to exhaust such a remedy.

The Commission has, in line with other international procedures, required the author of communication to adduce prima facie evidence that he has either exhausted all domestic remedies, or that the existing remedies are inadequate and ineffective. Once the author can establish the prima facie evidence, then the burden of proof shifts on to the defendant State.

- Communications are submitted within a reasonable period from the time local remedies are exhausted or from the date the Commission is seized of the matter.[98]

The Commission has not directly provided the details of the time frame in which communications are to be submitted after the exhaustion of domestic remedies requirement has been met, although some guidelines are available in the light of decisions. Thus in one case a Communication was held admissible despite the author having spent more than twelve years pursuing a discretionary remedy.[99] Similarly in another case a Communication was held admissible even though fifteen years had elapsed since the conclusion of the domestic proceedings.[100] This approach although apparently hugely favourable to the author is a realistic one and must be commended.

- Communications do not deal with cases which have been settled by the States involved in accordance with the principles of the United Nations Charter, or Charter of the OAU or the African Charter.[101]

In so far as restrictions relate to international procedures these limitation apply only to those Communications which have actually been *settled* by use of another procedure. Therefore, presumably, concurrent Communications are not barred from consideration by the Commission. Cases therefore have been held inadmissible when a decision has been made by such international

---

[98] Article 56(6).
[99] *Louis Emgba Mekongo* v. *Cameroon*, Communication No. 59/91 (1994).
[100] *John Modise* v. *Botswana*, Communication No. 97/93 (1997).
[101] Article 56(7).

bodies as the Human Rights Committee.[102] The Commission has decided to hold a communication inadmissible which received attention under UN ECOSOC Resolution 1503 procedure.[103] However, a change brought about in the rules of procedure, allowing the Commission only to preclude consideration 'to the extent to which the same issue has been settled by another international investigation or settlement body'[104] would arguably allow it to be more flexible in its approach.[105]

Article 58 communications

The Charter makes reference and elaborates upon the procedure regarding cases that are 'special'. According to Article 58(1), when it appears after deliberations of the Commission that one or more Communications relate to special cases which reveal the existence of a series of serious or massive violations of human and peoples' rights, the Commission shall draw the attention of the Assembly of the Heads of State and Governments of the OAU to these special cases. The Assembly of Heads of State and Government may then request the Commission to undertake a detailed study. This would result in making a report on the facts of the case, the findings of the Commission and its recommendations on the particular situation.[106]

According to Article 58(3) the Chairman of the Assembly is authorised to request an in-depth study in all the cases of emergency. However, there is no discussion of the position relating to those cases that are 'not special'. Two views can be put forward here. First, that the Commission has no role to play in these instances, thereby confirming the situation that the role of the Commission is to identify special cases and refer them to the Assembly in the hope that they will be passed back for further investigation. Hence any other case which does not fall within this category would be inadmissible. The second, more positive and forthright view is that in 'non-special' cases the Commission has the same functions as under Inter-State procedure, that is to conduct an investigation, attempt a reconciliation, and report the conclusions to the Assembly.

Article 59(1) establishes the requirement of confidentiality. It notes that all the measures undertaken in accordance with the provisions of Chapter III shall remain confidential until such time that the Assembly of Heads of State

---

[102] *Mpaka-Nsusu Alphonse* v. *Zaire*, Communication No. 15/88 (1993).
[103] See *Amnesty International* v. *Tunisia*, Communication No. 69/92 (1993); on Resolution 1503 procedure see above Chapter 2.
[104] Rules of Procedure R 104(1)(g).
[105] See Odinkalu and Christensen, above n. 9, at p. 268.
[106] Article 58(2).

and Government decides to disclose the measures. A report shall nevertheless be published by the chairman of the Commission upon the decision of the Heads of State and Government.[107] The report on the activities of the Commission is also published by its chairman after it has been considered by the Assembly of Heads of State and Government.[108]

Procedure

The procedure adopted by the Commission is that it brings any Communication received to the attention of the State party concerned. On receipt of a Communication, the Commission informs the concerned State party that a complaint has been lodged against it and requests the submission of the State party's comments as regards admissibility.[109] The rules of procedure allow the State party three months from the date of notification to respond.[110] Communications are considered in closed or private meetings.[111] Failing any response from the State concerned, at the end of three months, the Commission has the authority to hold the communication admissible. In practice, however, the Commission has not been particularly efficient, with the issue of admissibility being decided in a matter of years rather than months. The Commission has also shown a willingness to review the decision on admissibility if the State subsequently does decide to provide relevant evidence or information.

The Rules of Procedure require the Commission to notify both the author and the State party concerned if a decision has been made to hold a Communication admissible.[112] The Rules also allow for the seeking of additional supplementary information.[113]

If a Communication is held to be inadmissible, the case is closed with the parties being informed of such a decision.[114] However, upon being admissible, there is a time limit of three months provided to the State party to submit its views.[115] All submissions made by the States are to be disclosed to the author. The Assembly of Heads of State and Government is also entitled to receive information regarding the Communications that have been declared admissible.[116] More recently the Commission has decided to invite

---

[107] Article 59(2).
[108] Article 58(3).
[109] Rule 112.
[110] Rule 117(4).
[111] Rule 106.
[112] Rule 119(1).
[113] Rule 117(4).
[114] Rule 118.
[115] Rule 117(4).
[116] See Rules 113, 117.

State representatives as well as the author for oral hearings. It is also encouraging to note that States are attending the sessions of the Commission as a matter of routine and participating in the proceedings. After the presentation of all the available evidence and any oral hearings, the Commission deliberates in private, in accordance with the provisions of Article 59 of the Charter.[117]

ANALYSIS OF THE COMMISSION'S WORK AND THE PROBABLE CONTRIBUTIONS OF THE AFRICAN COURT OF HUMAN RIGHTS

From a survey of the existing jurisprudence, it would appear that the emphasis of the Commission has been on the amicable resolution of disputes. While such an emphasis is acceptable in the light of the provisions of the Charter, there have been occasions when this eagerness has led the Commission to overlook the admissibility and merit procedures altogether. The Commission has decided cases as being amicably resolved without consulting the author,[118] on the assumption that a new administration was likely to resolve the matter satisfactorily,[119] and in case of withdrawal of the case.[120] Another unsatisfactory aspect of the Commission's work is the reporting of its decisions. The approach taken by the Commission in a number of instances shows a considerable margin for improvement, particularly in relation to the substance and reasoning of the Communication. A survey of the Commission's work tends to suggest that in recent years some improvement has been made. Nevertheless:

> they do not make reference to jurisprudence from national and international tribunals, nor do they fire the imagination. They are non-binding and attract little, if any, attention from governments and the human rights community.[121]

Although the Commission has adopted a quasi-legal approach, as noted above, its decisions are non-binding.[122] Furthermore the Charter does not provide for any legally enforceable remedies nor have any procedures been established to obtain these remedies. The aforementioned weaknesses in the functions of the Commission and the desire to improve the system of protecting human rights, led to a widespread call for the establishment of the

---

[117] Odinkalu and Christensen, above n. 9, at p. 274.

[118] *Kalenga* v. *Zambia*, Communication No. 11/88 (admissibility) (1990).

[119] *Comité Cultural pour la Democratie au Benin, Hilaire Badjogoume, El Hadj Boubacare Diawara* v. *Benin* (merits), Communication Nos. 16/88, 17/88, 18/88 (1994).

[120] *Civil Liberties Organization* v. *Nigeria*, Communication No. 67/91

[121] Mutua, above n. 1, at p. 348.

[122] Naldi and Magliveras, above n. 16, at p. 432.

African Court.[123] The existence and successes of the European and Inter-American Courts also provided strong precedents to establish a regional human rights court for Africa.

The African Court represents the fruition of a process consisting of various meetings and draft protocols. The final Protocol (also known as the Addis Protocol) establishing the Court was adopted in June 1998.[124] The Court is granted substantial and in some senses unusual jurisdiction. According to the Protocol adopting the Court, actions may be brought before the Court based upon any instrument, including international human rights treaties, that has been ratified by the relevant State party. There is thus a major innovative feature. In its adjudication, in addition to the African Charter, the Court has the power to consider other human rights instruments accepted by the State concerned.[125] The Court will have the authority to decide whether it has jurisdiction in the case of a dispute.[126]

The Court has been granted contentious, conciliatory as well as advisory jurisdiction. In its advisory capacity it may issue opinions on 'any legal matters relating to the Charter or any other relevant human rights instruments'. This provision appears to be similar to Article 64(2) of the ACHR. A range of bodies including States parties to the OAU, the OAU or any of its organs, or African NGOs (provided they are recognised by the OAU) shall have the capacity to invoke the court's advisory jurisdiction.[127] The Court's advisory opinions would not be of a binding nature but, like the ICJ, it is assumed that they would carry substantial persuasive authority.

Upon ratification, the Protocol provides automatic access to the Court for the African Commission, State parties, and African intergovernmental organisations under Article 5(1).[128] However, no such 'automatic' facility is provided to individuals or the NGOs; their access is severely limited. Instead individuals and NGOs need to establish certain criterion before they may be granted access before the Court. The access is dependant in the first instance on the State party having made a declaration accepting the Court's jurisdiction to hear such cases. The jurisdiction to receive petitions from such complainants derives from Article 5(3).[129] Individuals and NGOs must also overcome the admissibility requirements as stated in Article 56 of the Charter. According to Article 6(2) of the Protocol,

---

[123] Ojo and Sesay, above n. 40, at p. 102.
[124] See *Protocol to the African Charter on Human and Peoples' Rights on the Establishment of an African Court on Human and Peoples' Rights* adopted 10 June 1998, OAU. Doc. CAB/LEG/66/5. Not yet in force. The Protocol requires 15 ratification before it came into force.
[125] Naldi and Magliveras, above n. 16, at pp. 434–435.
[126] Article 3(2) of the Protocol.
[127] Articles 3 and 10.
[128] See Article 34 of the Protocol.
[129] Article 34(6).

the Court shall rule on the admissibility of cases taking into account Article 56 of the Charter. One interpretation of this Article is that the admissibility requirement need not be satisfied in every case and that the Court would have a discretion to admit Communications with minor technical errors.[130]

The Court will consist of eleven judges, nationals of OAU member States[131] who will be elected in their individual capacity by the OAU Assembly of Heads of State and Government from among 'jurists of high moral character and of recognized practical, judicial or academic competence and experience in the field of human and peoples' rights'. Judges would serve for a six-year term and be eligible for re-election only once. All judges other than the President of the Court would work on a part-time basis. The judges would act in an independent capacity and would benefit from the international laws of diplomatic immunity. A judge of the court could only be removed by the unanimous decision of all the other judges of the Court.

The Court shall examine cases with a quorum of seven judges and would constitute a single chamber.[132] The Court's judgments, which will be final and without appeal, will be binding on States.[133] The OAU Assembly is authorised to monitor the execution of judgments delivered by the Court.[134] In its annual report to the OAU, the Court is to list specifically those States that have not complied with its judgments.

CONCLUSIONS

The continent of Africa represents a serious test for those wanting to ensure an effective system of protecting individual and collective group rights. The modern history of Africa has been an unfortunate one, and the transition from repressive colonial regimes to independent Statehood has not been satisfactory. In many instances, soon after independence, dictatorial and authoritarian regimes took charge of the newly independent States and showed little regard for human dignity and human rights. At the beginning of the twenty-first century, Africa continues to witness substantial violations of human rights; the recurrent genocidal campaigns in Burundi, Rwanda and Sudan confirm the existence of a major human tragedy.

---

[130] Naldi and Magliveras, above n. 16, at pp. 440–441.
[131] Article 11(1).
[132] Article 23.
[133] Article 28.
[134] Article 29(2). The actual monitoring would be conducted by the Council of Ministers on behalf of the Assembly. See Naldi and Magliveras, above n. 16, at p. 452.

This chapter has presented an overview of the African human rights law, which has been aptly described as:

the newest, the least developed or effective ... the most distinctive and most controversial of the three [i.e. the European, the Inter-American and the African] established human rights regimes.[135]

The African human rights system is primarily based on the African Charter which, as our analysis has revealed, contains a number of weaknesses. These weaknesses and limitations are derived not only from the substantive provisions of the Charter but also from the mechanisms of implementation. The African Commission, the principal executive organ, has performed a commendable task, although its work remains limited in many respects. More significantly the need for a body to deliver authoritative and binding judgments led to demands for the establishment of a Court of human rights.

The establishment of a Court is a very positive feature, although there continue to be many concerns. First there is a major question mark over the relationship between the African Commission and the new African Court. The (Adis) Protocol does not elaborate or clarify the situation and limits itself to noting that the Court will complement the protective role of the Commission. It will probably be the case that the Commission will have the initial more conciliatory jurisdiction, with the Court deciding the actual disputes. The precedents of the ECHR, with the merger of Commission and the Court, may indicate a long-term possibility. At the same time, a careful approach needs to be taken so as not to provoke conflicts similar to those generated between the Inter-American Commission on Human Rights and the Inter-American Court of Human Rights.[136]

The issue of the seat of the Court has been contentious, particularly after the *coup d'état* in Gambia.[137] An overarching concern about the African human rights system relates to the limitations of resources. Since its establishment, the African Commission has been under severe financial strain, with a lack of adequate equipment and supplies, and paucity of staff.[138] Similar financial difficulties are likely to be encountered by the new Court. The fate of the Rwanda tribunal, which was mandated by the United Nations' Security Council to hold trials for genocide and crimes against humanity, confirms that lack of financial backing can seriously hamper

---

[135] Steiner and Alston, above n. 1, at p. 920.

[136] D. Harris, 'Regional Protection of Human Rights: The Inter-American Achievement' in D.J. Harris and S. Livingstone (eds), *The Inter-American System of Human Rights* (Oxford: Clarendon Press) 1998, 1–29 at p. 3.

[137] Murray, above n. 58, at p. 29.

[138] Welch. Jr., above n. 14, at pp. 54–55.

efforts to vindicate human rights.[139] The requirement of confidentiality and privacy accorded to the deliberations has been a subject of criticism. According to two authorities:

> given the fact, that the decisions of the Assembly are often influenced by personal friendships and shared ideologies, it is possible that the matter may die in the Assembly. What the Commission needs are statutory provisions to enable it to carry out 'on-site' observations independent of the Assembly as is the case in Latin America.[140]

---

[139] See UN S.C. Res. 955, UN SCOR (3453rd mtg.) UN Doc S/RES/955. Reprinted 33 I.L.M. (1994) 1600. Discussed below Chapter 11.

[140] Ojo and Sesay, above n. 40, at p. 98.

IV

GROUP RIGHTS

10

EQUALITY AND NON-DISCRIMINATION[1]

INTRODUCTION

> Respect for human rights and fundamental freedoms without any distinction of any kind is a fundamental rule of international human rights law. The speedy and comprehensive elimination of all forms of racism and racial discrimination, xenophobia and related intolerance is a priority task for the international community.[2]

The principles of equality and non-discrimination represent the twin pillars upon which the whole edifice of the modern international law of human rights is established. The claim to equality 'is in a substantial sense the most fundamental of the rights of man. It occupies the first place in most written constitutions. It is the starting point of all liberties'.[3] This chapter considers the various mechanisms adopted by the international community to develop equality and non-discrimination as an established principle of international and constitutional law.

---

[1] See W. McKean, *Equality and Discrimination under International Law* (Oxford: Clarendon Press) 1983; N. Lerner, *Group Rights and Discrimination in International Law* (Dordrecht: Martinus Nijhoff Publishers) 1991; M. Banton, *International Action against Racial Discrimination* (Oxford: Clarendon Press) 1996; E.W. Vierdag, *The Concept of Discrimination in International Law–With Special Reference to Human Rights* (The Hague: Martinus Nijhoff Publishers) 1973; V. Van Dyke, *Human Rights, Ethnicity and Discrimination* (Westport, Conn. and London: Greenwood Press) 1985; N. Lerner, *The UN Convention on the Elimination of All Forms of Racial Discrimination*, 2nd edn (Alphen aan den Rijn: Sijthoff and Noordhoff) 1980; S. Skogly, 'Article 2' in G. Alfredsson and A. Eide (eds), *The Universal Declaration of Human Rights: A Common Standard of Achievement* (The Hague: Kluwer Law International) 1999, pp. 75–87.
[2] *Vienna Declaration and Programme of Action* (1993) UN Doc. A/49/668 (adopted 25 June, 1993) para 15.
[3] H. Lauterpacht, *An International Bill of the Rights of Man* (New York, Columbia University Press) 1945, p. 115.

Notwithstanding the enormous significance of the norm of equality and non-discrimination within general international law, this chapter recommends a cautious and critical approach for a variety of reasons. First, 'equality' and 'non-discrimination' are in themselves controversial terms with immense uncertainty as to their precise scope and content. Thus according to one authority 'equality is a notion exposed to different philosophical interpretations; its meaning in the various legal systems is not always the same'.[4] Secondly, there is a substantial debate as to the means of creating real and meaningful equality. Should affirmative action policies be approved or even enforced as a means of overcoming past inequality? Thirdly, it is important to realise that international law has not progressed dramatically to eradicate all forms of discrimination. Various facets of discrimination, in particular discrimination on the basis of religion or belief and gender remain neglected. The position in relation to gender-based discrimination is considered in Chapter 13. The position in relation to discrimination on the grounds of religion or belief is most unfortunate. Although there are references to religious non-discrimination in the United Nations Charter and the International Bill of Rights,[5] (unlike racial or gender discrimination) it has not been possible to draft a specific treaty condemning discrimination based on religion or belief.

EQUALITY AND NON-DISCRIMINATION WITHIN INTERNATIONAL LAW

Since the adoption of the United Nations Charter, the principles of equality and non-discrimination have proved to be the linchpins of the human rights regime. As noted earlier the references contained within the Charter concentrate on equality and non-discrimination – references which have been given meaning through the Universal Declaration on Human Rights.[6] Equality and non-discrimination are prominent features of both the ICCPR (1966) and the ICESCR (1966).[7] In addition to the general pronouncement condemning discrimination and upholding the norm of equality, the United Nations has also dealt with specific forms of discrimination through various treaties and instruments. The norms of racial equality and non-discrimination have been further strengthened by the International Convention on the Elimination of All Forms of Racial Discrimination (1966).[8] As we discuss in detail in due course,

---

[4] Lerner, above n. 1, at p. 25. M. Craven, *The International Covenant on Economic, Social and Cultural Rights: A Perspective on its Development* (Oxford: Clarendon Press) 1995, p. 154. Also see Judge Tanaka's dissenting opinion in *South West Africa* (Second Phase) 1966 ICJ Report 6.

[5] See above Chapters 1–5.

[6] See above Chapters 3–4.

[7] See above chapters 4–5.

[8] Adopted 21 December 1965. Entered into force, 4 January 1969. 660 U.N.T.S. 195, 5 I.L.M (1966) 352.

discrimination against women and against children has been condemned and outlawed by the Convention on Elimination of All Forms of Discrimination against Women[9] and the Convention on the Rights of the Child (1989)[10] respectively. Inequality and discrimination in education has been addressed by the UNESCO Convention against Discrimination in Education.[11] The theme of equality and non-discrimination has been most forcefully asserted by the United Nations in its more recent Declaration on the Rights of Persons Belonging to National or Ethnic, Religious and Linguistic Minorities[12] and the United Nations World Conference on Human Rights, Vienna Declaration and Programme of Action of the World Conference.[13]

Again as has been analysed already, equality and non-discrimination also form the critical mass of the regional instruments. These include the ECHR,[14] the EU[15] the Charter of the OAS,[16] the ADHR,[17] the AFCHPR.[18] Non-discrimination and equality has also been main concerns in the instruments adopted by the International Labour Organisation (ILO).

RELIGIOUS DISCRIMINATION AND INTERNATIONAL LAW[19]

Freedom of religion is a subject which throughout human history has been the source of profound disagreements and conflict.[20] The chronicles of humanity

---

[9] Adopted at New York, 18 December 1979. Entered into force 3 September 1981. UN GA Res. 34/180(XXXIV), GA. Res. 34/180, 34 GAOR, Supp. (No. 46) 194, UN Doc. A/34/830 (1979), 2 U.K.T.S. (1989); 19 I.L.M (1980) 33. See below Chapter 13.

[10] Adopted at New York, 20 November 1989. Entered into force 2 September 1990. UN GA Res. 44/25 Annex (XLIV), 44 UN GAOR Supp. (No. 49) 167, UN Doc. A/44/49 (1989) at 166; 1577 U.N.T.S. 3. 28 I.L.M (1989) 1448.

[11] Adopted 14 December 1960. Entered into force 22 May 1962. 429 U.N.T.S. 93.

[12] UN Doc. A/Res/47/35 Adopted by the General Assembly, 18 December 1992. See the Preamble, Articles 1, 2, 3(1), 4(1) of the Declaration. See below Chapter 11.

[13] *Vienna Declaration and Programme of Action* (New York: United Nations Department of Public Information) 1993 para 5 (pt 1). Adopted by the United Nations World Conference on Human Rights, 25 June, 1993.

[14] See above Chapter 6.

[15] See above Chapter 7. 261 UNTS 140; Cmnd 7461.

[16] See above Chapter 8.

[17] See above Chapter 8.

[18] See above Chapter 9.

[19] See B.G. Tahzib, *Freedom of Religion or Belief: Ensuring Effective International Legal Protection* (The Hague: Martinus Nijhoff Publishers) 1995; E. Benito, *Elimination of All Forms of Intolerance and Discrimination Based on Religion or Belief* (New York: United Nations) 1989; B. Dickson, 'The United Nations and Freedom of Religion' 44 *ICLQ* (1995) 327; R.S. Clark, 'The United Nations and Religious Freedom' 11 *NYUJILP* (1978) 197; D.J. Sullivan, 'Advancing the Freedom of Religion or Belief through the UN Declaration on the Elimination of Religious Intolerance and Discrimination' 82 *AJIL* (1988) 487; J. Rehman, 'Accommodating Religious Identities in an Islamic State: International Law, Freedom of Religion and the Rights of Religious Minorities' 7 *IJMGR* (2000) 65.

[20] See A. Krishnaswami, *Study of Discrimination in the Matter of Religious Rights and Practices*, UN Publication Sales E. 60.X.IV.2 1960; E. Benito, above n. 19; S.C. Neff, 'An Evolving International Legal Norm of Religious Freedom: Problems and Prospects' 7 *Cal. West ILJ* (1973) 543.

have seen the growth and extinction of many religions and beliefs. A promise of eternity, and of absolute truth and providence – hallmarks of many of the world religions – has acted as the great determinant of human existence. The overpowering nature of religion, however, has also been used as a weapon for generating intolerance, and as an instrument for the persecution and ultimate destruction of religious minorities. Religious intolerance and repression were the great predisposing factors of history.[21] Within the texts of religious scriptures, forms of genocide of religious minorities were sanctioned. The tragic wars of medieval times and the Middle Ages, the Crusades and the *Jihad*s, translated these religious ordinances to complete and thorough effect.[22]

Religious intolerance is, unfortunately, not simply a historical phenomenon. Intolerance based on religious beliefs continues to pose a clear and serious threat to the possibility of congenial human relationships.[23] During the modern era of the United Nations, the international community of States has made tremendous strides in formulating standards regarding the promotion of individual human rights. It is recognised that freedom of religion represents an essential concern for modern human rights law. Discrimination on the grounds of religion or belief is condemned and forms a necessary feature of the United Nations human rights regime.[24] The UDHR and the ICCPR contain specific provisions relating to freedom of religion. The United Nations Declaration on the Elimination of All Forms of Intolerance and of Discrimination based on Religion or Belief (1981) is dedicated entirely to the issue of religious freedom.[25] Freedom of Religion is also recognised by regional human rights instruments such as Article 9 of the ECHR,[26] Article III of the ADHR and Article 12 of ACHR;[27] and Article 8 of the AFCHPR.[28]

---

[21] See B. Whitaker, *Report on the Question of the Prevention and Punishment of the Crime of Genocide*, UN Doc E/CN.4/Sub.2/1985/6, pp. 6–7.

[22] L. Kuper, *International Action Against Genocide* (London: Minority Rights Group) 1984, p. 1; L. Kuper, *Genocide: Its Political Use in the Twentieth Century* (New Haven and London: Yale University Press) 1981, pp. 12–14; J. Kelsay and J.T. Johnson (eds), *Just War and Jihad: Historical and Theoretical Perspectives on War and Peace in Western and Islamic Traditions* (New York: Greenwood Press) 1991.

[23] For examples of religious intolerance and repression of religious minorities see K. Boyle and J. Sheen (eds), *Freedom of Religion and Belief: A World Report* (London: Routledge) 1997; Minority Rights Group (eds), *World Directory of Minorities* (London: Minority Rights Group) 1997.

[24] See Articles 1(3) and 13 of the United Nations Charter; Articles 1, 2, 18, Universal Declaration on Human Rights (1948); Article 2, Convention on the Prevention and Punishment of the Crime of Genocide (1948); Articles 2, 18, 26 and 27 of the International Covenant on Civil and Political Rights (1966); Article 2, International Covenant on Economic, Social and Cultural Rights (1966); UN Declaration on the Rights of Persons Belonging to National or Ethnic, Religious and Linguistic Minorities (1992).

[25] GA Res. 36/55, 36 UN GAOR Supp (No. 4) at 171 UN Doc A/36/51 1981.

[26] See above Chapter 6.

[27] See above Chapter 8

[28] See above Chapter 9.

INCONSISTENCIES WITHIN INTERNATIONAL STANDARDS AND DIFFICULTIES IN IMPLEMENTATION

The aforementioned provisions from the international instruments represent strong commitments undertaken by the international community. Alongside the provisions of the Declaration on the Elimination of All Forms of Intolerance and of Discrimination Based on Religion or Belief (1981) and the United Nations Declaration on the Rights of Persons Belonging to National or Ethnic, Religious or Linguistic Minorities (1992), they give an appearance of a strong consensus on issues regarding freedom of religion and protecting the rights of religious minorities. However, in reality, much of this consensus is superficial, as there are serious inconsistencies and disagreements regarding both the meaning and the substance of the right to freedom of religion.

Notwithstanding persistent references to the term 'religion' or 'belief' within international and national instruments, it has not been possible to explain the terms in a definitive manner. Attempts to incorporate a definition in the United Nations Declaration on the Elimination of All Forms of Intolerance based on Religion or Belief (1981) did not succeed.[29] The text of the Declaration represents a fragile compromise between States pursuing widely different ideological bases. Thus, at the insistence of the Eastern European States, the term 'whatever' was inserted between the words 'religion' and 'belief' in the third perambular paragraph as well as in Article 1. This insertion was aimed at extending the scope of the protection to theistic and non-theistic, and atheistic beliefs and values.[30] The lack of consensus on the definition of 'religion' or 'religious minorities' has produced unfortunate consequences. In some instances, States have denied the existence of religions and persecuted religious minorities as heretics and political enemies of the State. In other cases, certain groups have been forcibly excluded from mainstream religious faith and declared a religious minority. Thus, for example, the constitution of the Islamic Republic of Iran affords recognition to Jews, Christians and Zoroastrians as minorities. However, there is a complete refusal to accord any official and constitutional recognition to more than

---

[29] The European Commission on Human Rights has treated pacifism as a philosophy coming within the ambit of the right to freedom of though and conscience, *Arrowsmith* v. *United Kingdom*, App. No. 7050/75, 19 DR 5 (1980). Also see the United States Supreme Courts in *Davies* v. *Beason* 1889, 133 USS.Ct Report 333, at p. 342 and *The Commissioner, Hindu Religious Endowments Madras* v. *Sri Lakshmindra Thiratha Swamiar of Sri Shirur Mutt*, AIR 1954 SC 282. For scholarly views see Y. Dinstein, 'Freedom of Religion and the Protection of Religious Minorities' in Y. Dinstein and M. Tabory (eds), *The Protection of Minorities and Human Rights* (Dordrecht, London: Martinus Nijhoff Publishers) 1992, 145–169 at p. 146.
[30] See UN Doc A/C.3/SR. 43 (1981).

300,000 Bahais.[31] Conversely, notwithstanding a firm belief and insistence on the part of the Ahmaddiyyas of Pakistan that they are followers of Islam, they have been denounced as non-Muslims and relegated to the status of a religious minority.[32]

The next area of substantial controversy where international law has faltered is the issue of 'freedom to change one's religion or belief'. As noted earlier, the UDHR (1948) expressly authorises the right to change religion or belief.[33] The International Covenant on Civil and Political Rights, while not in a position to make as explicit a statement as the Universal Declaration, nevertheless grants the 'freedom to have or to adopt' a religion or belief.[34] The text of the 1981 Declaration, the most recent of the international instruments on religion, fails however to make any reference to the 'right' to change religion or belief.[35] The omission of such a provision is unfortunate, and represents what one commentator has termed as 'a downward thrust in the drafting process'.[36] The fact of the matter, however, is that during the drafting stages of the 1981 Declaration there had arisen major disagreements between various blocs; in order for this Declaration and subsequent treaties such as the Convention on the Rights of the Child to be adopted, it became necessary to omit all references to freedom to change religion or belief. The *travaux préparatoires* of the Convention on the Right of the Child and the reservations drawn to Article 14 of the Convention dealing with the issue of freedom of religion confirm this point.[37]

In terms of substance, a religion or belief often tends to be a conglomeration of various values, claims and rights. Religious freedom has several dimensions.

---

[31] According to Article 13 of the Iranian Constitution 'Zoroastrian, Jewish and Christian Iranians are the only recognised religious minorities, who within the limits of law, are free to perform their religious rites and ceremonies and to act according to their own canons in matters of personal affairs and religious education'. Constitution of the Islamic Republic of Iran of 24th October 1979, as amended to 28th July 1989. See A.P. Blaustein and G.H. Flanz, *Constitutions of the Countries of the World* (Dobbs Ferry: Oceana Publications) 1973 – Vol. viii.

[32] See C.H. Kennedy, 'Towards the Definition of a Muslim in an Islamic State: The Case of the Ahmaddiyya in Pakistan' in D. Vajpeyi and Y. Malik (eds), *Religious and Ethnic Minority Politics in South Asia*, (Glenn Dale: Riverdale Company Publishers) 1989, pp. 71–108; Dr. I. A. Ayaz, *Submission Made before the Working Group on Minorities* (Geneva) May 1998.

[33] Article 18 of the Universal Declaration of Human Rights. See above Chapter 3. It is important to note that tensions arose during the drafting of the UDHR. Proposals to incorporate the term 'nature' were eventually dropped because of anti-religious lobbying.

[34] Article 18 of the International Covenant on Civil and Political Rights.

[35] Article 8 of the 1981 Declaration however states that 'Nothing in the present Declaration shall be construed as restricting or derogating from any right defined in the Universal Declaration of Human Rights and the International Covenants on Human Rights'.

[36] B.G. Ramcharan, *Towards a Universal Standard of Religious Liberty in Commission of the Churches on International Affairs* (Geneva: 1987), 9.

[37] See D. Johnson, 'Cultural and Regional Pluralism in the Drafting of the UN Convention on the Rights of the Child' in M. Freeman and P. Veerman (eds), *Ideologies of Children's Rights* (Dordrecht: Martinus Nijhoff Publishers) 1992, 95–114 at p. 98. See Chapter 14 below.

A religion is not simply a personal belief but invokes teachings, practices, worship, observance and private as well as public manifestations of these beliefs and values.[38] There is a strong tendency among religions to invoke complete and absolute submission, and in the process they are likely to affect many aspects of human life including matrimonial and family affairs, family planning, care of children, inheritance, public order, food and diet, and freedom of expression and association.[39] The collective dimension of religious freedom raises complex issues within the individualistic framework of human rights in domestic and international law.[40]

A particularly serious difficulty arises from the claims made by religions or beliefs to have a complete and absolute 'monopoly of truth'.[41] It is this claim to a monopoly of the truth which has served 'as a basis of countless "holy, divine or just wars" and "crusades" waged against so-called "heretics" or "infidels"'.[42] Religions and beliefs also have the tendency of becoming rigid, and their followers intolerant towards other 'competing' religious values and philosophies. This intolerance, as Macaulay puts it, can lead a follower to the view that:

> [I] am in the right and you are wrong. When you are stronger, you ought to tolerate me; for it is your duty to tolerate truth. But when I am stronger, I shall persecute you; for it is my duty to persecute you.[43]

International law, like national laws, is confronted by the problem of religious extremism and rigidity. In view of the variance in State practices, international law has faced substantial difficulties in formulating established principles governing freedom of religion and non-discrimination for all religions. As one commentator has remarked:

> [t]he question of religion takes international law to the limits of human rights, at least in so far as the law functions in a community of States. It is quite meaningless, for example, to the adherents of a religion to have their beliefs or practices declared to be contrary to 'public morality'. To the believer, religion is morality

---

[38] See the General Comment by the Human Rights Committee, General Comment 22 on Article 18 of the ICCPR (48th Session), 20th July 1993.

[39] *Kokkinakis* v. *Greece*, Judgment of 25 May 1993, Series A, No. 260-A (proselytism); European Commission on Human Rights in *X* v. *UK*, App. No. 8160/78, 22 DR 37–38 (1981) (Time off work for Friday prayers); European Commission on Human Rights *Choudhury* v. *United Kingdom*, App. No. 17439/90, 12 HRLJ (1991) 172 (Blasphemy). See also IACHR Annual Report 1978–9, 251 (prosecution of Jehovah's witnesses for unwillingness to swear oath to military service, to recognise the State and symbols of the State). Also see the US Supreme Court in *Church of Lukimi Babalu Aye, Inc. & Ernesto Pichardo* v. *City of Hialeah*, 124 L.Ed.2d 472 (1993) (rituals) and the Indian Supreme Court in *Mohammed Ahed Khan* v. *Shah Bano*, 1985 AIR SC 945 (Muslim Personal Laws).

[40] See G. Gilbert, 'Religious Minorities and their Rights: A Problem of Approach' 5 *IJMGR* (1997) 97.

[41] Tahzib, above n. 19, at p. 30.

[42] Ibid. p. 31.

[43] T.B. Macaulay, *Cultural and Historical Essays* (London) 1870, 336.

itself and its transcendental foundation grounds it more firmly in terms of obligations than any secular rival, or the tenets of other religions. All religions are to a
greater or lesser extent 'fundamentalist' in character in that they recognise that
theirs is the just rule, the correct avenue to truth.[44]

The difficulties inherent in the issue of freedom of religion become prominent when contrasted with the international developments in relation to the
prohibition of racial discrimination and apartheid. While in its early years the
United Nations approached the issue of racial and religious discrimination
with equal vigour, with the emergence of new States it was the issue of racial
(not religious) discrimination which attracted international concern.[45] The
abolition of racial discrimination and the demolition of colonialism, apartheid
and racial oppression were less controversial subjects and suited the interests
of the majority of the member States of the United Nations. On the other
hand, the issue of freedom of religion and religious non-discrimination was
extremely sensitive; even an inquiry into the treatment of religious practice
within the General Assembly provoked angry responses. In its Resolution
1510 (XV) of 12 December 1960, the General Assembly condemned all manifestations and practices of racial, religious and national hatred in the political, economic, education and cultural spheres of the life of society as
violations of the Charter of the United Nations and the provisions of the
Universal Declaration of Human Rights. However, serious differences
emerged in relation to possible action to combat racial and religious discrimination. In the end, as a compromise, it was decided to create separate instruments dealing with race and religion. According to Tahzib:

> [t]he decision to separate the instruments on religious intolerance from those on
> racial discrimination constituted a compromise solution designed to satisfy a num-
> ber of conflicting viewpoints. Western states insisted on addressing both matters
> in a joint instrument. Communist states were not anxious to deal with religious
> matters. Arab states were eager to displace the question of anti-Semitism. African
> and Asian states considered the question of religious intolerance a minor matter
> as compared with racial discrimination. By separating the issues, the Communist,
> Arab, African and Asian states could obviously delay, if not prevent, the adoption
> of special instruments of religious intolerance.[46]

In 1962, the General Assembly requested the Economic and Social Council
to prepare a draft declaration and convention on the elimination of all Forms
of racial discrimination. The General Assembly in its Resolution 1904 (XVIII)
adopted on 20 November 1963, proclaimed the Declaration on the

---

[44] P. Thornberry, *International Law and the Rights of Minorities* (Oxford: Clarendon Press)
1991, at p. 324.
[45] Lerner, above n. 1, at p. 75.
[46] Tahzib, above n. 19, at p. 142.

Elimination of All Forms of Racial Discrimination. Two years later, the United Nations General Assembly adopted, with overwhelming support, the Convention on the Elimination of All Forms of Racial Discrimination. Efforts to draft an international treaty on the elimination of discrimination based on religion or belief have had a very difficult response.[47] The farthest the United Nations has gone in terms of drafting a specific instrument on religious freedom is a General Assembly Declaration adopted in 1981. In its capacity as a General Assembly Resolution, the Declaration is not a binding document *per se*. Even as a political and moral expression, the image of the Declaration has been tarnished by many deviations and disagreements among States.

It is probably the case that the constitutional provisions and legislation overwhelmingly satisfy the broad and generalised requirements of a non-discriminatory stance on the basis of religion, though even here a number of cases point in the opposite direction.[48] Freedom of religion or belief itself is a conglomeration of various rights and values and is capable of manifestation in innumerable ways.[49] 'Religion' or 'belief' is in many instances regarded as providing a complete code of life, determining every pattern of social behaviour. Its pronouncements affect every aspect of life, including matrimonial and family affairs, public order, freedom of expression and association, freedom to preach and freedom to manifest one's religion as matter of conscience and faith.[50] Domestic and international tribunals have often been confronted by the faithfuls of different religions and sects, all raising questions of a serious nature.[51] Therefore, although the plethora of international treaties since 1945 clearly reflects the view that the fundamental principle of the international law of human rights is that all individuals are to be treated equally and ought not

---

[47] P. Alston, 'The Commission on Human Rights' in P. Alston (ed.), *The United Nations and Human Rights: A Critical Appraisal* (Oxford: Clarendon Press) 1992, p. 134.

[48] Article 19 of the Iranian Constitution provides as follows 'the People of Iran, regardless of their ethnic, family or tribal origins shall enjoy equal rights. Colour, race, language or the like shall not be a cause for privilege'. Thus the Constitution excludes religion as a criterion for non-discrimination, an action which cannot be treated as non-deliberate. See Blaustein and Flanz, above n. 31.

[49] See the Human Rights Committee, *General Comment 22, Article 18*, 48th Session, 1993.

[50] See the cases before the Human Rights Committee e.g. *Karnel Singh Bhinder* v. *Canada*, Communication. No. 208/1986 (28 November 1989), CCPR/C/37/D/208/1986; *Coeriel et al.* v. *The Netherlands*, Communication No. 453/1991 (9 December 1994), UN Doc. CCPR/C/52/D/453/1991 (1994).

[51] See the US Supreme Court in *Church of Lukimi Babalu Aye, Inc.* & *Ernesto Pichardo* v. *City of Hialeah*, 124 L.Ed.2d 472 (1993); also see the jurisprudence under the European Convention on Human Rights (1950) e.g. *Kokkinakis* v. *Greece*, Judgment of 25 May 1993, Series A, No. 260-A; *Otto-Preminger Institute* v. *Austria*, Judgment of 20 September 1994, Series A., No. 295-A. Note also Pakistani and Indian case law see e.g. *Navendra* v. *State of Gujrat* AIR 1974 SC 2098; *Jagdishwar Anand* v. *P.C.*, Calcutta (1984) S.C 51; *Ratilal Panchad Ghandhi and Others* v. *State of Bombay and Others* AIR (SC.) (1954), 388; *Rev. Stainsislans* AIR 1975 MP 163; *Saifuddin Saheb* AIR 1962 SC 853; *Commissioner of Hindu Religious Endowments Madras* v. *Sri Lakshmandra* AIR (1954) SC 388; *Sarwar Hussain* AIR (1983) All 252; *State of Bombay* v. *Narasu Appa Mali* AIR 1952 Bombay 1984; *Mohammed Ahed Khan* v. *Shah Bano Begum* 1985 AIR SC 945.

to be discriminated against merely on the basis of their belonging to a certain ethnic, religious or linguistic group, it is argued that the strength of the prohibition in each case differs. Hence, while the legal norms in relation to the prohibition of racial discrimination are regarded as a fairly uncontroversial example of *jus cogens*,[52] the same cannot be said with equal conviction in relation to the prohibition of discrimination based on religion.

In view of the existing dissensions it is difficult to expect the emergence of a greater measure of consensus. There are no immediate prospects for the adoption of a specific treaty focusing on the elimination of religious discrimination. Having said that, while a radical shift in the existing position seems impossible to attain, the ingenuity of a number of human rights processes has led to positive developments towards reducing discrimination and intolerance on the grounds of religion. These processes include a more constructive usage of existing procedures, as well as a greater consciousness of the issues of religious discrimination in group rights discourses and standard-setting mechanisms. Using Article 18 of the ICCPR as its base, the Human Rights Committee has invoked the Reporting, individual Communication and General Comment procedures within the Covenant to elaborate upon the meaning and scope of the right to religious non-discrimination. Religious communities are the beneficiaries of the emerging jurisprudence on group rights. The United Nations General Assembly Declaration on the Rights of Persons Belonging to National or Ethnic, Religious and Linguistic Minorities 1992 places a special emphasis on non-discrimination and equality for members of religious minorities. The ILO Convention No. 169 on Indigenous and Tribal Peoples 1989 presents undertakings from States to protect and preserve the beliefs and spiritual well-being of indigenous peoples.[53] The States parties to the Convention on the Rights of the Child 1989 commit themselves not to discriminate against the child, irrespective of religious beliefs and his or her minority or indigenous background.[54]

A significant element in furthering the human rights norms has been the use of Rapporteurs, focusing on a thematic, geographical or territorial basis.[55] The role of institution of Rapporteurs has been particularly valuable not only in publicising instances of violations based on religious intolerance but also in persuading governments to follow the guidelines provided by the Declaration on the Elimination of All Forms of Intolerance and of Discrimination Based on Religion or Belief (1981) and the Declaration on the Rights of Persons Belonging to National or Ethnic, Religious and Linguistic Minorities (1992).

---

[52] I. Brownlie, *Principles of Public International Law*, 4th edn (Oxford, Clarendon Press) 1990, p. 513. See above Chapter 1.
[53] See Articles 5(a), 7(a) and 13. See below Chapter 12.
[54] See Articles 2 and 30. See below Chapter 14.
[55] See above Chapter 2.

In this regard the contributions made by the Special Rapporteur on Religious Intolerance, of the United Nations Commission on Human Rights, are of enormous significance and deserve fuller analysis. The initial appointment of the Rapporteur had been authorised by the Commission on Human Rights in its Resolution 1986/20.[56] This appointment was to last for a period of one year, during which period the Rapporteur was mandated *inter alia* to examine incidents and governmental actions in all parts of the world inconsistent with the provisions of the Declaration on the Elimination of All Forms of Intolerance and Discrimination Based on Religion or Belief. Resolution 1987/15 extended the mandate of the Rapporteur for a further year. This mandate has since been extended by subsequent Resolutions of the Commission.[57]

From 1988, the Special Rapporteur has submitted yearly reports which are extremely instructive not only in highlighting incidents of religious intolerance but also in providing constructive solutions and making valuable recommendations.[58] The work of the Special Rapporteur is characterised by a number of activities – these include sending Communications to various States and analysing their responses in the light of the prevalent human rights standards. The Communications also include urgent appeals where a particular individual or a group is under imminent threat. Another significant feature of Special Rapporteur's work is *in situ* visits and their follow-ups, which are valuable

> both for gathering opinions and comments on all alleged incidents and government action incompatible with the Declaration and for analysing and passing on the experience and positive initiatives of States pursuant to General Assembly Resolution 50/183 and Commission on Human Rights Resolution 1996/2B.[59]

The current Special Rapporteur, Professor Abdelfattah Amor, has made important visits to countries including China,[60] Pakistan,[61] Greece[62] and India.[63] Several meaningful objectives have been attained through these visits. Not only have they allowed the Special Rapporteur to form a clearer view of the nature and extent of the violations of the rights of religious communities,

[56] 10 March 1986 (42nd Session).
[57] See the Commission's Resolutions 1988/55; 1990/27; 1995/23.
[58] See E.CN.4/1988/45 and Add. 1; E.CN.4/198/44; E.CN.4/1990/46; E.CN.4/1991/56; E.CN.4/1992/52; E.CN.4/1993/62 and Corr and Add.1; E.CN.4/1994/79; E.CN.4/1995/91 and Add.1; E.CN.4/1996/95 and Add.1 and 2; E.CN.4/1997/91 and Add.1 and also the General Assembly at the 50th 51st and 52nd and 53rd Sessions (A/50/440; A/51/54/542 and Add.1 and 2; A/52/477 And Add.1) E.CN.4/1998/6.
[59] *Report submitted by Mr Abdelfattah Amor, Special Rapporteur in accordance with the Commission on Human Rights Resolution* 1996/23E/CN.4/1997/91, para 44.
[60] See E/CN.4/1995/91; November 1994.
[61] See E/CN.4/1996/95.Add.2 December 1995.
[62] See A/51/542/Add.1. June 1996.
[63] See E/CN.4/1997/91/Add.1. December 1996.

but in some instances the Rapporteur has been able to extract valuable concessions on religious equality from the governments concerned.[64]

RIGHT TO RACIAL EQUALITY AND NON-DISCRIMINATION IN INTERNATIONAL LAW

The international Covenants

As noted above, the underlying theme of the international bill of rights is the concept of equality and non-discrimination. The comment is particularly apt in its application to ICCPR. As one commentator has aptly stated 'equality and non-discrimination constitute the most dominant single theme of the [Civil and Political Rights] Covenant'.[65] According to Article 2(1) of ICCPR each States party undertakes to:

Respect and ensure to all individuals within its territory and subject to its jurisdiction the rights recognised in the Covenant, without distinction of any kind, such as race, colour, sex, language, and religion, political or other opinion, national or social origin, property, birth or other status.[66]

Article 3, while providing for equality for men and women, states:

The States Parties to the present Covenant undertake to ensure the equal rights of men and women to the enjoyment of all civil and political rights set forth in the present Covenant.

Article 25 provides that:

Every citizen shall have the right and the opportunity, without any of the distinctions mentioned in Article 2 and without unreasonable restrictions:

(a) To take part in the conduct of public affairs, directly or through freely chosen representatives;
(b) To vote and to be elected at genuine periodic elections which shall be by universal and equal suffrage and shall be held by secret ballot, guaranteeing the free expression of the will of the electors;
(c) To have access, on general terms of equality, to public service in his country

One of the primary articles on equality and non-discrimination is Article 26 according to which:

All persons are equal before the law and are entitled without any discrimination to equal protection of the law. In this respect, the law shall prohibit any discrimination and guarantee to all persons equal and effective protection against

---

[64] On the role of Rapporteurs see above Chapter 2.

[65] B.G. Ramcharan, 'Equality and Non-Discrimination', in L. Henkin (ed.), *The International Bill of Rights: The Covenant on Civil and Political Rights* (New York: Columbia University Press) 1981, 246–269 at p. 246.

[66] See above Chapter 4.

discrimination on any grounds such as race, colour, sex, language, religion, political or other opinion, national or social origin, property, birth or other status.

Article 2(2) of the ICESCR provides that:

> The States parties to the present Covenant undertake to guarantee that the rights enunciated in the present Covenant will be exercised without discrimination of any kind as to race, colour, sex, language, religion, political or other opinion national or social origin, property, birth or other status.[67]

Article 2(1) and 26 of ICCPR vary in their terminology. Article 2(1) uses the term 'distinction' while Article 26 invokes the phrase 'discrimination'. It also needs to be noted that Article 2(2) of the ICESCR relies upon the term 'discrimination'. The ambiguity generated by the differential use of the terms 'distinction' and 'discrimination' is exacerbated by the fact that there is no concerted attempt to define either of these terms,[68] although it is probably the case that the terms have been used interchangeably. While analysing the *travaux préparatoires*, Craven takes the view that the usage of the term 'discrimination' in the ICESCR (as opposed to 'distinction') was more suitably applied for setting into operation affirmative action policies.[69] Within the Covenants there is also an absence of any explicit provisions relating to policies of affirmative action, which tends to reinforce the anti-collective stance. The Human Rights Committee has, however, taken the view that affirmative action policies are provided for by the articles of the Covenant.[70]

International Convention on the Elimination of All Forms of Racial Discrimination (the Race Convention)

The adoption and entry into force of the Race Convention provided a significant step forward in the attempt to combat racial discrimination at the global level.[71] The Race Convention was adopted on 21 December 1965[72] and entered into force on 4 January 1969. The Convention was adopted by 106 votes to none. Although Mexico abstained initially, it later declared an affirmative vote in support of the provisions of the Convention.[73] The speed and number of State ratifications indicates the general consensus on

---

[67] GA Res. 2200 A, 21 UN GAOR, (Supp.No 16) 49–50.
[68] McKean, above n. 1, at pp. 148–152.
[69] Craven, above n. 4, at p. 161.
[70] See D. McGoldrick, *The Human Rights Committee: Its Role in the Development of the International Covenant on Civil and Political Rights* (Oxford: Clarendon Press) 1991, pp. 275–276.
[71] See T. Meron, 'The Meaning and Reach of the International Convention on the Elimination of all Forms of Racial Discrimination' 79 *AJIL* (1985) 283 at p. 283.
[72] UN GA Res. 2106A (XX).
[73] Thornberry, above n. 44, at p. 259.

the issues relating to the prohibition of Racial Discrimination. It currently stands as one of the most widely ratified treaties in the international arena.[74]

While the Declaration on the Elimination of Racial Discrimination provided the driving force for the incorporation of both substantive and normative articles of the Convention, it would be fair to suggest that the adoption of the Convention within two years of the Declaration had its roots in the political support of the newly emerging States of Africa and Asia, who have been particularly strong in condemning racial discrimination and apartheid.[75] The provisions of the Convention, although undeniably a major advance in the cause of eliminating racial discrimination, nonetheless raise a number of complex questions reflecting the existent weaknesses in international law relating to the prohibition of discrimination.

Complications in the definition of 'discrimination' and the scope of the Convention

The preamble to the Convention while introducing the matters under consideration, places emphasis on equality and upon the importance of removing racial barriers. Unlike the Declaration, the Convention does contain a definition of 'racial discrimination' which is:

> any distinction, exclusion, restriction or preference based on race, colour, descent, or national or ethnic origin which has the purpose or effect of nullifying or impairing the recognition, enjoyment or exercise, on an equal footing, of human rights and fundamental freedoms in the political, economic, social, cultural or any other field of public life.[76]

The importance of the contents of the definition need to be noted. 'Racial discrimination' is given a broad meaning; according to the terms of the Convention, it may be based on a variety of factors like race, colour, descent, and national or ethnic origin. According to the definition, four kinds of acts could be regarded as discriminatory: any distinction, exclusion, restriction or preference. For any of these acts to constitute discrimination they must be based on (a) race; (b) colour; (c) descent; (d) national origin or (e) ethnic origin and should have the purpose or effect of impairing or nullifying the recognition, enjoyment or exercise on an equal footing of human rights and fundamental freedoms in the political, economic, social, cultural or any other

---

[74] For the table of ratification see appendix II.
[75] See J.P. Humphrey, 'The UN Charter and the Universal Declaration of Human Rights' in E. Luard (ed.), *The International Protection of Human Rights* (London: Thames & Hudson) 1967, 39–56 at p. 56.
[76] Article 1(1).

area of public life.[77] The definition has been used as the basis of other human rights treaties.[78]

The Race Convention appears to have a broader perspective than the ICCPR, which is limited to rights addressed in that particular instrument. Article 1(1) of the Race Convention, in contrast, applies to racial discrimination 'which has the purpose or effect of nullifying or impairing, recognition, enforcement or exercise of all human rights and fundamental freedoms'.[79] However, in another respect the scope of the Race Convention is far more limited as it only deals with racial discrimination and any discrimination based on grounds of religion, sex or political opinion is prima facie outside its scope. The definition of racial discrimination raises a number of intriguing though controversial issues.[80] There is a constant debate over the nature of equality that is aspired to: how far is the separation of different groups on the basis of ensuring equality compatible with the provisions of the Covenant? How far does the Convention impose obligations or extend itself in prohibiting discrimination in private life as opposed to public life – with the meaning of what actually constitutes 'public life' itself being a subject of controversy.[81]

It is equally important to note the situations where the Convention (as provided in other paragraphs of Article 1) is not applicable. The Convention is not applicable in cases of 'distinctions, exclusions, restrictions or preferences' made by a State party between citizens and non-citizens and cannot be interpreted as affecting the laws regulating nationality, citizenship[82] or naturalisation, 'provided that such provisions do not discriminate against any particular nationality'.[83] Hence, while distinctions made solely on the basis of race, colour, descent, national or ethnic origin are not permissible,[84] the provisions of Article 1(2) appear objectionable as permitting de facto discrimination on the basis of nationality. The provisions of the Article represent the unfortunate reality that non-nationals can be denied equal treatment under international

---

[77] Ibid. p. 28.

[78] See the Convention on Elimination All forms of Discrimination Against Women (1979) below Chapter 13.

[79] Meron, above n. 71, at p. 286.

[80] See Vierdag, above n. 1.

[81] At first sight the usage of the terminology may restrict the activities contained therein to public life (see Article 1(1)). However a number of other provisions indicate a broader approach e.g. see Article 2(1)(d). Similarly Article 5 provides for a number of rights not necessarily coming within the ambit of public life. To reconcile these apparently conflicting approaches it has been suggested that the term public life is used in the wider sense encompassing all sectors of organised life of community, an interpretation presented in support of the rejection of draft proposal of the limiting of the scope of Article 1(1) of the Convention. See M.S. McDougal, H.D. Lasswell and L-C. Chen, *Human Rights and World Public Order: The Basic Policies of an International Law of Human Dignity* (New Haven, Conn.: Yale University Press) 1980, p. 593.

[82] Article 1 para 2.

[83] Ibid. para 3.

[84] Article 1(3).

law. The denial of citizenship as a tool for discrimination has been applied in several States.

Article 2 of the Race Convention sets out State obligations in detail with the aim of pursuing 'by all appropriate means and without delay, a policy of eliminating racial discrimination in all its forms and promoting understanding among all races'. The parties not only undertake to refrain from permitting discriminatory acts, but promise to take positive steps through legislative and administrative policies to prohibit and condemn racial discrimination. Article 2(1) reads as follows:

> States parties condemn racial discrimination and undertake to pursue by all appropriate means and without delay a policy of eliminating racial discrimination in all its forms and promoting understanding among all races, and, to this end
>
> (a) Each State Party undertakes to engage in no act or practice of racial discrimination against persons, groups of persons or institutions and to ensure that all public authorities and public institutions, national and local, shall act in conformity with this obligation;
> (b) Each State Party undertakes not to sponsor, defend or support racial discrimination by any person or organisations;
> (c) Each State Party shall take effective measures to review governmental, national and local policies, and to amend, rescind or nullify any laws and regulations which have the effect of creating or perpetuating racial discrimination wherever it exists;
> (d) Each State Party shall prohibit and bring to an end, by all appropriate means, including legislation as required by circumstances, racial discrimination by any person, group or organisation;
> (e) Each State Party undertakes to encourage, where appropriate, integrationist multi-racial organisations and movements and other means of eliminating barriers between races, and to discourage anything which tends to strengthen racial division.

Article 2(1) imposes a twofold obligation on parties: one positive and the other negative. The negative obligation prevents parties or their agents from undertaking acts or practices of racial discrimination against persons or institutions. The second – positive – obligation is conducted through effective, concrete measures to bring to an end any form of racial discrimination. Hence, while Article 2(1)(b) prevents a State party from sponsoring, defending or supporting racial discrimination by any persons or organisations, Articles 2(1)(c) and (d) impose on State parties positive obligations to take effective measures to eradicate the possibility of racial discrimination by any person, group of persons or organisation. Article 2(1)(e) perhaps reveals the essence of the whole section, stating that the aim of each State party is to encourage the integration of racial groups in the nation-State.

One of the most significant features of the Convention is the exception to the general rule of equality for all individuals. The provisions relating to affirmative action find expression in Articles 1(4) and 2(2).[85] According to Article 1(4):

Special measures taken for the sole purpose of securing adequate advancement of certain racial or ethnic groups or individuals requiring such protection as may be necessary in order to ensure to such groups or individuals equal enjoyment or exercise of human rights and fundamental freedoms shall not be deemed racial discrimination, provided, however, that such measures do not, as a consequence, lead to the maintenance of separate rights for different racial groups and that they shall not be continued after the objectives for which they were taken have been achieved.

This is complemented by Article 2(2), which represents a detail of the obligations undertaken by the States parties, who:

Shall, when the circumstances so warrant, take, in the social, economic, cultural and other fields, special and concrete measures to ensure the adequate development and protection of certain racial groups or individuals belonging to them, for the purpose of guaranteeing them the full and equal enjoyment of human rights and fundamental freedoms. These measures shall in no case entail as a consequence the maintenance of unequal or separate rights for different racial groups after the objectives for which they were taken have been achieved.

The two provisions are of potentially considerable significance for attempts to establish regimes of genuine equality for individuals. The insertion of these provisions are necessary as the Convention [aims] 'not only to achieve *de jure* equality but also de facto equality, allowing the various ethnic, racial and national groups to enjoy the same social development. The goal of de facto equality is considered to be central to the Convention'.[86] The essence of both these articles of the Race Convention is that, although they allow for special measures, they are designed to be of a temporary nature. Their essential purpose is to generate equality in real terms. McKean's view is that Articles 1(4) and 2(2) provide a synthesis

which incorporates the notion of special temporary measures, not as an exception to the principle but as a necessary corollary to it, demonstrates the fruition of the work of the Sub-Commission and the method by which the twin concepts of discrimination and minority protection can be fused into the principle of equality.[87]

---

[85] For similar provisions see Article 2(3) of the Declaration, Article 5 of the ILO Convention 328 U.N.T.S 247; Cmnd. 328. According to *UNESCO Convention* provision of separate schools by States parties will not be deemed discriminatory. Also see the 1978 *UNESCO Declaration on Race and Racial Prejudice* Article 9(2).

[86] A. Eide, *Possible Ways and Means of facilitating the Peaceful and Constructive Solution of Problems Involving Minorities* E/CN.4/Sub.2/1993/34, para.95.

[87] McKean, above n. 1, p. 159.

A number of provisions of the Convention have a very broad scope, and in practice may seem rather over-ambitious. For instance Article 4, primarily for this reason, has been regarded as one of the most controversial of Articles within the Convention.[88] According to it, State parties:

> Condemn all propaganda and all organisations which are based on ideas or theories of superiority of one race or group of persons of one colour or ethnic origin, or which attempt to justify or promote racial hatred and discrimination in any form, and undertake to adopt immediate and positive measures designed to eradicate all incitement to, or acts of, such discrimination and, to this end, with due regard to the principles embodied in the Universal Declaration of Human Rights and the rights expressly set forth in Article 5 of this convention *inter alia*:
>
> (a) Shall declare an offence punishable by law all dissemination of ideas based on racial superiority or hatred, incitement or racial discrimination, as well as acts of violence or incitement of such acts against any race or group of persons of another colour or ethnic origin, and also the provision of any assistance to racist activities, including the financing thereof;
> (b) Shall declare illegal and prohibit organisations, and also organised and all other propaganda activities, which promote and incite racial discrimination, and shall recognise participation in such organisations or activities as an offence punishable by law;
> (c) Shall not permit public authorities or public institutions, national or local, to promote or incite racial discrimination.

The provisions of Article 4 carry far-reaching implications. State parties not only take upon themselves only the prohibition of discriminatory acts, but also undertake to declare illegal and prohibit organisations and activities which attempt to disseminate opinions of racial superiority inciting racial discrimination. The scope of the obligations imposed are also far wider than those of other international provisions such as 20(2) of ICCPR. Article 4 uses a very wide and strong terminology and a question arises regarding the resolution of any conflict of rights which is inherent in the provisions of the Article.[89]

According to Article 5, States undertake to prohibit and to eliminate racial discrimination in all its forms and to guarantee the right of everyone without distinction as to race, colour or national or ethnic origin to equality before the law. The article then goes on to enumerate a number of rights, including both civil and political rights as well as economic, social and cultural rights. Article 6 provides remedies for those who have been involved in racial discrimination, be it in their official or unofficial capacity. It provides:

---

[88] M. Korengold, 'Lessons in Confronting Racist Speech: Good Intentions, Bad Results and Article 4(a) of the Convention on the Elimination of All Forms of Racial Discrimination' 77 *Minnesota Law Review* (1993) 719.

[89] Which right is to be given priority (freedom of expression as against non-discrimination) UN Docs E/CN.4/837, paras 73–83; E/3873, paras.144–188; A/6181, paras 60–74.

State Parties shall assure to everyone within their jurisdiction effective protection and remedies, through the competent national tribunals and other States institutions, against any acts of racial discrimination which violate his human rights and fundamental freedoms contrary to this Convention, as well as the right to seek from such tribunals just and adequate reparation or satisfaction for any damage suffered as a result of such discrimination.

It has been suggested that a liberal interpretation of the provisions of the article, particularly bearing in mind the phrase 'just and adequate reparation or satisfaction' for any damage suffered as a consequence of racial discrimination, would be a considerable advance on previous instruments such as Article 8 of the UDHR, Article 2 of the ICCPR, and Article 7(2) of the Declaration on the Elimination of All Forms of Racial Discrimination, that have dealt with the subject previously.[90] In accordance with Article 7, States parties undertake to adopt immediate and effective measures, particularly in the field of teaching, education, culture and information, with a view to combating prejudices which lead to racial discrimination; State parties also agree to promote understanding, tolerance and friendship among nations and racial or ethnic groups.

Issues of implementation

We have already noted that there exists a broad consensus on the issue of the prohibition of racial discrimination. This consensus is evidenced through an analysis of international treaty law as well as customary law. As far as the Race Convention is concerned, its unique position is reflected through the degree of its ratifications and by the readiness of States to endorse its provisions by the necessary amendments to their domestic legislation. A closer analysis of even the issue of racial equality, however, discloses a number of weaknesses in implementation. Discrimination based on race, colour, ethnicity, language, religion and culture is a historical as well as a contemporary phenomenon. The consequences of traditional practices of discrimination have produced complex problems in contemporary terms; it is largely recognised that legal prohibitions *per se* would not be completely effective in societies with an ancient history of rivalries between communities or where there are vast economic, educational and cultural differences among various groups.

The differences are generally a result of prejudice and past acts of discrimination. As Meron rightly points out:

Past acts of discrimination have created systematic patterns of discrimination in many societies. The present effects of past discrimination may be continued or even exacerbated by facially neutral policies or practices that, though not purposely discriminatory, perpetuate the consequences of prior, often intentional

---

[90] Lerner, above n. 1, at pp. 57–58.

discrimination. For example, when unnecessarily rigorous educational qualifications are prescribed for jobs, members of racial groups who were denied access to
education in the past may be denied employment.[91]

Craven makes a similarly valid point, that 'the concept of discrimination in
international law, while requiring strict scrutiny of any differential treatment
based on a suspect classification does not automatically prohibit differential
treatment if justified by some socially relevant objective'.[92]

In order to overcome past disabilities, a strong case can be made for affirmative action. However, if there is logic in the argument for overcoming past
acts of discriminatory behaviour, there is also a strong lobby which would not
be in favour of prima facie discriminatory treatment in order to compensate
for previous acts. In order to overcome past acts of discrimination going back
to earlier generations, would it be fair and just to give priority to contemporary, less meritorious claims?

The Race Convention, as has been seen, provides for affirmative action
policies. On the other hand, a closer analysis of the *travaux préparatoires* and
the reservations entered against the articles relating to the provisions of affirmative action adds complexity to the issues. It remains unclear whether the
broad consensus which is vested in the general principles of the Convention is
also reflected in support of the provisions related to affirmative action. It may
well be that at present, in view of the lack of clarity as to State practice, it is
difficult unequivocally to accept the view that the principles relating to affirmative action exist in customary international law. Another recurrent problem
which deserves attention is the nature of the political and administrative structures in various States. There are a number of patently undemocratic regimes
which perpetuate themselves and retain control by the exploitation of conflicts within their society. One has only to consider the problems confronted
by such States as Nigeria, Rwanda, Burundi and a number of other African,
Latin American and Asian States to appreciate the problems faced.[93]

The problems of racial, ethnic and religious tensions are confronted by most
States, regardless of their official admission. Whereas these tensions are
evident in the advanced industrialised States of North America and Western
Europe,[94] extreme forms of racial and ethnic divisions have taken place in
States which have recently gained their independence. Tribal, ethnic and racial
antagonism has been witnessed in many of the States of Africa. Similarly,
acute divisions have been evident in Asia, with the prime examples of
Sri Lanka, and India. In Malaysia for instance, as Van Dyke explains in some

---

[91] Meron, above n. 71, p. 289 (footnotes omitted).
[92] Craven, above n. 4, at p. 184.
[93] For a coverage of the pertinent issues see Minority Rights Group (eds), above n. 23.
[94] Consider e.g. the recent ethnic tensions and riots in Bradford, UK.

detail, the issues of religion, race and linguistic identity are intertwined and discrimination by the Malays, 'the Bumiputras', persists against the Chinese, Indians and others.[95] In Sri Lanka, through a culmination of discriminatory legislation and governmental policies, there has been a sustained effort to discriminate against the Tamils. The early restrictive and discriminatory laws relating to citizenship, and the linguistic and religious policies which continue to work against the Tamils, present an unfortunate picture.[96] In view of the socio-economic, political and historical difficulties it is not surprising that bringing about a complete end to all forms of racial discrimination remains an enduring and painstaking task. The implementation mechanisms which exist in pursuance of States' obligations under the Convention certainly provide a reflection of the difficulties inherent in combating racial discrimination.

The Committee on the Elimination of All Forms of Racial Discrimination (CERD)[97]

The key international implementation mechanism which has been devised as far as the elimination of racial discrimination is concerned is the procedure adopted under the Race Convention. The main vehicle for reviewing the performance of the Convention and measures of implementation is CERD. The rules providing for the constitution and the functions of the CERD are stated in Article 8 and supplemented by the Committee's Rules of Procedure. The CERD consists of eighteen individuals serving for a period of fours years. They are elected from a list of persons nominated by the State parties from among their own nationals. The experts are of high moral standing, elected by State parties from their nationals but acting in their personal capacity.[98] The Committee is involved in all the procedures concerned with implementation. These systems consist of (a) a reporting procedure, (b) an inter-State complaints procedure, (c) an ad hoc conciliation commission to deal with inter-State complaints, (d) petitions by individuals or groups on an optional basis, and (e) petitions by inhabitants of colonial territories. The key mechanism to

---

[95] Van Dyke, above n. 1, at p. 111.
[96] E. Nisan, *Sri Lanka: A Bitter Harvest* (London, Minority Rights Group) 1996; P. Hyndman, 'The 1951 Convention Definition of Refugee: An Appraisal with Particular Reference to the Case of Sri Lankan Tamil Applicants' 9 *HRQ* (1987) 49.
[97] See K.J. Partsch, 'The Committee on the Elimination of Racial Discrimination' in P. Alston (ed.), above n. 47, at pp. 339–368; N. Bernard-Maugiron, '20 Years After: 38th Session of the Committee on the Elimination of Racial Discrimination' 8 *NQHR* (1990) 395; N. Lerner, 'Curbing Racial Discrimination–Fifteen Years CERD' 13 *IYHR* (1983) 170; A.F. Bayefsky, 'Making the Human Rights Treaties Work' in L. Henkin and J.L. Hargrove (ed.), *Human Rights: An Agenda for the Next Century* (Washington, DC: American Society of International Law) 1994, pp. 229–296; T. Buergenthal, 'Implementing the UN Racial Convention' 12 *Texas International Law Journal* (1977) 187.
[98] Article 8(1).

date remains that of State reporting, upon which we shall focus our attention. Article 9(1) provides:

> State Parties undertake to submit to the Secretary-General of the United Nations, for consideration by the Committee, a report on the legislative, judicial, administrative or other measures which they have adopted and which give effect to the provisions of this convention:
>
> (a) within one year after the entry into force of the Convention for the State concerned; and
> (b) thereafter every two years and whenever the Committee so requests. The Committee may request further information from the State Parties

According to Article 9(2):

> The Committee shall report annually, through the Secretary-General, to the General Assembly of the United Nations on its activities and may make suggestions and general recommendations based on the examination of the reports and information received from State Parties. Such suggestions and general recommendations shall be reported to the General Assembly together with comments, if any, from the State Parties.

States who are overdue in their submission of reports can produce consolidated reports. CERD has insisted that the reporting obligation is a substantial one and imposes an obligation on State parties to provide detailed information on a range of governmental activities. Reports should be sufficiently exhaustive to inform of situations or circumstances which are outside of the ambit of the governmental activities.[99]

Procedure

The reporting procedure is designed to obtain information regarding legislative and administrative practices of the States parties. Reports also help in the identification of the overall policies which affect the position of racial or other less advantaged groups. Once a report is submitted it may take up to 12 months before it is considered. A confirmed list of reports due for consideration can be provided three months before the session. The Committee meets for two sessions a year, each of three weeks.[100] These sessions take place in March and August and are held in Geneva. There are two three-hour meetings each day. Once received by the Committee, each report is assigned to a Country Rapporteur. The Country Rapporteur may have specialist knowledge

---

[99] General Guidelines for the preparation of State Reports; see M. O'Flaherty, *Human Rights and the UN: Practice before the Treaty Bodies* (London: Sweet and Maxwell) 1996, p. 90.
[100] See M. Banton, 'Decision-taking in the Committee on the Elimination of Racial Discrimination' in P. Alston and J. Crawford (eds), *The Future of UN Human Rights Treaty Monitoring* (Cambridge: Cambridge University Press) 2000, pp. 55–78.

about the state of affairs of the particular country and will undertake a detailed study of the report and identify key issues arising from it. He also prepares a list of questions to be put to the State representative.

State reports are considered in public sessions. Reports are normally introduced by the representative of the State. After the report has been introduced by the State representative, the Country Rapporteur addresses the Committee and presents his (or her) views of the report. Then it is up to the discretion of the members of CERD to make comments on the report. Once comments have been made by members of CERD, it is conventional for the State representative to provide answers or brief explanations of the issues raised. Alternatively he may offer to provide answers to outstanding issues either in the form of additional information or in the next report.[101]

After having considered the report from the State, CERD adopts its 'Concluding Observations'. The concluding observations comprise a critique of the State report and of the response of the State representative to the scrutiny of the Committee, noting positive and negative features, and presenting suggestions and recommendations. Since 1995 the Committee has adopted 'Concluding Observations' in meetings which are open to the public. Despite the often considerable delay in receiving State reports, with frequent and significant omissions or lack of information, the flexibility and ingenuity with which the Committee has performed its task has made the reporting procedure a success. Its flexibility in receiving delayed reports, the use of a variety of sources of information alongside the content of the report, providing guidance as to the content of the State reports, and accommodating a system of examination of reports have all contributed towards a positive element.

The experience of CERD has revealed that a number of States regularly misconceive their obligations under the Convention. While some States have perceived no reporting obligations if they claim that racial discrimination does not exist within their States,[102] many others have felt under no obligation to report periodically if they have not instituted any further measures to combat discrimination.[103] Confusion has also been reported where a State declares that the ratification of treaty provisions is self-executory and the State party itself does not have to take any action to make changes in the constitutional or legal framework.[104] A frequent occurrence noted by CERD has been the delay in the preparation and submission of these reports. Thus, for example, Bangladesh's Seventh, Eighth and Ninth periodic reports have been due from July 1992–July 1996. Nepal submitted its (9–13) consolidated reports after

---

[101] See O'Flaherty, above n. 99, at p. 90.
[102] Note e.g. the position adopted by the Yemen and the comments given to its reports by CERD A/47/18 para 178. Banton, above n. 1, at p. 300.
[103] See generally Lerner, *The UN Convention*, above n. 1.
[104] Ibid. p. 116.

a delay of nine years. Concerns regarding incomplete and unsatisfactory information about legislative, judicial and administrative mechanisms relating to implementation have regularly been put forward by CERD.

Inter-State complaints procedure

The inter-State procedure under Articles 11–13 is supervised by CERD, with provisions for subordinate ad hoc conciliation commissions in the case of more serious disputes.[105] The provisions of the aforesaid Article are similar in nature to that of the ICCPR[106] and other regional human rights instruments. In the case of the ICCPR, however, the inter-State procedure applies only to States which have specifically recognised the competence of the Committee to receive reports.[107] This procedure has not been used frequently, although some States have made allegations against other States (non-parties) of having generated difficulties in their implementation obligations.

Individual or group Communications

Individual or group Communications under the Convention operate on the basis of an optional system, with States parties being required to make a Declaration accepting the procedure. In contrast to the Human Rights Committee, CERD has thus far considered very few Communications. Since 1984, the Article 14 mechanism has been in operation although its significance has not matched that of the first Optional Protocol under ICCPR. Article 14(1) provides for a provision whereby a State party:

> may at any time declare that it recognises the competence of the Committee to receive and consider communications from individuals or groups of individuals within its jurisdiction claiming to be victims of a violation by that State Party of any of the rights set forth in this Convention. No communication shall be received by the Committee if it concerns a State Party which has not made such a declaration.[108]

According to Article 14(1) individuals or groups may submit communications. 'Groups of individuals', however, does not mean organisations.[109] However according to Article 14(2) a State party agreeing to this procedure 'may establish or indicate a body within its national legal order which shall be competent to receive and consider petitions or group of individuals within its jurisdiction who claim to be victims'. Hence there exists the probability

---

[105] Articles 12 and 13.
[106] See Articles 41 and 42 of the ICCPR.
[107] Article 41.
[108] See the Optional Protocol to ICCPR 1966, Article 44 of ACHR 1969.
[109] See S. Lewis-Anthony, 'Treaty-Based Procedures for Making Human Rights Complaints within the UN System' in H. Hannum (ed.), *Guide to International Human Rights Practice*, 3rd edn (New York: Transnational Publishers) 1999, 41–59 at p. 50.

'of a double safeguard against the embarrassments which may be caused to a State party by individual or group petitions'.[110] The attenuated nature of the provisions of the Article are reflected through a careful reading, and the usage of the term 'petition' rather than 'communication' has led cynics to point out that the provisions are meant only 'to deliver the message'.[111] The Committee obtains all relevant information largely through written Communications. CERD, after having considered this information then decides, first, whether the complaint is admissible and if so it provides an 'opinion' on the merits of the case. CERD is not a court and does not provide binding judgments. All steps under Article 14 are confidential until the Committee adopts its opinion. Opinions are reported in CERD's annual report together with a summary of the information made available to the Committee. First, the applicant has to communicate the case through the Secretariat. Once a Communication has been submitted then the case is appointed a special rapporteur or a working group. The object of this exercise is to prepare the case for the admissibility process. A special rapporteur or a working group may seek further information and clarifications.

After the submission of a Communication, the special rapporteur or the working group undertakes a preliminary enquiry into the admissibility of the Communication. The admissibility requirements have strong similarities with other international procedures: the applicant must have exhausted all domestic remedies, and the Communication must not be an abuse of the right of petition. At the time of considering admissibility the government concerned is invited to comment on any relevant issues. The final decisions on admissibility are made in the plenary session of the Committee. An admissibility decision is sent to both the State and the individual.

In so far as the submission of the Communication is concerned, a duly appointed representative can bring an application on behalf of an alleged victim or victims. All (reasonable) domestic remedies must have been exhausted before a communication can be declared admissible. Article 14 stipulates a unique provision in that it has established national bodies to consider the petitions. It would appear that this provision is not obligatory; thus an application could still be successful even where such a procedure was not followed. There is no time limitation provided in the provisions of the Article itself although, according to the Rule of Procedure, the Communication must be submitted within six months after all domestic remedies have been exhausted, except in exceptional circumstances.[112]

---

[110] Thornberry, above n. 44, at p. 270.

[111] V. Bitker, 'The International Treaty against Racial Discrimination' 53 *Marquette Law Review* (1970) 68 at p. 79; 'According to the Canadian representative Article 14 could not be more optional than it was' UN Doc. A/C.3/SR.1357.

[112] Rules of Procedure of the Committee on the Elimination of Racial Discrimination, Rule 91(f) UN Doc CERD/C/65/Rev.3.

In line with recognised rules of international treaty law, a case can only be brought against a State party to the Convention, and the jurisdictional rules need to be complied with. While the identity of the applicant may be kept confidential, applications must not be anonymous. Similar Communications would be rendered inadmissible if they are deemed to be an abuse of the right to petition or are incompatible with the provisions of the Convention. The Committee may consider admissibility and merit at the same time.

Once deemed admissible, the State concerned is requested to offer its views on the Communication within three months.[113] There is also the possibility of interim measures to safeguard the individual concerned. Once CERD establishes a view that there is sufficient evidence to proceed on the merits of the case, it formulates its opinion and makes any recommendations.

The general practice of CERD has been to adopt opinions through consensus. Members are, however, entitled to append individual opinions if they wish to do so. CERD has no power to make pecuniary or non-pecuniary awards. However, it is entitled to – and does – make recommendations to the relevant State party. The State party is asked to inform CERD of the measures it has taken to comply with its opinions.

While the wording of the Article indicates the provisional nature of the presence of such a body with the obvious hurdle of State sovereignty, the provisions relating to petitioning provide a considerable advance since the procedure allows racial or ethnic groups the right to petition before an international tribunal. Although unlike the Optional Protocol group petitions are acceptable, the scope is narrow in comparison both to Article 34 of ECHR (as amended by Protocol 11) and Article 44 of ACHR, which allow any person, non-governmental organisation or group of individuals to address petitions to them.

CONCLUSIONS

Discrimination exists in various forms and its potentially evil manifestations are capable of affecting every member of society. As far as racial discrimination is concerned, it is highly persuasive to argue that there is now an absolute prohibition of it in international law. Discrimination based on race or ethnic origin is, however, only one facet of a wider phenomenon. Religious or linguistic discrimination, although associated with discrimination in general and categorised in the same bracket alongside racial discrimination, are evils in their own right with far-reaching implications.

It may well be possible to argue that the general prohibition existing in international law against discrimination on the grounds of *inter alia* sex, race, ethnicity, religion and language belongs to the category of peremptory norms

---

[113] Ibid. Rule 94, para 2, UN Doc CERD/C/Rev 3.

of *jus cogens*. However, in reality the consensus reached on the issue of the prohibition of discrimination based on the grounds of race and ethnicity cannot be said to be matched with similar concern regarding discrimination on the grounds of religion or sex. The issue of religion remains a difficult one in international law, as has been demonstrated.

Even in the case of racial discrimination, the apparent international consensus may have many elements of superficiality. We have already noted that, while unanimity lies in the ideal of equality and a non-discriminatory society, considerable differences exist in achieving genuine equality and overcoming previous discrimination. Despite the large number of ratifications to the Race Convention, the issue of affirmative action has remained divisive. It is submitted that State practice is equivocal without giving any firm guidelines on the position as regards customary law. The Race Convention makes explicit provisions regarding affirmative action and the issue is highly significant if progress is to be made in the direction of attaining genuine equality.

A number of tensions are precipitated when the matter of taking measures to prohibit racial discrimination is considered, more particularly that of obligations on the part of States to outlaw organisations which incite racial hatred. Article 4 of the Race Convention has already generated debate, controversies and reservations. There can often be a fine dividing line between racist expressions as opposed to rightful expressions based on freedom of speech. The liberties which a tolerant society bestows would surely include as much a right to free expression of views and values as it would aim to prevent racial abuse and violence. Despite the limitations of the Race Convention, CERD has adopted a number of positive and innovative procedures. Thus, for example, CERD has devised an early warning and urgent procedure. According to this system the Committee can examine a case which is a serious cause for concern. The procedure is not dependant on the State party having submitted a report. It has been invoked in a number of cases and allows the CERD to name the relevant party in public session and then, or later in the session, the situation is considered in public. Requests for further information can also be made. After its review of the situation CERD expresses its opinion and usually asks the relevant State to submit a report. It may also bring events to the attention of the High Commissioner for Human Rights, the Secretary-General of the United Nations or to the General Assembly, the Security Council and so on. Once a State is placed under this procedure it continues to remain under scrutiny for an apparently indefinite period.[114]

The role of CERD is in some ways analogous to that of the Human Rights Committee working under the auspices of the ICCPR, and the responses

---

[114] O'Flaherty, above n. 99, at p. 104.

which the States make to these two Committees are also similar.[115] However, in contrast to the individual petitions before the Human Rights Committee, the individual and group petitions before CERD have not so far been rigorously invoked. CERD only became competent to receive Communications in 1982.[116] Hence it still remains speculative as to what role these petitions might play in the enforcement procedures.

---

[115] See above Chapter 4.

[116] See S. Lewis-Anthony, 'Treaty-Based Procedures for Making Human Rights Complaints within the UN System' in H. Hannum (ed.), above n. 109, at p. 50.

11

THE RIGHTS OF MINORITIES[1]

Each nation has a unique tone to sound in the symphony of human culture; each nation is an indispensable and irreplaceable player in the orchestra of humanity.[2]

INTRODUCTION

Minorities as groups exist everywhere in varied forms and sizes. There are ethnic, linguistic, cultural, racial, religious, linguistic, sociological and political minorities in practically every State of the world. State practice has been inconsistent and incoherent in so far as protection of minority rights is concerned. Some States have adopted generous policies not only in recognising the existence of minorities but also in protecting their cultural and linguistic identity. However, there have been other States where genocide and the physical extermination of minority groups have taken place. In their practices, many States continue to refuse to recognise that minorities physically exist and have used forcible mechanisms of assimilation.[3] In view of the ambiguities emergent from State practices, international law has historically found it difficult to provide firm guidelines in defining 'minorities' and in articulating a detailed set of rights. An underlying theme in relation to the subject is that

---

[1] See J. Rehman, *The Weaknesses in the International Protection of Minority Rights* (The Hague: Kluwer Law International) 2000; S.S. Ali and J. Rehman, *Indigenous Peoples and Ethnic Minorities of Pakistan* (London: Curzon Press) 2001; P. Thornberry, *International Law and the Rights of Minorities* (Oxford: Clarendon Press) 1991; P. Thornberry, *Minorities and Human Rights Law* (London: Minority Rights Group) 1991; C. Brölmann, R. Lefeber and M. Zieck (eds), *Peoples and Minorities in International Law* (Dordrecht: Martinus Nijhoff Publishers) 1993; G. Alfredsson and A. de Zayas, 'Minority Rights: Protection by the United Nations' 14 *HRLJ* (1993) 1.
[2] I.L. Claude Jr., *National Minorities: An International Problem* (Cambridge, Mass.: Harvard University Press) 1995, p. 85.
[3] See R.G. Wirsing (ed.), *Protection of Minorities. Comparative Perspectives* (New York: Pergamon Press) 1981.

by way of contrast to individual human rights; minority rights – as collective rights – are also liable to pose more substantial threats to the territorial integrity of States or to those who form the government of those States.

At the time of the establishment of the League of Nations, an elaborate regime on minorities treaties was set. The mechanisms that were adopted by the League of Nations to protect minorities were limited in nature and the minority protection regime collapsed well before the start of the Second World War. With the establishment of the United Nations, emphasis shifted to the position of individual human rights. The United Nations Charter contains several references to human rights. The Universal Declaration is committed to promoting individual rights and non-discrimination. There is no reference to minorities in either the United Nations Charter or the UDHR.[4] The Human Rights Commission, one of the principal functional commissions of the ECOSOC, nevertheless established a Sub-Commission whose specific mandate included the promotion and protection of minority rights. Since the establishment of the Sub-Commission, efforts have been made to project the subject of minority rights in the international arena. However, such efforts have been stalled far too frequently not only because of divisions over substantive claims put forward by minorities but because the subject of definition and identification has proved an intractable one.

DEFINITION OF MINORITIES[5]

The issue of defining minorities in independent States has been a problematic one. In 1966 Special Rapporteur Franceso Capotorti was assigned to the task of preparing a study pursuant to Article 27 of the ICCPR. In producing a detailed examination of the Rights of the Persons Belonging to Ethnic, Religious and Linguistic Minorities, Capotorti also formulated a definition, which is generally regarded as authoritative. According to his definition a 'minority' is a:

> group numerically inferior to the rest of the population of a State, in a non-dominant position, whose members – being nationals of the State – possess ethnic, religious or linguistic characteristics differing from those of the rest of the population and show, if only implicitly, a sense of solidarity, directed towards preserving their culture, traditions, religion or language.[6]

---

[4] See A. Eide, 'The Non-inclusion of Minority Rights: Resolution 217C (III)' in G. Alfredsson and A. Eide (eds), *The Universal Declaration of Human Rights: A Common Standard of Achievement* (The Hague: Martinus Nijhoff Publishers) 1999, 701–723 at p. 723.

[5] J. Rehman, 'Raising the Conceptual Issues: Minority Rights in International Law' 72 *ALJ* (1998) 615; O. Andrýsek, *Report on the Definition of Minorities* (Utrecht: SIM, Netherlands Institute of Human Rights, Studie-en Informatiecentrum Mensenrechten) 1989; N.S. Rodley, 'Conceptual Problems in the Protection of Minorities: International Legal Developments' 17 *HRQ* (1995) 48.

[6] F. Capotorti, Special Rapporteur, *Study on the Rights of Persons Belonging to Ethnic, Religious and Linguistic Minorities* UN Sales No E. 78.XIV.2, 1991, 96.

This definition proposed by Capotorti has been challenged and criticised on a number of grounds. The primary feature of the definition seems to be a combination of both objective and subjective elements in ascertaining a minority group.[7] Objective criteria would involve a factual analysis of a group as a distinct entity within the State '[P]ossessing stable ethnic, religious or linguistic characteristics that differ sharply from those of the rest of the population'.[8] The subjective criteria would be found on the basis that there exists 'a common will in the group, a sense of solidarity, directed towards preserving the distinctive characteristics of the group'.[9] However, it could be argued that in view of the rather onerous considerations of evaluating both the objective and the subjective criterion, identification of a minority group might prove to be a difficult task.

The second proposition which needs to be addressed is that of the numerical strength of the group in question. It seems acceptable that the numerical strength must at least account for 'a sufficient number of persons to preserve their traditional characteristics',[10] hence a single individual could not form a minority group. On the other hand, it is contended that to put in place an absolute principle that in order to be recognised as a minority an entity must necessarily be 'numerically inferior' places an unnecessarily heavy burden on the group and may well be factually incorrect. The minority concept, controversial as it is, cannot be treated in such a restrictive manner. A consideration of the case of the Bengalis of East Pakistan clearly reinforces this point. At the time of its emergence as an independent State, Pakistan was divided into two 'wings' of unequal sizes: East Bengal (subsequently renamed East Pakistan) and Western Pakistan. East Bengalis constituted nearly 54 per cent of the total population and in this sense the provincial population formed a numerical majority. On the other hand, the Bengalis had very little share in the political and constitutional affairs of the State. They were heavily discriminated against and suffered from the characteristic minority syndromes.[11] This minority syndrome was also evident in the cases of the Black African majorities of South Africa and Rhodesia under the apartheid regimes.

Among the contemporary situations, the tragedies of 'ethnic cleansing' in the two Central African States of Rwanda and Burundi also defy this

---

[7] 'The prevailing approach to the definition of minorities [is one] which intermingles objective and subjective criteria'. M.N. Shaw, *International Law*, 4th edn (Cambridge: Grotius Publication) 1997, p. 222.

[8] L.B. Sohn, 'The Rights of Minorities' in L. Henkin (ed.), *The International Bill of Rights: The Covenant on Civil and Political Rights* (New York: Columbia University Press) 1981, pp. 270–289 at p. 278.

[9] Ibid. at p. 279.

[10] UN Doc. E/CN.4/703 (1953), para. 200.

[11] See Y. Dinstein, 'Collective Human Rights of Peoples and Minorities' (1976) 25 *ICLQ* 102 at p. 112.

conception of a minority being necessarily 'numerically inferior'. As a fact of *realpolitik*, minorities are possibly undermined not so much by their weaknesses in numbers, but by their exclusion from power. As one commentator has aptly pointed out, 'the distinction ... between nations and minorities is one of power. The element of power or powerlessness is the distinguishing characteristic of national and minority discourses'.[12] It may well be that a definition similar in nature to that of the one provided by Professor Palley, with its focus on the power-politics of a group may be more appropriate in these circumstances. According to her, a minority is 'any racial, tribal, linguistic, religious, caste or nationality group within a nation state and which is not in control of the political machinery of the state'.[13] Capotorti's insistence on numerical inferiority to the rest of the population would also generate difficulties in multi-minority situations where no single group forms an ascertainable majority. The *World Directory of Minorities* lists a number of States where it is difficult to isolate this straightforward majority–minority numerical relationship.[14]

The third issue to arise out of the Capotorti definition is that of the position of non-nationals within the State.[15] Non-nationals could form a significant proportion of a State's population, and although the main thrust of the development of the international law of human rights has devoted itself to a consideration of the plight of nationals within the State, the rights of non-nationals, as individuals, are also increasingly becoming a concern of human rights law. Indeed, as Lillich correctly points out:

> the question of rights of aliens is inextricably linked to the contemporary international human rights law movement because it poses a clear test of relevance and enforceability of international human rights norms which have developed since World War II.[16]

Non-nationals include migrant workers, refugees and Stateless persons and the phenomenal increase in their numbers in recent years has brought considerable

[12] H. Cullen, 'Nations and Its Shadow: Quebec's Non-French Speakers and the Courts' 3 *Law and Critique* (1992) 219 at p. 219.
[13] C. Palley, *Constitutional Law and Minorities* (London: Minority Rights Group) 1978, p. 3; also see J. Fawcett, *The International Protection of Minorities* (London: Minority Rights Group) 1979, p. 4; J.A. Laponce, *The Protection of Minorities* (Berkeley and Los Angeles: University of California Press) 1960, pp. 8–9.
[14] See Minority Rights Group (ed.), *World Directory of Minorities* (London: Minority Rights Group) 1997.
[15] See P. Weis, *Nationality and Statelessness in International Law*, 2nd edn (Alphen aan den Rijn: Sijthoff and Noordhoff) 1979.
[16] R. Lillich, *The Human Rights of Aliens in Contemporary International Law* (Manchester: Manchester University Press) 1984, p. 2; 'the whole human rights movement may be seen as an attempt to extend the minimum international standards from aliens to nationals' M. Akehurst, *A Modern Introduction to International Law*, 6th edn (London: Harper Collins Academic) 1987, p. 91.

attention to their position in international human rights law.[17] The *travaux préparatoires* of the ICCPR are not extremely helpful on the matter, though whatever guidance can be obtained points more in the direction of the exclusion of non-nationals from the category of minorities as envisaged in Article 27.[18] On the other hand, it must be noted that Article 27 of the International Covenant on Civil and Political Rights, unlike Article 25, refers to persons.[19] It is also significant to note the views put forward by the Human Rights Committee in its general comment on Article 27. According to the Committee:

> The term used in article 27 indicates that the persons designed to be protected are those who belong to a group and who share in a common culture, a religion and/or a language. Those terms also indicate that the individuals designed to be protected need not be citizens of the State party. In this regard, the obligations deriving from article 2.1 are also relevant, since a State party is required under that article to ensure that the rights protected under the Covenant are available to all individuals within its territory and subject to its jurisdiction, except rights which are expressly made to apply to citizens, for example, political rights under article 25. *A State party may not, therefore, restrict the rights under article 27 to its citizens alone.*[20]

The Committee's views on the position of those groups whose degree of permanence could be questioned are also interesting. The Committee spells out its views in para 5.2 of the Comment:

> Article 27 confers rights on persons belonging to minorities which 'exist' in a State party. Given the nature and scope of the rights envisaged under that article, it is

---

[17] See Weis, above n. 15; G.S. Goodwin-Gill, *The Refugee in International Law*, 2nd edn (Oxford: Clarendon Press) 1996; F. D'Souza and J. Crisp, *The Refugee Dilemma* (London: Minority Rights Group) 1985; J. Hathaway, *The Law of Refugee Status* (Toronto: Butterworths) 1991.

[18] See the additional draft clause to [Article 27] that was proposed by Yugoslavia limiting the Article to 'citizens', UN Doc. A/C.3/SR.1103 para 54; the Indian delegate Mr Kaslival 'wondered whether the committee would not prefer to replace the word "persons" by "citizens"'. According to Mrs Afnan, the Iraqi delegation understood 'the obligation of a state within its own territory could only be towards its own citizens. It was in that sense that she understood the word "person" used in the Article', UN Doc. A/C.3/SR.1104, para 7; also note the Pakistani position UN Doc. A/C.3/SR. 1104, para 17; cf. the position of the representative from Equador Ibid. para 45.

[19] Attempts to replace in Article 2(1) the term individuals with 'nationals' or 'citizens' could not succeed. UN Doc. A.C.3/SR. 1103, para 38; The exclusive focus of Capotorti has come under considerable academic criticism. According to Tomuschat 'One cannot fail to observe that the word employed [in Article 27] is "persons", not "nationals".' C. Tomuschat, 'Protection of Minorities under Article 27 of the International Covenant on Civil and Political Rights' (1983) *Völkerrecht als Rechtsordnung, Internationale Gerichtsbarkeit, Menschenrechte, Festschrift für Herman Mosler*, 945, at p. 960; similarly Dinstein is critical of this view of the special Rapporteur 'this interpretation cannot be endorsed'. Y. Dinstein, 'Freedom of Religion and the Protection of Religious Minorities' in: Y. Dinstein and M. Tabory (eds), *The Protection of Minorities and Human Rights* (Dordrecht: Martinus Nijhoff Publishers) 1992, 145–169 at p. 157.

[20] Para. 5.1. Italics added. Human Rights Committee, *General Comment No 23* (Fiftieth Session 1994) Report of the Human Rights Committee 1 GAOR 49th Session, Supp. No (A/49/40) pp. 107–110.

not relevant to determine the degree of permanence that the term 'exist' connotes. Those rights simply are that individuals belonging to those minorities should not be denied the right, in community with other members of their group, to enjoy their own culture, to practice their religion and speak their language. Just as they need not be nationals or citizens, they need not be permanent residents. *Thus, migrant workers or even visitors in a State party constituting such minorities are entitled not to be denied the exercise of those rights.*[21]

Notwithstanding these views put forward by the Human Rights Committee, confusion remains prevalent as to the national status of claimant groups. Several of the recent minority rights instruments make reference to the term 'National'. This includes the United Nations Declaration on the Rights of Persons Belonging to National or Ethnic, Religious and Linguistic Minorities (1992)[22] and the Council of Europe's Framework Convention for the Protection of National Minorities (1994).[23] This has provided some States with the opportunity to claim a limitation on the scope of minority status – a criticism reiterated in the fifth session of the Working Group on Minorities.[24] In the view of these States, nationality is the essential prerequisite for making any claims to the status of a minority. South Asia provides a number of examples, including those of the Biharis of Bangladesh, the Tamils of Sri Lanka and the Nepali-speaking Bhutanese, where the relevant State has exploited the nationality issue in order to discriminate against and persecute a minority group.

Another area on which Capotorti's definition could be challenged is its narrowness by concentrating almost exclusively upon what has been termed as 'minorities by will' and overlooking the position of 'minorities by force' – 'minorities by will' and 'minorities by force' are terms engineered by Laponce.[25] Explaining the distinctions between the two kinds of minorities, he comments: 'two fundamentally different attitudes are possible for a minority in its relationship with the majority: it may wish to be assimilated or it may refuse to be assimilated. The minority that desires assimilation but is barred is a minority by force. The minority that refuses assimilation is a minority by will'.[26]

---

[21] Ibid. para. 5.2; italics added.

[22] Adopted by the General Assembly 18 December 1992, GA Res. 135, UN GAOR 47 Sess. 49 at 210, UN Doc. A/Res/47/135. 32 I.L.M. (1993) 911.

[23] Opened for signature 1 February 1995, entered into force 1 February 1998. E.T.S. 157; 34 I.L.M. (1995) 351.

[24] See *Report of the Working Group on Minorities on its fifth Session* E/CN.4/Sub.2/1999/21 paras 19–20.

[25] Laponce, above n. 13, pp. 12–13.

[26] Ibid.

ANALYSING THE SUBSTANTIVE RIGHTS OF MINORITIES

It is well established that the rights of minorities are interrelated and are dependant upon the rights of the individual. Minority rights are built upon the existing framework of rights of the individual human being. The right to existence, the right to equality, non-discrimination, freedom of religion, expression and culture, therefore, are integral parts of individual and minority rights. The rights of minorities, however, have a collective dimension.[27] As we shall see in greater detail, the minority right to existence is not exclusive to the physical existence of members of a particular minority but would also include *inter alia* a cultural, religious, linguistic existence, without which the group in question would lose its distinctiveness.[28] In the context of groups, the right to equality and non-discrimination often raises issues of affirmative active and positive discrimination for the groups that have historically been deprived of equal opportunities.[29] Freedom of religion, and of cultural, linguistic and political autonomy for minorities is often related to notions of self-determination and possibly independent Statehood.[30] This latter claim of political self-determination leading to secession and independence poses a major threat to the existing world order – States and the governments in charge are very sceptical of encouraging any such claims.

Right to life and physical existence

The right to life and physical existence represents the most fundamental right of all individuals. The right is protected in all human rights instruments.[31] It is an unfortunate historical and contemporary feature of human existence that individuals have in many cases been deprived of their right to life because of their religion, culture, race or colour. Activity involving the physical destruction of minority groups has a long and painful history. In more modern times

---

[27] Thornberry, above n. 1, at p. 57.

[28] Ibid.

[29] See W. McKean, *Equality and Discrimination under International Law* (Oxford: Clarendon Press) 1983; N. Lerner, *Group Rights and Discrimination in International Law* (Dordrecht: Martinus Nijhoff Publishers) 1991; M. Banton, *International Action against Racial Discrimination* (Oxford: Clarendon Press) 1996. See above Chapter 10.

[30] See J. Rehman, 'Autonomy and the Rights of Minorities in Europe' in S. Wheatley and P. Cumper (eds), *Minority Rights in the New Europe* (The Hague: Kluwer Law International) 1999, pp. 217–231.

[31] See the UDHR Article 3; ECHR Article 2, and the Sixth Protocol (1983), ICCPR Article 6, ACHR Protocol to American Convention on Human Rights to Abolish the Death Penalty; AFCHPR, Article 4.

it has been labelled as genocide.[32] Raphael Lemkin, a Polish jurist of Jewish origin is accredited with developing the modern principles relating to the crime of genocide and for coining the term itself.[33]

In international legal discourse the use of the term 'genocide' is relatively new and appeared for the first time during the Nuremberg Trials in a separate category. Its recognition as a crime in international law was a direct consequence of the atrocities committed during the Second World War. After the establishment of the United Nations, international law confirmed genocide as a crime through the Convention on the Prevention and Punishment of the Crime of Genocide,[34] (hereafter called the Convention). According to Article 1 of the Convention:

> The contracting parties confirm that genocide whether committed in time of peace or in time of war, is a crime under international law which they undertake to prevent and to punish.

According to Article II, genocide consists of:

> any of the following acts committed with intent to destroy in whole or in part a national, ethnical, racial or religious group, as such

(a) Killing members of the group;
(b) Causing serious bodily or mental harm to members of the group;
(c) Deliberately inflicting on the group conditions of life calculated to bring about its physical destruction in whole or in part;
(d) Imposing measures intended to prevent births within the group;
(e) Forcibly transferring children of the group to another group.

Despite the coming into operation of the Genocide Convention, there have been several instances where minority groups have faced death and destruction.[35] A number of cases have highlighted weaknesses both in the substance and the implementation of the Convention. The protected groups in the Convention are 'national, ethnical, racial or religious...'.[36] The Convention makes no reference to the political and 'other' groups. Several cases reveal that political opponents have been a primary target of destruction and this

---

[32] Whitaker aptly describes this activity as 'the ultimate crime and gravest violation of human rights it is possible to commit'. Special Rapporteur B. Whitaker, *Revised and Updated Report on the Question of the Prevention and Punishment of the Crime of Genocide* UN Doc. E/CN.4/Sub.2/1985/6, 5.

[33] R Lemkin, *Axis Rule in Occupied Europe* (Washington: Carneige Endowment for International Peace) 1944, p. 79; J. Porter, 'What is Genocide? Notes towards a Definition' in J. Porter (ed.), *Genocide and Human Rights: A Global Anthology* (Washington D.C.: University Press of America) 1982, p. 5.

[34] Convention on the Prevention and Punishment of the Crime of Genocide, adopted 9 December 1948. Entered into force 12 January 1951. 78 U.N.T.S 277.

[35] Rehman, above n. 1, p. 58.

[36] Article II.

omission is particularly unfortunate. The Convention does not criminalise the destruction of a culture, language or a religion.[37] Thus individuals may be deprived of their cultural upbringing, their language or their faith and yet those responsible cannot be held accountable under this Convention. There is no explanation regarding the meaning of 'national' or 'ethnical', 'racial' or 'religious' group as used in Article II.

A further gap in the Convention is the absence of a prohibition on demographic changes which could transform the proportion of a population.[38] Forced expulsions are not within the ambit of the genocide Convention. Recent international instruments have covered some ground to condemn forced or mass expulsions. It is encouraging, therefore, to note that the Statute of the International Criminal Court regards mass expulsions as a crime against humanity. Similarly the forced expulsions are likely to breach the provision of ICESCR on the right to housing.[39] Modern day developments have created new threats to the survival of certain groups which were not covered by the provisions of the Convention. Activities such as the use of nuclear and chemical explosions, toxic environmental pollution, acid rain or the destruction of rainforests all threaten the existence of peoples in several parts of the world.[40]

The commission of the crime of genocide requires two necessary ingredients: *actus reus*, which is the physical action of destruction, in whole or in part, of a national, ethnic, racial or religious group; and *mens rea*, which is the mental element or the intent to commit such a crime. The crime of genocide requires a specific intent. Thus no offence would be committed, regardless of the ruthlessness of the act and the barbarity of its consequences, without a specific intent of committing genocide.[41]

At the level of implementation, several situations have confirmed the ineffectiveness of the Convention in the actual prevention and punishment of the crime of genocide. Genocide of minorities has taken place in a number of States. These States include both those which are parties to the Convention and those which have not ratified the Convention. A number of genocidal conflicts have taken place in the newly independent States of Asia and Africa. At the same time, the implementation mechanisms within the Genocide

---

[37] Rehman, above n. 1, p. 58.

[38] F. Ermacora, 'The Protection of Minorities before the United Nations' 182 *Rec. des cours* (1983) 251–366 at p. 314.

[39] See Article 11 Right to Adequate Housing. Discussion by M. Craven, *The International Covenant on Economic, Social and Cultural Rights: A Perspective on its Development* (Oxford: Clarendon Press) 1995, pp. 340–344.

[40] Whitaker, above n. 32, p. 17.

[41] N. Robinson, *The Genocide Convention: A Commentary* (New York: Institute of Jewish Affairs) 1960, pp. 58–59.

Convention have not come into operation or have proved fundamentally flawed.[42] According to Article V of the Convention:

> All Contracting parties undertake to enact in accordance with their respective constitutions, the necessary legislation to give effect to the provisions of the present convention and, in particular, to provide effective penalties for persons guilty of genocide or any other acts enumerated in article III.

This provision implies that each State party would introduce legislation that would meet the requirements of Article V. States are given considerable latitude as to the application of this provision within their constitutional framework. This has also meant differences in interpretation of the various provisions nationally, both by legislatures and judiciary. A number of States have not adopted any specific measures, implying that they regard the treaty as being self-executing. Finland and Poland are two key examples of States which have treated the Convention as directly applicable in their domestic laws.[43] Most States have claimed that their existing legislation satisfies the requirements of the Convention. The Special Rapporteur, M. Ruhashyankiko, in his report provides a number of examples where States have responded in this manner.[44] Egypt, for instance, stated: 'In application of these constitutional principles, Egyptian penal law contains provisions guaranteeing the individual's right to the physical and psychological safety of his person and the protection of his freedom. The penal code devotes a special chapter to the crimes of homicide and assault (Articles 230–251) and prescribes the death penalty for any person who leads such a band or holds a position of command therein. Any person who has joined such a band without taking part in its organisation or with holding a position of command therein is liable to a penalty of a term of hard labour or hard labour for life (Article 89).'[45] Ruhashyankiko's report similarly reveals that the domestic legislation introduced by a number of States is based on the provisions of the Convention. Indeed, in some cases the legislation uses the terminology of Article II verbatim.[46] The legislation incorporated by a few States, however, raises questions as to whether it complies with the provisions of Article II of the Convention.

---

[42] See H. Hannum, *Guide to International Human Rights Practice* (London: Macmillan) 1984; L.B. Sohn, 'Human Rights: Their Implementation and Supervision by the United Nations' in T. Meron (ed.), *Human Rights in International Law: Legal and Policy Issues* (Oxford: Clarendon Press) 1984, pp. 369–401.

[43] M. Ruhashyankiko, *The Study of the Question of the Prevention and Punishment of the Crime of Genocide*, UN Doc/CN.4/Sub.2/416, 141.

[44] Ibid.

[45] Ibid. p. 142.

[46] See the Legislation introduced by UK (*Genocide Act 1969*), Ch 12, 40 Halsbury's Statutes of England 387–90, 3rd edn also see the *War Crimes Act 1991*; A Richardson, 'War Crimes Act 1991' 55 *MLR* (1992) 73–87; G. Ganz, 'The War Crimes Act 1991: Why No Constitutional Crisis' Ibid. pp. 87–95; for Canada see *Can.Rev. STAT. Supp 1, 171–181,1970*.

The case of Israel is the classic example as its legislation, although similar to the Convention, is deemed to apply only to crimes committed 'against the Jewish people' with the implication that other groups are not covered by the law.[47]

In his report, the Special Rapporteur provides a detailed analysis of efforts made by a number of States to incorporate legislative measures to adopt the Convention in their domestic laws; this includes those States who have had a satisfactory record of protection of minority rights. In another, more recent study, Marschik surveys the penal codes of a number of European States to confirm that these States have legislated in accordance with the provisions of the Genocide Convention to prohibit and punish the crime of genocide.[48] There are a number of States which, although claiming to have incorporated the Genocide Convention, have failed to respect its provisions. Although a number of East European States could be cited in this respect, the main focus lies on the States of Latin America, Africa and Asia. One prime example in the context of Africa is that of Rwanda. Despite its unfortunate record on physical protection of minorities, Rwanda has maintained that its domestic legislation contains adequate protection against acts of genocide.[49]

As far as the implementation of the Convention is concerned, according to Article VI of the Convention 'Persons Charged with genocide ... shall be tried by a competent tribunal of the State in the territory of which the act was committed or by such international penal tribunal as may have jurisdiction with respect to those Contracting Parties which shall have accepted its jurisdiction'. The Convention in its final draft presents two alternatives: that of a trial in the territory where the offence took place or trial by an international penal tribunal.

In relation to trial in the territory of the offence, the primary problem is that genocide in most instances is committed by the governments in power, and as long as those governments remain in power, it is almost impossible to rely on this territorial principle. The case of Germany after the Second World War, as the defeated power, was an exceptional one in providing the allied powers a forum – probably a manifestation of the prerogative of the victors against the losers. However, in most cases of genocide, it is the governments within the States that are involved, and unless and until they are removed, there is a huge difficulty in trying those who have been involved in committing genocide. It is quite possible for a genocidal regime to stay in power for a long time and defy

---

[47] See the Nazi and Nazi Collaborators (Punishment) Law 1950.
[48] See A. Marschik, 'The Politics of Prosecution: European National Approaches to War Crime' in T.L.H. McCormack and G.J. Simpson (eds), *The Law of War Crimes: National and International Approaches* (The Hague: Kluwer Law International) 1997, pp. 65–101.
[49] Ruhashyankiko, above n. 43, pp. 150–151.

international law and municipal laws.[50] It is equally possible that the stance of successive governments might be based on the policy of genocide and forced assimilation of certain minority groups. Professor James Crawford recently reconfirmed this view by noting that '[t]he national jurisdiction envisaged by Article VI does not seem to work'.[51]

There also persists a strongly held view that the difficulties in the operation of the Convention are exacerbated by the apprehension of the accused: this point has recently been highlighted through the inability to arrest and try Radovan Karadzic and Ratko Mladic, two of the people indicted by the Yugoslav tribunal who have been 'on the run' for months.[52] Although, by Article VII, States parties to the Convention pledge to grant extradition wherever appropriate, political interests and subjective opinion seriously hamper the smooth operation of the provision. It is quite possible for the accused to flee to a State which is not a contracting party to the Convention. Since international law does not impose any specific obligations on States to cooperate with each other to extradite individuals, the last – and perhaps the only course of action – may be to resort to illegality to assume jurisdiction.[53] Even if the accused is captured and tried in the State in which the offences were committed, the sensitivity of the issue of genocide might make the possibility of a fair trial remote.

If the option of conducting trials on a territorial basis seems impractical, the second alternative – to have an international criminal court – has proved even more elusive. The large scale violations of human rights in the former Yugoslavia, Rwanda and elsewhere highlighted the need for a permanent international criminal court. In the absence of a permanent court, the United Nations Security Council acting under Chapter VII of the United Nations Charter in Resolution 827 (1993)[54] and Resolution 955 (1994),[55] established the ad hoc tribunals for former Yugoslavia and Rwanda.

The jurisdictional and territorial limitations of these ad hoc tribunals were obvious, generating an unprecedented momentum towards the creation of a

---

[50] The recent example of the arrest and extradition of the former President of Yugoslavia, President Milosovich also confirms this position. It has only been possible to extradite the former President after the overthrow of his government.

[51] J. Crawford, 'Prospects of an International Criminal Court' *CLP* (1995) 303 at p. 319.

[52] See *Prosecutor* v. *Karadzic*, Case IT-95-5-R61; *Prosecutor* v. *Mladic*, Case IT-95-18-R61.

[53] K. Harris and R. Kushen, 'Surrender of fugitives to the War Crimes Tribunals for Yugoslavia and Rwanda: Squaring International Legal Obligations with the US Constitution' 7 *CLF* (1996) 561 at p. 587; J. Bridge, 'The Case of an International Court of Criminal Justice and the formulation of International Criminal Law' 13 *ICLQ* (1964) 1255 at p. 1258. On Rwanda, C. Cissé, 'The End of a Culture of Impunity in Rwanda? Prosecution of Genocide and War Crimes before Rwandan Courts and the International Criminal Tribunal for Rwanda' 1 *Yearbook of International Humanitarian Law* (1998) pp. 161–188.

[54] See S.C Res. 827, 48 UN SCOR (3217th mtg) UN Doc S/RES/827 (1993) reprinted 32 ILM 1203.

[55] See S.C Roes 955, UN SCOR (3453rd mtg) UN Doc S/RES/955 (1994) reprinted 33 ILM 1600.

court with a universal jurisdiction. The General Assembly, which had requested the ILC in 1990[56] to draft a statute of an international criminal court, reiterated its request underlining the significance and urgency of the matter.[57] A draft produced by a working group of the ILC was discussed in 1993 by the General Assembly.[58] The revised draft was discussed again in 1994 by the Sixth Committee, by an ad hoc Committee on the Establishment of an International Criminal Court and by a Special Preparatory Committee on the Establishment of an International Criminal Court. The Special Preparatory Committee during its three sessions in 1996, 1997 and 1998 focused on the text of the draft statute.

The text submitted by the Preparatory Committee to the Rome Conference in June 1998 consisted of 116 Articles. A number of these Articles were essentially in draft format, with crucial details yet to be finalised.[59] It is thus to the credit of the participants of the Rome Conference that within the space of six weeks a Statute was adopted. Having said that, the Statute contains many weaknesses; there are a number of serious inconsistencies and agreement could not be reached on several key issues. It is also significant to note that many of the provisions within the Statute were heavily criticised by the United States, which also decided publicly to indicate that it had voted against the Statute.[60]

As regards the substantive issues, various criticisms could be made. The principle of complementarity which grants priority to national jurisdictions *vis-à-vis* the Court could seriously undermine the system of accountability. The priority accorded to national courts is also in stark contrast to the position adopted by the Yugoslavia and Rwanda Tribunals.[61] These jurisdictional requirements highlight the limitations with which the Court would have to operate. The Statute authorises the Court to exercise jurisdiction for crimes as stated therein if consent has been provided by the State with jurisdiction for the territory where the crime occurred or the consent of the State of which the accused is a national.[62] The point had strongly been resisted by the United

---

[56] GA Res. 45/41 UN GAOR, 45th Sess. Supp. No. 49, p. 363, UN Doc. A/RES/45/41 (1990).

[57] GA Res. 47/33 UN GAOR, 47th Sess. 73rd mtg, at 3, UN Doc. A/RES/47/33 (1992).

[58] J. Crawford, 'The ILC's Draft Statute for an International Criminal Tribunal' 88 *AJIL* (1994) 140 at p. 140; J. Crawford, 'The ILC Adopts a Statute for an International Criminal Court' 89 *AJIL* (1995) 404.

[59] P. Kirsch and J.T. Holmes, 'The Rome Conference on an International Criminal Court: The Negotiating Process' 93 *AJIL* (1999) 2 at p. 3.

[60] D.J. Scheffer, 'The United States and the International Criminal Court' 93 *AJIL* (1999) 12.

[61] GA Res. 47/33 UN GAOR, 47th Sess. 73rd mtg, at 3, UN Doc. A/RES/47/33 (1992). D. Sarooshi, 'The Statute of the International Criminal Court' 48 *ICLQ* (1999) 387 at p. 395. Sarooshi also highlights the position that 'decisions of the Court will not, in general terms, prevail over a State's other treaty obligations' at p. 390 and that 'there is no obligation under the Statute to waive [State or diplomatic] immunity' at p. 392 (footnotes omitted).

[62] See Article 12 of the Statute.

States as it would establish an arrangement whereby '[United States] armed forces operating overseas could conceivably be prosecuted by the ICC even if the United States had not agreed to be bound by the treaty. The United States took the position that such an overreaching by the ICC could inhibit its use of the military to meet alliance obligations and to participate in multinational operations, including humanitarian intervention to save civilian lives'.[63] Furthermore in the view of David Scheffer, the United States Ambassador at the Rome Conference, the position of non-parties was jeopardised through the amendment provisions as provided in Article 121(5). These provisions allow 'for the addition of new crimes to the jurisdiction of the Court or revisions of existing crimes in the treaty [entailing] an extraordinary and unacceptable consequence. After the states parties decide to add a new crime or change the definition of an existing crime, any state that is a party can decide to immunise its nationals from prosecution for the new or amended crime. Nationals of non-parties, however, are subject to potential prosecution'.[64]

The political dimension and role of the Security Council is underlined by the provision which authorises the Council to refer the matter to the Court even if crimes are committed in States that are non-parties, by the nationals of States not parties to the Statute and in the absence of any consent by the State of the nationality of the accused or by the territorial State.[65] In so far as the crimes over which the Court would have jurisdiction are concerned, these include genocide, crimes against humanity, war crimes and crimes of aggression.[66] While the list is limited to the 'most serious crimes', the emergent consensus is more apparent than real. The crime of genocide, encapsulating the definition accorded by the Genocide Convention, proved to be the least controversial. The Genocide Convention, however, as we have seen, presents serious limitations and weaknesses. Furthermore, notwithstanding the apparent inherent jurisdiction which is granted to the Court in the case of genocide, an uneasy relationship with the jurisdictional basis of the Genocide Convention would be formed. The position taken by the Statute is objectionable on two grounds. First, it tends to overlook the 'territorial jurisdictional' aspect in the Genocide Convention which, as we have noted, has hitherto remained the predominant one. Secondly, it brings into issue the position of States which are not parties to the Genocide Convention. Are they to be bound even by those treaty provisions from the Genocide Convention which are not settled and possibly do not form part of customary law? In addition, if the inherent jurisdiction of the International Criminal Court in matters of

---

[63] M. H. Arsanjani, 'The Rome Statute of the International Criminal Court' 93 *AJIL* (1999) 22 at p. 26.

[64] Scheffer, above n. 60, at p. 20.

[65] Arsanjani, above n. 63, at p. 26.

[66] Article 5 of the Rome Statute.

genocide could be sustained on the ground that Article 6 provisions had customary value, further explanation would need to be given for the position of States who decline to become parties to the Statute of the International Criminal Court.

In relation to other crimes, the expanded nature of crimes against humanity and war crimes raised considerable debate and disagreement. While the wider inclusive view is welcoming, the operations and actual reliance upon these aspects by the Court remains speculative. Finally the crime of aggression which, although incorporated, generated unacceptable levels of controversy over its definition. As a compromise position, it was decided that notwithstanding incorporation, the Court would only be able to exercise jurisdiction in relation to crimes of aggression once a definition had been agreed upon. Judging by the protracted and controversial history of definitional issues, a consensus definition of aggression may be a long way off. The aforementioned jurisdictional and substantive limitations constitute a considerable hurdle to attaining the ultimate objectives of the Statute – the accountability and punishment of individuals involved in serious crimes against international law. The final hurdle may be the lack of interest in the operations of the Court. Although the Rome Statute enters into force on 1 July 2002, there remain serious question marks over the position of the US, the superpower whose interest and support will be required if the Court is ever to operate effectively. In the meantime and in so far as the punishment of those involved in breaching the right to physical existence is concerned, the global situation cannot be taken to represent a serious note of optimism. Many minority groups continue to suffer as the provisions of international criminal law (and more specifically those of the Genocide Convention) remain insufficient to punish the perpetrators of these crimes.

The right to religious, cultural and linguistic autonomy[67]

Religious, linguistic and cultural autonomy is not a novel concept for minorities. Its history stretches to the time when minorities as distinct groups came to be recognised. Medieval and Modern History presents many revealing instances of the granting of autonomy to religious minorities. A clear example

---

[67] For useful commentaries on the subject see H. Hannum, *Autonomy, Sovereignty and Self-Determination: The Accommodation of Conflicting Rights* (Philadelphia, University of Pennsylvania Press) 1990; R. Lapidoth, 'Some Reflections on Autonomy', *Mélanges Offerts à Paul Reuter* (1981) 379; R. Lapidoth, *Autonomy-Flexible Solutions to Ethnic Conflicts* (Washington DC: United States Institute of Peace Press) 1997; G. Kardos, 'Human Rights: A Matter of Individual or Collective Concern?' in I. Pogany (ed.), *Human Rights in Eastern Europe* (Aldershot: Edward Elgar) 1995, pp. 169–183; see also the proceedings of the colloquium, *Autonomy and Self-Determination: Theories and Application*, at the Institute of International and European Law, University of Liverpool, England, 27 May 1997.

of autonomy was presented by the League of Nations through its system of minority rights at the end of the First World War. The intervening years between the two world wars saw a number of imaginative attempts to realise meaningful autonomy, for example, in the Aaland Islands, the Free City of Danzig and the Memel territory. The mechanisms installed to protect minorities proved defective and, along with minority treaties, collapsed well before the Second World War.[68]

The legal and political developments that took place after the Second World War more or less resulted in the erosion of any independent concern that had previously existed for ethnic, linguistic and religious minorities and for their aspirations to autonomy and existence as distinct entities. The interest in the position of minorities that could be ascertained was largely of an indirect nature, namely the United Nations' preoccupation with upholding individual human rights and concern with non-self-governing territories. In the present context the provisions of Chapter XI of the UN Charter need to be noted. Chapter XI concerns non-self-governing territories and Article 73 applies to territories 'whose peoples have not yet attained a measure of self-government'. A focus of this nature upon territorial elements meant a lack of consideration for ethnic, linguistic and religious groups who were without a territorial base.

The issue of self-government became almost synonymous with independence to former colonies. At the same time United Nations' bodies started relying heavily on the concept of individual human rights and non-discrimination, neglecting the subject and concerns of minorities.[69] The United Nations Charter – in solely confining itself to references to human rights and non-discrimination – appears to have taken the view that minority rights could be adequately protected in a regime of non-discrimination.[70] Despite the absence of any specific mention of minorities or their rights within the UN Charter or UDHR, minorities have been able to benefit from a number of concepts enshrined in these instruments.

Within the UDHR, there is mention of a number of rights which can be treated as forming the basis of minority protection. The Declaration specifically provides, in Articles 1 and 2, the right of equality and non-discrimination.[71] The right to freedom of thought, conscience and religion is stated in Article 18, the right to freedom of opinion and expression is provided in Article 19, the right to peaceful assembly and association in Article 20, the

---

[68] See Claude Jr, above n. 2; J. Kelly, 'National Minorities in International Law' 3 *JILP* (1973) 253–273 at p. 258.

[69] 'From the very beginning of the United Nations, emphasis has been put on the development of non-self-governing territories towards independence' L.B. Sohn, 'Models of Autonomy within the United Nations Framework' in Y. Dinstein (ed.), *Models of Autonomy* (New Brunswick and London: Transaction Books) 1981, 5–22 at p. 9.

[70] Claude Jr., above n. 2, at p. 211.

[71] See above Chapter 3.

right to education in Article 26 and the right freely to participate in the cultural life of the community.[72] All these right provide the necessary foundation for providing individual members with a natural claim for autonomy. Although the Universal Declaration has no explicit references to minorities, subsequent international instruments have given greater attention to minority or group rights. The International Convention on the Elimination of All Forms of Racial Discrimination,[73] while obviously emphasising the elimination of racial discrimination, also aims to protect racial minority groups. It provides an explicit recognition to affirmative action policies[74] and allows minority groups to institute a complaints procedure.[75] The ICESCR[76] represents a strong recognition of the value of cultural rights in the human rights context.[77] According to Article 15 of the ICESCR, States undertake to recognise that everyone has the right to 'take part in cultural life'.[78] There is also a recognition of legitimate differences in beliefs and traditions in Articles 13(3) and 13(4). Under Article 13, parents are given the right to establish and choose schools other than those established by the public authorities. The most significant of the international treaties with respect to protecting minority rights has been the ICCPR[79] Article 27 of the ICCPR is of special importance for minorities as it is the main provision in current international law which attempts to provide direct protection to ethnic, linguistic and religious minorities. Article 27 provides as follows:

> In those States in which ethnic, religious or linguistic minorities exist, persons belonging to such minorities shall not be denied the right, in community with

---

[72] Ibid, Article 27.
[73] Adopted 21 December 1965. Entered into force, 4 January 1969. 660 U.N.T.S. 195, 5 I.L.M (1966) 352. See above Chapter 10.
[74] See Articles 1(4) and 2(2).
[75] See Article 14(1).
[76] Adopted at New York, 16 December 1966. Entered into force 3 January 1976. GA Res. 2200A (XXI) UN Doc. A/6316 (1966) 993 U.N.T.S. 3, 6 I.L.M. (1967) 360. Craven notes that the Covenant 'arguably recognises the different needs of ethnic minorities particularly as regards their cultural identity'. Craven, above n. 39, at p. 188.
[77] See above Chapter 5.
[78] Ibid.
[79] Adopted at New York, 16 December 1966. Entered into force 23 March 1976. GA Res. 2200A (XXI) UN Doc. A/6316 (1966) 999 U.N.T.S. 171; 6 I.L.M. (1967) 368. There is no reference in the Covenant to according positive group rights or requirements that States should promote minority Rights, Craven, above n. 39, at p. 158. Craven however argues that the Covenant 'arguably recognize the different needs of ethnic minorities particularly as regards their cultural identity. Although article 15 merely states that everyone has the right to "take part in cultural life", a recognition of legitimate differences in belief and traditions is to be found in Article 13(3) and (4). Under that article, parents have the right to establish and choose schools other than those established by the public authorities. Similarly, the reference to self-determination in Article 1 of the Covenant may be interpreted as implying that minorities have a right to pursue their own "economic, social and cultural development" without excessive interference from the authorities'. Craven, above n. 39, at pp. 188–189.

other members of their group, to enjoy their own culture, to profess and practice their own religion, or to use their own language.

The Article, however, does not take a straightforward approach in extending protection to minorities. It is drafted in an awkward manner and appears to suggest that while the majority of States comprise of homogenous groups, the issue of minorities is confined to only a few. The aim behind such wording appears to be to provide protection only to the long established minorities and to prevent or discourage the formation of new minority groups. This phraseology invites States to deny the existence of minorities within their boundaries. Many States have, indeed, not hesitated to do so.[80]

The obligations in the Article require States 'not to deny the right [to persons belonging to minorities] to enjoy their own culture, to profess and practice their own religion, or to use their own language'. The wording of the provision, contrary to other articles, is negative in tone.[81]

The obligations that are to be imposed upon State parties have also been a matter of considerable debate. The text is not strong enough to place States and governments under the obligation of providing special facilities to members of minorities. The sole obligation that was placed on the States was not to deprive or deny members of the minority groups the status they were already enjoying.[82] Article 27 is not only weak in placing positive obligations on State parties, but it is also limited in scope as far as the issue of *locus standi* is concerned. The jurisprudence emanating from the operation of the first Optional Protocol confirms that the provisions of the article are limited to persons. Cases such *Sandra Lovelace* v. *Canada*[83] establish the possibility of vindication of minority rights using Article 27. At the same time, the article has proved inadequate in satisfying many of the claims put forward by minority groups, in particular when they may link across to the claims of self-determination.[84] Minorities as collective entities are not entitled to bring

---

[80] Mr Kaliswali of India had warned that such phraseology 'might encourage dictatorial States to refuse to recognise the rights of minorities living in their territory, simply by denying their existence' 9 UN ESCOR, Commission on Human Rights, UN Doc. E/CN. 4/SR. 368–71 (1951) para 37.

[81] In contrast see e.g. Article 18(1): Every one shall have the right to freedom of thought, conscience and religion. Article 24(3) Every child has the right to require a nationality.

[82] According to Capotorti during the discussions at the Commission 'It was generally agreed that the text submitted by the Sub-Commission would not, for example, place States and governments under obligation of providing special schools for persons belonging to ethnic, religious and linguistic minorities. Persons who comprised of ethnic, religious or linguistic minorities could as such request that they should not be deprived of the rights recognised in the draft article. The sole obligation imposed upon them was not to deny that right'. Capotorti, above n. 6, at p. 36.

[83] *Sandra Lovelace* v. *Canada*, Communication No. 24/1977 (30 July 1981), UN Doc. CCPR/C/ OP/1 at 83 (1984).

[84] See *Lubicon Lake Band* v. *Canada*, Communication No. 167/1984 (26 March 1990), UN Doc. Supp. No. 40 (A/45/40) at 1 (1990). Also see General Comment 23(50) Article 27, UN Doc. CCPR/C/21/Rev. 1/Add.5 (1994) at para 3.1.

actions before the Committee. Nor has it been possible to claim violations of Article 1 under the Optional Protocol to the ICCPR.[85]

MODERN INITIATIVES IN INTERNATIONAL LAW

Since the adoption of the ICCPR a number of recent initiatives have reinforced the international provisions relating to minority protection. The primary instrument at the global level is the United Nations General Assembly's Resolution 47/135 of 18 December 1992.[86] The Declaration represents a concerted effort on the part of the international community to overcome some of the limitations in Article 27 of the ICCPR.[87] According to Article 1(1), States

> shall protect the existence and the national or ethnic, cultural, religious or linguistic identity of minorities within their respective territories and shall encourage conditions for the promotion of that identity.

Article 2(1) confirms and elaborates upon the position of Article 27 of ICCPR. The provisions of this article present a more positive attitude compared with the tentative position adopted by Article 27. It provides:

> Persons belonging to national or ethnic, religious and linguistic minorities (hereinafter referred to as persons belonging to minorities) have the right to enjoy their own culture, to profess and practice their own religion, and to use their own language, in private and in public, freely and without interference or any form of discrimination.

Article 2(2) provides for wide-ranging participatory rights to persons belonging to minorities in 'cultural, religious, social, economic and public life'. The provision is significant as the recognition and authorisation of such rights form an essential element of the concept of autonomy. Similarly, Article 2(3) provides for effective participation at national and regional levels and on matters which necessarily affect the position of minorities. Article 2(4) authorises persons belonging to minorities to establish and maintain their own institutions, a matter indispensable to the autonomous existence of minorities. Hence, Article 2 as a whole, could be taken to bear significant value in recognising autonomy for minorities, even though the right to autonomy itself failed to be incorporated in the Declaration. Article 3 of the Declaration also carries a similar message. It reinforces the collective dimension with

---

[85] CCPR/C/33D/197/1985, 10 August 1988; Human Rights Committee, 33rd session; Prior decisions CCPR/C/WG/27/D/197 1985; CCPR/C/29D/197 1985 (admissibility 25 March 1987).
[86] UN Doc A/Res/47/135
[87] B. Dickson, 'The United Nations and Freedom of Religion' 44 *ICLQ* (1995) at p. 354.

encouragement of the communal enjoyment of rights without discrimination of any sort. Article 4 provides that:

(1) States shall take measure to ensure that persons belonging to minorities may exercise fully and effectively all their human rights and fundamental freedom without any discrimination and in full equality before the law.

(2) States shall take measures to create favourable conditions to enable persons belonging to minorities to express their characteristics and to develop their culture, language, religion, traditions and customs except where specific practices are in violation of national law and contrary to international standards.

(3) States should take appropriate measures so that, wherever possible persons belonging to minorities have adequate opportunities to learn their mother tongue.

(4) States should, where appropriate, take measures in the field of education, in order to encourage the knowledge of the history, traditions, language and culture of the minorities existing within their territory. Persons belonging to minorities should have adequate opportunities to gain knowledge of the society as a whole.

(5) States should consider appropriate measures so that persons belonging to minorities may participate fully in the economic progress and development in their country.

Articles 5, 6 and 7 also carry considerable value. According to Article 5, 'legitimate interests' of the persons belonging to minorities would be taken into account when formulating national policies or programmes of cooperation and assistance among States. The emphasis of Articles 6 and 7 is upon international cooperation in understanding the minority question in a more tolerant and rational manner. The Declaration has many positive elements. Aspects of ethnic, cultural and linguistic autonomy appear within the text of the Declaration and represent a considerable advance. The communal aspects of the existence of minorities are more pronounced; the references relating to State sovereignty and territorial integrity, although integral to the Declaration, are framed in a more accommodating manner. They are less confrontational to aspirations of autonomy and distinct identity.

The Declaration, however, is a General Assembly Resolution and its impact on the development of international law is not clear. Many of the substantive provisions of the Declaration are themselves framed in a rather general manner, enabling a number of States to claim that they already respect minority rights.[88] States may also prevent legitimate expression of minorities on the

---

[88] Hence the position adopted by Poland in the Human Rights Commission may be unduly optimistic according to which 'Even though the text, was not perfect, it did appear to fulfil two essential requirements: firstly, it constituted a comprehensive international instrument in the field of protection of minorities, all of whose rights were clearly specified, and secondly, it clearly set out the commitments by which States could universally agree to be bound in so sensitive a sphere. It was thus a sound document, in line with the general approach to the question of international standards for the protection of the rights of minorities, and which, while ensuring a satisfactory balance between the rights of the nation as a whole.' UN Doc. E/CN.4/1992/SR.18, para 20.

pretext of being 'incompatible with national legislation'.[89] Even as a political and moral expression there have been controversies as to the rights of minorities and concern for State sovereignty and territorial integrity resurfaced frequently. Right to autonomy was not acceptable and even the 'lower level' right to 'self-management' failed to be incorporated.[90] The manner and circumstances of the adoption of the Declaration, as its critics would argue, was probably more in response to the inability of the United Nations to take appropriate action to protect the rights of minorities, even after the East–West détente and the ending of the cold war.

One ingenious method of overcoming historical weaknesses in the implementation of minority rights mechanisms has been through the setting-up of a Working Group on Minorities. The Working Group, which was established in 1995, has helped to eradicate some of the criticisms regarding the weaknesses existent in the practical realisation and implementation of the Declaration. The Working Group on Minorities has also been influential in promoting the issue of minority rights at the global level, and notwithstanding its brief history has already created a lasting impression within the United Nations as an effective forum for deliberation and producing mutual understanding between minorities and their governments.

The origins of the Working Group can be traced through the recommendations of Professor Asbjørn Eide. These recommendations, initially presented in his report entitled *Possible Ways and Means of Facilitating the Peaceful and Constructive Solutions of Problems Involving Minorities*, were endorsed by the Human Rights Sub-Commission, which made a further recommendation to the Commission on Human Rights in its Resolution 1994/4 of August 1994.[91] The establishment of the Working Group was authorised by the Human Rights Commission,[92] and subsequently endorsed by the Economic and Social Council in July 1995.[93] The Working Group was initially authorised for a period of three years; it was to consist of five members of the Sub-Commission on Human Rights and to meet for five working days every year. The mandate of the Working Group is constituted as follows:

(a) Review the promotion and practical realisation of the Declaration;
(b) Examine possible solutions to problems involving minorities, including the promotion of mutual understanding between and among minorities and governments;

---

[89] See Articles 2(3) and 4(2) of the Declaration.
[90] P. Thornberry, 'International and European Standards on Minority Rights' in H. Miall (ed.), *Minority Rights in Europe: The Scope for a Transnational Regime* (London: Pinter) 1994, 14–21 at p. 20.
[91] See Sub-Commission on the Prevention of Discrimination and Protection of Minorities Res. 1994/4 (19 August 1994).
[92] See Commission on Human Rights Res. 1995/24 (3 March 1995).
[93] See ECOSOC Res. 1995/31 (25 July 1995).

(c) Recommend further measures, as appropriate, for the promotion and pro-
     tection of the rights of persons belonging to national or ethnic, religious and
     linguistic minorities.

In accordance with its mandate, the Working Group has held seven sessions, the most recent being held in May 2001. The sessions of the Working
Group consist of public meetings as well as private (closed) sessions. For the
most part the sessions are open to individuals belonging to minority groups,
representatives from intergovernmental organisations, non-governmental
organisations (NGOs), State representatives and scholars interested in the
subject. The sessions of the Working Group have not only succeeded in
promoting the practical realisation of the United Nations Declaration but
have also acted as an excellent forum for debate, deliberation and constructive
dialogue. Delegates representing various non-governmental organisations and
other bodies have been able to highlight their concerns and, where appropriate, make recommendations for necessary action. Issues of autonomy have
been at the forefront of a number of debates, both minority groups as well as
the State observers being participants in these debates.

The Working Group has been able to enhance the overall jurisprudence of
minority rights through a number of initiatives. Members of the Working
Group have produced commentaries on the Declaration, as well as on the
various rights contained therein. Professor Asbjørn Eide, the chairman of the
Working Group, has made a substantial impression on the proceedings and on
the continuing success of the Working Group.[94] Other members of the
Working Group have similarly provided valuable input. In March 1999,
Mustafa Mehdi presented a working paper on Multicultural and Intercultural
Education on the Protection of Minorities[95] as did another member of the
Working Group on Universal and Regional Mechanisms for Minority
Protection.[96]

In the Working Group's session of May 1999 numerous significant proposals were put forward, including the establishment of a database on minorities
and enhanced strategies for further involvement of regional and sub-regional
agencies.[97] At the present stage it appears premature to come to any conclusive views on the impact of the Working Group on the universal protection of
minority rights. Nevertheless, it has already become certain that in the global
framework, where there are substantial difficulties in the implementation
mechanisms, the Working Group has tremendous potential to advance the
cause of minority rights.

---

[94] E/CN. 4/Sub.2/AC.5/1998 WP. 1 and observations thereon from governments, specialised
agencies, non-governmental organisations and experts E/CN.4/Sub.2/AC.5/1999 WP. 1.
[95] E/CN.4.4/AC.5/1999 WP. 5.
[96] E/CN.4/Sub.2/AC.5/1999 WP 6 May 1999.
[97] E/CN.4/Sub.2/AC.5/1999 WP. 9.

REGIONAL PROTECTION OF MINORITY RIGHTS: AN OVERVIEW

Many of the difficulties which have characterised the United Nations approach towards minorities have been reflected at the regional level. The continents of Europe, America and Africa have established regional institutions for the protection of human rights, although concern for minority rights has not been a strength of any of these systems. The provisions of the European Convention on Human Rights as well as the jurisprudence arising from the Strasbourg institutions has reflected difficulties in advancing the cause of minorities as distinct entities; it is the absence of a focus on group rights that is problematic.[98] The ECHR contains a number of provisions relevant to protecting the interests of minorities. However, it is only in Article 14 (an article providing for a regime of non-discrimination) that a direct reference to minorities is made.

The European Court and Commission have not been forthcoming in advancing the cause of minorities. Efforts to adopt a minority rights protocol have, thus far, not borne fruit. The Council of Europe has however been successful in adopting two treaties which are directly relevant to minorities in Europe. The Framework European Convention for the Protection of National Minorities 1994[99] is the first binding instrument which has an exclusive focus on minorities. The treaty came into operation in 1998. The Convention emphasises the usual non-discriminatory norms. It provides for equality, prohibiting discrimination on the 'grounds of belonging to a national minority'.[100] The States parties also undertake to adopt 'measures in the fields of education and research to foster knowledge of the culture, history, language and religion of their national minorities and of the majority'.[101] There is an undertaking to promote minority languages,[102] and educational rights.[103] In accordance with Article 17, parties are also under an obligation 'not to interfere with the right of persons belonging to national minorities to establish and maintain free and peaceful contacts across frontiers with persons lawfully staying in other States, in particular those with whom they share an ethnic, cultural, linguistic or religious identity, or a common cultural heritage'.[104]

---

[98] See D.J. Harris, M. O'Boyle and C. Warbrick, *Law of the European Convention on Human Rights* (London: Butterworths) 1995, at p. 487; S Poulter, 'The Rights of Ethnic, Religious and Linguistic Minorities' 2 *EHRLR* (1997) 254.

[99] For the text of the Convention see 16 *HRLJ* (1995) 98.

[100] Ibid. Articles 3–4.

[101] Article 12(1).

[102] Articles 10–11.

[103] Articles 12–14.

[104] Article 17(1).

In spite of these positive features, the Convention has many weaknesses. The Framework Convention, like other minority rights instruments, fails to define the term 'national minority'. The Convention also does not detract from the path of according individual rights as opposed to collective group rights.[105] The authors of the text of the Framework Convention reiterate this point in an explanatory note, commenting that the application of the provisions of the Convention 'does not imply the recognition of collective rights'.[106] They also point out that the notion of collective rights is separate and distinct from the issue of enjoyment of rights by individuals who belong to minority groups.[107]

In addition, a number of provisions of the Framework Convention are structured in such a manner that there is an apparent distinction in the nature of obligations undertaken by States parties. For example, under Article 7, States parties undertake to ensure respect for the rights of persons belonging to a minority to enjoy freedom of peaceful assembly, association, expression, thought, conscience and religion. On the other hand, in a number of instances where positive action is required to promote the collective group rights dimension, the articles are framed in a manner which suggests an orientation towards 'progressive realisation' rather than an existence of immediate binding obligations – reminiscent of the principles enshrined in the ICESCR. Examples of the latter construction are apparent from the use of the terms such as 'undertake to recognise' or 'not to interfere with'.

There is little in the Convention for minorities from the standpoint of autonomy. The closest the Convention comes to the subject of autonomy is in the Article that provides that '[t]he Parties shall create the conditions necessary for the effective participation of persons belonging to national minorities in cultural, social and economic life and in public affairs, in particular those affecting them'.[108] The weak nature of the obligations contained in the Article have been the subject of criticism.[109] Furthermore this article represents a retreat from the statements already advanced through

---

[105] See S. Wheatley, 'The Framework Convention for the Protection of National Minorities' 1 *EHRLR* (1996) 583; 'The Framework Convention is predicated upon the rights of individuals and not collective rights of the minority group' Ibid. p. 584.

[106] See the Framework Convention for the Protection of National Minorities and Explanatory Report (1995) paras 13, 22.

[107] See E. Aarnia, 'Minority Rights in the Council of Europe: Current Developments' in A. Phillips and A. Rosas (eds), *Universal Minority Rights* (Turku/Åbo, London: Åbo Akademi University Institute for Human Rights, Minority Rights Group, International) 1995, 123–133 at p. 131.

[108] Article 15.

[109] Gilbert treats the provisions of Article 15 as 'somewhat timid' G. Gilbert, 'The Council of Europe and Minority Rights' 18 *HRQ* (1996) 160 at p. 186.

Recommendation 1201 (1993) of the Parliamentary Assembly of the Council of Europe.[110]

The final and most significant of weaknesses in the Convention is that it does not have a complaints procedure. The Convention establishes general principles which are not directly applicable at the national level, with implementation being the 'prerogative of the States'.[111] States parties are required to submit reports to an advisory committee of the Committee of Ministers on the measures, legislative and administrative, taken in order to ensure compliance with the treaty. It would be useful to advance further the possibility of NGOs and minority groups commenting, or State reports making suggestions, when State practices are being considered by the Advisory Committee.[112]

The Council of Europe has also adopted the European Charter for Regional or Minority Languages (1992). The Charter, a binding treaty, as its title suggests aims to protect the regional and minority languages spoken within Europe. States parties to the Charter undertake to encourage and facilitate regional and minority languages *inter alia* 'in speech and writing, in public and private life'. There is also an undertaking to encourage the usage of these languages in studies, in education,[113] in administration of justice,[114] in public services,[115] in the media,[116] and in social and economic life,[117] and to establish institutions in order to advise the 'authorities on all matters pertaining to regional or minority languages'.[118] Implementation of the treaty is to be conducted through periodic reports to the Secretary-General of the Council of Europe in a manner prescribed by the Committee of Ministers.[119] The first report is to be presented within a year following entry into force of the Charter with respect to the State concerned and thereafter at three-year intervals.[120] These reports are to be examined by a Committee of Experts, consisting of one member from each State party,[121] nominated by the relevant

---

[110] Article 11 of the Recommendation provided as follows: 'In the regions where they are in a majority the persons belonging to a national minority shall have the right to have at their disposal appropriate local or autonomous authorities or to have a special status, matching the specific historical and territorial situation and in accordance with the domestic legislation'.

[111] Wheatley, above n. 105, at p. 585.

[112] K. Boyle, 'Europe: The Council of Europe, the OSCE, and the European Union' in H. Hannum (ed.), *Guide to International Human Rights Practice*, 3rd edn (New York: Transnational Publishers) 1999, 135–161 at p. 155.

[113] Article 8.

[114] Article 9.

[115] Article 10.

[116] Article 11.

[117] Article 13.

[118] Article 7(4).

[119] Article 15(1).

[120] Article 15(2).

[121] Article 16.

State, appointed for a six-year term and eligible for reappointment.[122] Issues relevant to the undertakings of the State concerned may be brought to the attention of the Committee of Experts.

In the light of other information (including State reports) the Committee of Experts will prepare a report for the Committee of Ministers. This report is accompanied by comments which the Parties have been requested to make and may be made public by the Committee of Ministers. These reports are required to contain, in particular, the proposals of the Committee of Experts to the Committee of Ministers for the preparation of such recommendations of the latter body to one or more of the Parties, as may be required. The Secretary-General of the Council of Europe is required to make a biannual detailed report to the Parliamentary Assembly on the application of the Charter. The Committee of Ministers may, after the entry into force of the Charter, invite non-member States of the COE to accede to the Charter.[123]

In addition to work done by the Council of Europe, significant contributions in the field of minority rights are made by another intergovernmental organisation, the Organisation for Security and Cooperation in Europe (OSCE).[124] The concern shown for the subject of minority rights within the OSCE stretches back to the Helsinki Final Act. As was noted in an earlier chapter, significant progress was made in this direction during the course of the 'follow-up meetings' leading up to and beyond the Copenhagen Document.[125] The Copenhagen Document is valuable for the propagation of minority rights. There are important provisions relating to autonomy. Article 35 provides:

> The participating States note the efforts undertaken to protect and create conditions for the promotion of the ethnic, cultural, linguistic and religious identity of certain national minorities by establishing, as one of the possible means to achieve these aims, appropriate local and autonomous administrations corresponding to the specific historical and territorial circumstances of such minorities and in accordance with the policies of the State concerned.

Again, as has been discussed, the work of the OSCE High Commission on National Minorities has been of great value in promoting the interests of the minorities of Europe.[126] The post of High Commissioner was established in 1992 at the Helsinki meeting of the OSCE. The High Commissioner has performed a number of services for minority groups; his interventions to diffuse potentially volatile situations and his role as

---

[122] Article 17.
[123] Shaw, above n. 7, at p. 278.
[124] J. Wright 'The OSCE and the Protection of Minority Rights' 18 *HRQ* (1996) 190.
[125] See above Chapter 7.
[126] See Helsinki Document 1992, reprinted 13 *HRLJ* (1992) 284.

a mediator remain the most important ones. The African Charter on Human and Peoples Rights, as we have seen, contains a number of rights designated as People's rights.[127] These rights as group rights have the potential to be of great significance to minorities. On the other hand, it is equally true that individual State practice, the OAU as an organisation and the African Commission as the principal organ of the Charter have shown great reluctance in equating the terms 'minorities' and 'peoples'. The fear is, generally, that such an equation would lead minorities to claim a right of self-determination resulting in the break up of existing States. Latin America has seen problems arising out of minority rights, though a serious debate has arisen in relation to the rights of indigenous peoples – a subject to which we shall direct our attention in the next chapter.

CONCLUSIONS

Minority rights has been a problematic issue for international law to handle. Although international law primarily operates through the medium of States, and minorities generally have no *locus standi*, the treatment which minorities receive from their States has increasingly become a matter of international concern. International law, however, has historically found it difficult to deal with the problems around minorities. Like the poor, the weak and the inarticulate, they have since time immemorial been treated as natural victims of persecution and genocide. Even in the contemporary period of relative tolerance and rationality, minorities are often subjected to persecution, discrimination and genocide. The stance of international law remains tentative and extremely cautious, for minorities pose questions of a serious nature; they exist in myriad forms, with their own social, political, cultural and religious particularities. Often transcending national frontiers, minorities are extremely capable of appealing to the sensitivities of their international sympathisers. Most national boundaries are arbitrarily drawn and a number of States contain turbulent factions artificially placed within their borders, often cutting across frontiers.

After considerable hesitation, there are now a number of notable initiatives. At the UN level, Article 27 of the ICCPR continues to represent the leading provision dealing with minority rights. It is inadequate and there is need for reform. The UN Declaration on Minorities has been a positive step though much remains to be done. The Declaration needs to be converted in a binding treaty, and States must acknowledge more firmly their commitment to protecting minority rights. At the regional level, the Council of Europe's adoption of the Framework Convention for the Protection of

---

[127] See above Chapter 9.

National Minorities and the European Charter for Regional or Minority Languages represents two positive initiatives. It is, however, an unfortunate reality that the regions where some of the worst minority rights violations have taken place, for example, South-Asia, the Middle East and Africa, remain devoid of initiatives to protect minorities.

12

THE RIGHTS OF 'PEOPLES'
AND 'INDIGENOUS PEOPLES'[1]

INTRODUCTION

The identification of an entity as 'peoples' in international law, particularly in the post-colonial period, has proved to be controversial. The primary reason for this controversy is that if an entity is recognised as a 'people', it becomes a lawful claimant to the right of self-determination, a right which also includes independent Statehood.[2] The definitional debate as to the precise meaning of 'Peoples' has taken place ever since the term was used in the United Nations Charter. The Charter attaches the 'Right of Self-Determination to Peoples'.[3] The United Nations Secretariat commenting upon the term 'Peoples' in the Charter stated: 'Peoples refers to a group of human beings, who may or may not comprise States or Nations',[4] leading to the view, although a minority one, that the provisions of the Charter allowed secession for minorities.[5] International law is similarly moving towards allowing indigenous peoples a

---

[1] S.J. Anaya, *Indigenous Peoples in International Law* (New York: Oxford University Press) 1996; R. Barnes, A. Gray and B. Kingsbury (eds), *Indigenous Peoples of Asia* (Ann Arbor, MI: Association for Asian Studies) 1993; I. Brownlie, *Treaties and Indigenous Peoples: The Robb Lectures* (Oxford: Clarendon Press) 1992; W.S. Heinz, *Indigenous Populations, Ethnic Minorities and Human Rights*, (Berlin: Quorum Verlag) 1988; B. Kingsbury, '"Indigenous Peoples" in International Law: A Constructivist Approach to the Asian Controversy' 92 *AJIL* (1998) 414.
[2] Professor Malcolm Shaw appropriately points out '[t]he issue of what in law constitutes a "People" has proved to be one of the great controversies of the Post-World War II era. The reason for this has been the development of the concept of self-determination'. M.N. Shaw, 'The Definition of Minorities in international law' in Y. Dinstein and M. Tabory (eds), *The Protection of Minorities and Human Rights* (Dordrecht: Martinus Nijhoff Publishers) 1992, 1–31 at p. 2.
[3] See below.
[4] UNCIO Docs., XVIII, 657–658.
[5] UNCIO Docs., XVII, 142.

right to self-determination, and hence similar difficulties arise in identifying and defining 'indigenous peoples'.

Since the Charter became operational, the term 'peoples' has become a significant feature of many international and national instruments, though there has often been an inconclusive debate as to its meaning and scope. Notwithstanding the difficulties in identifying the term 'peoples' it is important to acknowledge and explore the meaning and content of the term 'People's Right to Self-Determination'. It is equally important to understand the relevance of considering the position of indigenous peoples in debates on self-determination. Indigenous peoples' claim to be recognised as 'Peoples' and their demand to self-determination includes a right to independent Statehood.

PEOPLES' RIGHT TO SELF-DETERMINATION

Self-determination in its modern form can be related to the experiences of the American, French and Bolshevik Revolutions, with their emphasis on popular sovereignty.[6] Though used widely by politicians and nationalists, in international law the concept remained in embryonic form until the events of the First World War when the United States President Wilson, the leading exponent of this ideal, attempted to assert his wishes in various forms.[7] However, as President Wilson was soon to discover, presenting Utopian ideals was one thing, putting them into practice was quite another. The fundamental difficulty with an otherwise attractive and even sensible proposition was the identification of its potential beneficiaries. Jennings' comments provide a fruitful analysis of this problem. He notes:

> Nearly forty years ago a Professor of Political Science who was also the President of the United States, President Wilson, enunciated a doctrine which was ridiculous, but which was widely accepted as a sensible proposition, the doctrine of Self-determination. On the surface it seemed reasonable: Let the people decide. It was in fact ridiculous because the people cannot decide until somebody decides who are the people.[8]

---

[6] T. Franck, 'Post-Modern Tribalism and the Right to Secession' in C. Brölmann, R. Lefeber and M. Zieck (eds), *Peoples and Minorities in International Law* (Dordrecht: Martinus Nijhoff Publishers) 1993, 3–27 at p. 6; M. Pomerance, *Self-determination in law and practice: the new doctrine in the United Nations* (The Hague: Martinus Nijhoff Publishers) 1982; A. Rigo Sureda, *The Evolution of the Right of Self-determination: A study of United Nations practice* (Leiden: Sijthoff) 1973, p. 17.

[7] M.N. Shaw, *Title to Territory in Africa: International Legal Issues* (Oxford: Clarendon Press) 1986, pp. 60–61; M. Nawaz, 'The Meaning and Range of the Principle of Self-Determination' 82 *Duke LJ* (1965) 82 at p. 82.

[8] I. Jennings, *The Approach to Self-Government* (Cambridge: Cambridge University Press) 1956, p. 56.

Hence, beset by the inherent contradictions of different though competing and equally worthy 'selves', the uncertainty in ascertaining the proper mode of 'determination' and its content and the conflict of self-determination with the cardinal principles of sovereign equality, duty of non-intervention, maintenance of status quo, preservation of peace and security and the sanctity of international treaties, the Wilsonian ideal failed to flourish.[9] On a universal level, its application could not be taken seriously, it was generally ignored at the Paris Peace Conference 1919 and was not even mentioned in the final draft of the Covenant of the League of Nations. Though the final territorial settlements proved disappointing, self-determination left some of its mark in the form of the mandate system,[10] minority rights treaties[11] and was sometimes reflected in the judgments of the Permanent Court of International Justice.[12]

Despite repeated references to it, by both politicians and lawyers during the inter-war years, self-determination failed to be recognised as part of General International law;[13] this position being confirmed by the Council of the League of Nations in the *Aaland Island Case*.[14] Although events in Europe in the 1930s and during the course of the Second World War forced the allied powers to focus on the issue of human rights, references to self-determination remained ambivalent, only rarely making an appearance. The Atlantic Charter of August 1941 makes reference to it, but the Dumbarton Oaks proposals do not.

The United Nations Charter makes express reference to self-determination on two occasions. According to Article 1, one of the purposes of the UN is to 'develop friendly relations among nations based on respect for equal rights and self-determination of peoples, and to take other appropriate measures to strengthen universal peace'.[15] The other reference is made in Article 55, according to which: '[w]ith a view to the creation of conditions of stability and well-being which are necessary for peaceful and friendly relations among nations based on respect for the principle of equal rights and self-determination of peoples, the United Nations shall promote' – followed by a

---

[9] Pomerance, above n. 6, at pp. 1–9.

[10] See Article 22 of the Covenant of League of Nations; 225 CTS 195; 112 BFSP 13, 316; 13 *AJIL* Supp 128, 361.

[11] P. Thornberry, 'Is there a Phoenix in the Ashes? – International Law and Minority Rights' 15 *Tex.ILJ* (1980) 421 at p. 453.

[12] See e.g. *Minority Schools in Albania* (1935) PCIJ Ser. A/B, No. 64, 17.

[13] F.L. Kirgis Jr., 'The Degrees of Self-Determination in the United Nations Era' 88 *AJIL* (1994) 304 at p. 304; P. Thornberry, 'Self-Determination, Minorities and Human Rights: A Review of International Instruments' 38 *ICLQ* (1989) 867 at p. 871.

[14] *The Aaland Island Case* (1920) LNOJ Special Supp No. 3 3 [H, 103–104], 5; L. Hannikainen and F. Horn (eds), *Autonomy and Demilitarisation in International Law: The Aland Islands in a Changing Europe* (The Hague: Kluwer Law International) 1997.

[15] Article 1(2) of the United Nations Charter (1945).

number of objectives. Chapter XI, which was subsequently to form the basis of decolonisation, also implicitly recognises the principle of self-determination, although the term itself is not used.

There seems to be some debate as to whether it was, in fact, the intention of the drafters of the UN Charter to provide for a legally binding right of self-determination,[16] although the view appears to be persuasive that Charter provisions in relation to self-determination did create binding legal obligations, albeit in a rather vague and imprecise manner. In any event, as Professor Higgins points out, the self-determination principle – as enunciated in the Charter – was inherently conservative and radically different from how it came to be understood subsequently. Whatever the legal position as regards self-determination may have been at the time the Charter became operational, the rapid changes in the UN have ensured its conspicuous existence as a legal right, though its primary focus has been directed towards decolonisation. Although a number of States have adopted a negative stance on the issue,[17] it seems certain that the right to self-determination is applicable even in the post-colonial world. As we have already noted this view is forcefully asserted in the common article of the ICCPR and ICESCR.[18] The right to self-determination has also been the subject of a General Comment by the Human Rights Committee. In its General Comment, emphasising the significance of this right, the Committee notes that:

> [i]n accordance with the purposes and principles of the Charter of the United Nations, article 1 of the International Covenant on Civil and Political Rights recognises that all peoples have the right of self-determination. The right of self-determination is of particular importance because its realisation is an essential condition for the effective guarantee and observance of individual human rights and for the promotion and strengthening of those rights. It is for that reason that States set forth the right of self-determination in a provision of positive law in

---

[16] H. Hannum, *Autonomy, Sovereignty and Self-Determination: The Accommodation of Conflicting Rights* (Philadelphia: University of Pennsylvania Press) 1990, p. 33; Y. Blum, 'Reflections on the Changing Concept of Self-Determination' 10 *Israel L.R.* (1975) 509 at p. 511; see also the views of Gross as discussed by Emerson, in R. Emerson, 'Self-Determination' 65 *AJIL* (1971) 459 at p. 461; I. Brownlie, *Principles of Public International Law*, 4th edn (Oxford: OUP) 1990, p. 596.

[17] See for example the Indian reservation to Article 1 of the ICCPR. According to this reservation, entered at the time of the ratification of the Covenant 'With reference to article 1 ... the Government of the Republic of India declares that the words 'the right of self-determination' appearing in this article apply only to the peoples under the foreign domination and that these words do not apply to sovereign independent States or to a section of a people or nation – which is the essence of national integrity' UN Centre for Human Rights, *Human Rights: Status of International Instruments* (1987) 9 UN Sales No. E.87.XIV.2; Although there are inconsistencies in India's position, the views expressed in the reservation were reaffirmed by her representative to the Human Rights Committee stating that 'the right to self-determination in international context [applies] only to dependent territories and people' UN Doc CCPR/C/SR. 498 (1948) 3.

[18] See above Chapters 4 and 5.

both Covenants and placed this provision as article 1 apart from and before all of the other rights in the two Covenants'.[19]

Claims to self-determination have also been invoked in a number of cases before the Committee.[20] In our survey of instruments we have analysed the role and position of the right to self-determination as enshrined in the AFCHPR.[21] The Convention Concerning Indigenous and Tribal Peoples in Independent Countries (ILO) No. 169[22] also provides for the right to self-determination, but without defining the concept.[23] The Organisation for the Security and Cooperation in Europe (OSCE) has laid down a particular emphasis on the continuing role of self-determination.[24] The Helsinki Final Act which has carried substantial influence affirms the right to self-determination. Article VIII of the Act provides as follows:

> The Participating States will respect the equal rights of peoples and their right to self-determination … By Virtue of the principle of equal rights and self-determination of peoples, all peoples always have the right, in full freedom, to determine, when as they wish, their internal and external political status, without external political interference, and to pursue as they wish their political, economic, social and cultural development

Customary international law affirms the view that self-determination is a binding legal right. We have already noted that General Assembly Resolutions are not *per se* binding, though they can be instrumental in providing evidence of State practice, and can in certain circumstances be regarded as interpreting the provisions of the Charter.[25] In this context it is important to note the highly authoritative UN General Assembly Resolutions which have been treated as authoritative interpretations of the Charter, and generally regarded as reflective of customary law, for example the Declaration on the Granting of Independence to Colonial territories and Peoples, GA Res 1514 (XV) and the Declaration of the Principles of International Law Concerning Friendly Relations and Co-operation Amongst States in Accordance with the Charter of the United Nations, GA Res 2625

---

[19] The Right to Self-Determination of Peoples (Art. 1). 13/04/84. CCPR General Comment 12. (General Comments) para 1.
[20] *Sandra Lovelace v. Canada*, Communication No. 24/1977 (30 July 1981), UN Doc. CCPR/C/OP/1 at 83 (1984); *Lubicon Lake Band v. Canada*, Communication No. 167/1984 (26 March 1990), UN Doc. Supp. No. 40 (A/45/40) at 1 (1990).
[21] Article 20(1) See above Chapter 9.
[22] 72 ILO Bulletin 59 (1989); 28 I.L.M. 1382.
[23] See N. Lerner, *Group Rights and Discrimination in International Law* (Dordrecht: Martinus Nijhoff Publishers) 1991, p. 29.
[24] See above Chapter 7; J. Wright, 'The OSCE and the Protection of Minority Rights' 18 *HRQ* (1996) 190; M. Koskenniemi, 'National Self-Determination Today: Problems of Legal Theory and Practice' 43 *ICLQ* (1994) 241 at p. 242.
[25] See above Chapter 3.

(XXV), 1970. There are many other General Assembly Resolutions which reaffirm this normative value.

Judicial discussion is heavily in support of this assertion. Dicta from the Advisory Opinion of the World Court in the *Namibia*[26] and the *Western Sahara cases*[27] are strong arguments to substantiate the point.[28] A further confirmation of this view came through the World Court's Judgment in the *Case Concerning East Timor (Portugal v. Australia)*.[29] In this case the Court found itself unable to look into the possible substantive breach of self-determination. According to the Court such a course would

> necessarily [involve ruling] upon the lawfulness of Indonesia's conduct as a prerequisite for deciding on Portugal's contention that Australia violated its obligation to respect Portugal's status as administering power, East Timor's status as a non-self-governing territory and the right of the people of the territory to self-determination and to permanent sovereignty over its wealth and natural resources.[30]

The Court, however, reconfirmed the value inherent in the right to self-determination. Thus according to the Court, 'Portugal's assertion that the right of Peoples to self-determination, as it evolved from the Charter and from the United Nations practice has *erga omnes* character is irreproachable ... it is one of the essential principles of international law'.[31] It could convincingly be argued that the inherent principles enshrined in the right to self-determination form part of the norms of *jus cogens*;[32] and their character of rights *erga omnes*[33] has been firmly engrained in the substance of international law.

---

[26] *Legal Consequences for States of the Continued Presence of South Africa in Namibia (South West Africa) notwithstanding Security Council Resolution 276 (1970)*, Advisory Opinion 21 June 1971 (1971) ICJ Reports 16.

[27] *Western Sahara*, Advisory Opinion 16 October 1975 (1975) ICJ Reports 12

[28] See the *Namibia* case 'the subsequent developments of international law in regard to non-self governing, as enunciated in the Charter of the United Nations, made the principle of self-determination applicable to all of them ... ' (1971) ICJ Reports, 6, 31; *Western Sahara*, Advisory Opinion 16 October 1975 (1975) ICJ Reports 12, pp. 31–33 and Judge Dillard's celebrated opinion especially at 122. For a succinct discussion see A. Cassese, 'The International Court of Justice and the Right of Peoples to Self-Determination' in V. Lowe and M. Fitzmaurice (eds), *Fifty Years of the International Court of Justice: Essays in Honour of Sir Robert Jennings* (Cambridge: Cambridge University Press) 1996, pp. 351–363.

[29] *East Timor Case (Portugal v. Australia)*, Judgment 30 June 1995 (1995) ICJ Reports 90.

[30] Ibid. para 33.

[31] Ibid. 29.

[32] See H. Gros Espiell, Special Rapporteur, *Implementation of United Nations Resolutions Relating to the Right of Peoples under Colonial and Alien Domination to Self-Determination*, Study for the Sub-Commission on Prevention of Discrimination and Protection of Minorities, UN Doc.E/CN.4/Sub.2/390, 1977, 17–19, paras 61–71; H. Gros Espiell, 'Self-Determination and *Jus Cogens*' in A. Cassese (ed.) *UN Law/Fundamental Rights: Two Topics in International Law*, (Alpen aan den Rijn: Sijthof and Noordhoff) 1979, pp. 119–135; ILC, *Draft Articles on State Responsibility*, Part I, Article 19 3(b). See above Chapter 1.

[33] See *Barcelona Traction, Light and Power Company, Limited Case (Belgium v. Spain)*, Judgment 5 February 1970 (1970) ICJ Reports 3.

A recent practical manifestation of the right could be found in the reunification of Germany, the break-up of the former Soviet Union and Yugoslavia, and the emergence of East Timor as an independent State.

INDIGENOUS PEOPLES IN INTERNATIONAL LAW: THE ISSUE OF DEFINITION

Indigenous peoples in a number of States occupy the position of minorities and, being weak and inarticulate, many of their demands coincide with those of other minority groups.[34] As their name reflects, being indigenous to the land, many of them were killed off, while survivors were conquered or subjugated.[35] However, just as genocide, persecution and discrimination form part and parcel of human history they have also tragically not been confined to a particular region or time but have been experienced as a global phenomenon.

The indigenous peoples, having been relentlessly victimised in the contemporary age, remain in conditions which governments of modern States regard as less developed. Efforts to retain their aboriginal and autochthonous life have cost a number of the groups dearly – from forced assimilation to genocide. Unfortunately, persecution and discrimination against indigenous peoples is still existent in many societies, and the continuation of a number of discriminatory laws provide a sad commentary on their state of affairs.[36] A United Nations document eloquently summarises the contemporary position facing indigenous peoples:

> Often uprooted from their traditional lands and way of life and forced into prevailing national societies, indigenous peoples face discrimination, marginalisation and alienation. Despite growing political mobilization in pursuit of their rights, they continue to lose their cultural identity along with their natural resources. Some are in imminent danger of extinction.[37]

While similar concerns are shared as regards both indigenous peoples and other minorities, there remains a pronounced view that indigenous peoples

---

[34] See e.g. H. O'Shaugnnessy and S. Corry, *What Future for the Armindians of South America*, (London: Minority Rights Group) 1987; J. Wilson, *Canada's Indians*, (London: Minority Rights Group)1982; I. Creery, *The Inuit (Eskimo) of Canada* (London: Minority Rights Group) 1983; N. Vakhtin, *Native Peoples of the Russians Far North* (London: Minority Rights Group) 1992; M Jones, *The Sami of Lapland* (London: Minority Rights Group) 1982; D. Stephen and P. Wearne, *Central America's Indians* (London: Minority Rights Group) 1984.

[35] J.H. Clinebell and J. Thomson, 'Sovereignty and Self-Determination: The Rights of Native Americans under International Law' 27 *Buff LR* (1978) 669; L. Kuper, *International Action against Genocide*, (London: Minority Rights Group) 1984, p. 5; J.S. Davidson, 'The Rights of Indigenous Peoples in Early International Law' 5 *Canterbury Law Review* (1994) 391.

[36] See International Labour Conference, *Report of the Committee of Experts on the Application of Conventions and Recommendations*, 64th Session, 1978.

[37] United Nations, *Indigenous Peoples: International Year 1993* (Geneva: United Nations) 1992.

belong to a distinct category.[38] This, in fact, is the established view of indigenous peoples themselves and is grounded on the argument that indigenous claims are far more substantial than minorities in general – ranging from collective rights to self-determination (including a possible right to secession). In some cases, there is also a reaction to State practice which refuses to accord any distinct and separate recognition to indigenous peoples. Bangladesh's approach towards the *adivasis* of the Chittagong Hill Tracts provides one clear example; the conventional stance put forward by successive governments is that while all Bengalis are indigenous, no further distinctions could be made out.[39] Other States are following a similar line.[40]

While several States have proved to be extremely sensitive on the definitional issue, many of the indigenous groups themselves have asserted a prerogative to define their 'nations'.[41] In the midst of these conflicts, it is not surprising to perceive tensions regarding whatever definition is accorded to the indigenous peoples or communities. Thus neither general international law nor regional custom provides a recognised and fully accepted definition of 'Indigenous Peoples'.[42] The most widely publicised definition of indigenous peoples and communities is the one put forward by the United Nations Special Rapporteur José R. Martínez-Cobo. According to him:

> Indigenous communities, peoples and nations are those which, having continuity with pre-invasion and pre-colonial societies that developed on their territories, consider themselves distinct from other sectors of the societies now prevailing in those territories, or parts of them. They form at present non-dominant sectors of society and are determined to preserve, develop and transmit to future generations their ancestral territories and their ethnic identity, as the basis of their continued existence as peoples, in accordance with their own cultural patterns, social institutions and legal systems.

---

[38] See the proceedings of the 11th meeting of the United Nations working group on indigenous rights 18 UN Doc E/CN.4/Sub.2/1992/33, 1992, 19; M.N. Shaw, 'The Definition of Minorities in international law' in Dinstein and Tabory (eds), above n. 2, pp.13–16; N. Lerner, 'The Evolution of Minority Rights in International Law' in Brölmann, Lefeber and Zieck, (eds), above n. 6, 77–101 at p. 81.

[39] For a confirmation of this view see *Report of the Working Group on Indigenous Populations on its Fourteenth Session* E/CN.4/Sub.2/1996/21, 14 para 34.

[40] Barsh mentions Bangladesh, Indonesia, the former USSR, India and China which have maintained that there are no 'indigenous' peoples in Asia only minorities epitomising former Soviet Ambassador Sofinsky's view before the Sub-Commission in 1985 that 'indigenous situations only arise in the Americas and Australasia where there are imported "populations" of Europeans'. R.L. Barsh, 'Indigenous People: An Emerging Object of International Law' 80 *AJIL* (1986) 369 at p. 375.

[41] Ibid. 376.

[42] Anaya, above n. 1, pp. 3–5; E. McCandles, 'Indigenous Peoples: The Definitional Debate' in Minority Rights Group (eds), *Outsider* (London: Minority Rights Group) 1996, p. 1.

The historical continuity may consist of the continuation, for an external period reaching into present, of one or more of the following factors:

(a) Occupation of ancestral lands, or at least of part of them;
(b) Common ancestry with the original occupants of the lands;
(c) Culture in general, or in specific manifestation (such as religion, living under a tribal system, membership of international community, dress, means of livelihood, life-style etc.);
(d) Language (whether used as the only language, as mother-tongue, as the habitual means of communication at home or in the family, or as the main preferred, habitual general or normal language);
(e) Residence in certain parts of the country, or in certain regions of the World;
(f) Other relevant factors.[43]

According to Article 1(1) of the ILO Convention 169, adopted in 1989, the Convention applies to:

(a) Tribal peoples in independent countries whose social, cultural and economic conditions distinguish them from other sections of the national community, and whose status is regulated wholly or partially by their own customs or traditions or by special laws or regulations;
(b) Peoples in independent countries who are regarded as indigenous on account of their descent from the populations which inhabited the country, or a geographical region to which the country belongs, at the time of conquest or colonisation or the establishment of present State boundaries and who, irrespective of their legal status, retain some or all of their own social, economic, cultural and political institutions.

Article 1(2) goes on to provide:

Self-identification as indigenous or tribal shall be regarded as a fundamental criterion for determining the groups to which the provisions of this convention apply.

A number of distinct features are evident in the definitions provided by Martínez-Cobo as well as by the 1989 Convention. These include self-identification, non-dominance, historical continuity with pre-colonial societies, ancestral territories and ethnic identity.[44] Other attempts that have been made to elaborate the concept of 'indigenous' also rely to an extent on these criteria. Thus according to Professor Anaya, '[t]oday, the term indigenous refers broadly to the living descendants of pre-invasion inhabitants of lands now dominated by others. Indigenous peoples, nations or communities are culturally distinctive groups that find themselves engulfed by settler societies born of the forces of empire and conquest'.[45] Similarly the World Council

[43] Special Rapporteur, José R. Martínez-Cobo, *Study of the Problem of Discrimination Against Indigenous Populations*, UN Doc. E/CN.4/Sub.2/1986/7/Add.4, 1986, 29, paras 378–380.
[44] B. Kingsbury, '"Indigenous Peoples" as an International Legal Concept' in R. Barnes, A. Gray and B. Kingsbury (eds), above n. 1, 13–34 at p. 26.
[45] Anaya, above n. 1, at p. 3.

of Indigenous Peoples defines indigenous peoples as '[N]atives, usually descendants of earlier population, of a particular country, composed of different ethnic or racial groups, but who have no control over the government'.[46] This discussion reveals the tensions and divisive nature of the probable definition of 'indigenous' peoples in international law. It is also the case that indigenous peoples, themselves, like other groups or communities, are capable of differing radically from each other.

RIGHTS OF INDIGENOUS PEOPLES

Many of the claims made by indigenous peoples coincide with those of other minorities. The desire for autonomy and recognition as collective entities forms part of the vocabulary of the indigenous peoples as well as other minority groups, although the thrust and vibrancy of these may differ significantly. Historical association with land and environment dispenses a distinct flavour to the demands made by indigenous peoples. Their claims include, *inter alia*, that of collective property rights to land and natural resources, the special nature and form of relationships between individual members and tribes, and the right to impose obligations on individual members which may not necessarily be aspired by other minorities.[47]

International instruments have, in recent years, attempted to consider the position of indigenous people and a number of specialist instruments have been adopted which aim to concentrate solely on the position of indigenous populations.[48] This rather sudden resurgence of interest may be taken as an acknowledgement, at least in part, that the cause of indigenous peoples raises specific issues of concern which ought to be focused on. The organisation which has shown a significant interest in the plight of indigenous peoples and more generally in its efforts to 'establish universal and lasting peace' through the means of social justice is the International Labour Organisation (ILO).[49]

---

[46] Cited in W. Roxanne, *What to Celebrate in the United Nations Year of Indigenous Peoples?* (Singapore: Department of Sociology, National University of Singapore) 1993, p. 5.

[47] G. Neithem, '"Peoples" and "Populations" Indigenous Peoples and the Rights of Peoples', in J. Crawford (ed.), *The Rights of Peoples* (Oxford: Clarendon Press) 1988, pp. 107–126; J. Rehman, 'International Law and Indigenous Peoples: Definitional and Practical Problems' 3 *Journal of Civil Liberties* (1998) 224.

[48] See e.g. Barsh, above n. 40; R.L. Barsh, 'Revision of the ILO Convention No. 107' 81 *AJIL* (1987) 756; R.L. Barsh, 'United Nations Seminar on Indigenous Peoples and States' 83 *AJIL* (1989) 599 at p. 762.

[49] Preamble to the Constitution of the ILO 62 Stat. 3485; TIAS No 1868; I. Brownlie (ed.), *Basic Documents in International Law*, 2nd edn (Oxford: Oxford University Press) 1981, p. 45; F. Wolf, 'Human Rights and the International Labour Organisation' in T. Meron (ed.), *Human Rights in International Law: Legal and Policy Issues* (Oxford: Clarendon Press) 1984, pp. 273–305.

The organisation, ever since its inception in 1919, has made evident its interest by establishing a Committee of Experts on Native Labour in 1926.[50] A natural projection of this agenda was reflected in the adaptation of various conventions and recommendations, including the Forced Labour Convention 1930 (ILO Convention 29),[51] the Recruiting of Indigenous Workers Convention 1936 (ILO Convention 50),[52] the Contracts of Employment (Indigenous Workers) Convention 1939 (ILO Convention 64),[53] the Penal Sanctions (Indigenous Workers) Convention 1940 (ILO 65)[54] and the Contracts of Employment (Indigenous Workers) Convention 1947 (ILO 86).[55]

A significant study for the protection of indigenous peoples was conducted under the auspices of the Organisation, Indigenous Peoples Living and Working Conditions of Aboriginal Population in Independent Countries.[56] The study published in 1953 has left its mark on the two texts adopted at the fortieth session of the organisation, culminating in Recommendations No 104 and the ILO Convention 107 Concerning the Protection and Integration of Indigenous and other tribal and Semi-tribal Populations in Independent Countries.[57] The adoption of the 1957 Convention was a significant step forward in projecting the views and aspirations of the indigenous peoples. The Convention, however, has been a product of its time with a considerable imprint of an assimilationist ideology. By its own admission it applies, *inter alia*, to those populations 'whose social and economic conditions are at a less advanced stage than the stage reached by other sections of the national community'. In 1986, the ILO organised meetings of representatives of indigenous peoples under the emblem of 'Meeting of experts'. The meetings forcefully advocated the case for revision of the Convention noting that 'the integrationist language of Convention No. 107 is outdated, and that the application of this principle is destructive in the modern world'.[58]

A prominent theme of Convention No. 107 is the emphasis on assimilation of indigenous peoples with other sections of the community, even at the cost of abandoning their heritage. The overwhelming feeling of discontentment with this provided the impetus to the adoption of a revised Convention Concerning Indigenous and Tribal Peoples in Independent Countries (ILO)

---

[50] See H. Hannum (ed.), *Documents on Autonomy and Minority Rights* (Dordrecht: Martinus Nijhoff Publishers) 1993, p. 8.
[51] 39 U.N.T.S. 55; Cmd 3693; 134 BFSP 449.
[52] 40 U.N.T.S. 109; Cmd 5305; 21 ILO Bull III.
[53] 40 U.N.T.S. 281; Cmd 6141; 8 Hudson 359.
[54] 40 U.N.T.S. 311; Cmd 6141; 8 Hudson 377.
[55] 161 U.N.T.S. 113; Cmd 7437; 148 BFSP 664.
[56] ILO, *Studies and Reports, New Series No, 35* (Geneva: International Labour Office), 1953.
[57] 328 U.N.T.S. 247.
[58] *Report of the Meeting of Experts*, para 46; See *Partial Revision of the Indigenous and Tribal Populations Convention, 1957* (No 107) Report 6(1), International Labour Conference, 75th Sess. (1988), 100.

Convention No. 169 (1989).[59] The 1989 Convention is a reflection of a more liberal attitude and is biased against hitherto prevalent integrationist and assimilation orientations; its moderating effect on what, according to its preamble, were 'the assimilationist orientations of earlier standards' is worthy of appreciation. In the words of one commentator the 1989 Convention is 'international law's most concrete manifestation of the growing responsiveness to indigenous peoples' demands. Convention No. 169 is a revision of the ILO's earlier Convention No. 107 of 1957, and it represents a marked departure in world community policy from the philosophy of integration or assimilation underlying the earlier Convention'.[60]

On the substantive front, a number of features of the 1989 Convention reflect a degree of promise. Article 2, for instance, while improving upon the 1957 Convention, reinforces the issue stating that governments shall have a responsibility to develop the participation of the peoples concerned and to act to protect their rights. It lays stress upon the participation of the peoples concerned, while actions to protect their rights puts emphasis upon the need to respect their social and cultural identity, their customs and traditions and their institutions. These acts shall ensure equality of rights and opportunities, full realisation of the social, economic and cultural rights of the indigenous peoples, and would eliminate the socio-economic gaps.

While Article 3, in line with the norm of non-discrimination in international treaties, prohibits discrimination in the enjoyment of human rights and fundamental freedoms, Article 4 enjoins special measures for safeguarding the institutions, property, labour, culture and environment of indigenous peoples in a manner which is not inconsistent with their freely expressed wishes. Article 5 reaffirms the fundamental principle of recognising, respecting and promoting the social, cultural and religious values. The significance of Article 6 lies primarily in the fact that it requires governments to consult indigenous peoples in matters affecting them, allowing and establishing means for free participation and for development of their institutions. Article 7 reflects the cherished ideals of autonomy by stating that peoples concerned shall have the right to decide their own priorities for the process of development as it affects their lives, beliefs, institutions and spiritual well-being and the lands they occupy or otherwise use. They shall also have the right to exercise control, to the extent possible, over their own economic, social and cultural development. In addition, they shall participate in the formulation, implementation and evaluation of plans and programmes for national and regional development which may affect them directly.

The advance of the 1989 Convention is considerable over its predecessor, and deserves our attention in so far as it relates specifically to the position of

---

[59] 72 ILO Bulletin 59 (1989); 28 I.L.M. 1382.
[60] Anaya, above n. 1, p. 47.

indigenous peoples and their rights. Having said this, the 1989 Convention falls short of providing an adequate expression to the claims of indigenous peoples in many ways. There are a number of issues where there is very little international consensus. These relate, *inter alia*, to land rights, the right to autonomy, self-determination and international personality. Although Chapter II of the Convention deals in considerable detail with the subject of land, in its drafting stages there emerged considerable disagreement with more than 100 amendments being presented, and in the final resort only reflecting a compromise among divergent interests.[61]

The right to self-determination has proved to be particularly contentious and it needs to be borne in mind that while the Convention does apply to 'peoples', a number of State representatives were unhappy with the use of the term 'peoples' with all its paraphernalia, and wanted it replaced with 'populations'.[62] The Convention itself has grudgingly granted indigenous peoples a limited recognition to the right to self-determination, although the adoption of this text was only possible through the addition of an extra paragraph curtailing the effect of whatever the right has to offer. This occurs in the form of Article 1(3) which provides:

> The use of the term 'peoples' in this convention shall not be construed as having any implications as regards the rights which may attach to the term under international law.

INDIGENOUS PEOPLES AND THE UN SYSTEM

Efforts on the part of other international organisations have of late begun to match those of the ILO. The issue of the rights of indigenous peoples has been canvassed strongly by the United Nations Working Group on Indigenous Populations. The creation of the Working Group on Indigenous Populations was proposed by the United Nations Sub-Commission on the Prevention of Discrimination and Protection of Minorities in September 1981,[63] a proposal endorsed and approved by the Commission on Human Rights in its Resolution of March 1982.[64] The ultimate authorisation to establish a Working Group was provided by the Economic and Social Council in 1982,[65] with the first annual meeting of the Working Group taking place in August of the same year.[66] The Working Group, as a subsidiary organ of the Sub-Commission on the Promotion and Protection of Human Rights (formerly the Sub-Commission

---

[61] See Lerner, above n. 23, p. 109.
[62] Ibid.
[63] See Sub-Commission Res. 2 (XXXIV) September 8, 1981.
[64] Commission on Human Rights Res 1982/19, March 10.
[65] See ECOSOC Res 1982/34, May 7.
[66] Hannum, above n. 16, p. 84; Barsh, above n. 40, p. 47

on the Prevention of Discrimination and Protection of Minorities), comprises five individuals who are members of the Sub-Commission (drawn from different regions) and who act in their capacity as independent experts and not as representatives of their governments. Since its creation, the Working Group has met every year with each session lasting for one or two weeks; its annual sessions taking place immediately prior to the annual session of the Sub-Commission. These sessions are conducted in the same conference room of the Palais des Nations where the Commission on Human Rights convenes.

The inspiration derived from the Rapporteur José R. Martínez-Cobo's study has been reflected in the activities of the Working Group, with many of the themes being used as a basis for developing international standard setting on indigenous rights. The original mandate of the Working Group comprised the following two parts:

(a) to review developments pertaining to the promotion and protection of the human rights and fundamental freedoms of indigenous populations;
(b) give special attention to the evolution of standards concerning the rights of indigenous populations throughout the world.[67]

For its first few sessions the Working Group concentrated on collecting useful data and information on the instances and forms of violations that take place against indigenous peoples. The information revealed killings, torture, inhuman and degrading treatment amounting to genocide and ethnocide. Serious violations of land rights of indigenous peoples all over the world through forcible occupation or destruction came to light. Indigenous peoples also used the forum of the Working Group sessions to publicise their experiences of forcible assimilation and erosion of their cultural and spiritual existence. The early successes achieved were a consequence of the enthusiastic and ingenious approach that was adopted by the Working Group. Thus at

> its first session, the Working Group took the almost unprecedented step of allowing oral (and written) interventions from all indigenous organizations which wished to participate in its work, not limiting such participation to those with formal consultative status. Approximately 380 persons took part in its sixth session in 1988, including representatives from over 70 indigenous organizations and observers from 33 Countries. As a result of this wide participation, the Working Group has provided a meaningful forum for exchange of proposals regarding indigenous rights and for the exposition of indigenous reality throughout the world. While the Working Group reiterates at each session that it is not a 'chamber of complaints' and has no authority to hear allegations of human rights violations, it has nevertheless permitted very direct criticism of government practices by NGOs, as a means of gathering data upon which standards will eventually be based.[68]

---

[67] ECS/ Res.1982/34, UN ESCOR, Supp. No.1, UN Doc. E/1982/82 (1982) pp. 26–27.
[68] Hannum, above n. 16, p. 84.

Although review of the developments pertaining to indigenous peoples has remained a significant feature of the sessions, since 1985 the Working Group has paid particular attention to universal standard setting for indigenous peoples. In this regard a valuable contribution of the Working Group has been its determined effort to draw up a Declaration on the Rights of Indigenous Peoples. In 1985 approval was given by the Sub-Commission supporting the Working Group to its decision to prepare a draft Declaration on the Rights of the Indigenous Peoples for adoption by the General Assembly of the United Nations.[69] Three years later, a first complete draft Declaration was produced, a document largely representing and favourable to the views of the indigenous peoples.[70] Further refinements and the views of governments were incorporated into the 1989 draft of the Declaration.[71] There then followed a period of deliberations and discussion within the Working Group, involving all the concerned parties-representatives from the indigenous groups as well as the concerned States. With the progressive development of the draft Declaration,

> more and more governments responded with their respective pronouncements on the content of indigenous peoples' rights. Virtually every state of the Western Hemisphere came to participate in the Working Group discussion on the declaration. Canada, with its large indigenous population took a leading role. States of other regions with significant indigenous populations also became active participants, especially Australia and New Zealand. The Philippines, Bangladesh and India are just three of the other numerous states that at one time or another made oral or written submission to the Working Group in connection with the drafting of the declaration.[72]

In 1993, the Working Group produced its final version of the draft Declaration.[73] A year later in 1994, the Sub-Commission approved and adopted – without any changes – the Working Group's draft which was then submitted for the consideration of the Human Rights Commission.[74] In March 1995 the Commission decided to establish an open-ended inter-sessional Working Group with a view to elaborating the draft Declaration.[75] The procedure for participation in the inter-sessional Working Group has been generous and has allowed virtually everyone interested to deliberate and contribute to its work without prior accreditation. The final progression of the

---

[69] Sub-Commission Res. 1985/22 (August 29 1985).

[70] Universal Declaration on Indigenous Rights: A Set of Preambular Paragraphs and Principles, UN Doc. E/CN.4/Sub.2/1988/25 at p. 2 (1988).

[71] See the first Revised Text of the Draft Universal Declaration on the Rights of Indigenous Peoples, UN Doc. E/CN.4/Sub.2/1989/33 (1989).

[72] See Anaya, above n. 1, at p. 52.

[73] See Annex to the Report of the Working Group on Indigenous Populations on its 11th Session, UN Doc. E/CN.4/Sub.2/1993/29 Annex 1 (1993).

[74] See UN Doc. E/CN.4/1995/2, E/CN.4/Sub.2/1994/56, p 105.

[75] See Commission on Human Rights Res. 1995/32 (3 March 1995).

Declaration, however, is proving to be a time-consuming and onerous task; by its third session, the inter-sessional Working Group had adopted at first reading two articles of the draft Declaration without any changes.[76] Further amendments have been proposed in subsequent sessions of the Working Group.

The draft Declaration in its existing form possibly represents the most substantial development in the move towards an international acknowledgement of the rights of indigenous peoples. Consisting of 19 preambular paragraphs and 45 substantive articles, the draft deals with a number of issues. It aims to ensure a number of the fundamental rights, such as the protection against genocide and ethnocide, preservation of ethnic and cultural characteristics, and the right to an autonomous development. More significantly, the draft Declaration accords indigenous peoples the right to self-determination,[77] without the apparent limitations contained in the ILO Convention No. 169.[78]

OTHER INITIATIVES

At the global and regional levels indigenous peoples continue to receive attention. A number of modern instruments contain articles with references to indigenous peoples. Rights of indigenous children are the subject of attention in the Convention on the Rights of the Child. According to Article 30 of the Convention:

> In those States in which ethnic, religious or linguistic minorities or persons of indigenous origin exist, a child belonging to such a minority or who is indigenous shall not be denied the right, in community with other members of his or her group, to enjoy his or her own culture, to profess and practise his or her own religion, or to use his or her own language.

Environmental concerns of indigenous peoples have been referred to by the Vienna Declaration and Programme of Action 1993, the 1992 Rio Declaration on Environment and Development,[79] and the 1992 Convention on Biological Diversity.[80] In many other instruments, while direct references are missing, the jurisprudence emanating from their implementation organs shows an interest in and growing concern for indigenous issues. The Human

---

[76] See Ms Erica-Irene A. Daes, E/CN.4/Sub.2/1998/16 para 19.

[77] According to Article 3: Indigenous Peoples have the right to self-determination. By virtue of that right they freely determine their political status and freely pursue their economic, social and cultural development. See also E/CN.4/2000/WG.15/CRP.4.

[78] Note, however, Article 45 of the Draft Declaration.

[79] 31 I.L.M. (1992) 874 (in particular principle 22).

[80] 31 I.L.M. (1992) 818 (in particular the preamble, Article 10 and 18). Also see UN Framework Convention on Climate Change (1992); and UN Convention to Combat Desertification in Countries Experiencing Serious Drought and/or Desertification, Particularly in Africa (1994).

Rights Committee has dealt with indigenous claims pertaining to non-discrimination, minority rights and the right to self-determination. Concern is also evident in United Nations treaties which do not deal directly with indigenous peoples. In its General Comment No. 14 on the right to health, the Committee on Economic, Social and Cultural Rights noted:

> In the light of emerging international law and practice and the recent measures taken by States in relation to indigenous peoples, the Committee deems it useful to identify elements that would help to define indigenous peoples' right to health in order better to enable States with indigenous peoples to implement the provisions contained in Article 12 of the Covenant. The Committee considers that indigenous peoples have the right to specific measures to improve their access to health services and care. These health services should be culturally appropriate, taking into account traditional preventive care, healing practices and medicines. States should provide resources for indigenous peoples to design, deliver and control such services so that they may enjoy the highest attainable standard of physical and mental health. The vital medicinal plants, animals and minerals necessary to the full enjoyment of health of indigenous peoples should also be protected. The Committee notes that, in indigenous communities, the health of the individual is often linked to the health of the society as a whole and has a collective dimension. In this respect, the Committee considers that development-related activities that lead to the displacement of indigenous peoples against their will from their traditional territories and environment, denying them their sources of nutrition and breaking their symbiotic relationship with their lands, has a deleterious effect on their health.[81]

We have already noted that the AFCHPR makes substantial references to 'peoples' rights; indigenous peoples may be able to claim many of these rights. Indigenous issues are also on the agenda of the African Commission on Human and Peoples' Rights. In its resolution on the rights of Indigenous Peoples/Communities, the commission reiterated and confirmed the decision to establish a working group to consider the concept of indigenous peoples and to devise mechanisms for their protection. The European and American human rights systems have also developed jurisprudence on indigenous rights. Within Europe although the problem of indigenous rights exists, it is less visible when compared with the situations in Australia and the Americas.[82] The issue of indigenous peoples has been elevated in the

---

[81] CESCR General Comment 14, *The Right to Highest Attainable Standard of Health*, (Article 12) General Comment No. 14 (11/08/00). (E/C.12/200/4). para 27.

[82] H. Hannum, 'The Protection of Indigenous Rights in the Inter-American System' in D.J. Harris and S. Livingstone (eds), *The Inter-American System of Human Rights* (Oxford: Clarendon Press) 1998, 323–343 at p. 325.

Inter-American Institute, a specialised agency of the OAS.[83] The Institute organises congresses and conferences on indigenous issues and has also provided technical and advisory services to members of the OAS and to indigenous peoples.[84] The Inter-American Commission on Human Rights has also addressed a number of cases from indigenous peoples[85] and has also engaged in country reports focusing on indigenous rights.[86] Since 1992 the Commission has also been engaged in the drafting of the American Declaration on the Rights of Indigenous Peoples. The proposed Declaration was approved by the Commission in its 95th regular session during 1997.

CONCLUSIONS

The right to self-determination forms a critical though controversial aspect of modern human rights law. As discussed in earlier chapters, this right has been incorporated into the international Covenants and other modern human rights documents.[87] While during the decolonisation phase the right to self-determination was deployed to claim independent Statehood, its meaning, purposes and objectives have been questioned by many States in the post-colonial era. The right to self-determination continues to be invoked by many dissatisfied minority groups, who often equate self-determination with secession or independent Statehood. Modern States, on the other hand, are extremely reluctant to grant an explicit right of self-determination to minority groups, fearing rebellion and claims to secession. This conflict arising out of the right to self-determination has been painful. It has led to destruction and more recently resulted in violations of human rights through terrorist activities.[88]

---

[83] See the Inter-American Commission on Human Rights, *Inter-American Year Book on Human Rights 1969–70* (Washington DC: OAS), 1976, 73–83; also see Inter-American Commission on Human Rights, *Report on the work accomplished by the Inter-American Commission on Human Rights during its 29th session* (October 16–27), 1972 OAS. Doc. OAS/Ser L/V/II.29 Doc.40 rev.1 1973, 63–65.

[84] H. Hannum, 'The Protection of Indigenous Rights in the Inter-American System' in D.J. Harris and S. Livingstone (eds), above n. 82, at p. 325.

[85] Case No. 1690 (Colombia), OEA/Ser.L/V/II.29, doc. 41, rev. 2, at 63; Case No. 1802 (Paraguay), OEA/Ser.L/V/II.43, doc. 21, 20 April 1978, at 36. Also see Report on the Situation of Human Rights of a segment of the Nicaraguan Population of Miskito Origin OAS OEA/Ser.L/V/II.62. doc 10 rev. 3 (1983) and OEA/Ser.L/V/II.62 doc 26 (1984), discussed by H. Hannum, 'The Protection of Indigenous Rights in the Inter-American System' in D.J. Harris and S. Livingstone (eds), above n. 82, at pp. 326–331.

[86] See IACHR Report on H. 332 fn. 48–52.

[87] See above Chapters 4 and 5.

[88] See below Chapter 16.

Indigenous peoples have a special claim to the right to self-determination. Being indigenous to the lands, their rights were violated by more powerful foreign forces. As this chapter has analysed, there is a growing recognition of the injustices that have been endured by indigenous peoples. International law has taken some steps, albeit very limited, to grant a measure of autonomy and land rights to indigenous peoples. A very significant step was undertaken through the adoption of ILO Convention 169. Some of the modern international law instruments have also shown a sensitivity towards issues which concern indigenous peoples. There is, however, much that remains to be done. The United Nations has struggled for decades to adopt a declaration on the rights of indigenous peoples. It is recommended that after the adoption of the declaration, the Commission on Human Rights must continue its work on the drafting of a treaty, aiming at the ultimate adoption of it as a legally binding instrument which would protect the rights of indigenous peoples.

13

THE RIGHTS OF WOMEN[1]

INTRODUCTION

From the very moment of her birth, the girl child confronts a world which values her existence less than that of boys. Girls face obstacles in education, nutrition, health and other areas solely because of their sex. They are viewed as having a 'transient presence' to be married young and then judged by their ability to pro-create. As they mature into women, they are thrust into a cycle of disempower-ment that is very likely to be their daughter's destiny as well.[2]

The issue of the rights of women remains highly divisive in most societies and regions of the world. These divisions are reflected in the developing norms of the international law of human rights. Discriminatory practices and violations of the rights of women are a historical as well as a contemporary

---

[1] See A.F. Bayefsky, 'The Principle of Equality or Non-Discrimination in International Law' 11 *HRLJ* (1990) 1; C. Tinker, 'Human Rights for Women: The UN Convention on the Elimination of All Forms of Discrimination Against Women' 3(2) *HRQ* (1981) 32; L. Reanda, 'Human Rights and Women's Rights: The UN Approach' 3(2) *HRQ* (1981) 11; R. Eisler, 'Human Rights: Towards an Integrated Theory for Action' 9 *HRQ* (1987) 287; N. Hevener, 'An Analysis of Gender Based Treaty Law: Contemporary Developments in Historical Perspective' 8 *HRQ* (1986) 78; R.J. Cook, 'Women's International Human Rights Law: The Way Forward' 15 *HRQ* (1993) 230; S. Wright, 'Economic Rights and Social Justice: A Feminist Analysis of Some International Human Rights Conventions' 12 *AYIL* (1989–90) 241; T. Meron, 'Enhancing the Effectiveness of the Prohibition of Discrimination Against Women' 84 *AJIL* (1990) 213; J. Morsink, 'Women's Rights in the Universal Declaration' 13 *HRQ* (1991) 229; M.E. Galey, 'International Enforcement of Women's Rights' 6 *HRQ* (1984) 463; H. Charlesworth, C. Chinkin and S. Wright 'Feminist Approaches to International Law' 85 *AJIL* (1991) 613.
[2] United Nations, *Human Rights and the Girl Child* (United Nations: Vienna) 1993.

344

phenomenon.[3] In contemporary terms the discriminatory nature of the treatment which women receive transcends national frontiers and can be visualised as a global issue rather than a regional or national concern. Even among social and cultural entities proud and confident of their human rights standards, women are more frequently victims of violence, abuse and discrimination of poverty and discrimination than men.[4] In many societies women are perceived as inherently inferior, intellectually deficient, and physically and emotionally subservient to men.[5] While in the scarcity of resources men's demands are given priority, women are often denied educational, professional and economic opportunities. There are also denials of inheritance and property rights, and discouragement for those women wishing to take part in public and social life – at the national as well as international level.[6]

If civic order breaks down, leading to anarchy and civil war, women are most vulnerable to torture, physical abuse and rape. The treatment accorded to women in domestic and international conflicts suggests that among the civilian population, it is the women who are most vulnerable to abuse: targets of torture, slavery, mass rape and other crimes against humanity.[7] Women

---

[3] M. Schuler (ed.), *Freedom from Violence Women's Strategies from Around the Globe* (New York: United Nations Development Fund for Women) 1992; 'significant numbers of the world's population are routinely subjected to torture, starvation, terrorism, humiliation, mutilation and even murder simply because they are female' C. Bunch, 'Women's Rights as Human Rights' 12 *HRQ* (1990) 486 at p. 486; M.S. McDougal, H.D. Lasswell and L-C. Chen, *Human Rights and World Public Order: The Basic Policies of an International Law of Human Dignity* (New Haven, Conn.: Yale University Press) 1980, p. 612.

[4] Charlesworth, Chinkin and Wright, above n. 1, at p. 639; McDougal, Lasswell and Chen, above n. 3, at p. 618; P.F. Marshall, 'Violence Against Women in Canada by Non-State Actors: The State and Women's Human Rights' in K.E. Mahoney and P. Mahoney (ed.), *Human Rights in the Twenty-First Century: A Global Challenge* (Dordrecht: Martinus Nijhoff Publishers) 1993, pp. 319–333; C.A. Mackinnon, 'On Torture: A Feminist Perspective on Human Rights' ibid. pp. 21–31.

[5] A. Dearden et al., *Arab Women* (London: Minority Rights Group) 1983; R. Jahan et al., *Women in Asia* (London: Minority Rights Group) 1983; O. Harris, *American Women* (London: Minority Rights Group) 1983; E. Ivan-Smith et al., *Women in Sub-Saharan Africa* (London: Minority Rights Group) 1988.

[6] M. Makram-Ebeid, 'Exclusion of Women from Politics' in K.E. Mahoney and P. Mahoney (eds), above n. 4, pp. 89–94; N. Wikler, 'Exclusion of Women from Justice: Emergency Strategies for Reform' ibid. p. 950–108; M. Waring, 'The Exclusion of Women from "Work" and Opportunity' ibid. pp. 109–117; McDougal, Lasswell and Chen, above n. 3, p. 616.

[7] See M. Tabory, 'The Status of women in Humanitarian Law' in Y. Dinstein and M. Tabory (eds), *International Law at a Time of Perplexity: Essays in Honour of Shabtai Rosenne* (Dordrecht: Martinus Nijhoff Publishers) 1989, pp. 941–951; C. Chinkin, 'Rape and Sexual Abuse of Women in International law' 5 *EJIL* (1994) 326; D. Petrovic, 'Ethnic Cleansing – An Attempt at Methodology' ibid. p. 342. On the violation of Rights of women during the Gulf War (1990–91) see F. Hampson, 'Liability for War Crimes' in P. Rowe (ed.), *The Gulf War 1990–1991 in International and English Law* (London: Routledge) 1991, 241–260 at p. 248. On former Yugoslavia see T.A. Salzman, 'Rape Camps as a means of Ethnic Cleansing: Religious, Cultural and Ethical Responses to Rape Victims in the former Yugoslavia' 20 *HRQ* (1998) 348; Z. Pajic, *Violations of Fundamental Human Rights in the Former Yugoslavia: The Conflict of Bosnia-Herzegovina* (London: Institute of International Studies) Occasional Paper No 2 (1993) p. 7.

constitute the greatest numbers of refugees world-wide, and as refugees are often subjected to abuse and victimisation.[8]

RIGHTS OF WOMEN AND THE HUMAN RIGHTS REGIME

Women face discrimination, intimidation, harassment, torture and physical abuse not simply from State organs but also from their own family and other private institutions. A major problem which has led to a negative impact on the position of women is the reluctance of international human rights law to intervene in what is perceived as private (as opposed to public) matters.[9] Attempts to combat discrimination and violence against women in the private domain have been met with substantial opposition. Intrusion into private and family life is not viewed as a desirable undertaking for legal establishments. Such an intrusion is seen as contrary to the social, cultural and religious values prevalent in many societies.[10] Within the sanctity of the home, women in many parts of the world are regularly subjected to mental and physical violence or sexual abuse, such as incest, rape, 'dowry deaths', wife battering, genital mutilation, prostitution and forced sterilisation.[11] In these social structures women have to undergo a persistent cycle of rejection, subordination and shame. Old age and disability have a substantially negative impact on the lives of women. Disabled women, as the Committee on Economic, Social and Cultural Rights has noted, suffer from 'double discrimination'.[12]

---

[8] A.C. Byrnes, 'The 'Other' Human Rights Treaty Body: The Work of the Committee on the Elimination of Discrimination Against Women' 14 *YJIL* (1989) 1–67 at p. 64; R.M.M. Wallace, 'Making the Refugee Convention Gender Sensitive: The Canadian Guidelines' 45 *ICLQ* (1996) 702.

[9] S.P. Subedi, 'Protection of Women Against Domestic Violence: The Response of International Law' 2 *EHRLR* (1997) 587; A. McGillivray, 'Reconstructing Child abuse: Western Definition and Non-Western Experience' in M. Freeman and P. Veerman (eds), *Ideologies of Children's Rights* (Dordrecht: Martinus Nijhoff Publishers) 1992, 213–236 at p. 213.

[10] A.C. Byrnes, 'Women, Feminism and International Human Rights Law – Methodological Myopia, Fundamental Flaws or Meaningful Marginalisation?' 12 *AYIL* (1988–90) 205 at p. 215.

[11] For a multitude examples of the literature see H.J. Steiner and P. Alston (eds), *International Human Rights in Context: Law, Politics, Morals: Text and Materials*, 2nd edn (Oxford: Clarendon Press) 2000, pp. 404–438; E. Dorkenoo and S. Elworthy, *Female Genital Mutilation: Proposals for Change* (London: Minority Rights Group) 1992; E. Dorkenoo, *Cutting the Rose: Female Genital Mutilation – the Practice and its Prevention* (London: Minority Rights Group) 1995; A. Slack, 'Female Circumcision: A Critical Appraisal' 10 *HRQ* (1988) 439; I. Gunning, 'Arrogant Perceptions, World Travelling and Multicultural Feminism: The Case of Female Genital Surgeries' 23 *CHRLR* (1991–1992) 189 at p. 238; S. Skrobanek, *Exotic, Subservient and Trapped: Confronting Prostitution and Traffic in Women* in M. Schuler (ed.), above n. 3, pp. 121–137; J. Seager and A. Olson (eds), *Women in the Third World An International Atlas* (London: Pluto Press) 1986; G. Van Bueren, *The International Law on the Rights of the Child* (Dordrecht: Martinus Nijhoff Publishers) 1995, pp. 262–292.

[12] Committee on Economic, Social and Cultural Rights, General Comment No. 5, *Persons with Disability* (Eleventh Session, 1994) UN Doc. E/C.12/1994/13 (adopted) 25 November, 1994.

It is encouraging to note that the United Nations has undertaken positive steps to combat discrimination and violence against women in both the public and private domains. The United Nations Convention on the Elimination of All Forms of Discrimination against Women, the primary focus of this chapter, prohibits discrimination in 'any other field'. At the same time it is important to note that difficulties have arisen in enforcing the norm of non-discrimination in the domestic sphere. Such difficulties are apparent through a large number of reservations to significant provisions contained in, for example, Article 16 of the Convention.

Violence against women, an action frequent within the confines of family and home, has been dealt with specifically by the United Nations. In December 1993, the United Nations General Assembly adopted a Declaration on the Elimination of Violence against Women. The United Nations has also appointed a Special Rapporteur on violence against women. An Optional Protocol to the Convention has recently been adopted by the United Nations General Assembly. The protocol would allow individuals to complain to CEDAW regarding violations of the rights contained in the Convention.

COMBATING GENDER-BASED DISCRIMINATION AND THE INTERNATIONAL HUMAN RIGHTS MOVEMENT

Attempts to combat discrimination against women and to establish *de jure* and de facto equality have a substantial history. As we have noted in this book the norm of equality and non-discrimination, especially gender-based equality and non-discrimination, represents the core of the modern human rights regime.[13] The international bill of rights is established on the principle of non-discrimination between men and women. The UDHR and the International Covenants contain various provisions confirming gender equality and non-discrimination.[14] As we considered in earlier chapters gender equality as a commitment is evident in the provisions of all regional human rights treaties.[15] By virtue of Article 1 of the ECHR, States parties undertake to 'secure to everyone' the rights contained in the Convention. According to Article 14:

> The rights and freedoms set forth in this Convention shall be secured without discrimination on any ground such as sex...

The guarantees on non-discrimination in ECHR are further strengthened by Protocol 12.[16] Protocol 12 extends beyond the rights provided in the

---

[13] See above Chapters 3, and 10.
[14] See above Chapters 3, 4 and 5.
[15] See above Chapters 6–9.
[16] Protocol No. 12 to the Convention for the Protection of Human Rights and Fundamental Freedoms ETS No.:177; (opened for Signature, Rome Date: 04/11/00). See above Chapter 6.

Convention to 'any right set forth by law'.[17] Such an extension is clearly to the benefit of disadvantaged groups such as women, who have suffered from various discriminatory norms which are not necessarily covered by the ECHR.

The African and American regional human rights systems also prohibit discrimination *inter alia* on grounds of sex. In 1994, the General Assembly of the OAS. adopted the Inter-American Convention on the Prevention, Punishment and Eradication of Violence against Women at Belem do Para.[18] The illegality and unacceptability of discrimination on the basis of sex is now regarded as a firmly accepted principle of general international law, and applied to all States as well as to international organisations. The European Union, although not a human rights institution, has taken an unequivocal stance on non-discrimination against women and gender equality.[19] There is a growing concern regarding matters of sexual discrimination and violation of women's rights among members States of the Arab League. The South-Asian Association for Regional Cooperation (SAARC) has frequently raised the issue of violations of the rights of children and women. The years 1991–2000 were designated as the 'SAARC Decade of Girl Child'.[20] In the light of the evidence presented, some jurists have adopted the view that discrimination on the basis of gender is a norm of *jus cogens*.[21] In our study we exhibit that while there is an overall consensus in prohibiting gender discrimination, there are also substantial disagreements on various aspects of women's positions in particular societies and States. Hence, a more cautious and realistic approach is recommended.

---

[17] Article 1, Protocol 12 provides as follows 'The enjoyment of any right set forth by law shall be secured without discrimination on any ground such as sex, race, colour, language, religion, political or other opinion, national or social origin, association with a national minority, property, birth or other status'.

[18] Signed 9 June 1994. Entered into force March 3 1995. 33 I.L.M. (1994) 1534. See above Chapter 8.

[19] See e.g. Article 141 TEC; Council Directive 75/117/EEC of 10 February 1975 on the approximation of the laws of the Member States relating to the application of the principle of equal pay for men and women; Council Directive 76/207/EEC of 9 February 1976 on the implementation of the principle of equal treatment for men and women as regards access to employment, vocational training and promotion, and working conditions; Council Directive 97/80/EC of 15 December 1997 on the burden of proof in cases of discrimination based on sex. See also the Community Framework Strategy on Gender Equality (2001–2005) Com (2000/335 Final Council Regulation 2836/98/EC on *Integrating of Gender Issues in Development Co-Operation*. Also see the proposed new Directive amending Equal Treatment Directive 1976.

[20] See J. Rehman, 'Women's Rights: An International Law Perspective' in R. Mehdi and F. Shahid (eds), *Women's Law in Legal Education and Practice: North–South Co-operation* (Copenhagen: New Social Science Monographs) 1997, 106–128 at p. 117; A. Ahsan, *SAARC: A Perspective* (Dhaka: University Press) 1991.

[21] For elaboration of the concept see above Chapter 2.

THE ROLE OF THE UNITED NATIONS

The United Nations Charter contains a number of references providing for gender equality and non-discrimination. According to Article 1 of the Charter one of the purposes of the Charter is:

> to achieve international cooperation in solving international problems of an economic, social, cultural, or humanitarian character, and in promoting and encouraging respect for human rights and for fundamental freedoms for all without distinction as to ... sex.

Soon after the establishment of the United Nations, the United Nations' Economic and Social Council, in accordance with Article 68 of the Charter, set up a Commission on the Status of Women (CSW). As we have noted CSW is one of the nine functional commissions.[22] The CSW was established as a functional commission of the ECOSOC to prepare recommendations and reports for the Council on promoting women's rights in political, economic, civil, social and educational fields.[23] The Commission also makes recommendations to the Council on urgent problems requiring immediate attention in the field of women's rights. The objective of the Commission is to promote implementation of the principle that men and women shall have equal rights. Its mandate was expanded in 1987 by the Council in its resolution 1987/22. Following the 1995 Fourth World Conference on Women, the General Assembly mandated the Commission to integrate into its work programme a follow-up process to the Conference, in which the Commission should play a significant role, regularly reviewing the critical areas of concern in the Platform for Action.

The Commission, which initially began with 15 members, currently consists of 45 members elected by the Economic and Social Council for a period of four years. Members are nominated by the governments. They are elected on the following geographical criteria: thirteen from African states; eleven from Asian states; four from Eastern European states; nine from Latin American and Caribbean states; and eight from Western European and 'Other' States. It is normal for the Commission to meet for eight working days every year.

The status of the members of the CSW resembles that of members of the Commission on Human Rights (in the sense that members act as representatives of States rather than in their personal capacity) and as in the case of the Human Rights Commission, the course of the proceedings and their outcomes reflect a general governmental stance on human rights issues.[24] Unlike the

---

[22] See above Chapter 2.

[23] By its resolution 11(II) of 21 June 1946.

[24] See ECOSOC Res. E/1979/36; S. Davidson, *Human Rights* (Buckingham: Open University Press) 1993.

Human Rights Commission, the CSW has not been able to develop its role much further than promotional, educational and standard-setting activities. Indeed, for sometime the future of the CSW remained under threat and there has been a pronounced resistance to the idea of expanding the scope and authority of CSW to receive and consider petitions similar in nature to the those received under the ECOSOC 1503 procedure. The specificity in the work of the CSW, with an exclusive focus on women's human rights, has also generated some concern and, as we note, there have been attempts to mainstream gender equality.

Notwithstanding its limitations the CSW should be given credit and commended for its contribution to establishing new standard-setting mechanisms. A number of international conventions were formulated under the sponsorship of the CSW, including the 1952 Convention on the Political Rights of Women,[25] the 1957 Convention on the Nationality of Married Women[26] and the 1962 Convention on Consent to Marriage, Minimum Age for Marriage and Registration of Marriages.[27] The most significant achievement of the Commission remains its role in the drafting of the Convention on the Elimination of All Forms of Discrimination against Women (1979).[28]

THE CONVENTION ON THE ELIMINATION OF ALL FORMS OF DISCRIMINATION AGAINST WOMEN

The Convention on the Elimination of All Forms of Discrimination Against Women was adopted by the General Assembly of the United Nations on 18 December 1979 and came into force on 3 September 1981. Like the Race Convention and the Convention against Torture, the Women's Convention was also preceded by a United Nations General Assembly Declaration. The Declaration on the Elimination of All Forms of Discrimination against Women was adopted in 1967.[29] The outcome of years of discussions, debates and ultimately compromises, the Convention asserts many of the fundamental rights of women.[30] It constitutes a comprehensive attempt at establishing

---

[25] UN GA Res. 640 (VII) 1952.

[26] UN GA Res. 1040 (XI) 1957.

[27] UN GA Res. 1763 (XVII) 1962; For a consideration of these instruments see M. Galey, 'Promoting Non-Discrimination against Women: The United Nations Commission on the Status of Women' 23 *International Studies Quarterly* (1979) 273.

[28] Adopted at New York, 18 December, 1979. Entered into force 3 September, 1981. UN GA Res. 34/180(XXXIV), GA. Res. 34/180, 34 GAOR, Supp. (No. 46) 194, UN Doc. A/34/46, at 193 (1979), 2 U.K.T.S. (1989); 19 I.L.M (1980) 33.

[29] However in the case of the Race Convention the time-span between the adoption of the GA Resolution and a binding treaty was shorter as compared to the Women's Convention.

[30] See Res. 5 (XXIV), 52 UN ESCOR Supp. (No 6), 70; UN Doc. E/5109 and E/CN. 6/568 (1972); 52 UN ESCOR Supp. (No 5); UN Doc. E/CN. 6/573.

universal standards on the rights of women. The convention is one of the widely ratified human rights treaties and can be regarded as a milestone on the path to the goal of standard-setting for gender-based equality.

In the preamble to the Convention the State parties acknowledge that 'extensive discrimination continues to exist against women'.[31] The preamble also acknowledges the detrimental effect that discrimination has on the development of nations, thereby linking gender equality with development. The family as well as society is hampered by the denial of women's full and adequate participation in the political, economic, social, legal and cultural activities. Significantly, within the preamble there is a recognition of the link between gender-based discrimination and exploitation for political and economic goals. Article 1, following the definition as provided in the Convention on Elimination of All Forms of Racial Discrimination,[32] defines discrimination as:

> any distinction, exclusion or restriction made on the basis of sex which has the effect or purpose of impairing or nullifying the recognition, enjoyment or exercise by women, irrespective of their marital status, on a basis of equality of men and women, of human rights and fundamental freedoms in the political, economic, social, cultural, civil or any other field.

The definition in the Convention differs from the Race Convention in that, first, it omits any reference to the term 'preference'. Secondly, the Women's Convention appears to have a wider sphere of influence, applying to the 'political, economic, social, cultural, civil or any other field' in comparison to the 'political, economic, social, cultural or any other field of public life' as stated in Article 1 of the Race Convention. This wider sphere includes eradication of distinctions and discrimination in private life.

Issues of discrimination and of de facto equality

Article 2 of the Women's Convention represents what has been aptly described as the 'core of the Convention'.[33] According to this Article States parties condemn discrimination against women in all its forms and agree to eliminate discrimination. The agreement is to eliminate discrimination 'by all appropriate means' and without delay follow a policy to this effect. The sub-sections of Article 2 spell out details of this undertaking. According to Article 2(a), States parties undertake to:

> embody the principle of the equality of men and women in their national constitutions or other appropriate legislation if not yet incorporated therein and to ensure, through law and other appropriate means, the practical realization of this principle.

---

[31] See Preamble to the Convention.
[32] See Article 1 of the Convention on the Elimination of All Forms of Racial Discrimination (1966).
[33] J. Nordenfield UN Doc. CEDAW/C/SR.35; UN Doc. A/39/45 Sec. 190.

In accordance with Article 2(b) States parties are under an obligation to 'adopt appropriate legislative and other measures, including sanctions where appropriate, prohibiting all discrimination against women' and Article 2(c) obliges States to 'establish legal protection of the rights of women on an equal basis with men to ensure through competent national tribunals and other public institutions the effective protection of women against any act of discrimination'. The underlying commitment of Article 2(d)–(g) is to prevent discrimination against women, and to ensure the abolition of all discriminatory laws, regulations, customs and practices.[34] Among the various sub-sections of the Article, Article 2(e) is worthy of specific mention. The Article represents an undertaking on the part of the parties to take 'all appropriate measures to eliminate discrimination against women by any person, organisation or enterprise'. In adopting a broad approach and condemning discrimination by any person or organisation, this provision further reinforces the reach of the Convention beyond the public sphere.

The provisions of Article 2 are particularly valuable in identifying and establishing a regime of non-discrimination and gender equality. As we see below, CEDAW has yet to deal with individual Communications under the Optional Protocol to the Convention. In its future analysis and application of Article 2, the Committee can usefully benefit from related jurisprudence of the ICCPR and ECHR. The discussion that follows, therefore, considers case law emerging from other human rights treaty provisions.

In *Shirin Aumeeruddy-Cziffra and 19 other Mauritian women* v. *Mauritius*[35] Aumeeruddy-Cziffra and nineteen women brought forward a claim against Mauritius under the first Optional Protocol to the ICCPR. These women complained that two pieces of legislation on immigration and deportation resulted in gender discrimination which violated the right to found a family and home and removed the protection of courts of law, breaching Articles 2–4, 17, 23, 25 and 26 of ICCPR. To further their complaints of the violation of norms of gender equality on non-discrimination, the authors argued that under the new laws:

> alien husbands of Mauritian women lost their residence status in Mauritius and must now apply for a resident permit which may be refused or removed at any time. These new laws, however, do not affect the status of alien women married to Mauritian husbands who retain their legal right to residence in the country. The authors further contend that under the new laws alien husband of Mauritian woman may be deported under a ministerial order which is not subject to Judicial Review.[36]

---

[34] See Article 2(f).
[35] *Shirin Aumeeruddy-Cziffra and 19 other Mauritian women* v. *Mauritius*, Communication No. 35/1978 (9 April 1981), UN Doc. CCPR/C/OP/1 at 67 (1984).
[36] Ibid.; also see above Chapter 4.

The Committee, while accepting that Mauritius could justifiably place restrictions on entry and expulsion of aliens, nevertheless found the pieces of legislation to be discriminatory since they subjected foreign spouses of Mauritian women to the restriction but not foreign spouses of Mauritian men.[37] The issue of gender discrimination was similarly raised in *Lovelace* v. *Canada*.[38] After finding violations of Article 27, the Committee did not feel the need to examine the subject of sex discrimination,[39] although in his individual opinion Mr Bouziri took the view that Canadian legislation discriminated against Indian women.[40]

Article 3 of the Convention represents a substantial obligation on the State parties to undertake all appropriate measures to 'ensure full development and advancement of women'. As an important provision, Article 3 has frequently been the subject of analysis of CEDAW in State reports. CEDAW in its review of reports has been critical of many States for failing to ensure compliance with this Article. In its Concluding Observations on the Report submitted by Cameroon, the Committee notes with concern

> that inadequate allocation of resources for the advancement of women, with the resultant incomplete execution of programmes and projects, seriously jeopardizes the improvement of women's living conditions.[41]

Article 4 of the Convention sanctions policies of affirmative action or reverse discrimination. According to this article temporary measures are required to accelerate the de facto equality while necessary steps are being taken to achieve *de jure* equality. In its General Recommendation No. 5, the Committee notes:

> the reports, the introductory remarks and the replies by States parties reveal that while significant progress has been achieved in regard to repealing or modifying discriminatory laws, there is still a need for action to be taken to implement fully the Convention by introducing measures to promote de facto equality between men and women [the Committee Recommends] that States Parties make more use of temporary special measures such as positive action, preferential treatment or quota systems to advance women's integration into education, the economy, politics and employment.[42]

---

[37] Ibid. para 9.2(b)2(ii)3.

[38] *Sandra Lovelace* v. *Canada*, Communication No. 24/1977 (30 July 1981), UN Doc. CCPR/C/OP/1 at 83 (1984). For commentaries see A.F. Bayefsky, 'The Human Rights Committee and the Case of Sandra Lovelace' 20 *CYBIL* (1982) 244; D. McGoldrick, 'Canadian Indians, Cultural Rights and the Human Rights Committee' 40 *ICLQ* (1991) 658.

[39] Paras 13.2–13.19.

[40] Ibid. p. 175. See above Chapter 4.

[41] Concluding Observations (Comments) of the Committee on the Elimination of All Forms of Discrimination Against Women: Cameroon 26/06/2000; A/55/38; para 47; Concluding Observations (Comments) of the Committee on the Elimination of All Forms of Discrimination Against Women: India 01/02/2000; A/55/38 para 56.

[42] General Recommendation No. 5 (seventh session, 1988), Special Temporary Measures.

However, these extraordinary steps to remedy past discrimination shall be discontinued 'when the objectives of equality of opportunity and treatment have been achieved'. A number of States including Bangladesh, India and Pakistan have a quota system for women in the fields *inter alia* of employment and higher education. Such initiatives representing affirmative action have been applauded by CEDAW in its consideration of State reports.[43] At the same time the subject of affirmative action is a controversial one. Article 4 is similar in nature and scope to Article 1(4) and 2(2) of the Convention on the Elimination of Racial Discrimination (save that it applies to women) and the debates arising out of its provisions have been similarly divisive.[44] Article 5(a) represents a significant commitment on the States parties to undertake 'all appropriate measures'

> to modify the social and cultural patterns of conduct of men and women, with a view to achieving the elimination of prejudices and other customary and all other practices which are based on the idea of inferiority or the superiority of either sexes or on stereotyped roles for men and women.

However, there is no specification as to what those 'appropriate measures' could amount to. Some elaboration has been provided by CEDAW in its General Recommendation No. 19 where the Committee observes that traditional attitudes representing stereotyped roles for men and women perpetuate practices of violence or coercion, forced marriages, dowry deaths and female circumcision.[45] The Committee goes on to observe that:

> Such prejudices and practices may justify gender-based violence as a form of protection or control of women. The effect of such violence on the physical and mental integrity of women is to deprive them of the equal enjoyment, exercise and knowledge of human rights and fundamental freedoms. While this comment addresses mainly actual or threatened violence the underlying consequences of these forms of gender-based violence help to maintain women in subordinate roles and contribute to the low level of political participation and to their lower level of education, skills and work opportunities. According to CEDAW comments these attitude also contribute to propagation of pornography and treatment of women as sexual objects.[46]

A number of States have been the object of criticism by CEDAW for their failure to comply with Article 5 or for entering reservations to the Article. Thus, for instance, the Republic of Ireland has been criticised for the provisions of Article 41.2 of the Irish Constitution, which according to the

---

[43] Concluding Observations (Comments) of the Committee on the Elimination of All Forms of Discrimination Against Women: Bangladesh 24/07/1997; A/52/38/Rev. para 415; Concluding Observations (Comments) of the Committee on the Elimination of All Forms of Discrimination Against Women: India 01/02/2000; A/55/38 para 32.
[44] See above Chapter 10.
[45] UN Doc. HRI/Gen 1/Rev. 1, 85–86
[46] Ibid. para 11.

Committee 'reflect a stereotypical view of the role of women in the home and as mothers'.[47] India is one of the States which has entered reservations to Article 5(a), representing tensions and male hegemony within the society.[48] Article 6 considers the important issue of female sexual slavery and the suppression of trafficking in women. In condemning such activities it requires States parties to take all appropriate steps to end trafficking in women and exploitation and prostitution of women.

Representation in public life and the issue of nationality

Article 7 of the Convention deals with the elimination of discrimination against women in the political and public life of a country. It attempts to ensure that women have the right to vote and have a right to be elected to office, with participatory rights in policy formulation, at all the governmental levels. It also attempts to ensure that women are able to participate in the activities of non-governmental organisations. While a majority of States accord equality to women in public life, there remain unfortunate remnants of legislative enactments and administrative policies barring women from political participation at the governmental level. This subject was recently raised by the Human Rights Committee in its analysis of the State Report from Kuwait. The Committee in its Concluding Comments expresses its concern that:

> in spite of constitutional provisions on equality, Kuwait's electoral laws continue to exclude entirely women from voting and being elected to public office. It notes with regret that the Amir's initiatives to remedy this situation were defeated in Parliament.[49]

CEDAW has shown concern on many occasions at the low levels of women in public office and women in ministerial posts.[50] It has elaborated on the provisions of the Convention through its General Recommendation No. 23 (1997) on women in political and public life.[51] In its recent consideration of Kazakhstan's initial report, the Committee expressed its concern at the very low representation of women in decision-making bodies, with only

---

[47] Concluding Observations of the Committee on the Elimination of Discrimination Against Women: Ireland. 01/07/99. A/54/38, paras 161–201. (Concluding Observations/Comments) para 193.
[48] The Indian reservation notes 'With regard to articles 5 (a) and 16 (1) of the Convention on the Elimination of All Forms of Discrimination Against Women, the Government of the Republic of India declares that it shall abide by and ensure these provisions in conformity with its policy of non-interference in the personal affairs of any Community without its initiative and consent'.
[49] Concluding Observations (Comments) of the Human Rights Committee Kuwait 19/07/2000. A/55/40, paras 452–497, at para 461.
[50] Concluding Observations (Comments) of the Committee on the Elimination of All Forms of Discrimination Against Women: Cameroon 26/06/2000; A/55/38; paras 56–57.
[51] General Recommendation No. 23 (sixteenth session, 1997).

an 11 per cent representation in the National Parliament.[52] Such views on gender equality unfortunately continue to invoke the displeasure of States, leading some of them to place reservations to the Article, particularly in relation to the representation of women in armed forces and national security systems.[53]

According to Article 8 of the Convention, State parties are under an obligation to take all appropriate measures to ensure that women have the opportunity to represent their governments at all international levels. In its General Recommendation on the Implementation of Article 8, the Committee notes that:

> States parties take further direct measures in accordance with article 4 of the Convention to ensure the full implementation of article 8 of the Convention and to ensure to women on equal terms with men and without any discrimination the opportunities to represent their Government at the international level and to participate in the work of international organizations.[54]

Article 9 deals with the complex though highly important issue of nationality rights, emphasising equal rights for women in acquiring, changing and retaining nationality. States parties are required to ensure that:

> neither marriage to an alien nor change of nationality by the husband during marriage shall automatically change the nationality of the wife, render her stateless or force upon her the nationality of the husband.

Issues relating to nationality are vexed and controversial ones in general international law. Matters concerning nationality and citizenship have traditionally been seen as falling within the jurisdictional domain of sovereign States. International consensus is particularly thin when it comes to the capacity of women to change or retain their nationality and to pass it on to their children.[55] It has thus not been surprising that Article 9 has attracted reservations from a number of States. Several States continue to insist on granting the child the nationality of the father.[56] Iraq has placed reservations to Article 9(1) and (2) while Egypt, Jordan, Morocco, Tunisia and Turkey have reserved this position as regards Article 9(2). An analysis of the available State reports reveals divergent rationales behind the imposition of reservations, though one possible unifying thread among these reservations would appear to be the argument in relation to preservation of family solidarity and cultural integrity. In relation to the inheritance of nationality,

---

[52] See the Initial Report of Kazakhstan CEDAW/C/KAZ/I, 490th, 491st and 497th meetings (18 and 23 January 2001).

[53] See UN Website (appendix 1)

[54] CEDAW (General Recommendation) Implementation of Article 8. Doc. A/43/38.

[55] For further analysis see *Unity Dow* v. *The Attorney General of Botswana*, [1992] Law Reports of the Commonwealth 623 (Count of Appeal). Case also considered in above Chapter 9.

[56] Article 9(1).

the arguments have less tenacity and indeed on occasions reflect a misunderstanding of the principles of gender equality.[57]

Educational, employment and health rights

Women frequently suffer from inequality of opportunities in education and vocational and professional training. Article 10 of the Convention attempts to eradicate such discrimination and inequality. Article 11 deals with elimination of discrimination in the workplace and in the field of employment. The Article recognises the right to work as an inalienable right of all human beings.[58] States parties undertake to adopt all appropriate measures to ensure equal opportunities in employment and to provide a free choice of profession and employment. There is also an undertaking to provide equal remuneration, right to social security and a right to protection of health and to safety in working conditions. Right to employment also needs to take account of the factors which concern women; in this context Article 11(2) is of enormous value. The provisions of Article 11(2) are also noteworthy since they move away from the sameness/equal treatment approach and recognise the biological uniqueness of pregnancy.

According to Article 11(2), States undertake to prohibit dismissals on grounds *inter alia* of pregnancy. Instead the commitment is to introduce maternity leave with pay or comparable social benefits without loss of former employment, seniority or social allowances. There is also an undertaking to provide special protection to women during their pregnancies, and to encourage the provision of necessary supporting social services to enable family obligations to operate in conjunction with obligations of employment. The provisions of this Article are enormously beneficial to women the world over. In many regions, women are deprived of equal opportunities of employment. Women of child bearing ages are particularly at a disadvantage as employers are reluctant to offer employment opportunities or have been known to terminate employment when these women become pregnant. Discriminatory actions are witnessed in the developing as well as the developed world. It is equally unfortunate to note that financially stable States such as Singapore have maintained reservations to Article 11.[59]

---

[57] Egypt, for instance, has justified inheritance to father's nationality alone 'to prevent a child's acquisition of two nationalities, since this may be prejudicial to his future' but goes on to plead that 'It is clear that the Child's acquisition of his father's nationality is the procedure most suitable for the child and that this does not infringe upon the principles of equality between men and women, since it is the custom for a woman to agree, on marrying an alien, that her children shall be of the father's nationality'. See UN Doc. CEDAW/SP/13Rev.Add 1, 18. See D.E. Arzt, 'The Application of International Human Rights Law in Islamic States' 12 *HRQ* (1990) 202 at p. 219.
[58] Article 11(1)(a).
[59] This reservation was raised as a subject of concern. See CEDAW, 25 session, 13 July 2001.

Article 12 of the Convention deals with the important subject of equality in health care, including family planning assistance. CEDAW has made a General Recommendation in pursuance of Article 12.[60] The right to health has also been a subject of General Comment by the Committee on the ICESCR.[61] In its General Recommendation, CEDAW has urged States parties to report on their health legislation and policies for women.[62] They are also required to provide information on health conditions, conditions hazardous to the health of women and on related diseases.[63] The Committee has recommended that States should draw up health care policies affecting women with particular regard, *inter alia*, to biological, socio-economic and psychological factors.[64]

The General Comment made by the Committee on ICESCR is a useful elaboration on women's health rights jurisprudence. The Committee notes:

> To eliminate discrimination against women, there is a need to develop and implement a comprehensive national strategy for promoting women's right to health throughout their life span. Such a strategy should include interventions aimed at the prevention and treatment of diseases affecting women, as well as policies to provide access to a full range of high quality and affordable health care, including sexual and reproductive services. A major goal should be reducing women's health risks, particularly lowering rates of maternal mortality and protecting women from domestic violence. The realization of women's right to health requires the removal of all barriers interfering with access to health services, education and information, including in the area of sexual and reproductive health. It is also important to undertake preventive, promotive and remedial action to shield women from the impact of harmful traditional cultural practices and norms that deny them their full reproductive rights.[65]

Social and economic rights

Article 13 represents important provisions related to economic and social rights. It emphasises equality of rights particularly the right to family benefits, the right to bank loans, mortgages, other forms of financial credit and the right to participation in recreational activities, sports and all other aspects of cultural life. Women often suffer from inequalities in obtaining benefits, loans and credit from governmental agencies, banks and building societies. The provisions of the

---

[60] CEDAW, General Recommendation 24, Women and Health (Article 12) Doc A/54/38/Rev. 1, chapter 1.

[61] ICESCR General Comment 14, *The Right to Highest Attainable Standard of Health*, (Article 12) General Comment No. 14 (11/08/00) (E/C.12/200/4).

[62] Ibid. para 9.

[63] Ibid. para 10.

[64] Paras 12(a)–(c).

[65] Para 21.

Article aim *inter alia* to prevent sex discrimination in the payment of social security and similar benefits. In *Broeks* v. *The Netherlands* Ms Broeks appealed to the Human Rights Committee under the first Optional Protocol claiming violations of Article 26 of the ICCPR and Article 9 of the ICESCR.[66] Ms Broeks had been dismissed by her employer because of illness. At first she received payments as unemployment benefits, but the Dutch government discontinued these since she was not the 'breadwinner' in her household as was required by the Netherlands Unemployment Benefits Act. The Human Rights Committee found violations of Article 26 of ICCPR, because the Statute was discriminatory in its treatment of women *vis-à-vis* men, and no grounds could be ascertained to justify such a distinction between men and women.[67] Similarly gender discrimination has been found by the Human Rights Committee where a woman was not allowed to claim before domestic courts in relation to matters arising from matrimonial property.[68] The offending legislation in Peru had provided that 'when a woman is married only the husband is entitled to represent matrimonial property before the Courts', a provision which violated the terms of Article 26.

Article 14 deals with the specific position of rural women whose work is often not acknowledged. The Article is a detailed expression of the rights belonging to women in rural areas and provides as follows:

1. States Parties shall take into account the particular problems faced by rural women and the significant roles which rural women play in the economic survival of their families, including their work in the non-monetized sectors of the economy, and shall take all appropriate measures to ensure the application of the provisions of the present Convention to women in rural areas.
2. States Parties shall take all appropriate measures to eliminate discrimination against women in rural areas in order to ensure, on a basis of equality of men and women, that they participate in and benefit from rural development and, in particular, shall ensure to such women the right

    (a) To participate in the elaboration and implementation of development planning at all levels;
    (b) To have access to adequate health care facilities, including information, counselling and services in family planning;
    (c) To benefit directly from social security programmes;
    (d) To obtain all types of training and education, formal and non-formal, including that relating to functional literacy, as well as, *inter alia*, the benefit of all community and extension services, in order to increase their technical proficiency;

---

[66] *S.W.M. Broeks* v. *The Netherlands*, Communication No. 172/1984 (9 April 1987), UN Doc. Supp. No. 40 (A/42/40) at 139 (1987).
[67] Ibid. para 12.1.
[68] See *Graciela Ato del Avellanal* v. *Peru*, Communication No. 202/1986 (28 October 1988), UN Doc. Supp. No. 40 (A/44/40) at 196 (1988).

(e) To organize self-help groups and co-operatives in order to obtain equal access to economic opportunities through employment or self employment;

(f) To participate in all community activities;

(g) To have access to agricultural credit and loans, marketing facilities, appropriate technology and equal treatment in land and agrarian reform as well as in land resettlement schemes;

(h) To enjoy adequate living conditions, particularly in relation to housing, sanitation, electricity and water supply, transport and communications.

According to Article 15, equality before the law in matters of civil law must be accorded to women, including the legal capacity to contract, to own and to administer property, and to move and to chose a residence and domicile. Under this Article, State parties are obliged to conform their national legislation to this rule. In addition any contract or legal document 'whose effect is directed at restriction of the legal capacity of women' shall be null and void. It is also important to note that such a significant Article has attracted reservations from many States. These reserving States continue to be reluctant to allow women legal and contractual capacity equal to that enjoyed by men. Women have often been excluded from inheritance and property ownership through legal disabilities. Women are thus, in some parts of the world, legally dependant in matters of contract and litigation. Among States entering reservations to the various provisions of Article 15 are Niger, Malta and Switzerland. The primary objection that has emanated from Islamic States – such as Algeria, Tunisia, Morocco and Jordan – relates to the application of Article 15(4). The apparent reasoning behind the reservations to Article 15(4) is the conflict with their personal laws.

In a recent observation, the Human Rights Committee has expressed its concern not only at the continued existence of the institution of polygamy but also deprivation of women from their due share in inheritance. In presenting its Concluding Comments to the report by Gabon, the Human Rights Committee expresses the following view:

> The Committee notes that there are customs and traditions in the State party, having a bearing on, among other things, equality between men and women, that may hamper the full implementation of some provisions of the Covenant. In particular, the Committee deplores the fact that polygamy is still practiced in Gabon and refers to its general comment No. 28, which states that polygamy is incompatible with equality of treatment with regard to the right to marry. 'Polygamy violates the dignity of women. It is an inadmissible discrimination against women' (CCPR/C/21/Rev.1/Add.10, para 24). The Committee also observes that a number of legislative provisions in Gabon are not compatible with the Covenant, including article 252 of the Civil Code requiring a woman to be obedient to her husband. Lastly, the Committee notes that, in the event of her husband's death, a woman inherits only the usufruct of a quarter of the property left by her husband, and only after her children.

The State party must review its legislation and practice in order to ensure that women have the same rights as men, including rights of ownership and inheritance. It must take specific action to increase the involvement of women in political, economic and social life and ensure that there is no discrimination based on customary law in matters such as marriage, divorce and inheritance. Polygamy must be abolished and article 252 of the Civil Code repealed. It is the duty of the State party to do everything necessary to ensure that the Covenant is respected.[69]

Marriage and family relations

In accordance with Article 16, States parties agree to undertake all appropriate measures to eliminate discrimination against women in all matters relating to marriage and family relations. Assurances are provided by States that men and women shall have the same right to enter into marriage, the same right freely to choose a spouse and to enter into marriage only with their free and full consent. States also agree that both parties to marriage would have the same rights and responsibilities during its existence and at the time of its dissolution. By virtue of this Article, States undertake to adopt measures to allow women (on the basis of equality) to plan a family, and to give women equal rights on the parenting of children and all other relevant issues such as guardianship, wardship, trusteeship and adoption of children, or similar institutions where these concepts exist in national legislation. According to Article 16(2) the betrothal and the marriage of a child shall have no legal effect, and all necessary actions, including legislation, shall be taken to specify a minimum age for marriage and to make the registration of marriages in an official registry compulsory.

Through the provisions of Article 16 State parties undertake to eliminate discrimination in matters relating to marriage and family relations. The Article lays emphasis upon equal rights in choosing a spouse and in the entering into and the dissolution of marriage. The Article also establishes equality of rights of men and women in raising of the family and in the ownership of family property. The rights granted to women in Article 16 raised opposition in many quarters, particularly from some Islamic States. A number of the Islamic States have registered their reservations to this Article. These States include Iraq (Article 16(1)(c)(f)), Jordan (Article 16(c)(d)(g)), Morocco (Article 16(c)), and Tunisia (Article 16(c)(d)(f)(g)(h)). The viewpoints of the State representatives and the text of the State reports reveal that the rights contained in this Article confront directly existing cultural and perceived religious norms. It is also the case that a number of Islamic States have treated the provisions of Article 16 as being contrary to the *Sharia* (Islamic law).

---

[69] Concluding Observations of the Human Rights Committee: Gabon. 10/11/2000. CCPR/CO/70/GAB, (Concluding Observations/Comments) seventieth session, para 9.

Kuwait provides a good example. It has put in the following reservations, which notes:

> The Government of the State of Kuwait declares that it does not consider itself bound by the provisions contained in Article 16(f) in as much as it conflicts with the provisions of the Islamic Shariah, Islam being the official religion of the State.[70]

RESERVATIONS AND THE ATTEMPTS TO FIND CONSENSUS ON THE PROVISIONS OF THE CONVENTION

During the course of this chapter we have come across a number of reservations that have been made by State parties to the various provisions. While international law does permit reservations and derogations to be made in certain circumstances, a question arises regarding the extent to which States can make such reservations without compromising their commitments to the Convention. The existing dissensions on women's rights are reflected vividly by the significant number of reservations. A complex though significant element in the entire debate surrounding this subject is the influence of socio-cultural and religious perspectives. While the impact of human rights law has been significant, many societies hold their distinct religious, cultural and societal ordinances in the highest esteem.

The prioritisation of international human rights norms faces the risk of being labelled as an attempt to impose western cultural imperialism. This view of it as imposition of cultural imperialism is evident from the State responses, and while such reaction can be discerned from many non-western States, the Islamic States have very strongly asserted the superiority of their religious and moral values. According to these States, Islam is not merely a religion, it is a complete code of life – a recipe for social and moral behaviour. Such an attitude prompted Bangladesh to enter a reservation noting that 'The Government of the People's Republic of Bangladesh does not consider as binding upon itself the provisions of articles 2, [...] and 16(1)(c) and [...] as they conflict with Sharia law based on Holy Quran and Sunna'. The reservation was withdrawn in 1997, although the spirit of the laws in Bangladesh very much represent the superiority of Sharia over any other law. The issue of compatibility becomes more complex, since there is neither a single unified view of the Sharia, nor are there any detailed official views on women's rights in Islam. Islamic States vary radically in their approaches towards the position of women in Muslim States. Thus the vision of the Talaban on the *Sharia* and women's rights in Afghanistan were very different from the position adopted by the governments of Turkey or Pakistan. Considering the position of women in a number of Islamic States, sceptics argue that religion has very often been

---

[70] See Reservations of the Government of the State of Kuwait to the Convention on the Elimination of All forms of Discrimination against Women (1979).

used as an instrument of domination and exploitation. This view appears to be substantiated when the breadth, plurality and accommodating nature of the *Sharia* is analysed.[71]

THE COMMITTEE ON THE ELIMINATION OF ALL FORMS OF DISCRIMINATION AGAINST WOMEN (CEDAW)[72]

Part V of the Convention establishes the Committee on the Elimination of Discrimination Against Women (CEDAW), a body of twenty-three experts. CEDAW is elected by State parties with individual members to serve in their personal capacity,[73] for four-year terms. CEDAW members are required to be 'of high moral standing and competence in the field covered by the Convention'.[74] The CEDAW Committee secretariat, unlike other treaty-based Committees, is not provided by the office of the High Commissioner of Human Rights. Instead the Division of Women provides technical and substantive support to both the Committee and CSW.[75] Like the Human Rights Committee and the Economic, Social and Cultural Rights Committee, the expenses of CEDAW are borne out of the UN budget. Prior to 1994 CEDAW met in New York and Vienna, although the New York sessions were more highly publicised. Since its thirteenth session in 1994, the Committee's sessions have always been held in New York.

According to Article 20, CEDAW is required to meet for a two-week session every year. However the rapid expansion of State membership meant that more time was needed to consider State reports. As of 1990, a pre-sessional working group has been used to review periodic reports. In the light of the unexpected workload, since 1990 the General Assembly has also allowed the Committee to meet on an exceptional basis for an extra one week per year. An amendment to Article 20 to enhance the meeting period was introduced in 1995. However the operation of such an amendment is dependant on a two-thirds majority of the States accepting this and it has not yet come into force.

---

[71] See the consideration on Universalism and Regionalism in the Introductory Chapter. See also S. Sardar Ali, *Gender and Human Rights in Islam and International Law: Equal Before Allah, Unequal Before Man?* (Boston: Kluwer Law International, 2000); J. Rehman, 'Accommodating Religious Identities in an Islamic State: International Law, Freedom of Religion and the Rights of Religious Minorities' 7 *IJMGR* (2000) 139.

[72] See Byrnes, above n. 8; R. Jackson, 'The Committee on the Elimination of Discrimination against Women' in P. Alston (ed.), *The United Nations and Human Rights: A Critical Appraisal* (Oxford: Clarendon Press) 1992, pp. 444–472; M.R. Busetlo, 'The Committee on the Elimination of Discrimination against Women at the Crossroads' in P. Alston and J. Crawford (eds), *The Future of UN Human Rights Treaty Monitoring* (Cambridge: Cambridge University Press) 2000, pp. 79–111. A.G. Martínez, 'Human Rights of Women' 5 *Washington University Journal of Law and Policy* (2001) 157.

[73] Article 17.

[74] Article 17(1).

[75] M.R. Busetlo, 'The Committee on the Elimination of Discrimination against Women at the Crossroads' in P. Alston and J. Crawford (eds), above n. 72, at pp. 81–82.

In the meanwhile the General Assembly has approved the holding of two, three-week sessions every year (pending the entry into force of the amendment) each preceded by a one week pre-sessional working group session, again pending entry into force of the amendment.[76] The sessional meetings of the Committee are held in January and June of each year.

CEDAW's overall structure and its composition resembles the Human Rights Committee, though the membership of the Committee is predominantly female. The Committee also has the largest membership of any of the United Nations treaties. The members of CEDAW come from a range of professions; they are nominated by States but serve in their personal capacity and not as government representatives. Until recently CEDAW has not had a judicial or quasi-judicial function. Its sole task has been to review the State reports; this will change when the Optional Protocol comes into operation.

The Committee's main task has been one of implementing the Convention, an exercise thus far conducted within the framework of reporting procedures.[77] An Optional Protocol to the Convention authorising communications from individuals or groups of individuals was adopted by the General Assembly on 6 October 1999.[78] As at 31 March 2002, there were thirty parties to the Protocol. The Protocol was opened for signature on 10 December 1999 and required 10 ratifications to come into operation. It came into force on 22 December 2000. In its twenty-fourth session (January–February 2001), the Committee adopted the rules of procedure for the Optional Protocol. The Protocol provides for an individual complaints procedure and also provides for a procedure under which the Committee can inquire into serious and systematic violations of the Convention. The overall pattern and the admissibility procedure are based on the first Optional Protocol of the ICCPR. A number of interesting variations and distinctions exist and should be noted. First, the Optional Protocol to the Women's Convention allows 'individuals or groups of individuals' to submit complaints to CEDAW. This represents a more generous rule when compared to the first Optional Protocol to the ICCPR which only allows 'individuals' to submit a Communication. In practice, however, as we have already considered, the Human Rights Committee using the existing rules of procedure has adopted a more flexible and realistic approach in relation to the submission of Communications.[79] Secondly, Article 8 establishes an inquiry procedure that allows the Committee to initiate a confidential investigation by

---

[76] GA Res 51/66.

[77] Article 29 provides that two or more States parties can refer a dispute arising from the interpretation and implementation of the Convention to arbitration and if the dispute is not settled, it can be referred to the ICJ. This procedure has thus far not been used.

[78] GA Res. 55/38.

[79] See above Chapter 4.

one or more of its members where it has received reliable information of grave or systematic violations by a State Party of rights established in the Convention. Where warranted and with the consent of the State Party, the Committee may visit the territory of the State Party. Any findings, comments or recommendations will be transmitted to the State Party concerned, to which it may respond within six months. There are no parallel provisions in the first Optional Protocol to the ICCPR. This procedure draws upon a similar procedure in the Convention against Torture.[80] Finally, no allowance is made within the Optional Protocol to the Women's Convention for reservations; a reaction to the difficulties that have arisen under the ICCPR with Trinidad and Tobago attempting to withdraw from their obligations.[81] In the twenty-fourth session the Committee also decided to set-up a working group to monitor the progress of the protocol. The meetings of this working group take place at the end of each session, the most recent meeting of the group being held during 23–28 July, 2001.

In pursuance of Article 18 of the Convention State parties undertake to submit reports of legislative, judicial, administrative and other measures adopted to give effect to the provisions of the Convention within one year as an initial report, and every four years thereafter. Article 21 provides for the reporting procedures. CEDAW reports annually to the General Assembly through ECOSOC. Its reports may be transmitted by the Secretary-General to the Commission on the Status of Women for information. Individuals and NGOs are not authorised to address the Committee directly; on the other hand, specialised agencies can be present at the time when reports are being submitted and considered by the Committee.

The present reporting procedure as provided in the Convention, in common with other reporting procedures, remains less than satisfactory. Reports are often delayed, outdated and inadequate with most State parties emphasising the legislative mechanisms relating to gender equality. We have already noted CEDAW's concern at the lack of information or data on issues related to women's rights. There is also the general complaint of reports being ineffective in their exposition of steps undertaken to eliminate de facto discrimination against women. To deal with the subject of outdated reports, in its sixteenth session in 1997, the Committee took a formal decision to encourage the submission of up to two consolidated reports.[82] In order to assist State parties in reporting, CEDAW has adopted guidelines for the preparation of initial and subsequent reports.[83] In the

---

[80] See below Chapter 15.
[81] See above Chapter 4.
[82] Report of CEDAW, GAOR 52nd Session, Supp. No. 38 (A/52/38/Rev.1), Part 1, Decision 16 (III).
[83] UN Doc. CEDAW/2/7/Rev. 3 (26 July 1996).

initial reports States need to pay particular regard to the criteria set out in paragraphs 4 and 5, as follows:

4. Part II should provide specific information in relation to each provision of the Convention, in particular:

    (a) The constitutional, legislative and administrative provisions or other measures in force;

    (b) The developments that have taken place and the programmes and institutions that have been established since the entry into force of the Convention;

    (c) Any other information on progress made in the fulfilment of each right;

    (d) The de facto position as distinct from the *de jure* position;

    (e) Any restrictions or limitations, even of a temporary nature, imposed by law, practice or tradition, or in any other manner on the enjoyment of each right;

    (f) The situation of non-governmental organizations and other women's associations and their participation in the elaboration and implementation of plans and programmes of the public authorities.

5. It is recommended that the reports not be confined to mere lists of legal instruments adopted in the country concerned in recent years, but should also include information indicating how those legal instruments are reflected in the actual economic, political and social realities and general conditions existing in the country. As far as possible, States parties should make efforts to provide all data disaggregated by sex in all areas covered by the Convention and the general recommendations of the Committee.

For the preparation of second and subsequent reports, the States need particularly to consider the following:

12. As a general rule States parties in their second and subsequent periodic reports should focus on the period between the consideration of their latest report up to the date of preparation of their last one.

13. In their periodic reports States parties should have regard to the previous report and to the proceedings of the Committee in regard to that report, and should include, *inter alia*, the following:

    (a) Legal and other measures adopted since the previous report to implement the Convention;

    (b) Actual progress made to promote and ensure the elimination of discrimination against women;

    (c) Any significant changes in the status and equality of women since the previous report;

    (d) Any remaining obstacle to the participation of women on an equal basis with men in the political, social, economic and cultural life of their country;

(e) Matters raised by the Committee which could not be dealt with at the time when the previous report was considered;

(f) Information on measures taken to implement the Beijing Declaration and Platform for Action.

General recommendations

In addition to considering State reports CEDAW may also make general recommendations and suggestions which are included in the report. CEDAW has made a number of General Recommendations on various significant though controversial issues. General recommendations are similar to the General Comments issued by the Human Rights Committee or those provided by the Committee on ICESCR. They are aimed at States parties and usually consist of the Committee's view of the obligations assumed under the Convention. General Recommendations have been used by CEDAW to expand into areas not covered by the Convention, for example, violence against women and female circumcision. Those General Recommendations adopted during the Committee's first decade of existence were short. They were frequently limited to dealing with issues such as the content of reports and reservations to the Convention and resources.

Since its tenth session the Committee has decided to adopt the practice of issuing General Recommendations on specific provisions of the Convention and on the relationship between the Convention Articles. This is what has been described by CEDAW as 'cross-cutting' themes. From this time onwards, CEDAW has issued a number of comprehensive and detailed General Recommendations offering States parties guidance on the application of the Convention in specific situations. Thus, for example, in its General Recommendation No. 5 (1988) the Committee called upon State parties to make greater use of 'temporary special measures such as positive action, preferential treatment or quota system to advance women's integration in to education, the economy, politics and employment'.[84] Its General Recommendation No. 14 (1990) called for the eradication of female circumcision,[85] General Recommendation No. 19 (1992) considered the issue of violence against women,[86]. General Recommendation No. 23 (1997) related to women in public life[87] and General Recommendation No. 24 (1999) was concerned with women and health.[88] During 2001, the Committee was working on formulating its Recommendation No. 25 which will address

---

[84] General Recommendation No. 5 (Seventh Session, 1988).
[85] General Recommendation No. 14 (Ninth Session, 1990).
[86] General Recommendation No. 19 (Eleventh Session, 1992)
[87] General Recommendation No. 23 (Sixteenth Session, 1997).
[88] General Recommendation No. 24 (Twentieth Session, 1999).

Article 4(1) of Convention on temporary special measures aimed at accelerating de facto equality between men and women. In addition to General Recommendations, the Committee has also adopted a number of Suggestions. Suggestions, as opposed to General Recommendation are usually aimed at United Nations entities. CEDAW has thus far adopted twenty-four general recommendations.

Procedure

At the end of each session, a decision is made on the States whose reports will be considered at the next session. The listing is published in the Committee report and available from the UN Secretariat. States are made aware of this listing and have until 1 September to withdraw from being considered should they wish to do so. Initial reports do not require the formation of a working group to scrutinise the contents of the reports. Subsequent reports are considered by a working group of CEDAW.[89] Pre-sessional working groups consist of four members, each drawn from a different regional group.

The purpose of the working group is to prepare a list of questions to be put before the State representative during the consideration of the report by CEDAW. In its scrutiny CEDAW is assisted by information from the Secretariat and non-governmental organisations. NGO documentation is made available to members of the working group. Initial reports are considered by up to three meetings. In relation to periodic reports, as already reviewed by a pre-sessional group and with questions already posed, the consideration is quicker (shorter period of up to one and a half meetings).

In common with other procedures, the Committee invites a representative from the State party to introduce the report prior to its consideration. After the presentation of reports, CEDAW members may ask additional questions, seek additional information or clarify certain points. Following the consideration of the report by CEDAW, it then proceeds to its 'Concluding Comments'. These typically include CEDAW's view of the report; an introduction to the comments; positive aspects in the report; factors and difficulties in the implementation of the Convention; and principal areas of concern and recommendations. The Concluding Comments are included in the annual report to ECOSOC, the General Assembly and the Commission on the Status of Women. From 1990, the Committee decided that it would review up to eight initial reports. Following the trend established by other treaty-based bodies, CEDAW has now rescheduled its working group sessions to take place at the end of each session. The intention for such rescheduling is that it will

---

[89] M. O'Flaherty, *Human Rights and the UN: Practice before the Treaty Bodies* (London: Sweet and Maxwell) 1996, p. 196.

allow the Committee to address issues properly and give States adequate time to respond.

From the seventeenth session (July 1997) the Committee decided that, while all members of the Committee could submit questions to be addressed by the relevant State, a group of three members – including the Country Rapporteur – would be assigned the primary responsibility for the preparation of questions with regard to each report, to assist the pre-sessional working group's consideration. The State party responds to those questions at a meeting several days later in the same session. Committee members may ask follow-up questions.

In common with other reporting procedures, State reports often characterise unsatisfactory coverage of issues. In many cases the reports are prepared by governmental officials who do not fully comprehend the provisions of the Convention. In these circumstances credit needs to be given to CEDAW for going beyond the strict parameters of its mandate. It has on a number of instances raised issues and concerns (for example in relation to abortion on the reports from the Republic of Ireland) upon matters not strictly covered by the Convention.

It is also the case that State reports vary in quality, volume and/or substance. Often there is little information on the implementation of the Convention with reports being excessively self-congratulatory and avoiding controversial areas. An uncompromising and unsympathetic attitude of governmental officials towards NGOs often results in little NGO involvement at crucial stages in compiling the report. To an extent, CEDAW can itself be criticised for having made insufficient use of information from other bodies. Within the Convention, there are no explicit provisions relating to the participation of NGOs. Article 22 of the Convention has thus far invoked limited interest from specialised agencies.

Recent initiatives

In light of the significant violations of women's rights, the international community has undertaken a number of initiatives. Women's rights as a subject has been considered in various contexts and by a number of recent international instruments. We have already considered the adoption of the Optional Protocol to the Convention on the Elimination of All Forms of Discrimination against Women. The Option Protocol forms part of a sustained campaign to ensure equality of treatment for women in all spheres of life, and also to provide impetus for addressing their needs. These campaigns include the Nairobi Forward-looking Strategies for the Advancement of Women (1985)[90] the

---

[90] See Report of the World Conference to Review and Appraise the Achievements of the United Nations Decade for Women: Equality, Development and Peace, Nairobi, 15–26 July 1985 (United Nations publication, Sales No. E.85.IV.10), chap. I, sect. A.

Vienna Declaration and Programme of Action adopted by the World Conference on Human Rights (1993),[91] the fourth World Conference on Women held in Beijing in September 1995.[92] The objectives of the Beijing Conference included, *inter alia*, reviewing the progress made since the Nairobi Conference and the adoption of a 'Platform for Action'. This 'Platform for Action' is intended to concentrate on key obstacles which are preventing the advancement of women. The document suggests and proposes to various agencies, including governments, NGOs, the private sector and individuals, strategies for the removal of barriers in the path of equality and the further progression of women's rights.

Further developments have taken place since the Beijing Conference. During its fifty-fifth session, the General Assembly adopted a resolution which is a follow-up to the Beijing Conference and was intended to review the progress made in the five years since the Conference.[93] The General Assembly also invited ECOSOC to continue to promote a coordinated follow-up pro-gramme for the implementation of the outcomes of the major UN Conferences and to ensure gender mainstreaming as an integral part of the activities of its mandate. At the same time there was a reaffirmation of the need to mobilise resources at all levels for the promotion of an active policy of adopting a United Nations gender perspective.

VIOLENCE AGAINST WOMEN

The Vienna Declaration focuses upon the rights of women as human rights. The Declaration notes:

> the human rights of women and of the girl child are an inalienable, integral and indivisible part of universal human rights. The full and equal participa-tion of women in political, civil, economic, social and cultural life, at the national, regional and international levels, and the eradication of all forms of discrimination on grounds of sex are priority objectives of the international community[94]

One of the recommendations made by the Vienna Declaration was to call upon 'the General Assembly to adopt the draft declaration on violence against women and [to urge] States to combat violence against women in accordance

---

[91] World Conference on Human Rights: The Vienna Declaration and Programme of Action, June 1993 (United Nations Department of Public Information, August 1993)

[92] A/CONF.177/20, 1995; 35 I.L.M. (1996) 401. The Beijing Conference as noted above was the fourth world conference on women. Earlier conferences had been held in Mexico City (1975), Copenhagen (1980) and Nairobi (1985) which adopted the Forward-looking Strategies for the Advancement of Women.

[93] GA./Res/55/71.

[94] Ibid. Section I.18, p. 34.

with its provisions'.[95] Much domestic violence goes on behind closed doors; the information that is leaked out to international monitoring bodies presents a horrific and regrettable picture. Reports of forms of domestic violence represent a source of serious concern. A serious criticism of the Women's Convention has been the absence of specific provisions condemning violence against women, an omission which is unacceptable in the light of the everyday instances of violence against women in every region of the world.[96] This criticism is visible in the analyses of such treaty-based bodies as the Human Rights Committee and the Committee against Torture.[97]

In order to overcome these lacunae, the United Nations General Assembly adopted a Declaration on the Elimination of Violence Against Women.[98] The Declaration provides an expansive definition of the term 'violence against women', taking it to mean:

> any act of gender-based violence that results in, or is likely to result in, physical, sexual or psychological harm or suffering to women, including threats of such acts, coercion or arbitrary deprivation of liberty, whether occurring in public or in private life.

Article 2, in elaboration upon the meaning of violence, provides examples such as physical, sexual and psychological violence occurring in the family, including battering, sexual abuse of female children in the household, dowry-related violence, marital rape, female genital mutilation and other traditional practices harmful to women, non-spousal violence and violence related to exploitation,[99] physical, sexual and psychological violence occurring within the general community, including rape, sexual abuse, sexual harassment and intimidation at work, in educational institutions and elsewhere, trafficking in women and forced prostitution,[100] and physical, sexual and psychological violence perpetrated or condoned by the State, wherever it occurs.[101]

The Declaration calls upon all States to condemn violence against women and not to invoke any custom, tradition or religious consideration to justify the continuation of any such violence.[102] This provision is particularly aimed

---

[95] Ibid. Section II.38, p. 54.

[96] Subedi, above n. 9, at p. 595; this point has been established by CEDAW in its consideration of State reports.

[97] See Human Rights Committee, Sixty-fourth session, *Concluding observations of the Human Rights Committee: Libyan Arab Jamahiriya.* 06/11/98. CCPR/C/79/Add.101. (Concluding Observations/Comments), para 17. On the Committee against Torture See A. Byrnes, 'The Committee against Torture' in P. Alston (ed.), above n. 72, 509–546 at p. 519; see below Chapter 15.

[98] GA Res. 48/104 of 20 December 1993.

[99] Article 2(a).

[100] Ibid. 2(b).

[101] Ibid. 2(c).

[102] Ibid. Article 4.

at those societies which continue to justify such policies as female circumcision, sati or dowry as part of divine ordinance or an integral part of their culture and traditions. In addition, the Declaration adopts a much wider approach in condemning psychological violence and marital rape. Marital rape remains a problematic family law issue in many States, including the United Kingdom.[103]

The UN Declaration is a General Assembly Resolution and is not *per se* a legally binding instrument.[104] However, as noted in an earlier chapter, General Assembly Resolutions present evidence of State practice which, alongside the requisite *opinio juris*, can lead to the establishment of customary international law. The fact that the Resolution was adopted without a vote, but by consensus among States has added to its weight and authority; subsequent developments, particularly since the Beijing Conference, may lead the provisions in the Declaration to represent customary law.

Whatever may be the precise legal position of the provisions contained in the Declaration, it is already obvious that the Resolution has had considerable impact in developing the law relating to women's rights and has provided substantial ammunition to CEDAW to scrutinise practices which contravene the provisions of the Declaration. CEDAW in its recent survey of reports has shown concern at the lack of available information on the incidence and types of violence against women, particularly at home.[105] It has expressed grave concern at the incidence of so-called 'honour killings',[106] acid throwing, stoning and dowry death,[107] dowry, sati and the *devadasi* system.[108] In a number of instances it has lamented the inability of governments to take effective action to enforce laws, or to provide immediate relief to women who are victims of such violence. The unfortunate position of women suffering from violence and the threat of violence, has led other courts and tribunals to extend human rights protection. There is, therefore, an increased willingness to recognise gender-based persecution as a ground for granting asylum. In a recent case before the House of Lords, their Lordships held that women suffering from domestic violence could be recognised as a 'particular social group' and thereby be able to rely upon the protection afforded under the Geneva

---

[103] See *R v. R (A Husband)* (CA (Crim. Div)) Court of Appeal (Criminal Division), 14 March 1991; Concern has been expressed at the subject of marital rape. See e.g. Concluding Observations/Comments by the Human Rights Committee for Uzbekistan. 26/04/2001 CCPR/CO/71/UZB, para. 19; see also Concluding Comments by CEDAW on the report by Egypt para 344, see Egypt's 3rd and Combined 4th and 5th periodic report, CEDAW/CIEGY/3 and CEDAW/C/EGY at its 492nd and 493rd meetings (4–19 January, 2001).

[104] On the value of General Assembly Resolutions see above Chapter 2.

[105] Iraq para 189.

[106] Ibid. para 193.

[107] Bangladesh, above n. 43, para 436.

[108] India, above n. 41, para 68.

Convention Relating to the Status of Refugees 1951 – and allowed their appeal.[109]

Given the widespread nature and growing concern over violence against women, the United Nations Human Rights Commission in 1994 appointed a Special Rapporteur on Violence against Women, for a period of three years. The mandate of the Special Rapporteur was extended in 1997 for a further term of three years. During her term in office the Special Rapporteur has made a number of visits to countries and produced several valuable reports. Violence against women was a subject that was highlighted as a particular source of concern in the Beijing Conference[110] and the follow-up to the Conference.[111]

CONCLUSIONS

The Convention on the Elimination of All Forms of Discrimination against Women has been described as the international bill of rights for women. Its many positive aspects include coverage of a fairly comprehensive range of rights and a useful State reporting mechanism which has more recently been supplemented by an individual complaints procedure. Despite these positive features the Convention still suffers from significant substantive and procedural weaknesses. The language of the Convention 'is considerably closer to that of a political declaration than that of an international treaty'.[112] The Convention fails to address some of the more fundamental issues such as violence against women: it does not makes any references to

---

[109] See Article 1A(2) Geneva Convention Relating to the Status of Refugees 1951. *Islam (A.P.)* v. *Secretary of State for the Home Department Regina* v. *Immigration Appeal Tribunal and Another Ex Parte Shah (A.P.) (Conjoined Appeals)* http://www.parliament.the-stationery-office.co.uk/pa/ld199899/ldjudgmt/jd990325/islam, 25 March 1999 (Internet edition: 27 October 2001). See also Wallace, above n. 8, at p. 702.

[110] 'Violence against women both violates and impairs or nullifies the enjoyment by women of human rights and fundamental freedoms. Taking into account the Declaration on the Elimination of Violence against Women and the work of Special Rapporteurs, gender-based violence, such as battering and other domestic violence, sexual abuse, sexual slavery and exploitation, and international trafficking in women and children, forced prostitution and sexual harassment, as well as violence against women, resulting from cultural prejudice, racism and racial discrimination, xenophobia, pornography, ethnic cleansing, armed conflict, foreign occupation, religious and anti-religious extremism and terrorism are incompatible with the dignity and the worth of the human person and must be combated and eliminated. Any harmful aspect of certain traditional, customary or modern practices that violates the rights of women should be prohibited and eliminated. Governments should take urgent action to combat and eliminate all forms of violence against women in private and public life, whether perpetrated or tolerated by the State or private persons' see above n. 92, para 224.

[111] See FWCW 'Platform for Action: Violence against women' Strategic objective D.1–D.3.

[112] L. Reanda, 'The Commission on the Status of Women' in P. Alston (ed.), above n. 72, 265–303 at p. 287.

sexual orientation or lesbian women, and apart from the reference in Article 12 to health, there is no particular recognition of reproductive rights. While some remedial attempts have been made by the United Nations, the absence of specific provisions – for example, prohibiting violence, and recognising sexual orientation and reproductive rights – within the treaty represents a significant omission.

It is also the case that the Convention was a product of years of debate and argumentation. Needless to say that the instrument that finally emerged was a product of political compromises, many of them fundamental to the entire debate relating to women's human rights.[113] A majority of the States would have been unwilling to proceed towards completion of the instrument if it contravened their fundamental precepts.

One lingering reminder of this conciliatory stance is the reservations clause, as provided in the Convention.[114] Out of all the human rights treaties, the Women's Convention has attracted the most number of reservations – some of them so sweeping and overriding in nature, that the issue of good faith and the principle of the integrity of the instrument inevitably comes into question.[115] The factors that have led States to place reservations include religious and cultural relativism and religious intolerance.[116] CEDAW has consistently encouraged States to review and withdraw their reservations. There have been disputes from a number of Islamic States on compatibility of provisions. Unlike the Race Convention, which provides that reservations are to be considered incompatible if at least two-thirds of the State parties object to it, the Women's Convention provides no similar provisions as to whether a reservation is valid except the possibility of reference to the International Court of Justice under Article 29. States which are unhappy with a reservation can enter an objection to the reservation and then raise the matter at meetings of State parties or other bodies such as ECOSOC or the General Assembly. The realisation of the purposes and principles set forth in the Convention through a system of periodic reporting has not been satisfactory. While the adoption of the Optional Protocol to the Convention (which would allow individuals to bring a complaint before CEDAW) is a very

---

[113] On definitional aspects see UN Doc E/CN. 6/589–591 (1974); UN Doc E/CN.6/AC.1/L.4. On Reservations see 54 UNESCOR Supp. (No. 5).

[114] B. Clark, 'The Vienna Convention Reservations Regime and the Convention on Discrimination against Women' 85 *AJIL* (1991) 281. Also see R.J. Cook, 'Reservations to the Convention on the Elimination of All forms of Discrimination against Women' 30 *Va.JIL* (1990) 643.

[115] S. Sardar-Ali and S. Mullally, 'Women's Rights and Human Rights in Muslim Countries: A Case Study' in H. Hinds, A. Phoenix and J. Stacey (eds), *Working Out: New Directions for Women's Studies* (London, Falmer Press) 1992, 113–123 at p. 118; Schabas regards the Women's Convention as 'the worst case'. See also W.A. Schabas, 'Reservations to the Convention on the Rights of the Child' 18 *HRQ* (1996) 472 at p. 474.

[116] H. Steiner and P. Alston (eds), above n. 11, at p. 441.

commendable undertaking, it is as yet too early to predict the extent to which this procedure will be relied upon.

There are other defects and weaknesses as well. In comparison to other treaty-based bodies, CEDAW has remained at a disadvantage when acquiring adequate information on violations of the rights set forth in the Convention. There is a need for greater formal and informal participation by NGOs and specialised agencies such as the International Labour Organisation.[117] The overall position of CEDAW (again when compared with other treaty-based bodies) is relatively weak. The Committee has had to adopt a more mundane and conciliatory stance, the reasons for which include a weaker threshold of implementing authority, limited resources in terms of time and finances, and often evident divisions among CEDAW members themselves.

---

[117] See O'Flaherty, above n. 89, at pp. 128–129.

14

RIGHTS OF THE CHILD[1]

INTRODUCTION

Violation of the rights of children represent a common occurrence in many parts of the world.[2] These violations take the form of torture, cruel, inhuman or degrading treatment, disappearances, excessive work and labour, prostitution, sexual abuse and slavery. Children also form a significant proportion of the global refugee or stateless population. Millions of children around the world are at serious risk of starvation and malnutrition; according to one estimate, malnutrition, starvation and disease leads to the deaths of 40,000 children every day.[3]

As a response to these violations efforts have been made to establish a regime of international protection of the rights of children. During the twentieth century the movement to protect children was given impetus by Save the

---

[1] See G. Van Bueren, *The International Law on the Rights of the Child* (Dordrecht: Martinus Nijhoff Publishers) 1995; M. Freeman and P. Veerman (eds), *Ideologies of Children's Rights* (Dordrecht: Martinus Nijhoff Publishers) 1992; D. McGoldrick, 'The United Nations Convention on the Rights of the Child' 5 *IJLF* (1991) 132; P. Alston, S. Parker and J. Seymour, *Children, Rights and the Law* (Oxford: Clarendon Press) 1992; D. Freestone (ed.), *Children and the Law: Essays in Honour of Professor H.K. Bevan* (Hull: Hull University Press) 1990.

[2] The Convention on the Rights of the Child confirming this point notes in its preamble that 'in all countries in the world, there are children living in exceptionally difficult conditions'. Preamble to the Convention on the Rights of the Child (1989). According to Freeman 'there are countries which today are systematically exterminating children as if they were vermin. Poverty, disease, exploitation are rife in every part of the globe'. M. Freeman, 'The Limits of Children's Rights' in Freeman and Veerman (eds), above n. 1, 29–46 at p. 31; W.S. Rogers and J. Roche, *Children's Welfare & Children's Rights: A Practical Guide to the Law* (London: Hodder & Stoughton) 1994.

[3] Van Bueren, above n. 1, at p. 293. G. Van Bueren, 'Combating Child Poverty–Human Rights Approaches' 21 *HRQ* (1999) 680.

Children International Union, an international NGO established shortly after the First World War.[4] In 1924, Save the Children International Union drafted a Declaration, which is more commonly known as the Declaration of Geneva or the Declaration of the Rights of the Child.[5] This Declaration was adopted by the Fifth Assembly of the League of Nations.[6] The Declaration provides for fundamental rights of children such as the right to normal development, the right to be fed, relief from distress and protection from exploitation, and proved to be the inspiration behind subsequent international child rights instruments.

Efforts to promote the rights of children continued after the Second World War. The United Nations Charter (1945)[7] though containing references to human rights does not refer to children's rights *per se*. The UDHR (1948) contains important provisions for children, although the emphasis is upon protection and non-discrimination, rather than granting specific, independent rights to a child as a person.[8] Article 25(2) of the Declaration provides that motherhood and childhood are entitled to special care and assistance. All children, whether born in or out of wedlock, shall enjoy the same social protection. Article 26 instructs compulsory and free education at elementary level. It also provides for parents to have a prior right to choose the kind of education that shall be given to their children.[9] The ICESCR (1966)[10] contains Articles regarding education and health, issues most intimately connected to children. The ICCPR also has several Articles which protect such valuable rights as the right to life, liberty and security of persons – rights that are applicable to all individuals including children.[11] The Covenant also addresses children's rights in Article 24, which provides that:

(1) Every child shall have, without any discrimination as to race, colour, sex, language, religion, national or social origin, property or birth, the right to such measures of protection as are required by his status as a minor, on the part of his family, society and the State.

(2) Every child shall be registered immediately after birth and shall have a name.

(3) Every child has the right to acquire a nationality.

---

[4] See C.P. Cohen, 'The Role of Non-Governmental Organizations in the Drafting of the Convention on the Rights of the Child' 12 *HRQ* (1990) 137. See Save the Children website: http://www.savethechildren.org/

[5] See C.P. Cohen, 'Natural Law and Legal Positivism' in M. Freeman and P. Veerman (eds), above n. 1, 53–70 at p. 60.

[6] Record of the Fifth Assembly, Supplement No. 23 LONOJ, 1924.

[7] UNTS XVI; UKTS 67 (1946); Cmnd. 7015; See above Chapter 2.

[8] Adopted 10 December 1948, GA Res. 217, U.N. Doc. A/810, 71; see above Chapter 3.

[9] Article 26(3) UDHR.

[10] Adopted at New York, 16 December 1966. Entered into force 3 January 1976. GA Res. 2200A (XXI) UN Doc. A/6316 (1966) 993 U.N.T.S. 3 (1967), 6 I.L.M. (1967) 360.

[11] Adopted at New York, 16 December 1966. Entered into force 23 March 1976. GA Res. 2200A (XXI) UN Doc. A/6316 (1966) 999 U.N.T.S. 171, 6 I.L.M. (1967) 368.

The Human Rights Committee, which implements the ICCPR, has also elaborated on the provisions of Article 24 through its consideration of State reports and its general comments on the Article.

INTERNATIONAL INSTRUMENTS ON THE RIGHTS OF THE CHILD

As far as children's rights as a distinct category of human rights law is concerned, the real impetus was provided with the adoption of the United Nations General Assembly Declaration on the Rights of the Child in 1959.[12] The Declaration, which consists of ten substantive principles and a preamble, enumerates the most fundamental rights of the child in international law. The principal aim is to provide for a range of rights including the right to a name and nationality, housing, recreation and medical services. The Declaration considers the position of physically, mentally and socially handicapped children and children without a family. It proved instrumental in developing concrete international standards and in particular the drafting of the Convention on the Rights of the Child. The year 1979 was designated by the United Nations General Assembly as the Year of the Child.[13] During 1979, the UN General Assembly authorised the Commission on Human Rights to draft a Convention focusing on the Rights of the Child. A working-group established by the Commission started work on drafting of the Convention, a task that culminated in the adoption of the Convention on the Rights of the Child in 1989.[14]

The Convention came into force in September 1990. It is the most valuable treaty in the armoury of human rights law with which to protect and defend the rights of children the world over. Notwithstanding the fact that the Convention is more comprehensive than any other human rights treaty, it has attracted the greatest number of ratifications.[15] The rights provided in the Convention have been extended by the Optional Protocol to the Rights of the Child on the Involvement of Children in Armed Conflicts[16] and the Optional Protocol to the Convention on the Rights of the Child on the Sale of Children, Child Prostitution and Child Pornography.[17] Children's rights have been

---

[12] Unlike the UDHR, this General Assembly Resolution was adopted without any abstentions; GA Res. 1386, XIV, November 1959.

[13] GA Res. 31/169.

[14] Adopted at New York, 20 November 1989. Entered into force 2 September 1990. UN GA Res. 44/25 Annex (XLIV), 44 UN GAOR Supp. (No. 49) 167, UN Doc. A/44/49 (1989) at 166; 1577 U.N.T.S. 3. 28 I.L.M (1989) 1448.

[15] There are currently 191 States parties to the Convention. All States apart from the USA and Somalia have ratified the convention. See Appendix II below.

[16] Adopted by the General Assembly 25 May 2000. GA Res. 263, UN GAOR, 54 Sess., Supp. 49; UN Doc. A/Res/54/263.

[17] Adopted by the General Assembly 25 May 2000. GA Res. 263, UN GAOR, 54 Sess., Supp. 49; UN Doc. A/Res/54/263.

expressly incorporated at the regional level through the European Convention for the Exercise of Children's Rights (1996) and the African Charter on the Rights and Welfare of the Child (1990).[18]

Children's rights have also been integrated into the wider human rights debate. We have already noted a developing human rights jurisprudence emergent from international bodies such as the European Court of Human Rights, and the Human Rights Committee.[19] The subject is increasingly being addressed by various international and regional bodies. The new international criminal court is authorised to consider specific aspects of child rights as it qualifies the conscription of children under 15 years of age as a crime.[20] International economic agencies and intergovernmental bodies such as GATT/WTO are increasingly reacting to sensitive issues of child exploitation and child labour.[21] The focus of this chapter is upon the Convention on the Rights of the Child, however, brief consideration is given to the jurisprudence emerging from regional or national instruments.

THE CONVENTION ON THE RIGHTS OF THE CHILD[22]

The basic thrust of the Convention is that the Child has independent rights and the primary focus of the Convention is to operate in 'the best interests of the Child'.[23] According to Professor Van Bueren the Convention is essentially about what she terms as the 'four Ps'. These are:

> the participation of children in decisions affecting their own destiny; the protection of the children against discrimination and all forms of neglect and exploitation; the prevention of harm to children; and the provisions of assistance for basic needs'.[24]

There are many positive features of the Convention. The Substantive Articles (Articles 1–41) are meant to cover all kinds of civil, political, economic, social and cultural rights. This is a detailed and comprehensive set of rights. The Convention not only provides a series of new rights for children, but also reiterates the fundamental rights which are applicable to everyone. It covers civil and political rights as well as social, economic and cultural rights.

---

[18] Adopted July 1990. Entered into force 29 October 1999. OAU Doc.CAB/LEGTSG/REV.1.

[19] See above Chapters 3 and 5.

[20] In its definition of 'war crimes' the Statute of the Court includes the offence of 'Conscripting or enlisting children under the age of fifteen years into armed forces or groups or using them to participate actively in hostilities' Statute of the International Criminal Court (1998) Article 8 (e)(vii).

[21] See D.E. Ehrenberg, 'The Labor Link: Applying the International Trading System to Enforce Violations of Forced and Child Labour' 20 *YJIL* (1995) 361.

[22] Adopted and opened for signature, ratification and accession by General Assembly Resolution 44/25 of 20 November 1989 (entry into force 2 September 1990, in accordance with Article 49).

[23] See Article 3(1).

[24] Van Bueren, above n. 1, at p. 15.

There is a detailed coverage of laws and regulations that affect children during armed conflicts. Rights, which are of a general character and have been applied in other human rights treaties, include the right to life, freedom of expression, freedom of religion, respect for privacy and the right to education. The Convention also establishes a regime of innovative rights. According to Cohen 'of the thirty-eight Articles ... which are devoted to substantive rights, at least ten of these have never been recognised for children in any other international instrument'.[25] The innovative rights, which shall be considered in due course, include those contained in Articles 8, 10, 12–16, 25, 37 and 40.

The Convention also provides children with fundamental protection such as the right to be shielded from harmful acts or practices, to be protected from commercial or sexual exploitation, physical or mental abuse, or engagement in warfare. The Convention allows for the participation of the child in various matters concerning his or her welfare, for example the right to be heard regarding decisions to be made affecting one's own life. It is fairly strong as regards provisional as well as protectional aspects. Within the Convention, the wishes of children are given much more prominence. Notwithstanding the many positive aspects in the Convention, there are also difficulties and tensions inherent in the text. The Convention represents tensions between the rights of parents, guardians and even the State *vis-à-vis* those of the child. The language of several articles is weak and vague. Furthermore, as this chapter explores, there are significant limitations in the machinery designed to implement the Convention.

ANALYSING THE SUBSTANTIVE PROVISIONS

The Convention can be broken down into three main parts: a preamble, the substantive articles (Articles 1–41) and measures of implementation (Articles 42–45). The preamble of the Convention spells out the principles and their interrelationship with other international human rights provisions. It makes reference to the human rights provisions of the United Nations Charter, to the UDHR and to the International Covenants on Human Rights. There are also references to the principles derived from the Declaration of the Rights of the Child of 1924 and to the Declaration of the Rights of the Children (1959).[26]

Definitional issues and the obligations of States parties to non-discrimination

The Convention accords the child with a definition. According to Article 1, for the purposes of the Convention a child is 'every human being below the

---

[25] See C.P. Cohen, 'Natural Law and Legal Positivism' in M. Freeman and P. Veerman (eds), above n. 1, 53–70 at p. 61.
[26] See the preamble to the Convention.

age of eighteen years unless, under the law applicable to the child, majority is attained earlier'. The provision represents a compromise since States parties differ in their views on the age of majority. At the same time the phrase 'unless, under the law applicable to the child, majority is attained earlier' puts the helpfulness of the article in doubt. According to McGoldrick:

> Article 1 clearly permits the national law of a State to provide that majority is attained at an age earlier than eighteen. Although that individual is then entitled to all the human rights of an adult, the special protection applicable to children no longer covers them. A minimum age limit for the declaration of majority by national laws should have been included.[27]

Article 1 uses the term 'human being' and the most common deduction appears to be that it is applicable to a child who is born; a foetus thus cannot be claimed to have rights under the Convention. At the same time, the Convention specifically incorporates in its preamble, the terminology from the United Nations Declaration (1959) which applies 'special safeguards and care, including appropriate legal protection before as well as after birth'.[28] The position, as we have noted already continues to remain ambiguous, and uncertainty exists in other regional and international human rights instruments.[29] Article 2(1) sets out the obligation of the States parties, which are to:

> respect and ensure the rights set forth in the Convention to each child within their jurisdiction without discrimination of any kind irrespective of the child's or his or her parents or legal guardian's race, colour, sex, language, religion, political or other opinion, national, ethnic or social origin, property, disability, birth or other status.

The reference to 'birth or other status' is aimed at according protection to children born out of wedlock. The Convention, in line with other human

---

[27] McGoldrick, above n. 1, at p. 133. Also see Human Rights Committee General Comment 17(35) adopted 5 April 1989, para 4.

[28] The strength of the preambular paragraph is however watered down by a statement in the *travaux préparatoires* which notes 'in adopting this preambular paragraph, the working group does not intend to prejudice the interpretation of Article 1 or any other provisions of the Convention by the States parties'. UN Doc E/CN. 4/1989/48, para 43. See P. Alston, 'The Unborn Child and Abortion under the Draft Convention on the Rights of the Child' 12 *HRQ* (1990) 156.

[29] Attempts to incorporate an article in the UDHR prohibiting abortion proved unsuccessful. See Å. Samnøy, 'The Origins of the Universal Declaration of Human Rights' in G. Alfredsson and A. Eide (eds), *The Universal Declaration of Human Rights: A Common Standard of Achievement* (The Hague: Kluwer Law International) 1999, 3–22 at p. 14. See Article 2 ECHR, Article 4(1) ACHR. In the context of inter-American human rights law see the *Baby Boy Case*, Case 2141 (USA), IACHR Annual Report 1980–81, 25; 2 *HRLJ* 110; for commentary on the case see D. Shelton, 'Abortion and the Right to Life in the Inter-American System: The Case of "Baby Boy"' 2 *HRLJ* (1981) *HRLJ* 309.

rights instruments[30] and case law emergent from treaties,[31] aims to eradicate all forms of discrimination against illegitimate children. The terms 'respect and ensure' impose positive obligations on the State. The usage of 'jurisdiction' as opposed to territory is also meaningful and, following Human Rights Committee jurisprudence, covers a wide range of activities which are not necessarily confined to the territorial boundaries of a State.[32] Article 2(2) goes on to provide that:

> States parties shall take all appropriate measures to ensure that the child is protected against all forms of discrimination or punishment on the basis of the status, activities, expressed opinions, or beliefs of the child's parents, legal guardians, or family members.

The Article is aimed at ensuring the norm of non-discrimination in so far as children are concerned. The Article relies upon conventional terms, although it is a more comprehensive expression of efforts to prohibit all forms of exclusions and discrimination. The terminology employed here is similar to the non-discriminatory provisions in other human rights treaties. It would appear that the use of the phrase 'birth' is meant to ensure that the child born through the process of artificial insemination also receives non-discriminatory treatment.[33]

Best interest of the child

As already noted, the Convention is built around the principle that all measures undertaken must take into account the best interest of the child. This point is clearly established by Article 3. According to Article 3(1):

> In all actions concerning children, whether undertaken by public or private social welfare institutions, courts of law, administrative authorities or legislative bodies, the best interests of the child shall be a primary consideration.

---

[30] See e.g. Article 25(2) Universal Declaration of Human Rights which requires treatment of all children 'whether born in or out of wedlock'; the ACHR also notes that the States 'shall recognise equal rights for children born out of wedlock and those born in wedlock'. For consideration of this Article see S. Davidson, 'The Civil and Political Rights Protected in the Inter-American Human Rights System' in D.J. Harris and S. Livingstone (eds), *The Inter-American System of Human Rights* (Oxford: Clarendon Press) 1998, 213–288 at p. 270. The ICCPR requires children not to be discriminated on grounds of birth and the ICESCR prohibits 'for reasons of parentage'. The European Social Charter (1961) accords rights 'irrespective of marital status and family relations'.

[31] See *Marckx* v. *Belgium*, Judgment of 13 June 1979, Series A, No. 31; *Johnston and others* v. *Ireland*, Judgment of 18 December 1986, Series A, No. 112; for discussion see J.S. Davidson, 'The European Convention on Human Rights and the "illegitimate" Child' in D. Freestone (ed.), above n. 1, at pp. 75–106.

[32] See jurisprudence of Human Rights Committee above Chapter 4.

[33] A. Lopatka, 'The Rights of the Child are Universal: The Perspective of the UN Convention on the Rights of the Child' in M. Freeman and P. Veerman (eds), above n. 1, 47–52 at p. 49.

The usage of the words 'a primary' instead of 'the primary' consideration allows for other factors to be taken into account.[34] In deciding what is in the best interest of the child, the wishes of the child are to be considered. Issues of cultural relativism do however enter the debate, making it difficult for international tribunals to formulate definitive judgments.[35] With regard to the application of the rights, the Convention, in line with the division produced by the International Covenants, distinguishes between civil and political rights of the child *vis-à-vis* economic, social and cultural rights; there is thus a difference between these two sets of rights of the child.[36] The civil and political rights obligations are of immediate application whereas in the case of economic, social and cultural rights, the State parties are to 'undertake such measures to the maximum extent of their available resources and, where needed, within the framework of international protection'.[37] The States in the reports have often relied on the lack of resources to justify their failure to meet the requirements of the Convention. This argument has, however, been criticised by the Committee on the Rights of the Child (the body in charge of supervising the implementation of the Convention) on numerous occasions.[38] According to Article 5:

> States Parties shall respect the responsibilities, rights and duties of parents or, where applicable, the members of the extended family or community as provided for by local custom, legal guardians or other persons legally responsible for the child, to provide, in a manner consistent with the evolving capacities of the child, appropriate direction and guidance in the exercise by the child of the rights recognised in the present Convention.

This is an important Article within the Convention. While accepting the realities of parental influences and rights and duties of the wider family, the Article is nevertheless reticent in dealing with situations where the interests, directions and guidance of parents are not 'appropriate' or 'consistent with the evolving capabilities of the child'. The 'evolving capabilities' themselves are not defined.

---

[34] Cf. The English Children's Act 1989, which makes the child's interests the paramount factor. In this comparison we see that the child's interests are not given as much weight in the Convention as under national law. This represent one significant criticism of the Convention.

[35] above Chapter 1.

[36] Cf. Van Bueren, above n. 3, at p. 692, where emphasising the interaction between civil and political rights she goes as far as to suggest that 'it is even arguable that the economic and social rights of children have become part of international customary law'.

[37] Article 4.

[38] See e.g. Consideration of Reports submitted by States Parties Under Article 44 of the Convention: Concluding Observations of the Committee on the Rights of the Child: Egypt, UN GAOR, Committee on the Rights of the Child 3rd Session UN Doc. CRC/C/15/Add.5 (1993); Jordan, UN GAOR, Committee on the Rights of the Child 6th Session UN Doc. CRC/C/15/Add.21 (1994).

Developmental rights of the child

The right to life (as noted throughout this book) is the most fundamental of all human rights.[39] In the case of children, the relevance of the right could not be overstated. Article 6 provides as follows:

1. States Parties recognize that every child has the inherent right to life.
2. States Parties shall ensure to the maximum extent possible the survival and development of the child.

The ambit of this right is very wide as it includes pre-natal and post-natal care, nourishment and proper development.[40] The right to life also includes freedom from malnutrition, starvation and disease. It is unfortunate that in some regions of the world, starvation has been adopted as a deliberate policy of extermination of certain individuals or groups.[41] In such situations children are the primary casualties. Article 7 of the Convention confers upon States parties the responsibility to ensure the important right to registration after birth, a right to name and to nationality, and the right to have knowledge of his parents. A 'right to identity', an unusual right, is accorded to the child by virtue of Article 8. This Article was sponsored by Argentina with its tragic experiences of the so-called 'Dirty War' and child disappearances.[42] It was prompted by the same feelings as those which led to the incorporation of Article 18 of the ACHR.[43] Article 8 (in combination with Article 30) would also be valuable to children belonging to minority or indigenous groups in preserving their family traditions as well their linguistic, cultural and religious identity.[44]

Article 9 reinforces a significant factor concerning the development of the child. It imposes an obligation on States to make sure that the child is never separated from his parents against their will, unless after due judicial determination it is considered necessary in the best interests of the child. Examples provided in the Article include situations where abuse or neglect

---

[39] See Article 6 ICCPR Article 2 ECHR, Article 4 AFCHPR, Article I ADHR and Article 4 ACHR. Article 19 ACHR provides that 'Every minor child has the right to measures of protection required by his condition as a minor on the part of his family, society and the State'.

[40] See Article 24.

[41] Leo Kuper points to Sudan where 'starvation [has been] deployed as a weapon against civilians'. See L. Kuper, 'Theoretical Issues Relating to Genocide' in G. Andreopoulos (ed.), *Genocide: Conceptual and Historical Dimensions* (Philadelphia: University of Pennsylvania Press) 1994, 31–46 at p. 42.

[42] D. Fottrell, 'Children's Rights' in A. Hegarty and S. Leonard (eds), *Human Rights: An Agenda for the Twenty First Century* (London: Cavendish Press) 1999, 167–179 at p. 172; D. Freestone, 'The United Nations Convention on the Rights of the Child' in D. Freestone (ed.), above n. 1, 288–323 at p. 290.

[43] See above Chapter 8.

[44] See J. Rehman, *The Weaknesses in the International Protection of Minority Rights* (The Hague: Kluwer Law International) 2000, at p. 173.

had been perpetrated by the parents or where the parents are living separately and the child's place of abode needs to be decided.[45] The Article also confers on the separated parents the right to maintain personal contact with the child.[46] The aims of Article 9 are further strengthened by Article 10 through encouraging States parties to allow the entrance and departure of parents in order to facilitate union or contact with their children. The rights of children and parents to leave any country and to enter their own country is only subject to such restrictions as are prescribed by law, which are necessary to protect national security, public order (ordre public), public health or morals, or the rights and freedoms of others and are consistent with other rights that are recognised in the Convention.[47] The applicability of this provision has been a problematic one in the immigration laws of many States including the United Kingdom.[48] Domestic legislation and administrative practices purporting to separate children from parents have received the attention of human rights tribunals. The ECHR does not include any articles establishing identical rights, but it has nevertheless been relied upon by individuals claiming that deportation or refusal to enter the State would mean separation from children.[49]

Article 11 ordains that States are to take appropriate measures to prevent the illicit trafficking of children, their abduction and non-return from abroad. Several important regional and international conventions to prevent child abduction have come into operation to reinforce international law concerning child abduction and child custody. These include the Hague Convention on the Civil Aspects of Child Abduction (1980)[50] and the European Convention on Recognition and Enforcement of Decisions Concerning Custody of Children and on Restoration of Custody of Children (1980).[51]

Another subject crucial to the development of children is that of adoption. Article 20 attempts to cater for adoption of the child, although as the provisions confirm there are widespread religious and cultural differences on this subject. Within the *Sharia*, (the Islamic legal system) adoption *per se* is not permissible, although the concept of *Kafalah* exists whereby the child can be taken care of in situations where the biological parents cannot do so. However *Kafalah* is a weaker concept as it does not permit the child to adopt the

---

[45] Article 9(1).
[46] Article 9(3).
[47] Article 10(2).
[48] M. Freeman, 'The Limits of Children's Rights' in M. Freeman and P. Veerman (eds), above n. 1, 29–46 at p. 40.
[49] See Article 8 ECHR. *Berrehab* v. *The Netherlands*, Judgment of 21 June 1988, Series A, No. 138; *Moustaquim* v. *Belgium*, Judgment of 18 February 1991, Series A, No. 193. Discussed above Chapter 6.
[50] Cmnd 8281 (1980).
[51] Cmnd 8155 (1980).

family's name and does not confer property or other rights.[52] The *travaux préparatoires* of the Convention reflect substantial disagreements between the Islamic bloc on the one hand and western States on the other.[53] As a consequence the original text, which was drafted in 1982, had to be altered.[54] The final text of the treaty represents a compromise applying only to those States which recognise the institution of adoption.[55] Article 21 while sanctioning inter-country adoption attempts to ensure that the interests of the child are upheld. States parties undertake to ensure the rights of the child in inter-country adoptions. They also guarantee that such adoptions will be undertaken by competent authorities who will safeguard the interests of everyone involved and that such placements are not going to result in 'improper financial gains' for any party.[56]

Children and their freedom of expression, association and religion

Articles 12 and 13 deal with the important rights to be heard and freedom of expression particularly in relation to the matters which affect the person and interests of the child. By virtue of Article 12(1), States undertake 'to assure to the child who is capable of forming his or her own views the right to express those views freely in all matters' which affect the child. Article 12(2) lays particular emphasis on the

> opportunity to be heard in any judicial and administrative proceedings affecting the child, either directly, or through a representative or an appropriate body, in a manner consistent with the procedural rules of national law.

Article 13 provides the child with the right to freedom of expression which includes:

> freedom to seek, receive and impart information and ideas of all kinds, regardless of frontiers, either orally, in writing or in print, in the form of art, or through any other media of the child's choice.

The exercise of the right is, however, subject to restriction. These restrictions are to be established by law and are to be laid down to ensure 'respect of the rights or reputations of others' or 'for the protection of national security or of public order (ordre public), or of public health or morals'. The provisions of Articles 12 and 13 can be criticised for the vague terminology, which allows

---

[52] Van Bueren, above n. 1, at p. 95.
[53] The issue of adoption has contributed to reservations from several Islamic States. See W.A. Schabas, 'Reservations to the Convention on the Rights of the Child' 18 *HRQ* (1996) 472.
[54] UN Doc E/1982/12/Add.1, C, para 76.
[55] D. Johnson, 'Cultural and Regional Pluralism in the Drafting of the UN Convention on the Rights of the Child' in M. Freeman and P. Veerman (eds), above n. 1, 95–114 at p. 105.
[56] Article 21(d).

States parties to apply their own standards to justify the exclusion of children from effective enjoyment of their rights.

Article 14 which deals with the right of the child to freedom of thought, conscience and religion is a problematic one. The article has attracted widespread reservations from Contracting States parties. As already noted, it is difficult to state if the right to freedom of religion or belief is fully established in international law – certainly in the light of divisions among States the parameters of any such rights are not clearly drawn.[57] Article 14(1) notes that 'States Parties shall respect the right of the child to freedom of thought, conscience and religion'. However, attempts to incorporate a right for the child to change his or her religion proved abortive.[58] Article 14(2) places an obligation on States to allow parents to direct their children to exercise the rights provided in Article 14(1) and Article 14(3) notes that freedom to manifest one's religion or beliefs can be subject only to minimalist limitations that are established by law and are necessary for public safety, public order, health or morals, or for the protection of fundamental rights and freedoms of others. There are substantial tensions inherent in the provisions of this Article. The Convention is reluctant to allow substantial rights to the child *vis-à-vis* the family, parents and the State. There is a worry for children living in societies which ordain submission – the State, society and parental pressure may force children towards cultural and religious extremism.

Article 15 provides for the recognition of the right to freedom of association and to freedom of peaceful assembly.[59] The limitation clause associated to Article 15 is taken from Article 22 of the ICCPR – right to peaceful assembly.[60] Article 16 prohibits arbitrary or unlawful interference with privacy, family, home or correspondence. The Article also makes it unlawful to attack the honour, dignity and reputation of the child. Article 17 ensures that the child has access to information and materials from a diversity of national and international sources. This is an innovative right and usefully highlights the significance of mass media in the development of the rights of the child. Article 18 obliges States parties to ensure recognition of the principle that both parents have common responsibilities for the upbringing and development of the child.[61]

---

[57] See above Chapter 9.

[58] UN Doc. E/CN.4/1984/71 (1984) paras 13–33. See Van Bueren, above n. 1, at pp. 157–58; D. Johnson, 'Cultural and Regional Pluralism in the Drafting of the UN Convention on the Rights of the Child' in M. Freeman and P. Veerman (eds), above n. 1, pp. 95–114.

[59] In its original format the Article included the right to privacy. However due to significant differences, two articles instead of one were drafted. See UN Doc. E/CN.4/1987/25 (1987) paras 111–118.

[60] McGoldrick, above n. 1, at p. 142.

[61] Article 18(1).

Measures to combat violence, abuse, exploitation and maltreatment of children

Article 19, obliges States parties to take the necessary appropriate actions to protect the child from all forms of physical or mental violence, injury or abuse, neglect or negligent treatment, maltreatment or exploitation including sexual abuse, while in the care of parent, parents or legal guardian. These appropriate actions include 'legislative, administrative, social and educational measures'.[62] Article 19(2) goes on to provide that:

> such protective measures should, as appropriate, include effective procedures for the establishment of social programmes to provide necessary support for the child and for those who have the care of the child, as well as for other forms of prevention and for identification, reporting, referral, investigation, treatment and follow-up of instances of child maltreatment described heretofore, and, as appropriate, for judicial involvement.

Article 19 is a very broad article as no definition is provided of 'physical or mental violence, injury or abuse, neglect or negligent treatment, maltreatment or exploitation, including sexual abuse'. According to Professor Van Bueren,

> the terms neglect and abuse are intentionally undefined in order to avoid the danger that a definition of child abuse and neglect could unwittingly be based upon either arbitrary or ethnocentric assumptions. In general terms child neglect involves either the inability or the deliberate refusal to care for a child with the result that a child's development is impaired. It is also clear that abuse and neglect includes all acts or omissions where the sole motivation is the desire to harm the child.[63]

Following the jurisprudence of the European Convention on Human Rights, States have a positive obligation to ensure the provision of civil and criminal proceedings against those involved in sexual offences against children.[64] Subsequent Articles of the Convention deal with unfortunate practices such as economic exploitation, illicit usage of drugs, sexual abuse and trafficking of children. Article 32 deals with some of most critical issues relating to the rights of the child. It provides as follows:

1. States Parties recognise the right of the child to be protected from economic exploitation and from performing any work that is likely to be hazardous or to interfere with the child's education, or to be harmful to the child's health or physical, mental, spiritual, moral or social development.
2. States Parties shall take legislative, administrative, social and educational measures to ensure the implementation of the present article. To this end, and

---

[62] Article 19(1).

[63] Van Bueren, above n. 1 at p. 88; *Costello-Roberts* v. *United Kingdom*, Judgment of 25 March 1993, Series A, No. 247-C; *A* v. *UK*, Judgment of 23 September 1998, 1998-VI RJD 2692.

[64] See *X and Y* v. *The Netherlands*, Judgment of 26 March 1985, Series A, No. 91. Discussed above Chapter 6.

having regard to the relevant provisions of other international instruments, States Parties shall in particular:

(a) Provide for a minimum age or minimum ages for admission to employment;

(b) Provide for appropriate regulation of the hours and conditions of employment;

(c) Provide for appropriate penalties or other sanctions to ensure the effective enforcement of the present article.

Notwithstanding the abolition of slavery and slave trade, child slavery and servitude is still being practiced in Africa and Asia. In addition there are millions of children employed in rigorous labour in many parts of the world. Children provide employers with a stable source of cheap labour. They are capable of putting in long hours and are unlikely to question their employers over working conditions and wages. It is estimated that 50 to 100 million children between the ages of 10 and 14 are currently in full-time employment.[65] Child labour is institutionalised in many regions of the world, for example Pakistan, Bangladesh and India. Article 32 not only complements existing human rights provisions but extends them to a significant extent. The UDHR and the ICCPR prohibit slavery, servitude and forced labour for everyone including children. Article 10(3) of ICESCR imposes a duty on States parties to protect children and young persons from economic and social exploitation. It requires States to set age limits below which it would be punishable to employ a child for labour. The Article also makes it punishable by law to employ children in work harmful to their morals or health. Child labour and exploitation for commercial and economic purposes has been an issue raised in a number of quarters. A useful study was prepared by Mr A. Bouhdiba in 1981, which prompted the UN Sub-Commission's working group on Contemporary Forms of Slavery to propose a '35-point Programme of Action for the Elimination of Exploitation of Child Labour'.[66] This proposal was adopted by the UN Commission on Human Rights in 1991.[67] The ILO Convention, Convention No. 138, places an obligation on States to ensure effective protection of children from labour.[68] There is also increasing pressure on international

---

[65] Van Bueren, above n. 1, at p. 263.

[66] A. Bouhdiba, Exploitation of Child Labour, E/CN.4/Sub.2/479/Rev.1 (1989); see also Sub-Commission Res. 1990/31 and Commission's Res. 1991/54, Pt II, para 10.

[67] See A. Eide, 'The Sub-Commission on Prevention of Discrimination and Protection of Minorities' in P. Alston (ed.), *The United Nations and Human Rights: A Critical Appraisal* (Oxford: Clarendon Press) 1992, pp. 211–264 at p. 234.

[68] Article 1. ILO Convention No. 138. Convention Concerning Minimum Age for Admission to Employment, 1973.

trading organisations to impose sanctions on States which allow the practice of child labour.[69]

Article 33 ordains States to take all necessary measures to protect children from the illicit use of narcotic drugs and psychotropic substances. Article 34 is also a very significant Article of the Convention. Children suffer from all forms of sexual exploitation and abuse which the Article designs to criminalise. Child pornography, prostitution, sale as servants and bonded labour, ritual and satanic abuse, or transcultural or transracial adoptions are also widespread contemporary phenomena. Article 34(a) aims to protect children from inducement or coercion to engage in any unlawful sexual activity. This includes sexual expatiation or abuse. Exploitation of children in activities such as prostitution, unlawful sexual practices and exploitation through pornography is also prohibited.[70] The international community has advanced further on prohibiting child pornography through the recent adoption of the Optional Protocol to the Convention on the Rights of the Child on the Sale of Children, Child Prostitution and Child Pornography.[71]

One of the more problematic areas within international and national family law relates to sexual abuse that takes place within the confines of the home and family. As with many other Articles in the Convention, international human right law provides protection for the child from sexual abuse conducted by non-State personnel. However, in practice these rights often remain ineffective largely due to lack of disclosure and detection. According to McGillivray:

> In a dysfunctional relationship [the] interpretive power displaces the child's view, making disclosure unlikely and detection difficult. The value given to the archetype of the family as a private cohesive unit joined by ties of blood, affection and economic interdependence contributes to the ideology of family loyalty. Children fear breaching the family compact by disclosing problems to outsiders and recant where family cohesiveness is threatened.[72]

By virtue of Article 35, States endeavour to take all appropriate and necessary action to prevent child abduction and the sale and trafficking of children. According to Article 36 'States Parties shall protect the child against all other forms of exploitation prejudicial to any aspects of the child's welfare'. Article 37 echoes the traditional human rights approach; it provides for the

---

[69] See Ehrenberg, above n. 21, at p. 361.

[70] G. Kent, 'Little Foreign Bodies: International Dimension of Child Prostitution' in M. Freeman and P. Veerman (eds), above n. 1, pp. 323–346; J. Ennew, *The Sexual Exploitation of Children* (Cambridge: Polity Press) 1986.

[71] Protocol on the Sale of Children, Child Pornography and Child prostitution GA Res. 54/263 Annex II (25 May 2000); see M.J. Dennis, 'Newly Adopted Protocols to the Convention on the Rights of the Child' 94 *AJIL* (2000) 789.

[72] A. McGillivray, 'Re-Construction Child Abuse: Western Definition and Non-Western Experience' in M. Freeman and P. Veerman (eds), above n. 1, 213–236 at p. 216.

prohibition of 'torture or other cruel, inhuman or degrading treatment or punishment' for the child. Widespread divergences exist on the subject of corporal punishment of children.[73] Distressing facts have emerged even from the developed world. Thus, for example, the Committee on the Rights of the Child, in its consideration of the report from the United Kingdom, has shown concern at the legislative provisions dealing with reasonable chastisement. The concern according to the Committee is that this so-called 'reasonable chastisement' may 'pave the way for subjective and arbitrary interpretation'.[74] It can be argued that following the cases from the European Convention on Human Rights a general norm is emerging in international law, which regards all forms of corporal punishment of children as violating the provisions of Article 37.[75]

Article 37 also provides for a ban on capital punishment and life imprisonment (without possibility of release) for offences committed by persons below eighteen years of age.[76] It also provides for prohibiting unlawful or arbitrary deprivation of liberty, and provides for requisite safeguards.[77] The prohibition of capital punishment for those under eighteen is a particularly valuable provision with implications for the issue regarding the point of majority, the definition of childhood and the overall campaign for the abolition of death penalty in international law. Notwithstanding the provisions of Article 37(a) and Article 6(5) ICCPR, capital punishment has been imposed on seventeen year olds. A number of such situations have arisen in the United States. In two cases filed in the United States and brought before the Inter-American Commission on Human Rights, the petitioners had argued that a norm of customary international law existed prohibiting the application of the death penalty to individuals below the age of eighteen.[78] While accepting the view that 'in the OAS member States there is a recognised norm of *jus cogens* which prohibits the State execution of children',[79] the Commission could not

---

[73] For further consideration see above Chapters 4–6.

[74] See UN Doc. CRC/C/15 Add. 34 para 16.

[75] See *Tyrer* v. *United Kingdom*, Judgment of 25 April 1978, Series A, No. 26 (judicial corporal punishment of 15 year old boy violating Article 3); *A* v. *UK*, Judgment of 23 September 1998, 1998-VI RJD 2692 (caning of a 9 year old boy by stepfather, violation of Article 3). See also the Human Rights Committee's General Comments (forty-fourth session 1992). In the Committee's view 'the prohibition in Article 7 (on torture, cruel, inhuman or degrading treatment or punishment) relates not only to acts that cause physical pain but also to acts that cause mental suffering to the victim. In the Committee's view, moreover, the prohibition must extend to corporal punishment, including excessive chastisement ordered as punishment for a crime or as an educative or disciplinary measure. It is appropriate to emphasize in this regard that Article 7 protects, in particular, children, pupils and patients in teaching and medical institutions' para 5.

[76] Article 37(a).

[77] See Article 37(b).

[78] Note Article 6(5) ICCPR which provides that 'Sentence of death shall not be imposed for crimes committed by persons below eighteen years of age'. USA was not a party to the ICCPR at that time.

[79] *Roach and Pinkerton* v. *United States*, Case 9.647, Res. No 3/87, OEA/Ser.L/V/II.71, Doc. 9 rev.1, at 147.

refute the United States contention on the absence of any customary rules for the determination of the age of majority.[80] It is also interesting to note that the United States, upon its ratification of the ICCPR, entered a reservation to Article 6(5) of the Covenant. This reservation has been considered as 'incompatible with the objects and purposes of the Covenant' by the Human Rights Committee which has called for its withdrawal.[81]

Children in wars and conflicts

Article 22 ensures that the child receives the protection of international refugee and humanitarian law. Article 22(1) provides that the States parties shall take appropriate measures to ensure that a child who is seeking refugee status or who is considered a refugee, receives appropriate protection and humanitarian assistance in the enjoyment of applicable rights under the present Convention and other international humanitarian and human rights treaties. The protection applies regardless of whether the child is accompanied by his parents.[82] According to Article 22(2) States are to cooperate with the UN and other intergovernmental agencies to trace the parents or other members of the family of any refugee child or to obtain information with a view to his reunification with his family.

Further safeguards are provided by Article 38 which aims to ensure the compliance and respect for the rules of international humanitarian law applicable to children in armed conflicts. The obligations of the Article are to prohibit the creation of child soldiers and ordains States not to allow those below the age of fifteen years to take a direct part in hostilities.[83] It is important to appreciate that during times of unrest and war, children need greater protection than during peace times. At the same time, it is also unfortunately the case that in times of war, children are more likely to be abused and are vulnerable to being coerced into becoming combatants.[84] A vast majority of contemporary armed conflicts are of a localised nature; examples of such internal conflicts can be

---

[80] The Inter-American Commission found the US in violation for its pattern of 'legislative arbitrariness throughout the United States which results in the arbitrary deprivation of life and inequality before the law' (para 173). For commentaries see D.T. Fox, 'Inter-American Commission on Human Rights finds the United States in Violation' 82 *AJIL* (1988) 601; D. Shelton, 'The Decision of IACHR of 27 March 1987 in the Case of Roach and Pinkerton: A Note' 8 *HRLJ* (1987) 355; D. Weissbrodt, 'Execution of Juvenile Offenders by the United States Violates International Human Rights Law' 3 *AUJILP* (1988) 339.
[81] See Report of the Human Rights Committee UN Doc. A/50/40 (1995) para 279; see also Amnesty International Report http://www.amnestyusa.org/abolish/juveniles.html (1 May 2002).
[82] Article 22(1).
[83] Van Bueren, above n. 1, at p. 275.
[84] J.G. Gardam, 'The Law of Armed Conflict: A Feminist Perspective' in K.E. Mahoney and P. Mahoney (eds), *Human Rights in the Twenty-First Century: A Global Challenge* (Dordrecht: Martinus Nijhoff Publishers) 1993, pp. 419–436; M. Elahi, 'The Rights of the Child Under Islamic Law: Prohibition of the Child Soldier' 19 *CHRLR* (1988) 259.

found in many regions of the world. In these armed conflicts children are used as combatants. Children also represent the highest number of casualties and suffer immensely. Until recently the Geneva Convention Relative to the Protection of Civilian Persons in Times of War (1949),[85] supplemented by the Protocols Additional to the Geneva Conventions of 1949 Relating to the Protection of Victims of International Armed Conflict (1977)[86] and the Protection of Victims of Non-International Armed Conflicts[87] have remained the most pertinent treaties protecting the rights of children in international humanitarian law. The combined effect of the aforementioned treaties is to accord protection to children living in occupied or unoccupied territories and to regulate child participation in hostilities. A further extension of humanitarian law has been through the adoption of the Optional Protocol on the Involvement of Children in Armed Conflict.[88] Among regional instruments, there exists the African Charter on the Rights and Welfare of the Child which takes a specific interest in protecting children in civil unrest and internal conflict. Article 22(3) of this chapter deals with children caught up in international and internal armed conflicts. States are required

> to protect the civilian population in armed conflicts and shall take all feasible measures to ensure the protection and care of children who are affected by armed conflicts. Such rules shall apply to children in situations of internal armed conflicts, tension and strife.

Concerns of disability and health

The Convention also accords rights to mentally and physically disabled children. In its Article 23, States parties recognise the rights of mentally and physically disabled children to have a decent living and to ensure that they live a life of dignity, self-reliance and are enabled to participate in the life of the community. This is an extremely important provision as disabled children are prone to abuse, violence and suffering. Inherent in the Article is the provision of non-discrimination as provided for in Article 2. The Article provides for special care and encourages the State to extend available resources.[89]

The rights in Article 24 are interrelated with those in Article 6, the right to life for the child. Article 24 expands on this right noting that the State parties recognise the right of 'the child to the enjoyment of the highest attainable standard of health and to facilities for the treatment of illness and rehabilitation of health'[90] and that they 'shall strive to ensure that no child is deprived

---

[85] U.K.T.S. 39 (1958), Cmnd 55.
[86] 1125 U.N.T.S. 3; Misc 19 (1977).
[87] Misc 19 (1977); 1125 U.N.T.S.
[88] GA Res. 54/263, Annex II, 25 May, 2000. See Dennis above n. 71, at p. 789.
[89] Article 23(2).
[90] Article 24(1).

of his or her right of access to such health care services'.[91] Particular emphasis is placed on diminishing the mortality rate of children,[92] and provision of medical and health care[93] to combat malnutrition and disease,[94] to provide maternal pre-natal and post-natal health care,[95] and to ensure that parents, children and others involved in the upbringing of children have the knowledge and education essential *inter alia* for the protection of child health and hygiene.[96] These provisions are much more specific than other human rights provisions including the right to health recognised by Article 12 of ICESCR.[97] While unlike Article 11 of the ICESCR there is no specific reference to the right to food, there is a recognition of the need to combat malnutrition.[98] Making reference to the Convention on the Rights of the Child in its General Comment on the right to health, the Committee on the International Covenant on Economic, Social and Cultural Rights has noted:

> The Convention on the Rights of the Child directs States to ensure access to essential health services for the child and his or her family, including pre- and post-natal care for mothers. The Convention links these goals with ensuring access to child-friendly information about preventive and health-promoting behaviour and support to families and communities in implementing these practices. Implementation of the principle of non-discrimination requires that girls, as well as boys, have equal access to adequate nutrition, safe environments, and physical as well as mental health services. There is a need to adopt effective and appropriate measures to abolish harmful traditional practices affecting the health of children, particularly girls, including early marriage, female genital mutilation, preferential feeding and care of male children. Children with disabilities should be given the opportunity to enjoy a fulfilling and decent life and to participate within their community.[99]

According to Article 24(3) State parties shall take all effective and appropriate measures with a view to abolishing traditional practices prejudicial to the

---

[91] Ibid.
[92] Article 24(2)(a).
[93] Article 24(2)(b).
[94] Article 24(2)(c).
[95] Article 24(2)(d).
[96] Article 9(2)(d).
[97] According to Article 12 States 'recognize the right of everyone to the enjoyment of the highest attainable standard of physical and mental health' and that steps are to be taken by States to the present Covenant to achieve the full realisation of this right shall include those necessary which are as follows: (a) The provision for the reduction of the still-birth rate and of infant mortality and for the healthy development of the child; (b) The improvement of all aspects of environmental and industrial hygiene; (c) The prevention, treatment and control of epidemic, endemic, occupational and other diseases; (d) The creation of conditions which would assure to all medical service and medical attention in the event of sickness.
[98] McGoldrick, above n. 1, at p. 146.
[99] ICESCR General Comment 14, *The Right to Highest Attainable Standard of Health* (Article 12) General Comment No. 14 (11/08/00) (E/C.12/200/4), para 22.

health of children. As an important improvisation, the intention had been to target such practices as female infanticide, male preferences, neglect and abuse of children and female circumcision. During the drafting of the treaty, the issue of female circumcision aroused significant tensions and disagreements.[100] In order to prevent holding up the work on this particular article, it was decided that no examples (including that of female circumcision) could be referenced in the text of the article itself.[101] As noted earlier, the practice of female circumcision continues to take place in many parts of the world, although there is equally a strong condemnation of this activity in many quarters. The abhorrence and condemnation of female circumcision has been so strong that in one case a girl fleeing from a country for fear of forced circumcision was entitled in principle to claim refugee status if she had a well-founded fear of being persecuted by reason of membership of a particular group.[102]

Article 25 of the Convention provides that 'States Parties recognize the right of a child who has been placed by the competent authorities for the purposes of care, protection or treatment of his or her physical or mental health, to a periodic review of the treatment provided to the child and all other circumstances relevant to his or her placement'. There is, however, no elaboration of 'competent authorities' or 'periodic review'. Article 26 recognises the right of children to State benefits such as social security and social insurance The right to social security as an important right has been recognised by Article 9 of the ICESCR and Article 12 of the European Social Charter. Article 27 of the Convention of the Rights of the Child (1989) provides that States 'recognize the right of every child to a standard of living adequate for the child's physical, mental, spiritual, moral and social development'. Articles 28 and 29 deal with various aspects of the educational rights of children.

Educational rights

According to Article 28(1) States parties recognise the right of the child to education, and with a view to achieving this right progressively and on the basis of equal opportunity, they shall, in particular:

(a) Make primary education compulsory and available and free to all;
(b) Encourage the development of different forms of secondary education, including general and vocational education, make them available and accessible to every child, and take appropriate measures such as the introduction of free education and offering financial assistance in case of need;

---

[100] For a multitude of literature see Chapter 13.
[101] UN Doc. E/CN.4/1986/42.
[102] See *Mademoiselle X* (9 September 1991). Case is considered in *Public Law* (1993) 197.

(c) Make higher education accessible to all on the basis of capacity by every appropriate means;
(d) Make educational and vocational information and guidance available and accessible to all children;
(e) Take measures to encourage regular attendance at schools and the reduction of drop-out rates.

The Articles develop the obligations inherited from Article 26(1) of the UDHR and Articles 13 and 14 of the ICESCR. As already noted, Articles 13 and 14 of the ICESCR have been the focus of substantial attention by the Committee on the International Covenant on Economic, Social and Cultural Rights, with the right to education being the subject of two General Comments by the Committee.[103] While commenting on the right to primary education the Committee noted:

> [i]n line with the clear obligations under article 14 [relating to primary education] every State party is under a duty to present to the committee a plan of action [which must cover all of the actions necessary in order to secure each of the requisite component parts of the right and must be sufficiently detailed so as to ensure the comprehensive realization of the right. Participation of all sections of civil society in the drawing up of the plan is vital and some means of periodically reviewing progress and ensuring accountability are essential] This obligation needs to be scrupulously observed in view of the fact that in developing countries, 130 million children of school age are currently estimated to be without access to primary education, of whom about two thirds are girls.[104]

The Article is important as many States, particularly those from Asia and Africa continue to invest poorly in education.[105] Although there is increasing emphasis on compulsory primary education, many children for economic or social reasons are forced to remain illiterate. The provisions of Article 28 are complemented by Article 29. The Committee on the Rights of the Child recently noted in its first General Comment that:

> Article 29(1) is not only complementing the right to education recognised in article 28 by a qualitative dimension which reflects the rights and inherent dignity of the child; it also insists upon the need for education to be child-centred, child-friendly and empowering; and it highlights the need for educational processes to be based upon the very principles which are recognised in article 29(1). The education to which every child has a right is one designed to provide the child with life skills, to strengthen the child's capacity to enjoy the full range of human rights and to promote a culture which is infused by appropriate human

---

[103] ICESCR General Comment 11, *Plans of Action for Primary Education (Article 14)* General Comment No. 11 (10/05/99) (E/C.12/1999/4); CESCR General Comment 13, *The Right to Education* (Article 13) General Comment No. 13 (8/12/99) (E/C.12/1999/10).
[104] Article 14, para 3.
[105] See HRCP, *State of Human Rights in Pakistan in 1998* (Lahore: HRCP) 1999, pp. 6–15.

rights values. The goal is to empower the child, through developing his or her skills, learning and other capacities, human dignity, self-esteem and self-confidence. 'Education' in this context goes far beyond formal schooling to embrace the broad range of life experiences and learning processes which enable children, whether individually or collectively, to develop their personalities, talents and abilities and to live a full and satisfying life within society.[106]

Article 30 is based on Article 27 of the ICCPR. It deals with the rights of minority children. It has attracted criticisms similar to those relating to Article 27: there is no definition of 'minorities' or persons of indigenous origins; the Article itself is drafted in a negative manner; and it is party to the same shortcomings that attach to Article 27.

Criminal justice rights

A number of the provisions within Article 40 draw inspiration from the Beijing Rules. Aspects of the Beijing Rules have developed into recognised rules of criminal law within domestic jurisdictions of States; there are, however, many others which do not have any such binding effect and belong to the regime of 'soft law'.[107] These 'soft laws' however, can prove significant in the development of norms of customary international law or binding treaty law. Article 40 caters for wide diversity in Penal systems. Some States have juvenile courts – separate regimes of administering offences conducted by children – whereas others treat children in more or less the same manner as adults.[108] The Article confirms many principles including the principle of non-retroactivity of penal law,[109] presumption of innocence,[110] being informed promptly of charges,[111] the matter being decided promptly by a competent, independent and impartial authority[112] and non-compulsion of confession.[113]

IMPLEMENTATION OF THE CONVENTION[114]

The second part of the Convention, dealing with its implementation, is provided for in Articles 42–45. Supervision of the Convention is conducted by

---

[106] Article 29(1): The Aims of Education 08/02/2001. CRC General comment 1.
[107] See above Chapter 1.
[108] Van Bueren, above n. 1, at p. 179–180.
[109] Article 40(2)(a).
[110] Article 40(2)(b)(i).
[111] Article 40(2)(ii).
[112] Article 40(2)(iii).
[113] Article 40(2)(iv).
[114] M. O'Flaherty, *Human Rights and the UN: Practice before the Treaty Bodies* (London: Sweet and Maxwell) 1996, p. 196; C.P. Cohen, S.N. Hart and S.M. Kosloske, 'Monitoring the United Nations Convention on the Right of the Child: The Challenge of Information Management' 18 *HRQ* (1996) 439.

a ten-member Committee called the Committee on the Rights of the Child.[115] The members of the Committee are drawn from States which are parties to the treaty. Members serve in their individual capacity.[116] They are 'of high moral standing and of recognised competence in the field'.[117] Each member's term of office is for four years, with the possibility of re-election.[118] The only mechanism for implementation of the Convention is through a system of periodic reports submitted by States parties.

Under Article 44 the Committee is obliged to forward a biannual report of its activities to the General Assembly via ECOSOC.[119] The Committee started with one session for the year; however, with the growing number of States, it soon became evident that this would be insufficient. Since 1995 three sessions per year have been the standard, these sessions being held in January, May–June and September–October in Geneva. Each of the sessions lasts for three working weeks and is followed by a meeting of one week's duration of a working group to prepare for the next session.

The Convention requires the reports to be submitted within two years of a State's entry and thereafter every five years.[120] According to Article 44(2), reports submitted by States 'shall indicate factors and difficulties, if any, affecting the degree of fulfilment of the obligations' of the provisions within the Convention. Reports are also aimed at providing adequate information of an analysis of the Convention's implementation. The first meeting of the Committee was held in 1991, and the scrutiny of reports started in 1993. During its sessions 1991–1992, the Committee concerned itself with practical issues such as drafting provisional rules of procedure and reporting guidelines. The first periodic report was examined in October 1997.[121]

In order to improve guidance on initial reports by State parties, the Committee has issued guidelines regarding the form and content of these reports.[122] These guidelines aim to provide a clear indication of the nature and depth of information required, and also to impose some degree of uniformity on the production of reports.[123] The Committee has also produced guidelines

---

[115] Article 43. An Amendment to increase the number of the committee to eighteen was adopted by the General Assembly – GA Res. 50/155 February 1996. The amendment requires acceptance of a two-third majority, and has as yet not come into operation.

[116] Article 43(2).

[117] Article 44(1).

[118] Article 43(6).

[119] Article 44(5).

[120] Article 44(1).

[121] Committee on the Rights of the Child, Report of the Sixteenth Session, CRC/C/69.

[122] General Guidelines regarding the form and Content of Initial Reports to be Submitted by States parties under Article 44, paragraph 1(a) of the CRC, UN Doc. CRC/C/5.

[123] G. Lansdown, 'The Reporting Procedure under the Convention on the Rights of the Child' in P. Alston and J. Crawford (ed.), *The Future of UN Human Rights Treaty Monitoring* (Cambridge: Cambridge University Press) 2000, 113–128 at p. 114.

on periodic reports.[124] In accordance with the provisions of the Convention, the Committee has asked governments to publish their reports within their own countries.[125] It has also been suggested by the guidelines that summary records of a State party's dialogue with the CRC, alongside the concluding observations, be published. The guidelines recommend a thematic approach for the reports adopting the following structure. Information should be provided with regard to the implementation of the following:

- General measures of implementation (Articles 4, 42 and 44(6)).
- Definition of the child (Article 1).
- General principles (Articles 2, 3, 6 and 12).
- Civil rights and freedoms (Articles 4, 8, 13, 14, 15, 16, 17 and 37(a)).
- Family environment and alternative care (Articles 5, 18(1), 18(2), 9, 10, 27(4), 20, 21, 11, 19 and 25).
- Basic health and welfare (Articles 6(2), 23, 24, 26, 18(3), 27(1), 27(2) and 27(3)).
- Education, leisure and cultural activities (Articles 28, 29 and 31).
- Special measures of protection (Articles 22, 38, 39, 40, 37(b), 37(c), 37(d), 37(a), 39, 32, 33, 34, 36, 35 and 30).

The guidelines highlight four underlying principles in relation to compliance and scrutiny of the Convention rights. These concern non-discrimination (Article 2); the best interest of the child (Article 3); the right to life survival and development (Article 6); and the right of children to participate in decisions affecting them (Article 12). In considering any issue these underlying factors must be central and relied upon. The Articles categorised in one band do not fall neatly in any single aspect of the rights of the child. Such a categorisation, however, places emphasis upon the integration of civil and political rights with those of social, economical and cultural rights – and the reaffirmation of the indivisibility of these sets of rights.

At the end of each session of the Committee, one week is allocated to consideration of the questions to be addressed to the States parties due to appear in the next session. A working group from among the Committee is established for the purpose of identifying areas within the report which raise concern or need further clarification. This pre-sessional working group meets in private; no government representatives are allowed to attend and no public record of the discussion is produced. NGOs are, however, invited to attend the pre-sessional working group. With the input of NGOs and other UN agencies, the Committee writes its list of issues to be presented to the relevant

---

[124] General Guidelines regarding the form and Content of Periodic Reports to be Submitted by States parties under Article 44, para 1(b) of the CRC, UN Doc. CRC/C/58.
[125] Article 44(6).

government.[126] A list of issues for transmission to the State parties is compiled with a request for written replies to be considered together with the issues drawn up by members serving as 'country rapporteurs'.[127] In addition, other sources of information derived from NGOs and agencies such as the ILO, UNICEF and the UNHCR are collated.

A State report once submitted is likely to be considered by the Committee within 18 months of submission, although it is difficult to predict at which session the report will be receiving consideration. A three-hour plenary session is allocated to each country report. At the plenary session the governmental representative appears before the Committee. At these sessions NGO representatives are invited to present their comments on the country reports and to identify major areas of concern. Those NGOs who wish to make submissions to the working group should inform the working group in advance and must provide evidence of the relevance of their intervention and interest.

Reports are considered in public sessions and are introduced by the State Representative. The proceedings of the Committee are based on the categorisation as provided within the Convention guidelines. The discussion on each of the categories is introduced by the comments of the State representative, followed by questions and comments of members and concluded by responses of the State representative. At the end of the consideration, the Committee members summarise their observations and make suggestions and recommendations. The State representative may make a final statement and provide a response to the Committee's observations.

After the completion of its review of the report, the Committee produces concluding observations in which the Committee presents its opinion on the adequacy or inadequacy of the report, positive as well as negative features of the report, and considers any possible difficulties of implementation. The Committee also puts forward the issues which it perceives to be a matter of concern and ends with suggestions and recommendations. The concluding observations are issued at the end of each session in the form of public documents and are included in the biannual report to the United Nations General Assembly. These concluding observations are also transmitted to UN specialised agencies such as UNICEF.

---

[126] See H. Cullen and K. Morrow, 'International Civil Society in International Law: The Growth of NGO Participation' 1 *Non-State Actors and International Law* (2001) 7 at p. 18.

[127] There are significant benefits derived from this procedure. With the NGO input the Committee members become much more aware of the actual situation. The Committee members can also raise concrete issues and criticises the misinformation within State reports. Government reports are often weak in terms of measures of implementing the Convention rights and the Committee is better placed to show their concerns in its concluding observations. The NGO-produced alternative reports underlines the weakness in the official position. The encouragement to NGO to submit this alternative report on behalf of the National NGO body as whole. The consolidated report is likely to be more authoritative and comprehensive and avoids duplication.

INNOVATIVE FEATURES AND OTHER INITIATIVES

In comparison to other reporting treaty-based procedures, the NGOs have a more prominent and formally acknowledged role to play. According to Article 45, the specialised agencies, the United Nations Children's Fund, and other United Nations organs are entitled to be represented at the consideration of the State reports. Thus, for example, when consideration is given to provisions related to employment or labour, the ILO can attend the proceedings of the Committee as of right. The Article also authorises the Committee to request submission of reports from the UN Children's Fund (UNICEF) and other UN bodies on areas falling within the scope of their activities. It can also invite these and other expert bodies (which implicitly includes the NGOs) to provide expert advice on areas falling within their respective mandates.[128] The Committee can consult, for example, the ILO on issues arising out of child labour in a particular State. This is a unique provision among human rights instruments and the Committee has responded by inviting NGOs to submit alternative reports which provide the Committee with a fuller and more critical analysis of the state of children's rights in a country.

The Convention also provides for NGOs to have a function, which is reflected in the rules of the procedure. The Committee has made use of the formal position of NGOs, as important providers of information. NGOs have also established a Group for the Convention on the Rights of the Child, with a full-time Geneva based co-ordinator facilitating the flow of information to the Committee and encouraging NGO contributions at the international and national level. This allows for a more effective contribution to the work of the Convention. Article 45(b) authorises the Committee to transmit at a State's request 'technical advice or assistance' to 'the specialised agencies, UNICEF, and other competent bodies'. The objective is to enable those States which are having difficulties in implementing the Convention to have access to and support from all the relevant competent bodies. In accordance with Article 45(c), the Committee may recommend to the General Assembly that it request the Secretary-General to undertake studies relevant to issues concerning child rights on its behalf. Article 45(d) allows the Committee to make suggestions and general recommendations based on information received through Articles 44 and 45. These suggestions and general recommendations are transmitted to the State party concerned and to the General Assembly.

The Committee has also adopted a number of initiatives. For some years now, for instance, the Committee has devoted one day every year to a general

---

[128] Article 45(a)(b); Cohen, above n. 4, at p. 146.

discussion of a specific issue. Rule 75 of the Rules of procedure sanctions such an activity. It provides:

> in order to enhance a deeper understanding of the content and implications of the Convention, the Committee may devote one or more meetings of its regular sessions to a general discussion on one specific article of the Convention or related subject.[129]

This provision has been used to set aside a series of 'Days of General Discussion' on a range of topics.[130] The first such discussion took place in 1992 on the subject of children in armed conflict; the second in 1993 related to the economic exploitation of Children; the third in 1994 focused on the role of the family. In 1998 the Committee devoted a day to discuss 'Children living in a world with HIV/AIDS'. The next days of general discussion were dedicated to State violence against children (2000) and violence against children within the family and in schools (2001). These discussions are attended by members of the Committee, NGOs and international organisations. They have been very useful in reaching a greater appreciation of the role of the Committee and in providing a forum of consideration and debate. Such debate may also influence international State practice and lead to the formulation of new standards regarding the Rights of the Child. Days of general discussion are normally announced in the report of the session immediately preceding that in which it is proposed they occur. The announcement may be accompanied by a paper by the Committee on the topic.[131] All those who are interested and concerned are invited to make written representations to the Committee.

Members of the Committee have also undertaken missions to various countries. These missions allow members of the Committee to consider and discuss issues arising out of the implementation of the Convention with the representative of the State, relevant organisations and NGOs. Traditionally all the Committee members have been able to participate on these missions. However, for the future, it is more likely that a selected group of members will be on each of these trips.[132]

CONCLUSIONS

Despite the many positives emerging from the work of the Committee there are concerns and there remains significant room for improvement. One of the outstanding concerns is the volume of work which the Committee is having to

---

[129] Rules of Procedure of the Committee on the Rights of the Child, Rule 75, UN Doc. CRC/C/4.
[130] O'Flaherty, above n. 114, at p. 196.
[131] Ibid.
[132] Ibid. p. 197.

deal with. The United Nations has agreed to provide further resources to the Committee. Five new posts have been created providing additional support to the Committee. It has also been proposed that the Committee's membership be increased to eighteen. In terms of substance of the State reports, many of the concerns that are reflective of other treaty bodies, for example the inadequacy, insufficient information, etc. is reflected in the observations of this Committee. With its enormous workload over the last decade, the Committee is increasingly under pressure. There is currently a backlog of reports. However, if the reports are being produced on time, it is inevitable that a delay in their consideration will take place. This will, in turn, lead to a situation where, by the time of their consideration the reports may be outdated.

Another concern regarding the Committee's consideration of the reports has been the inadequate attention given to some sets of rights. These include Articles 13–16 (freedom of expression, religion, conscience and thought, and privacy) and Article 23 (disability). It is important that the Committee pays attention to all the rights equally. On a procedural matter, the pre-sessional working groups have proved very useful. They allow for NGO input and for effective scrutiny. Even in this regard, however, there are some negative points. After a lengthy session of the Committee, members are often exhausted and frequently too few are present. The Committee members tend to show a relative lack of interest in these sessions, which is disappointing for the NGOs.

Having considered some of the weaknesses and limitations of the work of the Committee, the overall contribution of the Committee and the Convention must not be overlooked. The Convention has proved to be a stimulant to almost every State in the world to improve the position of children within its jurisdiction. As we have noted, serious disagreements remain on the scope and nature of many of the rights contained in the Convention. At the same time there is a fundamental recognition that the international community must act in the best interest of the child and must ensure his welfare, and respect his innocence and integrity.

V

CRIMES AGAINST THE DIGNITY OF MANKIND

15

TORTURE AS A CRIME IN INTERNATIONAL LAW AND THE RIGHTS OF TORTURE VICTIMS[1]

INTRODUCTION

> One of the most atrocious violations against human dignity is the act of torture, the result of which destroys the dignity and impairs the capability of victims to continue their lives and their activities.[2]

Throughout this book we have made references to the offences of torture, and inhuman and degrading treatment or punishment. A detailed consideration of the crime of torture and the rights of torture victims is therefore a fitting subject for this penultimate chapter. Actions amounting to torture unfortunately go back as far as human history itself, having been practised in all societies since time immemorial.[3] A historical legal analysis depicts a melancholy picture of the antiquity of this crime. During the twentieth century, torture was conducted in various forms. The two world wars provide tragic examples of torture being conducted during military operations as well as in non-armed conflicts against ordinary civilians.

---

[1] N.S. Rodley, *The Treatment of Prisoners in International Law*, 2nd edn (Oxford: Clarendon Press) 1999, A. Boulesbaa, *The UN Convention on Torture and Prospects for Enforcement* (The Hague: Martinus Nijhoff Publishers) 1999; J. Herman Bugers and H. Danelius, *The United Nations Convention against Torture: A Handbook on the Convention against Torture and Other Cruel, Inhuman or Degrading Treatment or Punishment* (The Hague: Martinus Nijhoff Publishers) 1988; D.J. Harris, *Cases and Materials on International Law*, 5th edn (London: Sweet and Maxwell) 1998, pp. 710–764.

[2] United Nations, *Vienna Declaration and Programme of Action* (New York: United Nations Department of Public Information) 1993 para 55 (pt II).

[3] On the historical analysis of acts of torture involving genocide see J. Rehman, *Weaknesses in the International Protection of Minority Rights* (The Hague: Kluwer Law International) 2000, pp. 51–54.

Since the end of the Second World War, there have been many gruesome acts of torture. It is also a crime that is currently practiced on a regular basis in many States of the world.[4]

Torture is an offence against human dignity and is rightly regarded as a crime against humanity.[5] Since the establishment of the United Nations in 1945 significant efforts have been made to eradicate acts of torture. The catalogue of international provisions condemning torture is so extensive that it would be impossible to give a comprehensive list here. There is currently an array of international documents prohibiting and condemning acts in the nature of torture. Among general human rights instruments torture, inhuman or degrading treatment or punishment is prohibited by the UDHR,[6] the ICCPR[7] and by the three regional human rights mechanisms.[8] The international machinery in the fight against those conducting torture has been supplemented by a variety of related instruments. The whole thrust of international humanitarian law is to attempt (in so far as is possible) to reduce pain, suffering and torture during international warfare and internal conflicts.[9] Specific human rights instruments dealing with *inter alia* genocide,[10] slavery and the slave trade,[11] racial discrimination,[12] apartheid,[13] children,[14]

---

[4] Boulesbaa, above n. 1, at p. 99.

[5] The Statute of the International Criminal Court incorporates Torture as a 'crime against humanity'. See Article 7(1)(f). It defines torture as 'the intentional infliction of severe pain or suffering, whether physical or mental, upon a person in the custody or under the control of the accused; except that torture shall not include pain or suffering arising only from, inherent in or incidental to, lawful sanctions' Article 7(2)(e).

[6] Article 5 provides that 'No one shall be subjected to torture or to cruel, inhuman or degrading treatment or punishment'.

[7] According to Article 7 'No one shall be subjected to torture or to cruel, inhuman or degrading treatment or punishment. In particular, no one shall be subjected without his free consent to medical or scientific experimentation'. The Human Rights Committee has established a substantial jurisprudence on this subject. See above Chapter 4.

[8] Article 3 ECHR (1950) see above Chapter 6; Article 5 ACHR (1969) see above Chapter 8; Article 5 AFCHPR (1981) see above Chapter 9.

[9] See the Geneva Conventions and the Protocols to these Conventions. In particular note the Common Article 3 of the Conventions.

[10] Convention on the Prevention and Punishment of the Crime of Genocide, adopted 9 December 1948. Entered into force 12 January 1951. 78 U.N.T.S 277. Considered above Chapter 11.

[11] The Supplementary Convention on the Abolition of Slavery, Slave Trade, and Institutions of Slavery and Practices Similar to Slavery (1956). Adopted by a Conference of Plenipotentiaries convened by ECOSOC Resolution 608 (XXI) 30 April 1956, Geneva 7 September 1956.

[12] International Convention on the Elimination of All Forms of Racial Discrimination (the Race Convention). See above Chapter 10.

[13] International Convention on the Suppression and Punishment of the Crime of Apartheid (1973) GA Res. 3068 (XXVIII). Adopted 30 November 1973. Entered into force 18 July 1976; 1015 U.N.T.S. 244.

[14] Convention on the Rights of the Child (1989) Article 37; see above Chapter 14.

women[15] and refugees[16] have also condemned acts of torture and violence. We have already noted that the Commission on Human Rights set up a working group on Enforced or Involuntary Disappearances in 1980.[17] In 1982 a UN Special Rapporteur was appointed on Arbitrary Executions followed by the UN Special Rapporteur on Torture in 1985.[18]

In addition to the aforementioned instruments and mechanisms the United Nations, as this chapter will consider in detail, has established a binding treaty which deals exclusively with the subject of torture, cruel, inhuman or degrading treatment or punishment. This United Nations Convention, known as the UN Convention against Torture and Other Cruel, Inhuman or Degrading Treatment or Punishment was adopted on 10 December 1984.[19] The adoption of the treaty at the universal level provided the impetus for other regional treaties concentrating on torture. In December 1985, the General Assembly of the OAS adopted the Inter-American Convention to Prevent and Punish Torture,[20] and in 1987 the European Convention for the Prevention of Torture and Inhuman and Degrading Treatment or Punishment was approved by the Council of Europe.[21]

The existing prohibitions in treaty law on the subject are strengthened by international customary laws. In an earlier chapter we considered that treaties provide evidence of State practice. An overwhelming acceptance of a treaty may lead to the formation of customary international law, which would be binding on all States. In the case of torture, the substantial number of ratifications to the treaties concerned with prohibiting torture (combined with the fact that neither the ICCPR nor any of the regional human rights treaties allow any derogations from those articles that deal with the prohibition of torture) provides persuasive evidence that the norm is binding in international law. Furthermore it can also be argued that the prohibition on

---

[15] The UN General Assembly's Declaration on the Elimination of Violence against Women (1993); the Inter-American Convention on the Prevention, Punishment and Eradication of Violence against women. See above Chapter 13.

[16] Convention Relating to the Status of Refugees. Signed 28 July 1951; entered into force 22 April 1954; 189 U.N.T.S. 150.

[17] See above Chapter 2.

[18] See discussion in this chapter.

[19] Adopted and opened for signature, ratification and accession on 10 December 1984 by GA Res. 39/46, 39 UN GAOR, Supp. No. 51, UN Doc. A/39/51, at 197 (1984). Entry into force 26 June 1987. 1465 U.N.T.S. 85; 23 I.L.M. (1985) 535.

[20] Signed 9 December 1985. Entered into force 28 February 1987 O.A.S.T.S.67, GA Doc/Ser.P, AG/doc. 2023/85 rev.1 (1986) pp. 46–54, 25 I.L.M. (1986) 519. See F. Kaplan, 'Combating Inter-American Convention to Prevent and Punish Torture' 25 *Brooklyn Journal of International Law* (1989) 399; S. Davidson, 'No More Broken Bodies or Minds: The Definition and Control of Torture in the Late Twentieth Century' 6 *Canterbury Law Review* (1995) 25.

[21] European Convention for the Prevention of Torture and Inhuman or Degrading Treatment or Punishment, E.T.S. 126, entered into force February 1 1989.

torture is a norm of *jus cogens*, a norm from which no derogation is permissible.[22]

States are bound under international law not only to refrain from torturing their citizens and other residents, but also to punish those involved in committing this act. Having made this universally accepted statement, there nevertheless remain a number of controversial issues. First, while consensus exists on the prohibition of torture, there are disagreements over the meaning and scope of the term 'torture'. Secondly, there are difficulties in identifying the nature of prohibitions involved in treatment or punishment that is cruel, inhuman or degrading. Societies as well as individuals differ in their perceptions. Thus, some societies view certain punishments as cruel, inhuman or degrading whereas others regard them as fair and just means of retribution.[23] Issues of cultural relativism are directly relevant to this debate.[24] Thirdly, there are difficulties in implementing and enforcing the prohibition of torture. As this chapter elaborates, while the UN Convention against Torture provides for implementation mechanisms, there are a number of limitations and weaknesses in the systems which need to be explored.

THE CONVENTION AGAINST TORTURE (TORTURE CONVENTION)

The Convention against Torture is the product of a sustained campaign to respond to growing instances of torture and violence. Many occurrences of torture including those relating to the treatment of political opponents in the East Bengal civil war (1970), in Chile (1973) and under regimes of men like Idi Amin of Uganda (1971–1979) and Francisco Marcias Nguema of Equatorial Guinea (1969–1979) highlighted the necessity of concerted international action. Like the Convention on Elimination of All Forms of Discrimination against Women and the International Convention for the Elimination of All Forms of Racial Discrimination, the Torture Convention was proceeded by a General Assembly Resolution.[25] In 1977 the Commission

---

[22] Professor Nigel Rodley makes the valid point that 'it is safe to conclude that the prohibition is one of general international law, regardless of whether a particular state is party to a treaty expressly containing the prohibition. Indeed, it may well be that the same reasons, especially the fact of non-derogability of the prohibition in the human rights treaties, permit acceptance of the view that the prohibition is itself a norm of *jus cogens* or a 'peremptory norm of general international law'. Rodley, above n. 1, at p. 74. On the meaning of *jus cogens* norms see above Chapter 1.
[23] See the Report of the 1982 Working Group, UN Doc. E/CN/1982/L/40 (1982) Text reproduced Addendum UN Doc E/1982/12/Add.1 (1982) p. 3. On capital punishment see above Chapter 4 and Chapter 6.
[24] See above introductory chapter.
[25] See Declaration on the Protection of All Persons from Being Subjected to Torture and Other Cruel, Inhuman or Degrading Treatment or Punishment adopted by GA Res. 3452 (XXX) of 9 December 1975.

on Human Rights was requested by the General Assembly to draft a convention against torture and other cruel, inhuman or degrading treatment. These negotiations in the Commission (and in later stages in the General Assembly) took place during 1977–1984. Debate centred around a number of areas; these included the implementation of the Convention, and jurisdictional issues such as universal jurisdiction.[26] Agreement was particularly difficult to reach on issues relating to implementation. In March 1984 the drafts of the treaty were transmitted to the General Assembly to finalise the Document. During much of 1984, the General Assembly worked on the improvement of the text and to agree on the implementation of the treaty. The Convention was adopted by the General Assembly on 10 December, 1984 – on the thirty-sixth anniversary of the adoption of the UDHR. The Convention came into operation in 1987 and currently has 128 State parties.[27] The Convention is divided into three sections. Substantive rights are contained in Article 1–16, implementation machinery is provided in Articles 17–24, and clauses relating to ratification, amendments, etc. are contained in the final part consisting of Articles 25–32. The preamble of the Convention, makes reference to the United Nations Charter,[28] to Article 5 of the UDHR and Article 7 of the ICCPR. It also refers to the Declaration on the Protection of All Persons from Being Subjected to Torture and Other Cruel, Inhuman or Degrading Treatment or Punishment, adopted by the General Assembly.[29]

Provisions contained in the convention

Article 2   Obligation on States to take effective legislative, administrative, judicial or other measures to prevent acts of torture

Article 3   Obligation on States not to return or expel people to countries where they may be subjected to torture

Article 4   Obligation upon States to criminalise all acts (and attempted acts) of torture with appropriately severe punishments

Article 5   Obligation upon States to establish jurisdiction over the offences of torture

Article 6   Obligation to take into custody alleged torturers

Article 7   Obligation to extradite or try alleged offenders

Article 8   Obligation to ensure that extradition is available for torturers

---

[26] A-M.B. Pennegård, 'Article 5' in G. Alfredsson and A. Eide (eds), *The Universal Declaration of Human Rights: A Common Standard of Achievement* (The Hague: Kluwer Law International) 1999, 121–146 at p. 130.

[27] It has been correctly pointed out that out of six human rights treaties with an implementing body, the Torture Convention has received the least ratifications thus far. Pennegård, ibid. at p. 130. For details of States parties see Appendix II.

[28] Particularly Article 55.

[29] Adopted by General Assembly resolution 3452 (XXX) of 9 December 1975.

Article 9   Obligation to afford assistance in connection with criminal proceedings in respect of torture, including supply of evidence

Article 10   Obligation to ensure education and information regarding the prohibition against torture

Article 11   Obligation to keep under review, interrogation rules and practices for the custody and treatment of persons subjected to any form of arrest, detention or imprisonment, to prevent torture

Article 12   Obligation to proceed to a prompt and impartial investigation in cases of torture

Article 13   Obligation to ensure the rights of torture victims (including the right to complain and have their case heard by competent authorities)

Article 14   Obligation to provide remedies

Article 15   Obligation to exclude evidence obtained through torture

Article 16   Obligation to prevent acts of cruel, inhuman or degrading treatment or punishment (not amounting to torture)

Defining the concept of 'torture', 'cruel' 'inhuman' or 'degrading treatment' or 'punishment'

A preliminary issue relates to the meaning of the terms of 'torture', 'cruel', 'inhuman' 'or 'degrading treatment' or 'punishment'. At the very outset of our survey of the Torture Convention, there appears to be a discrepancy; while the Convention defines 'torture', there is no detailed exposition of the terms 'cruel', 'inhuman' 'degrading treatment or punishment'. The Convention defines torture as follows:

> For the purposes of this Convention, the term 'torture' means any act by which severe pain or suffering, whether physical or mental, is intentionally inflicted on a person for such purposes as obtaining from him or a third person information or a confession, punishing him for an act he or a third person has committed or is suspected of having committed, or intimidating or coercing him or a third person, or for any reason based on discrimination of any kind, when such pain or suffering is inflicted by or at the instigation of or with the consent or acquiescence of a public official or other person acting in an official capacity. It does not include pain or suffering arising only from, inherent in or incidental to lawful sanctions.[30]

A number of issues emerge from this definition. First, the Convention defines and envisages 'torture' as a product of an 'act'. Could an omission with equally serious consequences amount to torture? While the matter was debated during the drafting of the convention, no clear position seems to have been established. It is submitted that omissions if intentionally conducted (for example, denial of food to prisoners) amount to torture. There is

---

[30] Article 1(1).

evidence to support this argument from case law emergent from human rights bodies.[31]

Similarly to the debate on the scope of 'an act', controversy surrounds the meaning of 'severe'. During the drafting stages several proposals were made in order to delete the term from the definition.[32] It was however retained, with some States expressing the view that pain or suffering must attain a certain threshold before it could amount to torture.[33] There are other limitations in the definition of torture as well. Pain and suffering must be inflicted intentionally and for the purposes listed in Article 1(1) to constitute torture. Pain and suffering administered as a 'lawful sanction' does not come within the definition of torture, although it may lead to 'cruel, inhuman or degrading treatment or punishment'.[34]

The ambit of torture is limited to when this activity is conducted 'by or at the instigation of' or 'with the consent or acquiescence of a public official or other person acting in an official capacity'. This definition only covers torture conducted by public officials (for example, police or other agencies established by the State). The public officials also include paramilitary organisations, vigilantes or death-squads. Torture may also be inflicted by private individuals provided they act on the instigation of, or with consent or acquiescence of State officials. The definition is, however, restrictive in that it excludes acts of torture conducted by non-State actors and private individuals against other individuals or State officials. This appears to be an unfortunate limitation as many instances of torture can be found where the act of torture is committed by non-State actors or private individuals.

The definition provided in Article 1 also raises the issue of the scope of the crime. The obvious intention of the Article is to protect the detainees in the custody of law enforcement agencies or security forces etc. The question has been raised as to the scope of torture outside of places of detention, for example, in public schools etc.[35] Andrew Byrnes, in suggesting a broader

---

[31] In *Denmark, Norway, Sweden v. Greece*, the European Commission on Human Rights held that 'the failure of the Government of Greece to provide food, water, heating in winter, proper washing facilities, clothing, medical and dental care to prisoners constitutes an "act" of torture in violation of article 3 of ECHR'. See the *Greek Case* Yearbook XII (1969) 1. Also see *Denmark, Norway, Sweden v. Greece*, 12 YB 1 (1969). Also see *Loizidou v. Turkey* (Preliminary Objections), Judgment of 23 March 1995, Series A, No. 310, para 62.

[32] See the Report prepared by the Secretariat on the fifth UN Congress on the Prevention of Crime of Torture and the Treatment of Offenders (1976) p. 38.

[33] See the summary prepared by the Secretary-General in accordance with the Commission Resolution 18 (XXXIV) containing the comments received from governments on the Draft Articles of the Convention on Torture, Commission on Human Rights, thirty-fifth session, UN Doc.E/CN/1314/Add.1(1979) p. 2.

[34] See Harris, above n. 1, at p. 715.

[35] A. Byrnes, 'The Committee Against Torture' in P. Alston (ed.), *The United Nations and Human Rights: A Critical Appraisal* (Oxford: Clarendon Press) 1992, 509–545 at p. 515.

approach, notes the possible application of torture to institutions which are *per se* not regarded as places of detention, for example State-run hospitals, offices and schools.[36]

Having pointed to the complexities in the definition of torture, the next issue concerns distinguishing torture from other forms of ill-treatment. These distinctions have been scrutinised by some human rights bodies more closely than others (see, for example, the ECHR as opposed to the ICCPR). Under the Torture Convention, while States are under an obligation to prevent acts amounting to cruel, inhuman, degrading treatment or punishment, the distinction is of significance since certain provisions can apply only to torture (see for example Article 20). A number of important provisions are only applicable when the offences attain the threshold of torture. These provisions are contained in Articles 3–9 and 14.

The absence of terms other than torture has already been alluded to; there is a similar dearth of analysis of these terms in the general corpus of international human rights law. One strategy adopted by some human rights treaty bodies is that of avoiding the issues of distinctions altogether. Thus the Human Rights Committee, the European Committee for the Prevention of Torture and the Inter-American Commission have generally avoided distinguishing torture from cruel, inhuman, degrading treatment or punishment.[37] This is possibly a result of the varying notions of torture; a generalised treatment of violations of particular articles is often seen as less controversial. Andrew Byrnes makes the following valid point:

> while it is obviously desirable that international bodies concerned with the prevention and punishment of torture not work at cross purposes, it is also important to keep in mind that there is no one, standard definition of torture and other ill-treatment that applies in every context. What 'torture' means for the work of one body will depend on the text, purpose and history of its enabling instrument, as well as on its own practice and the relevant practice of States.[38]

In the light of these complexities inherent in defining torture, a broad approach is recommended. It would also be useful for CAT (the Committee which implements the Torture Convention) to develop its jurisprudence in the light of related cases from other treaty bodies. The case law of the Human Rights Committee has been extensive and provides useful guidelines. The Human Rights Committee has classified physical acts such as punching and

---

[36] Ibid. 516.

[37] S. Davidson, 'The Civil and Political Rights Protected in the Inter-American Human Rights System' in D. Harris and S. Livingstone (eds), *The Inter-American System of Human Rights* (Oxford: Clarendon Press) 1998, 213–288 at p. 230.

[38] A. Byrnes, 'The Committee Against Torture' in P. Alston (ed.), above n. 35, at p. 513.

kicking,[39] forcible standing for hours,[40] electrocution and shocks,[41] and enforcement of malnutrition and starvation[42] as torture. Other regional bodies have established that physical beatings,[43] the death penalty,[44] disappearances,[45] prolonged periods of detention incommunicado,[46] rape,[47] putting hoods so as to suffocate the victim;[48] mock burials and mock executions,[49] amount to torture. It is also firmly established that torture results not only from physical force, but is also manifested by mental torture and suffering.

Non-expulsions and torture Convention

Article 2(1) of the Convention places an obligation on States parties to the Convention to 'take effective legislative, administrative, judicial or other measures to prevent acts of torture in any territory under its jurisdiction'. The obligation is immediate and the emphasis is upon *effective* measures to prevent acts of torture. While these provision are directed towards ensuring that State parties remain under an obligation to ensure effective prevention of torture within their own respective jurisdictions, complications have surfaced where a State decides to expel or extradite individuals to another State

[39] *Miguel Angel Estrella* v. *Uruguay*, Communication No. 74/1980 (17 July 1980), UN Doc. Supp. No. 40 (A/38/40) at 150 (1983).

[40] *Moriana Hernandez Valentini de Bazzano, Luis Maria Bazzano Ambrosini, Martha Valentini de Massera and Jose Luis Massera* v. *Uruguay*, Communication No. R.1/5 (15 February 1977), UN Doc. Supp. No. 40 (A/34/40) at 124 (1979).

[41] *Alberto Grille Motta* v. *Uruguay*, Communication No. 11/1977 (29 July 1980), UN Doc. CCPR/C/OP/1 at 54 (1984).

[42] *Raul Sendic Antonaccio* v. *Uruguay*, Communication No. R.14/63 (28 November 1979), UN Doc. Supp. No. 40 (A/37/40) at 114 (1982); *Roslik et al.* v. *Uruguay*, Case 9274, Res. No. 11/84, October 3, 1984, OAS/Ser.L/V/II.66, doc.10 rev 1, at 121.

[43] See *Denmark, Norway, Sweden* v. *Greece*, 12 YB 1 (1969), 504; *Raul Sendic Antonaccio* v. *Uruguay*, Communication No. R.14/63 (28 November 1979), UN Doc. Supp. No. 40 (A/37/40) at 114 (1982), paras 16(2) and 20.

[44] In its 1993 Resolution on Peru (IACHR) Annual Report 1993, 478, it noted 'For the Inter-American Commission on Human Rights, there is no premium that can be placed upon human life. The death penalty is a grievous affront to human dignity and its application constitutes cruel, inhuman and degrading treatment of the individual sentenced to death'.

[45] See *Lissardi and Rossi* v. *Guatemala*, Case 10.508, Report No. 25/94, Inter-Am.C.H.R., OEA/Ser.L/V/II.88 rev.1 Doc. 9 at 51 (1995) at 54.

[46] *Velasquez Rodriguez Case*, Judgment of July 29, 1988, Inter-Am.Ct.H.R. (Ser. C) No. 4 (1988).

[47] *Aydin* v. *Turkey*, Judgment of 25 September 1997, 1997-VI RJD 1885, para 86; *Caracoles Community* v. *Bolivia*, Case 7481, Res. No. 30/82, March 8, 1982, OAS/Ser.L/V/II.57, Doc. 6 Rev. 1, at 20 September 1982, at 36 (1994). and *Raquel Martí de Mejía* v. *Perú*, Case 10.970, Report No. 5/96, Inter-Am.C.H.R., OEA/Ser.L/V/II.91 Doc. 7 at 157 (1996) at 182–8.

[48] *Lovato* v. *El Salvador*, Case 10.574, Report No. 5/94, Inter-Am.C.H.R., OEA/Ser.L/V/II.85 Doc. 9 rev. at 174.

[49] *Barrera* v. *Bolivia*, Case No. 7824, Res. No. 33/82, Inter-Am.C.H.R., OAS/Ser.L/V/II.57, Doc. 6 Rev. (1982) 44.

in the knowledge that upon their return (to their State of residence or nationality) they are likely to be subjected to torture. Such expulsions of non-nationals have been the subject of intense debate in general inter-national law. We have already considered a number of cases where the Human Rights Committee and the European Commission and European Court of Human Rights have been confronted with this issue.[50] Article 3 of the ECHR has, in particular, led to some striking and exceptional decisions where the claimants have successfully relied on the argument that if expelled or extradited they would suffer from torture, or inhuman degrading treatment or punishment.[51] Article 3 of the Torture Convention, inspired by the case law of the ECHR, provides that:

(1) No State Party shall expel, return ('refouler') or extradite a person to another State where there are substantial grounds for believing that he would be in danger of being subjected to torture.
(2) For the purpose of determining whether there are such grounds, the competent authorities shall take into account all relevant considerations including, where applicable, the existence in the State concerned of a consistent pattern of gross, flagrant or mass violations of human rights.

Article 3 emphasises the fundamental right of non-refoulement, which is now considered part of customary international law.[52] Similar provisions can be found in Article 33 of the 1951 Convention Relating to the Status of the Refugees.[53] The significance of Article 3 of the Torture Convention is confirmed firstly by the fact that it has been the subject of regular scrutiny by the Committee against Torture (CAT) in its consideration of State reports. Secondly, CAT has thus far produced its only 'General Comment' on this Article and, thirdly and most significantly, a majority of cases dealt with by CAT relate to this particular Article.

An interesting example of the application of Article 3 is provided by *Alan* v. *Switzerland*.[54] In this case the author of the communication, Ismail Alan, was a Turkish national who had been involved in political activities in Turkey for the outlawed Marxist-Leninist group KAWA. During 1981–1983 he was detained a number of times during which he claimed to have been tortured by the Turkish authorities. He was sentenced in 1984 to two and a half years of imprisonment and was awarded a ten-month period of internal

[50] See above Chapters 4 and 6.
[51] See *Soering* v. *United Kingdom*, Judgment of 7 July 1989, Series A, No. 161; *Chahal* v. *United Kingdom*, Judgment of 15 November 1996, 1996-V RJD 1831.
[52] M. Kjǻrum, 'Article 14' in G. Alfredsson and A. Eide (eds), above n. 26, 279–295 at p. 285.
[53] Convention Relating to the Status of Refugees. Signed 28 July 1951; entered into force 22 April 1954; 189 U.N.T.S. 150.
[54] *Ismail Alan* v. *Switzerland*, Communication No. 21/1995, UN Doc. CAT/C/16/D/21/1995 (1996).

exile for his involvement with the militant organisation, KAWA. During 1989 and 1989 he was re-arrested. The author claimed that during this period he was tortured and his house was searched by the Turkish police. In 1990, after having left the Turkey on a forged passport, Ismail Alan sought asylum in Switzerland. Despite having produced medical evidence of scars on his body, the Swiss authorities turned down his application on the basis that there were too many inconsistencies in his claim for asylum. Ismail Alan, relying upon Article 3 of the Convention, then complained to the Committee against Torture (CAT). The Committee took account of all the relevant considerations as provided in Article 3(2) of the Convention.[55] It considered the existing consistent and systematic pattern of serious violations of human rights in Turkey, which had been confirmed by its own findings in its enquiry under Article 22 of the Convention.[56] According to the Committee, the critical factor in assessing the validity of the claims based under Article 3 was a determination that the person in question would be in danger of being subjected to torture upon his return to the country. Specific grounds must exist establishing that the individual concerned would be at risk personally.[57] In upholding the author's claim the Committee made the following observations:

> In the instant case, the Committee considers that the author's [Kurdish] ethnic background, his alleged political affiliation, his history of detention, and his internal exile should all be taken into account when determining whether he would be in danger of being subjected to torture upon his return. The State party has pointed out contradictions and inconsistencies in the author's story, but the Committee considers that complete accuracy is seldom to be expected by victims of torture and that such inconsistencies as may exist in the author's presentation of the facts are not material and do not raise doubts about the general veracity of the author's claim.[58]

In its General Comment adopted in 1997, CAT set forth the following guidelines as useful in determining the validity of the applicant's claim under Article 3 of the Convention:

(a) Is the State concerned one in which there is evidence of a consistent pattern of gross, flagrant or mass violations of human rights (see art. 3, para. 2)?

(b) Has the author been tortured or maltreated by or at the instigation of or with the consent or acquiescence of a public official or other person acting in an official capacity in the past? If so, was this the recent past?

---

[55] Para 11.2 and 11.5.
[56] Para 11.2; see below on Article 22 procedure.
[57] Ibid.
[58] Para 11.3

(c) Is there medical or other independent evidence to support a claim by the author that he/she has been tortured or maltreated in the past? Has the torture had after-effects?
(d) Has the situation referred to in (a) above changed? Has the internal situation in respect of human rights altered?
(e) Has the author engaged in political or other activity within or outside the State concerned which would appear to make him/her particularly vulnerable to the risk of being placed in danger of torture were he/she to be expelled, returned or extradited to the State in question?
(f) Is there any evidence as to the credibility of the author?
(g) Are there factual inconsistencies in the claim of the author? If so, are they relevant?[59]

In another more recent case, *A.S v. Sweden,*[60] CAT relied on the aforementioned guidelines to decide in favour of an asylum claim brought by an Iranian national. The case concerned an Iranian widow, whose husband had died while performing services for the State. After her husband's death, although provided with greater material support, the complainant was subjected to a strict Islamic code and was forced into a marriage with one of the high ranking Ayatollahs. This marriage, the author complained, was enforced through threats of physical harm to her and to her children. The author claimed that while not expected to live with the Ayatollah, she was used for sexual services whenever required. The author subsequently met a Christian man and in her attempts to elope with him was apprehended and allegedly severely beaten and tortured by the police. She was subsequently successful in leaving Iran and on arrival in Sweden submitted an application for asylum. She also submitted that since her departure from Iran she had been awarded the Islamic sentence for adultery (stoning to death) and was fearful of the execution of that sentence were she to be returned. The Swedish Immigration Board turned down her application for asylum, based on what they perceived as inconsistencies in the author's claim. On her communication before CAT, the Committee in upholding the authors' claim noted:

> Considering that the author's account of events is consistent with the Committee's knowledge about the present human rights situation in Iran, and that the author has given plausible explanations for her failure or inability to provide certain details which might have been of relevance to the case, the Committee is of the view that, in the prevailing circumstances, the State party has an obligation, in accordance with article 3 of the Convention, to refrain from forcibly returning the author to Iran or to any other country where she runs a risk of being expelled or returned to Iran.[61]

---

[59] Para 8.
[60] *A.S. v. Sweden*, Communication No. 149/1999. CAT/C/25/D/149/1999 (1999).
[61] Ibid. para 9.

Torture and the issues of sovereign immunity and universal jurisdiction

The criminalisation of torture is universally acknowledged and in this regard our earlier discussion needs to be recalled. Notwithstanding the prohibition and criminalisation of torture, two issues of fundamental importance remain to be considered. First, whether universal jurisdiction to try and punish those involved in crimes of torture exists. Secondly, to what extent can State or governmental officials rely upon their position to claim immunity from any challenges brought by their victims in domestic courts.

International law has struggled to provide definitive answers since both of these questions affect the very core of the international legal system which is based upon State sovereignty. Subsequent discussion aims to highlight the existing tensions through case law, State practice and the treaty provisions of the UN Convention. A frequently invoked case on the subject is *Filártiga* v. *Pena-Irala*.[62] The case concerned a claim of torture brought in the United States by two Paraguayan refugees against a Paraguayan (former police officer) who was apprehended in the United States. The applicants instituted civil proceedings for damages against the defendant even though the alleged acts of torture took place outside the United States. The plaintiffs claimed that the United States court had jurisdiction to deal with the case under the United States Judiciary Act 1789. The Act establishes federal court jurisdiction over 'all causes where an alien sues for a tort ... [committed] in violation of the law of nations'.[63] The United States Circuit Court of Appeal in confirming the United States courts' jurisdiction to try the case noted:

> A threshold question on the jurisdictional issue is whether the conduct alleged violates the law of nations. In the light of the universal condemnation of torture in numerous international agreements, and the renunciation of torture as an instrument of official policy by virtually all of the nations of the world (in principle if not in practice) we find that an act of torture committed by a State official against one held in detention violates established norms of international law of human rights and hence the law of nations.[64]

In the *Filártiga case*, although the defendant was a former police officer, any defences based on acts conducted in an official capacity were disregarded. The decision in *Filártiga*, in particular the recognition by the Court that torture is prohibited by customary international law, has been widely welcomed and publicised.[65] At the same time the views expressed by the court must be expressed with a hint of caution for two reasons. Firstly, because the Court was dealing with a

---

[62] 630 F. 2d 876 (1980); 19 ILM 966. US. Circuit Court of Appeals, 2nd Circuit.

[63] 28 U.S.Ct 1350.

[64] Per Circuit Judge, Kaufman.

[65] See J.M. Blum and R.G. Seinhardt, 'Federal Jurisdiction over International Human Rights Claims: The Alien Tort Claims Act after *Filártiga* v. *Peña-Irala*', 22 *Harvard International Law Journal* (1981) 53.

civil liability (as opposed to criminal liability) action, and secondly because it does not address the subject of universality of jurisdiction in the case of torture.[66]

In relation to torture claims, the defence based on sovereign or State immunity has been tested in the English courts. In *Al Adsani v. Government of Kuwait*,[67] the plaintiff, who had been tortured by the members of the Kuwaiti Royal Family, brought a civil action for damages against the Government of Kuwait (the first defendant) and individual members of the Royal Family (as second, third and fourth defendants). In dismissing the appeal in so far as it related to the first defendant, the Court of Appeal relied upon the limitations of State immunity as provided by the State Immunity Act 1978.

The enforcement of the Torture Convention appears to have addressed some of these uncertainties. The thrust of the Convention against torture is directed towards any individual committing acts of torture. The holding of official or public position is, therefore, not an excuse or justification for conducting torture. In other words, as Lord Browne-Wilkinson noted in the *Pinochet case*,[68] 'the notion of a continued immunity for ex-heads of States is inconsistent with the provisions of the Torture Convention' and that torture, as established by the Convention 'cannot be a State function'.[69]

The Convention also sets down jurisdictional principles. Article 5 in establishing a multi-jurisdictional system provides that:

1. Each State Party shall take such measures as may be necessary to establish its jurisdiction over the offences referred to in article 4 in the following cases:

   (a) When the offences are committed in any territory under its jurisdiction or on board a ship or aircraft registered in that State;
   (b) When the alleged offender is a national of that State
   (c) When the victim is a national of that State if that State considers it appropriate

---

[66] Rodley notes that the case 'did not deal, however, with the intractable question of when an international law prohibition, even one that requires penal action by States to repress violations, becomes one that requires or permits universality of criminal jurisdiction' and that 'it must be remembered that *Filártiga* case was one of civil, not criminal law. There is no reason to conclude that criminal liability would not also be the case, but as yet there is no state practice to endorse the point. Indeed, the chances of establishing such a practice will be rare: evidence is hard to come by in torture cases, especially in cases heard outside the country where the torture took place' Rodley, above n. 1, at pp. 128–129.

[67] *Al Adsani v. Kuwait* (1996) (CA) Court of Appeal 12 March 1996, *The Times*, March 29 1996; In the proceeding brought by Al-Adsani against the United Kingdom before the European Court of Human Rights, the Court recently decided that there were no violations of Article 3 and 6 of the European Convention on Human Rights. See *Al-Adsani v. United Kingdom* 21 November 2001, No. 35763/97 (2002) 34 EHRR 11.

[68] *R. v. Evans Ex p. Pinochet Ugarte (No. 1)* (HL) 25 November 1998 [1998] 3 WLR 1456; *R. v. Bow Street Metropolitan Stipendiary Magistrate Ex p. Pinochet Ugarte (No. 2)* (HL) 15 January 1999 [1999] 2 WLR 272; *R. v. Bow Street Metropolitan Stipendiary Magistrate Ex p. Pinochet Ugarte (No. 3)* (HL) 24 March 1999 [1999] 2 WLR 827.

[69] Ibid. at 114 J–115 a–e.

Under the provisions of Article 5(1) States parties are required to establish criminal jurisdiction in cases of torture where torture is conducted in their territory;[70] relying upon the nationality principle, when the offender is its national;[71] relying upon the passive personality principle, where the victims have the State's nationality.[72] The provisions in Article 5(1) are reinforced by Article 5(2) according to which '[e]ach State Party shall likewise take such measures as may be necessary to establish its jurisdiction over such offences in cases where the alleged offender is present in any territory under its jurisdiction and it does not extradite him pursuant to Article 8 to any of the States mentioned in paragraph I of this Article'. Article 5(2) and Article 7 of the Convention place an obligation upon the State either to extradite the alleged torturers or to try them on grounds of universal jurisdiction.[73]

The existence of the multi-State grounds of jurisdiction as provided in the Torture Convention have often been equated with 'universal jurisdiction'.[74] Such a view, however, remains questionable since in the absence of attaining a status of customary international law the jurisdictional provisions only bind States parties to the treaty.[75] Some commentators have suggested that under the Torture Convention the multi-State jurisdiction 'would permit all States, including those not parties to it, to prosecute or extradite torturers found in their territory'.[76] Others however have questioned this approach. According to Boulesbaa:

> The term 'universal jurisdiction' ... does not connote the same technical meaning as 'universal jurisdiction' over piracy in which any State may prosecute the pirate if it obtains personal jurisdiction over him regardless of whether it has any connection with the crime or the pirate. The multi-State jurisdiction in the Torture Convention merely connotes 'a multiplicity of jurisdictions' limited to the State parties of the Torture Convention which is intended to deny torturers any safe haven in such States. It does not include those States not party to the Torture Convention.[77]

Boulesbaa' s argument appears persuasive in the light of the recent high profile case concerning General Pinochet. In its second hearing in the House of Lords, although their Lordships relied upon a range of sources from general

---

[70] Article 5(1)(a).
[71] Article 5(1)(b)
[72] Article 5(1)(c).
[73] Rodley, above n. 1, at p. 129.
[74] See Burgers and Danelius, above n. 1, at p. 132–133; According to Professor Harris, '[s]ignificantly, the Convention grounds for criminal jurisdiction include universality jurisdiction; it is sufficient that "the alleged offender is present" in its territory for the Convention to apply Article5(2).' Harris, above n. 1, at pp. 715–716.
[75] On treaty provisions as binding in customary international law see above Chapter 1.
[76] G.C. Rogers, 'Argentina's Obligations to Prosecute Military Officials for Torture' 20 *Columbia Human Rights Law Review* (1989) pp. 289– 290, n. 154.
[77] Boulesbaa, above n. 1, at p. 205.

international law and came to deny a blanket immunity to General Pinochet, nevertheless they limited the scope of the offences of torture and conspiracy to commit torture to after 8 December 1988 – the date when the UK incorporated within its domestic law the Convention against Torture. The majority of their lordships recognised that jurisdiction, in so far as United Kingdom courts were concerned, was established from the time of the incorporation of the Convention into UK law.[78] However the issue also raised confusion. Thus according to Lord Brown-Wilkinson

> [t]he *jus cogens* nature of internal crime of torture justifies states in taking universal jurisdiction over torture wherever committed. International law provides that offences *jus cogens* may be punished by any state because the offenders are 'common enemies' of all mankind and all nations have an equal interest in their apprehension and prosecution ... In the light of the authorities to which I have referred (and there are many others) I have no doubt that long before the Torture Convention of 1984 state torture was an international crime in the highest sense.

Having made these substantial comments, he goes on to say:

> until there was some form of universal jurisdiction for the punishment of the crime of torture could it really be talked about as a fully constituted international crime. But in my judgment the Torture Convention did provide what was missing: a world wide universal jurisdiction. Further it required all member states to ban and outlaw torture.

A detailed consideration of the judgments delivered by their Lordships in the *Pinochet case* highlights the existence of a lack of clarity, particularly on issues of jurisdiction of domestic courts. Having said that, the articulation of rules through an international treaty is proving useful. The increasing number of ratifications to the Torture Convention and the equally insignificant number of reservations point towards a growing consensus that, in addition to treaty law, customary international law is moving towards a position where it is envisaged that States would be under an obligation to ensure the existence of universal jurisdiction in cases of torture.

THE COMMITTEE AGAINST TORTURE (CAT)[79]

Part II (Articles 17–24) of the Convention deals with the implementation of the treaty. Article 17, establishes a Committee against Torture (CAT) which

---

[78] Incorporation of the treaty effected through S.134 of the Criminal Justice Act 1998. The Act came into force on 29 September 1988.

[79] A. Dormenval, 'UN Committee against Torture: Practice and Perspectives' 8 *NQHR* (1990) 26; A. Byrnes, 'The Committee Against Torture' in P. Alston (ed.), above n. 35, at pp. 509–545; M. O'Flaherty, *Human Rights and the UN: Practice before the Treaty Bodies* (London: Sweet and Maxwell) 1996, p. 139.

consists of ten independent experts. CAT, alongside the Committee on the Rights of the Child, represents the smallest of the treaty-based bodies in the UN System. The small size of the CAT is arguably a consequence of its relatively specific mandate and increasing financial constraints. These members of CAT are of high moral standing and are well known for their knowledge and competence in human rights law. They serve on the CAT in their personal capacity and are elected for a term of four years. They are eligible for re-election if renominated.[80] The Committee members are elected by the States parties although consideration is provided to equitable geographical distribution and to the expertise (in particular legal experience) of the individuals.[81]

The Committee members are elected by secret ballot from a list of persons nominated by States parties.[82] Each State party is allowed to nominate one person from among its nationals.[83] In nominating individuals for membership to the Committee, States parties are required to consider the usefulness of persons who are also members of the Human Rights Committee established under the ICCPR and who are willing to serve on the CAT.[84] Unlike most other treaty-based bodies, it is the States parties and not the United Nations who are responsible for the expenses relating to the meetings of the Committee including staffing costs and other facilities. This feature was modelled on the CERD, although in the latter case the costs of the Secretariat are provided for from the United Nations budget.[85] The financial liabilities on State parties are a potentially discouraging factor in ratifying the treaty. There is also the danger that States could, in a way, hold the Committee 'to ransom'. As States parties go into arrears, there also remains the uncertainty about the prospect of future sessions. Article 18 authorises the Committee *inter alia* to formulate its own rules of procedures, which according to the Article must establish a quorum of six members. The decisions of the Committee are to be made by a majority vote of the members present.

IMPLEMENTATION MECHANISMS

Four methods of monitoring the implementation are provided in the Convention. These comprise: first the reporting procedure, secondly an inter-State complaints procedure, thirdly an individual complaints procedure and, fourthly, the initiation of enquiry and reporting into acts of systematic torture.

---

[80] According to Article 17(5) the term of five of the members elected at the first election shall expire at the end of two years; immediately after the first election the names of these five members shall be chosen by lot by the chairman of the meeting referred to in paragraph 3 of this article.
[81] Article 17(2).
[82] Ibid.
[83] Ibid.
[84] Ibid.
[85] A. Byrnes, 'The Committee Against Torture' in P. Alston (ed.), above n. 35, at p. 521.

The reporting procedure is the only compulsory procedure, the others being optional. We shall deal with each of these mechanisms in greater detail in the remainder of this chapter.

Reporting procedures[86]

Article 19 of the Convention deals with the reporting system. According to Article 19(1) each State party is obliged to submit a report within one year after the entry into force of the Convention. These reports are to be submitted to the Committee via the UN Secretary-General.[87] States parties are required to report on the measures they have taken to give effect to their undertakings under this Convention.[88] Periodic reports are to be submitted once every four years or at the request of the Committee. CAT is given *inter alia* the task of providing consideration to State Reports. In its initial phase CAT held two regular sessions every year, each lasting for two weeks. During each of the sessions, on average, five to seven reports were considered.[89] However, since its tenth session in May 1998 the duration of the sessions has been extended to three weeks, which has allowed the Committee to consider up to ten reports.[90]

As in the case of other treaty bodies there is an enormous amount of reluctance to submit reports as it opens the way for public criticism of State compliance.[91] At the same time, CAT also faces a backlog of examination of reports that have been submitted; and in the case of reports that are examined, pressure of time often does not allow a thorough or adequate discussion. In addition, the work of CAT has been criticised on a number of grounds. These include a failure to investigate the most pertinent questions, a superficiality and vagueness in consideration of reports and posing of questions, and inconsistencies in the approaching of issues among members of the Committee. These shortcomings remain, although the Committee members have, over time, gained more experience and there is now greater informal interaction with NGOs.

CAT like other human rights treaty bodies has issued reporting guidelines to States parties. The guidelines for initial reports are of a very similar nature

---

[86] R. Bank, 'Country-Oriented Procedures under the Convention against Torture: Towards a New Dynamic' in P. Alston and J. Crawford (eds), *The Future of UN Human Rights Treaty Monitoring* (Cambridge: Cambridge University Press) 2000, pp. 145–174.

[87] Article 19(1).

[88] Ibid.

[89] R. Bank, 'Country-Oriented Procedures under the Convention against Torture: Towards a New Dynamic' in P. Alston and J. Crawford (eds), above n. 86, at p. 147.

[90] Ibid. p. 149.

[91] CAT has considered (without implementing them) plans to discuss the Convention's implementation in relation to the States which have not submitted reports. Ibid. p. 148.

to those of the Human Rights Committee. In these guidelines, the request is made to States that reports should be divided into two parts: the first part outlining the general legal and constitutional structure within which the Convention is implemented and the second part should provide detailed information on the steps undertaken to implement individual Articles of the treaty. In the second part it is also anticipated that States would provide details of the difficulties experienced in the implementation of the Convention. The guidelines for periodic reports require the States to provide information on new developments in the period preceding their last report. Information that is sought in particular areas relates to institutional, legislative and administrative changes; to relevant case law and details of complaints of torture or other ill-treatment and their outcomes; and information requested by the Committee at the consideration of the previous report. As indicated earlier, CAT faces many of the issues confronted by other treaty bodies for example a growing backlog with overdue reports, inadequate reports or failure to provide additional information. The quality of reports that have thus far been submitted (like reports submitted to other treaty bodies) has been variable, both in terms of quality and relevance of information and length.

Procedure for the consideration of reports

The procedure for the consideration of the State reports is also similar to other treaty bodies. It is the norm that one member of the CAT acts as the Country Rapporteur and another as co-Rapporteur. The task of these members is to consider the reports in detail, to identify key issues, and to formulate a list of questions and comments to be put forward to the State representatives. In order to formulate his views, the Country Rapporteur relies upon the State report itself, on any previous reports, and on information received from the Special Rapporteur on Torture and from the NGOs.[92]

The CAT considers State reports in public sessions. It invites a State representative to introduce the report. The outline by the State representative is followed by questions put to him (or her) by the Committee members. These questions are usually initiated by the Country Rapporteur or a co-Rapporteur. The representative, if unable to answer the questions, appears before the Committee at a subsequent meeting (often held a few days later) to respond to the questions. At this subsequent meeting, CAT members may pose additional questions. The Committee then formulates what are termed 'Conclusions and Recommendations' or 'Concluding Observations/Comments'. These Conclusions and Recommendations, while synthesising the Committee's views

---

[92] O'Flaherty, above n. 79, at p. 147.

of the report and the overall situation pertaining to torture, consist of an introduction, positive aspects of the report, factors and difficulties impeding the application of the provisions of the Convention, subjects of concern and recommendations.[93] Like the Human Rights Committee and other treaty bodies, the CAT is authorised to make 'General Comments'.[94] The authority for formulating these General Comments is based on the same premise as the one provided for other treaties. The CAT has thus far utilised its authority in this regard very cautiously, adopting only a single General Comments on Article 3.

Inter-State procedure

Article 21 provides for an inter-State complaints procedure, and has distinct similarities to the provisions of Article 41 of the ICCPR. Although part of the same Convention, the procedure is optional with States interested in using this mechanism being required to make an additional declaration.[95] For the procedure to be operative, the complainant State and the State against whom the complaint is made must have made a declaration under Article 21.[96]

To pursue this procedure a State (A) that considers another State (B) is violating the Covenant can bring that fact to the attention of the State party concerned (that is, State B). State (B) must respond to the allegations within three months.[97] If, however, within six months after the receipt of the initial communication the matter has not been resolved, either State may bring the matter to the attention of the Committee.[98] The Committee must decide whether all local remedies have been exhausted (unless they are unreasonably prolonged or are unlikely to bring effective relief to the victim) before considering the case in closed sessions.[99] The Committee's task is to make an attempt to resolve the dispute through its good offices.[100] In order to pursue its functions of conciliation the Committee may appoint an ad hoc conciliation commission. The provision relating to the establishment of the commission is similar to the one provided in Article 41 of the ICCPR. However, unlike ICCPR, the procedures or mechanisms of the conciliation

---

[93] For recent examples see Conclusions and Recommendations of the Committee against Torture: Kazakhstan (17/05/2001) CAT/C/XXVI/Concl.7/Rev.1. (Concluding Observations/Comments); Conclusions and recommendations of the Committee against Torture: Slovakia (11/05/2001) CAT/C/XXVI/Concl.4/Rev.1. (Concluding Observations/Comments).

[94] See Article 19(3).

[95] Article 21(1).

[96] Ibid.

[97] Article 21(1)(a).

[98] Article 21(1)(b).

[99] Article 21(1)(c)(d).

[100] Article 21(1)(e).

commission are not addressed in this Convention. The Committee is obliged to produce a written report within twelve months of the date of receipt of notice of complaint. If a solution is reached then the Committee's report will be brief and confined to facts and the solution reached.[101] If a friendly solution has not been reached, the Committee is required to confine its report to a brief statement of facts. The written submissions and a record of the oral submissions made by the States parties are to be attached to the report.[102] In our study we have considered that inter-State mechanisms have been put in place in several human rights instruments.[103] While occasional usage has been made of the inter-State procedures (see for example, the ECHR), by and large States remain reluctant to use these procedure. This reluctance derives largely from a concern of straining diplomatic and political relations. Nor do States wish to establish a precedent which may ultimately be used against them.[104] It is therefore not surprising to note that the CAT has not received an inter-State complaint.

Individual complaints procedure

Article 22 provides for the individual complaints procedure. According to Article 22(1):

> A State Party to this Convention may at any time declare under this article that it recognises the competence of the Committee to receive and consider communications from or on behalf of individuals subject to its jurisdiction who claim to be victims of a violation by a State Party of the provisions of the Convention. No communication shall be received by the Committee if it concerns a State Party which has not made such a declaration.

The individual complaints procedure is optional and requires States parties to make an additional declaration to recognise the competence of the Committee to receive and consider communications. As at 1 March 2002, forty-six States had made a declaration under Article 22. Like the inter-State procedure described above, the individual complaints procedure is also modelled very closely on the first Optional Protocol to the ICCPR and the rules of procedure adopted by CAT largely mirror those adopted by the Human Rights Committee. There are a number of distinctions between the Optional Protocol and Article 22 which need to be highlighted. First, under Article 22(1) the Communication can be made either by or on behalf of the individual provided there is evidence that the Communication has the

---

[101] Article 21(1)(h)(i).
[102] Article 21(1)(h)(ii).
[103] See e.g. the ICCPR; Race Convention and the three Regional treaties.
[104] See S. Leckie, 'The Inter-State Complaint Procedure in International Law: Hopeful Prospects or Wishful thinking?' 10 *HRQ* (1988) 249.

authorisation of the victim.[105] By contrast the wording of the first Optional Protocol is restrictive in that it only allows the Human Rights Committee to consider communications from 'individuals'.[106] In practice, however, as we considered in an earlier chapter, the Human Rights Committee has allowed others to petition on behalf of the victim in circumstances where he is being held incommunicado, there is strict mail censorship, there is an incapacitating illness consequent to detention or death has occurred as a result of a State's actions or omissions.[107]

It is also noticeable that while the provisions of Article 22(1) of the Torture Convention authorise Communications to be made on behalf of the victims, the position regarding submissions by NGOs remains uncertain.[108] Thus far NGOs have been unsuccessful in submitting Communications before the CAT. CAT has also not allowed *actio popularis* submissions to be made. In *B.M'B* v. *Tunisia*,[109] a Communication on behalf of a dead victim was held inadmissible since the author of the communication was not able to establish sufficient evidence of authority to act on behalf of the deceased victim.

Secondly, according to the provisions of Article 22, the same matter must not have been (and must not currently be) under consideration through another international procedure.[110] Thus the CAT is unable to hear cases already examined by, for example, the European Court of Human rights or the Human Rights Committee. However it does not affect those situations considered under the ECOSOC Resolution 1503 procedure or those situations under the consideration of the Special Rapporteur on Torture. Similarly it would not be affected by a consideration of such bodies as the UN working group on indigenous peoples or the working group on minorities.[111] Finally, unlike the first Optional Protocol procedure whereby the Human Rights Committee is restricted to taking account of 'written' information, the CAT can consider all the information made available to it by or on behalf of the individual and the State party.[112]

---

[105] See above Chapter 4.

[106] Ibid.

[107] See *Herrera Rubio* v. *Colombia*, Communication No. 161/1983 (2 November 1987), UN Doc. Supp. No. 40 (A/43/40) at 190 (1988); *Miango* v. *Zaire*, Communication No. 194/1985 (27 October 1987), UN Doc. Supp. No. 40 (A/43/40) at 218 (1988). See P.R. Ghandhi, *The Human Rights Committee and the Right of Individual Communication: Law and Practice* (Aldershot: Ashgate Publishing Ltd.) 1998, at p. 85.

[108] According to one source NGOs may be entitled to take cases where they can 'justify their acting on the victim's behalf'. See UN Centre for Human Rights, *Fact Sheet No. 17, The Convention against Torture* (Geneva: United Nations).

[109] *B. M'B.* v. *Tunisia*, Communication No. 14/1994, UN Doc. A/50/44 at 70 (1995).

[110] Article 22(5).

[111] O'Flaherty, above n. 79, at p. 160.

[112] Article 22(4).

Article 22 also provides the admissibility requirements, which are similar to those of the other treaty bodies. Thus the communications must not be anonymous.[113] Nor should they be an abuse of the right of submission of such communications[114] or in any manner incompatible with the provisions of this Convention.[115] The individual, before making a communication must also have exhausted all domestic remedies unless they are ineffective or unreasonably prolonged.[116] The Committee has taken the view that a delay of fifteen months in investigating alleged torture is unreasonably prolonged.[117] As regards the burden of proof, while the CAT has refused to accept sweeping generalisations by authors as sufficient evidence of exhausting domestic remedies,[118] it has required the authors of the Communication to establish prima facie evidence of having exhausted domestic remedies. Those communications which are held inadmissible because of the non-exhaustion of domestic remedies can be re-submitted once domestic remedies have been exhausted.[119] At the same time a genuine (although ill-directed) effort to invoke domestic remedies has been held as satisfying the admissibility requirement.[120]

The procedure of handling communications is very similar to those operated for the Human Rights Committee. The Communication should provide all the material information. On receipt of the communication, it is screened by a member of the Secretariat and is allocated to a member of the CAT who is known as the Special Rapporteur. In practice the Special Rapporteur will seek out the information on both the admissibility and merits of the case. When the Special Rapporteur has collated all the relevant information, the case is put before the Committee. The Committee brings the matter to the attention of the State concerned. The State concerned is required to respond within six months by submitting written explanations or statements clarifying the matter and any remedies that have been undertaken.[121] The Committee then considers communications received under this article in the light of all information that is made available to it by or on behalf of the individual and by the State party concerned. There is an opportunity for the author of the Communication and the State party to further his case or to defend it both at the admissibility and merit stages. At the admissibility stage, the author of the Communication is given four weeks on issues regarding admissibility and six weeks at the merit stage to comment and to provide further evidence to

---

[113] Article 22(2).
[114] Ibid.
[115] Ibid.
[116] Article 22(5)(b).
[117] *Halimi-Nedzibi* v. *Austria*, Communication No. 8/1991, UN Doc. A/49/44 at 40 (1994).
[118] See *R.E.G* v. *Turkey*, Communication No. 4/1990 reported in UN Doc. A/46/44.
[119] See *I.U.P* v. *Spain*, Communication No. 6/1990 reported in UN Doc. A/48/44 Annex VI.
[120] See *Henri Unai Parot* v. *Spain*, Communication No. 6/1990, UN Doc. A/50/44 at 62 (1995).
[121] Article 22(3).

substantiate his case.[122] The CAT may also seek relevant information from other international agencies and UN specialised agencies.

The Committee makes its decisions to combine the judgment on the admissibility and merit stage. CAT goes on to consider the case on its merits in the light of all available information. The Committee makes decisions in closed meetings during its examination of the questions, and after consideration forwards its 'views' to the relevant State party and individual. There are no sanctions attached to the failure of the State concerned for not respecting the views of the CAT. The Committee reaches its decisions by consensus, although members are free to append individual opinions. Once the Committee has reached a decision, the views are forwarded both to the State party and the individual concerned. Under the provisions of Article 24, the Committee is required to submit an annual report on its activities and to the General Assembly of the United Nations. From a brief history of the CAT, it is apparent that the individual complaints procedure has not been used readily; the contrast between these procedures and those under the ICCPR and the ECHR is striking. A number of reasons can be advanced for this, including the fact that:

> The overwhelming majority of countries accepting the optional article 22 individual complaints procedure are also subject to one or more analogues procedures under the Optional Protocol to the International Covenant on Civil and Political Rights or the European or American Conventions on Human Rights, which potential applicants may feel provide more authoritative remedies ... there is little knowledge of the Convention and its protection system even among lawyers. It may well be that the procedure will only be of substantial use in respect of countries to which no other international procedure is applicable or as regards Convention provisions which are more convention-specific. In this connection it should be noted that the Committee has set up an expedited procedure for dealing with threatened expulsions[123]

Investigation on its own initiative (Article 20)

The CAT is unique among other international treaty-based bodies in that it is authorised to initiate investigations on its own initiative.[124] An essential

---

[122] S. Lewis-Anthony, 'Treaty-Based Procedures for Making Human Rights Complaints within the UN System' in H. Hannum (ed.), *Guide to International Human Rights Practice*, 3rd edn (New York: Transnational Publishers) 1999, 41–59 at p. 56.

[123] Rodley, above n. 1, at p. 157.

[124] S. Lewis-Anthony, 'Treaty-Based Procedures for Making Human Rights Complaints within the UN System' in H. Hannum (ed.), above n. 122, at p. 53; commenting on its potential Sir Nigel Rodley remarks 'there is no model for a procedure such as that provided by Article 20 in a United Nations human rights treaty. The innovative character of the procedure is particularly suited to the special elements of the systematic practice of torture. The uniformly clandestine circumstances in which torture occurs make it necessary for information to be compiled from a range of sources including families of victims and national and international Organizations.' Rodley, above n. 1, at p. 160.

prerequisite for initiation of this process is for the Committee to 'receive reliable information which appears to it to contain well-founded indications that torture is being systematically practised in the territory of a State Party'.[125] In practice CAT receives such information from NGOs and intergovernmental organisations. The CAT has provided an interpretation of 'systematic practice' according to which:

> Torture is practised systematically when it is apparent that the torture cases reported have not occurred fortuitously in a particular place or at a particular time, but are seen to be habitual, widespread and deliberate in at least a considerable part of the territory of the country in question. Torture may in fact be of a systematic character without resulting from the direct intention of a Government. It may be the consequence of factors which the Government has difficulty in controlling, and its existence may indicate a discrepancy between policy as determined by the central government and its implementation by the local administration. Inadequate legislation which in practice allows room for the use of torture may also add to the systematic nature of this practice.[126]

After having formulated a view that it has received reliable information about the systematic practice of torture, the Committee invites the State party concerned to cooperate through submission of observations on the alleged practices of torture.[127] It requests the State concerned to appoint a representative to meet with the members designated to conduct the inquiry so as to provide them with the relevant information. The inquiry on the part of Committee members may also include, with the consent of the State party, a visit to its territory by the designated members, who may gather evidence and proceed with hearings from witnesses.

In the light of all the available information, and if the Committee considers that there is sufficient evidence to proceed, it appoints one or more of its members to conduct further investigation and report to the Committee as a matter of urgency. After an inquiry has been conducted by its members, the Committee is required to submit its findings to the relevant State party along with its views, comments and suggestions.[128]

This innovative procedure is potentially of great significance for highlighting practices of torture.[129] Its broad nature and possible sources of information presents similarities with the ECOSOC Resolution 1503 procedure. However, unlike ECOSOC Resolution 1503, exhaustion of domestic remedies or other limitations do not apply.[130] The only crucial test is that the information

---

[125] Article 20(1).
[126] See Doc. A/48/44/Add.1, para 39.
[127] Ibid.
[128] Article 20(4).
[129] See Harris, above n. 1, at p. 716.
[130] See above Chapter 2.

provided contains well-founded indications that 'torture is being systematic-ally practised in the territory of a State Party'.[131] The possible sources of infor-mation include not only individuals but also NGOs and, occasionally, States parties themselves.

Despite the potentially broad nature of this procedure, there are a number of limitations that need to be noted. First, the procedure is confined to situ-ations of torture and is inapplicable to cruel, inhuman or degrading treatment or punishment. The procedure is confidential in nature and can be conducted only with the cooperation of the State. States parties are given a further option to opt-out of the procedure by making a declaration under Article 28(1). This op-out facility is available upon signature, accession or ratification but not once the procedure has been accepted. As at the end of 2001, only thirteen States had maintained a reservation to Article 20.

On the completion of an inquiry under Article 20, the CAT may at its dis-cretion produce only 'summary accounts' of the result, in its annual report which is published.[132] No other sanctions are attached to the Committee's findings under Article 20. Notwithstanding the enormous significance and potential of Article 20, the procedure has only been used three times. The CAT has employed this procedure against Turkey, Egypt and more recently against Peru. Only in the case of Turkey and Peru has it been possible to conduct a visit to the State.[133] In all these instances the published summaries varied sig-nificantly in terms of the qualities and issues addressed. In the case of Peru, two members of the CAT visited the State between 31 August 1998 and 13 September 1998. The Committee members came to the conclusion that:

> despite the existence of constitutional provisions protecting them, the rights of detained persons have been undermined by the anti-terrorist legislation, most of which was adopted in 1992 and is still in force, and which makes detainees par-ticularly vulnerable to torture. At the same time, the rights of persons detained for ordinary crimes have also been undermined under the legislation adopted in 1998 on a series of particularly serious offences.[134]

THE UN SPECIAL RAPPORTEUR, THE QUESTION OF THE RIGHTS OF TORTURE VICTIMS AND OTHER INITIATIVES TAKEN BY THE UN

A significant element in furthering the human rights norms has been the use of the institution of Rapporteurs, focusing on human rights on a thematic,

---

[131] Article 20(1).
[132] Article 20(1).
[133] R. Bank, 'Country-Oriented Procedures under the Convention against Torture: Towards a New Dynamic' in P. Alston and J. Crawford (eds), above n. 86, at p. 167.
[134] See Doc. A/56/54 (2001) para 164.

geographical or territorial basis. The present study has taken advantage of works conducted by several Rapporteurs; these include: Capotorti, Deschênes, Ruhashyankiko, Abdelfattah Amor, Whitaker, Eide, Krishnaswami and Benito. Of particular significance in the campaign against torture has been the role of the UN Special Rapporteur on Torture. The initial appointment of the Rapporteur had been authorised by the Commission on Human Rights in its Resolution 1985/33. This appointment was to last for a period of one year, and in 1986 the mandate was renewed for a further year. The Commission has since that time extended the mandate of the Special Rapporteur.[135] The first Special Rapporteur was Professor Kooijmans from the Netherlands, who was succeeded by Professor (Sir) Nigel Rodley from the United Kingdom. Sir Rodley gave up his position during 2001 in order to become a member of the Human Rights Committee.

The role of the Special Rapporteur on torture has been of great significance in *inter alia* 'examin[ing] questions relevant to torture'[136] and reporting 'on the occurrence and extent of its practice'.[137] The Special Rapporteur has been able to gain valuable insight into the nature of torture and its modern usage. Since his appointment the Special Rapporteur has submitted yearly and interim reports, which are extremely instructive not only in highlighting incidents of torture but also in providing constructive solutions and making valuable recommendations. His work is characterised by a number of activities – these include seeking information on torture from governments, specialised agencies, intergovernmental organisations and NGOs, responding effectively to the information he receives, sending communications to various States and analysing their responses in the light of the prevalent human rights standards. The communications also include urgent appeals where a particular individual or a group is under imminent threat. Another significant feature of Special Rapporteur work is *in situ* visits (with the consent of the State party concerned) and their follow-ups, which are valuable both for gathering opinions and comments on all alleged incidents of torture. The previous Special Rapporteur made a number of significant visits to several countries, including such afflicted areas as Rwanda (1994),[138] Pakistan (1996)[139] and Columbia (1994).[140]

While it is true that the findings and recommendations of the Special Rapporteur do not have any binding effect and *per se* cannot be enforced, they

---

[135] The latest renewal (for a period of three years) was conducted by the Commission on Human Rights in its Resolution 1998/38, 17 April 1998.
[136] Commission on Human Rights Resolution 1985/33 (para 1)
[137] Ibid. (para 7).
[138] See UN Doc E.CN.4/1995/34, para 7.
[139] See UN Doc E.CN.4/1997/7/ Add.2.
[140] See UN Doc E.CN.4/1995/111.

have nevertheless had an impact in raising awareness on the subject, and have been helpful in providing solutions to the problem of torture. Commenting on the value of the Special Rapporteur's contributions, Sir Nigel Rodley notes:

> His work confirms that a person who is tortured or threatened with torture is no longer outside the concern of main organisations of the world's States; on the contrary, the organisation now seeks to hold its members to account for the fate of that individual.[141]

A question that has often been raised relates to the overlap (and possible conflict) of the work of the CAT and the Special Rapporteur. Although CAT and the Special Rapporteur are pursuing the same goals (prevention of torture and punishment of those involved in torturing individuals), the ambit of the Special Rapporteur's mandate is in many respects much broader. First, unlike the CAT, he is not restricted to working with State parties to the Convention against Torture; the Special Rapporteur's mandate in this respect is global. Nor is he inhibited by the limited definition of torture as is provided in the Torture Convention. Secondly, the Special Rapporteur can respond to a call of torture almost immediately. He is not bound by the procedures that are set out in the Torture Convention (for example, exhaustion of domestic remedies etc.) under Article 22. A Special Rapporteur, unlike the Committee under Article 22, looks at situations rather than individual cases. In relation to the examination of investigations under Article 22, the situation has to reach a particular threshold before it is possible for the CAT to examine it; no such limitations apply to the work of the Special Rapporteur.

In addition to the appointment and continued retention of the Special Rapporteur, the United Nations has also established a special Fund called the United Nations Voluntary Fund for Victims of Torture. The fund was established by virtue of the General Assembly Resolution 36/151 of 16 December 1981.[142] The fund is aimed at providing aid to 'individuals whose human rights have been severely violated as a result of torture and to relatives of such victims'.[143] The fund is administered by a board of trustees. Although there are no geographical limitations, as such, to the origin of the beneficiaries, GA Resolution 36/151 provides that priority needs to be given 'to aid victims of violation by States in which the human rights situation has been the subject of resolutions or decisions adopted by either the Assembly, the Economic and Social Council or the Commission on Human Rights'.[144] At the start of the twentieth session of the Board of Trustees of the Fund (18 May–1 June 2001),

---

[141] Rodley, above n. 1, at p. 150.
[142] GA Res. 36/151 (16 December 1981).
[143] GA Res. 36/151 operative para 11(a).
[144] Ibid. Operative para 1(a).

the fund had received a total amount of US$1,079,516.[145] Attempts are also currently being made by the CAT for the adoption of an optional protocol to the Convention which would establish an international mechanism for carrying out visits to places of detention.[146]

CONCLUSIONS

A persistent point of reference in our study has been the international community's concerns over acts of torture, and cruel, inhuman and degrading treatment or punishment. We have noted that all international human rights instruments condemn and prohibit torture and other forms of ill-treatment. A number of treaty bodies have established substantial jurisprudence on the subject. In the fight against torture and gross violations of human rights, the enforcement of the Torture Convention represents a significant step forward. This chapter has, however, been critical of the narrow definition that has been given to the offence of torture by the Convention. It is recommended that wherever possible the CAT should take account of the jurisprudence emergent from related articles of other human rights instruments.

As this chapter has explored, the Convention against Torture contains a number of useful mechanisms to protect the rights of the individual. A particularly innovative procedure is provided by Article 20 where by the CAT may investigate a State on its own initiative after having received reliable information that torture is being systematically practised. Article 20 is subject to an opt-out clause, although it is fortunate that only a small minority of States has opted themselves out of this procedure. Despite this, the CAT has thus far been unable to utilise the procedure to its full potential and a greater use of Article 20 is recommended for the future.

On the whole, however, the CAT (since commencing its work) has performed a commendable job. The funding and resource problems which the CAT faces must be addressed. As noted in this chapter, the CAT is funded largely by States parties. However, the purpose of CAT would be much better served if it were funded out of the United Nations budget. Improvements are also required in the provision of resources to this Committee. The present Secretariat comprises of one part-time member, which is inadequate to deal with the substantial workload. While in the early years of the Convention NGO involvement was limited, various organisations have gradually shown an increasing amount of interest in the proceedings of the CAT, which has led to informed discussions of State reports and decisions on individual

---

[145] See Report of the Secretary-General, *Civil and Political Rights, Including the Question of Torture and Detention, United Nations Voluntary Fund for Victims of Torture*, Commission on Human Rights, E/CN.4/2001/59/Add.1 (4 April 2001).
[146] See Doc. A/56/54 (2001).

complaints. The role of the Special Rapporteur on Torture now seems necessary. Despite the limitations within which the UN system operates, the Special Rapporteur has examined the subject with great maturity and highlighted various instances of torture. His work has also been constructive for many governments in developing procedures and strategies to combat acts of torture. The UN Voluntary Fund for the Victims of Torture also represents a valuable initiative, although its overall impact has thus far been limited.

16

TERRORISM AS A CRIME IN INTERNATIONAL LAW[1]

We are all determined to fight terrorism and to do our utmost to banish it from the face of the earth. But the force we use to fight it should always be proportional and focused on the actual terrorists. We cannot and must not fight them by using their own methods – by inflicting indiscriminate violence and terror on innocent civilians, including children.[2]

INTRODUCTION

The consideration of international terrorism in the present chapter provides a fitting conclusion to a volume dedicated to the study of international human rights law. As the events of 11 September 2001 established, terrorism poses the most serious threat to international order and global human rights in the twenty-first century. The crime of international terrorism also represents the culmination of many other human rights violations. Whatever definition is accorded to terrorism, it violates fundamental human rights as enshrined in

---

[1] See R. Higgins and M. Flory (eds), *Terrorism and International law* (London: Routledge) 1997; M.C. Bassiouni (ed.), *Legal Responses to Terrorism: US Procedural Aspects* (Dordrecht: Martinus Nijhoff Publishers) 1988; Y. Alexander (ed.), *International Terrorism: Political and Legal Documents* (Dordrecht: Martinus Nijhoff Publishers) 1992; Y. Alexander (ed.), *International Terrorism: National, Regional and Global Perspectives* (New York: Praeger) 1976; J. Lodge (ed.), *Terrorism: A Challenge to the State* (Oxford: Martin Robertson) 1981; J. Lambert, *Terrorism and Hostages in International Law: A Commentary on the Hostages Convention 1979* (Cambridge: Grotius) 1990; L. Freedman et al., *Terrorism and International Order* (London: Routledge & Kegan Paul) 1986.

[2] Kofi Anan, United Nations Secretary-General addressing the United Nations General Assembly (18 November 1999).

the International Bill of Rights.[3] Terrorism also constitutes the violation of specific human rights treaties such as the Convention on the Prevention and Punishment of the Crime of Genocide,[4] the UN Convention against Torture and Other Cruel, Inhuman or Degrading Treatment or Punishment (Convention against Torture),[5] the Convention on the Elimination of All Forms of Discrimination against Women[6] and the Convention on the Rights of the Child.[7] Some of the case law arising out of human rights violations has already been considered in this book.[8] However, as this chapter elaborates, there is no established definition of the precise meaning and scope of the term 'terrorism'. The ambiguity in definition has been used by some States to deny their people's legitimate rights such as freedom of expression and religion, and collective group rights – particularly the right to self-determination.[9]

The present chapter advances the view that international law remains a difficult medium through which to address the subject of terrorism. There is first the difficulty in defining terrorism; perceptions vary, for example in differentiating a terrorist from a freedom fighter. Secondly, there is the

---

[3] See e.g. *United States Diplomatic and Consular Staff in Tehran (United States of America v. Iran)*, Judgment 24 May 1980 (1980) ICJ Reports 3, where the International Court notes 'Wrongfully to deprive human beings of their freedom and to subject them to physical constraint in conditions of hardship is in itself manifestly incompatible with ... the fundamental principles enunciated in the Universal Declaration of Human Rights' ibid. para 91. On the value of Universal Declaration on Human Rights see above Chapter 3.

[4] Convention on the Prevention and Punishment of the Crime of Genocide, adopted 9 December 1948. Entered into force 12 January 1951. 78 U.N.T.S. 277. For further analysis see above Chapter 11.

[5] Adopted and opened for signature, ratification and accession on 10 December 1984 by GA Res. 39/46, 39 UN GAOR, Supp. No. 51, UN Doc. A/39/51, at 197 (1984). Entry into force 26 June 1987. 1465 UN T.S. 85; 23 I.L.M. (1985) 535.

[6] Adopted at New York, 18 December 1979. Entered into force 3 September 1981. UN GA Res. 34/180(XXXIV), GA. Res. 34/180, 34 GAOR, Supp. (No. 46) 194, UN Doc. A/34/46, at 193 (1979), 2 U.K.T.S. (1989); 19 I.L.M (1980) 33. See also The UN General Assembly's Declaration on the Elimination of Violence against Women (1993); the Inter-American Convention on the Prevention, Punishment and Eradication of Violence against women. For further consideration see above Chapter 13.

[7] Convention on the Rights of the Child (1989) Article 37; see above Chapter 14.

[8] See above, Parts II and III.

[9] See M. Pomerance, *Self-determination in Law and Practice: The New Doctrine in the United Nations* (The Hague: Martinus Nijhoff Publishers) 1982; A. Rigo Sureda, *The Evolution of the Right of Self-Determination: A Study of United Nations Practice* (Leiden: Sijthoff) 1973; F.L. Kirgis Jr., 'The Degrees of Self-Determination in the United Nations Era' 88 *AJIL* (1994) 304; P. Thornberry, 'Self-Determination, Minorities and Human Rights: A Review of International Instruments' 38 *ICLQ* (1989) 867; H. Hannum, *Autonomy, Sovereignty and Self-Determination: The Accommodation of Conflicting Rights* (Philadelphia: University of Pennsylvania Press) 1990, p. 33; Y. Blum, 'Reflections on the Changing Concept of Self-Determination' 10 *Israel Law Review* (1975) 509; R. Emerson, 'Self-Determination' 65 *AJIL* (1971) 459; M. Koskenniemi, 'National Self-Determination Today: Problems of Legal Theory and Practice' 43 *ICLQ* (1994) 241.

complex issue of defining the meaning and scope of the so-called 'political offences' – should individuals who have committed acts of violence be exempted from prosecution or extradition because their actions are purportedly based on political motivations?[10] Thirdly, there is the difficulty of identifying perpetrators of the crime of terrorism – should the focus of international concern be individuals and other non-State organisations or should attention to be directed towards State-sponsored terrorism? If States are implicated in terrorism, how can international laws be made more effective? Finally, there is the subject of remedies for victims of terrorism. In a fragmented and incoherent system that deals with international terrorism, victims of this crime have frequently been denied access to national and international tribunals to claim their rights.[11]

This chapter is divided into six sections. After these introductory comments, the next section analyses the difficulties in defining international terrorism. This is followed by an overview of the historical developments and a further section that considers international efforts to formulate legal principles in dealing with this crime. The penultimate section looks at the subject in the light of the political events of 11 September. The final section provides a number of concluding observations.

THE DEFINITIONAL ISSUES[12]

As we have noted throughout our study, definitional issues have generated substantial complications in the formulation of international human rights standards.[13] The term 'terrorism' is probably the most difficult to define because of varied perceptions regarding the characterisation of terrorist acts, the purpose and motivation behind such acts and the inconsistent identity of the perpetrator. Indeed the issue has been so controversial that divisions have emerged not only in the proposed definitions but more fundamentally as to

---

[10] See C.L. Blakesley, 'Terrorism, Law and our Constitutional Order' 60 *University of Colorado Law Review* (1989) 471 at p. 514; L.C. Green, 'Terrorism, the Extradition of Terrorists and the "Political Offence" Defence' 31 *GYBIL* (1988) 337.

[11] Professor Dinstein correctly points out that 'the principal obstacle on the path of efforts to suppress international terrorism is that too many countries display a double standard in their approach to the problem. While concerned about acts of terrorism directly affecting their own interests (or those of their close allies) they demonstrate a marked degree of *insouciance* to the predicament of others. In the aggregate, the international community seems to lack the political will to take concerted action against terrorists of all stripes. As a result, terrorists frequently manage to get away with murder in the literal meaning of the phrase'. Y. Dinstein, 'Terrorism as an International Crime' 19 *IYHR* (1989) 55 at p. 56.

[12] See G. Levitt, 'Is "Terrorism" Worth Defining?' 13 *Ohio Northern University Law Review* (1986) 97; J.F. Murphy, 'Defining International Terrorism: A Way Out of the Quagmire' 19 *IYHR* (1989) 13.

[13] See, for example; above Chapter 11 (minorities); Chapter 12 (indigenous peoples).

whether it is worthwhile even attempting to define such an elusive concept.[14] Any attempt to reach a consensus on definitional issues is immediately confronted by significant complications.[15] An immediate and intractable question relates to the identification of 'terrorists'. In any ideological and political conflict, is it possible objectively to distinguish between a terrorist and a freedom fighter? In contemporary politics, our perceptions of acts of violence conducted by such groups as the Palestinians, the Kashmiris, the Northern Irish Catholics or the Tamil Tigers is variable. There is a great measure of truth in the well known cliché: One man's terrorist is another man's freedom fighter.

Furthermore, there is a difficulty in agreeing on the entities which could conceivably perpetrate this crime of torture. In this regard there has remained a major ideological conflict between the developing States on the one hand and the developed world on the other. While the developing States have emphasised State terrorism largely in the context of racial oppression and colonial regimes, the developed world has concerned itself with individual acts of terrorism.[16] From a human rights perspective it is arguable that every form of the taking of life, assassination, killings, bombings, hostage-taking and hijacking should be categorised as terrorist activity.[17] The motive, characteristics and underlying causes of any such actions ought not to provide a justification. On the other hand, depending on one's moral and political views, many of these actions have been justified or condoned.[18]

The controversies generated in the definitional debate have exercised the minds of many draftsmen and academics; a leading authority has noted that

---

[14] As Professor Bassiouni makes the point that 'there is ... no internationally agreed upon methodology for the identification and appraisal of what is commonly referred to as "terrorism"; including: causes, strategies, goals and outcomes of the conduct in question and those who perpetuate it. There is also no international consensus as to the appropriate reactive strategies of States and the international community, their values, goals and outcomes. All of this makes it difficult to identify what is sought to be prevented and controlled, why and how. As a result the pervasive and indiscriminate use of the often politically convenient label of "terrorism" continues to mislead this field of inquiry.' M.C. Bassiouni, 'A Policy–Oriented Inquiry into the Different Forms and Manifestations of "International Terrorism"' in M.C. Bassiouni (ed.), above n. 1, at p. xvi.

[15] R. Higgins, 'The General International Law of Terrorism' in R. Higgins and M. Flory (eds), above n. 1, 13–29 at p. 14.

[16] As Levitt correctly points out 'governments that have a strong political stake in the promotion of "national liberation movements" are loath to subscribe to a definition of terrorism that would criminalize broad areas of conduct habitually resorted to by such groups; and on the other end of the spectrum, governments against which these groups' violent activities are directed are obviously reluctant to subscribe to a definition that would criminalize their own use of force in response to such activities or otherwise'. Levitt, above n. 12, at p. 109.

[17] R. Higgins, 'The General International Law of Terrorism' in R. Higgins and M. Flory (eds), above n. 1, 13–29 at pp. 14–15.

[18] Examples are also put forward about possible justifications of the (hypothetical) killings of international criminals and gross violators of human rights such as Adolf Hitler. See Blakesley, above n. 10, at p. 474.

between 1936 and 1981 no less than 109 definitions of terrorism were purposed.[19] Within this timeframe, one of the earliest and most prominent definitions was advanced through the 1937 Convention for the Prevention and Punishment of Terrorism.[20] According to Article 1(2) of the Convention:

> In the present Convention, the expression 'acts of terrorism' means criminal acts directed against a State intended or calculated to create a state of terror in the mind of particular persons, or a group of persons or the general public.

To be subject to the provisions of this Convention an act had to come within the ambit of the aforementioned definition. It had to be directed against a State party and the concerned activity had to involve one of the enumerated actions in Articles 2 and 3 of the Convention, namely 'any wilful act causing death or grievous bodily harm or loss of liberty' to a specified category of public officials, 'wilful destruction of, or damage to, public property' or 'any wilful act calculated to endanger the lives of members of the public'.

In the event, the aforementioned definition of terrorism along with the remaining of the 1937 Convention failed to be adopted. Despite this abortive attempt, renewed efforts were made in the 1950s and 1960s to formulate a consensus definition of international terrorism. In 1972 the United States, presented a Draft Convention for the Prevention and Punishment of Certain Acts of International Terrorism.[21] Within this draft, offences of 'international significance' include offences committed with intent to damage the interests of or obtaining concessions from a State or an international organisation under certain enumerated transnational circumstances, and those consisting of unlawful killing, causing serious bodily harm, or kidnapping another person (including attempts and complicity in such acts).[22] These actions should have been 'committed neither by nor against a member of the armed forces of a State in the course of military hostilities'.[23]

The 1972 US Draft Convention, like the 1937 Convention, failed to gain the approval of the international community. Instead the United Nations General Assembly established an Ad hoc Committee on International Terrorism to 'consider the observations of States [and] submit its report with recommendations for possible co-operation for the speedy elimination of the problem ... to the General Assembly'.[24] A Sub-Committee of the Ad hoc

---

[19] W. Laqueur, 'Reflections on Terrorism' 64 *Foreign Affairs* (1986) 86 at p. 88.
[20] The Convention for the Prevention and Punishment of Terrorism, 16 November 1937, 19 League of Nations Official Journal (1938) 23 reprinted 27 UN GAOR, Annex I, Agenda Item No. 92, UN Doc. A/C.6/418 (1972).
[21] United States Draft Convention for the Prevention of Certain Acts of International Terrorism, UN Doc. A/C.6/L.850 (1972) reprinted in 67 Dep't State Bull. 431 (1972).
[22] Article 1.
[23] Ibid.
[24] GA. Res. 3034, 27 UN GAOR Supp. (No. 30) at 119, UN Doc. A/RES/3034, paras 9, 10.

Committee was established and within the deliberations of the Sub-Committee the following definition of 'international terrorism' was advanced

(1) Acts of violence and other repressive acts by colonial, racist and alien regimes against peoples struggling for their liberation ...

(2) Tolerating or assisting by a State the organization of the remnants of fascist or mercenary groups whose terrorist activity is directed against other sovereign countries;

(3) Acts of violence committed by individuals or groups of individuals which endanger or take innocent human lives or jeopardise fundamental freedoms. This should not affect the inalienable right to self-determination and independence of all peoples under colonial and racist regimes and other forms of alien domination and the legitimacy of their struggle ... ;

(4) Acts of violence committed by individuals or groups of individuals for private gain, the effects of which are not confined to one State.[25]

The contrast between this definition and the 1972 and 1937 definitions considered above is striking. The concern of the Sub-Committee is primarily focused on racist and alien regimes. There also appears to be some form of exception accorded to those activities which are conducted in pursuance of the inalienable right to self-determination. Within this definition, the issue of intent according to one commentator 'has been turned on its head':[26] private gain rather than political motives present the key determining factor.

Ideological divisions regarding the definition have hampered further efforts to draft a treaty dealing with international terrorism. As a consequence of these differences, the most effective way for the international community to proceed has been the consideration of specific aspects of the subject. Thus binding instruments have been adopted in areas of *inter alia* aircraft hijacking,[27] unlawful acts against the safety of civil aviation,[28] marine terrorism,[29] hostage-taking,[30] and theft of nuclear materials.[31]

---

[25] 28 UN GAOR Supp (1973).

[26] Levitt, above n. 12, at p. 100.

[27] See the Convention on Offences and Certain Other Acts Committed on Board Aircraft (1963) 704 U.N.T.S. 219; the Convention for the Suppression of Unlawful Seizure of Aircraft, (1970) 860 U.N.T.S. 105.

[28] See Convention for the Suppression of Unlawful Acts against the Safety of Civil Aviation (1971) 974 U.N.T.S. 177; 10 I.L.M. (1971) 1151.

[29] See the Convention for the Suppression of Unlawful Acts against the Safety of Maritime Navigation 27 I.L.M.668 (1988); the Protocol for the Suppression of Unlawful Acts against the Safety of Fixed Platforms Located on the Continental Shelf (March 1988). Text available (http://untreaty.un.org/English/Terrorism.asp) 31 January 2002

[30] See the Convention on the Prevention and Punishment of Crimes against Internationally Protected Persons, including Diplomatic Agents (1973) 1035 U.N.T.S. 167; International Convention against the Taking of Hostages 34 UN GAOR Supp. (No.39) at 23, UN Doc.A/34/39 (1979) 18 I.L.M. (1979) 1456.

[31] See Convention on the Physical Protection of Nuclear Materials (1980) 18 I.L.M. (1979) 1419.

Terrorism: a working definition

Before concluding the definitional debate, it must be emphasised that terrorism is a politically, ethically and morally divisive subject. In the existing global environment it may never be possible to arrive at a conclusive definition. An inability to define international terrorism in a comprehensive manner, however, must not be allowed to paralyse efforts to deal with the crime itself. Besides, it is fair to say that most rational and sensible individuals have a basic understanding of what the term entails. As Professor Oscar Schachter has noted, terrorism has a 'core meaning that virtually all definitions recognise'. By this he means:

> the threat or use of violence in order to create extreme fear and anxiety in a target group so as to coerce it to meet political (or quasi-political) objectives of the perpetrators. Such terrorist acts have an international character when they are carried out across national lines or directed against nationals of a foreign State or instrumentalities of that State. They also include the conduct defined in the international conventions against hijacking, ariel sabotage, sabotage at sea, hostage-taking, and attacks on diplomats and other internationally protected persons. Terrorist acts are generally carried out against civilians but they also include attacks on governmental buildings, vessels, planes and other instrumentalities. The objectives of the terrorist are usually political but terrorism for religious motives or ethnic domination would also be included. (However, violence or threats of violence for purely private motives should not be included.)[32]

Further elaboration has been provided by another leading authority, Professor Christopher Blakesley.[33] He takes the view that terrorism is 'the application of terror-violence against innocent individuals for the purpose of obtaining thereby some military, political or religious end from a third party'.[34] From the aforementioned academic definitions, it can be argued that – notwithstanding political and ideological divisions – a generalised and comprehensible meaning can nevertheless be formed.

TERRORISM AND INTERNATIONAL LAW

A historical analysis establishes an unfortunate picture of the antiquity of the crime of terrorism.[35] The phenomenon of terrorism is as old as human history;

---

[32] O. Schachter, 'The Lawful use of Force by a State against Terrorists in Another Country' 19 *IYHR* (1989) 209 at p. 210.
[33] Blakesley, above n. 10, at p. 473.
[34] Ibid.
[35] See W. Laqueur and Y. Alexander (eds), *The Terrorism Reader: A Historical Anthology* (New York: New American Library, Penguin) 1987; J. Rehman, *The Weaknesses in the International Protection of Minority Rights* (The Hague: Kluwer Law International) 2000, pp. 51–75.

on every leaf of the chronicle of human endeavours there are sad tales of terrorism and violence against the weak and the inarticulate. Many examples can be found where terrorism was accompanied by gross violations of human rights including torture and genocide. Among these one could mention the horrifying massacres resulting from the Assyrian warfare during the seventh and eight centuries BC, and the Roman obliteration of the city of Carthage and all its inhabitants.[36] Certain religious ideologies, and the wars that were conducted to further those ideologies, held a large imprint of terrorism and intolerance.[37]

In the more modern period the term 'terror' was associated with the Jacobin 'Reign of Terror' in the aftermath of the French Revolution.[38] The Jacobin 'Reign of Terror' led to 17,000 official executions, with several thousand deaths and disappearances.[39] The First World War was the product of an international act of terrorism – the assassination of Archduke Francis Ferdinand on 28 June 1914 by the Serbians.[40] Over the course of the next fifty years, the expression was broadened to include 'anyone who attempts to further his views by a system of coercive intimidation; especially applied to members of one of the extreme revolutionary societies in Russia'.[41] Throughout the twentieth century, the rise of nationalism, totalitarian ideologies such as Nazism and Stalinism, and the upsurge of racial, religious and linguistic extremism have all been accompanied by terrorism. It is also the case that the essence of colonialism was violence, intimidation and terrorism of indigenous peoples.[42] In the aftermath of the Second World War, State-sponsored terrorism was deployed to resist granting the right of self-determination to many of the oppressed nations and

[36] L. Kuper, *Genocide: Its Political Use in the Twentieth Century* (New Haven and London: Yale University Press) 1981, pp. 11–18; J.N. Porter (ed.), *Genocide and Human Rights: A Global Anthology* (Washington DC: University Press of America) 1982; L. Kuper, *The Prevention of Genocide* (New Haven: Yale University Press) 1985; L. Kuper, *International Action Against Genocide* (London: Minority Rights Group) 1984; H. Fein (ed.), *Genocide Watch* (New Haven and London: Yale University Press) 1992.

[37] L. Kuper, *Genocide: Its Political Use in the Twentieth Century*, above n. 36, pp. 12–14; See Special Rapporteur B. Whitaker, *Revised and Updated Report on the Question of the Prevention and Punishment of the Crime of Genocide* UN Doc. E/CN.4/Sub.2/1985/6B, pp. 6–7; also see I. Brownlie, *International Law and the Use of Force by States* (Oxford: Clarendon Press) 1963.

[38] See Murphy, above n. 12, at p. 14.

[39] Lambert, above n. 1, at p. 15.

[40] Dinstein, above n. 11, at p. 56.

[41] Cited in Green, above n. 10, at p. 337.

[42] See S. Qureshi, 'Political Violence in the South Asian Subcontinent' in Y. Alexander (ed.), above n. 1 pp. 151–193; see also the Reports of the sessions of the Working Group on Indigenous Populations and the Working Group on Minorities; Porter, above n. 36, at p. 16; Kuper, *International Action Against Genocide*, above n. 36, at p. 15.

peoples.[43] The terrorism of colonialism produced a backlash. Terrorism was often met with counter-terrorism: the colonisers used terror as an instrument to maintain their hold over their overseas territories, while the indigenous peoples and their national liberation movements resorted to terrorism and political violence as a means to gain emancipation and independence.[44] In their efforts to rid themselves of what they perceived as alien, foreign and unlawful domination, resistance movements were formed. Many of the so-called 'national liberation movements' such as the Algerian Liberation Movement (FLN),[45] the African National Congress (South Africa),[46] the Irish Republican Army (Ireland),[47] the Indian National Congress and Muslim League (British India) have at one point all been deemed terrorist organisations.[48]

At the height of the decolonisation movement, the issue of terrorism became a matter of serious contention between States with overseas colonies on the one hand, and the newly independent and communist States on the other. Even at the end of the decolonisation period, the legacies of colonial times render the subject often an unpalatable one. There is a substantial relationship with the right to self-determination for such groups or peoples as the Palestinians.[49] In this context it must be noted that Osama Bin Laden, the prime suspect for the attack on the World Trade Centre on 11 September 2001, has consistently emphasised the right of self-determination for the Palestinian people as a prerequisite to world peace and security. Another particularly controversial area is the right of the Kashmiri Muslims to self-determination, the conflict between India and Pakistan over the territory of Kashmir having already resulted in three wars.[50]

---

[43] O.Y. Elagab, *International Law Documents Relating to Terrorism* (London: Cavendish) 1995, p. iv.

[44] For a useful analysis see Minority Rights Group (ed.), *World Directory of Minorities* (London: Minority Rights Group) 1997.

[45] See L. Kuper, *The Pity of it All: Polarisation and Ethnic Relations* (London: Duckworth) 1977.

[46] See S. Dubow, *The African National Congress* (Sutton: Stroud) 2000; W. Beinart and S. Dubow, *Segregation and Apartheid in Twentieth-Century South Africa* (London: Routledge) 1995.

[47] See H. Patterson, *The Politics of Illusion: A Political History of the IRA* (London: Serif) 1997; M.L.R. Smith and M.L. Rowan, *Fighting for Ireland?: The Military Strategy of the Irish Republican Movement* (London: Routledge) 1995.

[48] P. Hardy, *The Muslims of British India* (Cambridge: Cambridge University Press) 1972; B.R. Tomlinson, *The Indian National Congress and the Raj, 1929–1942: The Penultimate Phase* (London: Macmillan) 1976; A. Jalal, *The Sole Spokesman: Jinnah, the Muslim League, and the Demand for Pakistan* (Cambridge: Cambridge University Press) 1985.

[49] On the complication generated by the definition of 'peoples' and 'indigenous peoples' see above Chapter 12.

[50] For further consideration see J. Rehman, 'Re-Assessing the Right to Self-Determination: Lessons from the Indian Experience' 29 *AALR* (2000) 454.

INTERNATIONAL EFFORTS TO FORMULATE LEGAL PRINCIPLES PROHIBITING ALL FORMS OF TERRORISM

The inter-war years 1919–1939

The absence of established judicial bodies, executive agencies and effective enforcement powers has led to particular difficulties in devising international legal norms to combat terrorism. Such a lacuna has also resulted in serious difficulties in the detection and punishment of terrorists. International terrorism was debated by the third (Brussels) International Conference for the Unification of Penal law held on 26–30 June 1930.[51] Parallel efforts were made by the League of Nations to formulate a binding instrument on international terrorism. Following the assassination of King Alexander of Yugoslavia and Mr Louis Barthou, Foreign Minister of the French Republic in Marseilles in October 1934, the League of Nations drafted a Convention for the Prevention and Punishment of Terrorism.[52] The treaty contained a number of positive elements. In addition to containing a definition, it obliged States parties to prevent and punish acts of terrorism. It imposed criminal sanctions for such acts as attacks on the lives and physical integrity of heads of States and other public officials, destruction of public property and acts calculated to endanger the lives of members of the public.[53] Despite its many positive aspects, the Convention failed to become operative. A prominent feature (which discouraged further ratifications) was the broad definition accorded to terrorism. The Convention remained ineffective, having received one ratification – that from British India. In any event the forces of aggression and terrorism emerged in Europe; the Second World War heralded the demise of the League of Nations, along with its Convention on Terrorism.

Post-1945 developments

At the end of the Second World War, there were renewed efforts to produce a consolidated instrument to deal with terrorism. However, the first two decades of the United Nations period were taken up by a range of issues within which the subject of terrorism formed only an incidental part. The Draft Code on Offences Against the Peace and Security of Mankind as prepared by the International Law Commission in 1954 dealt primarily with

---

[51] H. Labayle, 'Droit International et Lutte Contre Le Terrorisme' 32 *Annuaire Français de droit International* (1986) 114.

[52] The Convention for the Prevention and Punishment of Terrorism, 16 November 1937, 19 League of Nations Official Journal (1938) 23 reprinted 27 UN GAOR, Annex I, Agenda Item No. 92, UN Doc. A/C.6/418 (1972).

[53] Article 2.

the principles enshrined in the Charter of the Nuremberg Tribunal and with the Judgment of the Tribunal.[54] Article 2(6), however, defines an offence against the peace and security of mankind as:

> the undertaking or encouragement by the authorities of a State of terrorist activities in another State, or the toleration by the authorities in another State, or the toleration by the authorities of a State of organised activities calculated to carry out terrorist acts in another State.

Further progress on the completion of the code was hampered *inter alia* by disagreements over the definition of aggression. The General Assembly then turned its attention to the subject of the definition of aggression, an issue that was only resolved through the General Assembly Resolution on the Definition of Aggression (1974).[55] Article 3(g) of the Resolution includes in its explanation of acts of aggression:

> The sending by or on behalf of a State of armed bands, groups, irregulars or mercenaries which carry out acts of armed force against another State of such gravity as to amount to the acts listed ..., or its substantial involvement therein.

There was, however, a caveat which exempts national liberation movements in their struggle for self-determination.[56] Such an exemption, although a feature of this Resolution (and a number of subsequent UN General Assembly Resolutions), has added considerable uncertainty as regards the condemnation of terrorist activities. In 1979 the General Assembly passed its Resolution 34/145 which condemns all acts of terrorism. At the same time, the Resolution also condemned 'the continuation of repressive and terrorist acts by colonial, racist and alien regimes in denying people their legitimate right to self-determination and independence and other human rights and fundamental freedoms'. The title and the text of the Resolution also confirms that the focus of the Resolution is upon the 'underlying causes of those forms of Terrorism and Acts of violence which lie in Misery, Frustration, Grievance and Despair and which Cause Some people to Sacrifice Human Lives including their own in an Attempt to Effect Radical Changes'.[57] The same emphasis on the

---

[54] See UN GAOR Supp (No. 9) at 11–12; UN Doc.A/2693 (1972).

[55] GA Res. 3314 (XXIX) 14 December 1974. G.A.O.R 29th Sess., Supp. 31, 142; 69 *AJIL* (1975) 480.

[56] Article 7 of the Resolution provides 'Nothing in this Definition, and in particular Article 3, could in any way prejudice the right to self-determination, freedom and independence, as derived from the Charter, of peoples forcibly deprived of that right and referred to in the Declaration on Principles of International Law concerning Friendly Relations and co-operation among States in accordance with the Charter of the United Nations, particularly peoples under colonial and racist regimes or other forms of alien domination; nor the right of these peoples to struggle to that end and to seek and receive support, in accordance with the principles of the Charter and in conformity with the above-mentioned Declaration'.

[57] UN GA Res. 34/145 (1979).

underlying causes is placed in General Assembly Resolution 36/109 (1981)[58] and General Assembly Resolution 40/61 (1989).[59]

The debates within the United Nations General Assembly have represented fundamental divisions between the developing and the developed world. The developed world has insisted on the absolute prohibition of terrorism regardless of the motives and underlying causes. The developing world on the other hand has remained suspicious of this approach, claiming that underlying causes of terrorism need to provide the determining factors and that national liberation movements must be allowed to resort to every conceivable means to rid themselves of colonial or racist regimes. This conflict has been so severe as to seriously jeopardise any progress in devising international mechanisms to deal with terrorism.

Ending of the cold war and shift in policies

The ending of the cold war and a thaw in East–West relations has brought about a significant change in the policies of the former communist States. Many of these States have embraced the global human rights regime and have also renounced sponsorship of terrorist activities.[60] Over the years, the developing States themselves have shown signs of changing their position. This changing position can be attributed to a variety of reasons. First, with the independence of a vast majority of former European colonies the basis for supporting the national liberation movements has diminished. The case for liberation movements is confined to the struggle of pariah States such as Israel. Secondly, and perhaps more significantly, the new States which emerged from the rubble of decolonisation have themselves been challenged by secessionist movements represented by various groups. Among these groups one could cite the Tamil Tigers, the Sudanese Peoples Liberation Army and the Kashmiri Mujaheedaen.[61] These groups adopted similar tactics hitherto used by the nationalists seeking independent Statehood from European colonisers. Many of the new States, while emphasising the principle of territorial integrity, have treated these secessionist organisations as terrorist groups. Increasingly, these organisations have targeted diplomatic personnel and there have been hijackings of national aircrafts owned by developing States. The emergence of common concerns have led to a fluidity in the position of many countries in Asia and Africa.

---

[58] UN GA Res. 36/109 (1981).
[59] UN GA Res. 40/61 (1989).
[60] For the ratification of human rights treaties of the former communist States see Appendix II.
[61] For consideration of these and other cases see Minority Rights Group (ed.), *World Directory of Minorities* (London: MRG) 1997.

Signs of a common concern on terrorism were already emerging in the 1970s. According to the Declaration on Principles of International Law Concerning Friendly Relations and Co-operation Amongst States in Accordance with the Charter of the United Nations (1970):[62]

> Every State has the duty to refrain from organising, instigating, assisting or participating in acts of civil strife or terrorist acts in another State or acquiescing in organised activities within its territory directed towards the commission of such acts, when the acts referred to in the present paragraph involve a threat or use of force.

In 1979, the Ad Hoc Committee on Terrorism, a committee formed pursuant to General Assembly Resolution 3034[63] recommended *inter alia* that the General Assembly condemn attacks of terrorists, take note of the underlying causes contained in the Committee's reports, and that the States work towards the elimination of terrorism in compliance with their obligations under international law, refrain from organising, instigating, assisting or participating in terrorist acts in other States and refuse to allow their territory to be used for such acts and take all possible measures to cooperate with each other to combat international terrorism.

The General Assembly adopted these recommendations, although as noted above, these recommendations were tempered by the terminology of 'underlying causes' and the 'right to self-determination'. Further progress was made in 1985 when the UN General Assembly adopted a Resolution in which it urged States to take measures for the 'speedy and final elimination of the problem of international terrorism'.[64] The Assembly also took the position that it:

> Unequivocally condemns, as criminal, all acts, methods and practices of terrorism wherever and by whoever committed, including those which jeopardise friendly relations among States and their security [and] deplores the loss of innocent human lives which result from such acts of terrorism.[65]

A distinctive feature of the Resolution is that after a protracted debate of fifteen years, for the first time in the United Nations, this Resolution associated the term 'criminal' with terrorism.[66] Another Resolution (based along the lines of the 1985 Resolution) condemning terrorism was adopted by the

---

[62] GA Res. 2625 (XXV) (1970).
[63] See Report of the Sixth Committee, UN GAOR A/8969 (1972) at p. 5.
[64] GA Res. 40/61 (1985).
[65] GA Res. 40/61 (1985).
[66] C.Van den Wyngaert, 'The Political Offence Exception to Extradition: How to Plug the "Terrorists' Loophole" without Departing from Fundamental Human Rights' 19 *IYHR* (1989) 297 at p. 297.

General Assembly in 1987.[67] In 1994, the General Assembly adopted a Resolution entitled 'The Declaration on Measures to Eliminate International Terrorism'.[68] Peace, security and restraint of use of force represents the basis of the Declaration. In condemning terrorism the Declaration also calls upon States to refrain from organising, instigating, assisting or participating in terrorist activities, and from acquiescing in or encouraging activities within their territories directed towards the commission of any such acts.

It is noticeable that since the ending of the cold war, the General Assembly has been active in its condemnation of global terrorism. Such activism and unified views on the subject represent a positive development. At the same time it is important to recognise the fact that a significant reason for such activism is that General Assembly Resolutions are not legally binding *per se*; ambiguous terminology can be deployed to represent a show of unanimity in condemning terrorism.[69] The situation would be radically different if States were required to subscribe to any internationally binding agreement on global terrorism. The old differences and suspicions are certain to resurface.

Dealing with specific terrorist activities

As we have noted above, in the light of substantial disagreements over the definition, nature and scope of terrorism, the international community has been unable to formulate a single consolidated instrument dealing with terrorism. Progress has however been made in a number of related areas. A range of treaties have been entered under the auspices of the United Nations and regional organisations. In addition, the International Civil Aviation Organisation (ICAO) and the International Maritime Organisation (IMO) have also been successful in sponsoring conventions dealing with aeriel and maritime terrorism respectively. There are currently more than twelve conventions and protocols that deal with the various aspects of terrorism. These include the Convention on the Prevention and Punishment of Crimes against Internationally Protected Persons, including Diplomatic Agents, adopted by the General Assembly of the United Nations (1973),[70] the International

---

[67] GA Res. 42/159 7 Dec 1987. Writing in 1989, Lambert made the following useful points. 'The change in language in the most recent General Assembly Resolutions must be seen as some progress towards a universal consensus that acts of terrorism are not to be tolerated regardless of the cause. It must also be recognised, however, that the General Assembly continues to send out somewhat mixed signals regarding the issue of national liberation movements.' Lambert, above n. 1, at p. 44

[68] GA Res. A/Res/49/60.

[69] On the value of General Assembly Resolutions see above Chapter 2.

[70] 1035 U.N.T.S. 167; 13 I.L.M. 41 (1974).

Convention against the Taking of Hostages, adopted by the General Assembly of the United Nations (1979),[71] the International Convention for the Suppression of Terrorist Bombings, adopted by the General Assembly of the United Nations on 15 December 1997,[72] the International Convention for the Suppression of the Financing of Terrorism, adopted by the General Assembly of the United Nations on 9 December 1999,[73] the Convention on Offences and Certain Other Acts Committed on Board Aircraft (1963),[74] the Convention for the Suppression of Unlawful Seizure of Aircraft, signed at the Hague (1970),[75] the Convention for the Suppression of Unlawful Acts against the Safety of Civil Aviation (1971),[76] the Convention on the Physical Protection of Nuclear Material (1980),[77] the Protocol on the Suppression of Unlawful Acts of Violence at Airports Serving International Civil Aviation, supplementary to the Convention for the Suppression of Unlawful Acts against the Safety of Civil Aviation, signed at Montreal on 24 February 1988,[78] the Convention for the Suppression of Unlawful Acts against the Safety of Maritime Navigation (1988),[79] the Protocol for the Suppression of Unlawful Acts against the Safety of Fixed Platforms Located on the Continental Shelf (March 1988),[80] the Convention on the Marking of Plastic Explosives for the Purpose of Detection (1991).[81] There are also a number of regional conventions on terrorism, including the Arab Convention on the Suppression of Terrorism (1998),[82] the Convention of the Organisation of the Islamic Conference on Combating International Terrorism (1999),[83] the European Convention on the Suppression of Terrorism, concluded at Strasbourg on 27 January 1977,[84] the O.A.S. Convention to Prevent and Punish Acts of Terrorism Taking the Form of Crimes against Persons and Related Extortion that are of International Significance (1971),[85] the OAU

---

[71] 1316 U.N.T.S. 205; 18 I.L.M. 1460 (1979).
[72] Doc. A/Res/52/164; depository notification C.N.801.2001.TREATIES-9 of 12 October 2001.
[73] Resolution A/Res/54/109; depository notifications C.N.327.2000.TREATIES-12 of 30 May 2000.
[74] 2 I.L.M. 1042 (1963).
[75] 10 I.L.M. 133 (1971).
[76] 10 I.L.M. 1151 (1971).
[77] Text available (http://untreaty.un.org/English/Terrorism.asp) 31 January 2002.
[78] 27 I.L.M. 627 (1988).
[79] 27 I.L.M. 668 (1988).
[80] Text available (http://untreaty.un.org/English/Terrorism.asp) 31 January 2002.
[81] Ibid.
[82] Arab Convention on the Suppression of Terrorism, signed at a meeting held at the General Secretariat of the League of Arab States in Cairo on 22 April 1998. (Deposited with the Secretary-General of the League of Arab States).
[83] Text available (http://untreaty.un.org/English/Terrorism.asp) 31 January 2002.
[84] 15 I.L.M. 1272 (1978).
[85] 10 I.L.M. 255 (1971).

Convention on the Prevention and Combating of Terrorism, adopted at Algiers on 14 (1999),[86] the SAARC Regional Convention on Suppression of Terrorism (1987)[87] and the Treaty on Co-operation among States Members of the Commonwealth of Independent States in Combating Terrorism (1999).[88] Furthermore, a range of non-binding international instruments have been adopted. The following sections considers some of the international instruments that have been adopted at the international and regional levels to combat terrorism.

UN Conventions

Hostage-taking breaches all norms of dignity and human rights. It is a serious crime under international law, and has affected both the developed and the developing world. The crime of taking hostages was originally only confined to armed conflict. A number of indictments were brought forward in the Nuremberg Trials for acts of hostage taking.[89] The prohibition on hostage-taking during armed conflicts is incorporated in Article 3 and 34 of the Fourth Geneva Convention (1949).[90]

Since the end of the Second World War, hostage-taking of internationally protected persons as well as ordinary civilians has developed into a major concern. A proliferation of incidents led the international community to adopt binding instruments condemning and criminalising hostage-taking in all its forms. One unfortunate example of the violation of the rights of internationally protected persons was the murder of the Yugoslavian Ambassador to Stockholm in April 1971. Another more publicised instance involved was hostage-taking in Vienna during 1975 when terrorists seized sixty OPEC ministers. In 1973 the General Assembly adopted, by consensus, a Resolution attached to which is the New York Convention. The Convention, known as the Convention on the Prevention and Punishment of Crimes against Internationally Protected Persons, including Diplomatic Agents (1973)[91] represents the most far-reaching global instrument dealing with the crime of hostage-taking. The New York Convention protects certain categories of persons from the offences of murder, kidnapping or other attacks upon

---

[86] OAU Convention on the Prevention and Combating of Terrorism, adopted at Algiers on 14 July 1999. (Deposited with the General Secretariat of the Organization of African Unity).

[87] Text available (http://untreaty.un.org/English/Terrorism.asp) 31 January 2002.

[88] Treaty on Co-operation among States Members of the Commonwealth of Independent States in Combating Terrorism, done at Minsk on 4 June 1999. (Deposited with the Secretariat of the Commonwealth of Independent States).

[89] See Elagab, above n. 43, at p. 577.

[90] 75 U.N.T.S. (1950).

[91] 1035 U.N.T.S. 167; 13 I.L.M. 41 (1974).

their official premises, private accommodation and means of transportation. The category of persons protected includes heads of State (including members of a collegial body performing the functions of a head of State), heads of governments and ministers for foreign affairs, whenever such persons are in a foreign State – and their family members who accompany them.[92] Protection is also accorded to 'any representative or official of a State or any official or other agents of an international organization of an intergovernmental character who, at the time when and in the place where a crime against him, his official premises, his private accommodation or his means of transport is committed is entitled pursuant to international law to special protection from any attack on his person, freedom or dignity, as well as members of his family forming part of his household.'[93]

In 1979, the General Assembly adopted another convention, the International Convention against the Taking of Hostages. The adoption of the Convention was preceded by a range of incidents including the Entebbe raid[94] and the American hostage-taking by Iran.[95] According to Article 1 of this Convention any person who 'seizes or detains and threatens to kill, to injure or to continue to detain another person (hereinafter referred to as the "hostage") in order to compel a third party, namely a State, an international intergovernmental organisation, a natural or juridical person, or a group of persons, to do or abstain from doing any act as an explicit or implicit condition for the release of the hostage commits the offence of taking of hostages within the meaning of the Convention'. Article 1(2) goes on to classify attempts or participating in hostage-taking as offences. Article 2 places the States parties under an obligation to make offences set forth in Article 1 'punishable by appropriate penalties which take into account the grave nature of those offences'.[96] These provisions have similarities with other treaties dealing with grave human rights violations such as genocide.[97] There is a commitment on the part of States to attempt to secure the release of hostages, and to cooperate in the prevention of hostage-taking acts.[98] The Convention also provides a range of jurisdictional grounds including *lex loci*,[99] States with registration

---

[92] Article 1(1)(a).
[93] Article 1(1)(b).
[94] For further consideration see D.J. Harris, *Cases and Materials on International Law*, 5th edn, (London: Sweet and Maxwell) 1998, pp. 909–911.
[95] *U.S. Diplomatic and Consular Staff in Tehran Case (United States of America v. Iran)* ICJ Reports 1980, 3; Harris, above n. 94, at pp. 358–362.
[96] Article 2.
[97] See Article 1 of the Genocide Convention. Convention on the Prevention and Punishment of the Crime of Genocide, adopted 9 December 1948. Entered into force 12 January 1951. 78 U.N.T.S 277. For further analysis see above Chapter 11.
[98] Article 3(1).
[99] Article 5(1)(a).

of aircrafts and ships where the offence is committed,[100] nationality of the offender,[101] the nationality of the hostage,[102] or the presence of the offender in its territory.[103] In common with other treaties dealing with terrorism, the Convention affirms the principle of *aut dedere aut judicare*. The application of this principle means that in cases where the alleged offender is found in the territory of a State party, that State is under an obligation to extradite him or to submit his case before competent national authorities.[104] Following this principle, an attempt is made to ensure the trial of offenders. This provision, however, falls foul of the problem that States refuse extradition of certain individuals because of a variety of reasons. The point is further reinforced by the Discrimination Clause as contained in Article 9.

Regional Conventions

A number of regional instruments have been adopted to combat terrorism. The Council of Europe has passed a series of Resolutions and Declarations.[105] It has also adopted the European Convention on the Suppression of Terrorism[106] and the Agreement on the Application of the European Convention for the Suppression of Terrorism (Dublin Agreement).[107] The European Convention provides for cooperation on matters *inter alia* related to extradition and mutual assistance in criminal proceedings.[108] Article 1 lists a range of offences which are not to be recognised as political offences. These offences are already well-established in international criminal law and include those contained in the hijacking and hostage-taking Conventions. While according priority to the European Convention over previously entered extradition treaties and

---

[100] Ibid.

[101] Article 5(1)(b).

[102] Article 5(1).

[103] Article 5(2).

[104] Article 8(1).

[105] These include Recommendation 684 (1972) on International Terrorism; Recommendation 703 (1973) on International Terrorism; Declaration on Terrorism; Recommendation 852 (1979) on Terrorism in Europe; Recommendation 916 (1981) on the Conference on 'Defence of Democracy against Terrorism in Europe – Tasks and Problems'; Recommendation No. R (82) of the Committee of Ministers to Member States Concerning International Co-operation in the Prosecution and Punishment of Acts of Terrorism; Recommendation 941 (1982) on the Defence of Democracy against Terrorism in Europe; Recommendation of the Committee of Ministers to Member States on Measures to be Taken in Cases of Kidnapping followed by a Ransom Demand (1982); Recommendation 982 (1984) on the Defence of Democracy against Terrorism in Europe; Council of Europe Pledge to Step up Fight against Terrorism (1986); European Conference of Ministers Responsible for Combating Terrorism (1980).

[106] 15 I.L.M. 1272 (1978).

[107] 19 I.L.M. 325 (1982).

[108] C. Gueydan, 'Cooperation between Member States of the European Community in the Fight against Terrorism' in R. Higgins and M. Flory (eds), above n. 1, 97–122, at p. 101.

arrangements,[109] the Convention nevertheless allows for refusal to extradite where the requested State has 'substantial grounds for believing that the request for extradition for an offence has been made for the purpose of prosecuting or punishing a person on account of his race, religion, nationality or political opinion, or that that person's position may be prejudiced for any of these reasons'.[110] The Convention preserves the *aut dedere aut judicare* principle.

The European Union (EU) has also passed numerous Declarations, Resolutions and entered into treaty arrangements in order to deal with the problem of terrorism and terrorist activities.[111] The OAS, which has frequently encountered this problem, has also adopted numerous specialist instruments dealing with terrorism. These include the Convention to Prevent and Punish the Act of Terrorism Taking the form of Crimes against Persons and Related Extortion that are of International Significance (1971);[112] and the OAS General Assembly Resolution on Acts of Terrorism (1970).[113] The OAS Convention is of special significance in that it does not allow for the political offence exception. The Convention establishes a duty for States parties to cooperate in the prevention and punishment of 'acts of terrorism'. According to Article 2 of the Convention:

> Kidnapping, murder and other assaults on life or personal integrity of those whom the State has to give special protection according to international law, as well as extortion in connection with those crimes, shall be considered common crimes of international significance regardless of motive.

The Convention is based on the principle of *aut dedere aut judicare* and has provisions regarding extradition.[114] Article 6 provides for the right of asylum and a number of obligations are contained in Article 8 for the purpose of ensuring a general duty of cooperation in the prevention and punishment of the crimes covered. According to Article 9, the Convention is open to the participation of States other than members of the OAS.

In the contemporary debate on terrorism, a number of misconceptions have arisen concerning Islam, Islamic law and the State practices of Islamic States.

---

[109] Article 3.

[110] Article 5.

[111] See the Declaration by the European Council on International Terrorism (1976); Resolution on Acts of Terrorism in the Community (1977); European Communities: Agreement Concerning the Application of the European Convention on the Suppression of Terrorism among the Member States (1979); European Parliament Resolution on Problems Relating to Combating Terrorism (1989); also see the Treaty of European Union 1992 (Provisions on Co-operation in the Spheres of Justice and Home Affairs–Article A).

[112] 10 I.L.M. (1971) 255.

[113] 9 I.L.M. (1970) 1084.

[114] Articles 3, 5 and 7.

In order to eradicate some of these misconceptions, it is crucial to analyse the practices and arrangements made by the Organisation of Islamic Conference (OIC), the principal organisation representing the Islamic world. The membership of the OIC is exclusively Islamic. The organisation was formed in Rabbat, the Kingdom of Morocco in September 1969. It currently has a membership of fifty-six States. In view of the growing concerns regarding terrorism, the OIC adopted the Convention of the Organisation of the Islamic Conference on Combating International Terrorism (1999).[115] The Convention represents a strong condemnation of terrorist activities. It defines terrorism in a very clear and precise manner. Thus according to Article 1(2) of the Convention, Terrorism means:

> any act of violence or threat thereof notwithstanding its motives or intentions perpetrated to carry out an individual or collective criminal plan with the aim of terrorizing people or threatening to harm them or imperilling their lives, honour, freedoms, security or rights or exposing the environment or any facility or public or private property to hazards or occupying or seizing them, or endangering a national resource, or international facilities, or threatening the stability, territorial integrity, political unity or sovereignty of independent States.

While suggesting an exception in cases of self-determination, the Convention ensures that OIC members accept the established norms which prohibit and condemn international terrorism. The Convention lists major treaties on the subject and requires States parties to follow the principles established in these treaties. According to the Convention special preventive measures are to be introduced by State parties and members are to undertake to cooperate in combating international terrorism.

Aeriel terrorism

As recent events confirm, ariel terrorism poses a serious threat to international peace and security. Historically, there have been many instances of hijacking and sabotage. The first practical response to such forms of terrorism was the adoption of the Convention on Offences and Certain Other Acts committed on Board Aircraft, signed in Tokyo on September 14 1963. The Convention was adopted under the auspices of ICAO. It deals principally with crimes committed on board civilian aircraft. The principal purpose of the Tokyo Convention is to protect the safety of the aircraft and of the persons or property thereon, and to maintain good order and discipline on board.[116] The Convention authorises the aircraft commander, the crew members and

---

[115] Text available (http://untreaty.un.org/English/Terrorism.asp) 31 March 2002.
[116] http://untreaty.un.org/English/tersumen.htm#3 (31 March 2002)

the passengers to take reasonable actions in order to protect the safety of the aircraft, or that of persons or property on board.[117]

The Convention establishes a number of jurisdictional rules dealing with ariel hijacking. The State of registration has the principal jurisdiction to try offences committed on board the aircraft.[118] However, additional grounds of jurisdiction exist *inter alia* in cases of the territory of the State where the offence has effect on its territory,[119] where the offence has been committed by or against a national or permanent resident of such State[120] or the offence is against the security of such a State.[121]

For the purposes of extradition, Article 16 of the Convention provides that offences committed on board the aircraft shall be treated as if they were committed not only in the place where they occurred but also in the territory of the registering State. Other provisions of the Convention concern such matters as taking offenders into custody, restoring control of the aircraft to the commander and the continuation of the aircraft's journey.[122] The Convention represents an important development in international efforts to combat ariel terrorism. At the same time there are a number of shortcomings in the treaty. It does not define or list any offences which States parties are required to suppress; nor does it impose any obligations regarding the extradition or prosecution of offenders.

In order to overcome some of these weaknesses in the Tokyo Convention and to further consolidate international norms on the hijacking of aircraft, the Convention for the Suppression of Unlawful Seizure of Aircraft was adopted in 1970 in The Hague. According to the Convention an offence is committed when any person:

> who on board an aircraft in flight ... unlawfully, by force or threat thereof, or by any other form of intimidation, seizes, or exercises control of that aircraft; or is an accomplice of a person who performs or attempts to perform any such act.[123]

According to Article 2, States parties are obliged to make offences under the Convention punishable by severe penalties. Jurisdiction is granted *inter alia* to the State where the aircraft is registered, to the State where the aircraft lands once an offence has been committed on board and to the State or place of

---

[117] Article 6(1)(2).
[118] See D. Freestone, 'International Cooperation against Terrorism and the Development of International Law Principles of Jurisdiction' in R. Higgins and M. Flory (eds), above n. 1, 43–67 at p. 49.
[119] Article 4(a).
[120] Article 4(b).
[121] Article 4(c).
[122] Articles 6–15.
[123] Article 1.

business or residence of the lessee in the case of aircraft which are leases without crew.[124] If the offender is not extradited, the State party where the offender is found undertakes to prosecute him.[125] The Convention obliges parties to allow one another judicial assistance in criminal proceedings brought in respect of the offence.[126] It also requires States parties to report to the Council of ICAO any relevant information in their possession.[127] While both the 1963 and 1970 Conventions deal with aeriel hijacking, the subject of aeriel sabotage was left to be addressed by the Convention for the Suppression of Unlawful Acts against the Safety of Civil Aviation adopted in Montreal in 1971. According to Article 1 of the Convention a person commits an offence if he unlawfully and intentionally:

> performs an act of violence against a person on board an aircraft in flight if that act is likely to endanger its safety; destroys an aircraft or causes damage to it; places or causes to be placed on an aircraft in service a device or substance which is likely to destroy that aircraft or to cause damage to it which renders it incapable of flight or endangers its safety; destroys or damages air navigation facilities or interferes with their operation, if any such act is likely to endanger the safety of aircraft in flight or communicates information which he knows to be false, thereby endangering the safety of aircraft in flight.

Article 1 also makes it an offence to attempt to commit the aforementioned offences. The Convention provides for jurisdictional principles which are similar to the Hague Convention. Through a number of provisions, the Convention deals with such issues as custody, prosecution and extradition of the alleged offender. The Convention like the earlier Hague and Tokyo Conventions, does not apply to aircraft used in military, customs or police services. Article 5(1) attempts to provide a wide basis of jurisdiction, approaching the threshold of universal jurisdiction. The Convention follows the principle of *aut dedere aut judicare*.

A further treaty, the Protocol on the Suppression of Unlawful Acts of Violence at Airports Serving International Civil Aviation, supplementary to the Convention for the Suppression of Unlawful Acts Against the Safety of Civil Aviation, Montreal, was adopted in February 1988.[128] The Protocol is geared towards dealing with acts of violence which endanger or are likely to endanger the safety of persons at airports serving international civil aviation

---

[124] Article 41(a)(b)(c).

[125] Article 7.

[126] Article 10.

[127] Article 11.

[128] Protocol on the Suppression of Unlawful Acts of Violence at Airports Serving International Civil Aviation, supplementary to the Convention for the Suppression of Unlawful Acts Against the Safety of Civil Aviation, Montreal, 24 February 1988.

or which jeopardise the safe operations of such airports. The 1988 Protocol adds to the definition of offences as provided in Article 1 of the Montreal Convention, thereby providing for the punishment of any person who unlawfully commits an act of violence against a person at an airport serving international civil aviation which causes or is likely to cause death or serious injury by any device, substance or weapon. The jurisdictional issues are addressed in Article III, which also affirms the principle of *aut dedere aut judicare*.

Maritime terrorism

Under general international law, the crime of piracy has a universal jurisdiction allowing any State to prosecute the offenders.[129] Piracy as a crime, however, is distinguishable from Maritime Terrorism in the sense that the latter is conducted in order to pursue or achieve political ends (as opposed to private ends in the case of piracy).[130] While a number of instances of maritime terrorism have taken place, the *Achille Lauro* incident prompted the international community to take concrete action as regards formulating binding standards for the protection of ships from terrorists.[131] With this objective the Convention for the Suppression of Unlawful Acts against the Safety of Maritime Navigation was adopted in Rome during March 1988. The Convention defines a 'ship' as 'a vessel of any type whatsoever not permanently attached to the sea-bed'.[132] A positive feature in the definition of the offences is the inclusion of murder as a separate crime. As Malivana Halberstam points out, although exceptional when compared to the Convention against Airline Hijacking and Sabotage and the Convention against Hostage-taking, this inclusion was prompted directly by the murder of a crippled Jewish man Leo Klinghoffer on board the *Achille Lauro*.[133]

According to Article 3(1) of the Convention any person commits an offence if that person unlawfully and intentionally:

(a)   seizes or exercises control over a ship by force or threat thereof or any other form of intimidation; or

---

[129] See Article 101 of the Law of the Sea Convention (1982); M.N. Shaw, *International Law*, 4th edn (Cambridge: Grotius Publication) 1997, at p. 423; Elagab, above n. 43, at p. 465.
[130] Ibid. p. 465.
[131] For further consideration of the incident see J. McCredie, 'Contemporary Uses of Force against Terrorism: The United States Response to Achille Lauro–Question of Jurisdiction and its Exercise' 16 *Georgia Journal of Comparative and International Law* (1986) 435; Note, 'The Achille Lauro Incident and the Permissible Use of Force' 9 *Loyola of Los Angeles Journal of International and Comparative Law* (1987) 481; M. Halbertsam, 'Terrorism on the High Seas: The Achille Lauro, Piracy, and the IMO Convention on Maritime Safety' 82 *AJIL* (1988) 269.
[132] Article 1.
[133] M. Halbertsam, 'Terrorist Acts Against and on Board Ships' 18 *IYHR* (1989) 331 at p. 333.

(b)   performs an act of violence against a person on board a ship if that act is likely to endanger the safe navigation of that ship; or

(c)   destroys a ship or causes damage to a ship or its cargo which is likely to endanger the safe navigation of that ship; or

(d)   places or causes to be placed on a ship, by any means whatsoever, a device or substance which is likely to destroy that ship, or cause damage to that ship or its cargo which endangers or is likely to endanger the safe navigation of that ship;

(e)   destroys or seriously damages maritime navigational facilities or seriously interferes with their operation, if any such act is likely to endanger the safe navigation of a ship; or

(f)   communicates information which he knows to be false, thereby endangering the safe navigation of a ship; or

(g)   injures or kills any person, in connection with the commission or the attempted commission of any of the offences set forth in subparagraph (a) to (f).

The Convention does not cover ships used in military, customs or police service.[134] The jurisdiction of the Convention is very extensive and covers territorial waters as well as the high seas.[135] Equally, the treaty is applicable to ships navigating or scheduled to navigate into, through or from waters beyond the outer limit of the territorial sea of a single State, or the lateral limits of its territorial sea with adjacent States, or when the alleged offender is found in the territory of a State party. At the time of approving the Convention in March 1988, a Protocol was also adopted. This Protocol addresses acts committed against 'fixed platforms', fixed platforms being defined as an artificial island, installation or structure permanently attached to the sea-bed for the purpose of exploration or exploitation of resources or for other economic purposes. The offences under the Protocol are almost identical to those under the Rome Convention, differing only in so far as is necessary to take into account of the differences between ships and such platforms.[136] Despite the many positive features of the Convention and the Protocol on Maritime Terrorism, a number of weaknesses have been pointed out. These instruments do not deal with State terrorism; nor do they provide for universal jurisdiction, the absence of which is likely to generate problems where either the State is not a party to the treaty or the offence is committed by a national belonging to a State which is not party to the treaty.[137]

---

[134] Article 2.

[135] Article 4.

[136] Article 2.

[137] C.C. Joyner, 'Suppression of Terrorism on the High Seas: The 1988 IMO Convention on the Safety of Maritime Navigation' 19 *IYHR* (1989) 343 at p. 365.

INTERNATIONAL LEGAL DEVELOPMENTS SINCE 11 SEPTEMBER AND DIFFICULTIES RELATED TO COMPENSATION FOR VICTIMS OF INTERNATIONAL TERRORISM

On Tuesday 11 September 2001, four commercial planes were hijacked by terrorists. One hijacked passenger jet leaving Boston, Massachusetts crashed into the north tower of the World Trade Center at 8.45 a.m. setting the tower on fire. Eighteen minutes later, a second hijacked airliner, United Airlines Flight 175 from Boston, crashed into the south tower of the World Trade Center and exploded. Later that morning both the North and South towers collapsed, plummeting into the streets below. At 9.43 a.m., a third hijacked airliner (American Airlines Flight 77) crashed into the Pentagon sending up a huge plume of smoke. A portion of the building later collapsed. At 10.10 a.m. a fourth hijacked airliner (United Airlines Flight 93) crashed in Somerset county, Pennsylvania, south-east of Pittsburgh.[138] The crashing of these hijacked airliners into buildings and on land were the worst terrorist attacks in the history of the United States. They led to the loss of thousands of innocent lives and damaged property running into billions of dollars.

The terrorist attacks not only served as a chilling reminder of the dangers inherent in international terrorism, but have also sent shock waves around the world. The attacks have been unequivocally condemned by all States and by all international organisations. On 12 September 2001, the United Nations General Assembly passed a Resolution condemning the heinous acts which had resulted in the loss of lives and enormous destruction. While showing solidarity with the peoples of the USA, it called for international cooperation to bring to justice the perpetrators, organisers and sponsors of the crimes committed on 11 September. On 12 September, the United Nations Security Council also condemned the terrorist acts, expressing it to be a threat to international peace and security.[139] The Council called upon all States urgently to work together to bring to justice the perpetrators of the crime, organisers and sponsors of the terrorist attacks.[140] A further resolution, Resolution 1373 was adopted on 28 September 2001, requiring States to undertake a series of actions. Since the Council was acting under Chapter VII, all its decision were binding upon States.[141] Under this Resolution, the Council required States to adopt and implement the existing international legal instruments on terrorism. According to this Resolution States are under an obligation to

---

[138] Information taken from CNN. September 11 2001: Chronology of terror (http://europe.cnn.com/2001/US/09/11/chronology.attack/).
[139] S/RES/1368 Adopted by the Security Council at its 4370th meeting.
[140] Ibid. para 3.
[141] See above Chapter 2.

prevent and suppress the financing and the freezing of funds and financial matters. It also requires States to offer one another assistance for criminal investigations and proceedings related to the financing or support of terrorist acts.[142] According to the Resolution, States are also to prevent the movement of terrorists or their groups by effective border controls. The Council also determined that States shall intensify and accelerate the exchange of information regarding terrorist actions or movements; forged or falsified documents; traffic in arms and sensitive material; use of communications and technologies by terrorist groups; and the threat posed by the possession of weapons of mass destruction. In addition States are required to exchange information and cooperate to prevent and suppress terrorist acts and to take action against the perpetrators of such acts. By Resolution 1373, the Council established a Committee of the Council to monitor the implementation of the Resolution and called upon all States to report on actions they had taken to that end no later than 90 days from the date of the adoption of the Resolution (that is, 28 September 2001). On 4 October, Sir Jeremy Greenstock of the United Kingdom was named chair of the Security Council Committee on terrorism.

Immediately after the terrorist acts of 11 September 2001, there were calls for military action against the terrorists. While the United Nations Charter prohibits the use of force, it does expressly endorse an inherent right to self-defence for States.[143] The military action in and the bombing of Afghanistan that was commenced in October 2001 has principally been justified by the United States and the United Kingdom Governments on the basis of this inherent right of individual and collective self-defence. In the face of the heinous acts of 11 September, the loss and destruction of lives and property and the threat of future attacks by terrorists, there is some strength in reliance upon the principles of self-defence. However, the right to self-defence must be conducted in accordance with well-established principles of international law. According to these principles, which emanate from the *Caroline case* and are now accepted as forming part of customary international law, there must exist 'a necessity of

---

[142] Security Council SC/7158 (4385th Meeting) 28 September 2001.

[143] Article 51 provides that 'Nothing in the present Charter shall impair the inherent right of individual or collective self-defense if an armed attack occurs against a Member of the United Nations, until the Security Council has taken measures necessary to maintain international peace and security. Measures taken by Members in the exercise of this right of self-defense shall be immediately reported to the Security Council and shall not in any way affect the authority and responsibility of the Security Council under the present Charter to take at any time such action as it deems necessary in order to maintain or restore international peace and security'. The United Nations Charter Adopted at San Francisco 26 June 1945. Entered in to force 24 October 1945. 1 U.N.T.S xvi; U.K.T.S 67 (1946); 59 Stat. 1031.

self-defence, instant, overwhelming, leaving no choice of means, and no moment for deliberation'.[144] The right to self-defence, in order to be legitimate, must also comply with the requirement of proportionality.[145] In the present case there are the significant legal questions about the strength of evidence against Osama Bin Laden, and the responsibility of the Taliban and State of Afghanistan – issues which have been consistently raised since the commencement of the bombings in Afghanistan.[146] There have been claims that the US has used an indiscriminate bombing campaign in Afghanistan which has led to a huge number of civilian casualties.[147] A further disturbing feature (which as yet remains unresolved) is the treatment of the suspected terrorists who have been arrested by the United States and taken to its base in Cuba.[148]

While the condemnation of terrorism has been universal, some of the purported actions against the terrorists have been criticised as threatening civil liberties and human rights. Recent legislation adopted by the United States and the United Kingdom has raised substantial concerns;[149] similarly there is a fear that in the aftermath of the events of 11 September, minority groups – in particular Arab-Asian minorities in the western world – would be

---

[144] See the *Caroline case* 29 B.F.S.P. 1137–38; 30 B.S.F.P. 195–6 (1837). R.Y. Jennings, 'The Caroline and McLeod Cases' 32 *AJIL* (1938) 82; Shaw, above n. 129 at pp. 787–791.

[145] A. Conte, 'The Cost of Terror' *New Zealand Law Journal* (November 2001), 412 at p. 414; A. Cassese, 'Terrorism is Also Disrupting Some Crucial Legal Categories of International Law' 12 *EJIL* (2001) 993 at p. 995.

[146] International law allows for imputability of acts of private individuals where the concerned State endorses terrorist acts and fails to cooperate with the international community. See further the *Case Concerning United States Diplomatic and Consular Staff in Tehran (United States of America v. Iran)* 61 I.L.R. 559, para 74.

[147] http://news.bbc.co.uk/hi/english/world/south_asia/newsid_1740000/1740727.stm 'Pressure grows to stop Afghan bombing.' (4 January 2002) 'Continuing reports of civilian casualties in Afghanistan are raising questions about US military tactics and adding to a growing clamour for an end to the bombing. Evidence of civilian deaths in the village of Niazi Qalaye in Paktia province, struck in the early hours of 29 December, offers a direct challenge to the American military's version of the attack. The United Nations says it has an unconfirmed but reliable report from the area that 52 civilians were killed in the raid'.

[148] BBC South Asia, Head to Head (16 January, 2002) prisonershttp://news.bbc.co.uk/hi/english/world/americas/newsid_1763000/1763307.stm Head to Head Guantanamo. See the Statement made by United Nations High Commissioner for Human Rights Mary Robinson, 16 January 2002.

[149] On 13 November 2001, the United States President George W. Bush issued a Presidential Order, Detention, Treatment, and Trial of Certain Non-Citizens in the War Against Terrorism providing his administration the option of trying non-US citizens suspected of terrorism before special military tribunals as opposed to civilian courts. The composition and jurisdiction of these tribunals represent substantial curtailments of the rights of the accused. See President Issues Military Order Detention, Treatment, and Trial of Certain Non-Citizens in the War Against Terrorism (http://www.whitehouse.gov/news/releases/2001/11/20011113-27.html). For the position in the United Kingdom see the Anti-terrorism, Crime and Security Act 2001 c.24 (text available: http://www.hmso.gov.uk/acts/acts2001.htm) 31 January 2002.

discriminated against and their fundamental rights violated. Amidst the complexities in formulating legal principles to prevent terrorism and to punish perpetrators of this crime, a major disturbing feature is the absence of international mechanisms for providing remedies to the victims of terrorism. As we have considered throughout this book, international human rights law remains an unsatisfactory medium in according adequate remedies to victims of violations; nowhere is this more accurate than in the case of victims of international terrorism. In a handful of cases only have individual claimants been able to receive damages before international and national tribunals. In others, the existing State apparatus defies meaningful forms of remedies and compensation. This position can be confirmed through the events arising from the terrorist attacks of 11 September 2001. It would appear that some relatives and next of kin of victims of the attacks that took place in United States are entitled to compensation, though many others would be unsuccessful. A more unfortunate future awaits the millions of innocent men, women and children who have suffered for years under the terrorist regime of the Taliban and have endured the US bombings since October 2001.

CONCLUSIONS

The date of 11 September 2001 has gone down as one of the tragic days in the history of mankind. The hijacking of American airliners, their crash into the World Trade Center and the collapse of the twin towers continues to haunt not only the survivors of the tragedy but all those who believe in the inherent dignity and worth of mankind. The terrorist attacks of 11 September were followed by ariel bombardment (by the United States and the United Kingdom) which led to the unfortunate deaths of thousands of Afghani men, women and children. Although these events represent a tragedy of enormous magnitude, they also provide a number of lessons. First, the events reconfirm the view that international terrorism is a crime against humanity and that the international community of States should treat it as such. In this context it is interesting to note that during the drafting stages of the Statute of the International Criminal Court, attempts were made to provide the new court with a specific jurisdiction to try terrorist offences.[150] However, such efforts proved unsuccessful because of the opposition of many countries – including the United States. In hindsight such an approach can only be regarded as unfortunate. Despite the absence of a specific incorporation of the crime of terrorism, there is sufficient breadth in the definition of crimes against humanity to try crimes

---

[150] For further consideration of the Statute of the International Criminal Court see above Chapter 11. Conte, above n. 145, at p. 413.

of terrorism.[151] An international criminal court should provide a useful, impartial and internationally acceptable forum for trials of individuals indicted with the crime of international terrorism.

Secondly, the events of 11 September reinforce the need for an internationally binding agreement which condemns terrorism and provides for severe penalties for those involved in committing this crime.

This chapter has considered the enormous ideological and political differences that exist with regard to defining and conceptualising international terrorism. At the same time, a great measure of consensus exists on the absolute criminalisation of certain forms of activities such as hostage-taking of civilians and internationally protected persons, as well as the banning of aeriel and maritime terrorism. Although, as considered earlier, there are treaties criminalising these activities, the global prohibition would be more effective if the major offences were codified in the form of a single binding instrument. Finally, there is an important message in the political developments that led to the events of 11 September 2001. There is a strong connection between human rights violations and terrorist activities; in order to put an end to international terrorism, the international community of States must also address the underlying causes which lead individuals to resort to such extreme measures.

---

[151] G. Robertson, *The Guardian* 19 September 2001.

APPENDIX I: STUDYING INTERNATIONAL LAW OF HUMAN RIGHTS

SOURCES AND FURTHER RESEARCH IN HUMAN RIGHTS

Human Rights is an exciting and an extremely rapidly developing area of international law. To keep abreast with the latest developments students can consult:

Documents in print

a) International Human Rights Reports
b) International Legal Materials
c) United Nations Yearbook on Human Rights
d) United Nations Chronicle
e) Keesings Contemporary Archives

Significant journals

a) *European Human Rights Law Review (EHRLR)*
b) *International and Comparative Law Quarterly (ICLQ)*
c) *Human Rights Quarterly (HRQ)*
d) *American Journal of International Law (AJIL)*
e) *Netherlands Quarterly of Human Rights (NQHR)*

Internet sources (as at 5 April 2002)

a) **United Nations system and related websites**

International Court of Justice, the Hague, the Netherlands	http://www.icj-cij.org/
International Labour Organisation (ILO), Geneva, Switzerland	www.ilo.org
UN Children's fund, New York, USA (UNICEF)	www.unicef.org/
UN Environment Programme, Nairobi, Kenya (UNEP)	www.unep.org/
UN Headquarters, New York, USA (UN)	www.un.org/
UN High Commissioner on Human Rights, Geneva, Switzerland	www.unhchr.ch/

UN High Commissioner for Refugees,
Geneva, Switzerland   www.unhcr.ch/
UN University, Tokyo, Japan (UNU)   www.unu.edu/
UN Development Programme   http://www.undp.org/
UN Division for the Advancement
for Women   http://www.un.org/womenwatch/
daw/

b) **Other sources**
Council of Europe   http://www.coe.int/
Organization of American States   http://www.oas.org/
Organisation of African Unity   http://www.oau-oua.org/
International Criminal Tribunal for the
former Yugoslavia   http://www.un.org/icty/
International Tribunal for Rwanda   http://www.ictr.org/
University of Minnesota, Human
Rights Library   http://www1.umn.edu/humanrts/
York University Libraries Law School   http://www.info.library.yorku.ca/
depts/law/linkshr.htm
University of Essex, Library   http://libwww.essex.ac.uk/
Human_Rights/treaties.htm
US Department of State   http://www.state.gov/

c) **Non-governmental sources**
Save the Children   http://www.savethechildren.org/
Amnesty International   http://www.amnesty.org/
Human Rights Watch   http://www.hrw.org/
Human and Constitutional Rights   http://www.hrcr.org/
The International Committee of the
Red Cross   http://www.icrc.org/
Index on Censorship   http://www.indexonline.org/
Human Rights Internet   http://www.hri.ca/welcome.cfm
Minority Rights Group, International   http://www.minorityrights.org/

APPENDIX II: STATUS OF THE RATIFICATION OF THE PRINCIPAL INTERNATIONAL AND REGIONAL HUMAN RIGHTS TREATIES

INTERNATIONAL HUMAN RIGHTS TREATIES

Table of Ratifications (as at 1 March 2002)

State	ICCPR	ICESCR	OP 1	OP 2	Race C	Women C	Women-OP	CRC	OP-AC	OP-SC	Torture C
Afghanistan	24/01/83 a	24/01/83 a			06/07/83 a	14/08/80 s		28/03/94			01/04/87
Albania	04/10/91 a	04/10/91 a			11/05/94 a	11/05/94		27/02/92			11/05/94 a
Algeria	12/09/89	12/09/89	12/09/89 a		14/02/72*	22/05/96 a		16/04/93			12/09/89*
Andorra						15/01/97a	09/07/01 s	02/01/96	30/04/01	30/04/01	
Angola	10/01/92 a	10/01/92 a	10/01/92 a			17/09/86 a		06/12/90			
Antigua and Barbuda					25/10/88 d	01/08/89 a		06/10/93		18/12/01 s	19/07/93 a
Argentina	08/08/86	08/08/86	08/08/86 a		02/10/68	15/07/85	28/02/00 s	05/12/90	15/06/00 s		24/09/86*
Armenia	23/06/93 a	13/09/93 a	23/06/93		23/06/93 a	13/09/93 a		23/06/93 a			13/09/93
Australia	13/08/80	10/12/75	25/09/91 a	02/10/90 a	30/09/75*	28/07/83		17/12/90		18/12/01 s	08/08/89*
Austria	10/09/78	10/09/78	10/12/87	02/03/93	09/05/72	31/03/82	07/09/00	06/08/92	06/09/00 s	06/09/00 s	29/07/87*
Azerbaijan	13/08/92 a	13/08/92 a	27/11/01 a	22/01/99 a	16/08/96 a*	10/07/95 a	01/06/01	13/08/92 a	08/09/00 s	08/09/00 s	16/08/96 a
Bahamas					05/08/75 d	06/10/93 a		20/02/91			
Bahrain					27/03/90 a			13/02/92 a			06/03/98 a

State	ICCPR	ICESCR	OP 1	OP 2	Race C	Women C	Women-OP	CRC	OP-AC	OP-SC	Torture C
Bangladesh	07/09/00 a	05/10/98 a			11/06/79 a	06/11/84 a	07/09/00	03/08/90	07/09/00	07/09/00	05/10/98 a
Barbados	05/01/73 a	05/01/73 a	05/01/73 a		08/11/72 a	16/10/80		09/10/90			13/03/87
Belarus	12/11/73	12/11/73	30/09/92 a		08/04/69	04/02/81		02/10/90			
Belgium	21/04/83	21/04/83	17/05/94 a	08/12/98	07/08/75*	10/07/85	10/12/99 s	16/12/91	06/09/00 s	06/09/00 s	25/06/99*
Belize	10/06/96 s	06/09/00 s			14/11/01	16/05/90		02/05/90	06/09/00 s	06/09/00 s	17/03/86 a
Benin	12/03/92 a	12/03/92 a	12/03/92 a		30/11/01	12/03/92	25/05/00 s	03/08/90	22/02/01 s	22/02/01 s	12/03/92 a
Bhutan					26/03/73 s	31/08/81		01/08/90			
Bolivia	12/08/82 a	12/08/82 a	12/08/82 a		22/09/70	08/06/90	27/09/00	26/06/90		10/11/01 s	12/04/99
Bosnia and Herzegovina	01/09/93 d	03/03/92 d	01/03/95	16/03/01	16/07/93 d	01/09/93 d	07/09/00 s	01/09/93 d	07/09/00 s	07/09/00 s	01/09/93 a
Botswana	08/09/00				20/02/74 a	13/08/96 a		14/03/95 a			08/09/00
Brazil	24/01/92 a	24/01/92 a			27/03/68	01/02/84	13/03/01 s	25/09/90	06/09/00 s	06/09/00 s	28/09/89
Brunei Darussalam								27/12/95 a			
Bulgaria	21/09/70	21/09/70	26/03/92 a	10/08/99	08/08/66*	08/02/82	06/06/00 s	03/06/91	08/06/01 s	08/06/01 s	16/12/86*
Burkina Faso	04/01/99 a	04/01/99 a	04/01/99 a		18/07/74 a	14/10/87 a	16/11/01 s	31/08/90	16/11/01 s	16/11/01 s	04/01/99 a
Burundi	09/05/90 a	09/05/90 a			27/10/77	08/01/92	13/11/01 s	19/10/90	13/11/01 s	10/11/01 s	18/02/93 a
Cambodia	26/05/92 a	26/05/92 a			28/11/83	15/10/92 a	11/11/01 s	15/10/92 a	27/06/00 s	27/06/00 s	15/10/92 a
Cameroon	27/06/84 a	27/06/84 a	27/06/84 a		24/06/71	23/08/94		11/01/93	05/10/01 s	05/10/01 s	19/12/86 a*
Canada	19/05/76 a	19/05/76 a	19/05/76 a		14/10/70	10/12/81		13/12/91	07/07/00	10/11/01 s	24/06/87*
Cape Verde	06/08/93 a	06/08/93 a	19/05/00 a	19/05/00 a	03/10/79 a	05/12/80 a		04/06/92 a			04/06/92 a
Central African Republic	08/05/81 a	08/05/81 a	08/05/81 a		16/03/71	21/06/91 a		23/04/92			
Chad	09/06/95 a	09/06/95 a	09/06/95 a		17/08/77 a	09/06/95 a		02/10/90			09/06/95 a
Chile	10/02/72	10/02/72	28/05/92 a	15/11/01 s	20/10/71*	08/12/89	10/12/99 s	13/08/90	15/11/01 s	28/06/00 s	30/09/88
China	05/10/98 s	27/03/01			29/12/81 a	04/11/80		03/03/92	15/03/01 s	06/09/00 s	04/10/88
Colombia	29/10/69	29/10/69	29/10/69	05/08/97 a	02/09/81	19/01/82		28/01/91	06/09/00 s	06/09/00 s	08/12/87
Comoros					22/09/00 s	31/10/94 a	10/12/99 s	23/06/93			22/09/00 s
Congo	05/10/83 a	05/10/83 a	05/10/83 a		11/07/88 a	26/07/82		14/10/93 a			
Cook Islands								06/06/97 a			
Costa Rica	29/11/68	29/11/68	29/11/68	05/06/98	16/01/67*	04/04/86	20/09/01	21/08/90	07/09/00 s	07/09/00 s	11/11/93
Croatia	12/10/92 d	08/10/91 d	12/10/95 a	12/10/95 a	12/10/92 d	09/09/92 d	07/03/01	12/10/92 d			12/10/92 d*
Cuba					15/02/72	17/07/80	17/03/00 s	21/08/91	13/11/00 s	25/09/01	17/05/95
Cyprus	02/04/69	02/04/69	15/04/92	10/09/99 a	21/04/67*	23/07/85 a	08/02/01 s	07/02/91		08/02/01 s	18/07/91*

State	ICCPR	ICESCR	OP 1	OP 2	Race C	Women C	Women-OP	CRC	OP-AC	OP-SC	Torture C
Czech Republic	22/02/93 d	01/01/93 d	22/02/93 d		22/02/93 d*	22/02/93 d	27/02/01	22/02/93 d	30/11/01		01/01/93 d*
Côte d'Ivoire	26/03/92 a	26/03/92 a	05/03/97 a		04/01/73 a	18/12/95		04/02/91			18/12/95 a
Democratic People's Republic of Korea	14/09/81 a	14/09/81 a				27/02/01 a		21/09/90			
Democratic Republic of Congo	01/11/76 a	01/11/76 a	01/11/76 a		21/04/76 a	17/10/86		28/09/90			18/03/96
Denmark	06/01/72	06/01/72	06/01/72	24/02/94	09/12/71*	21/04/83	31/05/00	19/07/91	12/11/01	12/11/01	27/05/87*
Djibouti						02/12/98 a		06/12/90	07/09/00 s	07/09/00 s	
Dominica	17/06/93 a	17/06/93 a				15/09/80		13/03/91			
Dominican Republic	04/01/78 a	04/01/78 a	04/01/78 a		25/05/83 a	02/09/82	10/08/01	11/06/91			04/02/85 s
Ecuador	06/03/69	06/03/69	06/03/69	23/02/93 a	22/09/66 a*	09/11/81	10/12/99 s	23/03/90	06/09/00 s	06/09/00 s	30/03/88*
Egypt	14/01/82	14/01/82			01/05/67	18/09/81		06/07/90			25/06/86 a
El Salvador	30/11/79	30/11/79	06/06/95		30/11/79 a	19/08/81	04/04/01 s	10/07/90	18/09/00 s		17/06/96 a
Equatorial Guinea	25/09/87 a	25/09/87 a	25/09/87 a			23/10/84 a		15/06/92 a			
Eritrea	22/01/02 a	17/04/01 a			01/08/01 a	05/09/95 a		03/08/94			
Estonia	21/10/91 a	21/10/91 a	21/10/91 a		21/10/91 a	21/10/91 a		21/10/91 a			21/10/91 a
Ethiopia	11/06/93 a	11/06/93 a			23/06/76 a	10/09/81		14/05/91 a			13/03/94 a
Fiji					11/01/73 d	28/08/95		13/08/93			
Finland	19/08/75	19/08/75	19/08/75	04/04/91	14/07/70*	04/09/86	29/12/00	21/06/91	07/09/00 s	07/09/00 s	30/08/89*
France	04/11/80 a	04/11/80 a	17/02/84 a		28/07/71 a*	14/12/83	09/06/00	08/08/90	06/09/00 s	06/09/00 s	18/02/86*
Gabon	21/01/83 a	21/01/83 a			29/02/80	21/01/83		09/02/94	08/09/00 s	08/09/00 s	08/09/00
Gambia	22/03/79 a	29/12/78 a	09/06/88 a		29/12/78 a	16/04/93		08/08/90	21/12/00 s	21/12/00 s	23/10/85 s
Georgia	03/05/94 a	03/05/94 a	03/05/94 a	22/03/99 a	02/06/99 a	26/10/94 a		02/06/94 a			26/10/94 a
Germany	17/12/73	17/12/73	25/08/93 a	18/08/92	16/05/69*	10/07/85	15/01/02	06/03/92	06/09/00 s	06/09/00 s	01/10/90*
Ghana	08/09/00	08/09/00	08/09/00		08/09/66	02/01/86	24/02/00 s	05/02/90			08/09/00
Greece	05/05/97 a	16/05/85 a	05/05/97 a	05/05/97 a	18/06/70	07/06/83	24/01/02	11/05/93	07/09/00 s	07/09/00 s	06/10/88*

State	ICCPR	ICESCR	OP 1	OP 2	Race C	Women C	Women-OP	CRC	OP-AC	OP-SC	Torture C
Grenada	06/09/91 a	06/09/91 a			17/12/81 s	30/08/90		05/11/90			
Guatemala	06/05/92 a	19/05/88 a	28/11/00 a		18/01/83	12/08/82	07/09/00 s	06/06/90	07/09/00 s	07/09/00 s	05/01/90 a
Guinea	24/01/78	24/01/78	17/06/93		14/03/77	09/08/82		13/07/90 a			10/10/89
Guinea-Bissau	12/09/00 s	02/07/92 a	12/09/00 s	12/09/00 s	12/09/00 s	23/08/85	12/09/00 s	21/08/90	08/09/00 s	08/09/00 s	12/09/00 s
Guyana	15/02/77	15/02/77	10/05/93 a		15/02/77	17/07/80		14/01/91			19/05/88
Haiti	06/02/91 a				19/12/72	20/07/81		09/06/95			
Holy see					01/05/69			20/04/90			
Honduras	25/08/97	17/02/81	19/12/66 s	10/05/90 s		03/03/83		10/08/90	24/10/01	24/10/01	05/12/96 a
Hungary	17/01/74	17/01/74	07/09/88 a	24/02/94 a	01/05/67*	22/12/80	22/12/00 a	08/10/91			15/04/87*
Iceland	22/08/79	22/11/79	22/08/79 a	02/04/91 a	13/03/67*	18/06/85	07/03/01	28/10/92	02/10/01	09/07/01	23/10/96*
India	10/04/79 a	10/04/79 a			03/12/68	09/07/93		11/12/92 a			14/10/97 s
Indonesia					25/06/99 a	13/09/84	28/02/00 s	05/09/90	24/09/01 s	24/09/01 s	28/10/98
Iran (Islamic Republic of)	24/06/75	24/06/75			29/08/68			13/07/94			
Iraq	25/01/71	25/01/71			14/01/70	13/08/86 a		15/06/94 a			
Ireland	08/12/89	08/12/89	08/12/89	18/06/93 a	29/12/00*	23/12/85 a	08/09/00	28/09/92	07/09/00 s	07/09/00 s	28/09/92 s
Israel	03/10/91	03/10/91			03/01/79	03/10/91		03/10/91		14/11/01 s	03/10/91
Italy	15/09/78	15/09/78	15/09/78	14/02/95	05/01/76*	10/06/85	22/09/00	05/09/91	06/09/00 s	06/09/00 s	12/01/89*
Jamaica	03/10/75	03/10/75			04/06/71	19/10/84		14/05/91	08/09/00 s	08/09/00 s	
Japan	21/06/79	21/06/79			15/12/95 a	25/06/85		22/04/94			29/06/99 a*
Jordan	28/05/75	28/05/75			30/05/74 a	01/07/92		24/05/91	06/09/00 s	06/09/00 s	13/11/91
Kazakhstan					26/08/98 a	26/08/98 a	24/08/01	12/08/94	06/09/00 s	24/08/01	26/08/98 a
Kenya	01/05/72 a	01/05/72 a			13/09/01 a	09/03/84 a		31/07/90	28/01/02	08/09/00 s	21/02/97 a
Kiribati								11/12/95 a			
Kuwait	21/05/96 a	21/05/96 a			15/10/68 a	02/09/94 a		21/10/91			08/03/96 a
Kyrgystan	07/10/94 a	07/10/94 a	07/10/95 a		05/09/97 a	10/02/97 a		07/10/94 a			05/09/97 a
Lao People's Democratic Republic	07/12/00 s	07/12/00 s			22/02/74 a	14/08/81		08/05/91 a			
Latvia	14/04/92 a	14/04/92 a	22/06/94 a		14/04/92 a	14/04/92 a		14/04/92 a			14/04/92 a

State	ICCPR	ICESCR	OP 1	OP 2	Race C	Women C	Women-OP	CRC	OP-AC	OP-SC	Torture C
Lebanon	03/11/72 a	03/11/72 a			12/11/71 a	21/04/97 a		14/05/91		10/10/01 s	05/10/00 a
Lesotho	09/09/92 a	09/09/92 a	07/09/00 a		04/11/71 a	22/08/95 a	06/09/00 s	10/03/92	06/09/00 s	06/09/00 s	13/11/01 a
Liberia	18/04/67 s	18/04/67 s			05/11/76 a	17/07/84		04/06/93			
Libyan Arab Jamahiriya	15/05/70 a	15/05/70 a	16/05/89 a		03/07/68 a	16/05/89 a		16/04/93 a			16/05/89 a
Liechtenstein	10/12/98 a	10/12/98 a	10/12/98 a	10/12/98	01/03/00 a	22/12/95 a	24/10/01	22/12/95	08/09/00 s	08/09/00 s	02/11/90*
Lithuania	20/11/91 a	20/11/91 a	20/11/91 a	08/09/00 s	10/12/98	18/01/94 a	08/09/00 s	31/01/92 a			01/02/96
Luxembourg	18/08/83	18/08/83	18/08/83 a	12/02/92	01/05/78*	02/02/89	10/12/99 s	07/03/94	08/09/00 s	08/09/00 s	29/09/87*
Madagascar	21/06/71	22/09/71	21/06/71		07/02/69	17/03/89	07/09/00 s	19/03/91	07/09/00 s	07/09/00 s	01/10/01 s
Malawi	22/12/93 a	22/12/93 a	11/06/96		11/06/96 a	12/03/87 a	07/09/00 s	03/01/91 a	07/09/00 s	07/09/00 s	11/06/96 a
Malaysia						05/07/95		17/02/95 a			
Maldives					24/04/84 a	01/07/93 a		11/02/91	08/09/00 s	07/09/00 s	
Mali	16/07/74 a	16/07/74 a	24/10/01 a		16/07/74 a	10/09/85	05/12/00 a	21/09/90	07/09/00 s		26/02/99 a
Malta	13/09/90 a	13/09/90	13/09/90 a	29/12/94 a	27/05/71*	08/03/91 a		01/10/90			13/09/90 a*
Marshall Islands								05/10/93			
Mauritania					13/12/88	10/05/01 a		16/05/91			
Mauritius	12/12/73 a	12/12/73 a	12/12/73 a		30/05/72 a	09/07/84 a	11/11/01 s	26/07/90 a	11/11/01 s	11/11/01 s	09/12/92 a
Mexico	23/03/81 a	23/03/81 a			20/02/75	23/03/81	10/12/99 s	21/09/90	07/09/00 s	07/09/00 s	23/01/86
Micronesia (Federated States of)								05/05/93 a			
Monaco	28/08/97	28/08/97		28/03/00 a	27/09/95 a*		07/09/00 s	21/06/93 a	14/11/01	26/06/00 s	06/12/91 a
Mongolia	18/11/74	18/11/74	16/04/91 a		06/08/69	20/07/81		06/07/90	12/11/01 s	12/11/01 s	24/01/02 a
Morocco	03/05/79	03/05/79			18/12/70	21/06/93 a		22/06/93	08/09/00 s	02/10/01	21/06/93
Mozambique	21/07/93 a			21/07/93 a	18/04/83 a	16/04/97 a		26/04/94			14/09/99 a
Myanmar						22/07/97 a		15/07/91 a			
Namibia	28/11/94 a	28/11/94 a	28/11/94 a	28/11/94 a	11/11/82 a	23/11/92 a	26/05/00	30/09/90	08/09/00 s	08/09/00 s	28/11/94 a
Nauru	12/11/01 s		12/11/01 s		12/11/01 s			27/07/94 a	08/09/00 s	08/09/00 s	12/11/01 s
Nepal	14/05/91 a	14/05/91 a	14/05/91 a	04/03/98 a	30/01/71 a	22/04/91	18/12/01 s	14/09/90	08/09/00 s	08/09/00 s	14/05/91 a
Netherlands	11/12/78	11/12/78	11/12/78	26/03/91	10/12/71*	23/07/91	10/12/99 s	06/02/95	07/09/00 s	07/09/00 s	21/12/88*
New Zealand	28/12/78	28/12/78 a	26/05/89 a	22/02/90	22/11/72	10/01/85	08/09/00	06/04/93	12/11/01	07/09/00 s	10/12/89*
Nicaragua	12/03/80 a	12/03/80 a	12/03/80 a	21/02/90 s	15/02/78 a	27/10/81		05/10/90			15/04/85 s

State	ICCPR	ICESCR	OP 1	OP 2	Race C	Women C	Women-OP	CRC	OP-AC	OP-SC	Torture C
Niger	07/03/86 a	07/03/86 a	07/03/86 a		27/04/67	08/10/99 a		30/09/90			05/10/98 a
Nigeria	29/07/93 a	29/07/93 a			16/10/67 a	13/06/85	08/09/00 s	19/04/91	08/09/00 s	08/09/00 s	28/06/01
Niue								20/12/95 a			
Norway	13/09/72	13/09/72	13/09/72	05/09/91	06/08/70*	21/05/81	10/09/00 s	08/01/91	13/06/00 s	02/10/01	09/07/86*
Oman								09/12/96 a			
Pakistan					21/09/66	12/03/96 a		12/11/90	26/09/01 s	26/09/01 s	
Palau								04/08/95 a			
Panama	08/03/77	08/03/77 a	08/03/77	21/01/93 a	16/08/67	29/10/81	10/05/01	12/12/90	08/08/01	09/02/01	24/08/87
Papua New Guinea					27/01/82 a	12/01/95 a		02/03/93			
Paraguay	10/06/92	10/06/92 a	10/01/95 a		13/09/00 s	06/04/87 a	14/05/01	25/09/90	13/09/00 s	13/09/00 s	12/03/90
Peru	28/04/78	28/04/78	03/10/80 a		29/09/71*	13/09/82	09/04/01	05/09/90	01/11/00 s	01/11/00 s	07/07/88
Philippines	23/10/86	07/06/74	22/08/89 a		15/09/67	05/08/81	21/03/00 s	21/08/90	08/09/00 s	08/09/00 s	18/06/86 a
Poland	18/03/77	18/03/77	07/11/91 a	21/03/00 s	05/12/68*	30/07/80		07/06/91			26/07/89*
Portugal	15/06/78	31/07/78	03/05/83	17/10/90	24/08/82 a*	30/07/80	16/02/00 s	21/09/90	06/09/00 s	06/09/00 s	09/02/89*
Qatar					27/07/76 a			04/04/95		14/12/01 a	11/01/00 a
Republic of Korea	10/04/90 a	10/04/90 a	10/04/90 a		05/12/78*	27/12/84		20/11/91	06/09/00 s	06/09/00 s	09/01/95 a
Republic of Moldova	26/01/93 a	26/01/93 a			26/01/93 a	01/07/94 a		26/01/93 a			28/11/95
Romania	09/12/74	09/12/74	20/07/93 a	27/02/91	15/09/70 a	07/01/82	06/09/00 s	28/09/90	11/11/01	18/10/01	18/12/90 a
Russian Federation	16/10/73	16/10/73	01/10/91 a		04/02/69*	23/01/81	08/05/01 s	17/08/90	15/02/01 s		03/03/87*
Rwanda	16/04/75 a	16/04/75 a			16/04/75 a	02/03/81		24/01/91			
Saint Kitts and Nevis						25/04/85 a		24/07/90			
Saint Lucia					14/02/90 d	08/10/82 a		16/06/93			
Saint Vincent and Grenadines	09/11/81 a	09/11/81 a	09/11/81 a		09/11/81 a	05/08/81 a		26/10/93			01/08/01 a

State	ICCPR	ICESCR	OP 1	OP 2	Race C	Women C	Women-OP	CRC	OP-AC	OP-SC	Torture C
Samoa						25/09/92 a		29/11/94			
San Marino	18/10/85 a	18/10/85 a	18/10/85 a		11/12/01 s			25/11/91 a	05/06/00 s	05/06/00 s	
Sao Tome and Principe	31/10/95 s	31/10/95 s	06/09/00 s	06/09/00 s	06/09/00 s	31/10/95 s	06/09/00 s	14/05/91 a	08/09/00 s	08/09/00 s	06/09/00 s
Saudi Arabia					23/09/97 a	08/09/00		26/01/96 a			23/09/97 a
Senegal	13/02/78	13/02/78	13/02/78		19/04/72*	05/02/85	26/05/00	01/08/90			21/08/86*
Seychelles	05/05/92 a	05/05/92 a	05/05/92 a	15/12/94 a	07/03/78 a	06/05/92 a		07/09/90 a	23/01/01 s	23/01/01 s	05/05/92 a*
Sierra Leone	23/08/96 a	23/08/96 a	23/08/96 a		02/08/67	11/11/88	08/09/00 s	18/06/90	08/09/00 s	17/09/01	25/04/01
Singapore						05/10/95 a		05/10/95 a	07/09/00 s		
Slovakia	28/05/93 d	28/05/93 d	28/05/93	22/06/99	28/05/93 d*	28/05/93 d	17/11/00	28/05/93 d		30/11/01 s	28/05/93 d*
Slovenia	06/07/92 d	06/07/92 d	16/07/93 a	10/03/94	06/07/92 d	06/07/92 d	10/12/99 s	06/07/92 d	08/09/00 s	08/09/00 s	16/07/93 a
Solomon Islands		17/03/82 d			17/03/82 d			10/04/95 a			
Somalia	24/01/90 a	24/01/90 a	24/01/90 a		26/08/75						24/01/90 a
South Africa	10/12/98	03/10/94 s			10/12/98*	15/12/95		16/06/95	06/09/00 s	18/12/01	10/12/98*
Spain	27/04/77	27/04/77	25/01/85 a	11/04/91	13/09/68 a*	05/01/84		06/12/90	08/09/00		21/10/87*
Sri Lanka	11/06/80 a	11/06/80 a	03/10/97 a		18/02/82 a	05/10/81	06/07/01	12/07/91			03/01/94 a
Sudan	18/03/76 a	18/03/76 a			21/03/77			03/08/90			04/06/86 s
Suriname	28/12/76 a	28/12/76 a	28/12/76 a		15/03/84 d	02/03/93 a		02/03/93			
Swaziland					07/04/69 a			08/09/95			
Sweden	06/12/71	06/12/71	06/12/71	11/05/90	06/12/71*	02/07/80		29/06/90	08/06/00 s	08/06/00 s	08/01/86*
Switzerland	18/06/92 a	18/06/92 a		16/06/94 a	29/11/94 a	27/03/97	10/12/99 s	24/02/97	07/09/00 s	07/09/00 s	02/12/86*
Syrian Arab Republic	21/04/69 a	21/04/69 a			21/04/69 a			15/07/93			
Tajikistan	04/01/99 a	04/01/99 a	04/01/99 a		11/01/95 a	26/10/93 a	07/09/00 s	26/10/93 a			11/01/95 a
Thailand	29/10/96 a	05/09/99 a				09/08/85 a	14/06/00	27/03/92 a			
The Former Yugoslav Republic of Macedonia	18/01/94 d	18/01/94 d	12/12/94 a	26/01/95	18/01/94 d*	18/01/94 d	03/04/00 s	02/12/93 d	17/07/01 s	17/07/01 s	12/12/94 d
Togo	24/05/84 a	24/05/84 a	30/03/88 a		01/09/72 a	26/09/83 a		01/08/90		15/11/01 s	18/11/87*
Tonga					16/02/72 a			06/11/95 a			
Trinidad and Tobago	21/12/78 a	08/12/78 a			04/10/73	12/01/90		06/12/91			

State	ICCPR	ICESCR	OP 1	OP 2	Race C	Women C	Women-OP	CRC	OP-AC	OP-SC	Torture C
Tunisia	18/03/69	18/03/69			13/01/67	20/09/85		31/01/92			23/09/88*
Turkey	15/08/00 s	15/08/00 s			13/10/72 s	20/12/85 a	08/09/00 s	04/04/95	08/09/00 s	08/09/00 s	02/08/88*
Turkmenistan	01/05/97 a	01/05/97 a	01/05/97 a		29/09/94 a	01/05/97 a		20/09/93 a			25/06/99 a
Tuvalu				11/01/00 a		06/10/99 a		22/09/95 a			
Uganda	21/06/95 a	21/01/87 a	14/11/95		21/11/80 a	23/07/85		17/08/90		30/11/01 a	03/11/86 a
Ukraine	12/11/73	12/11/73	25/07/91 a		07/03/69*	12/03/81	07/09/00 s	28/08/91	07/09/00 s	07/09/00 s	24/02/87
United Arab Emirates					20/06/74 a			03/01/97 a			
United Kingdom of Great Britain and Northern Ireland											
Ireland	20/05/76	20/05/76		10/12/99	07/03/69	07/04/86		16/12/91	07/09/00 s	07/09/00 s	08/12/88*
United Republic of Tanzania	11/06/76 a	11/06/76 a			27/10/72 a	20/08/85		11/06/91			
United States of America	08/06/92	05/10/77 s			21/10/94	17/07/80 s		16/02/95 s	05/07/00 s	05/07/00 s	21/10/94*
Uruguay	01/04/70	01/04/70	01/04/70	21/01/93	30/08/68*	09/10/81		20/11/90	07/09/00 s	07/09/00 s	24/10/86*
Uzbekistan	28/09/95 a	28/09/95 a	28/09/95 a		28/09/95 a	19/07/95 a	26/07/01	29/06/94 a		28/09/95 a	
Vanuatu						08/09/95		07/07/93			
Venezuela	10/05/78	10/05/78	10/05/78	22/02/93	10/10/67	02/05/83	17/03/00 s	14/09/90	07/09/00 s	07/09/00 s	29/07/91*
Vietnam	24/09/82 a	24/09/82 a			09/06/82 a	17/02/82		28/02/90	20/12/01	20/12/01	
Yemen	09/02/87 a	09/02/87 a			18/10/72 a	30/05/84 a		01/05/91	08/10/01 s	08/10/01 s	05/11/91 a
Yugoslavia	12/03/01 d	12/03/01 d	06/09/01	06/09/01 a	12/03/01 d*	26/02/82		03/01/91 d			12/03/01 d*
Zambia	10/04/84 a	10/04/84 a	10/04/84 a		04/02/72	21/06/85		06/12/91			07/10/98 a
Zimbabwe	13/05/91 a	13/05/91 a			13/05/91 a	14/05/91 a		11/09/90			

International Human Rights Treaties	ICCPR	ICESCR	OP 1	OP 2	Race C	Women C	Women-OP	CRC	OP-AC	OP-SC	Torture C
Total Signatories (among non-State parties)	7	7	4	7	9	3	45	1	77	76	11
Total State parties	148	145	101	46	161	168	30	191	14	17	128

Notes:

ICCPR = International Covenant on Civil and Political Rights

ICESCR = International Covenant on Economic, Social and Cultural Rights

OP 1 = The First Optional Protocol to the International Covenant on Civil and Political Rights

OP 2 = The Second Optional Protocol to International Covenant on Civil and Political Rights aimed at the abolition of the death penalty

Race C = International Convention on the Elimination of All forms of Racial Discrimination

Women C = The Convention on the Elimination of All forms of Discrimination against Women

Women-OP = The Optional Protocol to the Convention on the Elimination of All forms of Discrimination against Women

CRC = Convention on the Rights of the Child

OP-AC = The Optional Protocol to the Convention on the Rights of the Child on the involvement of children in armed conflict

OP-SC = The Optional Protocol to the Convention on the Rights of the Child on the sale of children, child prostitution and child pornography

Torture C = The Convention against Torture

a = accession

d = succession

s = signature

* indicates that the State party has recognised the competence to receive and process individual communications of the Committee on the Elimination of Racial Discrimination under Article 14 of the Race Convention (total States Parties) or the Committee against Torture under article 22 of Torture Convention (total 46 States Parties).

Table adapted from the information taken from the Office of the United Nations High Commissioner on Human Rights. I am very grateful to Maria Eugenia Freitas for her support in the completion of this table.

KEY REGIONAL HUMAN RIGHTS TREATIES

European Convention for the Protection of Human Rights and Fundamental Freedoms (1950)

State party	Date of signature	Date of ratification	Date of entry into force
Albania	13/07/95	02/10/96	02/10/96
Andorra	10/11/94	22/01/96	22/01/96
Armenia	25/01/01		
Austria	13/12/57	03/09/58	03/09/58
Azerbaijan	25/01/01		
Belgium	04/11/50	14/06/55	14/06/55
Bulgaria	07/05/92	07/09/92	07/09/92
Croatia	06/11/96	05/11/97	05/11/97
Cyprus	16/12/61	06/10/62	06/10/62
Czech Republic*	21/02/91	18/03/92	01/01/93
Denmark	04/11/50	13/04/53	03/09/53
Estonia	14/05/93	16/04/96	16/04/96
Finland	05/05/89	10/05/90	10/05/90
France	04/11/50	03/05/74	03/05/74
Georgia	27/04/99	20/05/99	20/05/99
Germany***	04/11/50	05/12/52	03/09/53
Greece**	28/11/50	28/11/74	28/11/74
Hungary	06/11/90	05/11/92	05/11/92
Iceland	04/11/50	29/06/53	03/09/53
Ireland	04/11/50	25/02/53	03/09/53
Italy	04/11/50	26/10/55	26/10/55
Latvia	10/02/95	27/06/97	27/06/97
Liechtenstein	23/11/78	08/09/82	08/09/82
Lithuania	14/05/93	20/06/95	20/06/95
Luxembourg	04/11/50	03/09/53	03/0953
Malta	12/12/66	23/01/67	23/01/67
Moldova	13/07/95	12/09/97	12/09/97
Netherlands	04/11/50	31/08/54	31/08/54
Norway	04/11/50	15/01/52	03/09/53

State party	Date of signature	Date of ratification	Date of entry into force
Poland	26/11/91	19/01/93	19/01/93
Portugal	22/09/76	09/11/78	09/11/78
Romania	07/10/93	20/06/94	20/06/94
Russia	28/02/96	05/05/98	05/05/98
San Marino	16/11/88	22/03/89	22/03/89
Slovakia*	21/02/91	18/03/92	01/01/93
Slovenia	14/05/93	28/06/94	28/06/94
Spain	24/11/77	04/10/79	04/10/79
Sweden	28/11/50	04/02/52	03/09/53
Switzerland	21/12/72	28/11/74	28/11/74
The Former Yugolsav Republic of Macedonia	09/11/95	10/04/97	10/04/97
Turkey	04/11/50	18/05/54	18/05/54
Ukraine	09/11/95	11/09/97	11/09/97
United Kingdom	04/11/50	08/03/51	03/09/53

Notes:

1. Opened for Signature in Rome 4 November 1950. Entered into force 3 September 1953.
2. As of 5 April 2002 total number of ratifications/accessions: 41. Total number of signatures not followed by ratification: 2.

* Date of signature and ratification by the former Czech Republic and Slovak Federal Republic.
** Ratification 28 March 1953 – Denunciation with effect on 13 June 1970.
*** Ratification by Saarland 14 January 1953 – Saarland became an integral part of Germany on 1 January 1957.

Source: Treaty Office Council of Europe http://conventions.coe.int/

American Convention on Human Rights 'Pact of San Jose, Costa Rica'

(Signed at San José, Costa Rica, 22 November 1969, at the Inter-American Specialised Conference on Human Rights)

State party	Date signed	Date deposit/ ratification	Date of acceptance of the jurisdiction of the Court
Argentina*	02/02/84	05/09/84	05/09/84
Barbados	20/06/78	27/11/82	04/06/00
Bolivia		19/07/79	27/07/93
Brazil		25/09/92	10/12/98
Chile*		21/08/90	21/08/90
Colombia*		31/07/73	21/06/85
Costa Rica*		08/04/70	02/07/80
Dominica		03/06/93	
Dominican Republic	07/09/77	19/04/78	25/03/99
Ecuador*		28/12/77	24/07/84
El Salvador		23/06/78	06/06/95
Grenada	14/07/78	18/07/78	
Guatemala		25/05/78	09/03/87
Haiti		27/09/77	03/03/98
Honduras		08/09/77	09/09/81
Jamaica*	16/09/77	07/08/78	
Mexico		02/03/81	16/12/98
Nicaragua		25/09/79	12/02/91
Panama		22/06/78	03/05/90
Paraguay		24/08/89	11/03/93
Peru*	27/07/77	28/07/78	21/01/81
Suriname		12/11/87	12/11/87
Trinidad and Tobago		28/05/91	28/05/91
United States	01/06/77		
Uruguay*		19/04/85	19/04/85
Venezuela*		09/08/77	24/06/81

Notes:

1. The entry into force: 18 July 1978, in accordance with Article 74.2 of the Convention.
2. * (denotes) States that have accepted the competence of the Inter-American Court of Human Rights to receive and examine communications in which a State party alleges that another State party has violated the human rights set forth in the American Convention: Argentina (05/09/84); Chile (21/08/90); Colombia (21/06/85); Costa Rica (02/07/80); Ecuador (13/08/84); Jamaica (07/08/78); Peru (21/01/81); Uruguay (19/04/85) and Venezuela (09/08/77).
3. All States (with the exception of those whose date of signature is cited in the Table) signed the Convention on 22 November 1969.

Source: Adopted from the Inter-American Commission on Human Rights: Organization of American States http://www.cidh.oas.org/Basicos/basic4.htm

African Charter on Human and Peoples' Rights (1981)

State	Date of signature	Date of ratification/ accession	Date deposited
Algeria	10/04/86	01/03/87	20/03/87
Angola		02/03/90	09/10/90
Benin		20/01/86	25/02/86
Botswana		17/07/86	22/07/86
Burkina Faso	05/03/84	06/07/84	21/09/84
Burundi		28/07/89	30/08/89
Cameroon	23/07/87	20/06/89	18/09/89
Cape Verde	31/03/86	02/06/87	06/08/87
Central African Republic		26/04/86	27/07/86
Chad	29/05/86	09/10/86	11/11/86
Comoros		01/06/86	18/07/86
Congo	27/11/81	09/12/82	20/07/87
Congo (RD)	23/07/87	20/07/87	28/07/87
Côte d'Ivoire		06/01/92	31/03/92
Djibouti	20/12/91	11/11/91	31/03/92
Egypt	16/11/81	20/03/84	03/04/84
Equatorial Guinea	18/08/86	07/04/86	18/08/86
Eritrea		14/01/99	15/03/99
Ethiopia		15/06/98	22/06/98
Gabon	26/02/82	20/02/86	26/06/86
Gambia	11/02/83	08/06/83	13/06/83
Ghana		24/01/89	01/03/89
Guinea	09/12/81	16/02/82	13/05/82
Guinea Bissau		04/12/85	06/03/86
Kenya		23/01/92	10/02/92
Lesotho	07/03/84	10/02/92	27/02/92
Liberia	31/01/83	04/08/82	29/12/82
Libya	30/05/85	19/07/86	26/03/87
Madagascar		09/03/92	19/03/92
Malawi	13/11/81	17/11/89	23/02/90
Mali	13/11/81	21/12/81	22/01/82
Mauritania	25/02/82	14/06/86	26/06/86
Mauritius	27/02/92	19/06/92	01/07/92
Mozambique		22/02/89	07/03/90

State	Date of signature	Date of ratification/ accession	Date deposited
Namibia		30/7/92	16/09/92
Niger	09/07/86	15/07/86	21/07/86
Nigeria	31/08/82	22/06/83	22/07/83
Rwanda	11/11/81	15/07/83	22/07/83
Sahrawi Arab Democratic Republic	10/04/86	02/05/86	23/05/86
Sao Tome and Principe		23/05/86	28/07/86
Senegal	23/09/81	13/08/82	25/10/82
Seychelles		13/04/92	30/04/92
Sierra Leone	27/08/81	21/09/83	27/01/84
Somalia	26/02/82	31/07/85	20/03/86
South Africa	09/07/96	09/07/96	09/07/96
Sudan		03/09/82	11/03/86
Swaziland		15/09/95	09/10/95
Tanzania	31/05/82	18/02/84	09/03/84
Togo	26/02/82	05/11/82	22/11/82
Tunisia		16/03/83	22/04/83
Uganda	18/08/86	10/05/86	27/05/86
Zambia	17/01/83	10/01/84	02/02/84
Zimbabwe	20/02/86	30/05/86	12/06/86

Notes:

1. The African Charter on Human and Peoples' Rights adopted by the eighteenth session of the Assembly of Heads of State and Government, June 1981.
2. Entered into force on 21 October 1986.

Source: Adapted from the University of Minnesota, Human Rights Library Web Site (on 25 March 2002) www1.umn.edu/humanrights/index.html

INDEX